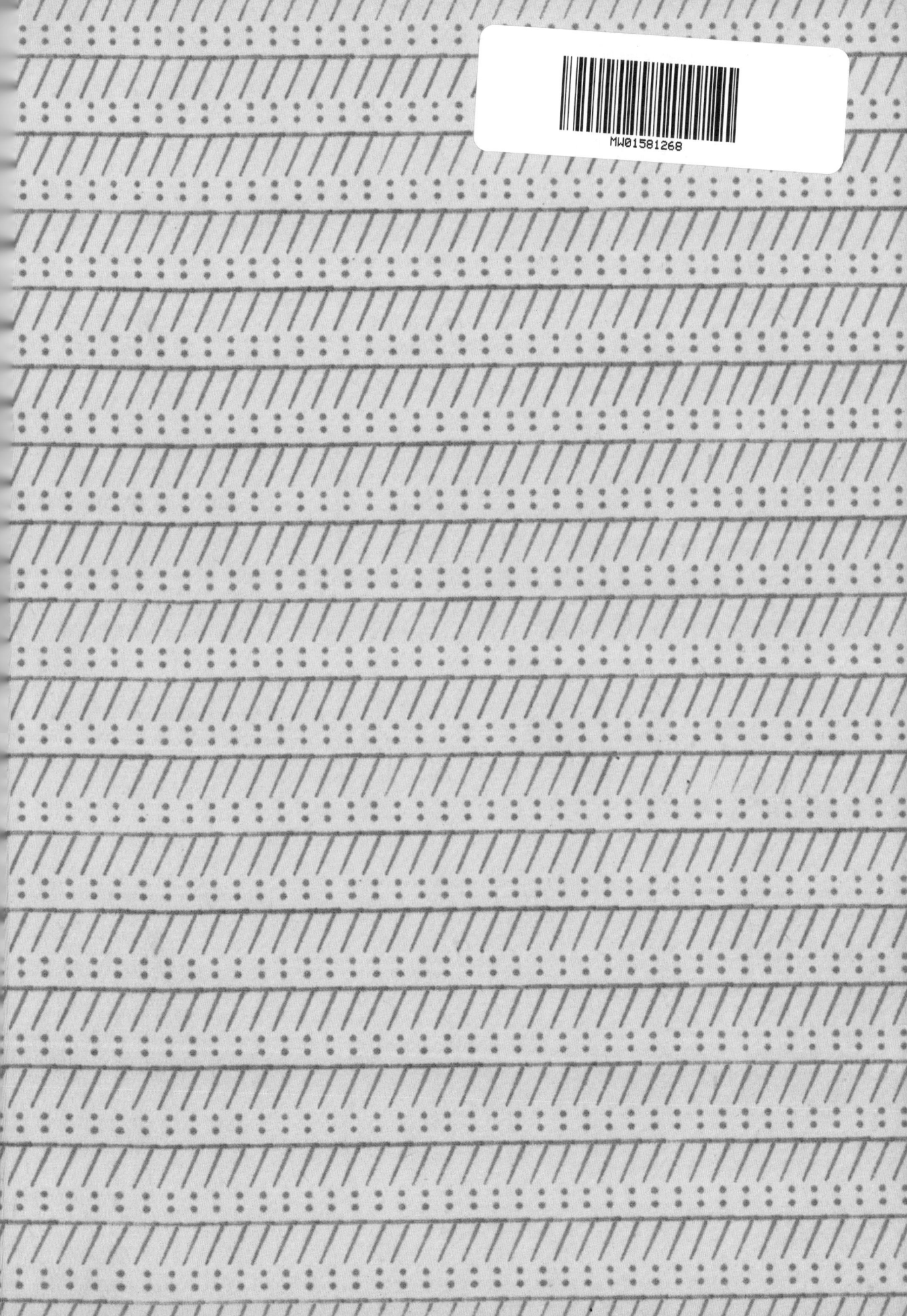

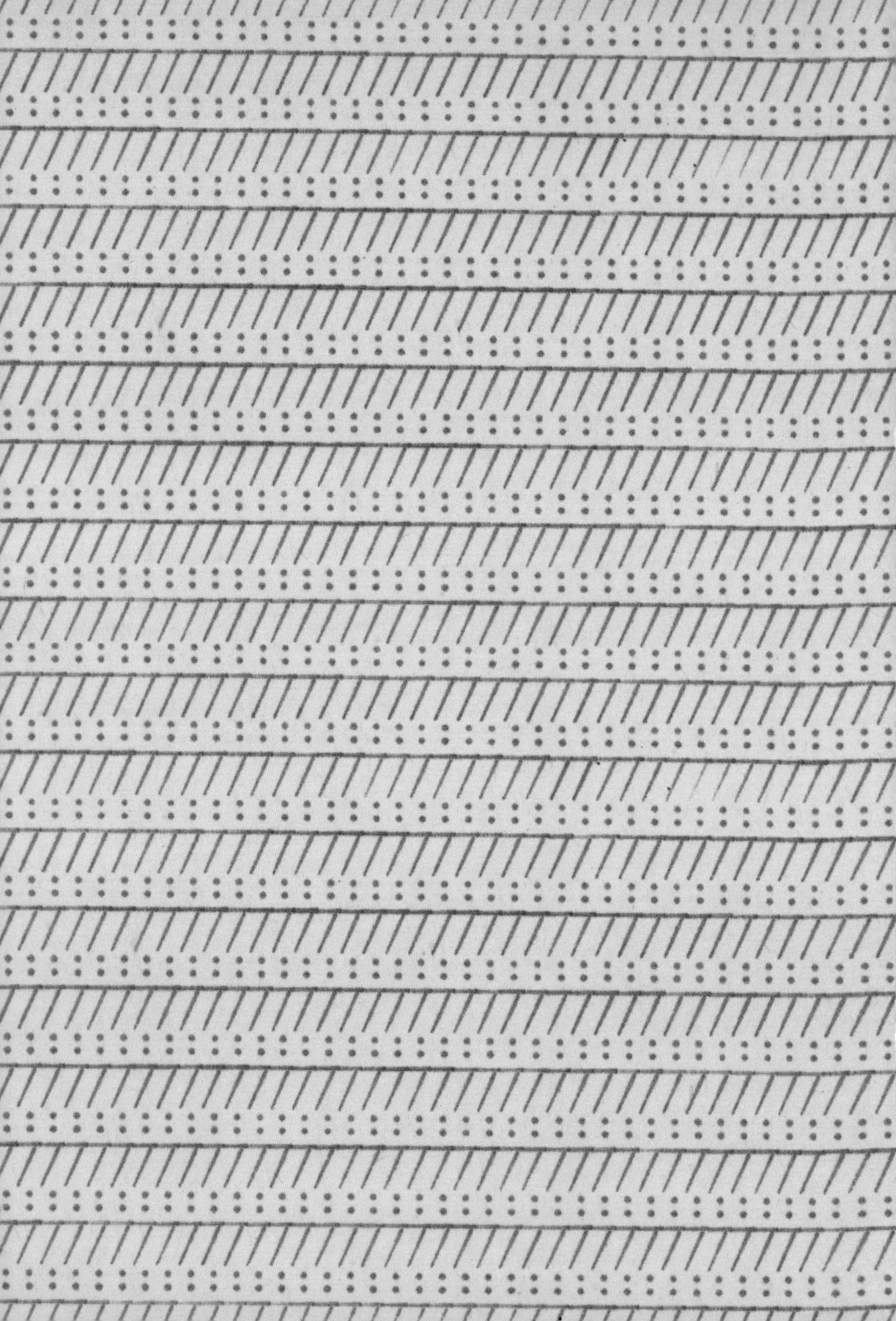

OBJECTS IN EXILE

Robin Schuldenfrei

OBJECTS IN EXILE

Modern Art and Design
across Borders
1930–1960

Princeton University Press
Princeton and Oxford

Contents

1   Introduction   Dislocation, Modernism, and the Materiality of Exile

Transposition

20   Chapter 1   Architecture's Material Abstraction: László Moholy-Nagy and the Industrial City

56   Chapter 2   Minimal Dwelling: Walter Gropius, Marcel Breuer, and László Moholy-Nagy at Isokon in England

Contingent Conditions

96   Chapter 3   Images in Exile: Lucia Moholy's Bauhaus Negatives and the Construction of a Modernist Legacy

124   Chapter 4   Assimilating Unease: László Moholy-Nagy and the Wartime/Postwar Chicago Bauhaus

154   Chapter 5   Domesticating the Grid: Ludwig Hilberseimer's Housing

Remediation

206 **Chapter 6** Exigencies of Materializing Vision: Josef Albers's Glass Paintings to *Homage to the Square*

242 **Chapter 7** Anni Albers's Design Theory and Its Objects: Typewriter Studies to Architecture's Pliable Plane

274 **Chapter 8** Herbert Bayer's Expanded Vision and the Instrumentalizing of Design

300 Acknowledgments

303 Notes

335 Index

344 Photo Credits

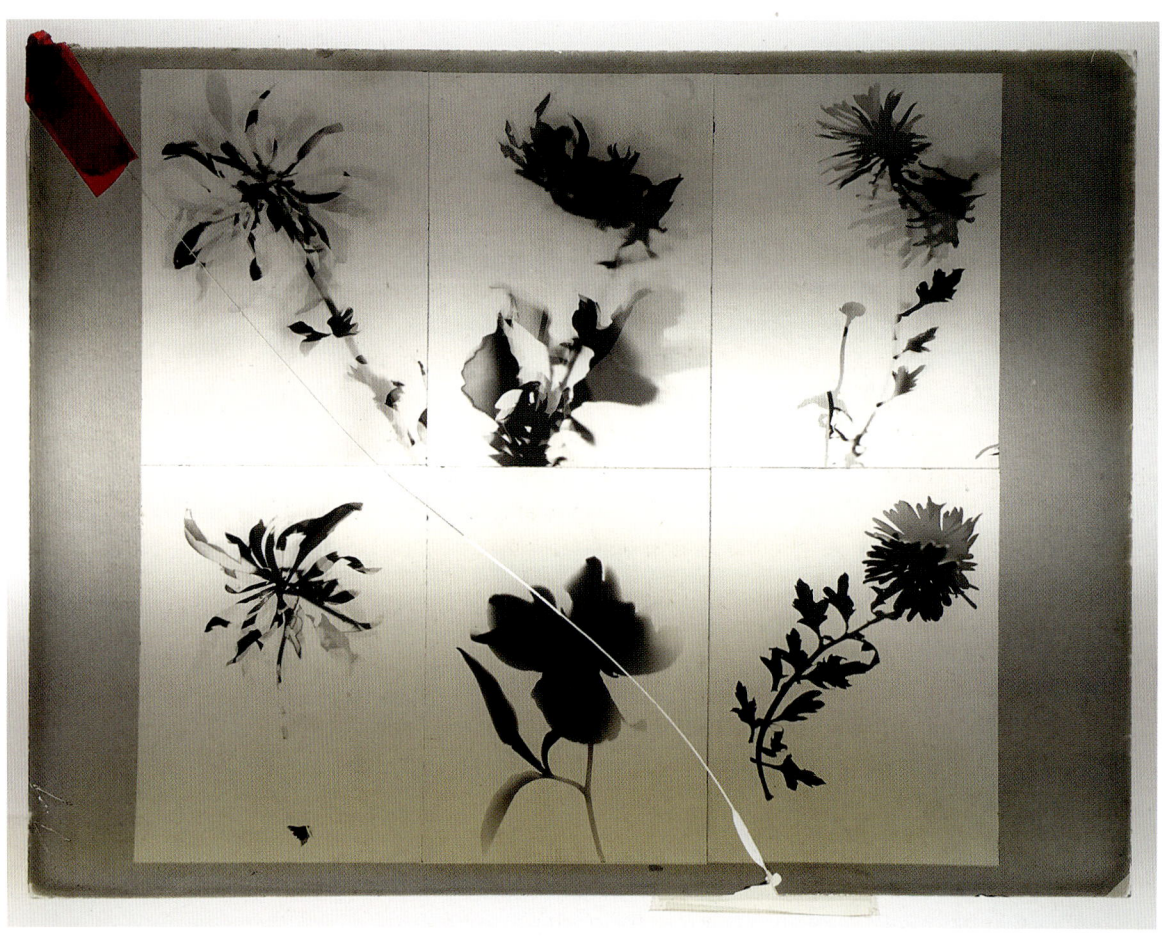

Fig. I.1 László Moholy-Nagy, *Six Flowers*, 1925–26, glass negative (broken) of six photograms (fgm 148, fgm 150–52, fgm 154, fgm 155). Photograph by Lucia Moholy.

Introduction

Dislocation, Modernism, and the Materiality of Exile

Modernism, as we understand it today, could only coalesce after a period of international mobility—a process of exile, emigration, and resettlement from continental Europe to Great Britain and America, in the interwar, wartime, and postwar period. In examining how an influx of émigrés profoundly shaped the direction of modernism, *Objects in Exile* argues that modernism gained coherence only *after* it passed through conditions of exile.[1] Spanning the period 1930–60, this book looks at the trajectory not just of people, or objects, but also how ideas surrounding modernism traveled – and were diverted and reshaped in new contexts. It resituates modern works produced at a crucial point of historical, cultural, and artistic interchange, allowing for a new and wider understanding of the theorizing and production of modernism in the twentieth century.

Objects in Exile examines modernism in the context of its materiality (and absence), its objects, its evolving theorization, and the pressures and contingencies exile placed on its practitioners and their designs and artworks. Owing to the conditions of exile, Marcel Breuer's bent metal chairs became bent wooden chairs for the Isokon company in England, and Walter Gropius instrumentalized the short, fourteen-year lifespan of the Bauhaus for its afterlife as a modernist legacy, usurping Lucia Moholy's glass negatives in order to do so. While the *Six Flowers* photographs did not accompany László Moholy-Nagy on his exilic perambulations, and the individual photographs are now lost (with one exception), he did retain a glass plate negative, now cracked, of the grouping, which gave him the possibility of making reproductions (fig. I.1).[2] Josef Albers's flat glass artworks, shattered in transit to the United States, reemerged as commercial paint on smooth Masonite for his *Homage to the Square* paintings (fig. I.2).

Although France and the Soviet Union, for example, were important loci of modernist activity during this same period, they took a different form and trajectory. This book trains an eye on a specific strand of exile within the history of modernism: the movement of architects and visual artists from Germany to the United Kingdom and the United States. Germany had been a fertile ground for modernism's conceptual ideas and works of art and architecture – its protagonists had initially amalgamated there from across central Europe, and thus many were displaced from Germany to new sites, often via circuitous routes. And it should not be forgotten that many modern artists and designers never

Fig. I.2 Josef Albers, *Homage to the Square*, 1969, oil on Masonite. The Josef and Anni Albers Foundation, 1976.1.198.

made it out of Germany at all. With the uncertainties of exile, modern ideas took on urgency. This critical assessment pays particular attention to ways in which modernist strands, developed in Europe, could be implemented to address wartime demands and other urgent needs in the United States. During the war, European modernism proved its usefulness by introducing new typographies and highly legible graphic design for effective communication in instructive US government war posters, camouflage and other wartime design, and exhibitions intended to bolster confidence and cohesion (fig. I.3).

Avant-garde ideas would come together and emerge as mainstream modernism in the vibrant postwar period, thereby securing a future for modern objects and their originators alike. Raw, open possibilities in the United States gave the émigrés unique opportunities to build in a manner that had merely been a photomontaged dream in Europe and for their pedagogies to be well-received at America's highest echelons – at Harvard, Yale, and the New Bauhaus in Chicago – for their product designs to be mass-produced, and for their art to enter prominent collections.

Objects in Exile argues that the substantial body of innovative work produced by key twentieth-century European modernists in the United States in the years 1930–60 was both informed by the places left behind and a reaction to, and molding by, the new sites of exile, thereby changing the course of modernism. Exilic modernism was formed by a set of diverse ideas and aesthetics,

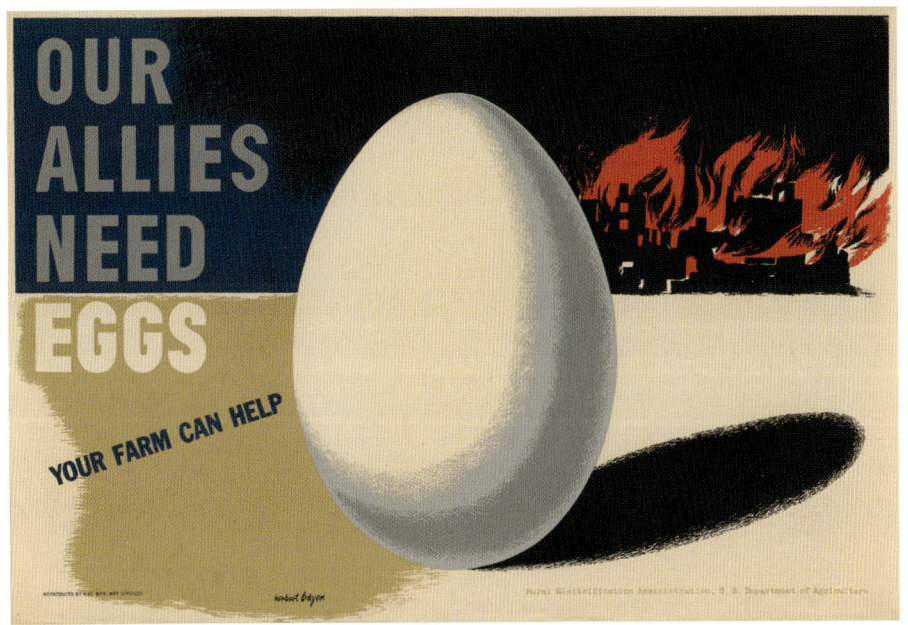

Fig. I.3 Herbert Bayer, *Our Allies Need Eggs*, 1942, poster for Rural Electrification Administration, reproduced by NYC WPA War Services. Bauhaus-Archiv, Berlin.

brought together by happenstance of world events that caused a mass migration of people generally, and the evacuation of key members of the avant-garde from continental Europe. Through focused reexamination of this artistic production in the work of Anni and Josef Albers, Herbert Bayer, Marcel Breuer, Walter Gropius, Ludwig Hilberseimer, Ludwig Mies van der Rohe, Lucia Moholy, and László Moholy-Nagy, many of whom taught at the Bauhaus, *Objects in Exile* appraises the results of the radically different contingencies that exile placed on architecture, art, and design.[3] While institutions such as the Bauhaus and groups such as the Werkbund were essential to constituting the modern movement, this book argues that modernism only fomented in exile. The chapters that follow offer a new picture of the powerful impact that the circumstances of exile had on the mid- to late twentieth century, concentrating on questions of materiality in modernism, while exploring issues of transnationalism, assimilation, translation, pedagogy, abstraction, and new concepts of seeing and cultural production.

Over the course of eight chapters, this book will explore the circularity of modernism in motion — examining how émigrés brought ideas and aesthetics to America that had often originated there. Fordism, grain silos, large-scale factory production, the bustle of New York City, the 1890s skyscrapers of the Chicago school, and the work of Louis Sullivan and Frank Lloyd Wright all had a profound impact on German modernists in the 1910s and 1920s, many of whom made their own pilgrimages to the United States or consumed its ideas and images via publications. Erich Mendelsohn's book *Amerika* and Sigfried Giedion's *Mechanization Takes Command* are just two examples that arose from interaction with America — the publication of which, in turn, further influenced European artists and architects of the period. This early exposure to the United States formed a crucial foundation for the later success the émigrés found as architecture and art school faculty, as artists and architects, and as freelance designers. They already had internalized much of its previous development and could adapt to American circumstances, not all of which were new to them. While French exiles

The Materiality of Exile

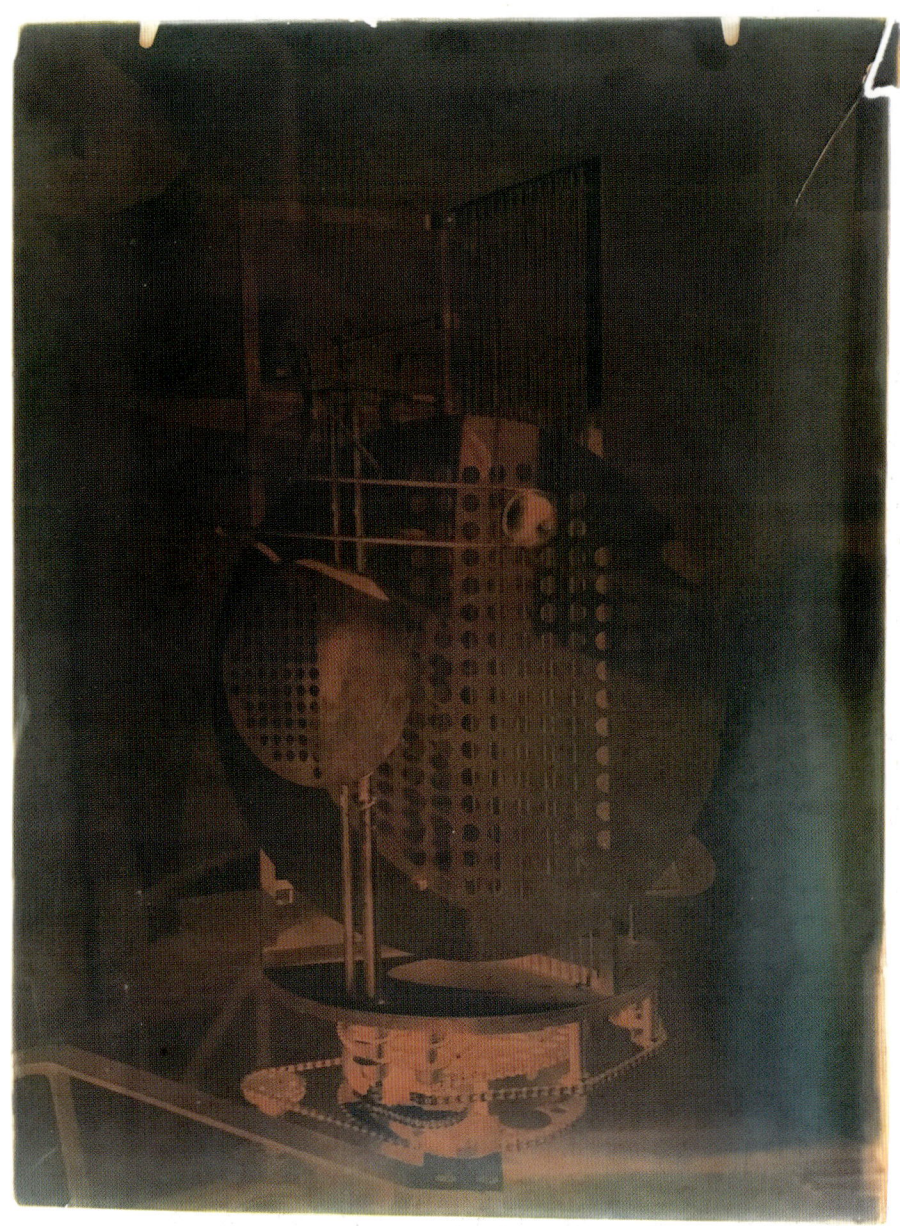

Fig. I.4 László Moholy-Nagy, *Light Prop for an Electric Stage* (*Light Space Modulator*), 1930, glass negative (broken).

such as Fernand Léger, Marc Chagall, and André Breton all returned to Europe, German exiles, especially, made the decision to stay in the United States. With premonitions of the postwar opportunities they were to find there, eventual architectural commissions such as the Seagram Building for Mies van der Rohe and the Pan Am Building for Gropius, both in New York, bore this out.

Modernism's own discourse of universalism and internationalism forms a key question here. Internationalism in modern architecture was always, to a certain degree, belabored; architects could see the opportunity afforded by advancing the movement through cohesion. This is represented, for example, by the reluctant agreement with Mies van der Rohe's dictate that the buildings of the 1927 Werkbund-sponsored Weissenhof Settlement be painted white. Likewise, friendships had been formed — between Le Corbusier and Gropius, for example — out of a shared sense of the utility of consolidating interests.

Moreover, nationalism was always a present, if understated, aspect of the so-called International Style; local materials and traditions were subtly incorporated in order to make modernism more palatable to a national audience. Groups such as the Werkbund, backed by the government, were set up specifically to advance Germany's economy, via design, into international markets. Focusing on the interwar, war, and postwar periods, *Objects in Exile* delves beyond the superficial eliding of modernist concerns to upend this narrative of internationalism. It instead seeks to add nuance and layers of complexity to the argument, asserting that often modernism, especially as it came to be defined and practiced in the United States, can be better understood as *transnationalist* in nature, that is, related to the flow of people, ideas, designs, and artworks across borders.

Exiled artworks and objects form the crux of a paradox between the history of specific modern objects and a reduction in the status of the object. What émigrés were able to bring with them would enable them to set up their new lives — Gropius transported models of his architecture as well as all of Lucia Moholy's glass plate negatives of the Bauhaus products and buildings, thereby denying her the use of them, while employing them to establish himself in America. Moholy-Nagy decided to ship, with great effort, his unwieldy *Light Space Modulator*, a work critical to articulating his theories; he also brought the glass negative that allowed him to make photographic reproductions of it (fig. I.4). For years following his emigration, Mies van der Rohe took great pains — paying multiple lawyers in several countries — to maintain his own and the Bauhaus's furniture patents, the rights to which he retained as the school's final director; this gave him much-needed funding during the lean, early years. Objects, and, even more important, protagonists' ownership over them, form a materialist basis for the successful employment and commissions that the émigrés were then able to obtain in their new contexts.

<u>This book is a history of objects' agency — modernism is read via its material output, a history of works that had been hastily packed or carefully shipped.</u> And yet, much could not be taken with them, and these lacunae, too, will form a crucial element of what was to take place upon arrival. A reality of exile is the straightforward fact that while photographs and representations of architecture could be brought along, the actual buildings could not. Likewise, Moholy-Nagy was forced to leave behind many canvasses, which were subsequently destroyed by a caretaker sympathetic to the Nazis. The mechanics of movement, what émigrés chose — or were forced — to leave behind, the things they carried, the representations they brought or subsequently constructed, all have a place in this narrative. Thus *Objects in Exile* points to how a range of conditions created the circumstances for a certain anti-materiality, an anti-objectality, and how form and reproducibility were privileged over specific materials and objects. Albers's shattered crate of glass paintings informed his subsequent artistic acts; Anni Albers's lack of a functional weaving workshop upon her arrival had important implications for the development of her teaching methods; and Breuer's deft reinterpretation of his metal furniture into plywood — all represent a denial of the specificity of material, which brought forth key new works for these exiles (fig. I.5). It is this fundamental tension — between the role of specific objects

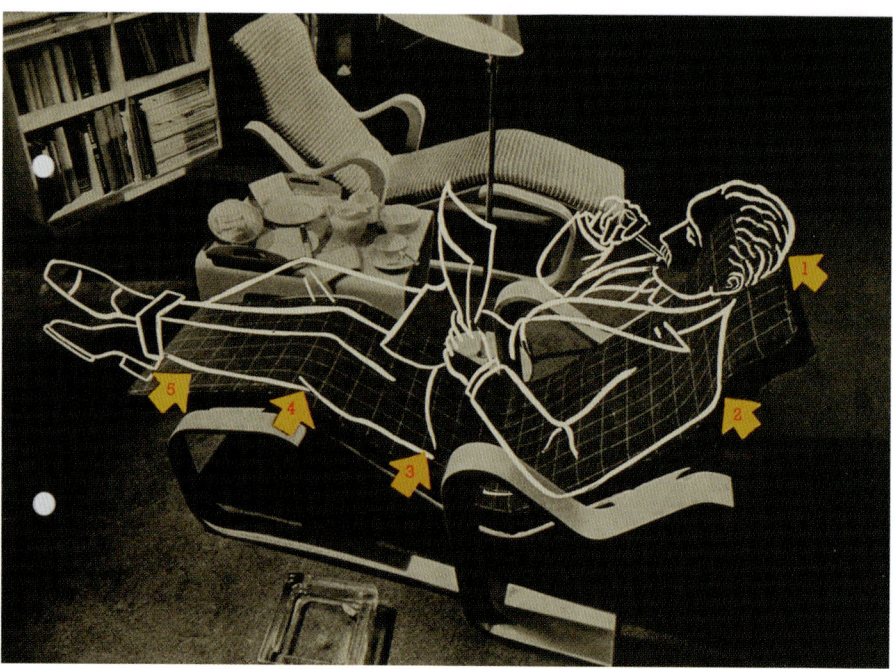

Fig. I.5 Marcel Breuer (chair design), Isokon Long Chair, 1936; as shown in László Moholy-Nagy (graphic design), brochure, *The New Isokon Chair* (detail).

and an anti-materiality — informed by the exigencies of exile, that allows for this book's critical new reading of modernism itself.

This interdisciplinary study reveals the concentrated effort by émigrés to bring modern aesthetics, ideologies, and methods to a new audience, via art, architecture, and exhibitions. To do so, I look afresh at canonical works of the period as well as previously underexamined archival documents, photographs, drawings, artworks, prototypes, and final products. In addition to their makers, this book understands objects themselves as being in exile, and as having agency and meaning within society. In doing so, this study views objects as crucial carriers of meaning, looking to the social life of things to connect them to people. It thus aims to offer a broader historical context for objects' existence, in order to offer, in turn, a nuanced explication and theorization of the social and political conditions of their making and subsequent reception.

The protagonists of this book, although networked with each other, worked in varying media with diverging modernist goals. What unified them, I argue, was not their output, but rather a fundamental belief in modernism's productive social impact. Overall, this transnational study aims to give insight into continuities in design, methods, and materials between the pre- and postwar periods that are often viewed as starkly demarcated. Some of the connecting threads discussed include a wrestling with architecture in Moholy-Nagy's oeuvre and the use of the grid and the unit in Hilberseimer's urban plans and designs for housing, from Berlin to Chicago. Forced into exile by circumstances beyond their control, this book shows how émigré designers, and their objects, necessarily changed unexpectedly to meet the new needs and contexts of a rapidly altering world, using crucial objects and points of interchange to understand modernism anew. Despite having to change course radically, oftentimes the new work builds compellingly on earlier ideas or theories, with stronger resulting outcomes; fresh attention is paid to these arcs of continuity.

While it is generally agreed that this influx of émigrés profoundly shaped the direction of modernism in America, this study situates the locus of change in the very circumstances of exile itself. These conditions include the necessity of substituting certain materials for others, the use of remediation as a means of improved expression, the rationing and standardizing of minimal subsistence needs, issues of assimilation, and, most crucially, changing ideas of materiality and visuality under modernism. The ruptures and breaks that the experience of exile engendered in the work of Josef and Anni Albers, for example, in their move to Black Mountain College in North Carolina from Berlin, impacted the working methods and materials of both artists. Issues of translation are inevitably bound to studies of exile, but this book frames translation not only as a stark, linguistic problem but, moreover, a concrete, material one. It examines the instrumental intermediate years spent in England by several of the protagonists, crucial translations of their texts into English, and how earlier avant-garde designs were converted and adapted to an American context. The book is not teleological in nature; it specifically counters a narrative of the smooth advancement of art and ideas from Europe to the United States in order to productively examine the fissures and schisms that exile placed on art and design. Contingency and the conditions on the ground, as the émigrés experienced them, have an important place in this study, highlighting the productivity of friction and the unexpected events that changed the course of modernism.

European modernism, especially as developed and practiced by artists and architects who had coalesced in Germany by the 1920s and early 1930s, grew out of a complex political, social, and cultural situation and was subsequently received into a very different context in terms of (broadly) unacclimated British and American audiences.[4] Part of the challenge émigrés faced was to explain a complicated set of modernist ideas. This book not only examines the trajectory of artists and designers, and their objects, but also how modernism's theories, as articulated by its protagonists, changed and developed. It asserts that displacement itself irrevocably shaped key concepts of modernism. And yet, *Objects in Exile* is not a recounting of paths and journeys, but rather it gives central agency to the very objects and theoretical formulations that emerged as a result of the contorted trajectory of the twentieth century, allowing for a nuanced reading of modernism's key tropes: materiality, abstraction, surface, and reproduction.

While the approach here is to carefully situate the material in its historical, cultural, and social contexts, this book does not seek to smoothly arrive at a unified notion of postwar modernism; instead, the varying degrees of assimilation and ensuing successes of the figures under examination were a result of the unique emigration circumstances and the varied landing places and paths they followed thereafter. It emphasizes the contingencies of exile that caused the uneven unfolding of modernism's ascent and also seeks to build on recent work on the criticality and logistics of movement.[5] *Objects in Exile* thus resituates modern works produced at a crucial point of historical, cultural, and artistic interchange, allowing for a new and wider understanding of the theorizing and production of modernism in the twentieth century.

The Materiality of Exile

∎ ∎ ∎

The book is organized under three main sections that have been identified as primary conditions of exilic modernity. Each chapter depends on a deep engagement with artworks, objects, and visual and textual archival sources, then synthesized to explicate a set of works through a conceptual analysis of broader period issues. The three overarching modes of inquiry into exilic modernism are organized under the terms "transposition," "contingent conditions," and "remediation."

Transposition

The section on transposition proposes that exile was crucial to what we know as modernism, precisely because of the need to constantly face – and transcend – the materiality of things via the transfer of one material or idea for another in the design and artistic process. Chapter 1, "Architecture's Material Abstraction," traces a long arc across László Moholy-Nagy's investigations into ephemeral surface effects and the materiality of the modern metropolis in order to examine what might be understood as the architectural in Moholy-Nagy's work. It begins with his early 1920s paintings of abstract shapes and the materials of the city streets, which represented a sustained engagement with the architectural possibilities of glass and its role in modern abstraction. From painted planes that simulated glass and metal, to three-dimensional relief works that incorporated these actual materials gathered from the city streets, a continual process of material simulation – and material transfer – took place in his work. In the 1930s, Moholy-Nagy began to paint directly on new, modern materials, beginning with Trolit (an early plastic) and aluminum (fig. I.6). He also took up mechanization and moving form with his metal, glass, and wood *Light Prop for an Electric Stage*. He conducted other artistic experiments in three-dimensional space, which he termed "light architecture," concluding with his late Plexiglas works, the *Space Modulators*. This chapter argues that in Berlin and Chicago alike, crucial components of Moholy-Nagy's modernism were formed by his investigations into the potential of the metropolis's basic components – metal and glass – and by using the city's effects to demonstrate, in differing valences, the materiality of light and the problem of surface. In doing so, it explores the wider period tensions his works mediate – between darkness and light, production and reproduction, concrete form and abstraction, contained space and projected space, movement and architectural stasis.

In his resonant objects, Moholy-Nagy reinstigated three-dimensional form only to dematerialize it into representations of surface and light. These concerns posit a new reading of his engagement with modern architectural space and, simultaneously, its seeming breakdown into abstraction. However, these supposed "abstract" works by Moholy-Nagy are understood anew as the results of his deep investigations into the city's representative value. His transposition of materials, that is, his interchanging and transferring of substances intended for one use into new forms, results in new meanings. Across Moholy-Nagy's oeuvre, the value of modernity is not read for its increasing abstraction but as a

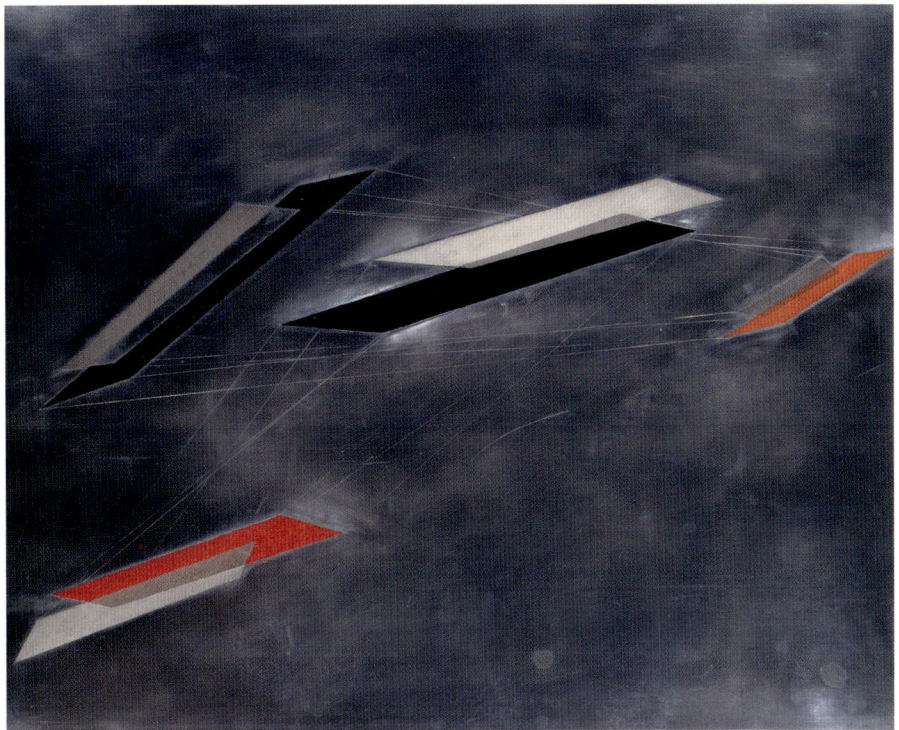

Fig. I.6 László Moholy-Nagy, *Sil 2*, 1933, oil and incised lines on silberit. Solomon R. Guggenheim Museum, New York.

form of communication; contra Marshall Berman (and Marx), not all that is solid melts into air. Moholy-Nagy's abstraction is instead understood in terms of the continued presence of – albeit constantly transubstantiated – materiality, and an engagement with the city and its forms, from Berlin to Chicago. This chapter argues that abstraction was not always abstract and that abstraction can be understood materially, as representative of socially meaningful transpositions.

Chapter 2, "Minimal Dwelling," examines the British company Isokon's employment and housing of Walter Gropius, Marcel Breuer, and László Moholy-Nagy at its Bauhaus-inspired building, the Isokon Flats (also known as Lawn Road Flats) in London. It trains a lens on an important formative period, before members of the trio were selected to lead important institutions in the United States – Harvard's architecture program for Gropius, who brought Breuer with him to the Graduate School of Design, and the newly constituted New Bauhaus in Chicago for Moholy-Nagy. This chapter focuses on these Bauhaus members' time in England in the 1930s, asking how furniture designs and the spaces for which they were intended can be better understood as objects of exile. It examines how exile itself informed design processes – centered on the direct material transposition that gave rise to the objects produced there. This British interlude has been downplayed to date, but as this chapter argues, the London period is crucial for understanding how modernism was translated for an Anglophone audience from the German, via techniques and materials, as well as linguistically.

The chapter also examines Breuer's conversion of his modern metal furniture into plywood versions for Isokon and how Moholy-Nagy's previous work in exhibition design and photography informed his graphic design for the firm. In this same period, Gropius published his first book in English, *The New Architecture and the Bauhaus* (1935, with a striking cover conceived by Moholy-Nagy), introducing the school and modern architecture to an English-speaking audience. Gropius's main project at Isokon was to translate his high-rise architecture, with its scaled-down individual apartments balanced by expansive communal amenities, into an English context. This chapter examines Gropius's engagement with the idea of the "minimal dwelling," an important subject of architectural discourse in the 1930s, first in Germany and shortly thereafter in Britain. In considering the preceding and concurrent debates in architecture surrounding *Existenzminimum* (minimal existence), it argues that through their carefully designed interiors, related to Bauhaus members' exigencies of exile, new notions of an architectural *Gesamtkunstwerk* (total work of art) reemerged as part of the modern movement, albeit in changed form from its turn-of-the-century predecessors. Therein, it uses a critical and multivalent notion of material transposition to show how these designers utilized this period to productive ends, reconverting modern ideas and materials into new designs. Although they would ultimately not find a permanent home in Britain, these activities, especially those tied to processes of material change, would favorably situate these émigrés for their future in America, signaling the way in which modernism might be viewed as a perpetual condition of productive change.

Contingent Conditions

The chapters that focus on contingent conditions look at the changed courses of events resulting from exile and its impact on artworks and design. This section examines how modernism's visual and material objects were disrupted because of the circumstances surrounding departure and new landings, resulting in significant new directions for modernism, including designs for a society and future beyond war. Chapter 3, "Images in Exile," begins with the simple observation that when Bauhaus members fled Germany in the 1930s, what they were able to take with them formed a disproportionate part of their oeuvre thereafter; what was no longer extant was often lost to the footnotes of history. What we now know as "modernism" was often contingent on a given situation, defined by a selection of works removed from their country of origin that was dependent on the events and conditions of exile. This oeuvre could be further built up and expanded once the destination was reached. Objects and works left behind – such as Mies van der Rohe's erasure of his early Berlin oeuvre by purposefully leaving that material in Germany, or by happenstance owing to the haste or mode of departure, such as Moholy-Nagy's early canvasses – could no longer serve to form modernism's core visual and material archive.

This chapter argues that photographs taken by Lucia Moholy of the Bauhaus – its architecture and design objects – played a key role in establishing the school during the short period of its existence, but that these images took on heightened significance in exile, especially during the 1930s and 1940s when the Bauhaus's legacy was being solidified (fig. I.7). In 1933, Lucia Moholy was forced to leave behind her entire collection of original glass negatives when she fled into exile from Berlin. What followed – in which the negatives she thought lost became the core of the visual archive deployed by Walter Gropius in the subsequent narration of the Bauhaus – demonstrates the exigencies of exile,

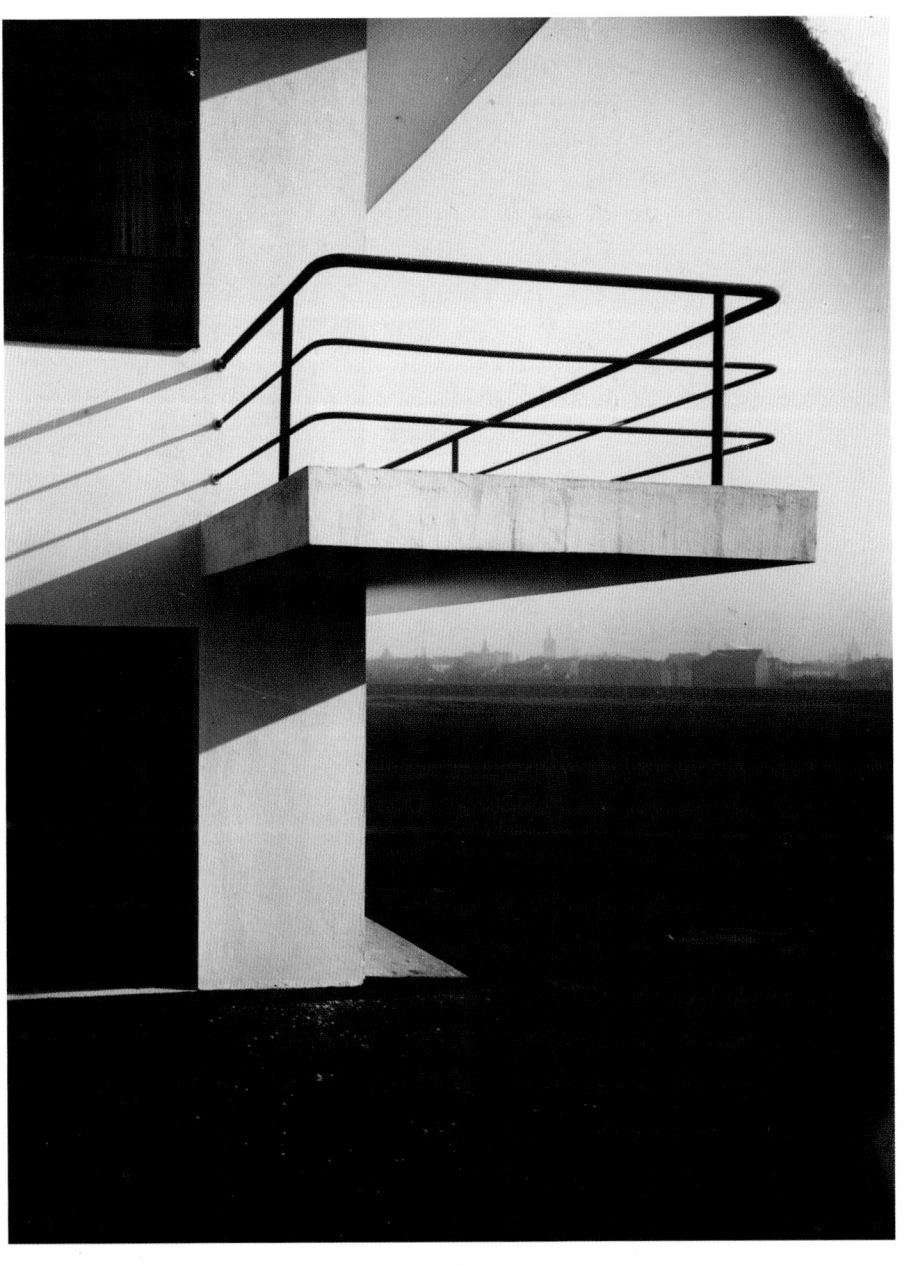

Fig. I.7 Lucia Moholy (photographer), Bauhaus Building by Walter Gropius (architect), detail of studio wing balcony, 1926, gelatin silver print. Harvard Art Museums/Busch-Reisinger Museum, Gift of Walter Gropius, BRGA.20.56.

especially the lacunae created by objects left behind upon emigration, and how photography as a medium became crucial to the later reception of the closed school and what had been produced there. By examining this constellation of circumstances, the chapter illuminates shifts in notions of authorship and in the signification of objects. It argues that processes of meaning-formation for exiled artists of the Bauhaus were closely tied to the power involved in the ability to reproduce photographs, specifically Lucia Moholy's photographs, and for the importance of the photograph as a stand-in for that which was no longer accessible or extant.

"Assimilating Unease," chapter 4, focuses on Moholy-Nagy's leadership of the New Bauhaus in Chicago, the school's designs for the war effort, and how this emergent design simultaneously looked to a society and future beyond war. World War II forced certain émigré protagonists to reposition their design and teaching to more constructive ends and, via these efforts, this chapter argues, provided them an opportunity for more rapid assimilation. While the adaptation of European modern forms and ideas to American circumstances is a crucial element in the story of the Bauhaus's continuation in America, the adeptness with which former members of the Bauhaus plunged into their new American cultural milieu is noteworthy. Gropius, Mies van der Rohe, Moholy-Nagy, and others, almost immediately after emigration, won over government bureaucrats, private businessmen, and other officials to see their projects to fruition, a task that had earlier proven difficult in prewar Europe.

This chapter demonstrates how the contingent conditions of their arrival in the United States gave rise to critical work for the war effort and helped pave the way for the postwar acceptance of modernism in America. In this changed context the New Bauhaus in Chicago, under the leadership of Moholy-Nagy, took up the German Bauhaus's linking of "art and technology" anew through courses on camouflage, rehabilitation therapy, and "visual propaganda in wartime," out of which came practical solutions that were immediately put to use by the US military. Only just established, and chronically underfunded, the fledgling American Bauhaus, unlike its predecessor, was not engaged in speculative projects nor broadly conceived solutions but worked closely with US government agencies to meet material needs brought about by wartime conditions.

During the war years, Moholy-Nagy forged crucial partnerships with various official programs, such as the Office of Civilian Defense, the Works Progress Administration (WPA), the Veterans' Administration, and the Illinois State Department of Public Welfare. Important portions of the Chicago Bauhaus's technical research and the new inventions it generated were then presented to the public in an exhibition titled *War Art*. While demonstrating continuity between wartime efforts and the postwar boom, this chapter illuminates the ways in which these activities directly addressed the contingent conditions in which émigrés found themselves. And it shows how they contributed to the increased acceptance of the kind of modernism that these former Bauhaus members were offering in their new context in America.

"Domesticating the Grid," chapter 5, considers the architect, critic, and urban planner Ludwig Hilberseimer, focusing on his long-standing interest in the relationship between the unit and the grid, and its application for urban infrastructure. In Germany, his 1920s speculative projects for city development envisioned a future based on the unit, from the individual dwelling cell to the skyscraper to an entire urban grid; his accompanying photomontages and drawings had been laid out as an imagined rational grid imposed on Berlin's earlier built environment. But in the years prior his leaving Germany, and once he arrived in America, he focused on the mass-reproducible, L-shaped single-family dwelling. Mies van der Rohe's final years in Germany and work in the United States likewise had examined the possibilities for courtyard houses, but this shortly gave way to an interest in mass-reproducible buildings.

This chapter examines what occurred (the specific, local conditions and their contingencies) when Mies van der Rohe and Hilberseimer emigrated to Chicago and designed for—and upon—the American grid: in Chicago's South Side, at Detroit's Lafayette Park, and elsewhere. Chicago's nineteenth-century design had earlier exerted a profound influence on a whole generation of German architects; in this context, Hilberseimer's arrival in the city provided a unique opportunity, one for which he was ostensibly prepared (fig. I.8). Yet the ideas, buildings, and urban plans that he brought there were also distinctly tied to his unrealized modern visions from Weimar-era Germany. In interwar and postwar Chicago, with its building boom and workers migrating north to toil in its factories, there was an alignment between objects being mass produced and the building-out of the grid into housing units for the producers of those goods. Processes of reproduction can be read in both the objects and the visions for the spaces those objects might be consumed in—ideas that had their roots in important earlier discourses in Germany. In this equation, Hilberseimer's unit and grid emerge as significant theoretical—and material—objects, related to the unit's scalability from room cell to apartment, to block, to planned city. The grid is analyzed as both subject and object, forcing us to think about the non-neutrality and contingency of nominally neutral and universal tools, such as a grid. These considerations bring full circle, in Hilberseimer's case, the contingent conditions and exilic tensions in the dialectical relationship between the place left behind and the new site of habitation.

Remediation

Chapters in the section on remediation examine the materiality of media and changes wrought in a productive transfer between media forms. Chapter 6, "Exigencies of Materializing Vision," argues that in the move from the Bauhaus to Black Mountain, and on to Yale, the diverse practice of Josef Albers can at first glance be seen to shift from the patently material to the purely visual. In a period of the ascendency of Jackson Pollock, Albers's teaching at Yale focused on the drawn line and the interaction of colored papers placed flatly against one another, away from the rich tactility that had constituted the classroom exercises and his own artworks during his German Bauhaus years. Tactile content was replaced by another experience offered up by Albers, a new kind of visuality embodied by the experience of seeing itself. By interacting with the viewer's subjective eye, and distorting perceptions through color, the objects he produced, and those resulting from his pedagogical exercises, called into question

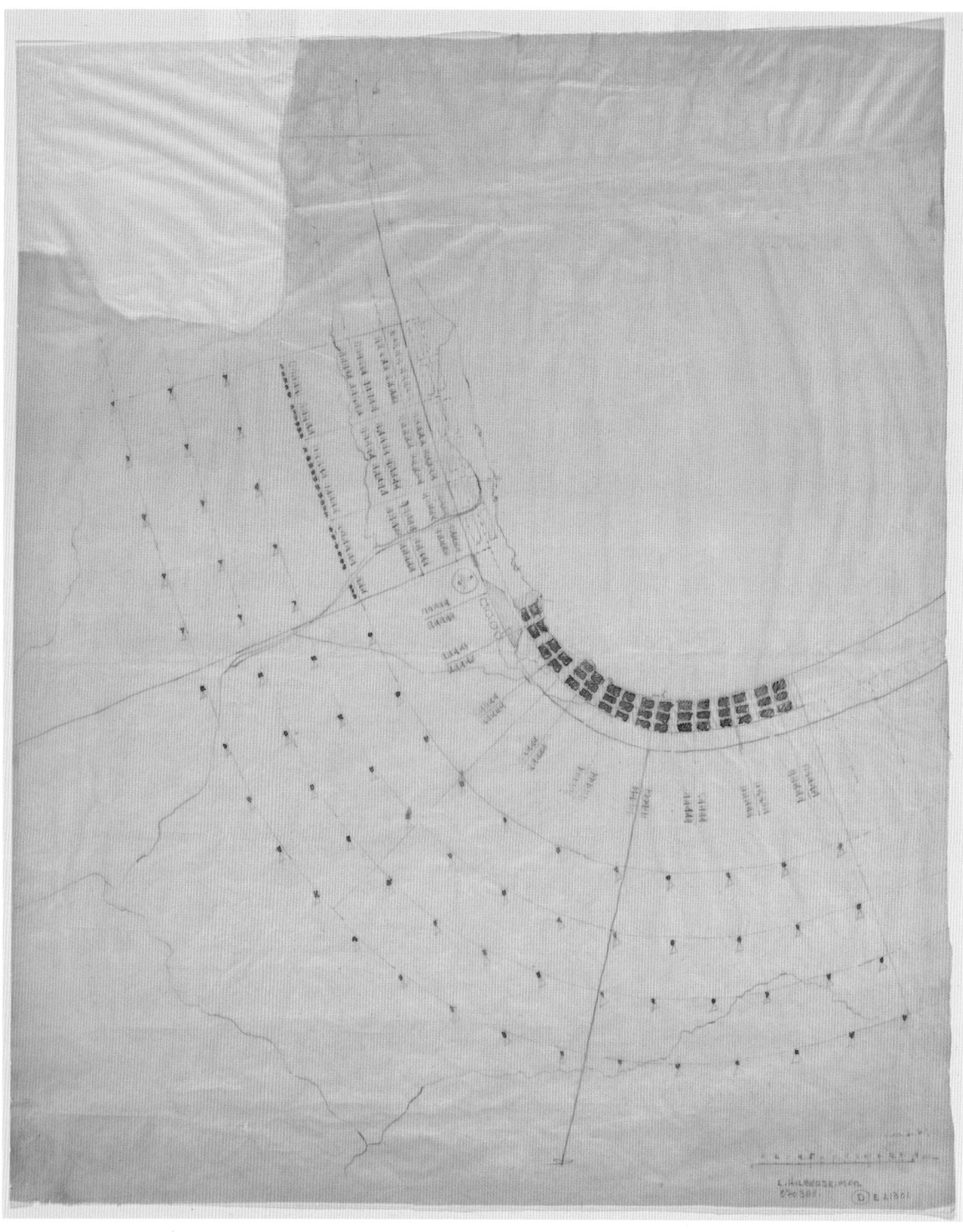

Fig. I.8 Ludwig Hilberseimer, replanning diagram, Chicago, Illinois, 1940, preliminary sketch, ink on paper. Art Institute of Chicago.

the beholder's ability to understand them in stable, objective, and purely visual terms. They almost seem to project their own agency; these precise and circumscribed art objects are read, in this chapter, as contemplations on the material – and subjective – nature of vision itself.

Their instability also makes them contingent objects. During the years in Germany, Albers had been intensely involved with making objects, not only furniture and domestic objects, but also artworks that had a deep materiality and object-ness, as evidenced by the jagged glass shards roughly held together by metal wire in his *Lattice Pictures* (*Gitterbilder*) and in his thick, layered sand-blasted glass works of abstracted factories and urban skyscrapers. In the United States, after the shipment of his glass paintings arrived as shattered fragments, he abruptly changed course – a radical reduction in materiality, form, and subject matter took place, as evidenced in the planar visual surface of the flat panels of his *Homage to the Square* series. These works, painted under the controlled conditions of fluorescent light and using factory-mixed colors, the details of which Albers neatly charted on the paintings' versos, are the flattened summation of an artistic praxis exchanging – remediating – a rich materiality in glass for one of painted surface on Masonite.

Albers's *Homage* panels are examined as whole artifacts, with their carefully controlled, flat surfaces read as an essential, compellingly material component. Albers draws our attention to the surface of things; in doing so, this chapter contends, he calls attention to both surface and thing. In the radically reduced *Homage to the Square* works, conceptions of materiality and visuality are understood as interrelated, with an important role played by subjectivity therein. In moving away from the material toward an emphasis on the visual surface, designed to be, in Albers's terms, an "evocation of vision," the resulting flat surfaces of his works are evaluated afresh to understand surface, even vision, in distinctly material terms. With this examination of the underlying move from the material to the visual in Albers's art practice, from Germany to the United States, this chapter theorizes the varying strands of visuality in his work. However, it argues that the end result of this seemingly visual turn are ultimately remediated evocations of the materiality of the abstract surface itself.

Chapter 7, "Anni Albers's Design Theory and Its Objects," considers Albers's use of materiality toward ends that were both deeply theoretical and object-oriented. As a weaver, materiality was critical to – and at the forefront of – her work, but this chapter looks at the ways in which weaving's materiality was a springboard for other output, especially when brought into dialogue with her theoretical writing on design. Often, unusual materials were used out of necessity during periods of transition in which the Black Mountain College weaving workshop was not available. Albers designed assignments, such as typewriter studies, that aided the students in developing critical design thinking appropriate for weaving, as well as encouraging creativity that expanded the realm of possibility in the medium of weaving. Significant, in this context, are the alternatives she used in conjunction with the teaching and production of weaving – such as typewriter patterning, and samples from nature such as grasses and kernels of corn – each embodying different types of materiality. In her own work, she also made jewelry from hardware store parts and woven room dividers that were architectural in nature, or, as she termed them, "pliable planes." At first blush seemingly at a distant remove from her core output of weaving, these other media are deployed by Albers – in a process of remediation – in order to better express the theoretical stakes of her weaving praxis.

The concluding chapter, "Herbert Bayer's Expanded Vision and the Instrumentalizing of Design," examines Bayer's graphic design and wartime displays to consider the ways in which he used processes of remediation to deploy critical wartime information, from which a groundbreaking, dynamic viewing experience emerged. Tracing an arc from his initial research in Germany to its materialization in the United States, this chapter analyzes his intensified turn toward the social usefulness of art. Bayer was deeply invested in reaching viewers – he experimented with new and visually arresting techniques of display and graphic design as a means of communicating visually in new ways. In Europe, beginning with the German Werkbund's contribution to the 1930 Paris exhibition, Bayer installed large-scale photographs of modern architecture suspended at tilted angles from floor to ceiling, presenting his sweeping vision for a new mode of exhibition display – one that sought to activate the full range of optical angles of the viewer's eye, which he termed "expanded vision." The Paris exhibition catalog's illustration of a large, all-seeing eye placed on a man in a three-piece suit and tie, depicted how this radical exhibition design could alter the very basic act of seeing.

Upon arrival in the United States, Bayer continued to deploy innovative techniques that forged new kinds of connections between viewers and the objects under examination in a series of exhibitions he designed for the Museum of Modern Art, beginning with the 1938 Bauhaus show, followed by the museum's 1942 *Road to Victory* exhibition (in collaboration with the US Office of War Information), and its 1943 *The Arts in Therapy* exhibition (developed with the Red Cross). For these exhibitions, Bayer used large-scale photographs, photomontages, oversize text, floor patterning, ramps, and other structures that framed content in a process of continual remediation that vividly conveyed wartime messages to its audience. His Bauhaus-era graphic design was also deployed for the American war effort, namely, in his posters for the WPA and his contributions to campaigns led by the Container Corporation of America, a paperboard company that supported an international roster of artists who brought striking modern design to the broader public in the form of moving wartime public service messages. These initiatives simultaneously introduced the Bauhaus's typography and graphic design to a widespread US audience. In wartime America, the stakes surrounding this new, dynamic viewing experience were higher than they had been in prewar Europe, because the design was intended to convey critical information or uplift spirits in support of the war effort. This chapter argues that Bayer's designs, especially those related to his "expanded vision" and his other theories of communication – often dependent on processes of remediation – can be understood as emerging out of the unique circumstances of the exilic wartime condition and the imperative of social design in this period.

∎ ∎ ∎

Through architecture, art, photography, graphic design, and exhibition design, this volume examines the various modalities by which the twentieth-century phenomenon of exile impacted modernism's trajectory. Across its chapters, overarching areas of attention train a lens on the use of materials, visuality, questions of surface and depth, new spatial conceptions and bodily experience, and the role of subjectivity therein. It hones in on turning points in the work and discourse of key figures of the modern movement, especially the role of materiality and the meaning of abstraction. In doing so, it brings forth a new framework for understanding this fraught period of modernism. Taken together, the following chapters strive to explicate the complex relationship between the places left behind and the new sites of habitation for these artists and designers, along with the exilic tensions raised. *Objects in Exile* sheds new light on the context in which modernist ideas were received and shows how modernism came to coalesce into a set of cohesive ideas at midcentury.

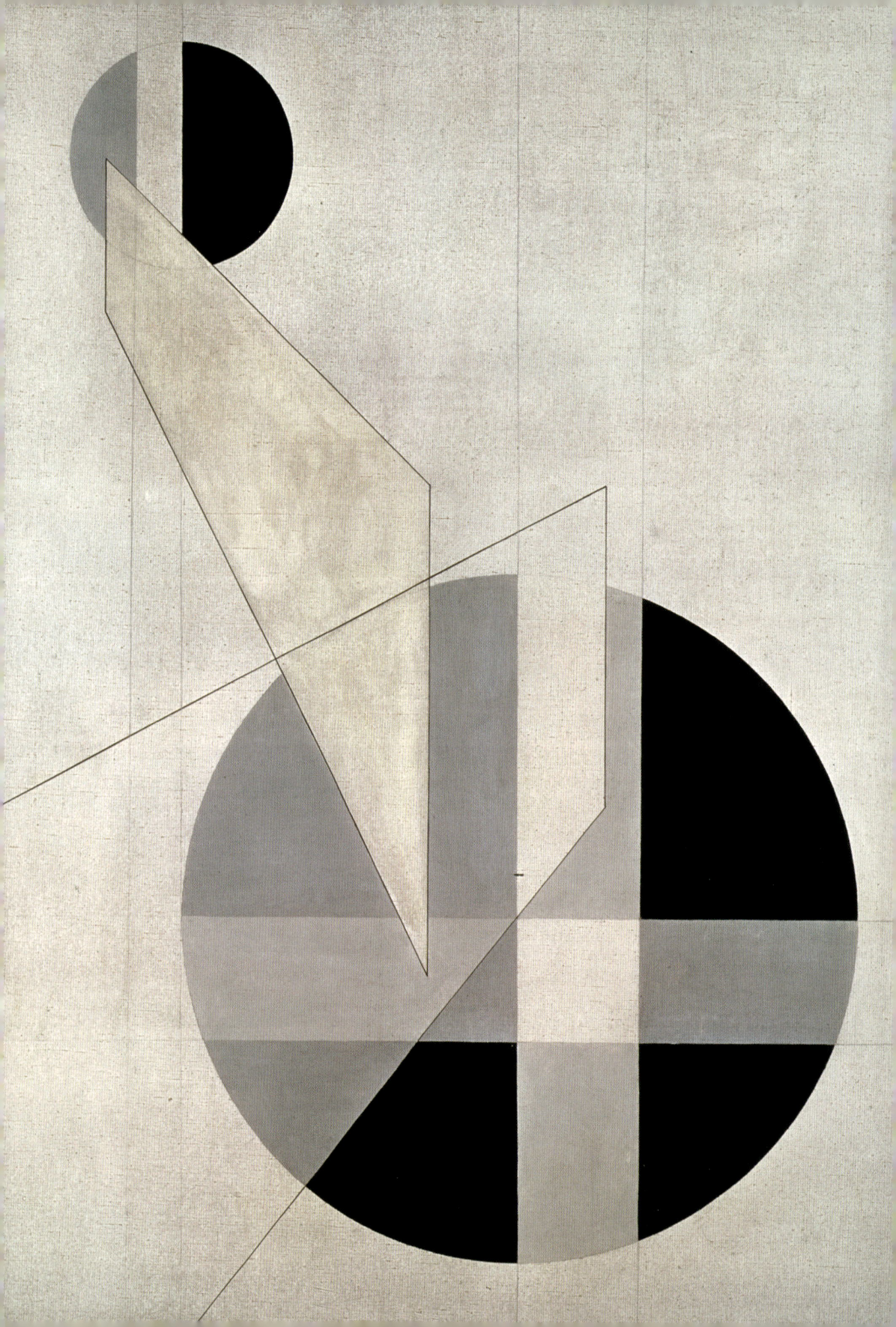

TRANSPOSITION

Chapter 1

Architecture's Material Abstraction

László Moholy-Nagy and the Industrial City

Writing in 1946, László Moholy-Nagy might as well have been reflecting back on the entire industrial history of his adopted city, Chicago: "The metamorphosis of the world through mass production, mass distribution, and mass communication forced man to think in economic terms and organize his business affairs on a global scale. . . . He absorbed the technological and economic aspects of the industrial revolution with surprising speed but without an understanding of their manifold implications."[1] He continues, "Creative abilities, concentrated on limited problems, produced stunning results, expanding the boundaries of the capitalist economy. The wheels of industry turned fast."[2]

When the newly emigrated Moholy-Nagy encountered Chicago's exhilarating built environment and its exceptional space of commerce—with its framework for the production, distribution, and movement of vast quantities of goods—he had already been evoking, from his earliest days in 1920s Berlin, the rationalization of industry for art. In Chicago, Moholy-Nagy reinstigated the primacy of the industrial materiality of the city and its representations, as surface and as light.[3] Across media and an extraordinarily varied artistic output, these ideas had absorbed him in Berlin—where he arrived in February 1920 and which represents his first city of extended immigration—and continued at the Bauhaus in two locations (Weimar and Dessau), during his return to Berlin, in London, and then in Chicago, where he arrived in 1937. This chapter traces a long arc across Moholy-Nagy's protracted investigations and analysis of the materials, the ephemeral surface effects, and conceptions of space in the urban environment, from 1920s Berlin to 1940s Chicago. Its aim is to consider afresh Moholy-Nagy's artistic engagement with the modern metropolis in order to argue for what might be understood as the *architectural* in his work.[4]

It will do so, however, by examining Moholy-Nagy's sustained engagement with urban experience via his perpetual process of transposition, in which he works in one media and then transfers the same concepts into another media. In these terms, abstracted forms of the city in pigment on canvas were supplanted by industrial materials, and, eventually, projected light. Likewise, his photographs, theater sets, and pedagogical exercises in a range of materials, each, in turn, took up these concepts. Whereas the major locational moves by other artists and architects resulted in deep ruptures in their practice, unlocking new directions and uncertainties in their oeuvres, Moholy-Nagy presents solid consistency in the artistic questions he posed to his urban environments, from 1920s Berlin to postwar Chicago. His is a story of continuity, a cohesive underlying quest across varied materiality. It forms a solid base against which subsequent chapters will throw into relief the nature of rupture, of division, of works separated from their makers, of concepts that greatly shift as they travel from Europe to the United States. From Berlin to Chicago, the overarching theoretical questions Moholy-Nagy posed regarding relationships within the city remained constant. What changed were his modes of representing a diversity of urban impressions and his materials, from solid industrial materiality to ephemeral surface effects, which gave rise to changes in artistic form—these media were transposed from one to another as he traveled through an astonishing range of materials, as he simultaneously changed location—Berlin, Weimar, Dessau, Berlin once more, Amsterdam, London, and Chicago—in a peripatetic search for a stable landing place. Across these borders, he brought a material abstraction of modern architecture.

From Urban Streets to Works of Art: Industrial Materiality and Its Effects

How do you make meaning of the experience of the early-twentieth-century metropolis, especially 1920s Berlin, as a new arrival? How might one capture, in appropriately modern ways, the fragmentary experience of its light and materiality or convey its exhilarating pace? Moholy-Nagy's paintings from his earliest days in Berlin represent a deeply embodied urban experience, its attendant architecture, and its visual ramifications. Crucial components of Moholy-Nagy's modernism were formed, I argue, by his investigations into the potential of the metropolis's basic components – metal and glass – and demonstrated, in differing valences, the materiality of light and the problem of surface.

The role of architecture and its material effects in the industrial city were key organizers of Moholy-Nagy's artistic forays, both in the eye-opening initial years in vibrant, modern Berlin (preceded by his studies in bustling Budapest and short stay in Vienna) and throughout his career, closing in Chicago. Unlike many of his Bauhaus peers such as Georg Muche, Oskar Schlemmer, or Josef Albers, almost without exception the artistic polymath Moholy-Nagy never expanded his multivalent art practice directly into architecture, architectural drawings, interior design, or even large-scale architectural elements. And yet, his work must be understood as distinctly *architectural*, and that architecture itself was an organizing framework for him. Although he does not make architecture per se, this chapter argues that Moholy-Nagy directly co-opts architecture, and its agency, for modernism. His art and theory share with architecture crucial aspects, such as inquiries into varying materials' space-forming qualities, as well as their effects of transparency, surface, and light. As art historian James Merle Thomas perceptively writes, Moholy-Nagy "envisioned systemic, habitable space at the cusp of sculpture, architecture, and urban design by navigating what might best be understood as the *abstraction of space*, a concept that simultaneously encompasses, on the one hand, a sense of artistic or 'designed' abstract composition, and on the other, a representational logic drawing upon (or even conjuring) a more scientific or 'cosmic' sense of outer space as found in the artist's formal abstract paintings."[5]

These phenomena were noted by Moholy-Nagy's peers. Ernő Kállai, writing in 1924, described Moholy-Nagy's art of the period as being "nurtured by the regulated and controlled current of motion of huge metropolises, the dynamism of Paris, Berlin, New York and London – whirling, rushing, uncontrollably expanding and multiplying."[6] Moholy-Nagy would point out, "The same driving force that incessantly pounds innovations into the consciousness of every newspaper reader, every telephone user, every radio listener, every ordinary consumer, is also behind modern art.... We are witnessing today the pressure of a tremendous increase in intellectual and technological development which is transposed into the first groping attempts at sublimation through contemporary means of form and expression."[7] And as Sigfried Giedion recalled, 1920s Berlin "was a focus of artistic activity ... for those imbued with the desire to enlarge the field

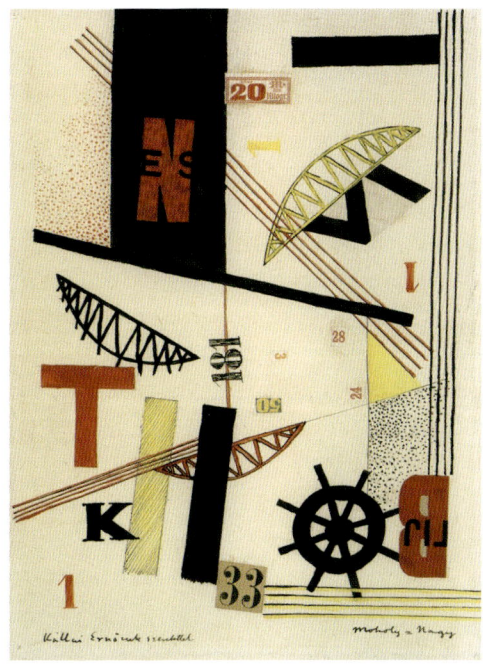

Fig. 1.1 László Moholy-Nagy, *Bridges 1 K 33*, 1920, gouache and collage on paper.

of our optical perceptions. . . . One of the most important studios in which these people were continually meeting, was that of Moholy-Nagy. The emotive values latent in modern industry and in the realities of modern life in general," Giedion felt, impacted Moholy-Nagy more, given his rural roots, such that "a steel bridge, an airplane hangar, or the mechanical equipment of a modern factory is, as a rule, far more stirring to the imagination of those who do not see such things every day of their lives."[8] *Bridges 1 K 33*, a 1920 work in gouache and collage on paper by Moholy-Nagy, illustrates the manner in which he brings together the elements of the city that these commentators had noted in his work (fig. 1.1). A dynamic composition of bridges, factory elements such as a cog wheel, and parallel lines reminiscent of tension wires, it revels – like the many other similar works he produced in this period – in the technical forces and mechanisms of the modern city. With its letters and numbers scattered across the page, sometimes placed against a black form, as if in nighttime illumination, the work also alludes to the modern advertising that so distinguished Berlin, and, more generally, to the cacophony of the urban experience.

Moholy-Nagy's prints of the early 1920s, made during his earliest days in Berlin, likewise press into paper the striking dominant forms of the modern city, their relationships to one another emboldened by dramatic light and shadow engendered by the printing process. A print from this period, *Two Circles with Beam* (ca. 1922–23), appears abstract in nature; it is composed of circles bisected by long rectangles, but its title underscores its key architectural components. Other similar prints in this series repeat the same elements. Early paintings, abstractions of Berlin's urban architectural relationships, also directly communicate their content with titles such as *Architektur 1* (1922) and *Architecture (Eccentric Construction)* (ca. 1921). The pared-down geometric shapes in these paintings are reminiscent of industrial building silhouettes, crossed by parallel streets or tracks, and connected by rounded arches suggesting railroad

Architecture's Material Abstraction

bridges. His use of metallic paint references Berlin's modern surfaces and the interaction of metal machine parts and light, or perhaps tall buildings or smokestacks. Other works from this period, prints and paintings alike, feature similarly suggestive urban forms, underscored by titles that reference glass architecture, such as the print *Untitled (Glass Architecture Series)*, the cover for *MA* (*Today*) magazine, and the painting *Glass Architecture III*, all from the period 1921–22 (fig. 1.2). These works do not use metallic materials but rather rely on concentrated pigment or black-and-white lines, their solid shapes suggesting the form of imaginary tall buildings, factories, and other modern structures. Critic Ernő Kállai, writing in 1921 about Moholy-Nagy's early painting, aptly describes these works: "The projection of the tremendous diagonal of a factory chimney leaning left, the leaning, resting forces, forces pressing tensed into [the] vertical, are gathered into a compact architecture of form. Details of bridges and architectural structures, having lost all their utilitarian references and practical functions, freely elevate themselves into a self-willed order, an existence meaningful in itself."[9] The result is "the exultation over a million possibilities of forms and motion which only the metropolis and modern technology can create."[10]

Taken together, these artworks are highly influenced by modern architecture and the urban experience of Berlin. But Moholy-Nagy also provocatively suggested that the compositions of these architectonic forms and materials, could, in turn, double back and influence the built environment. In his book *Malerei, Fotografie, Film* (*Painting, Photography, Film*, 1925, second edition 1927), in a section headed "Easel Painting, Architecture and 'Gesamtkunstwerk,'" Moholy-Nagy proposes, first, that the composition of artworks derives from architectural elements, "on the basis of a theory of composition which says that a work of art should be created solely out of means proper to itself and forces proper to itself; the next step would be an architectonic composition arising as a synthesis out of the functional elements proper to architecture." The resulting work could then suggest the final architectural scheme; he states, "Such composition would make it possible to obtain the desired color-scheme of the rooms and building complexes . . . since functional use of the building material: concrete, steel, nickel, artificial materials, etc., can unequivocally provide the color-scheme of the room and of the whole architecture."[11]

Writing Architecture: Capitalism and the Industrial City

The modern architecture of this period was organized around the materials and capitalistic enterprises of industry. Significant, for Moholy-Nagy, especially expressed in his writings, were architecture's concomitant economic and political relations and ramifications. In an early 1922 essay, "On the Problem of New Content and New Form," he says, "slowly we are moving towards architecture" and our task is to "clarify what is requisite for giving birth to it (in politics, economics, education, the medical and natural sciences) as well as for consciously shaping the physical components of construction (matter, space, form, color)."[12] His interest in the architectural and its tropes, as a means by which to bring his diverse practice into cohesion, was noted by his peers. Period critic Ernő Kállai, writing in 1924, cited Moholy-Nagy's use of color and industrial materiality—

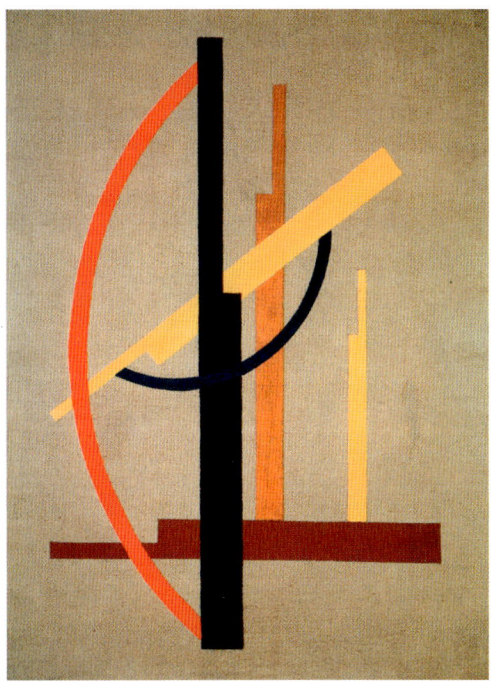

Fig. 1.2 László Moholy-Nagy, *Glass Architecture III*, 1921–22.

iron, glass, and nickel – as the means by which he "succeeded in organizing a comprehensive and animated reality from geometric forms. Thus, *with architecture* he established such a formal and structural unity, which even without any ornaments is a vital creation beyond its practical purpose – and simultaneously is precise, economical, and also true to the material."[13]

Beyond the city's architecture as directly experienced by Moholy-Nagy, his early publications, numerous articles as well as books, illustrate his familiarity with modern architecture and its industrial sources. He and coauthor Lajos Kassák, in their 1922 *Buch neuer Künstler* (*Book of New Artists*), included photographs of factories, grain silos, and bridges, preceding Le Corbusier's canonical 1923 book, *Toward a New Architecture*, illustrating how conversant Moholy-Nagy was with modern architectural tropes.[14] Likewise, in all of Moholy-Nagy's single-authored books – *Painting, Photography, Film*, (1925), *Von Material zu Architektur* (1929, *From Material to Architecture*), *The New Vision* (1938), and *Vision in Motion* (1947) – modern architecture is richly illustrated and discussed.[15]

His first book, *Painting, Photography, Film*, published as part of the Bauhaus book series, concludes with *Dynamik der Gross-Stadt* (*Dynamic of the Metropolis*) a visual film script developed in 1921–22, which he hoped to bring to fruition with his friend Carl Koch.[16] Consisting of an activated typographical layout interspersed with photographic images of modern metropolitan spaces and their constitutive elements (communication towers, factory chimneys, illuminated streets at night) as well as its urban protagonists (showgirls, circus performers, a marching military parade, boxers, and other athletes), it recreates the pace and tempo of Berlin as Moholy-Nagy experienced it.[17] The words and phrases that constitute the script likewise reflect the contemporary city's activities: a "crane in motion . . . hoisting bricks," a "car dashing," "shunting yard sidings," "scrap is converted into factory work," an airplane, and a "shot of a train taken from a

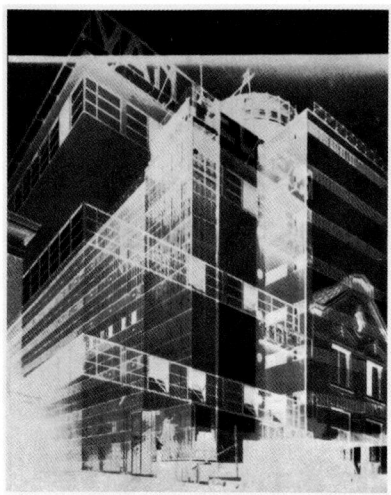 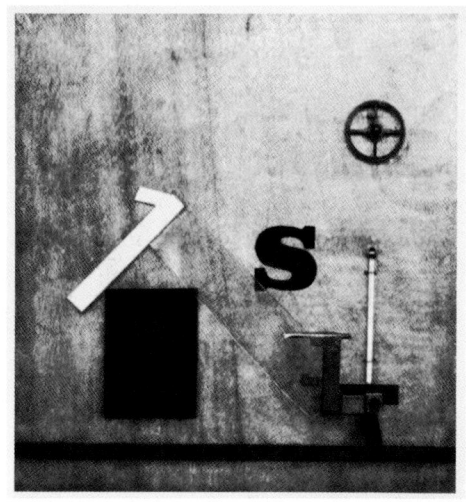

Fig. 1.3 László Moholy-Nagy, *Von Material zu Architektur*, 1929, image captioned "Architecture," page 236. Photograph by Jan Kamman.

Fig. 1.4 László Moholy-Nagy, *Relief S*, 1920.

bridge" and "from the trench" between the rails below. Particular attention is paid to glass and transparency, with references to a "glass lift in a warehouse," a "glass telephone box with man telephoning," and instructions for a "shot of the ground floor through the glass panes." The quality of urban light is also scripted – "flickering," "darkness," "light reflected in the water" – and its light-giving objects specified: an "arc-lamp," "fireworks," "electric signs with luminous writing which vanishes and reappears."

From Material to Architecture, another volume within the Bauhaus book series, traces Moholy-Nagy's pedagogical theory, paying particular attention to issues of materiality. The book then moves to a discussion of volume, predominantly sculpture, before concluding with an important, well-illustrated section on space ("Raum," expansively defined by Moholy-Nagy, who includes a list of forty-two types of space) and architecture. Moholy-Nagy includes Charles Sheeler's striking image of the Ford Motor Company's factory complex, part of a series that had been made by Sheeler just prior to the publication of the book. With its dynamic crisscrossed conveyors, water towers, and bevy of looming smokestacks in the background, the industrial forms of Sheeler's photograph find correspondence in Moholy-Nagy's paintings. The book's last caption reads: "Architecture: from two superimposed photos (negatives) the illusion of spatial penetration emerges, as the next generation may yet experience it – as glass architecture – in reality."[18] It is placed under a double negative image of the modern Van Nelle factory in Rotterdam and a traditional nineteenth-century building (fig. 1.3). Moholy-Nagy's artistic forays directly correlate with the architecture of modernism, the optical creation of space, transparency, and more.

Concurrent with his prints and paintings of architecture, Moholy-Nagy began a series of relief works that brought urban industrial materials directly into his art (fig. 1.4). Rather than suggestive skylines in paint or ink, the *Reliefs* more concretely allowed him to showcase his artistic conception of "glass architecture" materially, for example, by incorporating glass and metal fragments in the works. Moholy-Nagy best explains the creative influence of Berlin on the conceptual trajectory of their formation:

I went to Berlin. Many of my paintings of that period show the influence of the industrial "landscape" of Berlin. They were not projections of reality rendered with photographic eyes, but rather new structures, built up as my own version of machine technology, reassembled from the dismantled parts. Soon these dismantled parts appeared in my *montage* pictures.

On my walks I found scrap machine parts, screws, bolts, mechanical devices. I fastened, glued and nailed them on wooden boards, combined with drawings and painting. It seemed to me that in this way I could produce real spatial articulation, frontally and in profile.... I planned three-dimensional assemblages, constructions, executed in glass and metal. Flooded with light, I thought they would bring to the fore the most powerful color harmonies. In trying to sketch this type of "glass architecture," I hit upon the idea of transparency. This problem has occupied me for a long time.[19]

These urban fragments of glass, metal, wheels with ball bearings, and single letters (alluding to commercial advertising), which gave each work its title, were composed in dynamic groupings, at points connecting diagonally or at right angles, in other places set off from each other. Moholy-Nagy, in these works, was undoubtedly influenced by Berlin Dadaists who were creating and exhibiting assemblage works in this period, and especially Kurt Schwitters, with whom he shared a studio in the winter of 1922–23.[20] In addition to the urban materiality they engendered, Moholy-Nagy saw these works as a means by which light and depth could interact as surface and in abstract space, foregrounding his later light space modulators. *Relief S*, for example, he explains in *From Material to Architecture*, was made out of various materials to exploit height and depth as a means of "achieving light and shadow effects," such as the multiple shadows projected onto its base that were cast from the glass strip protruding out by several centimeters, secured by metal rods.[21] Moholy-Nagy's artistic goals were lauded by his peers. As one critic noted in the period, he "arrived in a logical manner at the idea that industrial materials should be integrated into the creative process and be made into forms. It is wonderful how he managed to elevate to such a degree of beauty and intensity the material-sensory qualities of iron, glass, wood and nickel by the various combinations of these materials."[22] As designer Jan Tschichold pointed out in 1925, more generally, "The new art was forced through its choice of material (steel, plaster, glass, etc.) to adopt an equally mechanical technique, similar to Industrial technique. The new art does not create pictures, but rather objects, material objects."[23]

If paintings such as *Architecture (Eccentric Construction)* or the *Glass Architecture* series are Moholy-Nagy's own suggestive collection of disparate urban shapes rendered in flat geometries painted (including with metallic paints) onto the canvas, composed in relation to each other to suggest an abstracted cityscape as a whole, then the *Reliefs* series addresses the urban industrial materiality in a wholly different manner (see figs. 1.2, 1.4).[24] The *Reliefs*, composed of found elements affixed to a substrate, bring together fragments of the city into material dialogue with each other. Although approaching the industrial

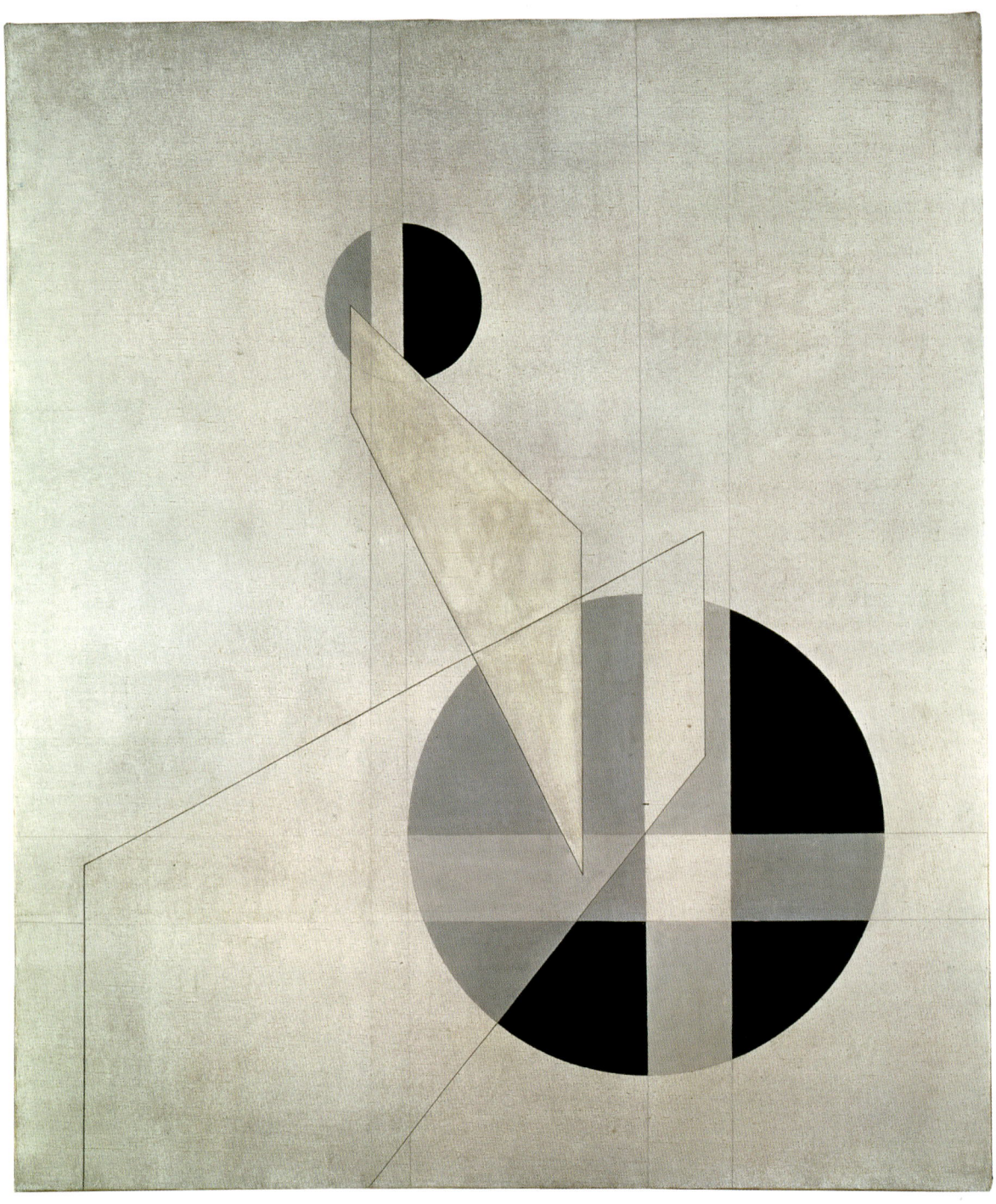

Fig. 1.5 László Moholy-Nagy, *A XX*, 1924. Musée National d'Art Moderne / Centre de Création Industrielle, Centre Pompidou, Paris.

materiality of the city from two directions, both categories of works arrive at the same place: representations of the urban as ephemeral surface, as a modulator of light, or through glass (real or implied) as a means to express transparency. And these qualities of (urban, architectural) ephemerality and transparency were consistently rendered through a conscious attention to (urban, industrial) materiality. This was recognized and acknowledged in the period. For example, the architect and critic Ludwig Hilberseimer wrote in 1922 about Moholy-Nagy: "He attempts to synthetically form both the industrialism and what is impersonal and collective in our technological civilization. . . . [He] wields his artistic means with ascetic transparency, leaving them to completely persist in their materiality."[25] A persistence of materiality in the face of a life-long quest to deeply engage light and transparency—this sums up Moholy-Nagy's ongoing artistic investigations. He enacts these inquiries into artistic production over and over, their essential ideas transubstantiated from material or object to surface, to paper and canvas, to relief and sculpture, to film and photography.

Paintings: Layered Transparency and the Spatial Relationships of the City

Moholy-Nagy's interests in the effects of light, transparency, surface planes, and the creation of space translated into his compositions and painting techniques of the same period.[26] Wandering the streets of Berlin, Moholy-Nagy took in the city's built forms and its industrial force, purposefully abstracting out the projective, spatial relationships of metropolitan architecture. In the resulting finely layered paintings, such as *A IX* (1923) or *A XX* (1924), solid geometric forms intersect with overlapping, abstract planes of varying simulated transparency, floating in a groundless space (fig. 1.5). His results were important enough to warrant an entry in Ise Gropius's diary, who took pains to explain his method: "Moholy is in the best of spirits and has been unbelievably productive. His paintings, for which he has found a whole new production technique, now have their own original style; he works in multiple layers, each separated by a transparent material, one above the other. The finished picture makes a perfectly precise, clear impact."[27] As Moholy-Nagy himself explains about his 1924 painting *A II* (*Construction A II*), but which could describe many of his paintings from the early 1920s, "Transparency is used here as a new medium of spatial relationship."[28] "One dominating factor in all these paintings, although they are so different, is that there is no horizon line," noted Sibyl Moholy-Nagy. "All of these paintings, no matter what the material, are floating in space. To him this idea of perspective and the horizon line was finished. Man now was capable of projecting himself into a space that was no longer limited."[29]

It is this relationship—the unique spatial forms created through representations of transparency in Moholy-Nagy's paintings, and in the use of large expanses of glass against the solid elements of urban architecture (built and speculative, lit and unlit)—which captures the experience of dematerialization in the face of the shifting surfaces of hard urban materials. This is what makes these paintings, and similar works on paper, so architectural and so strikingly modern. The painting *K VII* (1922), the "K" of the title standing, aptly,

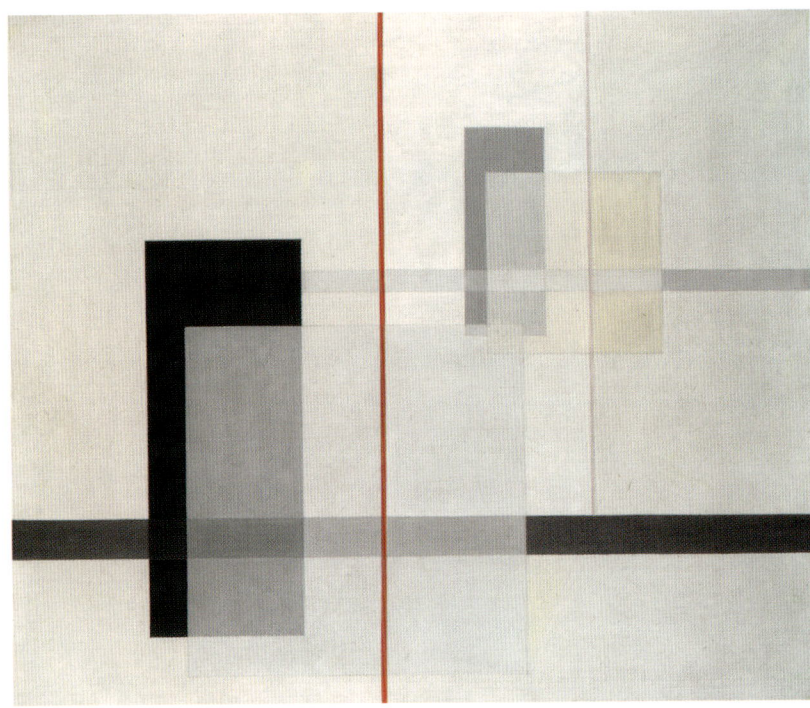

Fig. 1.6 *Left*, László Moholy-Nagy, *K VII*, 1922, oil and graphite on canvas. Tate, London. *Right*, Martin Höhlig (photographer), BVG-Wartehalle (waiting room, Berlin urban transit), ca. 1929, Berlin.

for *Konstruktion* (construction) depicts solid and luminous layered rectangles—some glowing a gentle yellow, others shades of white and gray—reminiscent of structural beams, doorways, and plate glass windows, or other architectonic elements, especially the illuminated nocturnal experience of the modern city as captured in nighttime photographs featuring luminous shop windows, kiosks, and the waiting rooms of the transit system (fig. 1.6).[30] *K VII*'s elements are duplicated and appear to be receding in space, suggesting illuminated interior depth, or perhaps the smaller and lighter elements represent subtle reflections on glass panes. From the upper right corner, insinuating a light source, projecting rays shine downward in delicate, barely perceptible pencil lines. Sibyl Moholy-Nagy described this painting as "most characteristic for the period in the artist's development when he translated his research into pictorial non-perspective space from paper collages on the canvas. He refers in one of his later articles to the problem of 'luminous layers rather than dense planes of vision.'"[31] And Moholy-Nagy is setting this ephemerality into dialectical tension with representations of form. This was noted by period critics. Ernő Kállai, writing in 1924, described Moholy-Nagy's works as confronting one with

> modern, technically-economically and scientifically-intellectually motivated objectivity.... However, Moholy-Nagy freed himself even of those elements of objective structure.... Moholy-Nagy experiences the intellectually governed consciousness and its domain extending over technology, transport, industrial and public health organization, city-planning and the domination over Nature as a world of infinite possibilities leading to newer and newer miracles. Because of this, his forms are floating and finely articulated, the layers of colors are transparent and the structure of the picture is gradually relieved of

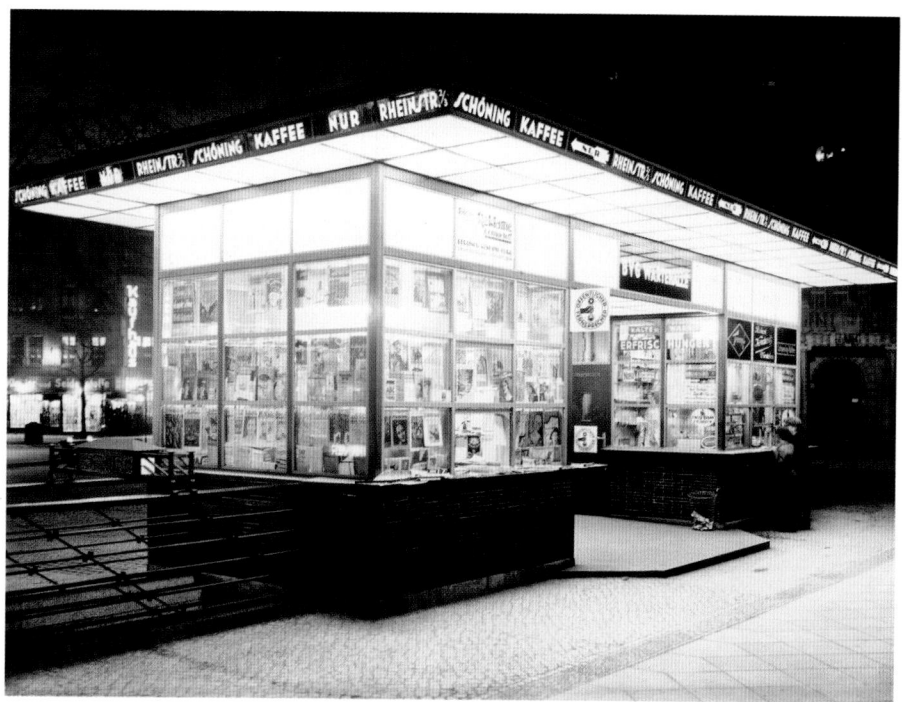

all burdens. There was a period for Moholy-Nagy when his works were imbued with the experience of statics of architectural severity. These forms were only partly fixed in concrete expansion. Yet they appeared still too heavy for the artist. . . . While in the earlier works one sensed still a certain pathos of the upward thrust and the stability of the kind of equilibrium we are accustomed to on earth, his latest pictures convey a sense of unrestrained floating. . . . The effect of dematerialized tension is increased by the elongated rods, the barely perceptible lines and the delicately applied light colors. Nevertheless, a structure of complete and clearly definable forms is organized here within the picture.[32]

The paintings from this period show these interactions of form and light and surface, suspended in space. Moholy-Nagy would clarify his objectives in this way, setting the path for his later investigations: "I became interested in painting-with-light, not on the surface of canvas, but directly in space. . . . I painted as if colored light was projected on a screen, and other colored lights superimposed over it. I thought this effect could be enhanced by placing translucent screens of different shapes, one behind the other, and projecting the colored lights over each unit. Although at the time I was without the necessary skill and means, this idea was responsible, with some changes, for my later experiments with stage sets and with molded transparent plastics."[33] Projected light—whether represented in two-dimensional artworks or later, with his *Light-Space Modulator*, a sculptural machine that beamed light outward as it was set in mechanical motion—was put into almost ineffable space.[34]

And yet that undefined space was urban, suggestive of the city's lights and their projective forms. Several paintings feature circles and converging lines

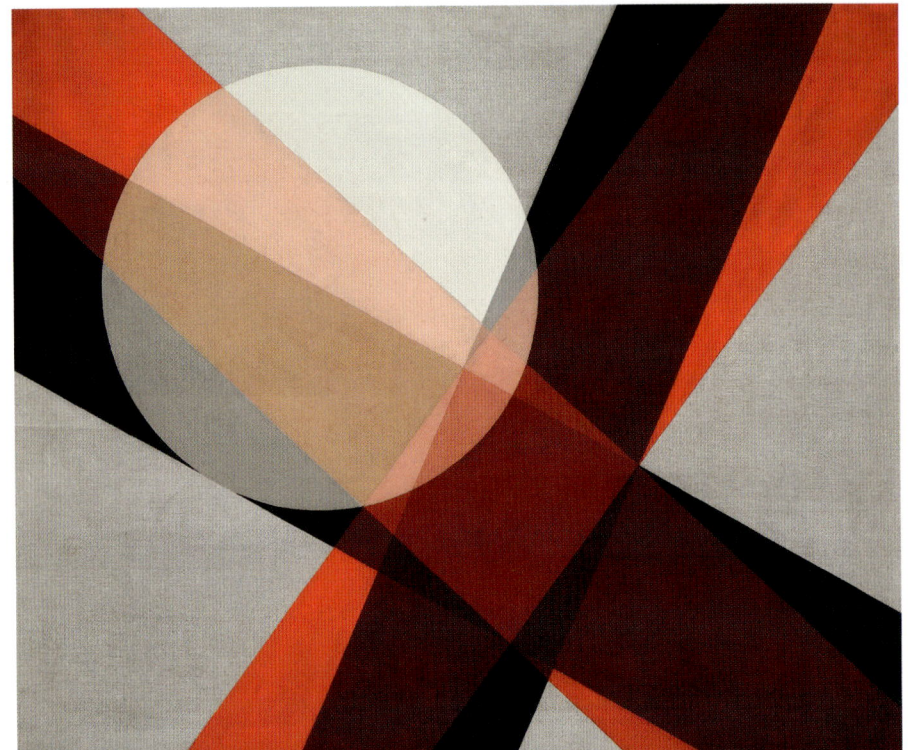

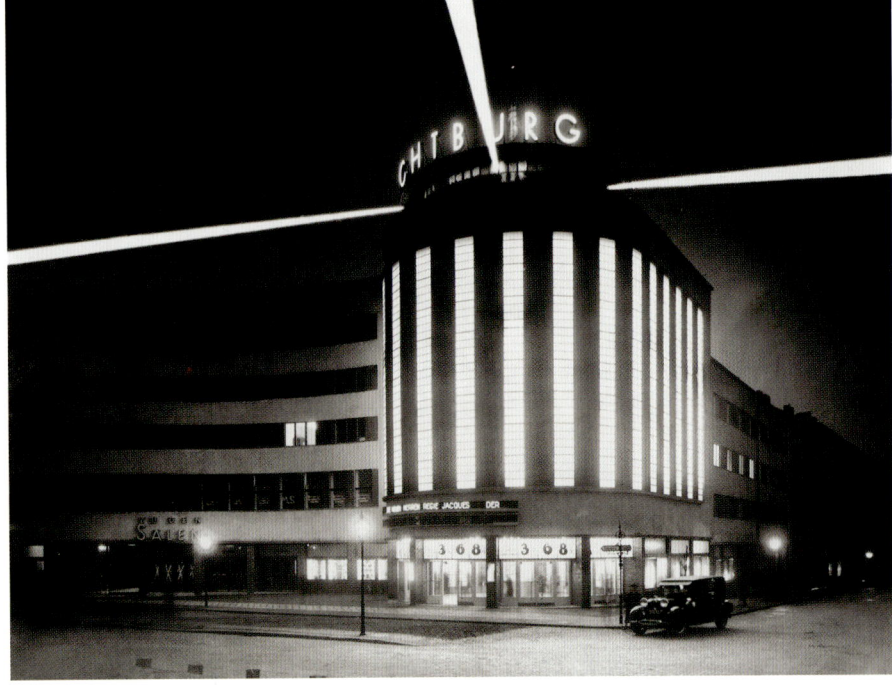

Fig. 1.7 *Top*, László Moholy-Nagy, *A 19*, 1927, oil on canvas. Collection Hattula Moholy-Nagy. *Bottom*, Martin Höhlig (photographer), Lichtburg Kino (Lichtburg movie theater), Rudolf Fränkel, architect, ca. 1929, Berlin.

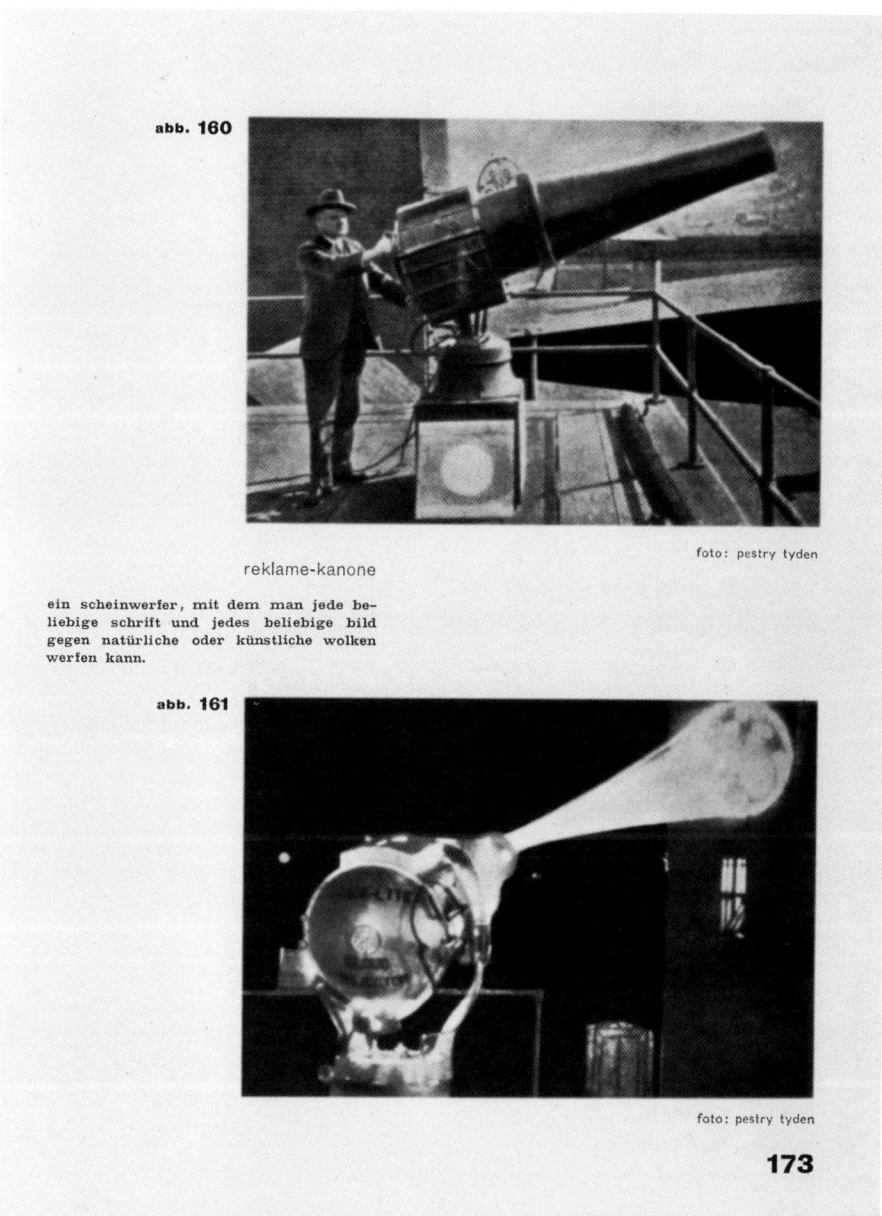

suggestive of projecting light beams, such as *Z II* (1925), *AXL II* (1927), and *A 19* (1927). *A 19*, particularly, is evocative of the moving, crossing light beams that in 1920s Berlin were regularly projected into the night sky as advertising or on celebratory occasions, such as for a film premier or the opening of a new commercial building (fig. 1.7). In *From Material to Architecture*, Moholy-Nagy published images of the machines that beamed advertising into the night sky, noting that the machines allowed for any desired image or lettering to be projected out, and that the size of the letters could be up to fifty meters high (fig. 1.8).[35] Works such as *Construction* (1922, oil and graphite on panel), with its forms suggestive of beams of light illuminated upward against a black background, appears to illustrate one example of this projection of light (fig. 1.9). *Die Lichter der Stadt* (*City Lights*), a photocollage from 1926 (although possibly made in 1927–28),

Fig. 1.8 Night advertising projectors, as published in László Moholy-Nagy, *Von Material zu Architektur*, 1929, page 173.

Architecture's Material Abstraction 33

places diminutive figures at the top of a similar construction (fig. 1.10). Here the transparent forms are crossed at right angles, suggestive of tall glass panes or beams of light – the title, *City Lights,* could equally refer to urban projective light beams or the glass panes of the illuminated tall buildings of the city.[36]

Resonating with both the solid forms and transparent geometries evocative of panes of glass in the painting *K VII*, as well as the projective geometry suggested by *City Lights*, is Moholy-Nagy's 1925 photomontage *Human Mechanics (Variety)*, which layers on dynamic figures: leaping and hanging among architectonic elements (fig. 1.11). Here, ideas of space and transparency have been transubstantiated from paint into photomontage, for an updated modern version of a variety show, a popular entertainment genre in Berlin in this period. Moholy-Nagy published this image to accompany his essay "Theater, Circus, Variety," in *The Theater of the Bauhaus*.[37] He linked the experience of the modern city – montages of images and light – with the source of the metropolis's attendant economic engines, industry and commerce. As he wrote elsewhere, "the regulative principles of color configuration, the discovery of the specific psycho-physical role of each color value, the combination of manual skill with mechanical devices, the conception of montage and the introduction of direct light, all provide a subconscious parallel to modern industry"; moreover, art could stimulate activity, "pressing for the solution of the urgent social and economic problems of today."[38]

From his representations of the cityscape as a whole, in his *Architecture* and *Glass Architecture* series (as well as other works that directly reference "architecture," or its elements, such as factory smokestacks), to his use of the actual materials of city, as seen in his *Relief* series, to his collages and photomontages, Moholy-Nagy can be understood as directly engaging the metropolis's key materials and effects – architecture's material abstraction. Whether by insinuating the city's forms and spatial dynamics via carefully layering paint, or simulating light shining through, or onto, the surface of glass and metal, or directly incorporating glass and metal, with characteristic calculated precision Moholy-Nagy's artworks perceptively hone in on the materiality and the experience of the modern city. In doing so, he abstracts it, but in a manner that encapsulates the overwhelming cacophony of light and motion that heightens the sensations of the urban experience itself.

The Industrial Metropolis in the Atelier: Scratched Surfaces, "Production-Reproduction," and Modern Industrial Materials

From his translation of the industrial city into dematerialized architectural forms on the standard artistic formats of paper, canvas, or wood discussed thus far, Moholy-Nagy began to directly engage, as the basis for the works themselves, the actual materials of modern industry – aluminum, steel, enamel, and new opaque and transparent plastics. The varying surfaces that these new materials offered gave rise to an inventive range of possibilities for their artistic manipulation and resulting effects. As Moholy-Nagy explained in a 1926 letter about this body of work, "I use, instead of paper and canvas, materials which are most homogenous and able to be worked in to highly polished or dull or pressed or

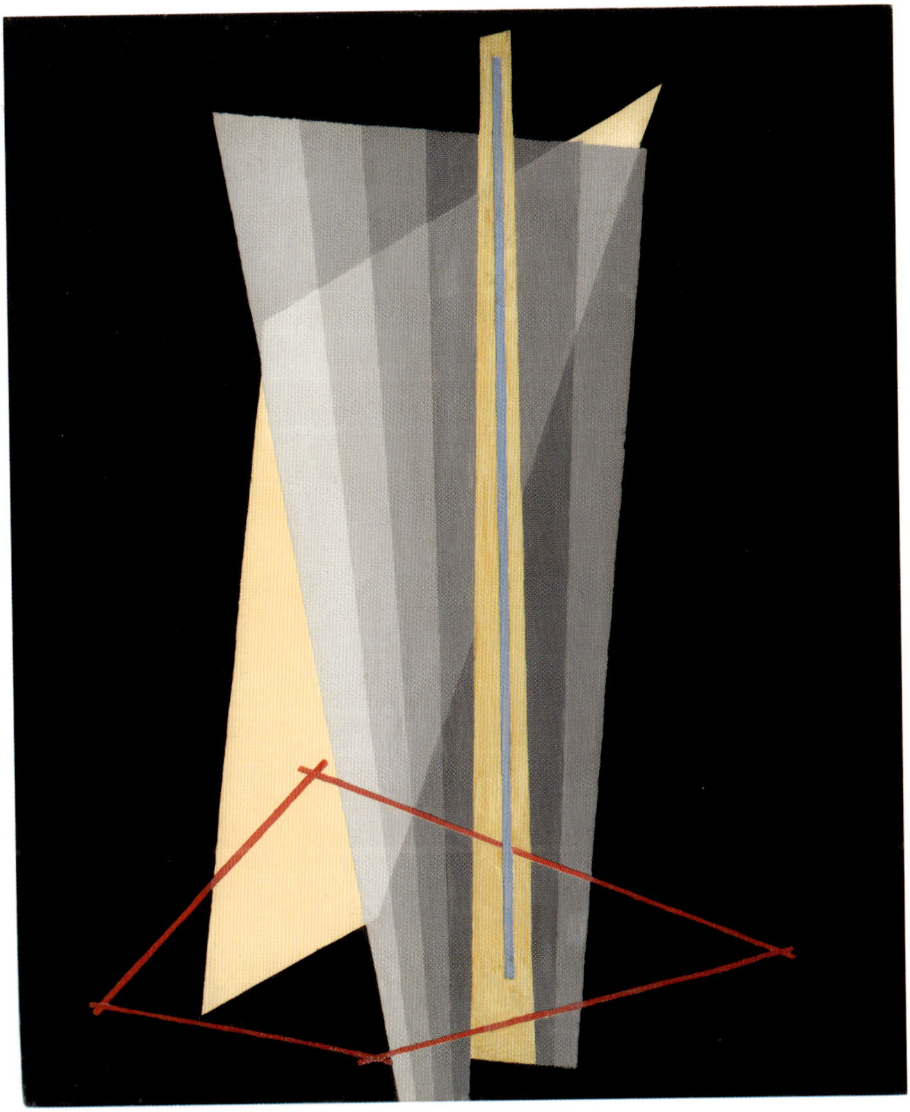

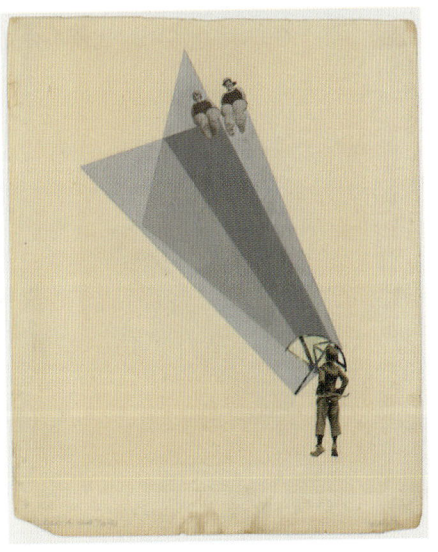
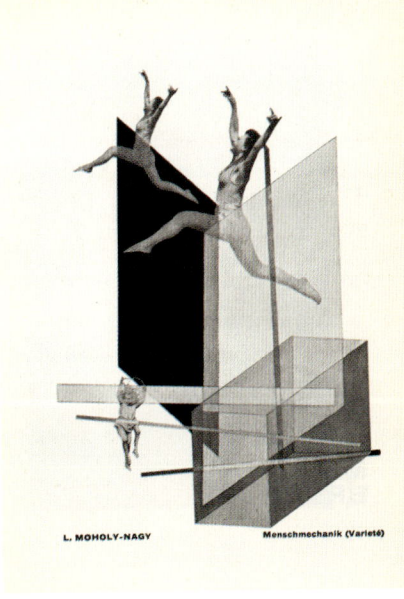

Fig. 1.9 László Moholy-Nagy, *Construction*, 1922, oil on panel. Harvard Art Museums/Busch-Reisinger Museum, Gift of Lydia Dorner in memory of Dr. Alexander Dorner.

(LEFT)
Fig. 1.10 László Moholy-Nagy, *City Lights*, dated 1926 [1927–28], photocollage. Bauhaus-Archiv, Berlin.

(RIGHT)
Fig. 1.11 László Moholy-Nagy, *Human Mechanics (Variety)*, 1925, photomontage (photomechanical reproduction) on paper. Published in *Die Bühne im Bauhaus*, Bauhausbücher 4 (Munich: Albert Langen Verlag, 1925), 65.

Architecture's Material Abstraction

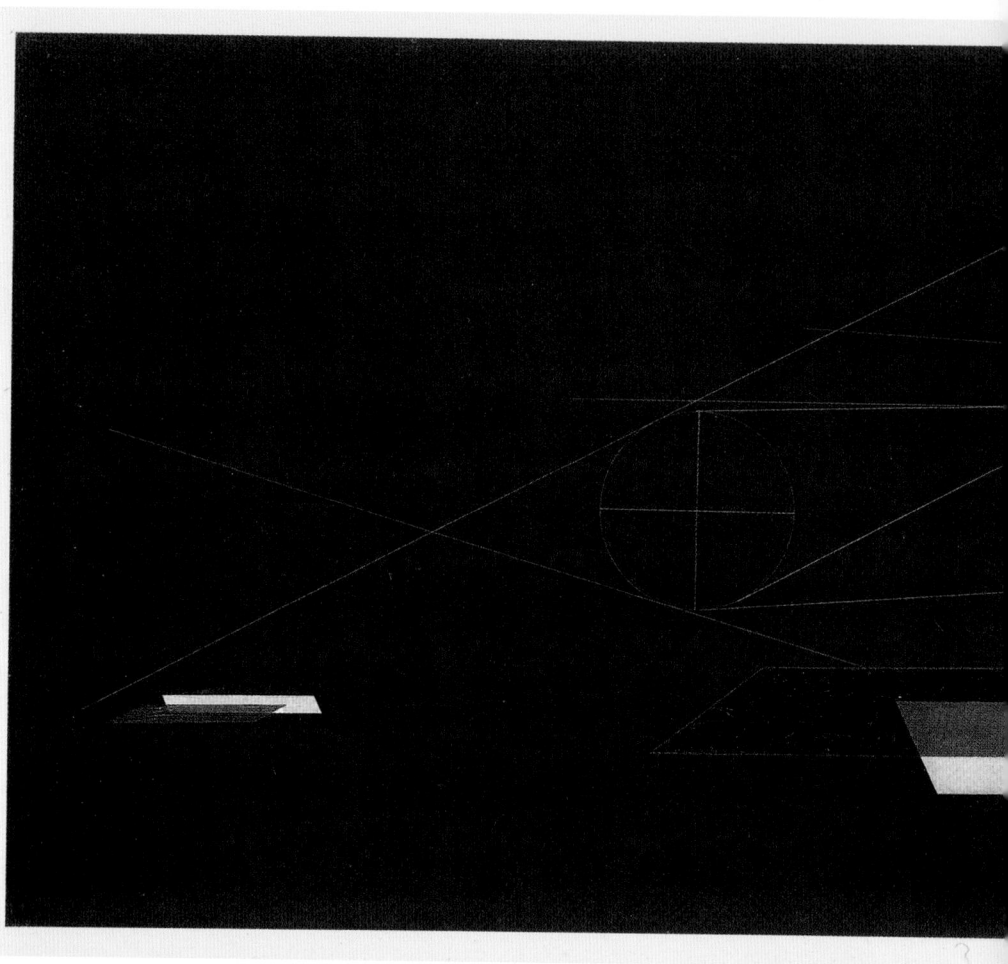

Fig. 1.12 László Moholy-Nagy, *Tp 2*, 1930, oil on Trolit. Solomon R. Guggenheim Museum, New York.

roughened surfaces, such as galalith [casein formaldehyde, an early plastic], trolit [cellulose nitrate or cellulose acetate, another early plastic], cellon [cellulose acetate, a clear early plastic], and aluminum."[39] To work on these man-made materials, he also noted his development of "precise new painting techniques."[40]

In the modern surfaces they offered, these industrial materials resonated through the meaning of — as well as their actual — materiality. *Tp 2*, on Trolit plastic, and *Sil 2*, on silberit aluminum, feature abstract planes in space, akin to earlier canvasses with the same forms and themes, but these artworks are also, importantly, entirely composed of industrial materials (fig. 1.12; see also fig. I.6). Trolit and silberit, a nearly pure aluminum, both offered luminous, reflective surfaces. Moholy-Nagy wrote with enthusiasm to art historian and photography colleague Franz Roh about the architectonic forms of his new silberit works, which create "an interesting effect: the colored planes float in an abstract space that is constituted only through reflections and mirrorings."[41] Carefully incised lines on the paintings' surfaces form transparent planes, suggestive of glass, which assist in the formation of an evocatively three-dimensional space. The floating effect of the colored and transparent planes was aided by the material of the substrate. In *Painting, Photography, Film*, Moholy-Nagy writes of experiments "with painting on highly polished black panels (trolite) [sic], on colored transparent and translucent plates (galalith, matt and translucent cellon)" that produce

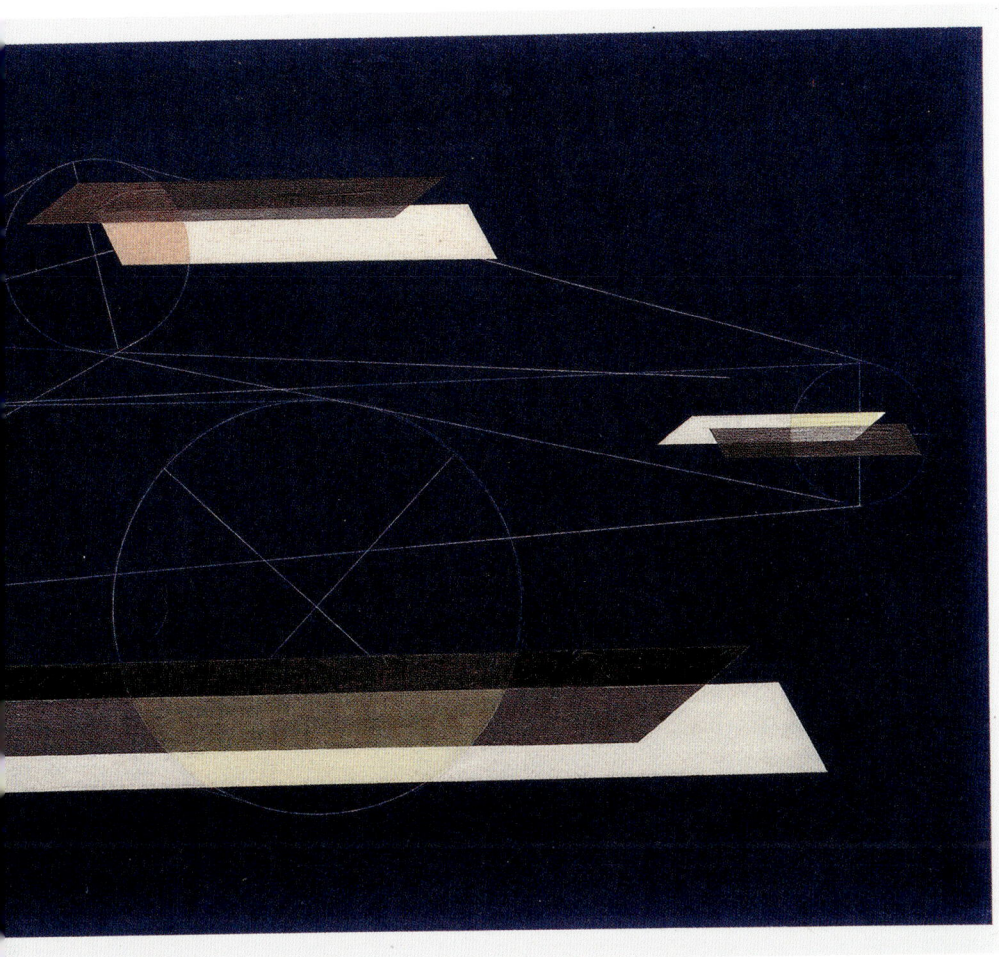

"strange optical effects: it looks as though the color were floating almost without material effect in a space in front of the plane to which it is in fact applied."[42]

Trolit and silberit were new materials with a plethora of potential uses, especially for the modern building industry (Trolit) and aircraft manufacture (silberit). Trolit offered the ability to install factory-smooth modern walls or room dividers, unlike the installation of earlier wall materials, such as plaster, which showed the vagaries of the worker's hand (present in low-quality work) or entailed the hiring of a master craftsman (for high-end work). Moholy-Nagy, in one of his rare architectural installations, had in fact already used multicolored, reflective Trolit panels for the demountable walls in his cinematic Room 2, produced for Germany's section at the 1930 Paris exhibition of the Société des artistes décorateurs (fig. 1.13).[43] Here Moholy-Nagy used Trolit in black, red, gray, yellow, and white.[44] His mounted slide projector is left exposed, celebrating the machine itself, with its light projected forward to the screen and also on the wall behind. In addition to the Trolit dividers, Moholy-Nagy created a graceful undulating glass wall inserted into shimmering nickel-chrome framing elements, recalling the abstracted colored walls and transparent windows depicted in artworks such as *K VII* and *Human Mechanics (Variety)* (see figs. 1.6, 1.11).

The oscillation here between literal walls and abstracted notions of them in works of art — between drawing attention to the materiality of the surface in

Architecture's Material Abstraction

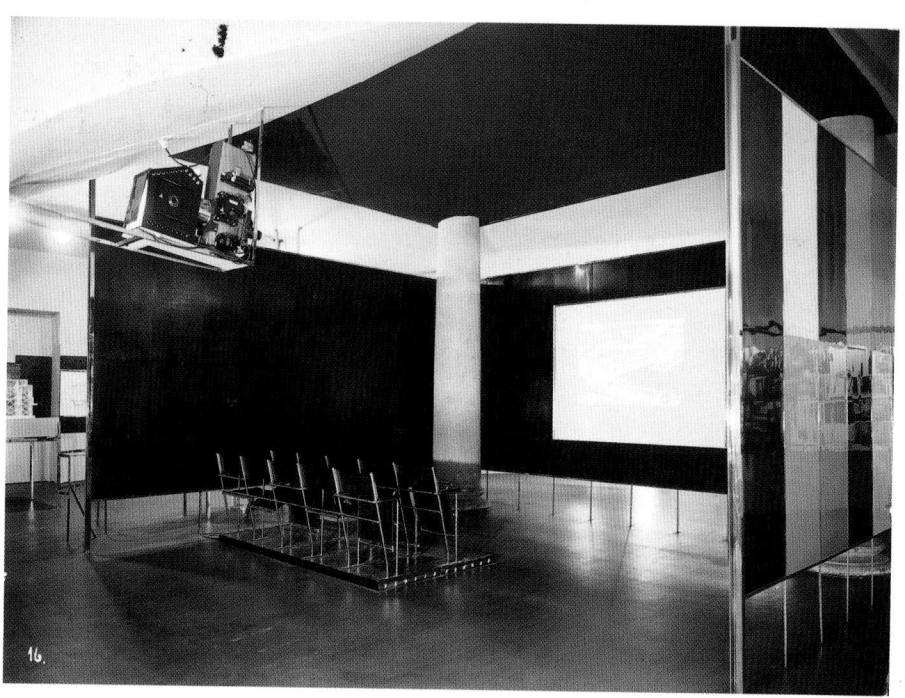

Fig. 1.13 László Moholy-Nagy, Room 2, featuring dividing walls made of Trolit, German section of the Société des artistes décorateurs exhibition, 1930, Paris.

its reflectiveness and incised lines and the suggestiveness of three-dimensional space — creates a visual and perceptible instability. This instability is fruitful for understanding period tensions of production and reproduction in relation to modern art. The operations performed on these modern surfaces allow for a revisiting of Moholy-Nagy's canonical "Production-Reproduction" essay, written with his first wife, Lucia Moholy, in 1922.[45] Both Moholy-Nagy and Lucia Moholy subscribed to the notion that when an artistic medium, or media form, was thoroughly understood, it could be made "productive" by doing different things with it, throwing it into new situations, pushing the boundaries of expected limits or meanings. The insight of the essay was that media used for what Moholy-Nagy calls "reproduction," a "reiteration of already existing relations," could instead service "production."

The essay thus calls for the use of instruments normally used for reproductive purposes to be used for productive purposes. Moholy-Nagy suggests that instead of the usual intervention by mechanical means to "reproduce already existing acoustic phenomena" onto the surface of a record album (usually merely a reproductive media), one should instead scratch it by hand, changing its material form for unique productive artistic results and "hitherto unknown" relations. The result is a new effect and a new meaning. By using base materials such as Trolit, for *Tp 2*, and silberit, for *Sil 2*, he connects his artworks to architecture and industry. The Trolit and silberit represent both the literal materials of infinitely reproducible walls (their "reproduction," in Moholy-Nagy's terms) *and* the picture's "productive" artistic content (again, in Moholy-Nagy's sense of the term), namely, the abstracted planes and implied walls within the artwork (see figs. 1.12, I.6). And by incising lines into them by hand, as with the hand-scratched record album in the "Production–Reproduction" essay, Moholy-Nagy calls attention to his artistic intervention on this material intended for industrial use. He

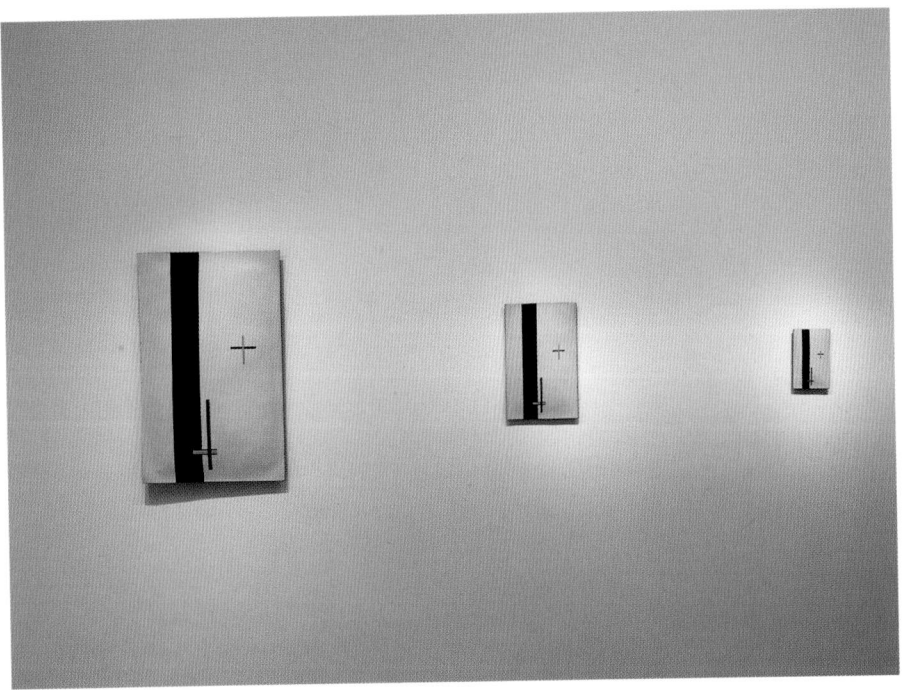

Fig. 1.14 László Moholy-Nagy, *EM 1, EM 2, EM 3* (*Telephone Paintings*), 1923, porcelain enamel on steel. Left to right: *Construction in Enamel 1* (also known as *EM 1*); *Construction in Enamel 2* (also known as *EM 2*); *Construction in Enamel 3* (also known as *EM 3*). Museum of Modern Art, New York.

regularly hand-incised lines into many of his works, not only on Trolit and silberit, but also into his photograms and Plexiglas pieces.

Another critical example of Moholy-Nagy's bringing into dialogue new relations between medium, artistic practice, and the technical reproduction enabled by industrial developments are his enamel paintings, *EM 1, EM 2*, and *EM 3*, also known as *Konstruktionen in Emaille* (*Constructions in Enamel*) and more informally, as *Telephone Paintings*, from 1923 (fig. 1.14).[46] It is not the abstract, crossed forms on a white enamel background that give the works their meaning but rather the concept that one could theoretically order a painting, in any proportional size, from a factory, disrupting an essential relationship – that between the artist's hand and a canvas. The *reproduction* that the factory is capable of has been made *productive* for art via a new set of relations surrounding the process of making. For these works Moholy-Nagy again takes a reproductive technique and makes it productive for art – namely, a painting made in a factory according to a grid. The factory that can reproduce enamel signs, standardizing corporate identity in advertising signage, or other goods, through Moholy-Nagy's intervention could make this technology useful for the production of art. Only a total of five enamel paintings were actually made, but the productive potential, Moholy-Nagy realized, was enormous. The meaning lay in the idea of the *Telephone Paintings*' technical production – the supposed phoning in of the painting's gridded coordinates to a factory, devoid of the direct hand of the artist himself. Moholy-Nagy writes: "I was not at all afraid of losing the 'personal touch,' so highly valued in previous painting. On the contrary, I even gave up signing my paintings. I put numbers and letters with the necessary data on the back of the canvas, as if they were cars, airplanes, or other industrial products."[47]

The reproductive potential of the *Constructions in Enamel* has long overshadowed discussion of their actual materiality, but the enamel itself is important

Architecture's Material Abstraction

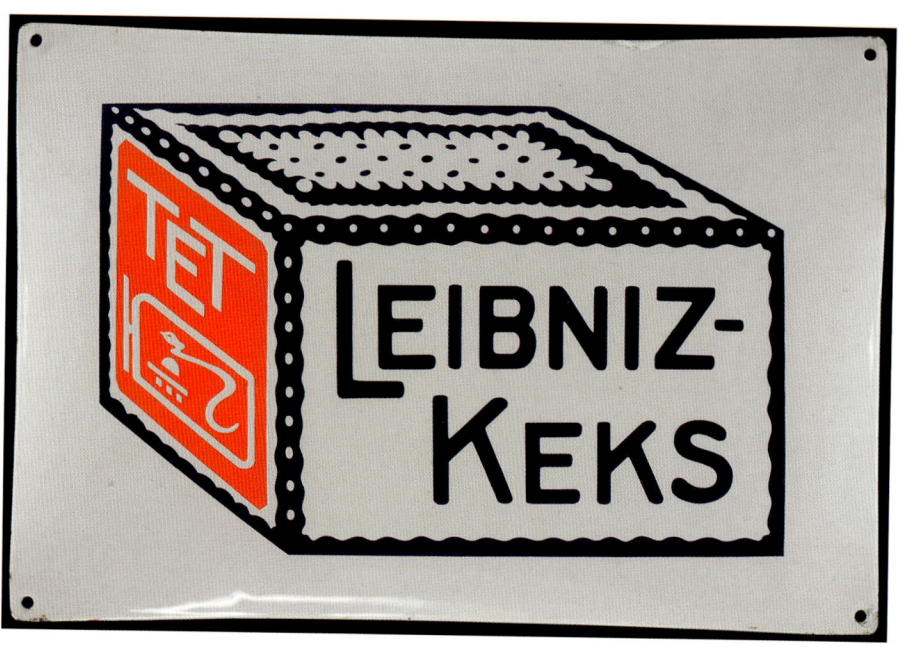

Fig. 1.15 Enamel sign for Leibniz-Keks butter cookies, ca. 1920.

in this context. The individual short titles—*EM 1*, *EM 2*, and *EM 3*—stand for "enamel" in German—*Emaille*. In a period in which groups such as the Werkbund were active in helping to bring the standardization and mass production of well-designed, high-quality German products to the market, there was a concurrent emphasis on trademarks and standardizing advertising.[48] Whereas earlier store signs in different cities would have been hand-painted locally, leading to slight differences in the rendering of the trademark, given the vagaries of the hand, in the 1910s, companies sought to homogenize their visual representations nationally and internationally. This had a strong visual effect in cities, which became flooded with signs and symbols, linked to the vast increase in the number of standardized, industrial products newly available in urban centers. Signs in porcelain enamel on steel, such as those for Leibniz-Keks brand butter cookies, provided a durable, weather-stable advertising medium and allowed for companies to ensure their logos and trademarks were identical wherever they were encountered (fig. 1.15). Moholy-Nagy's paintings should be read in that context: as the Leibniz-Keks sign advertises factory-produced cookies, the *EM 1, 2*, and *3* advertise factory-produced, modern painting. Moreover, their means of coming into being is an artistic representation of—reflection on—the products and state of modern industry itself. As Moholy-Nagy stated, "As far as I know, I am the first one who has comprehensively attempted to bring painting to a desubjectivization and to a basis which corresponds to today's technology. This effort comes down to becoming factory-wise or ultimately to the production of painting of pictures by ordering them at the factory."[49]

The paintings respond to the metropolis's mass-produced material output and its connected visual landscape of signs and symbols, highlighting their potential for new relations between industrial production and art production. To read the works again through the "Production-Reproduction" essay, the factory-produced *EM* paintings, identical but in three sizes, are representative of

Moholy-Nagy's ideas of "reproduction," and they are also about "production" – not only as an artistic response to the output of industry, but their making of *reproductive* technologies, *productive* for art. This *productive reproduction* attempts to capture for art – and relates directly to – similar processes occurring in the modern metropolis in industrial and architectural contexts – from the rampant reproduction of goods on the factory floor to the dizzying glass facades of the modernism's new architecture.

Space Articulation: Photograms, Space Modulators, and Other Means of Making Space

Throughout the 1920s, Moholy-Nagy became increasingly interested in the effects of light for the production of art, a focus that intensified in the 1930s with his experiments in film, photography, and with the light-producing machine known as *Lichtrequisit*, 1928–30 (*Light Prop for an Electric Stage* or *Light Space Modulator*). These investigations continued through his immigration to England and to the United States, especially during the Chicago years, when he created a wide variety of what he termed "light modulators." I would like to draw attention to the ways in which his work with light was also motivated by an interest in the articulation of space, and by extension, directly connects to his other forays into the material abstraction of architecture and its representations in the industrial metropolis. Especially in his new approaches in the use of direct light to express his ideas of creating or manipulating space, light was transubstantiated from an expression in paint to one of direct projection. Moholy-Nagy also began to fold in a notion of time in both his theoretical formulations and artworks. As he writes in *The New Vision*, under the heading "The play of refracted light": "We undoubtedly must come to the manipulation of moving, refracted light (color); we must 'paint' with flowing, oscillating, prismatic light, in lieu of pigments. This will allow us a better approach to the new conception of space-time."[50]

One early result of Moholy-Nagy's intense exploration of the effects of light was the photogram, produced purely by training light on diverse materials and small objects lying on light-sensitive paper. The paper darkens where it was exposed to light and remains white where the solid objects had been placed; when fixed through immersion in a water bath, the process gave rise to an artwork. His experiments with photograms represent a sustained artistic practice that spanned his entire oeuvre, from his earliest experiments in 1922 until his death in 1946.[51] For his photograms, like his *Reliefs* series, Moholy-Nagy often used the urban detritus he had gathered from the Berlin streets – scrap machine parts, gear wheels, screws, bolts, and small sheets of metal and glass – and worked directly with these objects on photosensitive paper to create photograms that reflected the materiality of the built environment. His photograms are also often composed of geometrical shapes – quadrilaterals, circles, and spirals – that constitute the basic forms of the city. Moholy-Nagy carefully modulated the light so that the same objects placed on paper produced different outcomes depending on the strength and duration of the light, and if he chose to move the objects during the exposure period – sometimes resulting in hard-edged, black-and-white forms, and at other times generating soft contours, a

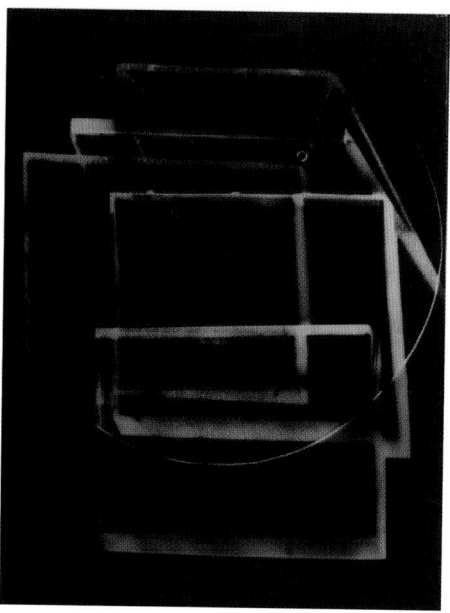

Fig. 1.16 László Moholy-Nagy, *Untitled*, ca. 1924, enlarged photogram (original lost). Museum of Modern Art, New York.

range of tonal grays, and fluctuating transparency. As he would formulate it, "All concrete shapes dissolve in light."[52]

For these photograms or "cameraless pictures," Moholy-Nagy removes the intermediary—the camera—for a direct engagement between object and surface; he exploits the transparency and materiality of objects that are modulated only by light. By tilting small plates of glass or folding paper to create gradate planes, to cite just two examples, through the mere application of light itself, Moholy-Nagy created photograms that are similar not only in form and composition to his abstract painting but also his theoretical formulations (fig. 1.16). Though the resulting photogram depended in a small measure on an object's transparency and opacity, in the main, the emphasis for Moholy-Nagy was on an object's eventual abstraction, on its representative value as a mediator of light. Photograms are, as he framed it, direct "records of forms produced by light," but more important, they are not just abstract art, but for him, what he called a way of "abstract seeing."[53] As he notes, "the photogram opens up perspectives of a hitherto wholly unknown morphosis governed by optical laws peculiar to itself. [By removing the camera] it is the most completely dematerialized medium which the new vision commands."[54] To this formulation he layers in the component present in all of his other work discussed thus far, an articulation of space. He writes, "Cameraless pictures are also direct light diagrams recording the actions of light over a period of time, that is, the motion of light in space.... Photograms, however, bring a completely new form of space articulation. It no longer has anything to do with the record of an existing space (or space-time) structure.... The photogram for the first time produces space without existing space structure only by articulation on the plane with the advancing and receding values of half-tones in black and gray and with the radiating power of their contrasts and their sublime gradations."[55]

Moholy-Nagy also noted, "If one would like to go into the more complex explanation then one could say that a photogram is a motion diagram of the

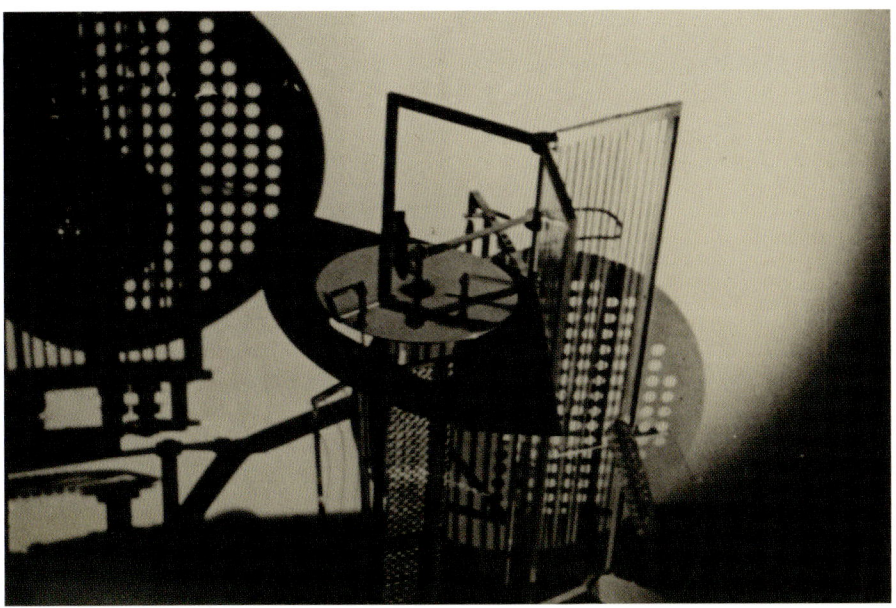

Fig. 1.17 László Moholy-Nagy (photographer and inventor), *Photograph (Light Prop)*, 1930, gelatin silver print.

movements of light."[56] Crucially, as with his paintings, these experiments with photograms are to be understood as a means by which to use light to articulate space, even to, as he frames it, *produce space without existing space structure*. As early as 1929, he explains about his photograms, "One of the aims was to create a new space, which was to be produced through the relations of the elemental material of visual expression — a new space created with light directly, subordinating even paint (pigment) — or at least sublimating it as far as possible."[57] The photograms of tilted glass plates or folded pieces of paper exemplify Moholy-Nagy's notion of abstract space, both visually (the resulting prints seem to suggest glass architecture and architectural planes), and in his articulated theoretical formulations concerning space in his photogram

Moholy-Nagy's ideas of using light to articulate new space reached a critical point in another series of experiments and ongoing adjustments to a work that was initially called the *Light Prop for an Electric Stage*, but is now often known as the *Light Space Modulator*, the initial piece in a larger series of light space modulators that occupied him throughout the rest of his artistic career (fig. 1.17; see also fig. I.4). First intended as a stage lighting device, the *Light Prop* projected various effects depending on its siting and the box it was encased in over the years, the rear panel of which could be removed; it later became a freestanding work, a kinetic sculpture that was allowed to project light displays onto walls.[58] According to Moholy-Nagy, the *Light Prop* "originally served as an experimental apparatus for 'painting with light.'"[59] Paintings were the gateway to these radical experiments in light: he first simulates in paint what he will later achieve with his stand-alone light modulators. Sibyl Moholy-Nagy articulated the crucial role painting played for his other artistic investigations, observing in an interview,

> It's interesting that he had hoped for all sorts of new art media, for instance, enormous light displays from large Klieg lights and things like that which would play on clouds and create outdoor spectacles…

Architecture's Material Abstraction

and so on, and then he often said, "Why do people say, Why do I still paint in addition to doing all these new things?" And he said, "I always have to come back to the canvas for . . ." he called this incubation, "For the incubation of my ideas, I always have to come back." It was the point of departure, so to speak. And from there he could project these things. You see here in this painting before you, which belongs to Mrs. Paepcke, you see it is actually two light beams crossing. This is what he had in mind, two enormous light beams.[60]

Sibyl Moholy-Nagy is not referring to *A 19*, but here, too, urban light beams are likely being depicted (see fig. 1.7). Indeed, the *Light Prop* comes out of Moholy-Nagy's interest in "light painting," which he describes as an investigation in "the effects of light hitting a surface, whether plain or curved (you can call this surface also the 'screen'), instead of thinking in terms of pigments only. Hence my experiments with synthetic materials, plastics, and with photography, motion picture and kinetic sculpture."[61]

Premiering in Germany's section at the 1930 Paris exhibition of the Société des artistes décorateurs, in its first iteration the *Light Prop* was contained in a dark flashed glass box and meant to produce light effects outward on the theater stage. In its next incarnation, it was housed in a box with a single, cut-out hole, intended to be displayed in Moholy-Nagy's 1930 installation, the *Raum der Gegenwart* (Room of the Present) in Hanover.[62] Thereafter, it would be displayed, and run, freestanding in a room. As Jack W. Burnham has observed, it "created both shadow and substance; it supported Moholy-Nagy's feeling that light, if rendered into art, must first be *transmitted* and *transformed* through materials — not projected directly at the viewer."[63] In addition to light, it thus furthered his engagement with modern materiality, ideas of surface, and articulated space. Moreover, the *Light Prop* also relates to the city in two important ways. First, it suggests, akin to the earlier *Reliefs*, the materiality of the city through its visible constituent parts (glass, metal, and other mechanical elements), and second, it projects the moving light and forms outward, performing, in abstraction, the urban experience itself.

Once he resumed painting, in 1930, he never gave it up again. Following his interest in the effect of light, materiality, and space — as exemplified by the photograms and the *Light Prop* — Moholy-Nagy, from the mid-1930s and into the 1940s, produced a group of works that he referred to as "space modulators." His experiments with this concept resulted in artworks in diverse materials, from straightforward oil and graphite pencil on linen (*Space Modulator*, 1938–40), to oil on perforated zinc and composition board with glass-headed pins (*Space Modulator L3*, 1936), to oil and incised lines on Formica (*Space Modulator CH for Y*, 1942).

Alongside canvas and other opaque substrates, Moholy-Nagy worked increasingly on translucent materials. For the transparent works, predominantly two types of newly available, clear material formed the substrate: Rhodoid (invented in 1917, an early thermoplastic derived from cellulose acetate) and Plexiglas (developed in 1928, sheets of which became available in the United States in 1934). He had experimented with Rhodoid as early as 1935, when he created a model city with transparent skyscrapers for the film adaption of H. G. Wells's *Things to Come*, while living in London.[64] A notable additional material that he used much less often is acetate (for example, *CH 1*, 1938). From his translucent base, he built up multiple layers of media, often applied by hand either above or below the transparent sheet, into which he also incised lines. Layers of paint were sometimes thinly sprayed, so that a reflecting layer beneath was left visible. To certain Rhodoid and Plexiglas pieces, which are hung at a slight remove from the wall, he applied painted shapes. They read as color forms on the work's surface, but they also cast shadows onto the wall behind it, projecting the shape from the artwork to wall, transposing it from solid to shadow. This also occurs with his delicately incised lines—some of which are left as bare scratches in the Plexiglas, while others have color rubbed into them—which delicately project the lines onto the wall. See, for instance, *Space III* from 1940 (fig. 1.18). This tension—between an articulation of the artwork's surface and its projection of form onto the space of the wall behind it—is exemplified in works spanning the duration of his light modulator investigations, which lasted until the production of his final works; for example, *Space Modulator (Rhodoid)* (1935, Rhodoid), *Space III* (1940, oil and incised lines on Plexiglas), *CH P Space Modulator or Iridescent Space Modulator* (1940, oil and incised lines on Plexiglas), and *Space Modulator* (1946, oil on Plexiglas). With Plexiglas, he could also warm and bend a work before adding color or other treatments to it (for example, *B-10 Space Modulator*, 1942, oil and incised lines on Plexiglas).

Again, as with earlier artworks, here Moholy-Nagy is using modern materiality and the effects of light to articulate and draw the viewer's attention to the surface, while simultaneously creating space. Extra depth is further added, in some cases, by suspending the paintings at a distance from the wall by using metal pins or slotted wooden framing blocks. This caused transparent works such as *Space III* to cast a delicate but delineated projective architecture onto the surface behind it. This is a gathering in, in a sense, to the picture plane (as a Heideggerian "thing" gathers; the bridge that gathers the banks).[65] As Moholy-Nagy himself would frame it, "the reflections and refractions bring the surroundings into the picture surface, attaining the surface flexibility striven for ever since the first days of impressionism. . . . The surface becomes a part of the atmosphere, of the atmospheric background, in that it sucks up the light phenomena produced outside itself. . . . This stage . . . represents the mastery of the surface, not for plastic but for clearly spatial ends."[66] He sums up, "One of the results of the investigations in modern art is that we can articulate space in the same way as we are able to articulate color, tone, volume, etc. To articulate and modulate space was old knowledge to architects."[67] Indeed, with the space modulators, once again he holds in dialectical tension these aspects, also so key in architecture, of surface and space, and a materiality that served these ends.

The City Takes Center Stage: Toward a Future of Screens and Other Speculative Display

If Moholy-Nagy's painting can be understood as the abstractions and relationships of the city's materials, forms, and architecture, his ultimate goal can be

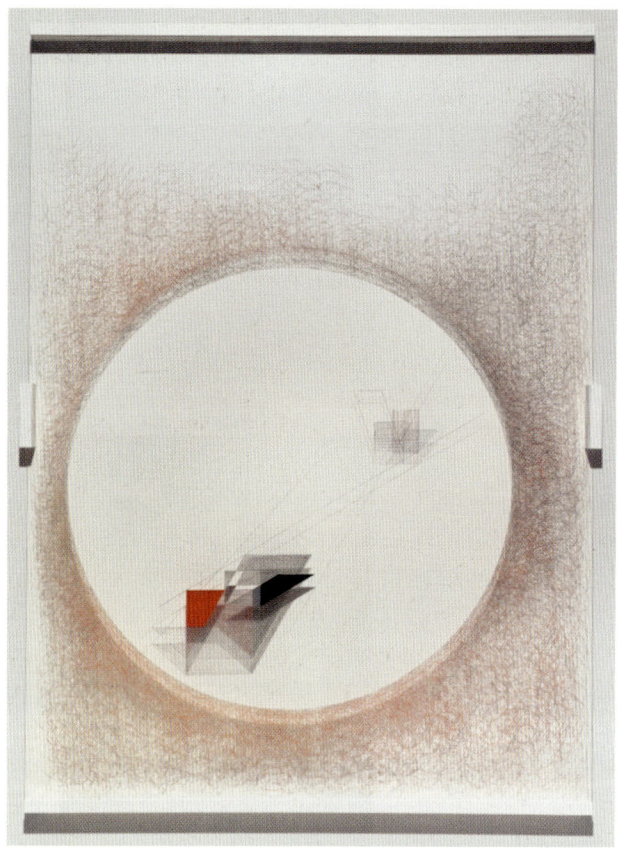

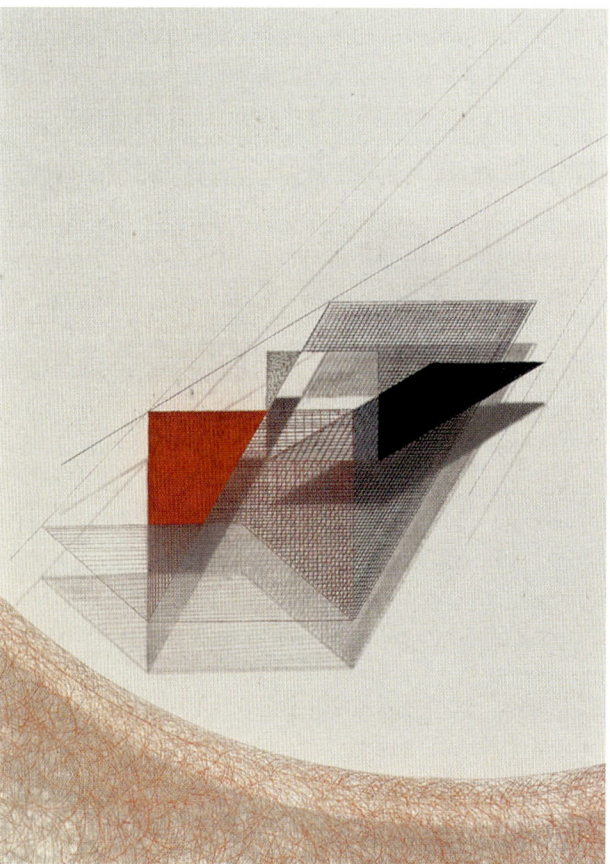

Fig. 1.18 László Moholy-Nagy, *Space III* (and detail, *below*), 1940, oil and incised lines on Plexiglas.

understood as one of a continuous pursuit of light. As he framed it, as early as 1926, his interest was in the "sublimation of pigment to pure light effects, from pigment to light with painterly construction."[68] In the introduction to *Painting, Photography, Film*, Moholy-Nagy proposed, "Moving light displays side by side with easel-painting, instead of frescos – films in all dimensions; outside the film theatre, too, of course."[69] His pursuit of light took many other artistic forms beyond painting, from photograms made by concentrated rays that darkened photosensitive paper, leaving the abstracted white forms of objects that had been placed there, to the dancing light play of the *Light Space Modulator* (and the photographs and films that extended it), to the refracted light bouncing off the surfaces of Trolit, silberit, Rhodoid, and Plexiglas artworks. But Moholy-Nagy also conceptualized much larger, much more dazzling, and much more *architectural* harnessing of light, for artistic ends. Light was a key material with which to produce artworks at large, beyond the confines of the picture plane, and even the interior itself. Writing in 1934, he stated, "Ever since the invention of photography, painting has advanced by logical stages of development 'from pigment to light.' We have now reached the stage when it should be possible to discard brush and pigment and to 'paint' by means of light itself. We are ready to replace the old two-dimensional color patterns by a monumental *architecture of light*."[70]

In Sibyl Moholy-Nagy's first encounter with him in 1931 at her place of work, a large motion picture company in Berlin, he presented a sketch to her, with a concave and convex refraction scheme and proposed that two plate glass mirrors be mounted on an open truck. A film camera was to be directed at each mirror. She recounted his concept: "As the truck was driven through the streets of Berlin, each camera would photograph the happenings of a single day – between dawn and dusk. City life would be reflected, distorted, broken up, concentrated, through the medium of the mirrors."[71] Titled *Reflected Image*, Moholy-Nagy wrestled with the film's sequencing, viewing as too trite an ordering of morning, noon, and night or of awakening, activity, and relaxation. He placed the emphasis not on the diurnal but on light. He clarified, "The rhythm of this film has to come from the light – it has to have a light-chronology.... Light beams overlap as they cross through dense air; they're blocked, diffracted, condensed. The different angles of the entering light indicate time. The rotation of light from east to west modulates the visible world. Shadows and reflexes register a constantly changing relationship of solids and perforations."[72] Although unrealized, this film proposal was one of the more potentially viable of Moholy-Nagy's ideas.[73]

In letters and in articles such as "Light Architecture," Moholy-Nagy envisioned a series of speculative works in which, through the use of projectors, reflectors, and search lights, light would interact strikingly with the built environment,[74] revealing "ever-changing planes and angles."[75] He foresaw light frescos that would "animate vast architectural units, such as buildings, parts of buildings or single walls, by means of artificial light focused and manipulated according to a definite plan."[76] He wrote, "I longed to have at my disposal a bare room containing twelve projectors, the multi-colored rays of which would enable me to animate its white emptiness."[77] Screens particularly preoccupied him. The definition of a screen, to Moholy-Nagy, was very open-ended; a photogram, he noted in 1929, was "the recording of light as it hit a projection screen – in this case, the sensitive layer of the photographic paper."[78] More speculatively, he proposed a number of projectors concentrating on a single screen, filling it with simultaneous images, or those same images expanded, covering all walls of a room.[79]

Moholy-Nagy went further, envisioning displays that eschewed the screen, or even a fixed material projection surface altogether. In the mid-1920s he imagined a probable future in which a kinetic, projected composition, with "interpenetrating beams and masses of light" would float "freely in the room without a direct plane of projection."[80] Even more evocatively, he desired to beam light into an ineffable space until it reached some other substance – such as gas, fire, smoke, or vapor:

> I have often dreamed of hand-controlled or automatic systems of powerful light generators enabling the artist to flood the air – vast halls, or reflectors, of unusual substance – such as fog, gaseous materials or clouds, with brilliant visions of multicolored light. I elaborated innumerable projects – but no patron ever commissioned me to create a monumental fresco of light, consisting of flat and curving walls covered with artificial substances, such as galalith, trolit, chromium, nickel – a structure to be transformed into a resplendent symphony of light . . . while the controlled movements of the various reflecting surfaces would express the basic rhythm of the piece.[81]

He wrote of an expansive future in which "light displays of any desired quality and magnitude will suddenly blaze up, and multicolored floodlights with transparent sheaths of fire will project a constant flow of immaterial, evanescent images into space by the simple manipulation of switches."[82] He also proposed that "astonishing effects might be obtained by simultaneously focusing a number of projectors on to gaseous formations, such as smoke clouds, or by the interplay of multiform luminous cones."[83]

As discussed in detail in chapter 4, at the School of Design in 1940s wartime Chicago, Moholy-Nagy was able to put into instrumental use many of his ideas about lighting and the city. Specialists and the school's students carefully studied the built environment and worked on potential methods of changing the appearance of Chicago in order to camouflage it enough to confuse the enemy. Many of the proposals that the school wished to prototype for the war effort stem from Moholy-Nagy's earlier concepts developed as artworks. The school proposed a "moving-light" plan using "halation units" that would place lamps in strategic locations around the city to create disorientating light patterns and cast strong, confusing glows over or near potential target areas. This would render them invisible under a blinding light system, filling the sky with luminous haze, even disguising the location and contour of Chicago's distinctive lakefront.[84] Other proposals investigated the possibility of using lights and shadows, fog and smoke to obfuscate targets; for example, one idea was to project green floodlights onto the red flames of the steel mill flares.[85] The role of artificial light and light manipulation in obscuring targets drew on one of Moholy-Nagy's own long-standing, primary artistic interests, giving him an opportunity to capitalize on his previous experiments.

Moholy-Nagy's oeuvre had developed from an interaction with the city and industry, with its references to concrete materials, architecture and space, to a future of abstracted images and effects composed purely of light. He extended the application of these phenomena to the theater stage, for which he envisioned similar projections and spatial effects. He suggested, in a 1925 essay, a future for theater in which

> films can also be projected onto various surfaces and further experiments in space illumination will be devised. This will constitute the new ACTION OF LIGHT, which by means of modern technology will use the most intensified contrasts to guarantee itself a position of importance equal to that of all other theater media. We have not yet begun to realize the potential of light for sudden or blinding illumination, for flare effects, for phosphorescent effects, for bathing the auditorium in light synchronized with climaxes or with the total extinguishing of lights on the stage. All this, of course, is thought of in a sense totally different from anything in current traditional theater.[86]

Moholy-Nagy was able to try out some of these ideas in his work for Berlin-based avant-garde director Erwin Piscator. Piscator, who had his own theater, conceptualized a new type of theatre experience and end goals in his book *Das Politische Theater*, for which Moholy-Nagy designed the cover. For Piscator's 1929 production of Walter Mehring's *Der Kaufmann von Berlin* (*The Merchant of Berlin*), Moholy-Nagy designed the set, a pared down modern stage with curving ramps and simple architectonic structures.[87] On the stage, an enormous screen allowed for the projection of a photomontage featuring a cacophony of urban images: buildings (including train stations and tunnels, apartment houses, illuminated department stores, factory smokestacks), vehicles (trains, cars, airplanes), and urban crowds (shoppers, parades, formations of revue girls). He elaborated on his methods: "It is possible to enrich our spatial experience by projecting light on to a succession of semitransparent planes (nets, trellis-work, etc.). I did this in my scenic experiments for the 'Kaufmann von Berlin' [Merchant of Berlin] performed at Piscator's theatre in 1929. It is also quite possible to replace a single flat screen by concave or convex sections of differing size and shape that would form innumerable patterns by continual change of position. One might also project different films on to all the walls of the cinema simultaneously."[88]

Another stage set design by Moholy-Nagy, also from 1929, in which his aims for the theater aligned neatly with his paintings and photograms in terms of similarly focusing on the harnessing of light and creating space, was *Les contes d'Hoffmann / Hoffmanns Erzählungen* (*The Tales of Hoffmann*), written by Jacques Offenbach.[89] The drawings for the stage design include many architectural elements, including a bar with tall, tubular steel stools, small tables and chairs, block-shaped club chairs and couches, and a winding circular staircase. Moholy-Nagy employed a looming white screen onto which changing projections appeared, while light also illuminated and bounced off of the other modern materials on stage – furniture in tubular steel and wood, other metal and wooden structural elements, cloth, cellophane, and transparent screening panels. *The*

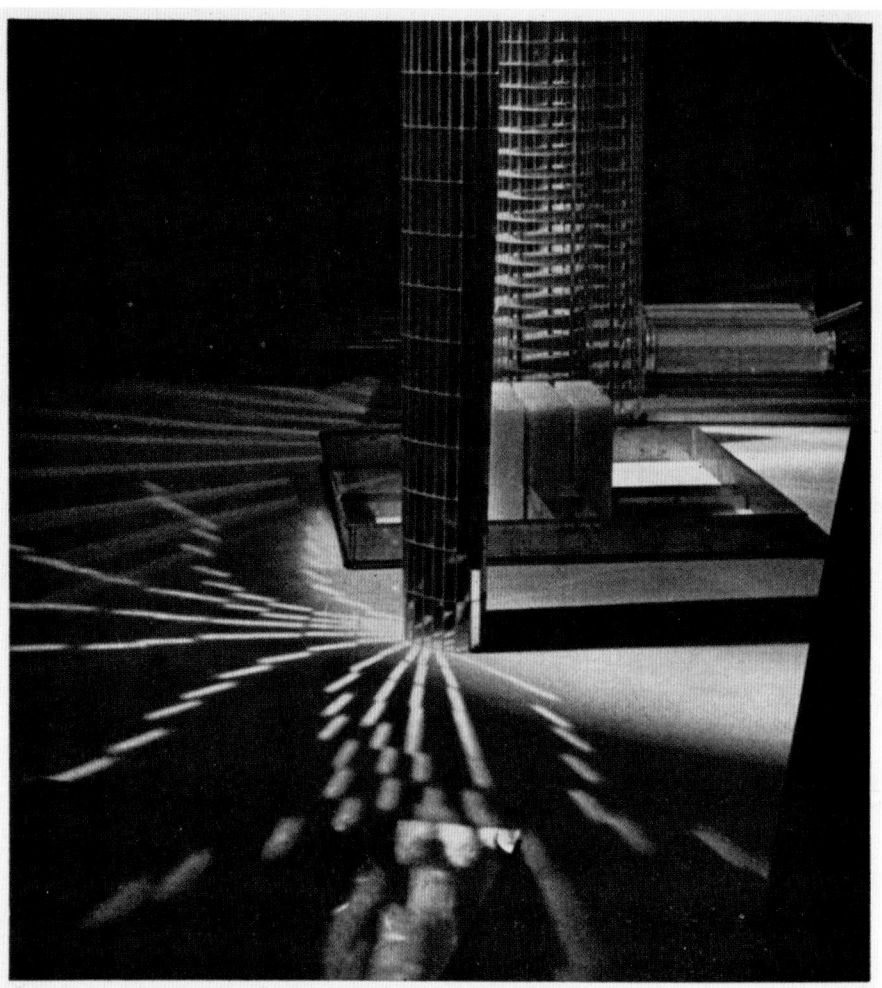

Fig. 1.19 László Moholy-Nagy, set design, *Things to Come*, 1935.

Tales of Hoffmann's set, Moholy-Nagy explained, was "an experiment with the problem of creating space from light and shadow. Among other devices, the wings are employed here to create shadows. Everything is transparent, and all the transparent surfaces work together to make an organized and well perceptible space arrangement."[90]

Perhaps the apotheosis of Moholy-Nagy's handling of these concepts was not on stage but in the set designs he contributed to the 1936 film by H. G. Wells, *Things to Come*, created during his time in London (fig. 1.19).[91] Here he imagined a transparent urban landscape akin to Mies's glass skyscraper designs. Moholy-Nagy dreamed of eliminating solid form in his utopian city of the future, as Sibyl Moholy-Nagy writes of his designs: "Houses were no longer obstacles to, but receptacles of, man's natural force, light. There were no walls, but skeletons of steel, screened with glass and plastic sheets."[92]

New Techniques for an Architectural Future

Moholy-Nagy also reflected on domestic architecture's relationships and the creation of space for dwelling. In his 1929 essay "Man and His House," Moholy-Nagy discusses "the *construction of space*," which he considers a "special architectonic consideration," noting that "beyond the satisfaction of his elementary bodily needs, man must also experience space in his home – at least, he must learn to experience it. The home must not be allowed to be an escape from space but a living-in-space, an honest relationship with it ... first and foremost the *experience of space*, which is the basis of the mental as well as the physical well-being of the inhabitants."[93] For Moholy-Nagy, the space created – not the architecture itself – was the meaningful element: "Architecture – all the functional parts taken together – must be conceived as a whole. Without this, a building becomes a piecing together of hollow bodies, which may be technically practical, but can never serve in creating space."[94] Yet, he notes, through the work of photographers and modern architects, "we have attained an enlargement and sublimation of our appreciation of space, the comprehension of a new spatial culture."[95]

Though the Bauhaus did not add a formal architectural course until 1928, the year Gropius and Moholy-Nagy would leave, architecture was seen as an end goal for the school. The *Vorkurs*, or Foundation Course, taught by Josef Albers and Moholy-Nagy, not only involved the study of new materials, or new approaches to handling familiar substances and understanding their creative and industrial potential; it encompassed a larger conceptualization of making, of space and spatial perception, via a teaching praxis grounded in abstract principles. Moholy-Nagy prepared students via a series of spatial exercises in his Foundation Course at both the German and Chicago Bauhaus, where students used varied materials to experiment with concepts of equilibrium, transparency, surface effect, and relationships between elements.[96]

In this context, Moholy-Nagy played an important part in readying students for architecture. He set the students the task of creating works in equilibrium and assigned them other exercises in spatial conceptualization that emphasized the optic and the material; haptic tasks involved Moholy-Nagy's oft-discussed touch panels and other tactile exercises.[97] Other works emerging from the students emphasized ideas of surface and materiality, space and light, such as Charlotte Victoria's study of volume and space (1923, glass and muslin) and Lotte Gerson's architectural construction with sections of glass (ca. 1928), both of which approach modern architecture, especially glass curtain walls, from within the *Vorkurs* (fig. 1.20). Suggestive of cantilevered balconies, roof overhangs, and other structural elements favored by modern architects of the period, other student exercises showed an awareness of, and a measured working toward, the design of contemporary architectural components. August Brauneck's facture exercise is reminiscent of Gropius and Adolf Meyer's widely reproduced entry for the Chicago Tribune Tower competition of 1922. Likewise, a 1924 construction by Anni Wildberg, in metal and glass, reflects the dynamism and new architectural forms of the period, particularly Gropius's memorial to the workers killed in the Kapp Putsch.

The *Vorkurs* exercises were meant to tackle modern issues that were also distinctly architectural in nature, such as dematerialization, weightlessness, and overcoming gravity; visual aesthetics (of scale, proportion, static and dynamic tension); and the fundamental properties of the materials themselves (elasticity, strength).[98] Other exercises probed certain relationships of material to space,

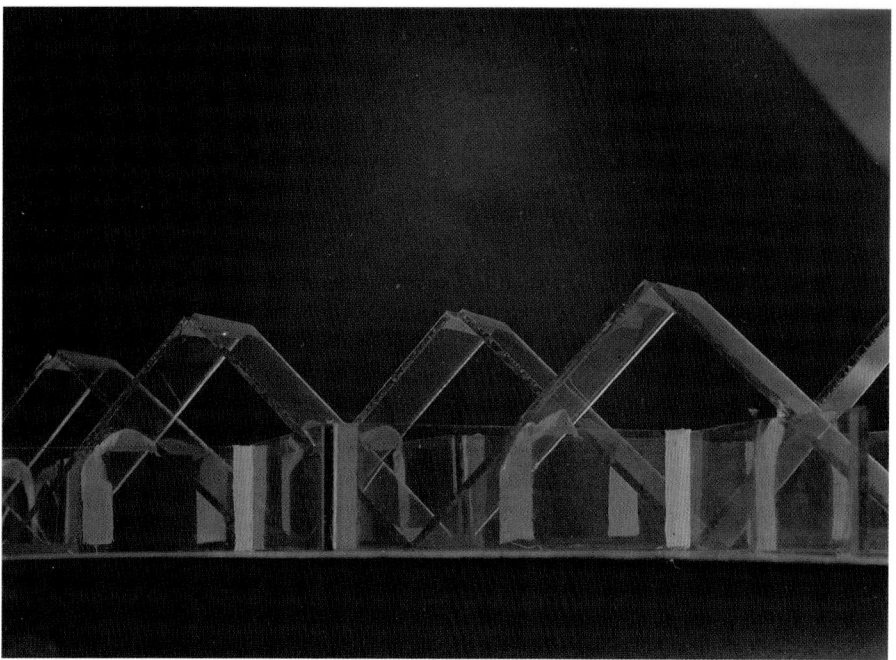

Fig. 1.20 Lotte Gerson, Bauhaus Dessau, Architectural Construction with Sections of Glass, ca. 1928.

such as those aimed at demonstrating tension (using strips of wood veneer), studies of diagonals in space, and exercises involving concepts of interconnecting planes.[99] For studies in equilibrium, students focused on proportion and the weight of varying materials, balancing them on a single point. For example, a perfectly calibrated equilibrium exercise by student Toma Grote, based on the specific density of differing types of wood, employed heavier wood on the work's lower front, equalizing, in perfect balance, the projection of the less-dense upper portion.

    The work produced in the Foundation Course was part of a whole that comprised the Bauhaus's main goals as an institution and what the school saw as its contribution to society and culture at large. Moholy-Nagy's mode of teaching the *Vorkurs* was essential for preparing the next generation and also for his own thinking about a world to come. Via the underlying concepts that the specific exercises were meant to elucidate — tension, equilibrium, new relations between materials, untethered space — students discovered how a praxis in modernism might unfold for future work envisioned as multidirectional and open-ended. The exercises emerged from an imperative of new relationships in the modern world — of materials to each other, of forms in space, of change in the material through the working of it — not just as a pedagogical practice on a prescribed route to a future Bauhaus workshop and architectural training, but as a kind of generative modern-making in its own right. The Foundation Course exercises were aimed at a retooling of human perception, based not on representational image or even a basic knowledge of materials (although these were important steps along the way) but on a new set of relationships between the viewer and the abstract world, however it might come to be shaped. And this, too, is Moholy-Nagy's insight: he was not just trying to come to grips with his age or predict future needs; his work and his pedagogy should instead be read as a prolonged investigation in productive, and productively changing, modern relationships. In a period of accelerated development of technology, manufacturing techniques, and materials, Moholy-Nagy's *Vorkurs* was also astute preparation and attuning of the individual for an unknown future.

■ ■ ■

Moholy-Nagy's works in a plethora of media — with their geometric regularity of planes and surfaces reflecting modern architecture, their range of opacities of glass, and their shifting and projective lighting — emerged from an engagement with the abstract qualities of the metropolis, beginning in 1920s Berlin and ending in 1940s Chicago. Moholy-Nagy brought urban materiality into and onto the painted picture plane, abstracting both its modern materials and its forms; and he reversed this process, using light, in his theater sets and the light space modulators to project outward, into the surrounding space. But what he very much envisioned, and worked toward, was to effect visual change at the level of the metropolis, with the idea of projecting still further out, onto the city itself, onto the facades of large-scale buildings or even more nebulous substances, such as clouds. Both in these realized works and unrealized visions, Moholy-Nagy presented abstractions without, paradoxically, losing sight of the industrial materiality of the modern city. Surface, in this equation, was both substance (regardless of painted content, the material of the artworks' surface was always already part of his paintings' meaning) and projective receiver — receiver of image, of light. His writing, his photography, set designs, and teaching reflected these goals, too. Held in a dialectical relationship of surface and projection, the city's materiality — metal, glass, searchlights — was brought in and abstracted onto the flat picture plane, while in Moholy-Nagy's projective works, the metropolis itself was envisioned as a surface for art. From these investigations, Moholy-Nagy conjured abstracted visions of space and of architecture.

Moholy-Nagy's prodigious, re-mediated output has cemented his importance across the many fields his work encompasses — for art historians, graphic and design historians, photo historians, and media theorists. Although he generally escapes the notice of architectural historians, his work also takes as its center essential components of the modern architecture of its period. Moholy-Nagy created paintings that represented the architectural interactions of the city in pigment, and then engaged its industrial materiality as substrate, which became three-dimensional form — only to dematerialize it into representations of surface and light. Moholy-Nagy can be seen as having a prolonged engagement with modern architectural space and, simultaneously, its breakdown into abstraction.

Moholy-Nagy's objects resonate. They can be seen as part of a long arc of twentieth-century investigations into abstraction and objecthood, the materiality of light, and the problem of surface, representation, and space. A 1941 painting such as *CH 7*, in oil and graphite on canvas, illustrates the continuity of his problematics (fig. 1.21). It might just as well represent the urban lights on planes in his early 1920s work in Berlin, or his avant-garde stage set work of the late 1920s, or the desire for multi-screen projections that he began to formulate in the 1930s, as it does his Chicago period, where he continued to grapple with the effects of light on smoke and vapor (against a darkened sky) for the wartime defense of his

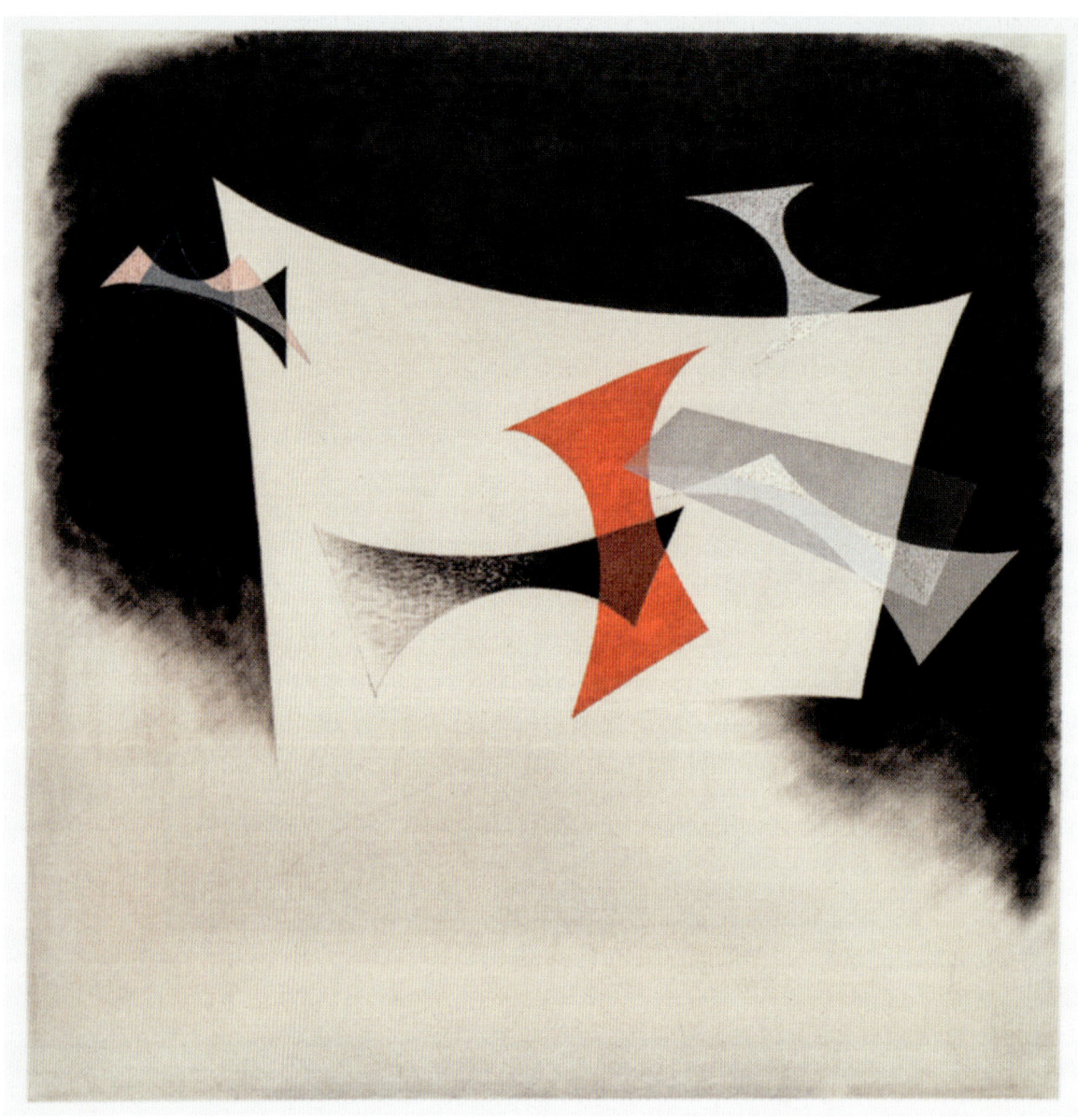

Fig. 1.21 László Moholy-Nagy, *CH 7* (or *Chicago Space 7*), 1941, oil and graphite on canvas. Solomon R. Guggenheim Museum, New York.

adopted city. As Walter Gropius reflected, "Those who may believe that Moholy-Nagy's wide range of activities, in the fields of photography, stage design, art, film, typography, and advertising, dissipated the power of Moholy-Nagy the painter, are mistaken. All his successful activities in these territories were after all nothing but necessary diversions conducted so that he could move up to conquer new conceptions of space in painting."[100] Or as Moholy-Nagy himself asserted in a 1936 speech before the Royal Institute of British Architects, "Often one is questioned about the content" of an abstract picture or a sculpture. "The only comprehensive answer, and a very simple one, is, however, that all modern works of art represent the battle to achieve a new relation to space."[101] Materiality and its dematerializing effects, through the application of light, are held in interconnected tension. Moholy-Nagy desired to use new industrial materials for productive and reproductive ends. He strove to dematerialize the artwork's surface in pursuit of depicting space, constructed via interactions with light. As Moholy-Nagy cycled through differing artistic materials, he used a process of transubstantiation to resolve productive tensions within his own work—between darkness and light, production and reproduction, contained space and projected space, movement and architectural stasis.

Denizens of the burgeoning twentieth-century metropolis faced radical alienation. Yet Moholy-Nagy's abstraction, which could have been alienating, instead investigated—and celebrated—the new urban industrial environment. He connected his abstraction to humanity, writing, "I believe that abstract art not only registers contemporary problems, but projects a desirable future order, unhampered by any secondary meaning.... Abstract art, I thought, creates new types of spatial relationships, new inventions of forms, new visual laws—basic and simple—as the visual counterpart to a more purposeful, cooperative human society."[102] His works allowed for a mode of desubjectivization, a flattening out, a dematerialization—as a way to connect and to create meaning in modern space. And his resonant objects might also ask us to take stock of the city for ourselves—its multiple shifting meanings and the experience it engenders for each of us.

Chapter 2

Minimal Dwelling

Walter Gropius, Marcel Breuer, and László Moholy-Nagy at Isokon in England

At perhaps the culmination of his career to date, on December 4, 1926, Walter Gropius opened the expanded Bauhaus school in its new hometown of Dessau to much fanfare and acclaim. The magnificently designed and outfitted modern building included a theater, canteen, workshops, and student accommodations; nearby stood a row of masters' houses—three double houses and Gropius's own expansive director's house. Gropius left the school in 1928, and six years later he and his wife, Ise, found themselves nearly penniless in England—living in a single-room accommodation at the Lawn Road Flats in the Hampstead area of London (figs. 2.1, 2.2).[1] Although Gropius had faced hardships in Germany's tumultuous 1920s, his beginnings in England were more challenging—he hardly spoke any English at the time of his arrival, and hard currency could not be brought out of Germany (fig. 2.3). A letter from Gropius to his benefactor, Jack Pritchard, presumably composed by Ise, who did speak English, awkwardly but vividly describes his situation:

> Your extraordinary generous invitation for my wife and myself to stay at your house for the period of my first permit has been a really decisive help for our start in England. We are both very thankful not only for having been so very well lodged and boarded but particularly for the extremely warm heartiness [he means, heartedness] and friendship. . . . I am sure . . . our [design] collaboration will soon become productive. . . .
>
> All the more I am ashamed not to be on my own legs yet after six months' work. . . . In two or three weeks . . . I shall be able to pay at least our board. As to the rent it occurred to me today that it might be possible to pay it in German marks. Perhaps it could be done with the help of "Venesta" [the firm that supplied plywood to Pritchard's company, Isokon] provided that your firm has any negotiations with Germany and could use marks without exchanging them, since the export of any German currency is prohibited. This solution would be a great help for me, otherwise I should have to ask you whether you would be prepared to grant a delay in paying my rent. . . . May I ask you to give me your reply very frankly.[2]

In response to another entreaty from Gropius later that autumn, Pritchard would reassure him:

> Dear Gropius,
> Thank you very much for your charming letter.
>
> No, I am not going to let Number 15 at present in any case, so you may as well stay there.
>
> Molly and I would like you to stay on at present, but I expect you would prefer to contribute, and doing your own catering would help. So just do as you like (but of course not till your wife is fit again.)
>
> You must not worry about the risk I took and lost. The risks you have to take are so much bigger than mine which are in the ordinary way of business.

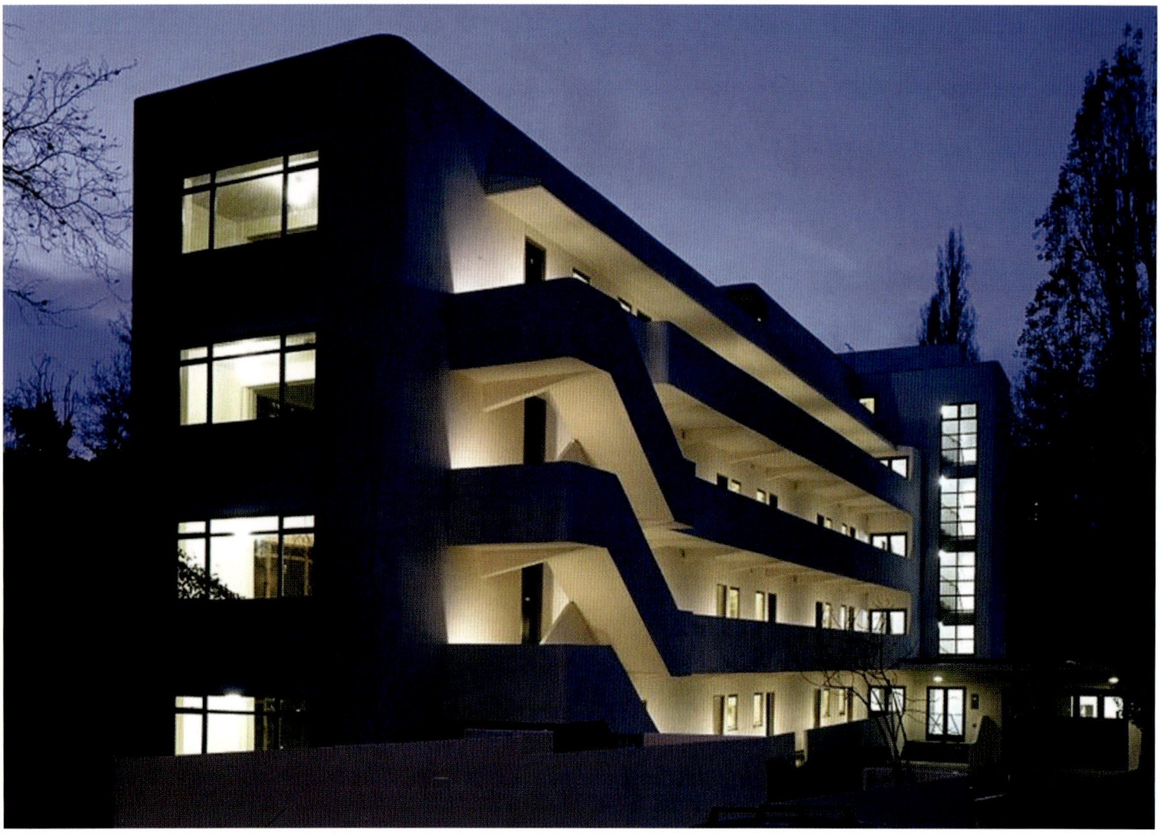

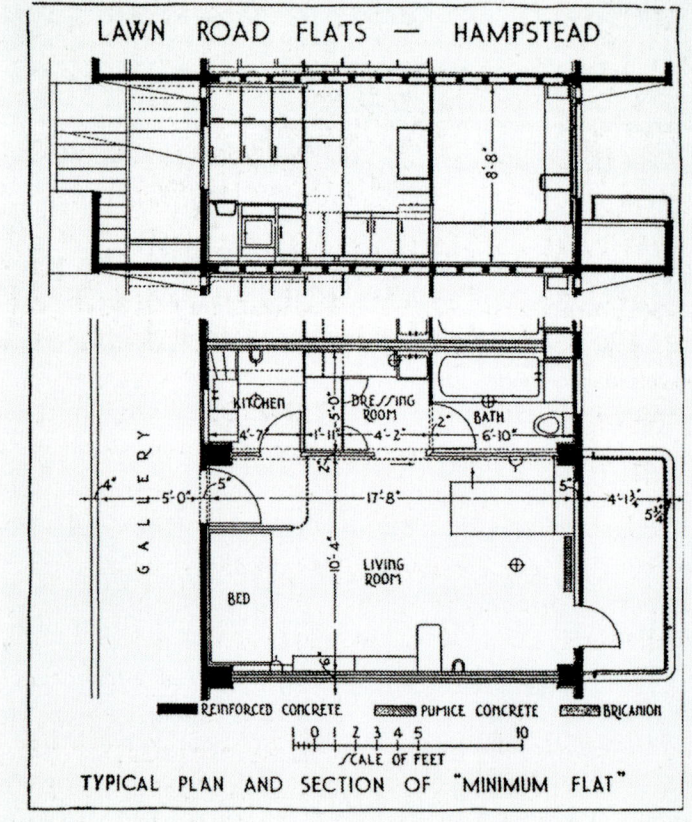

Fig. 2.1 Wells Coates (architect), Lawn Road Flats / Isokon Flats, 1934, London.

Fig. 2.2 Wells Coates, Lawn Road Flats, typical plan and section of a "minimum flat," 1934.

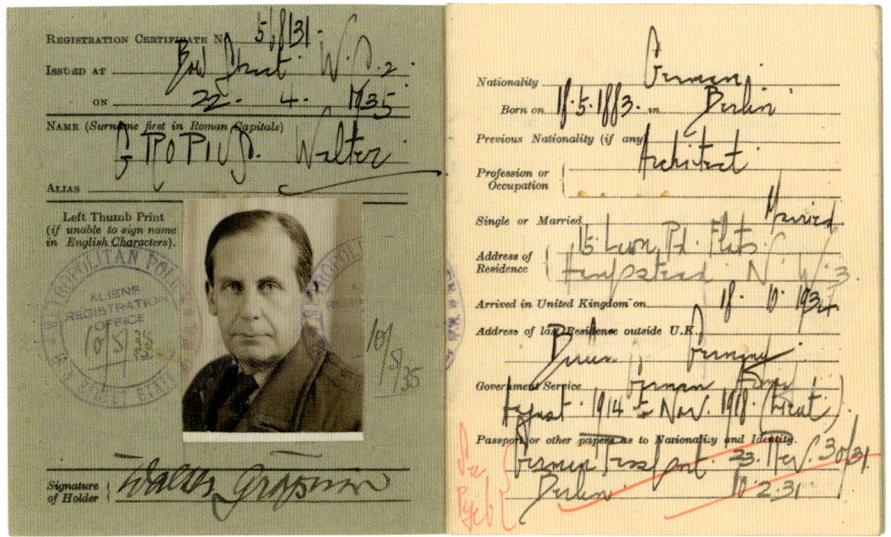

Fig. 2.3 Walter Gropius's certificate of registration to reside in the United Kingdom, 1935.

You have been a tremendous help to us already and I hope that in the near future we can begin to put it on a profitable basis. So please don't decide to start paying for the flat just yet.

It is grand having you in any case and I feel very hopeful that things will begin coming well again soon.[3]

As modern designers fled Germany in the 1930s, many came to find shelter and work under the auspices of the Isokon Furniture Company, a British firm that designed modern furniture and housing featuring new materials, especially plywood (fig. 2.4). Under the patronage of Isokon founder Jack Pritchard, Gropius designed architectural projects; both he and Marcel Breuer were commissioned to design furniture pieces for Isokon; while László Moholy-Nagy contributed to the graphic design of the firm's publicity materials. The British authorities (as overseen by the Royal Institute of British Architects) specified that foreign architects wishing to practice in the United Kingdom had to do so in partnership with a British architect — and that they must be employers, not employees. Therefore Gropius formed a partnership with Maxwell Fry (in 1936), Marcel Breuer with F.R.S. Yorke, and Erich Mendelsohn with Serge Chermayeff (a Russian émigré who had received British citizenship in 1928).

As period documents and archival letters indicate, in no way should Gropius be considered having been forced into political exile, nor, as is sometimes ascribed to him, was he a "refugee" from Nazi Germany. As has been documented by scholars, Gropius did try to remain in Germany and practice under the National Socialists, with little success.[4] His was an artistic and economic emigration, and he was very careful not to ever say or write anything against the Nazis in these years. Breuer and Moholy-Nagy, neither of whom ever attempted to design for the Nazis, each made the decision to move to England as their livelihoods were quickly evaporating in Germany. Moholy-Nagy's description of the modernists' growing artistic isolation in Germany is also illustrative of the early 1930s climate: "The situation of the arts around us is devastating and sterile. One vegetates in total isolation, persuaded by newspaper propaganda

Minimal Dwelling

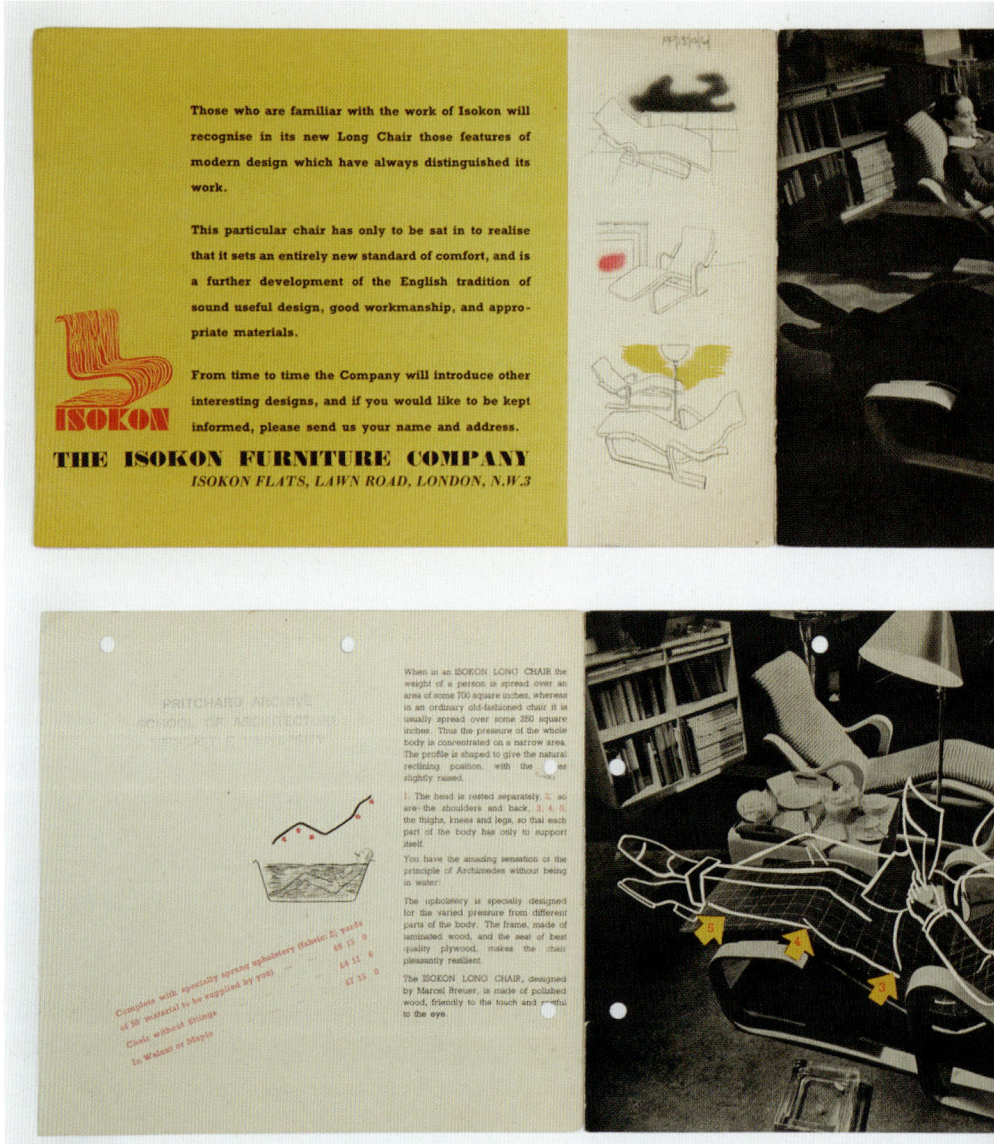

Fig. 2.4 László Moholy-Nagy (graphic design), brochure *The New Isokon Chair*. Marcel Breuer (chair design), Isokon Long Chair, 1936.

that there is no longer any place for any other form of expression than the emptiest phraseology.... One is forced into an insane solipsism."⁵ Moholy-Nagy moved to London following a short stint of work in Holland.⁶ Thus the term "émigré" is used explicitly in this chapter to describe the status of Gropius, Breuer, and Moholy-Nagy in England, instead of the stronger terms "exile" or "refugee."

As opposed to others who made the decision to come to England under severe distress or who had been banished or fled under dangerous conditions (such as Moholy-Nagy's first wife, Lucia Moholy, who fled Germany overnight after the Gestapo raided her apartment), these designers had emigrated willingly. They had time to settle their affairs as best they were able and arrived in London with the requisite letters of invitation to work collaboratively with British citizens, which secured their official status and legal right to work—although their financial situation often remained tenuous. However, these émigrés, once

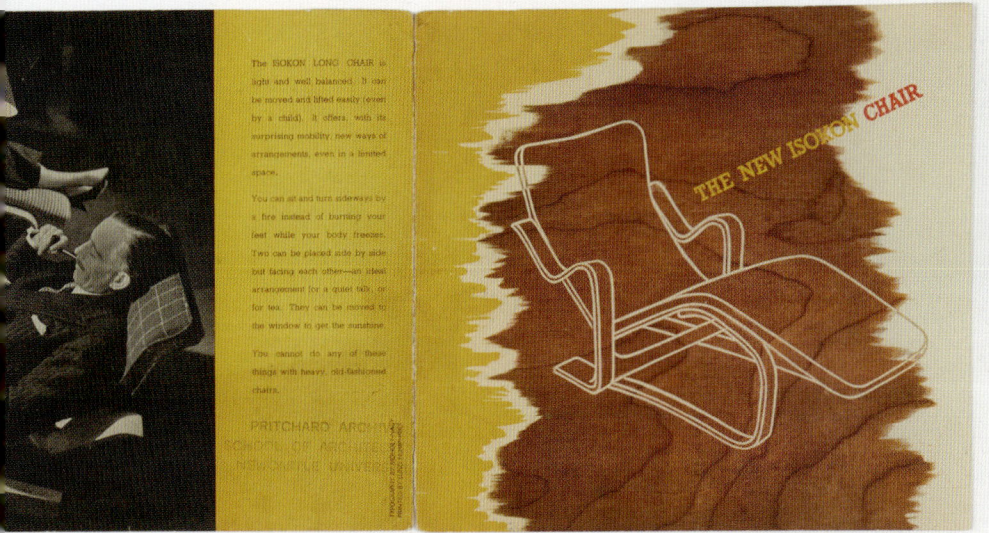

in England, can be understood as in a "state of exile" using the milder sense of the term, in that the political and artistic climate of Germany was such that once they had left, they would have faced difficulties had they tried to return and likely would not have been able to make a living or have a normal day-to-day existence under the Nazis. This is not meant to put them in the same category as political exiles, for whom return would have meant severe persecution or punishment.

This chapter examines the émigrés' 1930s design in terms of the preceding and concurrent debates surrounding "minimal existence" in architecture. It uses the changed circumstances and status of the émigrés themselves – focusing on three leaders of the modern movement in Germany who arrived nearly destitute and lived in greatly reduced quarters – to contextualize ideas of the minimum dwelling anew. Its aim is not to look at the objects designers brought with them *into* exile, rather to examine how conditions and contingencies of exile *itself* informed the design of objects produced in exile.

Minimal Dwelling

It asks how furniture designs, and the spaces for which they were intended—whether in the context of the existing furnished Lawn Road Flats by Wells Coates (himself an expatriate Canadian whose minimalist design was influenced by the childhood he had spent in Japan), or in the similar dwellings Gropius proposed for Windsor, Birmingham, and Manchester—can be better understood as "objects of exile." That is, not only as objects created by designers *in* exile, but related to the *conditions of* exile. Questions surrounding the possibility of translation will be one factor. This chapter looks at the experience of exile and the financial crisis of émigrés like Gropius to contextualize how they failed to come to terms with the economic and social realities of their new surroundings in England. Finally, it examines the ways in which the notion of the total environment implicit in turn-of-the-century theories of the architectural *Gesamtkunstwerk* persisted into the minimalist modernism of the 1920s and 1930s, and into the postwar period, even as architects reconsidered the relationship of luxuries and necessities, individual artistic output and machine production, art and politics.[7] This chapter argues that through these carefully designed interiors, new notions of an architectural *Gesamtkunstwerk* can be found in changed form from its earlier predecessors, arising from the period's difficult economic strictures and the circumstances of emigration.

Dwelling Minimally: *Existenzminimum* in Architecture

Gropius had begun to contemplate the move to England only four months prior to his permanent landing there, writing to British architectural critic Morton Shand in June 1934, "I have seriously been thinking about looking for work in England. The difficulties which oppose this are however considerable, mainly for material reasons. . . . I shall be forced to undertake something because here there are no prospects of work."[8] Pritchard's subsequent invitation was enthusiastic, "When Morton Shand told me that you might consider coming here . . . I was delighted especially as I understand that you would be prepared to work with my friend Maxwell Fry. . . . I am very hopeful that you will be able to come, and I shall be very glad to put one of our flats at your disposal."[9] Gropius accepted the invitation in a letter postmarked a mere three days after the date of Pritchard's letter.[10]

Walter and Ise Gropius arrived at London's Victoria Station on October 18, 1934, and were met by Jack Pritchard, who housed them in unit 15 of his building, Lawn Road Flats (also known as the Isokon Flats or Isokon Building). László Moholy-Nagy joined them in May 1935, taking apartment 16.[11] And Marcel Breuer moved into apartment number 1 that October.[12] The Isokon building, whose accommodations were furnished, proved a particularly useful arrangement for émigrés who arrived with few belongings. Famously Agatha Christie, Henry Moore, and other notable cultural figures lived at Lawn Road, including Sigfried Giedion in 1940.[13] Because they were originally intended as furnished housing for working professionals, the one-room flats were thought a sufficient amount of dwelling space, especially as sliding doors partitioned some units, so they could function as two rooms (fig. 2.5). The modern furniture designed by key architects and designers for Isokon was intended to be mass produced,

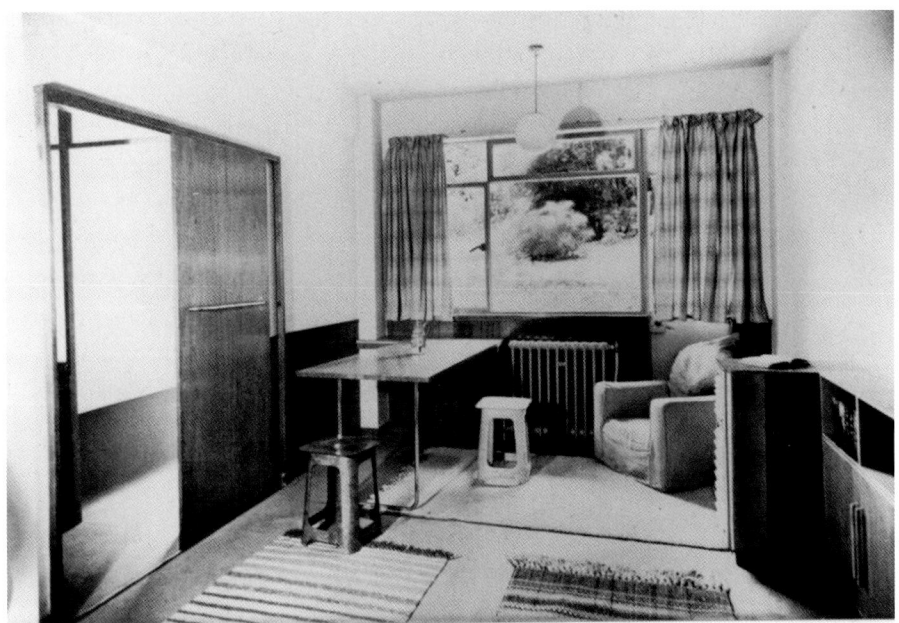

Fig. 2.5 Wells Coates, interior, Isokon Flats, 1934, London. Photograph by Sydney Newbery.

and these pieces also made up the furnishings of Lawn Road Flats. Longtime promoters of a "minimum standard," these émigré modernists now experienced its constrictions through firsthand experience in their move from Germany to London.

For the exiles, the furnishing of the "minimal dwelling" and the architectural "unit" suddenly took on new relevance. In the late 1920s and early 1930s, in response to crowded and unfit housing conditions, the question of the minimal dwelling, framed in the German-speaking realm as *Existenzminimum* (literally, "the minimum requirement for living" or subsistence-level living), was a topic of immense architectural attention, resulting in numerous projects, exhibition displays, conferences, and publications. Modern architects such as Gropius had long worked with the notion of the "minimal dwelling," which encompassed both single-room spaces of inhabitation and whole building systems aggregated from single units. The architectural unit's long history in domestic modernism (and its antecedents) can been seen in such projects as Gropius's *Baukasten* — single building block elements that he intended be combined to construct two- to three-story single and multifamily houses — that he had been working on in Germany as early as 1922.[14]

Elsewhere in Germany, small apartments, intended for working women or childless couples, were also being designed, such as those on display at the 1927 Weissenhofsiedlung exhibition in Stuttgart, or the rooms designed by Lilly Reich, and others, for the 1931 Berlin exhibition, *The Dwelling in Our Time*. There was also a concurrent shrinking and compartmentalizing of domestic space within the dwelling, especially a newfound emphasis on separate sleeping spaces for family members in multiple small rooms, carefully and economically laid out. Other period innovations in this vein, such as the design of the compact and efficiently laid-out kitchen used solely for cooking, exemplified by the Frankfurt Kitchen designed by Margarete Schütte-Lihotzky in 1926, superseded the larger communal living-sleeping-eating-cooking space that had been the norm.

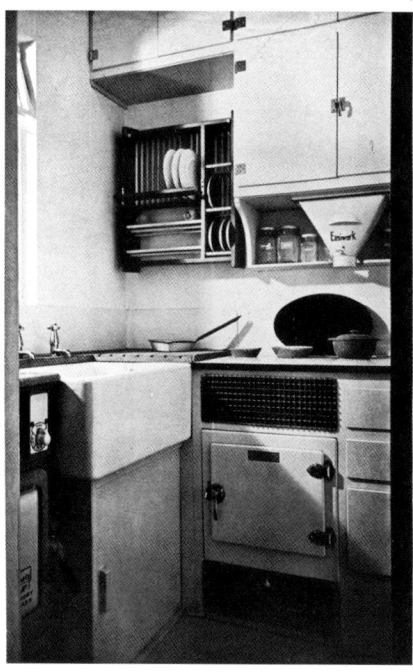

Fig. 2.6 Wells Coates, kitchen, Isokon Flats, 1934, London. Photograph by Sam Lambert.

The Frankfurt Kitchen and other concurrent prototypes influenced the miniscule and minimally provisioned kitchens in the Isokon Building (fig. 2.6).

Other 1920s German architects, such as Ludwig Hilberseimer, likewise considered the pared down architectural unit of minimal dwelling; his multiplicator cells, and what he termed the "living minimum" (*Wohnminimum*), are considered further in chapter 5.[15] In the context of building the metropolis, Hilberseimer outlined two interrelated elements, "the individual cell of the room" and the "collective urban organism."[16] He proposed apartments that were fully outfitted with built-in furniture such that tables and chairs were the only movable furniture, and thus residents could relocate with merely a suitcase, rather than a moving van.[17] The "total design" of these units, Hilberseimer opined, demanded utmost care and specificity — he called for the small apartment to be "meticulously designed" and similarly expressed admiration for "meticulously furnished" cooking alcoves.[18]

Architect (and successor to Gropius as director of the Bauhaus) Hannes Meyer charted similar changes in his proposed "living cells" (*Wohnzellen*) — minimum-size dwellings with thirty-two to fifty-four square meters of living space.[19] For these cells, Meyer reduced the number and size of rooms of the typical middle-class dwelling, eliminated corridors, and devised a "sleeping bunk system" to replace bedrooms. The kitchen was systematically and successively condensed from a "combined kitchen-living room" to a "galley kitchen," to a "kitchen recess," to a "kitchen cupboard." He, like Hilberseimer, saw the organization of standardized elements — forming technical, economic, and social norms — as leading to standard organic architectural entities, that is, as the building up of elements to a total architecture, which, in turn would constitute practical life.[20] But, he stipulated, "The building itself is not a work of art. Its size is determined by the dimensions and functions of its program and not by the shallow pathos of any trimmings."[21]

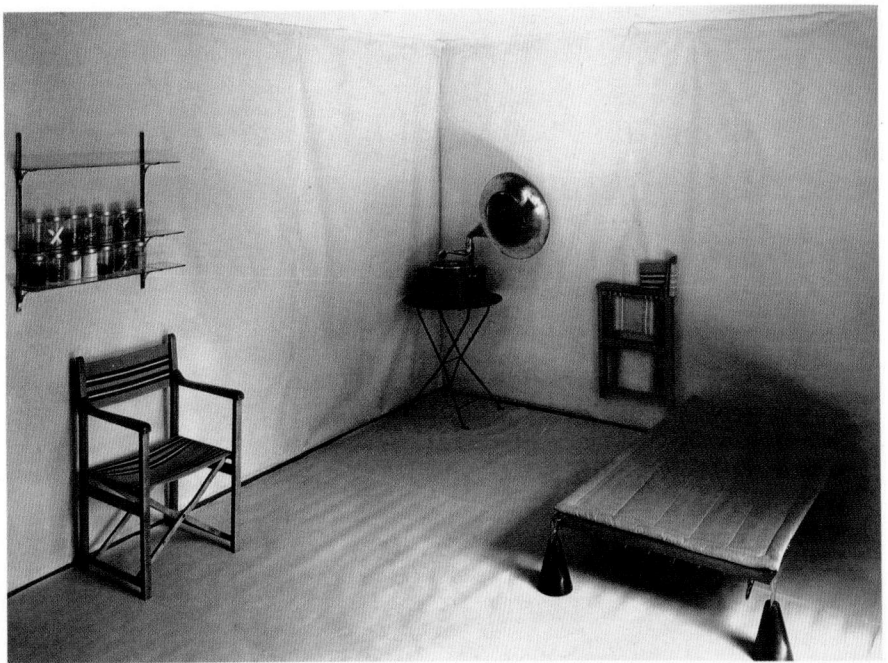

Fig. 2.7 Hannes Meyer (architect), Co-op Interior, 1926. Deutsches Architekturmuseum, Frankfurt am Main.

One of the most visually evocative and early examples is Meyer's Co-op Interior, as seen in a photograph he published in 1926 as part of a larger essay and photo spread titled "The New World" (fig. 2.7).[22] In this proposal, a single room for habitation responds to the peregrinations of modern citizens and their basic necessities: bed, folding chairs, foodstuffs organized in rows, and music. Via mass production with its norms, types, and standards, Meyer argued that "the same needs" can be met for everyone by fulfilling the collective demand with the "standard product" – "the folding chair, roll-top desk, light bulb, bathtub and portable gramophone." As typical standard products manufactured internationally and uniform in design, they would constitute the "apparatus in the mechanization of our daily life."[23] Mass production would both satisfy needs and facilitate collectivity for modern subjects.

Meyer declared, "Dead is the work of art as a 'thing in itself' as 'art for art's sake': our communal consciousness will not tolerate any individualistic excesses."[24] Therein he makes a nuanced move from the traditional notion of the architectural *Gesamtkunstwerk* of the preceding period, to the total environment, proclaiming: "The new work of art is a totality, not an excerpt, not an impression. The new work of art is an elemental creation made by primary means."[25] By reducing living to its essentials, a new, basic totalized environment, as exemplified by the *Co-op Interior*, was put forth by Meyer, replacing what he saw as the prior "artistic" environment. A differing aesthetic emerged, and a language of technocratic rationality replaced what Meyer viewed as an earlier emotionality, but both environments – old and new – can be understood as cohesive *Gesamtkunstwerke*: total works of art. As modern iterations, *Existenzminimum* dwellings arose from detailed systems and analyses, diminutive total environments – *Gesamtkunstwerke* – that were meticulously conceived by architects.

In his writings of the late 1920s and the 1930s, Meyer continued to search for socially concordant means of dwelling through architectural solutions. His

Minimal Dwelling

propositions, albeit aesthetically distanced from the art nouveau *Gesamtkunstwerk* interiors of architects such as Henry van de Velde and others, share essential, underlying ideals of harmonious architecture. In "Bauhaus and Society" (1929) Meyer writes:

> All life is an urge toward harmony. . . . The new theory of building is an epistemology of existence. . . . As a theory of society it is a strategy for balancing co-operative forces and individual forces within the community of a people. This theory of building is not a theory of style. It is not a constructivist system, it is not a doctrine of technical miracles. It is a system for organizing life, and it likewise clarifies physical, psychological, material and economic concerns. It explores, delimits and orders the fields of force of the individual, the family and society. Its basis is the recognition of the living space and the knowledge of the periodicity of the process of living.[26]

The interior, therefore, was to be the basic element of modern life. It was to be a total environment that was standardized and reproducible. Meyer called for "a doctrine of standardization embracing technical, economic and social standards, types and norms . . . to analyze the processes of life and . . . give organic unity to this knowledge in the building."[27] This paring down to essentials had important social repercussions in Meyer's formulation. "Because of the standardization of his needs as regards housing, food, and mental sustenance," Meyer argues, "the semi-nomad of our modern productive system has the benefit of freedom of movement, economies, simplification and relaxation," while "the degree of our standardization is an index of our communal productive system."[28] The result, Meyer suggested, was "true community," achieved through the provision of all basic needs within a single, easily reproducible unit intended to befit a condition of heightened mobility. The minimum dwelling, a meticulously designed *Gesamtkunstwerk* for the modern age, would facilitate modern movement by meeting the total needs of the perambulating modern human. It would also, in Meyer's formulation, foster community and social collectivity, even in the face of displacement that was to come to characterize 1930s Europe. Indeed, the ideas promoted by Meyer and Hilberseimer, of elemental units aggregated into a living community, were part of a widespread interest among German architects in modular dwelling and in the underpinnings of how architecture might give rise to community. Indeed, a spirit of shared community arose among the occupants of the Isokon Flats.

The interest in these issues was pervasive, as other texts published in same period show. Books such as *The Minimum Dwelling* (1932) by the Czech critic and architect Karel Teige focused entirely on this problem. Teige defined the "minimum dwelling" as "the central problem of modern architecture and the battle cry of today's architectural avant-garde. . . . It sheds light on a situation that has reached a point requiring the radical reform and modernization of housing."[29] Like Meyer, Teige saw "a new conception in the culture of dwelling" linking architectural form to social content, whereby "particular types of small apartments, such as those with a live-in kitchen, a small kitchen, or a living room with a cooking nook," were "not simply commensurate variants and alternatives," but rather, each corresponded to differing "social content" and represented "a manifestation of a different cultural level and a different socially determined world."[30] Teige and Meyer both desired to induce political change by refuting bourgeois individualism – they, like other modern architects, believed that meeting common needs via carefully designed spaces would allow for a new kind of society to emerge.

Existenzminimum was also discussed collectively by architects and planners in professional environments. For example, in 1929 the second CIAM (Congrès internationaux d'architecture moderne) met in Frankfurt, taking up as its theme "Die Wohnung für das Existenzminimum," the problem of the minimal dwelling.[31] There, an international group of modern architects and urban planners offered solutions. Le Corbusier and Pierre Jeanneret promoted "standardization, industrialization, and Taylorization," while Frankfurt architect and city planner Ernst May appealed for affordable rental units "just satisfying the material and mental needs of their occupants."[32]

Gropius, lecturing at the congress with a talk titled the "Sociological Foundations of the Minimum Dwelling," described a process in which households were moving away from a model built on larger, intergenerational groups to smaller, nuclear units; he called for a commensurate increase in the number of ever-smaller, self-contained dwelling units.[33] He also acknowledged the inherent difficulties in getting the populace to embrace architects' and planners' new proposals for modern living, noting that the contemporary industrial population of the city originated from the countryside, and while this group lived in a reduced form in the city, it retained "its primitive demands upon life," rather than adhering to a modern totality "of the new form of life."[34]

Gropius's architectural office, too, had been working on these issues just before his emigration in 1934 (although in a vein more directed toward meeting needs pragmatically through modern means, without quite as strong a set of political convictions as those behind Meyer or Teige's assessment of society, mass housing, and production). He developed a standard unit concept, publishing it as the "Gropius Standard": the prototype floor plan shows a diminutive kitchen, bathroom, bedroom, and living-dining room, as well as furnishings and ample storage (fig. 2.8).[35] The end wall, along the bedroom and living room, is entirely glazed and opens onto an outdoor space. In a manuscript produced around the same time, "Minimal Dwelling and Tower Block" (1934), Gropius called for an "objective minimum and a standard dwelling unit."[36] He advocated for a decrease in overall room size, the negative impact of which was to be mitigated by increasing the size of the windows. Like Meyer and Teige, Gropius did believe that modern life might be transformed through mass production, standardization, and the design of a totalized interior environment in which the individual unit connected to a more collective whole and community. These discussions had also reached England by the 1930s.

Isokon and the Minimum Flat

Lawn Road Flats can be viewed as a minimum dwelling within this context, though one focused on convenience for the unencumbered urban professional

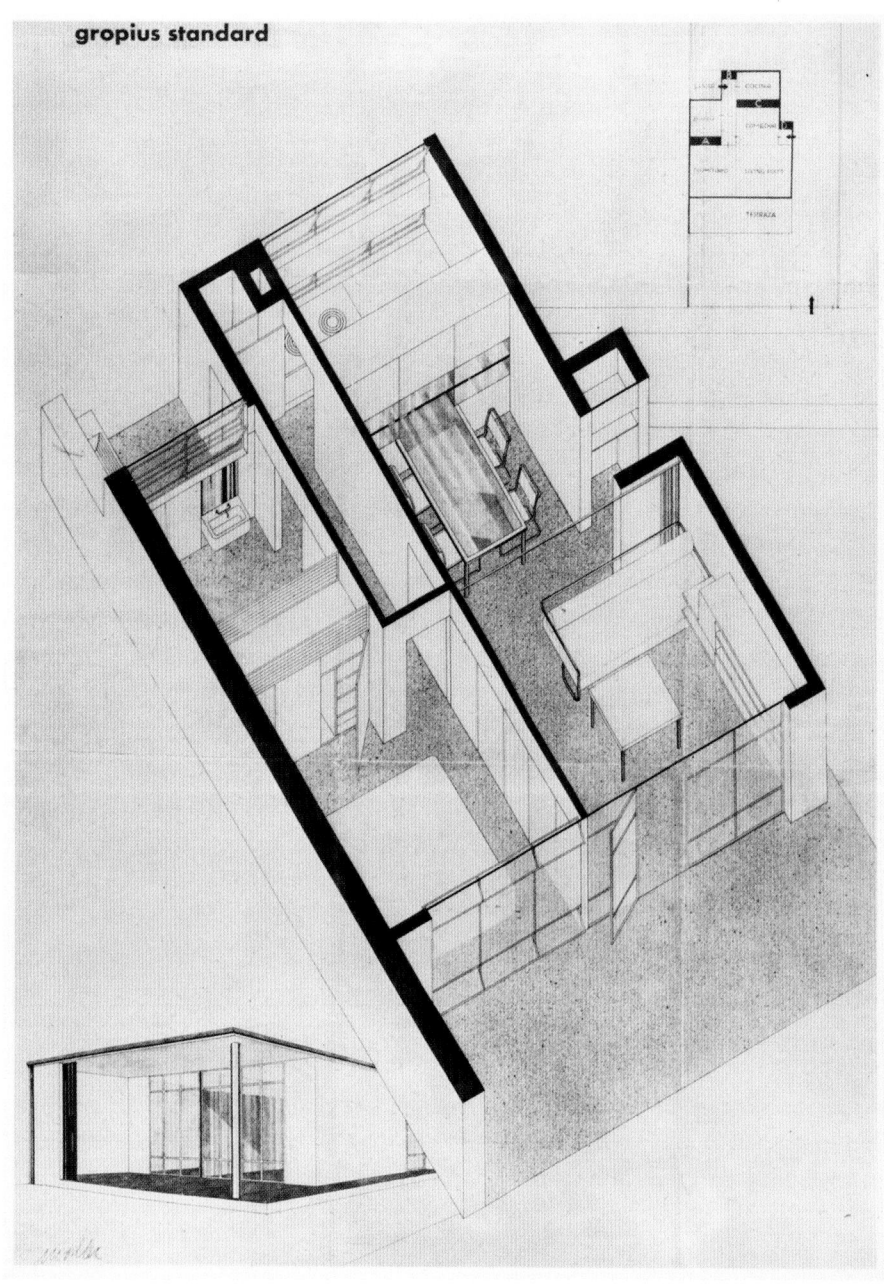

Fig. 2.8 Walter Gropius (architect), Gropius Standard (design for standard apartment), 1934.

class rather than conceived for the working poor. Indeed, an early published plan referred to each unit as a "Minimum Flat" (see fig. 2.2). Molly and Jack Pritchard initially intended to put two single-family houses on the empty site that the couple had purchased in Hampstead. They had found a sympathetic architect in Wells Coates, whom they met and hired in 1929. In spring 1932, Molly Pritchard devised a new brief for a building with multiple apartments. In addition to themselves, it was intended for young professionals with few possessions and simple needs — sleeping, cooking, eating, storage of clothes — with an attendant domestic service providing amenities such as window cleaning, dusting, and bedmaking, as well as simple meals to be supplied by a manager.[37] The Pritchards also specified unit construction, built-in furniture, and modern

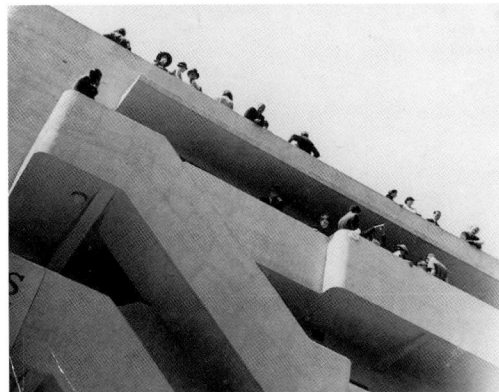

Fig. 2.9 Isokon opening ceremony, July 9, 1934. Photograph by Edith Tudor-Hart.

equipment. For his part, Coates described his idea in a letter to Jack Pritchard, "this idea of property — so much of this little garden is for you m'dear and this tweeny little wishy bit is for me so there! — is dead, dead, dead.... My scheme provides a place which every actor in this drama can call his own place and further than that my Idea of property does not go. This is the room where I sleep, this is where I work and this is where I eat."[38]

Ideas similar to those of Hannes Meyer can be found in Coates's idea of modern mobility: "We don't possess our homes in the old, permanent, settled sense; we move from place to place, to find work or to find new surroundings.... We cannot burden ourselves with permanent tangible possessions, as well as our real new possession of freedom, travel, new experience — in short, what we call life."[39] And Molly Pritchard asked expansively, "How do we want to live, what sort of framework must we build around ourselves to make that living as pleasant as possible?"[40] Together they formed a company — Isokon — in December 1931. The name was a shortened form of "Isometric Unit Construction," an amalgam of the isometric perspectives favored by Coates and the intended modular units of the building.[41] Coates displayed a full-scale Minimum Flat at an exhibition — *British Industrial Art in Relation to the Home* — at Dorland Hall in London in 1933, gaining enough committed interest to move the project forward.[42] The Isokon building opened on July 9, 1934 (fig. 2.9).

As Jack Pritchard describes the period, "We met Wells [Coates] at exactly the right moment. We had just been hit by the Bauhaus, which in fact we went to see with Wells and [Serge] Chermayeff. We were very much bowled over by that episode."[43] Their 1931 research trip to Germany, during which period Coates was working on the architectural designs for the Pritchards, was to investigate potential uses for plywood in architecture and furniture. The group visited Gropius's Bauhaus buildings in Dessau, among other modern architectural sites in Germany. The amenities of the Bauhaus's student dormitory rooms — dwelling cells with individual balconies and simple common tea kitchens on each level, serviced by a ground floor central kitchen and canteen for meals — seem to find an apt successor in Coates's solution for Lawn Road (figs. 2.10, 2.11). In total, the Isokon Building comprised twenty-nine apartments, each with a sitting room with sliding table and single or double bed, plus a bathroom and adjacent dressing room (fig. 2.12; see also fig. 2.5).[44] The double apartments differed only in that a sliding partition created a separate bedroom, and a larger bed was

Minimal Dwelling

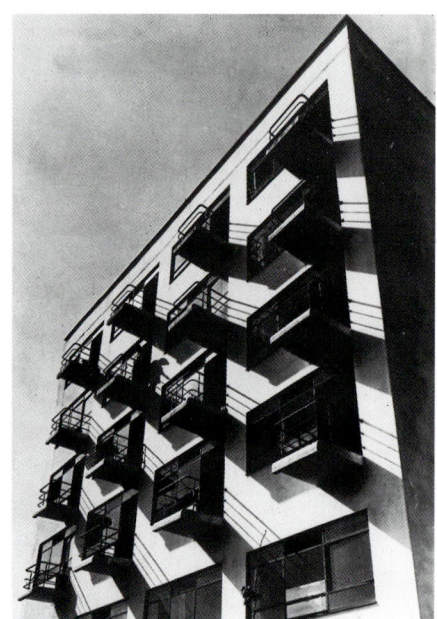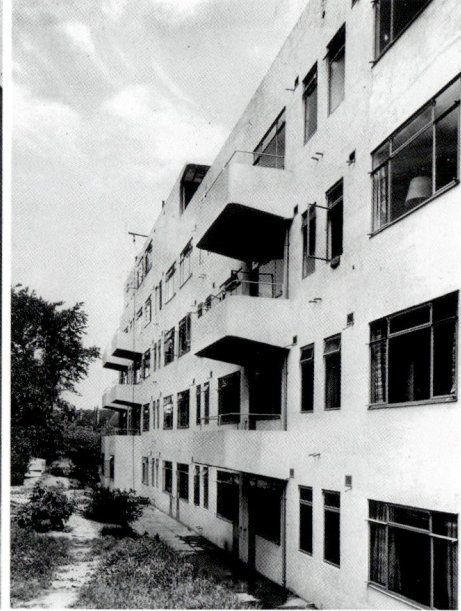

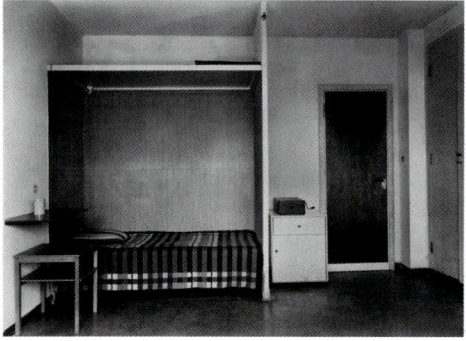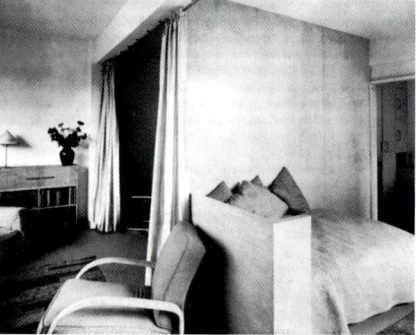

Fig. 2.10 *Top left*, Walter Gropius, Bauhaus Building, Dessau, 1925–26, studio wing balconies from the northeast, gelatin silver print, ca. 1925–26, printed later. *Top right*, Wells Coates, Isokon Flats showing rear balconies, London, 1934.

Fig. 2.11 *Above left*, Walter Gropius, Bauhaus Building, student room in dormitory wing, Dessau, 1925–26, gelatin silver print. Photograph by Walter Peterhans, ca. 1926. *Above right*, Wells Coates, Apartment of Ise and Walter Gropius (no. 15) at the Isokon Flats, 1934, London.

Fig. 2.12 *Right*, Wells Coates, dressing room, Isokon Flats, 1934, London. Photograph by Sydney Newbery.

Fig. 2.13 *Far right*, Wells Coates, combination electric radiator–cocktail cabinet–radio unit in mahogany, 1933. As exhibited in the Minimum Flat for Lawn Road Flats, *British Industrial Art in Relation to the Home* exhibition, Dorland Hall, 1933. Later installed at Lawn Road Flats.

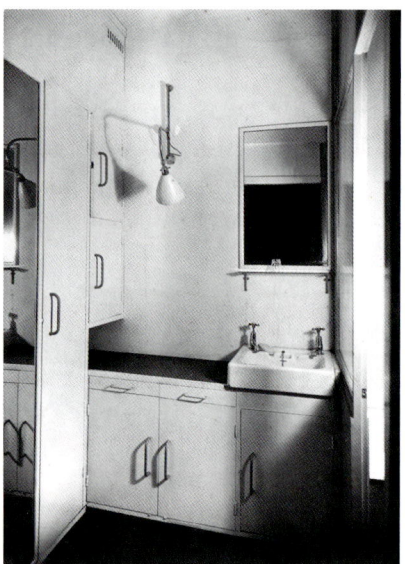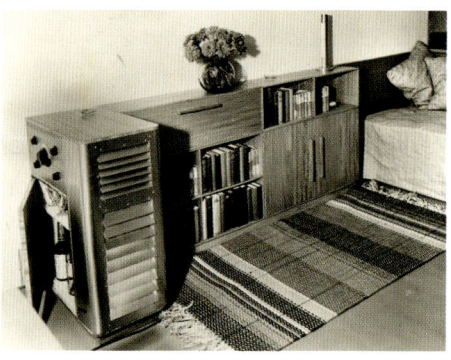

provided. Each floor had a common pantry and service trolley with electric hot plates, with telephones in each apartment to connect to the central kitchen and order food; every unit also had its own rudimentary kitchen (see fig. 2.6).[45] Additional furniture, well-fitted to the spaces, could be arranged via a hire-purchase agreement with Isokon, including plywood unit bookshelves, cupboards, and an ingenious combination electric radiator-cocktail cabinet-radio unit (fig. 2.13).[46] Residents needed to merely insert light personal belongings into this domestic realm. As Coates noted, "Very soon it will be considered quite as fantastic to move accompanied by wardrobes, tables and beds, as it would seem today to remove the bath, or the heating system, including all the pipes."[47]

This arrangement proved particularly convenient for émigrés who, like Walter and Ise Gropius, arrived with only suitcases. Space constrictions notwithstanding, Gropius sought to meticulously set up his apartment as a highly productive space to entertain, woo potential clients, and work. To make his flat "more efficient for social purposes," Gropius inquired from Pritchard whether he "could hire from Isokon some more furniture, i.e. a sofa matching the existing fauteuil [armchair], a lampstand (both as in [apartment] number 7), a writing board of 18" to 48" fixed to the wall (or on legs) and two more stools. Further we should like to exchange the existing large bed with a small one, and the existing round table with a rectangular one. Altogether this would bring about great improvement of the flat."[48] In this work-living environment, in which so much had to take place and so much was at stake for the Gropiuses, careful and efficient design were key to meeting needs.

One reads in these suggested amendments the importance of the unit's functioning for social business and its use as a workspace, over the Gropiuses' day-to-day living comforts, as evidenced by the addition of significantly more seating, in an already tight space, and the request by a large man for a smaller bed. This aspect, namely, the relationship of social connections to the acquisition of architectural commissions, is key, especially in an exilic context, where Gropius and his fellow émigrés needed to establish themselves anew in an entirely foreign situation. These cultural circumstances had a direct impact on the design produced in this period. Gropius came from a well-established, elite Prussian family and had always enjoyed every social advantage — especially over newcomers and architects from more workaday backgrounds, such as Ludwig Mies van der Rohe. Here, perhaps for the first time in his life, Gropius was nearly a complete outsider.

While the social network among the exiles themselves was robust and needed no special accommodation, connecting to British architects and potential clients was something that required the tools of social assimilation and astute attention to local conditions. Gropius's carefully inserted, extraneous sofa and his rapidly diminishing bed, are seemingly small, yet critical details that he deployed to function in his new surroundings. Telling, perhaps, is the reply Gropius gives to Pritchard regarding the alcohol supply at Lawn Road Flats, presumably used to entertain. Pritchard had inquired of Gropius:

> Some of our tenants have asked us if it would be possible for us to make arrangements to carry a stock of wine, beer, and whiskey on the premises.

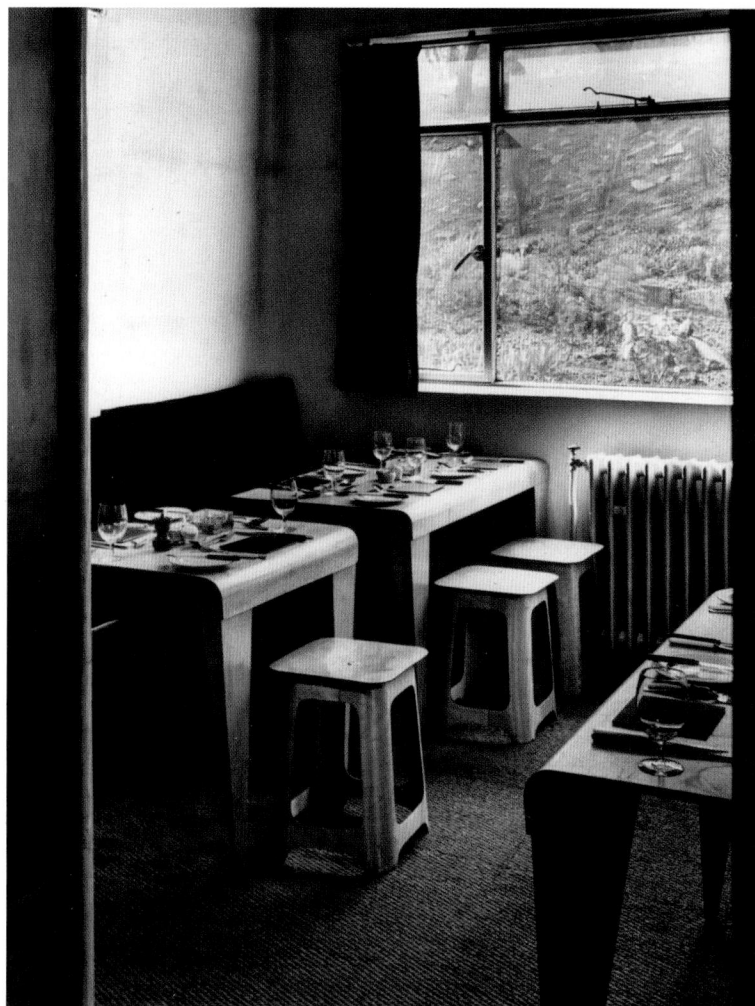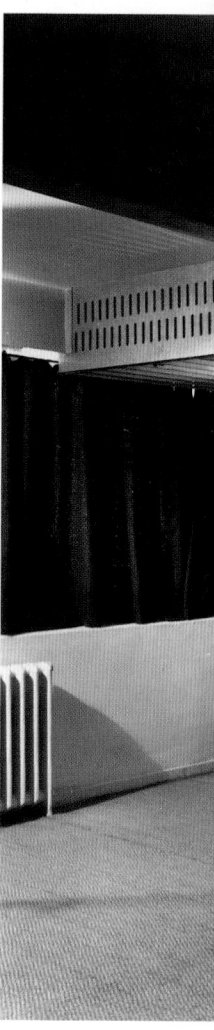

Fig. 2.14 *Left*, Marcel Breuer and F.R.S. Yorke (designers), dining area of the Isobar, 1937, London. *Right*, bar area of the Isobar, 1937. Photographs by Dell and Wainwright.

As there are certain legal points to be got over before we can do this, it would be of great help to us if tenants would give us some idea of their probable requirements by answering the following questionnaire:

1. Would it be a convenience to you to be able to purchase wine, beer and spirits on the premises instead of having to have it brought in specially?

2. Are your special requirements likely to be:

a. Wine b. Beer c. Spirits

3. Could you give us some idea of the probable quantities you would be likely to require?

4. If wine, the ideal stock to be held?[49]

Gropius replied affirmatively, estimating his need at "about 20 half bottles of Bass Ale per month, about 20 half bottles of Milk Stout per month, about 1 bottle of whiskey (J. Haig) per month."[50]

The Isobar opened in November 1937 in the basement of Lawn Road Flats and proved to be a significant social space for the building. It was divided into a restaurant with seven tables (it took over the building's central kitchen,

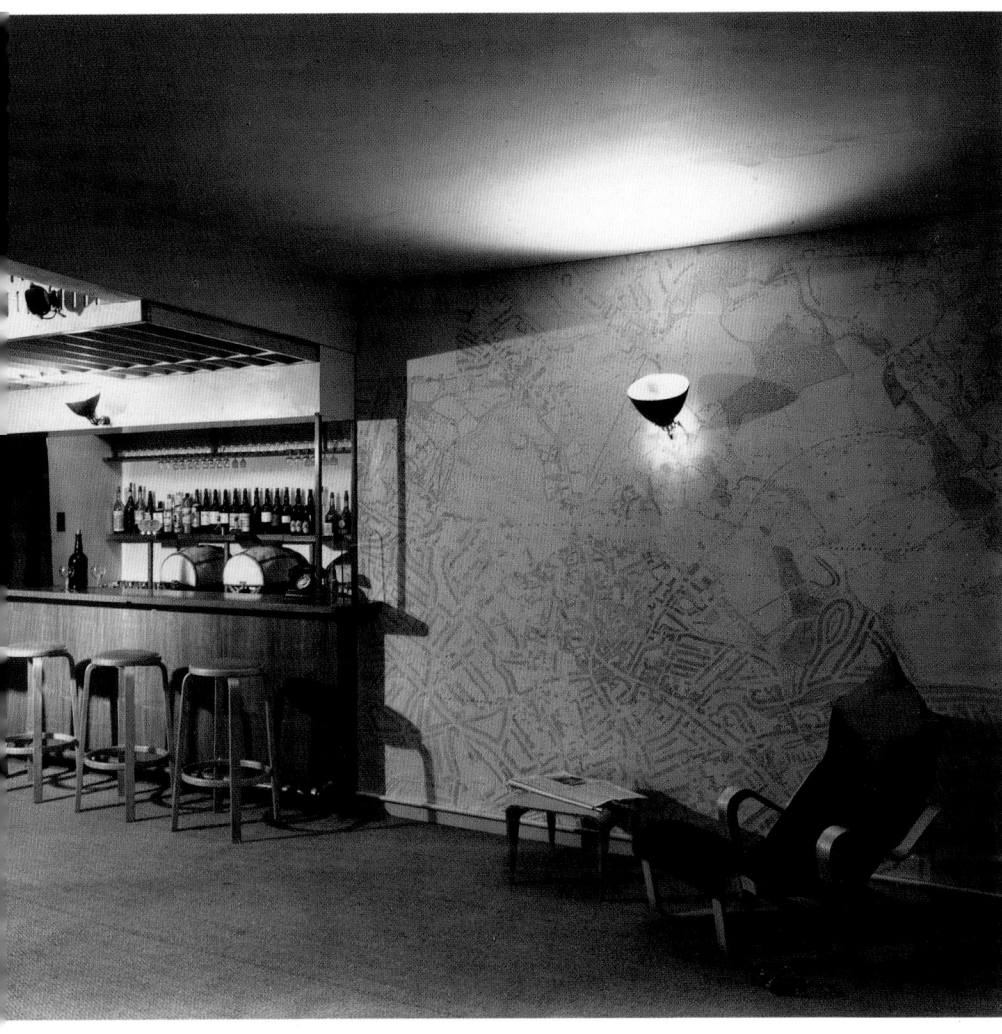

superseding the earlier arrangement of ordering up meals) and a larger club room with a fully stocked bar (fig. 2.14).[51] Designed by Marcel Breuer (with F.R.S. Yorke), the space was modern, warm, and inviting, and showcased natural materials, especially plywood. The bar was made of teak and white-painted deal wood, a birch screen was fitted between the bar and the restaurant, and the tables, chairs, and stools were in birch plywood.[52] There was a prominent barograph for taking weather readings, as well as a wall-mounted surface pressure chart. A large-scale map of Hampstead graced the wall, with its streams and ponds painted in blue.

The Isobar galvanized Lawn Road's dwellers, as well as local artistic and architectural figures, forming a stimulating hub and center of gravity for the exile community in the surrounding area, who gathered regularly at its tables – both genuine exiles and those whose ideals differed from 1930s mainstream British thought. Community was fostered by shared interests in food, science, and culture – in addition to a Supper Club, the Isobar had a General Committee; a Wine Committee (which also evaluated and served high-quality, rare beers); an Arts Committee, which exhibited and sold artworks; a Weather Committee, which tracked and provided information from the Air Ministry and whose leadership included Molly Pritchard; and a Literature Committee, which held subscriptions to a wide variety of international periodicals and newspapers.[53] Sibyl Moholy-Nagy fondly remembered the "'ever-open Lawn Road flats and the endlessly generous companionship they offered."[54] And historian Fiona MacCarthy has noted that the Isobar in its early years "had a unique quality, inseparably related to that time and place and purpose. An atmosphere of serious intention, solemn subjects being bandied to and fro beneath the barograph. And at the same time a kind of quality of craziness, a sense of dislocation, broken accents, broken marriages. An irresponsibility engendered by the number of arrivals and departures, set against a background of political uncertainty."[55] Indeed, the exilic condition – one marked by uncertainty, hard work, a positive belief in modernism, and an attempt to form a new community – is aptly described by, and reflected in, the situation of the building and its occupants.

Isokon Expands into the Housing Market

After the success of Lawn Road Flats, Pritchard laid out his ideas for an expansion of the Isokon idea in architecture and furnishings. He extended his mission for the firm and redefined "Isokon" as a proprietary word denoting the application of modern functional design to houses, apartments, furniture, and fittings and the idea of standard unit construction, not just for units of housing, but for their contents. His plan was to first build and manage a number of Isokon service apartments, each with Isokon furniture and fittings, then follow with private houses built to householders' specifications from Isokon units, with interiors to be fitted out and furnished by Isokon.[56] With these plans in mind, Pritchard worked closely with Gropius and his fellow émigrés to bring these ideas to fruition.

Isokon's initial focus was on housing at a variety of scales. A diminutive building, referred to as "Isokon 1½," was planned for a small site to the north of the Lawn Road Flats, to be designed by Gropius. The project underwent several iterations. Pritchard, envisioning a small timber building, instructed Gropius, "I have in mind a small sitting room, dining room, one or two sleeping spaces, and large studio. Alternatively something much smaller, say living room and bedroom."[57] Another proposal was for offices, two studio apartments, and a restaurant for twenty to thirty people.[58] Neither idea came to fruition. Over the course of late winter and spring of 1935, Isokon had also unsuccessfully sought to acquire and build on land to the west of the Isokon Building where there were existing workshops and a yard known as "1–5 Lawn Road stables," as well as attempting to annex other adjacent properties.[59]

In 1934, Pritchard commissioned Gropius, before he had even arrived in London, to design an apartment building known as Isokon 2 for a riverfront property in Manchester. Eventually, because of immigration requirements, it would be in partnership with the British architect Maxwell Fry.[60] As Fry would write to the more established Gropius, "I know from Morton Shand that you have accepted Pritchard's offer to design a block of flats in Manchester with me as a collaborator. I feel very honored and glad to be able to work with you. I have talked to Pritchard and gather from him that as soon as the Lawn Road Flats are 80% let he will get finances for the new project."[61] Photographs of the proposed site, taken in preparation for the development of the project, show a garden with mature trees, ferns, pathways, a pergola walk, and lawns, including existing lawn tennis courts.[62] Fry visited the site and reported back to Gropius, "[It] is at the end of a cul-de-sac development built about 1880 at a bad, dull period. It is about 3 acres most of which is low lying. At the bottom of the garden is the river Mersey heavily embanked and not visible. . . . Pritchard thinks we should build bigger flats than at Lawn Road with a preponderance of two and three room flats, and some even larger, with a few 1-room bachelor flats on top."[63]

A report was prepared in November 1934 that assessed (through meetings with local agents, owners of flats, estate agents, and the city surveyor) competing existing serviced flats in Manchester; among equivalent offerings evaluated, the report noted amenities such as the location of telephones (in the hall or in each flat), whether the flats came with fitted furniture, rents, terms of the lease, and so forth.[64] For Isokon 2, the report's author determined that "flats for two people or a couple with one, or even two, children is the mark—that is, two young men sharing or a young couple. The flats should have, say, two beds, one sitting room, kitchen and bath. This would make the cost per person low enough for Manchester (i.e. lower than each person having a single flat with kitchen and bath) and enable us to compete. . . . I doubt if more service than stair cleaning, central heating and water should be given."[65] Thus, with a sitting room separate from one, or even two, bedrooms, the apartments envisioned were larger and contained more rooms than those at the Isokon Building. Pritchard, however, struggled to find financial backing for the project.

Soon thereafter, in March 1935, plans for Isokon 4 in Birmingham were begun by Gropius and Fry. Similar to the development in Manchester, Pritchard proposed that each flat in the Birmingham project have three rooms, plus a kitchen and bathroom; additionally "constant hot water," central heating, and a porter were foreseen.[66] Gropius produced a drawing with a curved building set near a lake, with a multitude of pathways and plantings around the irregular lot.[67] He carefully sited and shaped the apartment block to preserve the old trees, envisioning a single large building comprising twenty-four apartment units, each nearly identical in size (30–35 square feet), with balconies and three communal staircases.[68] By July, Pritchard reported to Gropius that he was ready to move forward; because it was smaller than Manchester, they could move more swiftly.[69]

As with Isokon 2 in Manchester, comparative market research was conducted in Birmingham, and an estimate was made of the projected costs of cleaning, management, fuel, lighting, and employing a porter and his wife to work on the premises.[70] The design progressed in earnest, with Pritchard asking Gropius to create three apartment types: flats with three bedrooms (accommodating small families: husband, wife, child, and a nursemaid); single flats (for a man or a woman, similar to those at Lawn Road); and one or two "special flats," which were penthouse units on the roof.[71] Proposed amenities, to be costed separately, included squash courts, a swimming pool, internal telephones from the flats to the porter's quarters; and "arrangements for wireless aerials for each tenant to plug in his own apparatus."[72] A Birmingham surveyor and appraiser employed by Isokon determined, "I am of the opinion that a scheme for sixteen flats with a small swimming pool would succeed on this site if built . . .

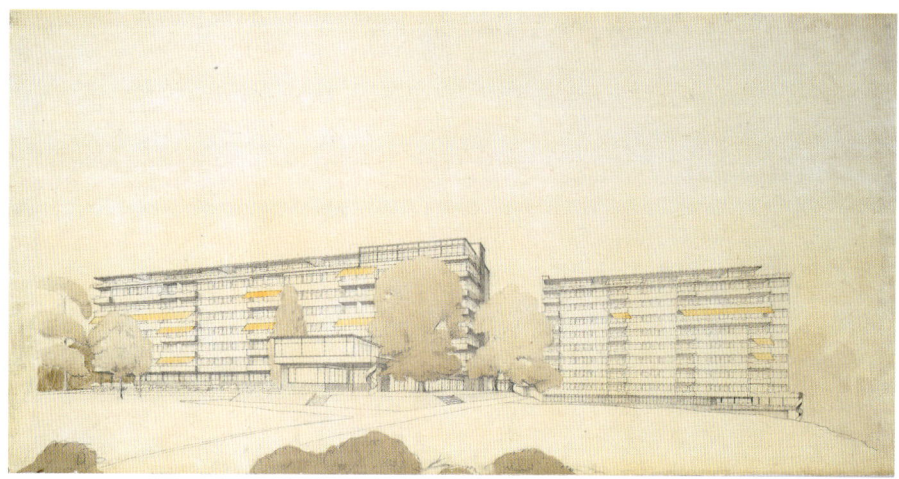

Fig. 2.15 *Above*, Walter Gropius and Maxwell Fry (architects), design for Windsor Apartment Complex / Isokon 3, Windsor, 1934–35. *Opposite*, interior design for Windsor Apartment Complex.

in blocks of four."[73] However, Isokon 1½, Isokon 2, and Isokon 4 all ultimately proved unviable.

Isokon 3 represents the most developed foray into housing by the Isokon Company. Known as the St. Leonard's Hill "Windsor Apartment Complex," designed by Fry and Gropius (although in practice this was mainly Gropius's project), its luxury apartments were upscale in scope from other Isokon initiatives (fig. 2.15). It was to be located on a large, countryside estate just outside the town of Windsor, a lengthy commuting distance from London. The justification for this development was made via a new angle; rather than build a new suburban town of small, single-family houses on the thirty-three-acre estate, which was the predominant mode of housing expansion in England in this period, Gropius argued for "preservation by concentrated development," proposing to conserve the countryside by building three high-rise apartment blocks to house five hundred people.[74]

Gropius's "country apartment houses," as the American architectural historian Henry-Russell Hitchcock referred to them, were a unique solution in the context of the United Kingdom. In his text on modern architecture in England, Hitchcock noted that building in such density would preserve, as landscape, the integrity of "magnificent private estates that are perpetually coming on the market . . . instead of breaking them up into garden suburbs of small lots. . . . Otherwise the entire southeast of England will become one unbroken dormitory of two-story villas."[75] As the development could potentially be seen from Windsor Castle, permission had to be obtained from King George V, who surprisingly gave preliminary approval, although his royal representative noted, "while there is no objection to flats being built there, it would be an advantage to have the flats as low as possible, because they are clearly seen from the windows of the Castle that are looking that way."[76]

At different phases of development, the scheme varied in dimension and scale, from two blocks of 69 apartments to a later plan for three towers with 110 units.[77] Each apartment block was sited so that every dwelling unit would enjoy stunning views of Windsor Forest and the Royal Park; the idea expressed by the architects was that the land would be "preserved for all time" and that the view "belongs to everybody."[78] The tenants would enjoy a myriad of amenities,

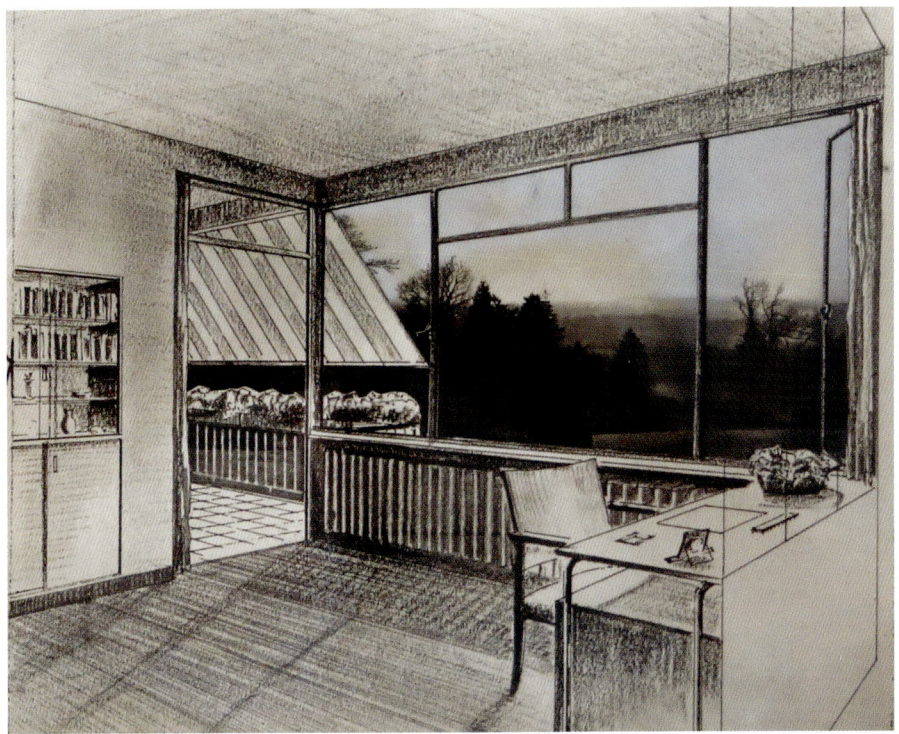

including tennis and squash courts, a swimming pool, a cocktail bar, a ballroom, a "completely equipped Turkish bath," a barber's shop, a film screening room, and a darkroom, as well as "good stabling for horses."[79] In the apartments themselves, plans were mounted for very modern (for 1935 England) domestic appliances such as kitchens with refrigerators, electric stoves, and a garbage disposal system; in terms of infrastructure, the buildings were to have both central heating and electric radiators, an internal telephone system, a post office system, and "express, smooth-running automatic passenger lifts."[80] The available housekeeping services included window cleaning once per month, shoe cleaning, daily dusting and weekly cleaning, and more.[81]

With the hope of funding the development through advance subscriptions, Isokon prepared shares for the project, which were released on July 1, 1935.[82] To meet the cost of the land, roads, the architectural plans, constructing the initial apartment block of sixty-nine units, as well as the amenities of the restaurant, tennis courts, and swimming pool, the funding goal was set at £135,000.[83] Pritchard sought to publicize the project and obtain potential shareholders through an arrangement with Harrods department store. He proposed that Harrods host a launch event (either a luncheon or a "sherry party") with models of the Windsor development, explanatory texts, and large-scale photographs; additionally, he suggested a longer-term exhibition in Harrods' furniture showrooms displaying the sitting and dining room of a typical flat, to be fully furnished by Harrods.[84] The windows' prospective countryside views could be simulated by strategically mounting photographic enlargements in the display. Pritchard also proposed that once the apartments were built, Harrods would install a shopping service at the new building with a booth for taking orders — so that from the comfort of home Windsor tenants could shop at Harrods.[85] However, the department store rejected all of these ideas as taking up too much floorspace and likely resulting in too little income. Pritchard was able to appeal to another tony establishment, Hampton's, located at 20 St James's Square in London, who did hold an exhibition in summer 1935, of models, plans, and photographs "illustrating a new method of saving the fine old country estates around the big cities."[86]

Ultimately, all of the Isokon building projects, including Isokon 3 at Windsor, faced local opposition and failed—neither investors nor individual dwellers, it seemed, were ready to accept the Isokon idea. As Pritchard wrote to Gropius, in July 1935 to break the news about Isokon 3:

> We have been unable to raise the money required for No 3. . . . You will think me a broken reed. First No 2 . . . then No 3 . . . and you will think that we have asked you to England for nothing. I have now pushed ahead with No 1½ and hope to purchase the land to the north of the Lawn Road Flats, and we hope that you will design a building on the new land for us. Meanwhile my wife and I would like to ask you both to stay with us anyway for a few months until we know what the position is.[87]

Fortunately, Gropius was busy on other projects in this period. He drew up plans for a student dormitory for Christ's College of Cambridge University. For this complex project he envisioned ten street-level shops, fifty-one dormitory rooms on three floors, and two rooftop penthouses for the college's Fellows. He was also working on other mixed-use and dormitory buildings, also not built, such as that for Black Mountain College in North Carolina, a school at which other former Bauhaus members had found employment.[88] His experience living in a situation that could almost be described as a dormitory surely had an impact on his architectural visions for dwelling in this period and beyond.

A commission that did come to successful fruition was Gropius and Fry's Impington Village College, a school and community center completed in 1939. The duo also built two private houses in this period, the Benn Levy House in the Chelsea area of London and the Wood House, in Kent.[89] The two-story, cedar clapboard Wood House was well-sited on a prospect with sweeping views of the countryside. It featured indoor-outdoor living with a covered terrace off the dining room, sheltered children's play area with a glass and steel screen, and second-story sleeping porch, accessible internally and from an exterior staircase.[90] It combined many of the features of his own Bauhaus director's house in Dessau, while folding in natural materials, such as a flint stone fireplace.

The Wood House, which by Fry's own account, was not co-designed with Fry, would prove an important influence on the subsequent house that Gropius would design for himself (with Marcel Breuer) in Lincoln, Massachusetts, once he was established at Harvard University (fig. 2.16). Like the Wood House, Gropius's subsequent US home would feature a large entrance overhang, horizontal windows, covered indoor-outdoor living spaces, as well as a second-floor sleeping porch, similarly accessible by an exterior staircase, and many other similar details. The Gropius Residence in Lincoln is often thought to be influenced by New England vernacular architecture, but it bears many of the elements of the Wood House, reflecting the roots and origins of New England's buildings in England.

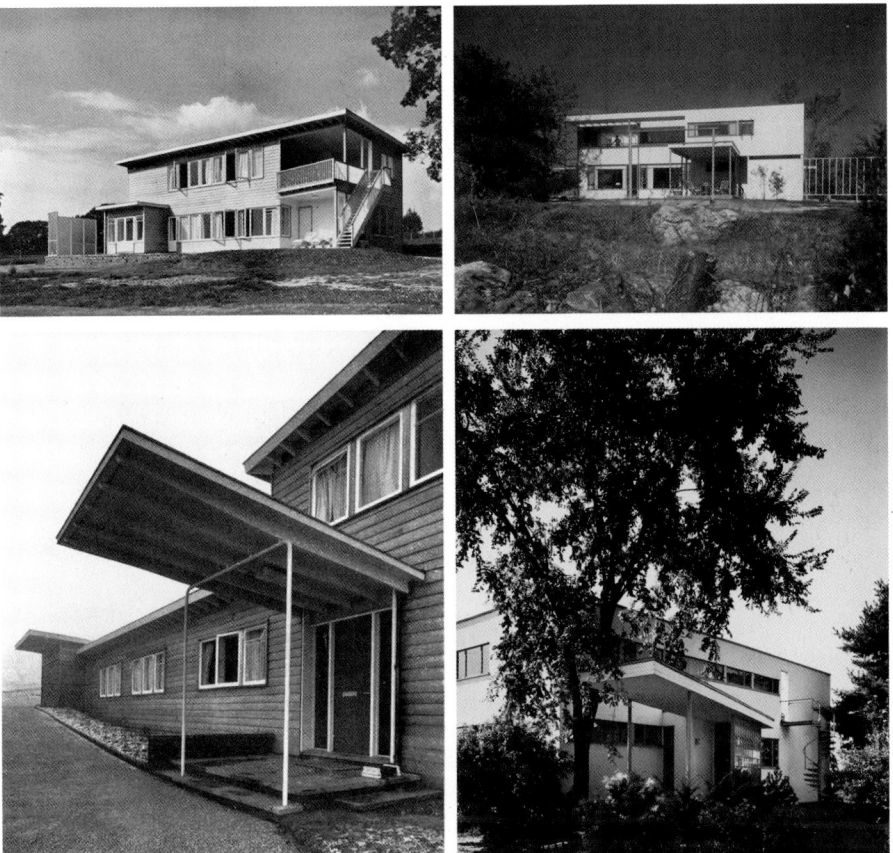

Fig. 2.16 *Left, top and bottom*, Walter Gropius and Maxwell Fry, Wood House, Shipbourne, Kent, 1936–38. Photographs by Millar & Harris. *Right*, Walter Gropius and Marcel Breuer, Gropius Residence, 1937–38, Lincoln, Massachusetts, rear view (*top*) and view from east (*bottom*).

Another key project was Gropius's "Flat of 1937," a furnished, full-scale modern apartment that was part of an exhibition of show rooms for the Kendal Milne Department Store, which opened in February 1937 in Manchester (fig. 2.17).[91] The full-sized, one-bedroom apartment with a separate kitchen and an open living-dining room and balcony, showcased branded modern materials, such as Venesta plywood, which was used for the walls, floors, and doors.[92] It also featured mass-produced objects that were tied to the department store's merchandise and modern furniture designs, including several well-placed exemplars of Isokon furniture. For the apartment, Gropius custom-designed several furniture pieces: a mirror glass fireplace, a large, three-cushion couch, two large armchairs, and an upholstered wing chair. The brochure published to accompany the exhibition details many convenient amenities such as a serving table, "collapsible tea trolley," a dining table featuring a "built-in turn-table," and a partition curtain described as "fadeless" chenille.[93] The color palette of the furnishings and rugs was soothing, a combination of white, ivory, cream, beige, browns, and yellows; explained Gropius, "the quiet colors are restful to the eye."[94] The promotional brochure noted that the apartment "achieves economy of space yet attains complete comfort without enervating luxury."[95] Gropius clarified his underlying ideas for the apartment: "I have designed this Flat to satisfy one's need for relaxation and stimulating diversion, so essential in these distracting days and to enable one by its free and easy atmosphere to lead a natural and unconstrained life. I consider that living free from the friction caused by

Minimal Dwelling 79

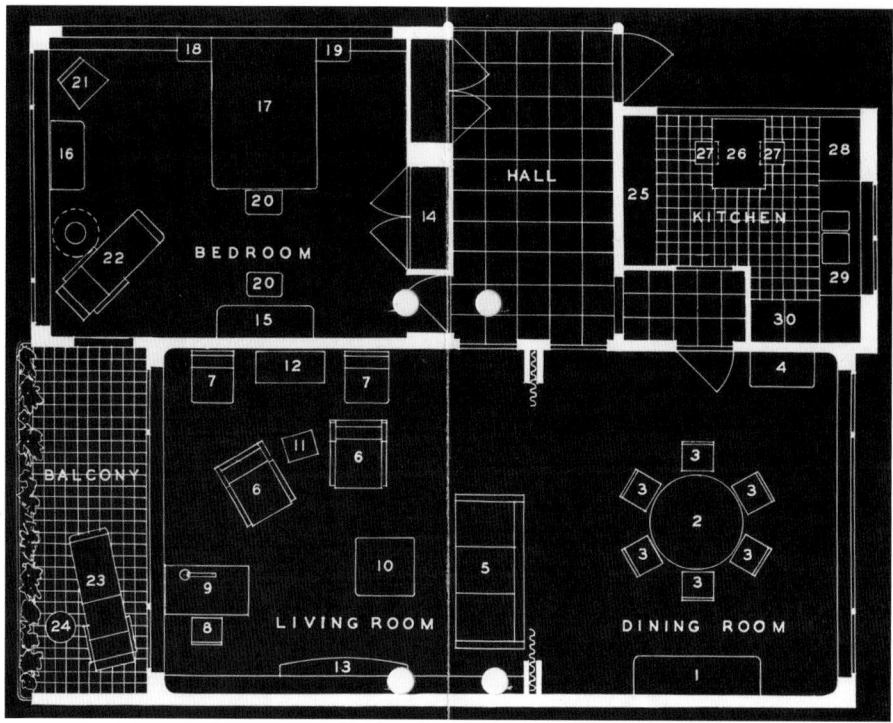

Fig. 2.17 Walter Gropius, *The Flat of '37*, brochure, 1937, Manchester, England.

unpractical surroundings is essential for the attainment of the maximum amount of personal liberty and independence. The modern mind calls for directness and harmony both in the shapes and in the arrangement of our daily surroundings."[96]

As English design critic John Gloag observed in his speech at the exhibition's opening, "It is felt by many people that the modern movement makes things bleak; that coziness becomes impossible in an ultra-modern room; but I think this Exhibition completely refutes that suggestion. Professor Gropius, looking at us as a national problem; asking himself more searchingly than many English people will ask, what makes an Englishman comfortable, what gives him this feeling of coziness, Professor Gropius asking these questions, has studied us, has done research work into our likes and our dislikes; and he knows, perhaps a little more clearly than most of us, what we will accept, and what we won't have at any price."[97] Gropius's work, Gloag noted, proposes "so many agreeable solutions to the problems of providing a background for modern life," and addresses "the very difficult task of making English people feel comfortable and at home."[98]

The question of "Englishness" with regard to modernism was a lively one in this period. In December 1937, the *Architectural Review* ran a two-part article showcasing recently built modern architecture in the United Kingdom, focusing on the topic of "the minimum" for workplaces and dwellings.[99] As the accompanying article intoned, "In our participation in an architectural movement which derives largely from foreign influences it is appropriate to consider . . . certain qualities that are essentially English . . . certain attitudes which English architecture has been prone to abjure in its periodical prostrations to cultural movements from the Continent, but have always painfully reasserted themselves."[100]

The article predominantly singled out and published the built projects of continental Europeans working in Britain (and their partners) – such as Gropius and Fry, Lubetkin and Tecton, Breuer and F.R.S. Yorke, Mendelsohn and Chermayeff. However, rather than a strict minimum aesthetic or modest footprint, the accompanying text suggested techniques such as designing multi-use rooms, flexible and convertible spaces appropriate for different activities, and using fabrics and furnishings to change the character of rooms. Notably, the Isokon Building – with its interiors genuinely set at the minimum – was not featured in the issue.

The radical implications in proposals by Hannes Meyer, Ludwig Hilberseimer, and others, for dwelling minimally, to which Gropius, too, had earlier contributed, had faded by the time he began working on the Flat of 1937. Where Meyer wanted to raise living standards for the masses and serve their needs, as part of a larger political agenda, Gropius now espoused a modernism supportive of personal liberty and individual independence. Though their ideas and designs for modern dwellings diverged, their architectural works found common ground as total designs – *Gesamtkunstwerke*, in which every operative detail had been carefully considered for its contribution to the interior as a whole, and in the service of a greater enhancement of life – as differently envisioned and articulated by each designer.

Eventually, the contradictions in Gropius's design of this period could not be resolved; even though he had been thinking, lecturing, and working on *Existenzminimum* projects in the years prior to his arrival in England and himself lived in a minimal dwelling once there, the modern multifamily apartments Gropius designed for Isokon reflected a more expansive, and ultimately financially unfeasible, architecture. He was not emphatic during this period about whether multifamily dwellings were more desirable than single-family houses. In a 1934 article, "The Formal and Technical Problems of Modern Architecture and Planning," he noted that opinion was still very divided about "the ideal form of dwelling for the bulk of the population."[101] He argued, "It is indisputable that to most people the separate house seems the most tempting haven in which to take refuge from the stony ocean of a great city. The direct communication with the garden, the greater seclusion, and the delicious sense of complete possession are obvious advantages which everyone can realize."[102] Ultimately, however, he came to the conclusion that the apartment block was the housing type that was the "truer embodiment of the needs of our age."[103] Gropius, in exile, sought an architectural amalgamation of standardization – the basis of his own *Existenzminimum* dwelling circumstances at Lawn Road Flats and his new proposals for Isokon, and one of sleek modernism and luxurious amenities, apparent in designs such as the Flat of 1937 and Isokon 3 at Windsor. In the end, neither conceptual direction was embraced by prospective inhabitants or financial backers, thus rendering his architectural visions untenable on the market, especially in the darkening time of international events leading up to World War II.

Furnishing and the Minimum

The minimal dwelling had such constrained physical dimensions that the specificity of its objects, especially its furnishings, and their relationship to the space as a whole, were of heightened importance to the smooth functioning of its interior. The euphoric, "frictionless" modern life that Gropius was championing, so seemingly carefree and enjoyable, seems furthest from his own dramatic professional and economic situation in this period, and that of many others. The modern objects that he and the other newly arrived émigrés designed for the pared-down, minimal interior must be understood in light of an emphasis on mobility and a deemphasis on significant personal belongings.

At Isokon, the trio of émigré designers—Gropius, Breuer, and Moholy-Nagy—were highly engaged in the prototyping of modern furnishings and products, experimenting in their new context with new materials, especially plywood. Isokon was uniquely situated to exploit its possibilities. Jack Pritchard's work, from 1925 onward, with Venesta (a British firm importing Estonian plywood) meant that he was deeply familiar with the material's qualities and its potential for modern furnishings, as well as a building material. Wells Coates's plywood furnishings for the Lawn Road Flats were developed with the intention of also being mass produced and sold more widely. Other modern architects working in England, such as Serge Chermayeff, Gerald Summers, and Gordon Russell, also successfully experimented with the material. In addition to designs developed and sold under Isokon's name, Pritchard also imported and marketed a few other modern pieces of furniture. For example, via Isokon he retailed a lightweight, stackable plywood stool—available finished in black cellulose or an oak or birch veneer—manufactured by the Estonian company A. M. Luther and imported by Venesta; the stool was also widely used to furnish the Lawn Road Flats and its Isobar restaurant.[104]

Isokon's experiments were influenced by continental European designers already working in plywood. Of particular importance were the Finnish architects Alvar Aalto and his wife Aino Marsio-Aalto, who cofounded a company, Artek, to distribute their modern furniture products.[105] Alvar Aalto's pioneering forms and fabrication methods in plywood were well known to modernists working in Britain in this period. This was due not only to the publicity generated by his plywood furniture for the Paimio Sanatorium, but also by the influential exhibition *"Wood Only": The Exhibition of Finnish Furniture*, held in November 1933 at the Fortnum & Mason department store, organized by the *Architectural Review* and Morton Shand. Based on the success of that show, Shand went on to cofound (with Geoffrey Boumphrey) the company Finmar to import Aalto furniture to the United Kingdom.[106]

Moholy-Nagy, who had previously come to know Aalto during a month-long trip to Finland in 1931, was in London on an exploratory visit—he was considering a move—and was able to help the Aaltos arrange their furniture in the *"Wood Only"* exhibition, attending the opening on November 13.[107] The Aaltos, in fact, had postponed the exhibition in London in order to meet up with Moholy-Nagy,[108] whom they had recently seen at the CIAM congress in Athens that summer.[109] Aalto furniture was soon stocked in progressive stores, such as Heal's and the London shop of designer Gordon Russell.[110] As Henry-Russell Hitchcock would observe in the MoMA's 1937 exhibition catalog *Modern Architecture in England*, the "predilection for blond wood coloring is soundly based upon the Finnish birch veneer furniture designed by Aalto which is readily obtainable in London."[111]

Shand, with Pritchard, had visited the Aaltos and toured the Paimio Sanatorium in August 1935.[112] Following that visit, Pritchard set up the Isokon Furniture Company, which focused on bent plywood furniture designs, many of them by Marcel Breuer. The influence between Aalto and Breuer was bi-directional—Aalto had previously furnished his apartment with Breuer's bent metal Bauhaus-era furniture before going on to develop his own cantilevered, bent wood furniture, while Breuer would draw on Aalto's expertise when he translated his bent metal designs into structurally sound, molded plywood during his time in London.[113] In designing chairs, both utilized a supportive framework formed by a continuous length of plywood that extended from the arms downward to constitute the chair legs, to which a suspended seat was attached. This gave the chairs a weightless, modern quality. Writing in 1937, Hitchcock would prefer Aalto's results: "The furniture designed by Breuer . . . despite his long preoccupation with furniture, is less satisfactory than the imported Finnish product [by Aalto]."[114] Indeed, Aalto furniture was specified for significant UK buildings throughout the 1930s—it was used at the Highpoint apartments designed by the Tecton Group, at the De La Warr Pavilion by Chermayeff and Mendelsohn, in the London Theatre Studio commission by Yorke and Breuer, and at Impington Village College by Fry and Gropius.[115] Pritchard (promoting Breuer and others' designs at Isokon) and Shand (importing Aalto designs for Finmar), would ultimately cooperate informally—showing their wares together in an interior furnishings exhibition by Gropius at John Lewis's Manchester store, and furniture exemplars by both Breuer and Aalto were on display in a show house for the firm P. E. Gane designed by Breuer and Fry.[116]

When Pritchard hired Gropius to be the consultant for a new initiative in 1935, Isokon Furniture, Gropius's fee was conveniently set at the equivalent of the rent of his apartment at Lawn Road.[117] While still in Germany, Gropius had already made copious drawings for furniture prototypes in tubular aluminum, including cupboards, bookshelves, and a desk. In England, he designed in both metal and wood. For the London Aluminum Company, Gropius produced an aluminum waste basket, a teapot, a heater, and a table, as well as a prototype for an aluminum bed.[118] Some of these products—such as the waste can—were then sold via Isokon, through an agreement between the two firms.[119] Gropius also developed an aluminum table dumb waiter, wireless radio, and electric water kettle.[120] For Isokon, he focused on plywood, designing a plywood desk and chair set, a plywood table, shelves, and a school desk with a steel frame.[121] Gropius and Pritchard were also in dialogue about developing a plywood tray and bedroom furniture, among other plywood prototypes.[122] Although it never came to fruition, one of Gropius's most visually stimulating ideas was for what he called "corrugated plywood," sheets of plywood with a tight, undulating ripple, which he envisioned for use in the design of cupboards, chairs, and as paneling.[123]

Pritchard asked Moholy-Nagy to design a new trademark for Isokon, requesting for it to be "simple so that, where necessary, it can be fixed to our products" (fig. 2.18).[124] As the Isokon initiative grew, Gropius suggested that Marcel Breuer, with whom he had worked closely at the Bauhaus, and who had continued to distinguish himself with important modern furniture designs, be invited to design for the firm. Pritchard negotiated agreeable terms that brought

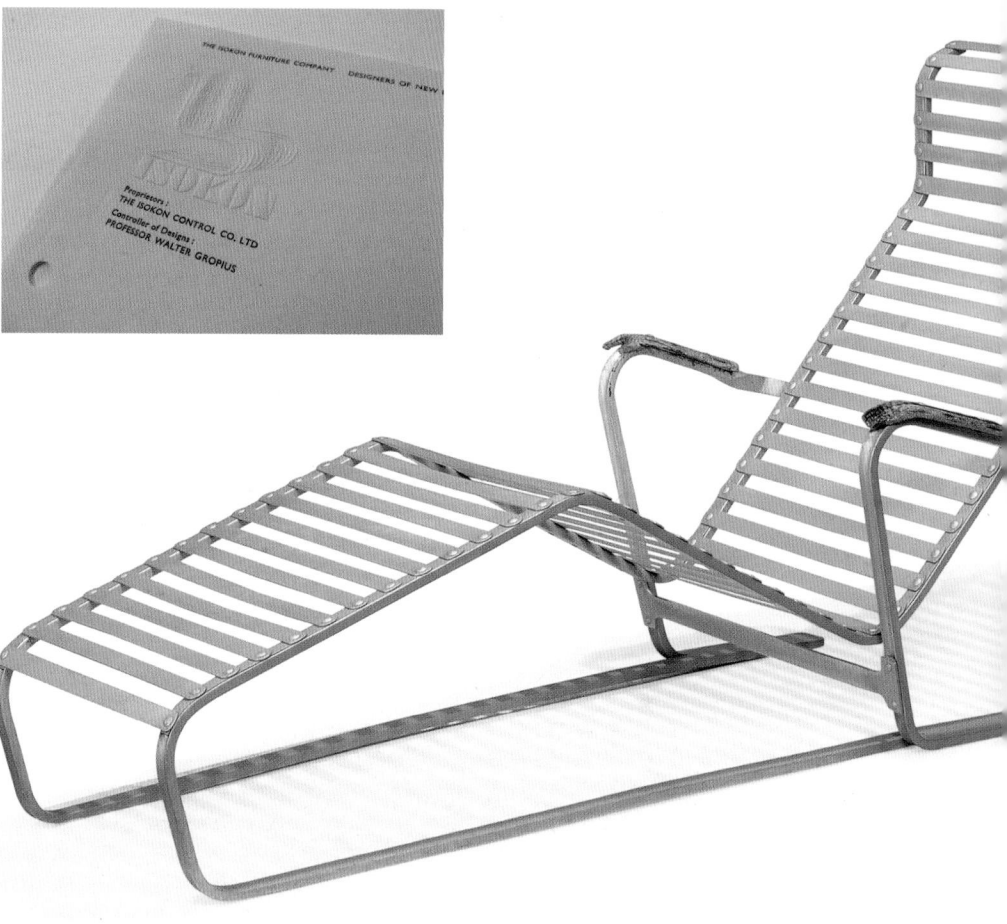

Fig. 2.18 *Top*, László Moholy-Nagy, Isokon logo, 1936.

Breuer to London.[125] Breuer began in December 1935, making drawings for dining tables, side and "occasional" tables, chairs, stools, and other basic pieces for the company, mainly intended to be made of Isokon's signature material, plywood, but with some designs specifying aluminum- and chromium-plated steel tubes.[126] Breuer also set about creating a chaise longue in plywood, inspired by his previous aluminum chaise longues, which were manufactured by the Swiss company Embru (and by other companies representing the market in Germany, France, and Italy). Not limiting his materials to plywood, he also began developing an aluminum nesting chair for Isokon (fig. 2.19).[127] It was composed of a light frame made of sheet metal, part of a collection of metal furniture prototypes by Breuer, all designed to be "stacked together in nesting fashion."[128]

For the chaise longue in plywood, Isokon offered two Breuer-designed models – a full-sized lounge chair (named the Isokon Long Chair) and a shorter one (the Isokon Short Chair) – which were available in basic birch plywood, walnut or maple veneer, and topped with an optional upholstered cushion in a fabric supplied by the purchaser (fig. 2.20).[129] The molded cushions to fit the chairs were fabricated by agreement with two outside firms, Dunlop Rubber Co. and Hairlok.[130] The Isokon chair was a significant piece of furniture that allowed the occupant to relax in a recumbent position, legs fully extended in a "new standard of comfort," as the Isokon sales brochure proclaimed (see fig. 2.4).[131] It was

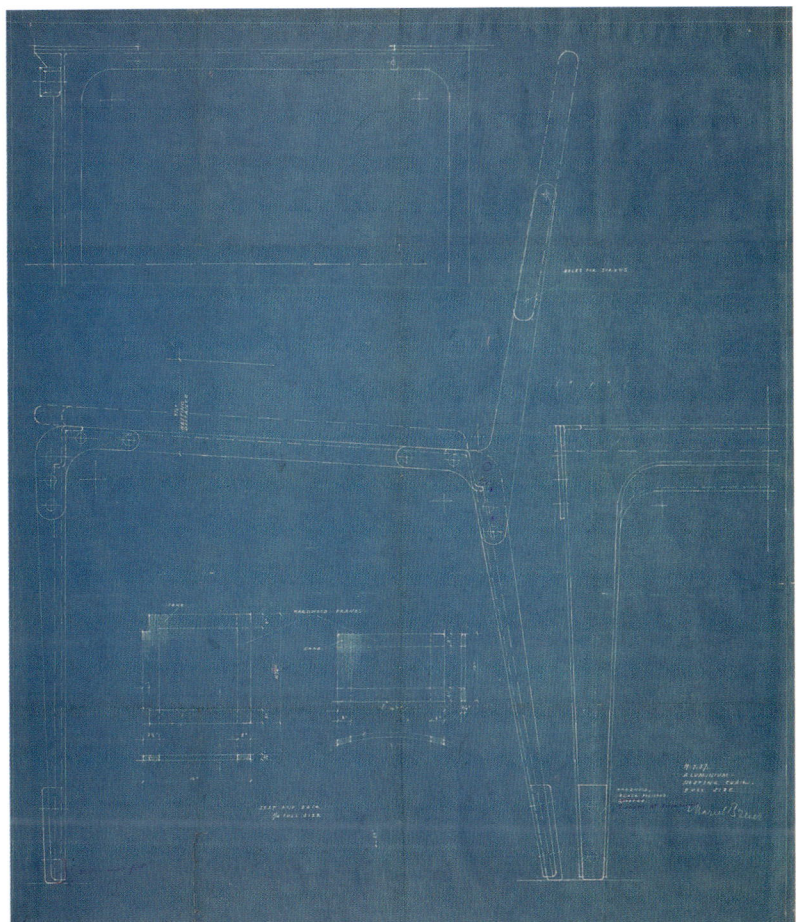

also flexible and easily moved, and thus suitable for the Isokon Flats and other modern spaces, as it allowed the occupant to turn "sideways by a fire instead of burning your feet while your body freezes. Two can be placed side by side but facing each other – an ideal arrangement for a quiet talk, or for tea. They can be moved to the window to get the sunshine. You cannot do any of these things with heavy, old-fashioned chairs."[132] After some initial production issues were resolved, the chair became one of Isokon's most successful and best known products. Breuer would go on to design, and patent, a further ten lounge chair variants, which were never put into production.[133]

Breuer similarly translated other earlier metal furniture into plywood – his tubular steel B9 Nesting Tables from 1925 found a corollary in his laminated bent plywood Isokon Stacking Tables of 1936 (fig. 2.21). However, in an essay, "Architecture and Material," published in 1937, Breuer sought distance from his tubular steel precedents. About this innovative new design he wrote, "Here the plywood is not used merely as a panel or as a plane surface borne by separate structural members; it performs two functions at one and the same time – it bears weight and forms its own planes. Here we have a new material and a new form which has very little resemblance to the tubular steel furniture shapes from which it was originally derived. Here, the usual joinery construction gives place to the new bending technique."[134]

Fig. 2.19 *Opposite*, Marcel Breuer, Model 313 chaise longue, 1932, manufactured by Embru-Werke AG and retailed by Wohnbedarf AG, Zurich, forged and extruded aluminum, wooden armrests. *Above*, Marcel Breuer, blueprint for aluminum nesting chair, July 19, 1937.

Minimal Dwelling

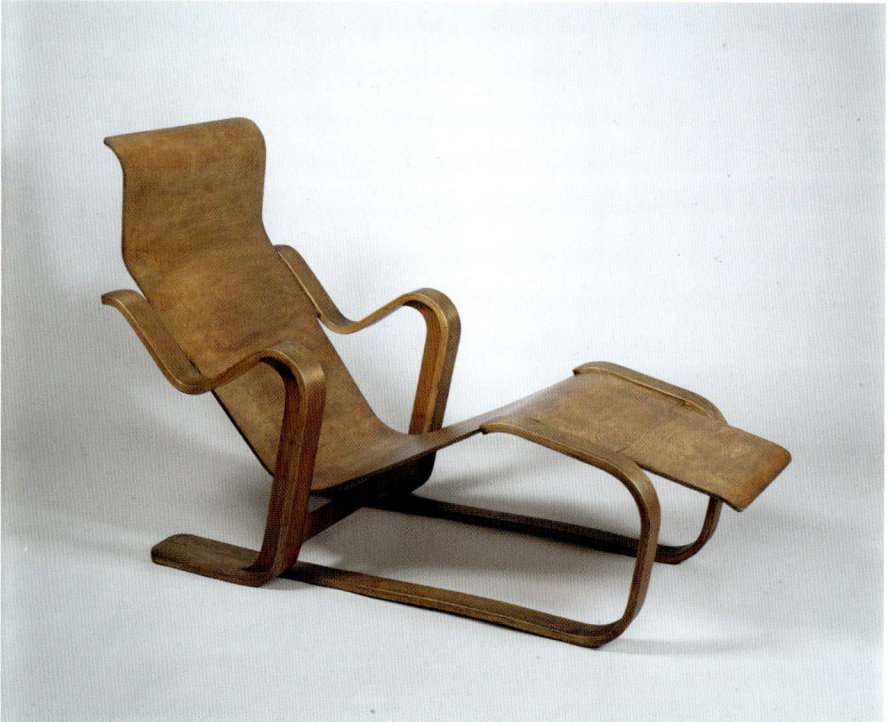

Fig. 2.20 *Top*, Marcel Breuer, blueprint for Isokon Short Chair, May 25, 1937. *Bottom*, Marcel Breuer, Isokon Long Chair, 1936, bent laminated birch veneers, bent plywood.

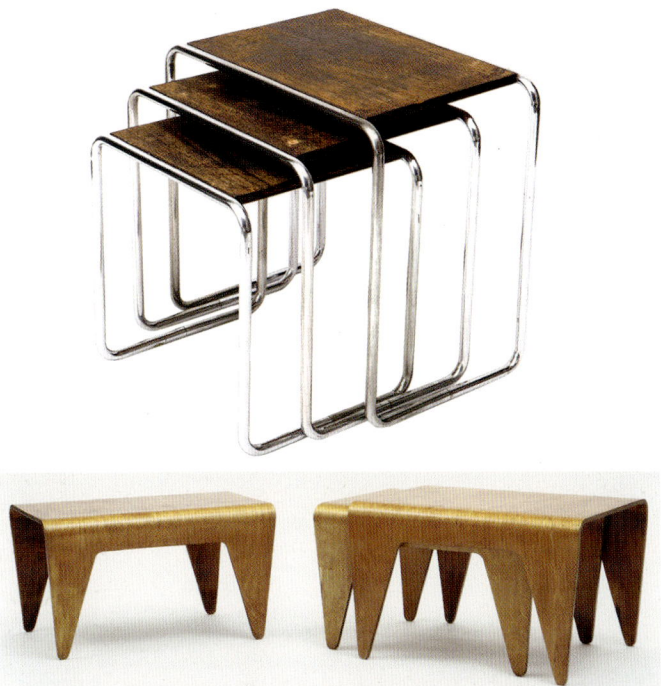

Experiments in "nesting" or "stacking" plywood furniture particularly occupied him; optimal for saving space in the small, modern apartments for which they were intended, stacked chairs and tables could then be scattered around a room when entertaining guests (fig. 2.22). Where previously multiple furniture parts were necessary, Breuer bent the plywood to form continuous elements from one sheet, such that table tops extended down to form stable table legs and seatbacks were elongated downward to become chair seats. This reduced the number of plywood elements to be cut out and bent, as well as the labor needed to assemble the furniture. These innovations were formalized in a patent under the title "Improvement in Furniture," which encompassed Breuer's designs across several furniture types. The patent application asserted, "According to the invention a chair, table, stool or like piece of furniture comprises a single piece of sheet material, preferably ply-wood, so bent as to form a flat surface spanning the distance between two substantially vertical parts constituting legs. The flat surface constitutes the seat of a chair or the top of a table or stool."[135] The application document goes on to specify how the furniture might be easily stacked, as an "important feature of the invention."[136] In August 1937, Breuer was successful in obtaining a patent for his nesting plywood furniture.[137]

With his impending departure for America, Gropius would recommend Breuer as his successor as controller of designs for Isokon.[138] Breuer, however, would follow Gropius to the United States. Combined, the work of Gropius, Breuer, and Moholy-Nagy in England was part of a sustained effort to assist Isokon in creating modern, reproducible furniture and housing. Although ultimately their expertise and design was not enough to successfully develop Isokon into an economically viable or widely accepted design style, their time in England allowed them to transition from the German context into a new one by adapting their ideas.

Fig. 2.21 *Top*, Marcel Breuer, B9 nesting tables, 1925, wood and tubular steel. *Bottom*, Marcel Breuer, Isokon stacking tables, 1936, manufactured by Venesta for Isokon Furniture Company, laminated plywood, birch veneer.

Minimal Dwelling

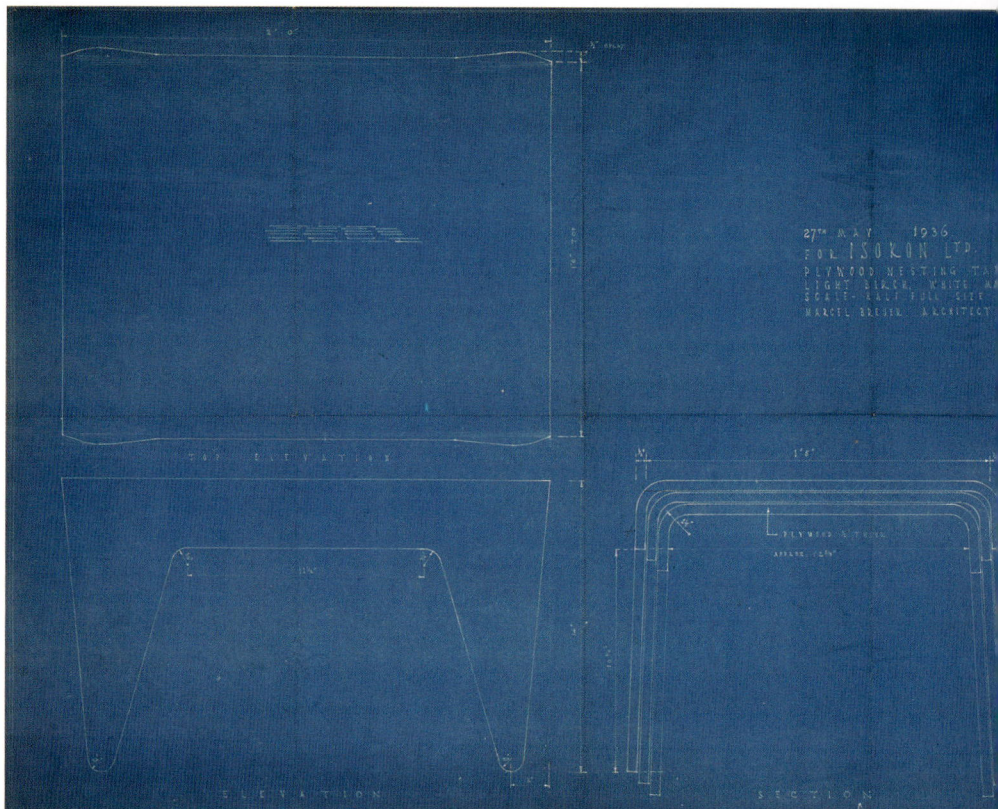

In designing interiors and fittings alike, modern architects such as Gropius and Meyer explicitly denounced the bourgeois individualism of art nouveau designs by architects of an earlier period; yet they drew on similar ideas of a total work of art, or *Gesamtkunstwerk*, in pursuit of their totalized, rationalized environments. It is true that Meyer's texts, for example, abound in revolutionary pronouncements such as, "Dead is the work of art as a 'thing in itself' [*Ding an sich*] as 'art for art's sake' [*L'art pour l'art*]: our communal consciousness will not tolerate any individualistic excesses."[139] Nevertheless, in the process, Meyer repurposed the preceding period's architectural *Gesamtkunstwerk*, transforming it into a minimal, total environment, proclaiming: "The new work of art is a totality, not an excerpt, not an impression. The new work of art is an elemental creation made by primary means."[140]

In opposition to prior "artistic" and "individualized" design solutions, these architects reduced living to its essentials, deploying techniques of standardization and rationalized forms, to give rise to the totalized modern dwelling. While at the turn of the century the *Gesamtkunstwerk* in architecture had been represented by a unique, totally designed environment, in the 1920s and 1930s the modern dwelling unit can also be understood as a *Gesamtkunstwerk* – one that emerged in the meticulous design of a totalized cell. In the former, the design was *singular*, a total work of art that was not intended to ever occur more than once, whereas in the latter, the single design was to be carefully perfected such that it was appropriate for *infinite reproducibility*. Also explicit in the latter solution to dwelling – whether housing the worker, the arriving émigré, or the modern working professional – were underlying ideas of the individual as a member of a

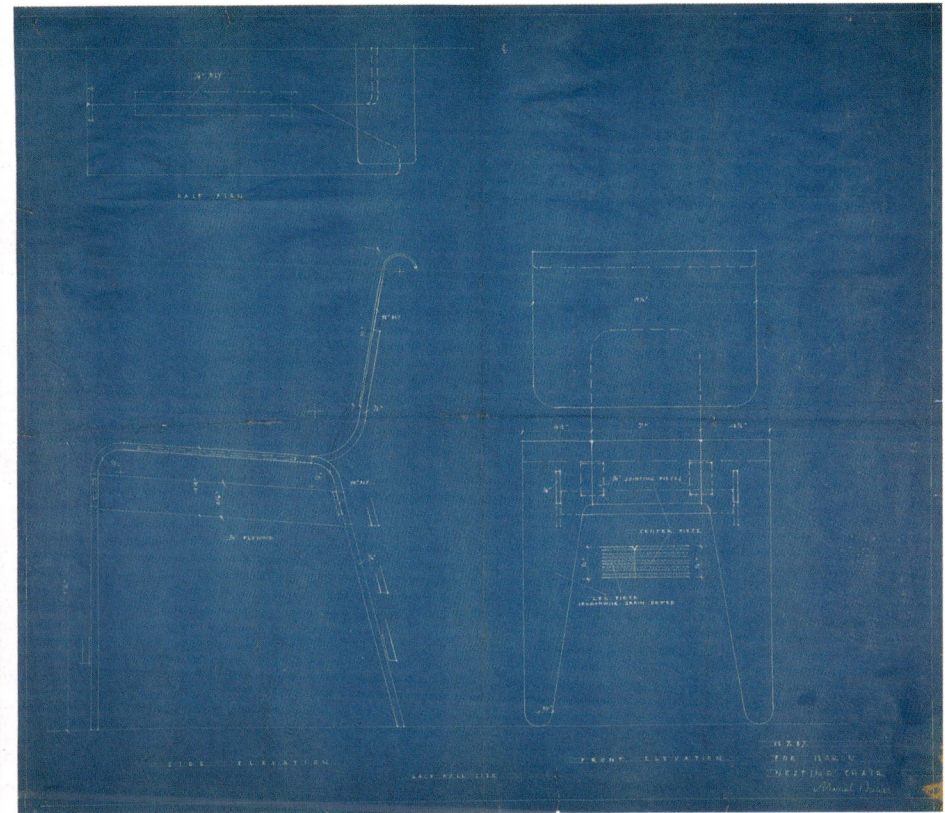

Fig. 2.22 *Left*, Marcel Breuer, blueprint for plywood nesting table, light birch, matte finish, May 27, 1936. *Right*, Marcel Breuer, blueprint for plywood nesting chair, July 13, 1937.

collective, and that of an architectural cell within a larger metropolitan organism. This, too, is a key underlying idea of the more socially integrated *Gesamtkunstwerk* of the modern era.

Translation as a Mode of Transfer

His small successes in England notwithstanding, Gropius eagerly took up the call to Harvard University's Graduate School of Design and left London on March 12, 1937. Breuer and Moholy-Nagy followed shortly thereafter. The time spent by these three in England has often been seen as, if not an outright failure to entrance their hosts with modern architecture and design, then as a brief interlude en route to success elsewhere: a tidy teleology. However, their years in England should be understood as a period of crucial translation. As the architectural historian Robin Evans has noted, "to translate is to convey."[141] The America that these modernists moved to was one in which the locals were, equally, if not more, skeptical about – and more removed from – the modern architectural movement in Europe. Although these exiles did not find their final success in England, it proved to be a fruitful milieu in which to stop and translate their ideas and design for an Anglophone audience; England proved a site of transfer, via translation.

The most literal aspects of the exiles' period of translation was a simple question of language. It must be remembered that Gropius could hardly speak English on his initial visit to England in 1934 for the opening of his exhibition at the Royal Institute of British Architects (RIBA). His lecture on "The Formal and Technical Problems of Modern Architecture and Planning" had been translated for him by Morton Shand.¹⁴² British architect Maxwell Fry, although full of admiration for Gropius's ideas on modernism presented in the RIBA speech, noted that he addressed the audience "awkwardly in a language that he had yet to adopt."¹⁴³ Indeed, the typescript of this speech and others Gropius gave during his years in England are full of penciled diacritical marks in his hand indicating where the emphasis of particular words should lie: "inévitable," "enábles," "áspect," and so on.¹⁴⁴

Back in Germany following the RIBA exhibition, Gropius would assure Shand, "I will now make strenuous efforts to learn English, so that I can get along better during my next visit."¹⁴⁵ Once he accepted the invitation to move to the United Kingdom, Gropius would again assert to Shand, "I'm desperately trying to learn English, so that when I come to England I will be somewhat better equipped linguistically."¹⁴⁶ Shand's advice back to Gropius was kind and also useful, "I hope that learning English is not causing you too much trouble. I think, for a German things progress most quickly and easily, if one resolves always to simplify one's sentences and thoughts. The spirit of this language is always – do not be over explicit; leave something to the imagination of the person you are speaking to. Do not use more adjectives than you need to."¹⁴⁷ As Gropius himself recalled of his time in England, "I stumbled along, murmuring a language meant to be English."¹⁴⁸ This small point, about obtaining the necessary language skills, is important because it gave Gropius the platform upon which to acquire and practice English before he arrived on US shores. Indeed, it must not be forgotten that Gropius was in direct competition for the Graduate School of Design position with the arguably more architecturally talented Mies van der Rohe, and the fact that Gropius could already competently speak English by that point gave him a significant edge over Mies, who could not.¹⁴⁹

The second important instance of translation in this period was the 1935 publication of Gropius's first book in English, *The New Architecture and the Bauhaus*.¹⁵⁰ Morton Shand translated it for him, with Moholy-Nagy designing the cover. The slim volume sold briskly and was widely reviewed.¹⁵¹ Importantly, it served as the first English language introduction to the newly closed Bauhaus and reiterated Gropius's role as founder and instigator of the ideas behind the school, simultaneously situating both the Bauhaus and his own architectural praxis as a dominant force in the field of modern architecture. By no means fresh, this text had originated in German ten years earlier, but the publication was a timely and crucial "translation" in more than one sense – literal, situational (in that it positioned Gropius for what was to follow), and disseminational (introducing a new audience to his ideas and work).

Just prior to leaving England, Gropius was showcased in a television feature, "Architecture Today"; an accompanying article about the broadcast noted the circularity of the new architecture's ideas, "The historians of the movement will tell you that it is to English pioneers that the Continent turned, in the first instance to William Morris, Mackintosh, and others. But it was in Germany and Austria that these ideas took strong roots, were nurtured and ripened to fullness."¹⁵² This cycle continued, in which the architecture and product designs by Bauhaus members and other German modernists were interpreted by Wells Coates at Isokon for an English idiom, namely, for the furnished efficiency apartment for the working professional (see fig. 2.2). The Isokon Building was inhabited by former Bauhaus members, who then used their British years to transpose and further reflect their ideas back to an English and an eventual American audience. A long thread connecting designs for minimal housing can be traced through successive translations and reinterpretations: beginning in 1860s England with the arts and crafts movement's rejection of Victorian clutter and excess in favor of a stripped-down "truth to materials"; moving to 1920s Germany with its dormitory cells to accommodate students at the Bauhaus and other proposals for standard units; to Gropius's designs for Isokon 2, 3, and 4; to, finally, the units he would propose in America in the form of worker and military housing and graduate student dormitories at Harvard. Key to the architecture that spans this entire period, from the 1860s to the 1950s, was its ability to be continuously translated, improved on within its new social, cultural, and material context, and then pushed out into the world again for its next adaptation.

In Gropius's English period, one finds pointed moments of architectural translation, from buildings such as the Wood House in Kent, to the later house Gropius would build for himself in Lincoln, Massachusetts (see fig. 2.16). The Lincoln house is usually viewed as adapting modernism to building forms found in America, such as the use of vertical timber, but American vernacular architecture is also, itself, a general translation from the British precedent.

Similarly, in order to develop the Isokon plywood long chair from his earlier aluminum chaise longue, and his nesting tables from tubular steel to bent plywood, Marcel Breuer required many iterations — technical and visual — to arrive at the translated form (see figs. 2.19, 2.20, 2.21). Like any good translation, it was not too literal but rather took into account subtle changes and nuances necessary to arrive at a complete and satisfying final result. Or, as Walter Benjamin somewhat nonchalantly framed it in his essay "The Task of the Translator": "It is self-evident how greatly fidelity in reproducing the form impedes the rendering of the sense."[153]

For any exile, contending with issues of displacement, language, idiom, and translation becomes a daily imperative. After fleeing dictatorship, financial difficulties and an uncertain future hovered over the émigrés in these years. In photography and painting, practitioners could more quickly get set up and begin work with a minimum of impediments. But for those working in design and architecture, there were more concrete hurdles to surmount: linguistic (essential to the courting of clients), material (concrete to timber, aluminum to plywood), and contextual (in the severe limitations of what the émigrés could bring with them to secure future commissions, when traveling to view extant work was no longer possible).

Only in translation, according to Benjamin, does the life of the original attain "its latest, continually renewed, and most complete unfolding."[154] Following Benjamin's logic, the British period was neither a junction nor an interlude; rather, it introduces an element of time and an open-endedness to our understanding. Benjamin points out that "a translation comes later than the original, and since . . . important works . . . never find their chosen translators at the time of their origin, their translation marks their stage of continued life. The idea of life and afterlife in works of art should be regarded with an entirely unmetaphorical objectivity."[155] Thus, these years should not be seen as a transitional moment of interaction between continental European designers and British modernists but a crucial intersection in which ideas and forms underwent semi-simultaneous translation, making both sides the richer for it.

■ ■ ■

Gropius's route from the Bauhaus into successive emigrations offers a picture, too, of the itinerary traveled by the *Gesamtkunstwerk* in modern twentieth-century interiors. A minimal dwelling, in which every object was carefully conceived or calibrated to contribute to the functioning of a self-contained and greatly reduced environment can be understood as a *Gesamtkunstwerk*. Not only can the interior of a building such as the Lawn Road Flats be understood as a minimalist total work of art, but it can be seen as a prototype of an idea that continued long after the Bauhaus members departed from Great Britain—that is, for the next generation of architects.

In the post–World War II period, flexible and mobile units of architecture continued to capture the imagination of architects. In 1947, Wells Coates designed a prefabricated living component system, a concept that he termed "Room Unit Production." He envisioned six different standardized types while giving the purchaser the agency to determine the location of the walls, windows and doors, as well as the layout of the furniture, before delivery to the site. The unit could be used as a stand-alone house on a private plot of land, which Coates called "Rooms in a garden," or slotted into a frame, to become part of a multidwelling building that he publicized as "Rooms into Frame."[156] He proposed that residents could add further dwelling units as their needs expanded and also suggested that owners might slide a unit out of the frame on a Friday, lower it onto a truck, and drive it to a frame located in the countryside for the weekend.[157]

Capsule Homes (1964) by members of the British architecture group Archigram, and The Environment Bubble (1965), a membrane-enclosed proposal by the British architect and critic Reyner Banham and his French colleague, François Dallegret, are two other examples of the many works of this period that envisioned flexible, prefabricated units.[158] These two very different designs each enveloped and immersed their occupants in a totalized world. The Environment Bubble contained a fluid and playful selection of objects, services, and technologies, as an alternative to a monumental architecture imposed by an architect. Although Banham wrote that he borrowed the term "standard-of-living package" from Buckminster Fuller to describe his dwelling, he was indebted to ideas from 1920s and 1930s Europe.[159] With all amenities, especially technological needs, envisioned within their membranes, these spare environments of the postwar period proposed to meet the needs of their dwellers on their global peregrinations—updating architectural proposals of the earlier period.

Works by Archigram, such as Cushicle (1966–67)—a thin membrane enclosing a chassis that supported appliances and other apparatus—and the Suitaloon (1967–68)—a suit that enveloped the wearer, devised by Michael Webb—similarly conveyed immersion in a totalized world. Like an updated version of Hannes Meyer's collapsible room of amenities and entertainment, the Co-op Interior, the Cushicle was described by the group as "a complete environment" or "complete nomadic unit," "fully serviced" with food, water, radio, and a miniature projection television.[160] Webb clarified that he was thinking in terms of the minimal dwelling: "The space suit could be identified as a minimal house.... The suit provides all the necessary services."[161] So too did Archigram's 1966 Living-Pod Dwelling Capsule and the Inflatable Suit-Home (1968), both by David Greene; in the latter, a "suit package" (made by Pat Haines) was inflated around the wearer to form a large, pumpkin-shaped membrane housing.[162] In these designs, the experience of immersion sat within a paradigm of a new, technically inflected and more nomadic existence. They were totalized environments whose constituent objects and elements aspired to meet the necessities of life, whenever and wherever their inhabitants might need them.

Growing from the cell-like apartments of the *Existenzminimum* movement in Germany, the fully furnished, diminutive Isokon apartments served a crucial function for their inhabitants — offering shelter, time to assimilate and to translate — in a key period of social, political, and economic urgency. More generally, dwelling environments that addressed the housing minimum with efficiency and careful design came to the fore as a critical solution to housing in the fraught period of displacement in the period leading up to World War II, during the war, and in the postwar period, until society and the economy could reestablish themselves and the postwar period of growth commenced.

Modernism's spartan proposals of this period feature a careful redesign or reduction of objects in space. But, this visual contrast obscures a more essential continuity. The judicious outfitting of interiors represented by the precise stagings of *Existenzminimum* in such works as Hannes Meyer's Co-op Interior, more luxurious proposals by Gropius in England, or mobile architectural projects of the 1960s, can and should be seen in light of continued notions of architecture's total work of art. Each dwelling attempts to address the perceived needs, as inflected by period concerns, of its inhabitant through design. Each transposes those needs into architectural form and provides integrated interior objects intended to respond to those needs.

Although architects of the 1920s were scathing in their excoriation of art nouveau, their interiors were total environments too — total works of art — in much the same way as their predecessors; they now reflected modernist emphases on mass production, standardization, economy, and politics rather than artistic expression and bourgeois individualism. The communal ideals of Hannes Meyer and Karel Teige and the private, personal freedoms envisioned by Walter Gropius, Reyner Banham, and Archigram, owe something to the new role for design that their nineteenth-century forebears envisioned. The modern movement's political and social content was positioned in the totalized interiors of modernism, especially in the uneasy period on the cusp of World War II. Focused on the minimal requirements of life — simplified and perhaps democratized — these totalized environments of modern architecture, precisely in their showcasing of carefully considered interior objects, were intended as a response to basic living needs, social harmony, and communal needs. The Isokon Flats provided the émigrés precisely that respite — a base from which they could design a better future.

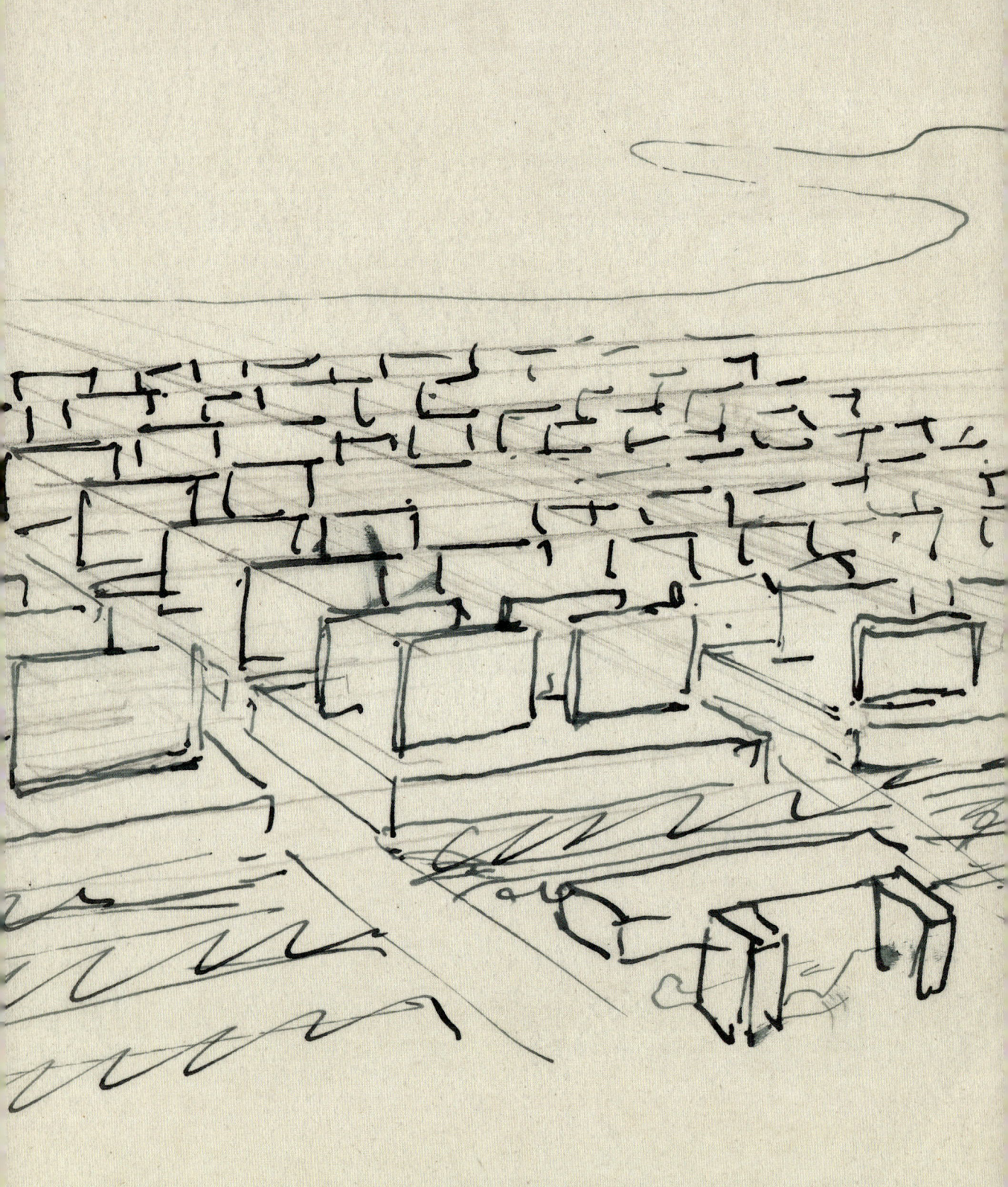

CONTINGENT CONDITIONS

Chapter 3

Images in Exile

Lucia Moholy's Bauhaus Negatives and the Construction of a Modernist Legacy

Lucia Moholy's photographs of the Dessau Bauhaus complex, masters' houses, and Bauhaus products, taken between 1924 and 1928, formed an essential part of the Bauhaus's documentation during its years of operation – and they played an inestimable role in the construction of the Bauhaus's legacy, which was largely formed after the school was closed in 1933 and its members had gone into exile.[1] Though Lucia Moholy was neither a pupil nor faculty at the Bauhaus, one might see her as a crucial participant and collaborator during the period that her then-husband, László Moholy-Nagy, taught there. The crisp, black-and-white images themselves, made from large-format glass plate negatives, have earned a place in the history of photography, as representative of the *sachlich* (objective) photography of the 1920s (figs. 3.1, 3.2; see also fig. I.7). During the years of divided Germany, when foreign scholars and architects had little access to the Bauhaus's buildings in Dessau, Moholy's iconic images of the school – made just after its completion, before the grass had a chance to grow – continued to be those through which generations of art history and architecture students were taught. These images, which carefully documented the school building and the masters' houses, widely reproduced in their day and beyond, cemented these edifices in the history of architecture (figs. 3.3, 3.4, 3.5).

This chapter explores the life in exile of these images. By considering the circumstances of the separation of the negatives from Moholy – both she and they went into exile, at separate times and to two different places – and their eventual return, it interrogates the meaning of the role these photographs played for the Bauhaus's former members in creating the school's history for posterity. It was precisely due to the exigencies of exile, especially the lacunae created by objects left behind at the time of emigration, that photography as a medium became crucial to the later reception of the closed school and what had been produced there. But while other exiled protagonists were able to establish their reputations anew, often on the basis of the images, Moholy was denied this opportunity because of the inaccessibility of the negatives – even as photography, through her work, assumed a role in the Bauhaus's mythos that it had not been granted at the school under Walter Gropius's direction.

Bauhaus Photographs

Moholy's photographs are sophisticated images. She painstakingly composed them so that architectural lines were in sharp focus, underscoring the rectilinearity – or sometimes playing up the dynamic visual diagonals – of the buildings' architecture. Blacks, whites, and grays additionally defined the buildings, while shadowing was also carefully considered. Moholy's photographs of the Bauhaus were multivalent tools, serving specific needs through seemingly straightforward shots that communicated basic information about the edifices themselves while simultaneously enunciating the buildings' architectural innovations and Gropius's architectural ideals. For example, the dematerialization of the Bauhaus building's corners, while physically and materially a provision of the steel and glass of their construction, is especially distinctly registered and remembered owing to the angle and flat light of Moholy's photograph (see

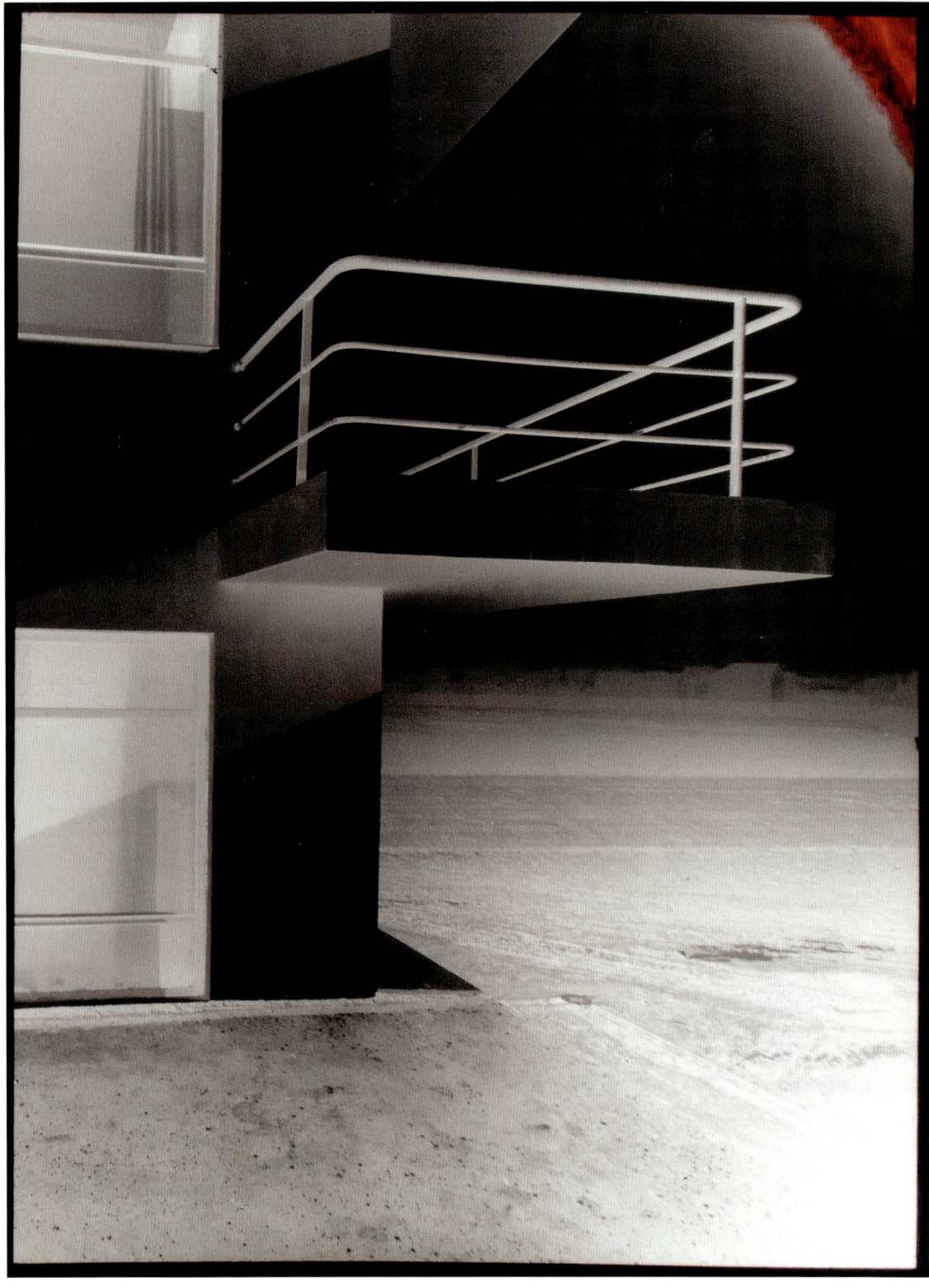

Fig. 3.1 Lucia Moholy (photographer), Bauhaus Building by Walter Gropius (architect), studio wing balcony (detail), 1926, glass negative. Bauhaus-Archiv, Berlin.

fig. 3.4).[2] The photographs are not neutral entities but rather helped express the modernist goals of the buildings' designer.[3]

It is important to note that in this period, Lucia Moholy also collaborated actively on many of the photographic works, such as the photograms, for which László Moholy-Nagy is singly credited. It was a rich period of experimentation, in which the husband and wife built on each other's ideas, resulting in a prodigious output of photographic and written work. The pair depended entirely on Lucia Moholy's darkroom and technical skills. She had begun training with a local photographer after her husband was appointed to his position at the Weimar Bauhaus in April 1923 and then attended the "Principal Course in Reproduction Technology" at the art academy in Leipzig, which, notably, had opened a photography department as early as 1893.[4] Upon moving into the masters' houses in Dessau with Moholy-Nagy in 1926, Moholy set up her first darkroom, in the ground-floor guest room.[5] As Moholy later explained, "The working arrangements between Moholy-Nagy and myself were unusually close, the wealth and value of the artist's ideas gaining momentum, as it were, from the symbiotic alliance of two diverging temperaments."[6] As Moholy-Nagy's collaborator, she failed to receive credit for her contributions, but it was only after their separation, when she was again on her own, that she regretted the secondary role she allowed herself to take, though this was the norm at the Bauhaus and in Weimar German society generally.[7]

But Moholy-Nagy and Lucia Moholy also worked independently, and there are distinctive differences in their individual oeuvres, which can be perceived, for example, in photographs of the Bauhaus Building. Moholy-Nagy's 1926–27 photographs of the Bauhaus balconies are extreme compositions, isolating the balconies and taken from the ground almost directly beneath them at an angle that produces a sensation of vertigo in the viewer. Often this feeling is accentuated by the inclusion of a silhouetted figure in what appears to be a precarious position, looming over the viewer. In these images, Moholy-Nagy deploys elements of "New Vision" (*Neues Sehen*) that almost force the viewer to see differently via photography.[8] On the other hand, Lucia Moholy's straightforward images should be understood under the tenets of "New Objectivity" (*Neue Sachlichkeit*), in which she uses equally carefully crafted shots, devoid of figures, that seemingly strive to make the object they depict more comprehensible. Although the individual, repetitive Bauhaus balconies are among the most visually compelling aspects of the school building, often photographed by others from below in the manner of Moholy-Nagy, she does not feature them prominently in her photographs of the building; with the exception of one cropped image of a single balcony photographed straight on, balconies are only seen from afar in her photographs. Where Moholy-Nagy photographs of this period feature unusual angles, extreme heights, or parts of wholes isolated to such an extent that the object is sometimes no longer discernable and becomes a series of abstract patterns, in Lucia Moholy's images, even where only a portion of an object or building is in view, the sense of its entirety is still conveyed.

Lucia Moholy's images of Bauhaus products, intended for the practical purposes of demonstrating the Bauhaus workshops' virtuosity and the (hoped-for) mass production of their objects, were similarly carefully composed, lighted,

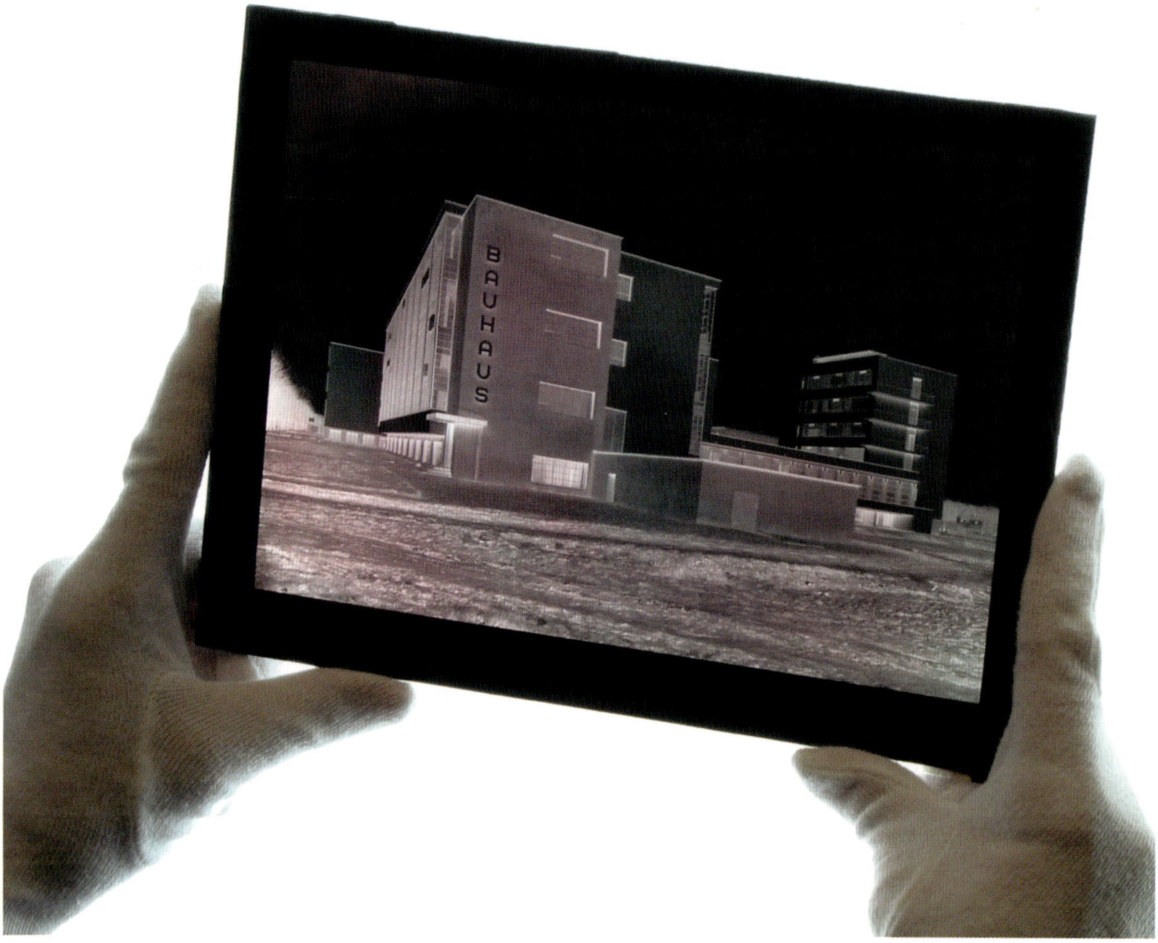

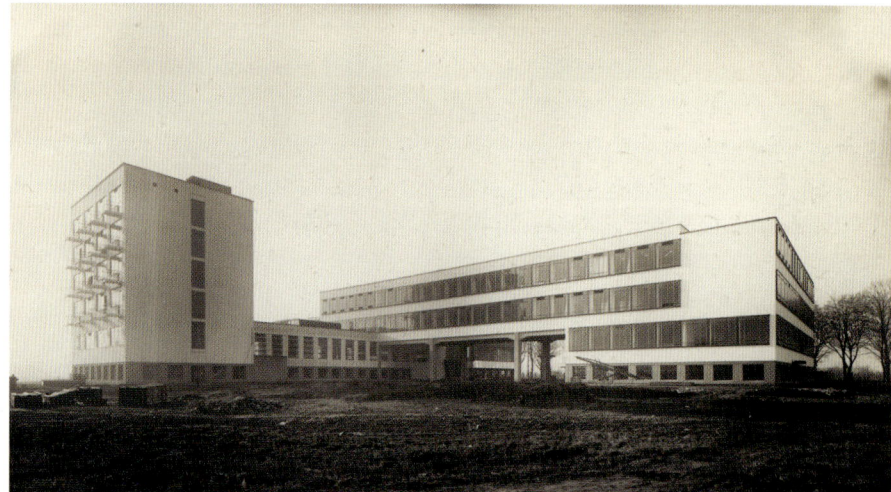

Fig. 3.2 Lucia Moholy, Bauhaus Building by Walter Gropius, view from southwest, 1927, glass negative. Bauhaus-Archiv, Berlin.

Fig. 3.3 Lucia Moholy, Bauhaus Building by Walter Gropius, view from northeast, 1926, gelatin silver print. Bauhaus-Archiv, Berlin.

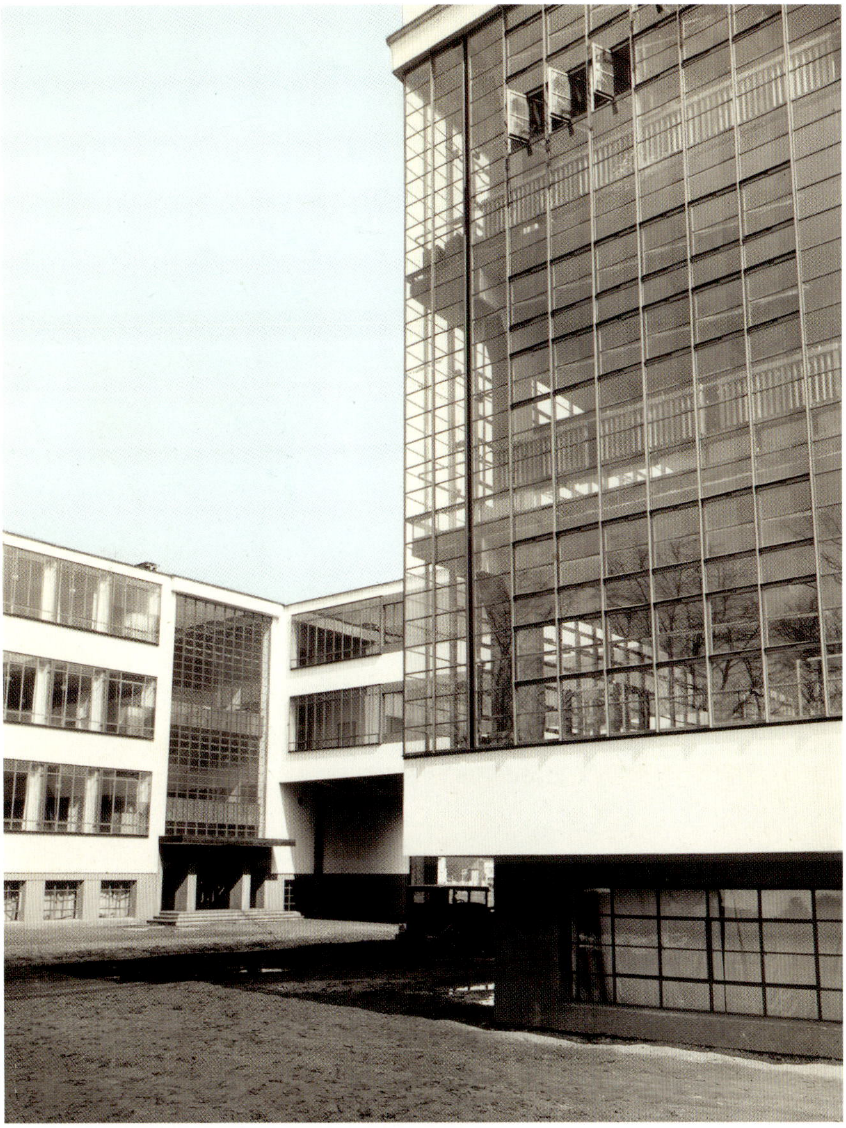

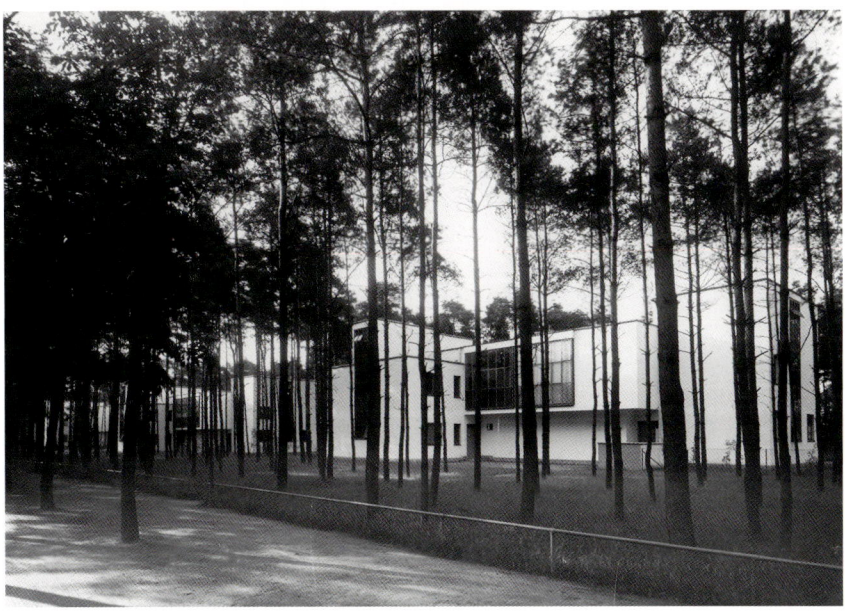

Fig. 3.4 Lucia Moholy, Bauhaus Building by Walter Gropius, northwest corner of the workshop wing, 1927, gelatin silver print. Bauhaus-Archiv, Berlin.

Fig. 3.5 Lucia Moholy, masters' houses by Walter Gropius, view from northwest, 1927, modern gelatin silver print (1994) from original glass negative. Bauhaus-Archiv, Berlin.

Images in Exile

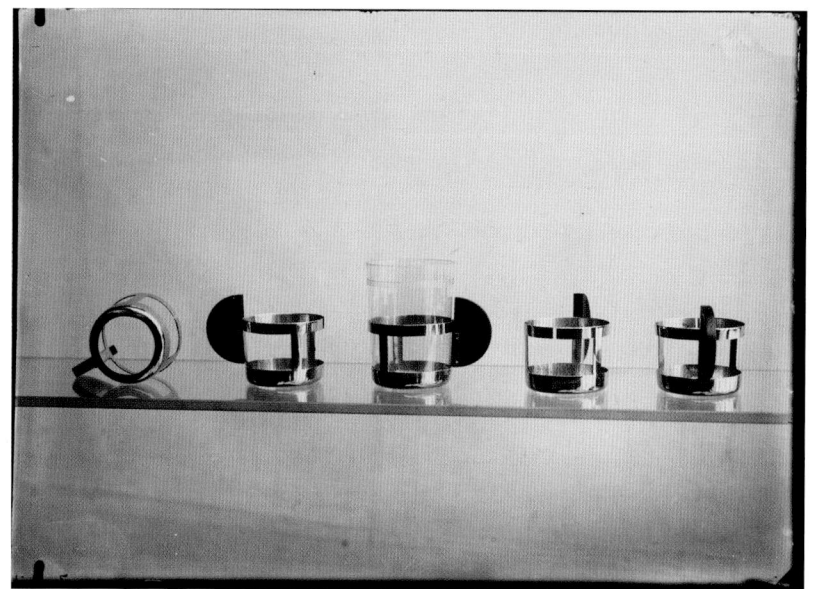

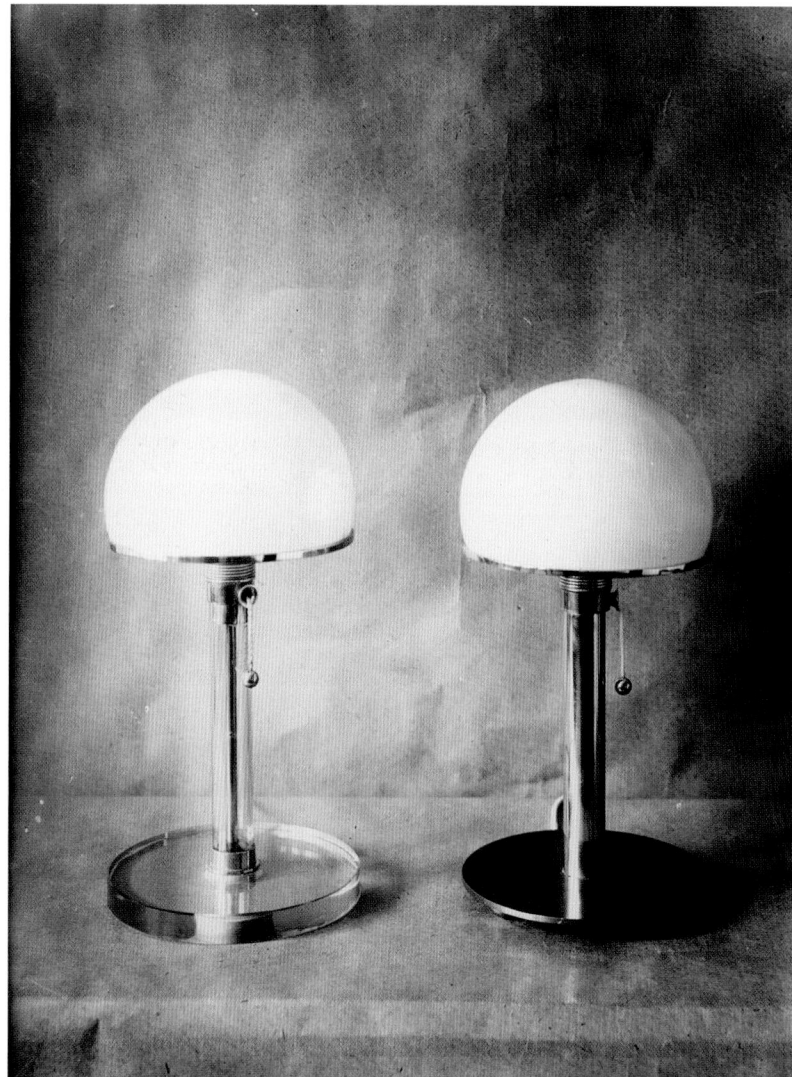

Fig. 3.6 Lucia Moholy, tea glass holders by Max Krajewski (designer), 1924, gelatin silver print (printed ca. 1950 by the Busch-Reisinger Museum). Harvard Art Museums/Busch-Reisinger Museum, Gift of Walter Gropius, BR50.107.

Fig. 3.7 Lucia Moholy, two table lamps by Carl J. Jucker and Wilhelm Wagenfeld (designers), ca. 1924–25, gelatin silver print (printed ca. 1950 by the Busch-Reisinger Museum). Harvard Art Museums/Busch-Reisinger Museum, Gift of Walter Gropius, BR50.86.C.

Fig. 3.8 Lucia Moholy, verso with German-period stamps: Lucia Moholy (stamped twice), "Reproduction forbidden without permission," and Cambridge, MA–period stamp: "Walter Gropius, Registered Architect," of photograph of Bauhaus Building by Walter Gropius (architect), view of the workshop wing from under the bridge, 1926, gelatin silver print. Harvard Art Museums/Busch-Reisinger Museum, Gift of Ise Gropius, BRGA.20.454.

and printed.[9] The products' modernity is underscored in the photographs themselves: in the shiny reflective surfaces, lit so that they gleam but do not over-reflect; in the clear lines; and in their staging against a neutral background, often on thick sheets of glass (fig. 3.6). The images served as professional portraits of the objects themselves as individual works of art, in line with Moholy's simultaneous documentation of sculpture and other Bauhaus student output (fig. 3.7). Moholy executed this extensive body of photographic work over the course of a number of years. There are no surviving documents to indicate that she was officially hired; it seems, rather, that she took up the task in oral agreement with Gropius and in support of the school. Not paid for her work, she kept the negatives and subsequently charged a small image-usage fee, at her discretion, to non-Bauhaus affiliated users.[10] Copies were available at no charge to school members and for Bauhaus publications and other publicity measures. Moholy would stamp the verso of copies that she made with two stamps: one with her name and another that stated "Reproduction forbidden without permission" (fig. 3.8).

The photographs played various roles within the Bauhaus during its operation. In-house, the object and architectural photographs were reproduced in the Bauhaus's newspaper and the Bauhaus book series, where Moholy also assisted the two editors, her husband, and Gropius, in the editing, copyediting, and other production tasks. Certain photographs also doubled as illustrative materials for the school's sales catalog, known as the *Katalog der Muster*, through which the Bauhaus GmbH marketed its products. Her photographs also served as publicity material for the school, sent out for use by newspapers, art and architectural journals, and other publications.

Even products that were never put into production during the years that the Bauhaus was in operation, such as Theodor Bogler's storage jars, remain in the collective Bauhaus memory in large part thanks to her iconic images (fig. 3.9).

Images in Exile

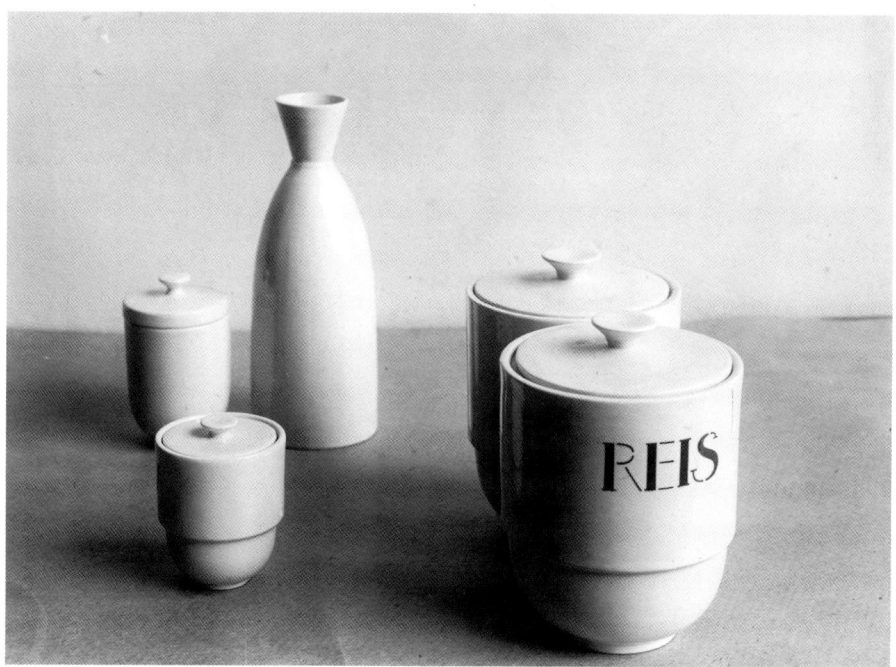

Fig. 3.9 Lucia Moholy, kitchen containers by Theodor Bogler (designer), ca. 1924, modern gelatin silver print (1994) from original glass negative. Bauhaus-Archiv, Berlin.

Beyond their function as documentation of Bauhaus products, they helped to set the artistic and visual standards for modern products in their time and subsequently, as well as for the ongoing legacy of the Bauhaus itself.

The images are didactic: through their objective-seeming, straightforward nature the photographs visibly serve to underscore ideas about *Sachlichkeit* and mass production promoted by the school. Seriality, in particular, is visualized in images where several examples of one object type were set up to provide multiple perspectives of the product within a single image.[11] Seriality was also implied in the photographs showing multiplications and proliferations of single objects, sometimes aided by the doubling produced by projected shadows (figs. 3.10, 3.11). Because only a limited number of these objects were produced (many only exist as a single prototype or as a small, hand-reproduced series), it is the photographs that give the objects an aura of mass reproducibility.[12] But they stop short of representing mass production itself: the number of exemplars remains limited — with a few exceptions featuring at most three to four single objects or views — and the Moholy photographs are entirely devoid of suggestions of industrialization or the tools of manufacture. Images by other photographers who captured the Bauhaus workshop output, such as Erich Consemüller, also depicted a circumscribed number of goods available on view.[13]

This is in stark contrast to the seemingly unending vertical stacks or diagonal rows of goods that *Neue Sachlichkeit* (New Objectivity) photographers, such as Albert Renger-Patzsch, used to illuminate factory products such as metal bathtubs or shoe lasts — though Renger-Patzsch's precise attention to the material, texture, and structure of objects and architecture, especially as evidenced in the use of shadow and diagonal forms, is replicated in her work of the same period.[14] But during the short time the school was in operation and, certainly, following its closure, physical access to Bauhaus objects remained elusive. Moholy's photographs, then, made these items visually available and

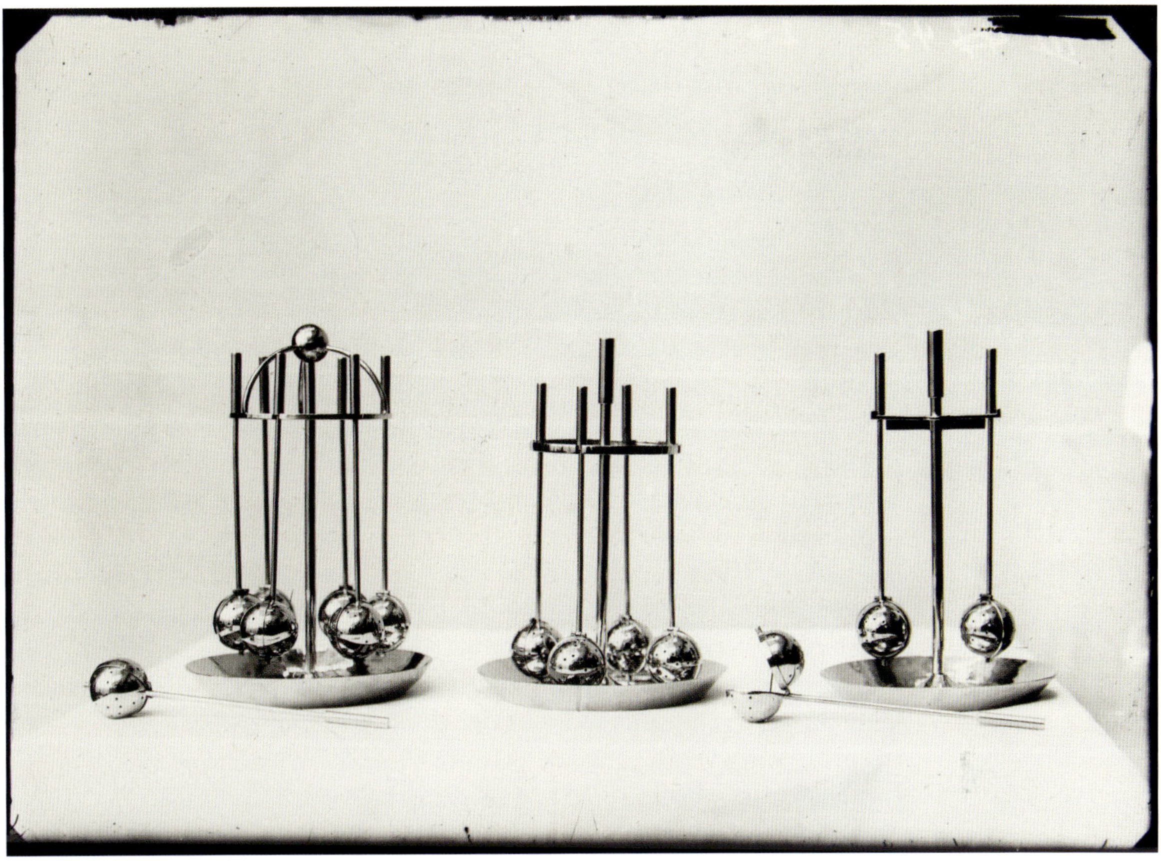

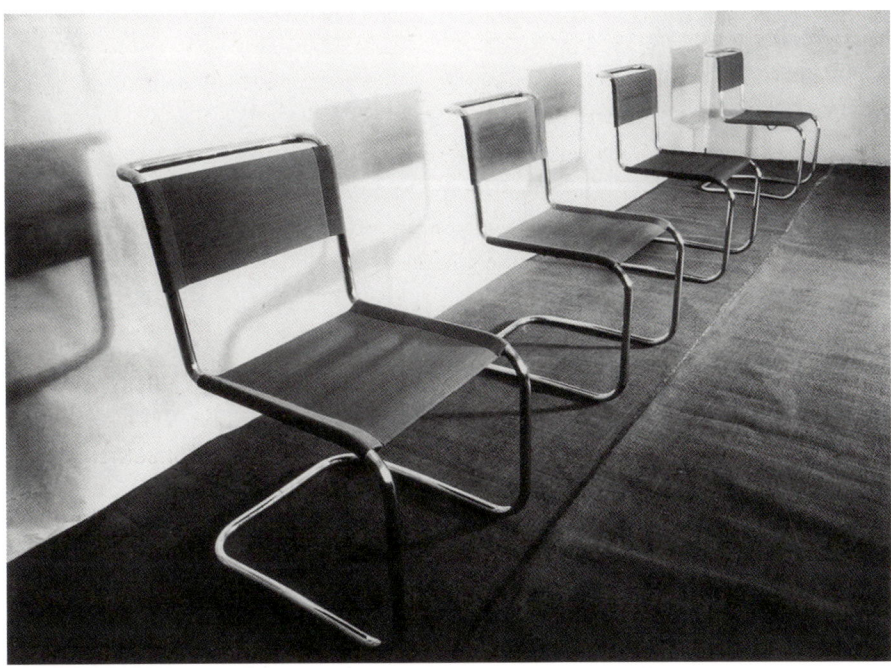

Fig. 3.10 Lucia Moholy, stands with tea infusers by Otto Rittweger (designer, executed by Wolfgang Tümel), 1925, gelatin silver print, (printed ca. 1950 by the Busch-Reisinger Museum). Harvard Art Museums/Busch-Reisinger Museum, Gift of Walter Gropius, BR50.120.

Fig. 3.11 Lucia Moholy, tubular steel chairs (B33) by Marcel Breuer (designer), 1928, modern gelatin silver print (1994) from original glass negative. Bauhaus-Archiv, Berlin.

thus served to convey the ideas they were meant to instantiate. The photos, in contrast to the physical objects depicted in them, were fully reproducible and able to circulate (in the objects' stead) as their designers originally intended.

Exile Photography

For the majority of her Weimar-era photographs Moholy used a large-format wooden camera mounted on a tripod with 13 × 18 cm or 18 × 24 cm glass plates, mainly Perutz dry plates.[15] When she and her husband left the Bauhaus, following the resignation of Walter Gropius in 1928, Moholy took all of her Bauhaus negatives with her. Exile for so many *Bauhäusler* was an exercise in leaving art and possessions behind, in making difficult decisions, in trusting those who were to remain. László Moholy-Nagy was ultimately forced to leave metal constructions and early canvasses showing his development from representational to abstract painting with a housekeeper and her husband, who subsequently turned them to kindling wood and threatened to have him arrested for *Kulturbolschewismus* (cultural bolshevism).[16] However, he was fortunate in that he was able to bring his furniture and works such as the cumbersome *Lichtrequisit* (also known as the *Light Prop for an Electric Stage* or *Light Space Modulator*) on his peregrinations in Europe and then to the United States.[17] Gropius, too, was able to ship everything from Germany to America, including his model of the Bauhaus Building and the custom-designed double-desk at which he and Ise worked. Lucia Moholy's loss of access to her negatives meant that she was not only barred from swiftly building on her past work and reputation but also from utilizing her expertise as a witness to those productive years at the Bauhaus, where she had been both a bystander and participant in that remarkable period of creativity.

That Moholy found herself in London in 1934 without her belongings, especially without her photographic negatives or any examples of her work, was a consequence of the circumstances under which she was forced to flee Germany. Following the disintegration of her marriage to Moholy-Nagy in 1929, she had entered into a relationship with Theodor Neubauer, a Communist Party parliament member and activist. It was in Moholy's apartment that Neubauer was arrested on August 3, 1933. She would never see him again; he was imprisoned in the Zuchthaus Brandenburg prison, then at Esterwegen (a prison for political opponents, where he was forced to do hard labor in the peat bogs), followed by the Lichtenburg and Buchenwald concentration camps. Released in 1939, he was arrested again in 1944 and executed in February 1945 in the Zuchthaus Brandenburg.[18]

After Neubauer's arrest, in accordance with the plan they had previously formulated, Moholy went immediately into exile, leaving her well-appointed apartment and its contents, taking practically nothing with her.[19] She fled first to Prague, then to Vienna, and then via Paris to London, where she arrived in June 1934. In her haste, she was forced to leave behind between five hundred and six hundred glass negatives, representing her entire photographic oeuvre to date, in the care of her ex-husband, László Moholy-Nagy. Her negatives, or even one set of good prints, would naturally have been useful in establishing herself in England, for, as she noted, "they not only showed the quality of my earlier work, but they also were my only tangible asset."[20] Instead she found

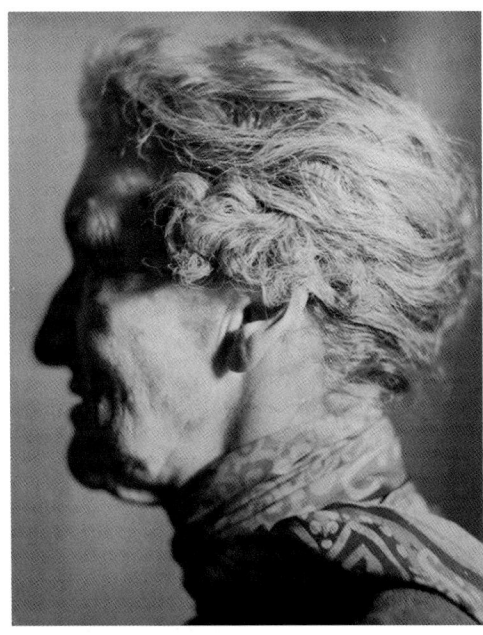

Fig. 3.12 Lucia Moholy, *Portrait of Emma, Countess of Oxford and Asquith*, 1935, gelatin silver print. Bauhaus-Archiv, Berlin.

herself penniless, a foreign national in a country on the brink of war with the one she had just left.[21] Unlike many of her Bauhaus colleagues, whose roles at the school would become the basis for their post-Bauhaus careers in England, the United States, and elsewhere, Lucia Moholy was forced to begin more or less anew in exile.

Fortunately for Moholy, her photographic work at the Bauhaus had also included the development of her skill in formal portrait photography, which she would now come to rely on. Unlike the candid snapshots popular at the Bauhaus, hers were formal undertakings with careful attention to the technical aspects – composition, lighting, and background. In their artistic ambition they attempted to capture the character of the sitter and his or her artistic milieu. For example, her iconic photograph of her husband Moholy-Nagy, wearing what appears to be a machinist's coverall (*Monteuranzug*) over his crisp shirt and tie, presented an image of the *Monteur* or artist-constructor at work, which played an important role in the development of his artistic persona.[22]

In exile in England, she built on her Bauhaus portraits by taking photographs of prominent sitters: barons, lords, countesses, academics, literary figures (writers, publishers, editors), and politicians (fig. 3.12). Predominantly taken in the time span 1935–38, most of these insightful, luminous portraits have entered the National Portrait Gallery collection in London. Although she had qualified as a German and English teacher, had studied art history and philosophy, and had significant experience as an editor and copy editor, in England the strict rules governing the employment of foreign nationals in the years leading up to World War II meant that Moholy was only able to obtain permission to set up as an independent photographer.[23] Through this work she was nonetheless able to assimilate quickly into English society and found success; her photographs were well liked by her eminent sitters. As the Countess of Oxford and Asquith wrote, "I think your photographs quite wonderful, so do all my friends. They are different from the modern photography which goes in for what might be called 'beauty parlors.' Your photographs make real men and women, and will be contributions to the biography of great and famous people in the future."[24]

In this period she also compiled the photographs and wrote the text for her history, *A Hundred Years of Photography*, which was published in 1939 by Penguin Books.[25] She had begun research for it in 1929, while still teaching at the Itten School in Berlin. By 1930, she had developed a short concept paper, "Kulturgeschichte der Fotografie" (A cultural history of photography), outlining her ideas for the book, followed, in 1932, by a more concrete précis.[26] In these two working papers, she describes the project very specifically as a "cultural history" of the medium, consciously rejecting a "history of photography" and an "art history of photography." By "cultural history" she meant both the development of a culture of photography in and of itself and a wider cultural life as reflected in photography (e.g., changes in taste, concepts of morality).

In other preparatory documents she considers the way photographs represent or reflect society and, in turn, how they exert an influence on that society.[27] She ruminates on the ways in which an economic situation might be mirrored in photographs and whether this might be so in every age or only at certain junctures, concluding that photographs are an untrustworthy such measure in that merely a selection of images is ever available and is therefore not broadly representative. Moholy also reflects on the ways in which photography functions as a means of reproducing reality (*Wirklichkeit*) and on whether photographs accompanying a text make the text more factual (*sachlich*). After examining new publications, she determines that photographs are no guarantee for objectivity but rather too dependent on authorial choice and interpretation. She also theorizes the subject-object relationship in the context of photography as well as the autonomy of photography as an art form, first questioning the character of photographs as *objects* themselves, subject to the influence of outside pressures, and then considering how they might move to become *subjects*, and as such, exert an independent influence outward. The role of technology on the medium is also contextualized by Moholy, who sees the development of photography running parallel with the advancement of other modern technologies.

However, as published, the resulting book, *A Hundred Years of Photography: 1839–1939*, is a consolidation of material packaged for a very general readership. Less a theoretical consideration of the place of photography in culture than a remarkably succinct technological and artistic history of the field, it encompasses developments and practices in the medium from the standpoint of the professional and the amateur photographer alike. The slim volume was just under two hundred pages and priced at only 6 pence. In its initial two years, about forty thousand copies of the book were sold.[28]

In the book, Moholy provides descriptions of contemporary movements in photography that illuminate her own photographic practice. She thus characterizes 1920s *Neue Sachlichkeit*, or what she also terms "modern object photography," as an artistic movement in photography in which "the object, by being isolated from its natural surroundings, was endowed with a much greater importance than it originally possessed," arguing that as photography became more "object-conscious" its objects became more "self-assertive," granting significance to all of their details.[29] This sheds particular light on Moholy's Bauhaus photographic practice, indicating her awareness of the complexity of the object/photograph relationship in this work and the agency that the things represented could take on specifically via the photographs that reproduced them, something that would become more poignant in exile, as the Bauhaus objects depicted in Moholy's photographs took on increased significance through repeated reproduction. The image section of the book, which contains only thirty-five photographs in total, nonetheless elides the period from the 1900s to the 1930s, omitting any photographs representing *Neue Sachlichkeit*, other developments that she describes occurring in the 1920s, or others' or her own work from that period — which, in any case, she would have been unable to reproduce. Although the photographs appear grainy because production costs were held down so as to keep the book inexpensive, the reproductions were all made from originals housed in such institutions as the Victoria and Albert Museum, the London Science Museum, and elsewhere, mainly in Great Britain, representing both the care she took in finding high-quality images and the limitations posed by publishing in this period.

She does, however, situate her new work by naming herself among other practitioners as part of a new, "realistic" type of portrait photography and reproducing one of her recent commissions, the Countess of Oxford and Asquith from 1935 (see fig. 3.12). Seeing the two developments as aligned, she writes that the new direction in portraiture grew out of object photography in which "not only the shape, delineation and expression of the human face, but the sculptural details of the head and the texture of skin, hair, nails and dress . . . became attractive subjects to the photographer."[30] Though the book served to secure her as an authority on photography, she uses it only subtly as a podium to assert her own place — as photographer — in the history of photography and to further her own concurrent photographic career.

Although aimed at a lay audience, *A Hundred Years of Photography* was also notably an important contribution to the work of a circle of authors and photographers in the 1930s who were attempting to draw up histories of photography from multiple angles — aesthetic, technical, historical, cultural, and theoretical.[31] Moholy-Nagy's 1925 *Malerei, Photographie, Film*, which was an intellectual collaboration between Moholy-Nagy and Lucia Moholy and which relied heavily on Lucia Moholy's literary skills in German, was an important precursor to both the photographic discourse and to histories of photography of the 1930s.[32] *A Hundred Years of Photography* would influence practicing photographers working in London, such as Helmut Gernsheim, who would go on to write extensively about the history and theory of photography.[33] Moholy's text furthered important discussions under way in this period concerning the role of photography as an independent art with its own creative process and photographic vision as a distinct form of seeing.

Commercially and critically, *A Hundred Years of Photography* was a success. As an exile who had been in England for only a few years, the accessibility and popularity of the book helped Moholy to establish herself as an expert on the medium. A decade later, in 1948, this status was recognized with her admittance to the Royal Photographic Society.[34] Despite these successes, however, the strains of being in exile took their toll on Moholy, as they did on other

Bauhäusler and non-artist immigrants alike. One glimpses this only fragmentarily, from letters such as one she wrote to a potential patron in 1937 to postpone a portrait sitting:

> All kind[s] of old suffering came back after this flu, and I had to fight them for several weeks, till at last it was found that I am not strong enough to get rid of these things here at present, and that I shall go to Switzerland for a few weeks. Well, this was rather a difficult problem, for not only is it a grave financial matter for me, but, being away, it means, in addition, losses of work.... In fact, I believe, there is some sort of wound on the bottom of the heart with such people as I am — and one has [to] try very hard to react normally again after all the worry of the last years.... Excuse, in addition to all the rest, please, my typing. Some days I am too nervous to write by hand.[35]

The perils of Moholy's existence were also made clear when her home in London was bombed in September 1940, and, once again, she was forced to flee on short notice, able to take only a few belongings with her.[36]

Multiple Exiles

While in exile, a wide circle of former Bauhaus members leaned on each other for logistical help, companionship, reprieve from the constant challenge of exile, and retreat to something like the normalcy of former times. In the United States especially, former Bauhaus members visited each other for pleasure and on work pretenses — continuing to collaborate on various projects and lecturing at one another's new institutional homes. In 1940, when World War II was in full force and London was often under severe bombardment, Moholy appealed to many of them to help her make a new start in the United States. Gropius agreed to serve as a reference in her pursuit of a position with MIT's library; during this period she was involved with the reproductive and preservation processes of microfilm. Moholy's brother — a successful playwright and screenwriter in Hollywood — attempted to sponsor her visa.[37] Moholy-Nagy endeavored to help by offering her a position at the New Bauhaus in Chicago, by then called the School of Design. Sibyl, Moholy-Nagy's second wife, wrote to Lucia: "You may be sure, that we shall do everything we can, to help you. But of course this is not very much. We shall send you a contract with the School of Design in Chicago, appointing you as teacher for photography and possibly history of art.... There will always be a couch for you to house you long enough, till you have found enough means to live on your own, and I may add that all of us shall be very glad, to tide you over as long as it is necessary."[38]

A week later the contract was sent. However, Moholy was turned down by US immigration officials on the grounds that she could not prove that her principal occupation in the past had been that of professor of photography but rather only that she was a practicing photographer and writer.[39] Forced to stay in England, Moholy initially depended on the kindness of Quakers, who had helped her flee Germany and establish herself in London, and on fellow Czech exiles. She was soon integrated into a circle of British friends and professional colleagues, principally centered in Bloomsbury, where she lived, as well as the exiled Bauhaus community.

In London she also had contact with circles of photographers and those in photography-related fields, such as photojournalists, editors, agents, and leaders of photographic documentation projects (such as activities sponsored by the Warburg Institute), a group that was predominantly Jewish.[40] Within this context, and given the circumstances of her displacement, first willingly, from Prague to Wiesbaden, Germany (she left at age twenty and entirely supported herself), and later as a refugee, from Berlin to London, Moholy's Jewish background, even though she had been brought up in an entirely assimilated context, is not insignificant.[41] Of affluent, upper-class Jewish parentage, Moholy's birth certificate stated "mosaischen Glaubens" (literally, "of Mosaic faith," i.e., Jewish), but she was brought up as an atheist and would otherwise reject her Judaism throughout her life.[42] Yet Donald Kuspit has noted that art critic Harold Rosenberg argued that "anxiety about identity" was the most serious theme in Jewish life, while Clement Greenberg saw "alienation" built into Jewish existence.[43]

These themes, hardly unique to the assessments of these art critics, were indeed pressed again upon individual Jews with particular force by the events of the mid-twentieth century, and they are also present in Moholy's biography, both metaphorically and also practically, if not necessarily ever as a direct consequence of her Jewish background: as a citizen of Prague born in 1894, she was of Austrian nationality, subsequently Czechoslovak (1918), and she became Hungarian upon her marriage to Moholy-Nagy (1921). Following her divorce (1934) the Hungarian authorities refused to extend her passport, leaving her stateless and without a valid passport until she became a British citizen in 1947, a process she had begun in 1936.[44] In the postwar period, through her lawyer, Lucia Moholy filed a series of formal claims for compensation from the German government for persecution under the Nazi regime, seeking recompense for her livelihood and the loss of her household goods left behind in Berlin. In a complicated, drawn-out series of lawsuits, Moholy ultimately lost all claims except one, which resulted in a single payment of 10,000 marks. In the lawsuit paperwork she excised her relationship with the communist Neubauer and based her claims and reason for fleeing on her Jewish status and her loss of employment when she was let go from Itten's art school, earlier that year, following election of the National Socialists.[45]

The Gropiuses arrived in England in 1934 and the Moholy-Nagys in 1935. In the shipment of their goods to England, the Moholy-Nagys had included a number of Lucia's belongings, including miscellaneous pieces of furniture, but not her negatives. The circumstances surrounding the loss of Lucia Moholy's Bauhaus-era negatives are particularly difficult to clarify.[46] When she left Berlin, Lucia had stored her glass negatives with the Moholy-Nagys, who, in turn, brought them to Walter Gropius's house in Berlin. From there they were shipped to the United States with Gropius's belongings in 1937 and then stored in his basement.[47] Both the Gropiuses and the Moholy-Nagys had left England for America in 1937, and Lucia subsequently remained in frequent contact with both couples. At the conclusion of the war, she wrote to Moholy-Nagy, only months before his death: "You remember that after I left, you and Sybil [sic] took care of my things, and among them were all my negatives.... You left them somewhere. Can you remember where? Perhaps they could be retrieved.... Was there anything else left behind which might be of value now? Did I not have some of your paintings also?"[48] Sibyl, apparently not knowing the negatives had been shipped to the United States, subsequently informed Lucia that Gropius's house had been fire-bombed during the war.[49] Thus, Lucia believed that her negatives had been destroyed, not knowing that a large portion of them had survived and were safe.

For Moholy, the subsequent, accidental tracing of her negatives' continuing existence started in June 1950 with a last-minute letter to Walter Gropius looking for generic Bauhaus photographs—because she did not have any of her own—to illustrate a lecture she was to give at the London School of Printing and Graphic Arts. She wrote: "I have been invited to give a talk on the Bauhaus on June 15—only two weeks from today. I know it is very short notice, but if you or Ise could send me some photographs from which to prepare lantern slides, it would be a great help.... It is shockingly short notice, I know, do you think it worth trying just the same? What I should like are some two dozen pictures from various periods to give an overall picture for one 50 minute lecture to people who know nothing about it."[50]

She simultaneously sent a telegram with the plea: "Can you airmail photographs or slides for my lecture Bauhaus 15th June uninformed audience. Apologies short notice Thanks Love Lucia Moholy."[51] A cable from Gropius follows: "Cannot send only original photographs suggest asking *Architectural Review* Sorry, (Signed) Walter Gropius."[52] Gropius also replied by letter with a further explanation: "I was sorry that I couldn't help in the very short time to send you material over for a lecture on the Bauhaus. The few photographs I have are last copies which I cannot replace. The negatives, as far as I have them, have been given to the Germanic Museum [later renamed the Busch-Reisinger Museum] for their newly built-up Bauhaus collection. It would have taken too much time to have copies made which would have reached you in time before your lecture. I hope that in spite of it it went all right."[53] Moholy wrote back: "I really must apologize again for troubling you with the telegram about Bauhaus work. Of course I understand that you cannot part with your only copies even for a short time. I made many attempts to secure slides or photographs from all the likely organizations including the *Architectural Review*, but the total result is astonishingly poor. That is why I wired. However, I shall just have to manage, and make up by describing what I should have preferred to show."[54]

This short exchange between old friends leaves out crucial elements of what was to be revealed four years later. Gropius did not say that he was in possession of her negatives, only that he had photographic prints, and he did not say that the "negatives" that he had promised to the museum were her negatives. Moholy's negatives, stored in his Lincoln basement, it transpires, were used by Gropius to make prints upon request, which were then given away by him, along with the permission to use them, without crediting Moholy. He also had a large supply of prints that Moholy had made in Germany, which were stamped clearly with her name, sometimes in duplicate, and the text "Reproduction forbidden without permission," upon which he added his own architecture firm's stamp (see fig. 3.8).

The fact that Bauhaus imagery was in such scarce supply in England after the war that Moholy had to ask Gropius for prints underscores just how important Moholy's negatives were (and were increasingly to become) for establishing the Bauhaus legacy. Her images played a significant role in the 1938 large-scale exhibition at the Museum of Modern Art, titled *Bauhaus, 1919–1928*, whose catalog became the standard text in English on the school. Postwar publications, both those about the Bauhaus and monographs on individual artists, such as Marcel Breuer, frequently used her photographs, too. This usurpation of her property put a significant strain on Moholy, a single woman trying to support herself; commenting later on the affair, she mentioned her "extreme poverty" in these years.[55] She recalled that during the war her "mind was occupied with other, more acute worries. I began to feel the loss later on, increasing with the demand for lectures and articles which needed illustrating."[56]

Forced to bypass crucial opportunities — invitations for lectures and articles continued to be extended to her throughout the 1950s — and as new publications with good reproductions of her photographs began to emerge, Moholy began to sense that her negatives might have survived. She thus wrote again to Gropius in January 1954:

> I have been invited to collaborate, and in particular provide documentary material, for a series of articles on a subject close to our hearts: the relation between architecture, painting, sculpture, textiles, stained glass etc. and the entity [entirety] of the result achieved by their organized use, or in other words: team spirit. . . . It is therefore essential to . . . show what the Bauhaus has done.
>
> . . . [I] should like to make another attempt at locating my own collection of documentary material, i.e. the considerable number of photographs (original negatives) which I took during my Bauhaus years. I wonder if there is anything you can recall, possibly from discussions with Moholy who took care of them when I left in 1933.
>
> It did not occur to me to ask you earlier, or at any rate not until Sybil [*sic*] told me the negatives were stored in the house where you and Ise lived in Berlin. Is this correct? If so, can you remember when they were deposited there and, whether they were left there when you decided to come to England? Or were they moved elsewhere? . . .
>
> So: if there is the slightest hope that my negatives may still be intact, I must do what I can to trace them. But how do I go about it? These negatives are irreplaceable documents which could be extremely useful, now more than ever. I am prepared to look into the matter myself, or request friends in Germany to do this for me. But I can do nothing unless I have a line to work on. Do you think you could advise me on this? I should be extremely grateful.[57]

It is ironic that it was in preparation for a lecture on Bauhaus "team spirit" that Moholy discovered that news of the survival of her negatives had been withheld from her. Gropius's reply, for the first time, seventeen years after bringing the negatives with him to the United States, finally, definitively informed Moholy that he was in fact in possession of them:

> Long years ago in Berlin, you gave all these negatives to me. I have carefully kept them, had copies made of all of them and have given a full set of copies to the Busch-Reisinger Museum at Harvard which has built up a special Bauhaus Department which is steadily growing. I have promised them the original negatives with your name attached as soon as I do not need them any more myself. Both Ise and myself remember this clearly. You will imagine that these photographs are extremely useful to me and that I have continuously made use of them; so I hope you will not deprive me of them. Wouldn't it be sufficient if I sent you contact prints of the negatives? There are a great many, but I certainly understand that you want to make use of them yourself. Anyhow it will be a relief to you to know that they are in existence and in good shape. I have never left them out of hand.[58]

A number of letters between Moholy and the Gropiuses ensued. Moholy replied at length: she had never given the negatives away, and she was appalled that Gropius had promised them to a museum and was only now offering her contact prints, a paltry substitute that might have been proposed earlier, under circumstances that should have prompted the return of the negatives; she concluded by registering this betrayal as a "shattering experience" by someone she had "always considered one of my truest friends."[59] Moholy then spent several years consulting a series of international lawyers.[60] In 1957, after three years of legal negotiations, Moholy ultimately received a large crate of negatives.[61] Today, the Bauhaus Archive in Berlin has 230 of the 560 Bauhaus-era negatives she took, while 330 negatives, according to Moholy's own card catalog, are still missing.[62]

Trust and Restitution

In the context of exile and the circumstances of fleeing into exile, the issue of trust, in its multiple senses of meaning, takes on a special role. As Moholy wrote to Gropius,

> You must have realized that my case was one of many hundreds of thousands, if not millions of people who had no alternative but to leave their belongings on trust (*zu treuen Händen*) with [that is, in the trust of] someone whose position was less precarious than one's own. It was neither possible nor necessary to come to an understanding regarding the return of one's property, since to take care on trust firmly implies the obligation to return it to its owner as soon as circumstances permit. Surely you did not expect me to delay my departure in order to draw up a formal contract stipulating date and conditions of return? No formal agreement could have carried more weight than our friendship. It is this friendship I have always relied on, and which, also, I am now invoking.[63]

In reference to a claim from Gropius that she should be thankful that he saved the negatives from bombardment in Berlin, and to his subsequent reluctance to return them, Moholy's lawyer wrote: "Do you believe that because you had the negatives which were entrusted to you sent to the U.S.A., and thus saved them from destruction in Germany, you had a good excuse for depriving her of their use . . . ? Do you subscribe to the proposition that the fireman who puts out a fire in a house should keep as prize the treasures of the house?"[64]

In times of emergency, under conditions of dictatorship or war and under the circumstances of exile, in particular, as the laws and norms of society lose their effect, individuals are forced more than ever to rely on trust and friendship to endure and counter hardship. Former members of the Bauhaus were no exception to this; to assist their colleagues still in Europe the Gropiuses set up a special "Bauhaus Fund," while Mies, the Moholy-Nagys, the Gropiuses and the Bayers sent countless CARE packages and financial donations. As Sibyl commiserated in a letter to Lucia Moholy, "The reports from England are very depressing and I would be very happy to send you whatever you need to supplement your obviously meager diet. Please Lucia don't hesitate to let me know what you need."[65] But when it came to the photographs Moholy had taken, with their indispensable role to play in the construction of the Bauhaus story, this rule gave way. Owing to the circumstances surrounding this inaccessibility of her negatives, Moholy was also thrown into an oppositional position vis-à-vis her former Bauhaus colleagues and friends. This further loss of trust, friendship, and the support of the exile network compounded the more tangible losses she suffered through this episode.

There was also an overall negative impact on her career, like that often suffered by exiles forced to leave behind important portions of their prior lives. As she wrote to Gropius, "All my negatives, those you have used more and others you may have used less, have been completely out of reach as far as I am concerned. Consequently I have been prevented from carrying out any requests, orders, commissions, projects and other activities depending on having access to my negatives and have suffered considerable harm in terms of loss of face and loss of income and potential income."[66] The outsize role that her images played, in exile from her, in the growing attention paid to the Bauhaus indeed compounded this isolation, separating her from a collaborative project in which she had been an important participant – even as the significance of her particular contribution now grew markedly.

Because she was not credited for her essential role in collaborative work with László Moholy-Nagy, these photographs represent the only contribution during the Bauhaus years that can be attributed to Lucia Moholy alone. This lack of acknowledgment was stinging. In the midst of the effort to retrieve them, she wrote: "Everybody, except myself, have used, and admit to having used my photographs . . . and often also without mentioning my name. Everyone – except myself – have derived advantages from using my photographs, either directly, or indirectly, in a number of ways, be it in cash or prestige, or both."[67] Indeed, in an era in which it was somewhat unusual to do so, especially in the context of the collaborative atmosphere and friendship circles of the Bauhaus, Moholy had always taken care to maintain her copyright over the images – asserting the relative autonomy of the photographic works from their subject matter. Until the point at which she lost control of them, all prints made from the negatives had been stamped with her name and her copyright on the verso. The negatives themselves were generally not marked, however, except for the negative's number, which Moholy sometimes wrote on the black tape around the glass negative's edges, as they were never intended to be separated from their owner.[68]

In the Weimar period she had been, for the main part, credited for her images when they were published – such as in the Bauhaus book *Walter Gropius Bauhausbauten Dessau* (*Walter Gropius Bauhaus Building Dessau*), which credited fifty-five photographs to her, or the 1926 inaugural issue of the *Bauhaus* magazine, which prominently featured a photograph of the Bauhaus Building by her on its cover and several more within. But in the post-1933 period, when she lost control of the negatives, her name increasingly did not appear in the photograph credits. During the same period, books such as Gropius's *The New Architecture and the Bauhaus* made heavy use of her negatives for its images as did the 1938 Museum of Modern Art exhibition catalog, *Bauhaus, 1919–1928*, which uses at least forty of Moholy's images, supplied by Gropius.[69]

Indeed, the MoMA exhibition, which took place only five years after the school's closure, played a particularly critical role in establishing its enduring legacy.[70] By focusing exclusively on the years of Gropius's own tenure, the show allowed him, very shortly after his arrival in the United States, to begin to construct a framework for the reception of the school and the work produced there.[71] The exhibition was a major success for the museum, at least as reported by Alfred H. Barr Jr.: "We were very doubtful whether the exhibition would be a popular success because of the complexity and difficulty of the subject.... To our surprise we were completely mistaken. We have had a far larger attendance at the exhibition than at any previous show in our present quarters."[72]

The exhibition design by Herbert Bayer featured many large-scale photographs by Moholy, likewise unattributed. In a room focusing on the Bauhaus workshops, for example, a few extant physical examples were on display (two vitrines of metal objects, two chairs, and a chess set), but the most informative feature of the room was the rear-wall photographic mosaic of product designs from the furniture workshop (fig. 3.13). As in the exhibition generally, because there were few available objects (most could not be shipped out of Germany or were not otherwise accessible), and especially in the case of large pieces of furniture, photographs served to fill the lacunae. Indeed, in a letter to Herbert Bayer, who was coordinating the loans, Gropius enumerated the materials in his possession that might be of use for the exhibition, noting that he had a great many original photographic plates of the Bauhaus buildings and workshop objects, in fact, "so many that I haven't had the chance to view them all."[73] (After the show closed, Gropius was anxious to get the photographs back in his possession, writing to the registrar, "there are about 80 photographs which I sent to Mr. Bayer [for the exhibition] for which I received no receipt from you.... Will you please talk these over with Mr. Bayer, as almost all the items I have sent are unique and cannot be replaced.")[74]

Even the MoMA press release elaborated that photography compensated for the lack of objects: "Under existing conditions in Germany it was not

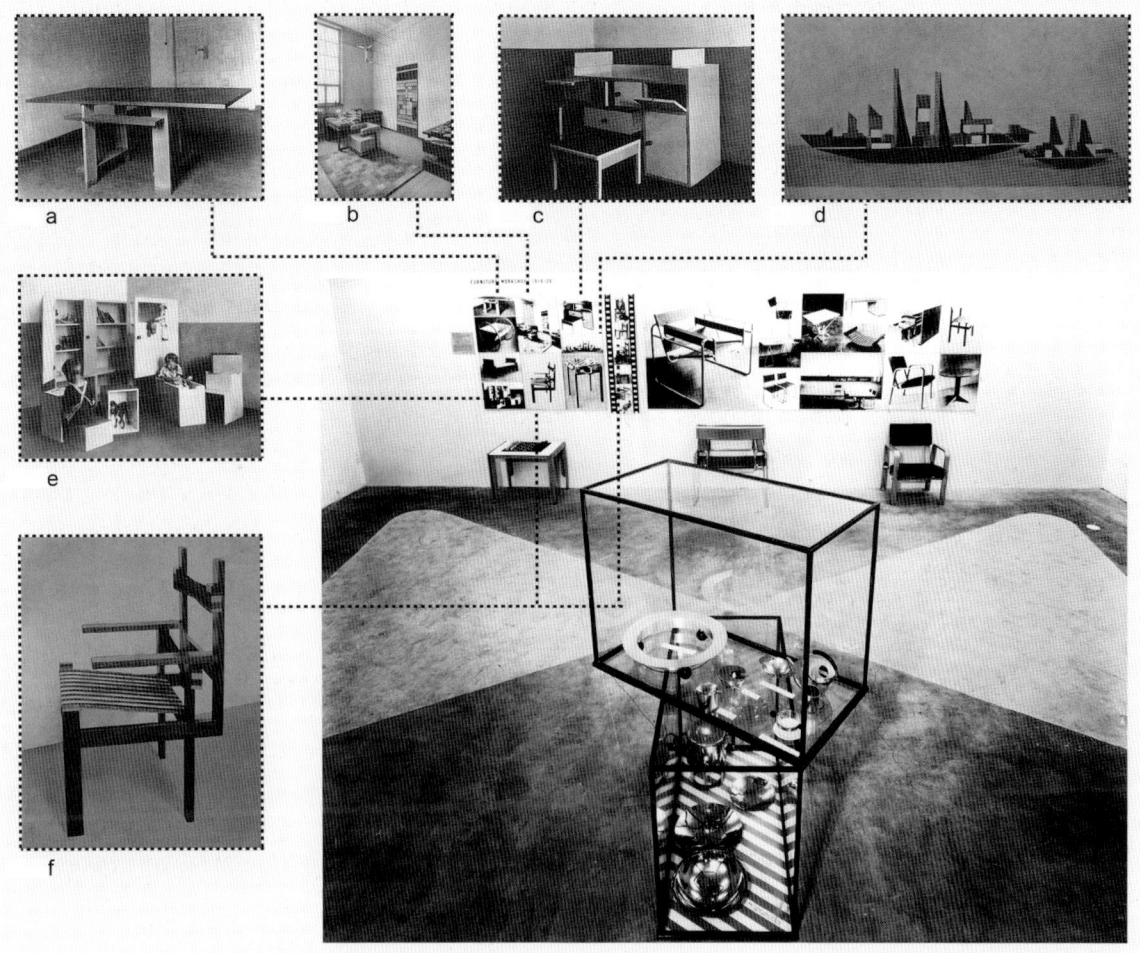

Fig. 3.13 Installation view of *The Bauhaus, 1919–1928*, Museum of Modern Art, 1938, gelatin silver print. Photograph by Soichi Sunami. Bauhaus-Archiv, Berlin.

a. Photograph, Lucia Moholy, ca. 1924, conference table, Josef Albers (designer), 1923.

b. Photograph, Lucia Moholy, ca. 1924, Bauhaus director's office, 1923, Weimar.

c. Photograph, Lucia Moholy, 1924, changing table, Alma Buscher (designer), 1924.

d. Photograph possibly Lucia Moholy, ship toy, Alma Buscher (designer), 1923.

e. Photograph probably Lucia Moholy, for Atelier Eckner, toy cabinet, Alma Buscher (designer), 1923.

f. Photograph, Lucia Moholy, ca. 1924, armchair (later titled TI 1a), Marcel Breuer (designer), 1922.

Images in Exile

possible to bring more actual objects to this country for the exhibition," and it pointed out that the show was "supplemented by enlarged photographs."[75] Of the photographic objects making up the furniture workshop mural, six images are likely by Moholy. They exhibit a documentary nature combined with a vitality that breathed life into the designs. Three-quarter profiles were utilized for the furniture, creating "portraits" that showed off the joinery and planes extending out into space, as evidenced in photographs of the Conference Table and Armchair (figs. 3.13a, 3.13f). Gropius's office recedes into a one-point perspective that allowed for the maximum of furnishings to be glimpsed (fig. 3.13b). All of the various drawers are jauntily angled open to show the Changing Table's versatility (fig. 3.13c), while children demonstrate the multitude of possibilities of the Toy Cabinet (fig. 3.13e). The photographs on the wall do not function as mere illustrative material of what could not be shown in three dimensions but rather convey these and other innovative aspects of the school's designs through distinctly photographic imagery — acting as equal pendants to the physical objects on display.

The accompanying catalog, published in 1938, just before the outbreak of World War II effectively halted the publication of books on modern architecture, served as the most important text on the school until the translation of Hans Maria Wingler's magnum opus *The Bauhaus* appeared in 1969. Although there were also many other images that were not by Moholy in this richly illustrated catalog, her photographs were of immense assistance in conveying the school's unique output, especially Gropius's architecture. On a two-page spread, for example, a mere five photographs by Moholy succinctly convey the most vital information about the masters' housing: key aspects are dynamically depicted, such as the striking siting of the houses in a grove of mature pines, the buildings' cubic forms, flat roofs, projecting cantilevers, modern materials, especially the expanses of glass, and the exceptionally light-filled interiors, replete with modern fittings and furniture (fig. 3.14). The images themselves give an air of coherence, functioning remarkably well together, as can be seen in the way in which the two interior photographs' ceilings recede into nearly identical one-point perspective, with the furnishings also falling visually into line.

A survey of other Bauhaus literature demonstrates how important her images were in laying a foundation for the school's reception in its day and to the subsequent construction of its history through a heavy reliance on photographic evidence, in addition to textual description. These books span a wide swath of time: thirty-eight of Moholy's photographs appeared in 1925 in *Neue Arbeiten der Bauhauswerkstätten* (*New Work of the Bauhaus Workshops*), as part of the Bauhaus's own book series. Hans Maria Wingler's canonical *The Bauhaus: Weimar, Dessau, Berlin, Chicago* (first published in 1962 in German, 1969 in English) likewise featured thirty-eight of her images. More recently, the catalogs produced in conjunction with the major 2009–10 international Bauhaus exhibitions — *Bauhaus 1919-1933: Workshops for Modernity* and *Bauhaus: A Conceptual Model* — and the 2019 centennial catalog, *Original Bauhaus*, included ample Moholy images, employed as straightforward (vintage) illustrative material but also discussed as artistic photography in its own right.

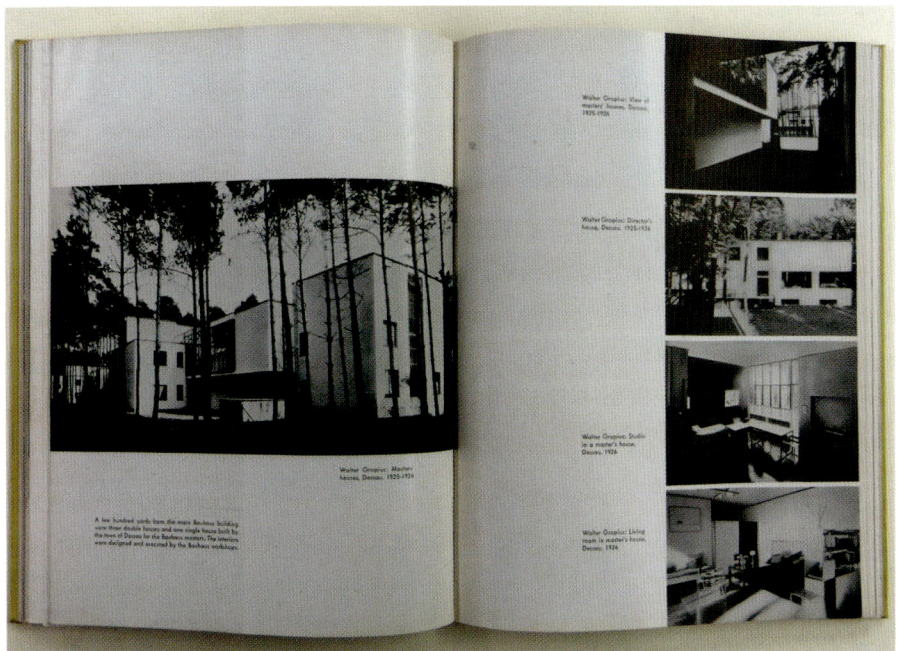

Fig. 3.14 Lucia Moholy, five unattributed photographs featured on pages 108–9 of the exhibition catalog *Bauhaus, 1919–1928*, edited by Herbert Bayer, Walter Gropius, and Ise Gropius (New York: Museum of Modern Art, 1938).

In combination with the 1938 exhibition and its catalog, the general books on the Bauhaus were immensely important in publicizing the school beyond avant-garde art and architectural circles. The Bauhaus was a "well-advertised" movement, noted one period reviewer in his estimation of the 1938 MoMA exhibition.[76] This publicity provided a pedigree for the school's former members in their new exile contexts. In sum, Moholy's photographs depicted the architecture and output of the school in a dynamic and visually straightforward manner; at the same time, it was a function of their calculated virtuosity that they subtly advanced a stylized, idealized version of the Bauhaus, one that would become canonical precisely through their intensive use.

Once Moholy's negatives were back in her possession, she set to work seeking compensation for the multiple publications that had reproduced her photographs in the interim, for new books in process, and for books being prepared for reissue or translation, of which there were many in the 1950s and 1960s—such as the reissue of the Bauhausbücher series and the MoMA exhibition catalog.[77] At this point she also attempted to charge modest fees for the use of her photographs in new publications, but she met with continual opposition. To Sigfried Giedion, who balked at paying a fee for his book *Walter Gropius: Work and Teamwork*, she alluded to the disadvantages she had endured as a result of Gropius's appropriation of the images: "It need hardly surprise you that I expect to be paid for my contributions as a matter of course. You know, and other people know too, that it is exclusively my work I have to rely on for my living. . . . While other former members of the Bauhaus built their continued successes on what pictorial records they had or could get hold of, I was debarred from making such use, and indeed any use, of my own photographs."[78]

Marcel Breuer also proved recalcitrant, stating bluntly, "While the publication fees you ask for are not worth a lot of correspondence and trouble, I could not, with the best will, create a precedent and recognize your rights, which I believe are non-existent. As far as consulting you before the photographs were published, again I feel that this is unjustified."[79] To his publishers, Breuer retorted that he would not pay a fee, stating, "To check up on my own point of view in this matter I was in touch yesterday with Professor Walter Gropius . . . [who] completely confirmed my own stand in this matter, stating that Mrs. Moholy has no right whatsoever to demand such publication fees."[80] Breuer's position is especially remarkable given that, during the Dessau years, it was Breuer who, against Gropius's wishes, had lobbied hard for designers to hold the rights to – and reap the profit from – copies made of their designs for furniture and other objects, arguing convincingly that other Bauhaus members, such as Klee and Kandinsky, retained ownership of their work.[81] This question of the relative individuality of artistic ownership and participation in a collaborative project – one that notably also sought to turn a profit through the marketing and sale of products of its workshops – was a very live issue at the Bauhaus.

Moholy's photographs were also distributed without her permission in Germany and abroad by the Franz Stoedtner Archive.[82] Stoedtner was an art historian who had pioneered an early imaging service based in Berlin that provided prints and slides, predominantly for educational and editorial use. Moholy only became aware of the archive's circulation of her images in the postwar period, although her images likely entered the Stoedtner Archive's collection around 1927 and appear in a catalog that was assembled by the archive prior to 1932. Ottilie Stoedtner, widow of Franz Stoedtner, concluded that Gropius himself must have contributed the print images that were used for reproduction and distribution purposes. The Moholy images in the Stoedtner archive were not marked with – or distributed with – her name.[83]

Even into the 1960s, when the negatives had been returned to Moholy, Gropius continued to give out copies of her photographs to authors writing on the Bauhaus without naming her. For example, Ludwig Hirschfeld-Mack apologized to Moholy for not knowing photographs were hers, and thus not crediting her in his book, *The Bauhaus: An Introductory Survey*. He explained that in sending twenty-nine original Bauhaus photographs, Gropius had noted that they all came from his archive, "so I have the right to decide about their publication. Please feel free to make use of them."[84] Slowly, through her lawyer and with perseverance, reprints and new texts on the Bauhaus began to appear with her photo credit and with modest usage fees paid to her.

Meaning-Formation in Exile

During Gropius's tenure as director, photography was not granted official status at the school (that came only after Gropius's departure, in 1929, when Hannes Meyer engaged Walter Peterhans to teach there), but its role was more than documentary. Significantly, Gropius never formally acknowledged photography or granted it status as an independent artistic medium, although many of his colleagues were intensively working with it. As Annemarie Jaeggi has pointed out, Gropius was well aware of the significance of good photography; he was very selective about commissioning renowned photographers to capture his buildings and subsequently distributed certain sanctioned photographs from his personal archive to those writing about his work.[85] From an early point in his career Gropius utilized specific photographs to promote his built work and already by the late 1920s and early 1930s a select range of images came to illustrate his ideas about modernism.[86] It is likely in this light that he came to see the Moholy photographs of his Dessau oeuvre as somehow "his," especially after historical circumstances allowed the negatives to come into his possession.

Perhaps, then, the best way to view his actions is not in terms of the ownership of the negatives (which he did not seem to perceive as Moholy's property), but, crucially, over what they showed, which is to say the Bauhaus and its buildings and output under his directorship—namely, his own creation. Architectural authorship, in this way, extended to the photography of it. Not only did Gropius refuse to acknowledge Moholy's artistic agency in creating the images, he did not acknowledge the crucial role of photography in the history of the Bauhaus more generally, even as he was using it for his own ends. Gropius and his colleagues relied on photography to tell the story of the Bauhaus. And thus photography from the school, despite its lack of official recognition, contributed materially to the perception of the Bauhaus's modernism, then and today.

As the various *Bauhäusler* fled Germany throughout the 1930s, what they were able physically to take with them formed a disproportionate part of their oeuvre thereafter. What was no longer extant—unable to be displayed at the 1938 MoMA exhibition, for example—was often lost to the footnotes of history or only accessible through grainy reproduction images, especially in the immediate postwar period. Unlike writers, composers, or similar types of creative exiles, for Bauhaus protagonists, photographic imagery had to stand in for art objects left behind. In exile, the role of images and their reproduction necessarily became even more outsized than they otherwise would have been. Especially where material art objects no longer played the role originally asked of them, processes of meaning-formation were transmuted: *object*—be it ashtray, painting, or building—regained its relevance in exile by means of *image*.[87] This potent image, standing for an unapproachable object—the Bauhaus school building in a divided Germany, for example—had a host of meanings formed around it, not only original ideas of new architecture in the 1920s but also the postwar ideologies about the school formulated by former *Bauhäusler* in exile during the Cold War. This image was often the last tangible asset, the last link, to the inaccessible or destroyed work. But what happens when the objects were, in fact, photographs themselves? Without the negatives, Moholy was also without the means of reproduction. Photographs often acted as a stand-in for works that many Bauhaus members no longer had access to (such as a large oil painting); thus photographs reproduced and circulated images of artworks as if they were the work itself, able to further an artist's postwar reputation. Because her works were already images, Moholy—through the loss of her negatives—was singularly denied a chance at this transmutation of meaning and subsequent new meaning-formation.

Even more important was the photographic image for Bauhaus-designed objects that were intended for reproduction—objects like the individual tea infusers, which have become key signifiers of the Bauhaus project and its supposed aspirations to revolutionize modern life — but that did not achieve it, often owing specifically to their conservative material properties (luxury materials, handwork, and so forth). These objects became singularly reproducible in the photographs of them (see figs. 3.6, 3.7, 3.9, 3.10, 3.11). Indeed, it was their wide photographic reproduction that made the objects themselves seem like modern, mass-produced articles — which is the way that they have been handed down to history in the Bauhaus myth that the photographs enabled Gropius to cultivate.

Importantly, the immortalization of the Bauhaus took place in the postwar period, led in particular by Gropius as the school's founder and most powerful director and by former members generally. Gropius's position of power at the architecture school at Harvard gave him a pulpit from which to further strengthen the school's legacy. His generosity toward the Germanic Museum at Harvard, later named the Busch-Reisinger Museum, established a home for Bauhaus objects and collections at a time when they were not yet essential collectible items. His tireless work in maintaining the school's public profile after its closure — not letting it be forgotten as a brief example of Weimar-era art and politics — allowed him to instrumentalize its existence in a way that strengthened his own reputation and practice in postwar America, played a role in Cold War politics, and helped build up support for modernism in American architecture. Other former Bauhaus members, too, considered a furthering of the Bauhaus's mission while in exile to be necessary and desirable, apart from what any of them stood to gain individually. As Herbert Bayer wrote to Moholy, he and Gropius had "acted in good faith, making use of the photographs in Gropius's and Moholy [-Nagy]'s files for the benefit of the Bauhaus Movement."[88] This bolstering of the Bauhaus legacy, in turn, helped launch the careers of Bauhaus members in exile.

The uneven power equation between Gropius, as former director of the Bauhaus and head of the architecture department at Harvard, and Moholy, with little wherewithal in London and rendered virtually anonymous without her negatives, was one that both were distinctly aware of. Gropius had, of course, long lost control of the Bauhaus buildings in Dessau, but he would tighten control — to the point of usurping control — over its architectural image. Under the circumstances of exile and then the Cold War, not just the *images themselves* but the *means of their reproduction* became an oversize method of distribution and control, of power, of authorship, of ultimate signification.

Moholy's authorship was overwritten as a result of her loss of control over the negatives and thus over the means of their reproduction. This was a straightforward consequence, albeit one that need not have occurred had Gropius continued to insist on credit lines. But authorship was also overwritten in the way that the physical objects signified within the photographs — Bauhaus buildings and products — were considered to be more important referents than the media that carried them (glass negatives, printed reproductions). Although the power of the photographic image was well-known and used to its full effect by Bauhaus members in the pre- and postwar periods, ultimately the circulation of the *object* photographed took precedence over the authored *photograph* as object. Owing to its inaccessibility, and precisely via these canonical photographs, the Bauhaus Building more strongly signified itself, or, again as Moholy formulated it: isolating the object through photography was to endow it with greater significance than it previously possessed.[89] This was indeed in keeping with the attainment of "self-assertion" by the objects of the photographs of *Neue Sachlichkeit* that Moholy herself had theorized in *A Hundred Years of Photography*, if also at odds with the becoming-subject of photographs that she had similarly contemplated.

■ ■ ■

Moholy's photographs, and Gropius's handling of them, contributed decisively to the development of the iconic status that Bauhaus objects have today. Notably, Bauhaus products are often still viewed collectively as generic "Bauhaus" objects, as Gropius desired that they be, rather than objects by specific designers (although Gropius did not erase designers' authorship as readily or thoroughly as he did Moholy's). This was done in the name of the Bauhaus, helping to secure its legacy, to all of its former members' benefit perhaps, except for one. However, the intention of this chapter is neither to demonize Gropius nor to bring this story to light — Moholy herself published a guarded version in 1983 — but to use this episode to think about how notions of authorship are changed under conditions of exile, how photographs can be the most important means of communication for work no longer extent or accessible, and how their importance *as photographs* can as a result and perhaps especially under such conditions be overtaken by what they depict and what it comes to signify, by their subject matter and its photographically enabled properties of signification.

An exceedingly large part of the Bauhaus legacy, explicitly formulated in exile, was visual and in the form of photographs, especially photographs taken by Lucia Moholy. The very essence of her photographs — seemingly straightforward, clean, spare, *sachlich* — provided viewers with a picture of the school as Gropius desired to project it — and as he did, relying on them. The images served his goals in shoring up support for modern architecture in the United States in the nascent postwar period, when modernism was certainly not embraced with open arms by all Americans. These photographs created a highly legible, accessible image of the Bauhaus, both in its day and, more important, and to a far greater extent than anyone might have imagined when they were made, solidifying its place in history. Lucia Moholy's photographs would remain essential to the Bauhaus's standing and reception. These images played a crucial role in processes of meaning-formation surrounding the school. And they did so largely in and through their multiple exiles — that is, on the various conditions that exile imposed on them and the ways these conditions affected and facilitated the functioning of the photographic art form.

Chapter 4

Assimilating Unease

László Moholy-Nagy and the Wartime/Postwar Chicago Bauhaus

László Moholy-Nagy's debut as leader of the New Bauhaus in Chicago was auspicious (fig. 4.1).[1] A high-profile *New York Times* article in September 1937, "America Imports Genius," hailed his arrival along with that of three other men of "genius": Albert Einstein, Thomas Mann, and Walter Gropius. The article cautioned, "The hospitality that America extends to these men should not be merely physical, but spiritual. We should not be in too great haste to 'Americanize' them—in the sense of attempting to indoctrinate them with all the beliefs we already hold. To make the most of their presence here we must think not only of what we have to tell them but of what they have to tell us."[2] Despite this plea, Moholy-Nagy was quick to claim America as his own. Especially as Europe plunged into war, Moholy-Nagy's unambiguous public statements reflected his desire to ingratiate himself with the country that he hoped would move the world beyond the war: "The present world crisis will bring unforeseen problems to all of us. We shall have to make decisions of great consequences, both to ourselves and to the nation. Whether or not Hitler wins, whether or not we get into the war, we shall undergo great strains because an equilibrium has been disturbed. Europe has lost the leading position which it had in culture and technics. America is now the country to which the world looks."[3] This last observation is an early iteration of a position that would be taken up by a number of critics of art and architecture in the postwar period, but a tension can nonetheless be detected in Moholy-Nagy's language—an uneasiness with which émigrés, understandably, conducted themselves, underscored here by Moholy-Nagy's references to "us," "we," and "the nation." The émigrés' unease about their status in the United States was often palpable; their anxiety about the war that Europe brought to the world propelled their efforts to continue their work in spite of that uncertain status.

When the New Bauhaus opened in October 1937 as the self-proclaimed successor of the famed German institution, which had itself gone through several iterations, lastly in Berlin, before closing in 1933, the United States was still emerging from its Great Depression, while—from the perspective of the emigrant former members of the German Bauhaus—the situation in Europe was becoming more dire.[4] When World War II broke out, the European *Bauhäusler*, who had experienced the darkening situation firsthand, were more politicized and also ready to contribute to the war effort in more practical ways, perhaps, than their American counterparts; although individual architects and artists took varied positions on the swiftly changing situation, the American public generally remained wary of entering another major war after the experience of World War I. Many of the original Bauhaus members now plunged adeptly into their new American cultural milieu, winning over government bureaucrats, private businessmen, and other officials, later capitalizing on these relationships during the postwar boom. As America welcomed fleeing members of the Bauhaus, as well as other modern artists and architects from across Europe, an assimilation of European modern forms and ideas to American conditions took shape.[5] This assimilation occurred over a relatively short period of time, as Moholy-Nagy reflected in 1946: "When I came to this country ten years ago, I had to relearn completely my ideas about design. I had thought that European measures could be applied to America immediately with the same results as over there.... I never

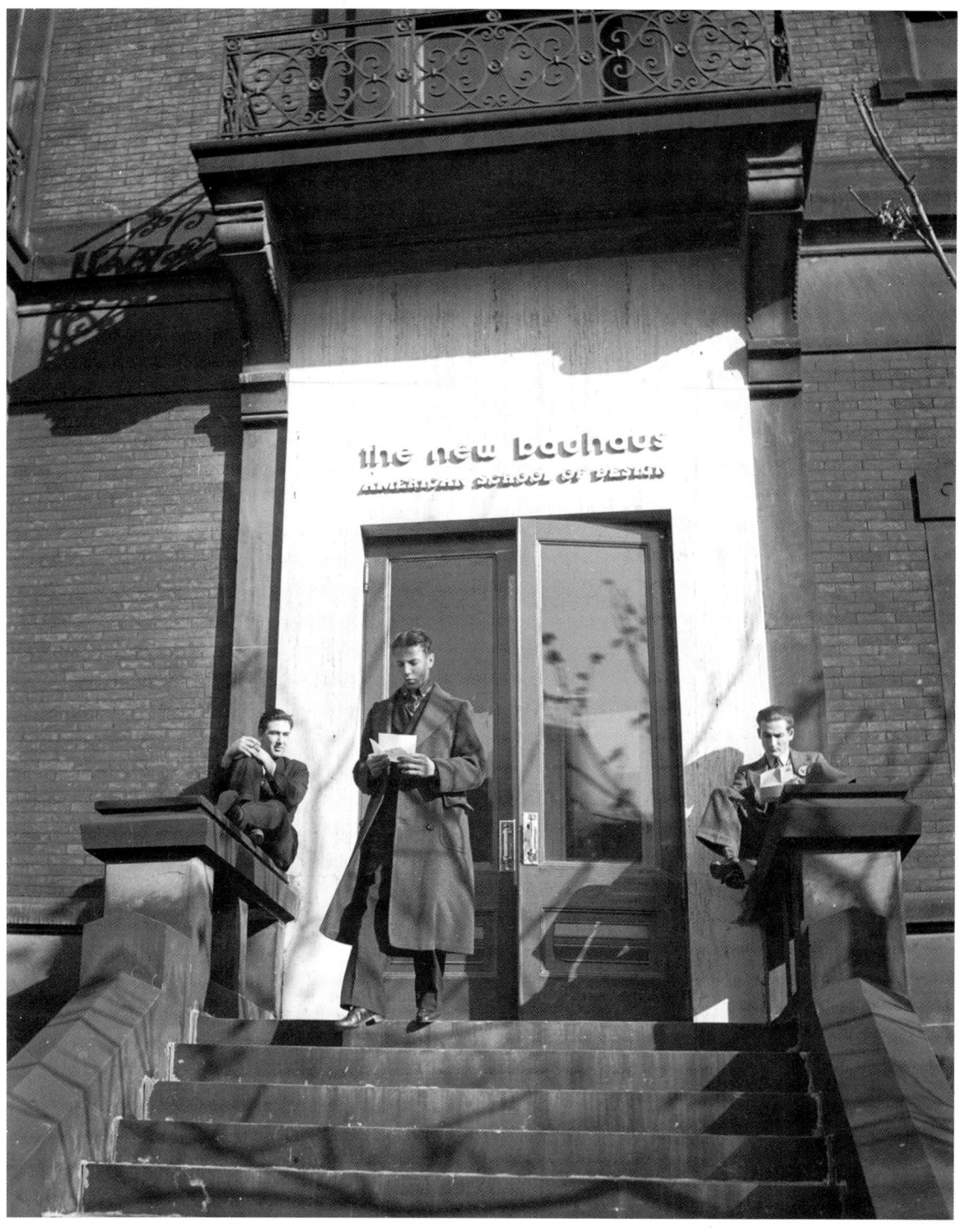

Fig. 4.1 The New Bauhaus, 1937, Chicago. Photograph by Herbert Matter, 1938.

would have believed that a grown-up person could learn as much as I had to learn in this country."[6]

In Moholy-Nagy's case at the New Bauhaus and its successor, the School of Design in Chicago, it is striking how the exigencies of the circumstances in which he found himself in America, and the very anxiety that this new situation generated, carried him almost overnight from a left-leaning artistic milieu to American government collaborations and very pragmatic assistance to his new country.[7] Gropius was later able to assert, "When Moholy-Nagy built up the Institute here in Chicago, he had the vision to lay its foundations in such a way that indigenous American design could be stimulated and developed."[8] During the war years, I argue, the protagonists of the New Bauhaus – by now, the School of Design – laid the groundwork for their acceptance in postwar America, both in terms of design research and connections established with American individuals and institutions. The school began to prepare for possible entry into war very early on, before Pearl Harbor, and, while the country was still in the midst of the war, looked to a planned transition from its wartime work to preparations for the postwar period, declaring as early as 1942 that it was adapting its program for "the present emergency as well as to the problems of postwar production."[9] Indeed, the school's ability to contribute novel, practical solutions to the war effort aptly positioned its mode of modern design for participation in postwar technological progress and the boom-time affluence that accompanied it.

In the process, under Moholy-Nagy, the attempt to revive and continue the Bauhaus experiment in America necessarily altered the project that the German institution had pursued.[10] Perhaps paradoxically, this transformation was marked by an intensified turn toward the usefulness of design. This chapter situates that development, and Moholy-Nagy's school's contribution to postwar modernism in America, in the context of its involvement in the nation's war effort and the opportunities for assimilation of émigrés like Moholy-Nagy that it afforded. While demonstrating the continuity between wartime efforts and the postwar boom, this chapter examines the ways in which these activities contributed to the increased acceptance of modernism in America, and the Chicago school's role therein – as well as the ways in which this connection to the war was formative for American postwar design.[11] The project Moholy-Nagy pursued through the series of wartime design schools he directed in Chicago was indeed one of designing, and teaching, during war for a time and circumstance beyond war.

Anxiety, Assimilation, Integration

Although they had been given plum positions of power in institutions of higher learning, an act that in and of itself indicates a large amount of faith in them, former members of the Bauhaus had reason to be anxious about their tenuous status.[12] For the most part, the newcomers arrived with just the material possessions and artworks that they could bring with them, often with larger art collections left in trust behind with the hope of eventual exportation; with very little money (savings, if there were any, generally had to be left behind in Germany); and with varying levels of proficiency in English – and they faced very different educational structures, cultures, and expectations in their new positions.[13] Hal

Foster has asserted that Moholy-Nagy's prior critique of capitalism became muted after his arrival in the United States, and that the American version of the Bauhaus ideal revealed a belief on the part of Moholy-Nagy that the "modernist evolution in abstract styles was commercial design."[14] This is undoubtedly largely so. Yet for Moholy-Nagy, this assimilation to American capitalism and the realm of the business owner–supported, nonprofit institution (rather than government support, which had been the – tenuous – mainstay of the German Bauhaus) was likely engendered more by pragmatism than core belief.[15] Dismayed by the commercial world's reaction to the work of his fellow artists, he worried privately, "the provocative statement of modern art is constantly annulled by checkbook and cocktail party. Am I on the same way?"[16]

The tangible design contributions that he and his colleagues were able to make in their new country thanks to a partial but rapid assimilation were one palliative for the anxiety created by their uneasy status. Once America entered the war, more uncertainty ensued, as Sibyl Moholy-Nagy's diary entry of December 11, 1941, starkly captures: "War with Germany – that means severing the last connections with my family. No more letters."[17] Beyond physical and economic hardship, there was also the continuing emotional hardship of emigration, to which an entry in Sibyl's diary from the end of the war gives further insight: "Laci [Moholy] came home. There is an unwritten code among emigrants – even when you are married. Every reference to Europe or to the past is guarded, casual, uttered only after the emotion behind it has been secured safely with an enforced dose of self-control. There is an emigrant etiquette, and Laci has adhered to it the same as I."[18]

Part of the wartime and postwar endeavors of the Bauhaus circle, such as Ludwig Mies van der Rohe, Gropius, and Moholy-Nagy, were activities related to, understandably, simply trying to help family, friends, and colleagues who remained in Germany.[19] Former Bauhaus members were also quick to serve the US government in more concrete ways. They were asked to join committees to which they gave generously of their expertise and time. For example, Gropius was a key member of the Harvard Group of the American Defense Committee, work for which he was personally thanked by the group's leader in a letter of 1941: "I want to tell you how grateful we are for your contribution to the work of the Group and above all for your personal interest and sympathy."[20] Likewise, Moholy-Nagy served on the city of Chicago's Civil Defense Commission, was a key member of the Chicago Metropolitan Area camouflage section, and worked closely on various initiatives with the Office of Civilian Defense in Washington, DC.

During the war years, and thereafter, the relationship between the émigrés and their new government was not based on open trust. The Federal Bureau of Investigation kept extensive files on Gropius, Mies, and others.[21] Moholy-Nagy's citizenship process was held up for several years by the FBI's investigation of him, which prevented the Naturalization Service from granting him citizenship until the bureau closed its case, nor could the Naturalization Service put pressure on the FBI to expedite the case.[22] Gropius was obliged to report his travel itinerary to the authorities every time he left Cambridge.[23] Yet he worked closely with American government officials to further their postwar aims. As Karen Koehler has brought to light, by 1944, in collaboration with the United States War Information

Bureau, Gropius allowed a propagandistic radio play to be written about him for a series called *America, the Haven*.[24] A work of fiction, it was intended to reach retreating German working-class soldiers and was meant to be aired in areas of Germany liberated by the Allies.[25] The play celebrated his life's work, touting a "cultural trust" placed in him and the accomplishments that he would continue to achieve in America. The text, written under the auspices of the War Information Bureau, frames Gropius's position in this manner: "I am an exile and yet I shall live. I will continue my work.... For there is a trust placed in me. A cultural trust."[26] It was perhaps this idea of "cultural trust" that formed the lens through which American officials saw the usefulness of the European émigrés and, in turn, what émigrés saw as their offering to America: the importation of their ideas, forms, and educational working methods. But they also quickly offered pragmatic new design-objects and inventive solutions to wartime problems.

Of the émigrés' many responses to the instability of their position in America, a crucial one was to anchor and stabilize themselves not only through their design contributions and their teaching positions, but through their formal and informal social networks. They used a web of connections between themselves to share information and opportunities in a foreign land and culture. And they helped each other to connect themselves to prominent Americans in the cultural sphere, such as Philip Johnson at the Museum of Modern Art, as well as in the business realm, through figures such as Walter Paepcke, head of the Container Corporation of America (CCA), who backed the New Bauhaus financially and fostered further support for the institution through his network of contacts. Through Moholy-Nagy and the school, Gropius and Herbert Bayer came to know Paepcke closely, who, for his part, awarded them design commissions under the auspices of his company. These important Americans could help stabilize the positions of the newcomers, through key introductions, via direct financial support for their projects, by providing help in obtaining financial backing via a third party, or by lending expertise in navigating governmental and other systems that could help to establish them.

It is also significant that designers who moved from Germany, such as Gropius, Mies, Moholy-Nagy, Marcel Breuer, Ludwig Hilberseimer, and Erich Mendelsohn, showed little desire to return after the war, despite the fact that the rebuilding of Germany would have afforded them many opportunities to practice. Instead they were particularly committed to forging a career in their new country and pursuing the opportunities they saw for their work in America. This was in contrast to other groups of émigrés in the realm of art and culture, such as George Grosz, Bertolt Brecht, Theodor Adorno, and Max Horkheimer. Moholy-Nagy, in New York in 1945 for a meeting of the American CIAM organization (Congrès internationaux d'architecture moderne), which was promoting postwar planning, was astounded to find "most French refugees dead-set on going back to France and England at the first possible moment."[27] He felt that it was "a great pity that we cannot bind them (with love and money) to this country."[28] This "binding" to his new country, through as rapid an assimilation as possible, was of especial importance to Moholy-Nagy.

Moholy-Nagy frequently used the idea of "integration" to describe his vision of the design process, and this vision might be seen to correspond to the situation faced by these designers in America too. Registering the anxiety surrounding technology in this period, Moholy-Nagy wrote often of a sought-for integration of the human and the technical world: "We feel that after the war, conditions will have a task of greatest importance for us: the integration of the neglected values of art and humanities with a hypertrophic technology."[29] Such an integration was also foundational to his teaching aims: "By now technology has become as much a part of life as metabolism. The task therefore is to educate the contemporary man as an *integrator*, the new *designer* able to re-evaluate human needs warped by machine civilization."[30] In war, the use of new materials and technologies clearly had devastating consequences. In Moholy-Nagy's view, this reality increased the need to use new knowledge and new design to positive wartime ends that could mitigate these consequences, from designing camouflaged shelter for citizens during attacks, to new safety equipment for those on the battlefields, to using the design process for restorative occupational therapy for those returning from war, all to be discussed here. The anxiety that followed the Great War in response to the devastation wrought by technological prowess, which had been largely replaced by excitement in 1920s Weimar Germany, including at the original iteration of the Bauhaus, once again resurfaced for many during World War II.[31]

The *Chicago Sun* aptly captured the school's wartime ethos in this manner: "The work carried forward by this group can no longer be described as revolutionary, but rather as a unified and imaginative approach to both fine arts and design technology. Some changes in emphasis have come about in response to American ways of living."[32] For Moholy-Nagy, adapting to America while integrating technology to serve human needs would also require an attempt to counteract the horrors of war. An era that had held so much promise seemed to have reached an impasse. Moholy-Nagy characterized the situation in this manner: "To state the case is almost too simple: The industrial revolution opened up a new dimension – the dimension of a new science and a new technology which could be used for the realization of all-embracing relationships. Contemporary man threw himself into the experience of these new relationships. But saturated with old ideologies, he approached the new dimension with obsolete practices and failed to translate his newly gained experience into emotional language and cultural reality. The result has been and still is misery and conflict, brutality and anguish, unemployment and war."[33]

In response, Moholy-Nagy called for a well-balanced social organization to come out of a form of education in which everyone was utilized to his or her highest capacity. Although many designers, companies, and industries articulated their eager preparedness for the promised postwar boom ahead, in terms of retooling for peacetime production and consumption, Moholy-Nagy saw the need, even during war, to design *beyond* war not just in terms of material goods, that is, but to envision a future with a place for design and design education in a *society* beyond war.

This was the basis for the American version of the Bauhaus in Chicago – a stated repositioning toward the cultural realm and toward a concern for humanity. While the nexus of technology and culture had always been part of the Bauhaus's aims, it is the true concern for pragmatic design solutions and the humane use of technology in aiding civilization—areas in which so much went so wrong during World War II—that ultimately distinguishes the American institution during the war years from the Bauhaus in its series of prewar iterations in Germany, where it did not broadly succeed in designing for a different society, despite its efforts to engage new industrial technology.

The objects produced at the German Bauhaus under Gropius, when Moholy-Nagy was teaching there (he left in 1928, following Gropius's resignation), represent the successful *visual* iteration of ideas about modernism that that institution embodied—indeed, its symbolically resonant objects are much more likely to be found in museum vitrines today than any products of the New Bauhaus/School of Design—but the German Bauhaus was nonetheless still profoundly shaped by the nineteenth-century heritage of *Kunstgewerbe*, or arts and crafts, and its post–World War I revival, which explicitly attempted to recover that heritage via the high-quality art object of the craftsman. The New Bauhaus, on the other hand, partly by virtue of lacking a strong anchoring tradition but also owing to the exigencies of the coming war, would serve to cement and intensify a tendency away from craftsmanship toward further engaged, practical experimentation and pedagogical innovation. This was reflected in its first curriculum, which added "scientific subjects" (which included the fields of geometry, physics, chemistry, mathematics, and economics, including statistics and marketing) as one-third of the Foundation Course program, a weighting on par with the two other categories of "basic design workshop" and "analytic and constructive drawing." As Moholy-Nagy wrote in the institution's first catalog, the school's ambitious task was "to contrive a new system of education which, along with a specialized training in science and technique leads to a thorough awareness of fundamental human needs and a universal outlook."[34]

The German Bauhaus had harbored lofty goals for its design with regard for the masses, but even these declared aims were outstripped by the new focus formulated by Moholy-Nagy in Chicago, which implied the extent to which a new social mode of design would require radically changed foundations. The iconic modernist designs that came out of the German Bauhaus during Moholy's time there were represented by luxury objects in ideology, form, and type (silver and ebony tea services, chess sets, and ashtrays) that remained out of reach for many. Ostensibly intended for mass production, they were expensive, difficult to fabricate, and never sold on a widespread basis. Reflecting the altered economic realities and challenges of manufacturing and purchasing modern mass-produced objects, Moholy-Nagy's Chicago school went much further to put a new production paradigm for design into institutional and pedagogical practice.[35] While other émigrés were important facilitators of the Bauhaus legacy in America, in the American phase of their careers these key protagonists were notably focused on either art-related issues at art schools (Anni and Josef Albers at Black Mountain College, followed by Yale) or architectural concerns at schools of architecture (Gropius and Breuer at Harvard, Mies at IIT). The housing and urban solutions proposed by these latter architects and their students for the postwar period were arguably as grounded in offering real solutions as those of Moholy-Nagy's school's were for design. However, as the leader of a newly founded, independent school of *design* (and not as a division of a larger, less flexible, institution), Moholy-Nagy had a special, if notably precarious, platform from which to attempt to bring about a – of course, vastly altered – version of what he and his colleagues in Dessau had sometimes envisioned.

Moreover, Moholy's singular commitment to – and practice of – the Bauhaus labor-intensive educational working methods permitted him to conceive of changed design practices in the pragmatically charged context of the realities of the wartime situation while actively undertaking the kind of transformations he thought this new practice would require. War and precarity provided the impetus to achieve a form of practical, problem-driven design that the original, still elite-oriented Bauhaus had never fully managed to put into practice. The uniqueness of the New Bauhaus/School of Design lay in its particularly remarkable unification of this effort in a school (like the former Bauhaus) and its community-oriented pedagogical practices, along with the singular way that it integrated contingent war-related demands into these modes of learning. In doing so, the school's activities were always looking to a time and condition beyond the war. Not least for this reason, the research engaged in on behalf of the war effort, and their products, also had implications for change in design processes in the postwar period.

War Efforts

As the nation's circumstances changed – initially on the brink of war, then at war, and then facing the transition to postwar, peacetime production – the new Bauhaus reacted (while going through its own institutional reorganizations into the School of Design). The school retooled its existing courses and introduced many new ones in order to focus on the evolving practical problems facing the country. Keeping the idea of working with industry at the forefront of its mission, Moholy-Nagy used the phrase "war industry" to refer to the war-related work in this period.[36] By this he meant efforts to design with and for industry in such a way as to directly aid the war effort: students worked on portable runways for temporary airfields and air-raid shelters, shock-proof helmet construction and a shock-absorbing wire-cloth pillow for helmets, an infrared baking oven that cooked food at four times the usual rate, and parachute clothes.[37] An airplane door was designed in plywood, and the school experimented with a new system of friction welding of clear acrylic plastics intended for the swifter repair, in the combat zone, of the easily shattered Plexiglas and Lucite domes and blisters of airplanes.[38] Another useful product developed at the school was a new kind of wire, sent to Washington for testing, intended for repairing holes in the plastic gunners' hoods on bombers.[39] Also devised during this period were life belt units by student Elic Nekimken, which were rubberized cloth units that could be connected by notebook rings to form a lifebelt or raft (fig. 4.2). George Marcek contributed a ventilated helmet for a patient with skin disease, which also could potentially protect healthy men from the sun's rays. A "mobile machine gun unit" by student Nolan Rhoades was intended to be constructed out of a few structurally simple parts welded together in an assembly line using standard automobile power, allowing for mass production at low cost; it was also designed to be light enough for two men to handle and to break down into stackable

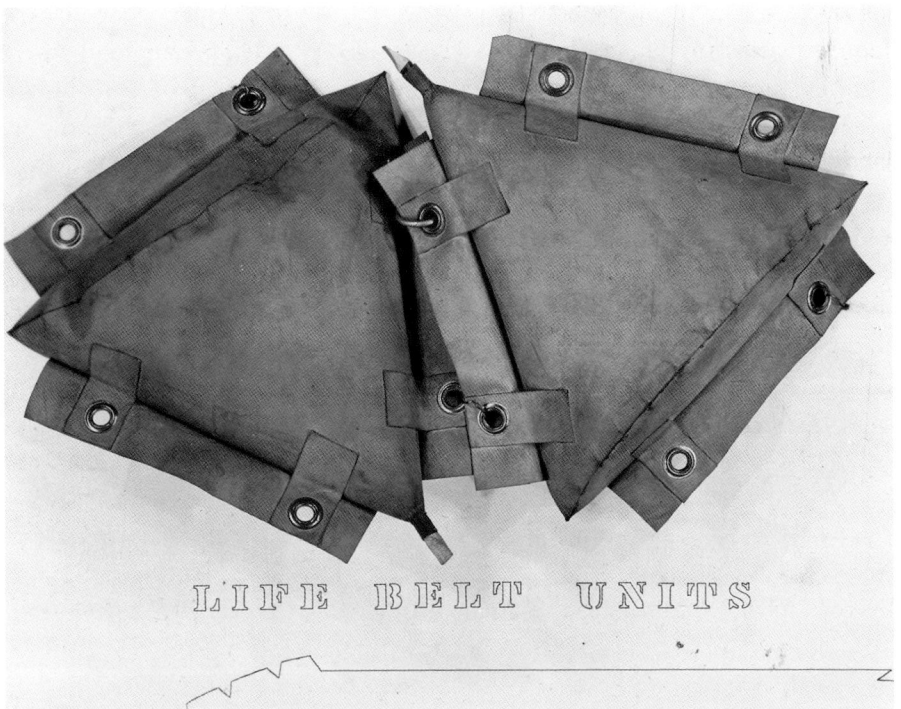

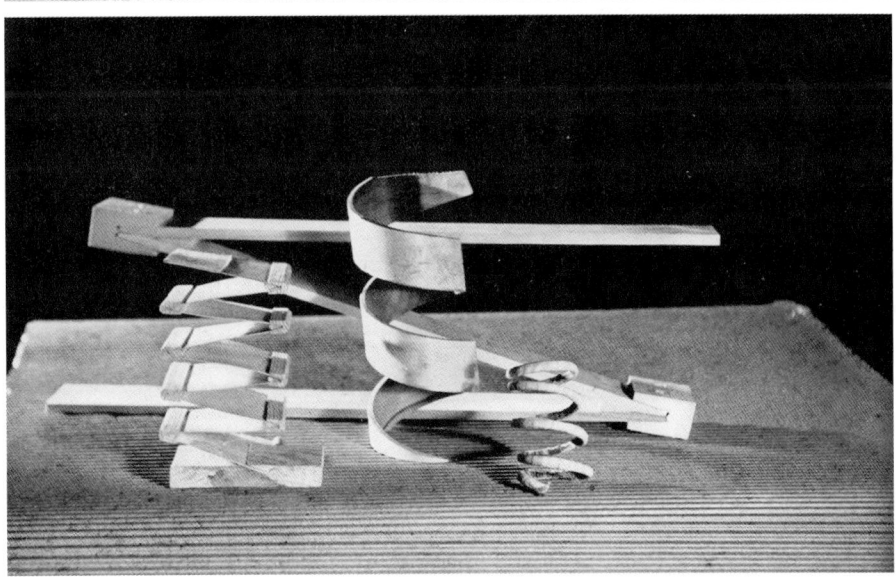

units for shipment. Rhoades's design of a "guerrilla supply bomb" and "plastic balloon skin" made out of "weather proof cellophane and cheesecloth bound by alternate rectangular patterns of glue" illustrate the school's investigations in materials studies.

These objects reached varying levels of actualization—some remained innovative ideas and never developed further than the design phase—but they show the school reacting systematically and creatively to perceived needs. Other ideas progressed to the prototype stage, exhibited as mock-ups both at the school and beyond. Finally, some inventions advanced to the degree that they could be manufactured and tested at the school, and then sent on to contacts in industry or to defense officials.

Fig. 4.2 *Top*, Elic Nekimken, life belt units, student work, School of Design, 1942. *Bottom*, four types of wooden springs ("V-spring" shown front left), student work, School of Design, 1941– early 1940s.

Assimilating Unease

Wooden springs were perhaps one of the school's biggest developments (see fig. 4.2). Beginning in June 1941, students, working with faculty, designed a number of viable prototypes, devising at least twenty-four different wooden springs in plywood or laminated wood.[40] The threat of a metal shortage stimulated this project, and it was successfully carried out before the ban on metal went into effect.[41] Wood ceased to be viewed as a mere substitute for steel and came to be appreciated as a structural material in its own right, especially because it withstood specific pressures and, unlike metal, could recover from fatigue when rested.[42] One of the school's prototypes, the V-spring (for "victory"), was found to hold the same amount of compression weight and to withstand ten years' wear, proving as durable as metal springs.[43] Importantly, the V-spring was made not of large sheets of plywood, which was quickly being rationed for war use, but rather of small strips of veneer sealed with resins that conserved its moisture content and protected it from variations in humidity.[44] These strips were hinged at alternate ends and folded over wedges, zigzag fashion, at the joint of each "V," so that the size and shape of the wedges determined the amount of elasticity in the spring.[45]

The wooden spring represents the school's first attempt at direct cooperation with industry; after it developed a prototype, a manufacturer conducted large-scale tests that led to its perfection and use.[46] Here as elsewhere Moholy-Nagy maintained a concomitant desire to articulate wartime designs toward postwar hopes, as is evidenced by his report to Nikolaus Pevsner in March 1943: "Through our success with the wood spring experiments . . . a large furniture manufacturer is interested in our bent wood solutions. This type of furniture can be seen as a forerunner of simplified and healthier design, having the potentialities of replacing the over-stuffed upholstered furniture."[47] A model wooden spring mattress was displayed by the Seng Company, a large furniture firm, at the 1942 Chicago furniture fair.[48] Moholy-Nagy reported that the school received its first check for $2,500 in November 1942, as advance royalty payment on the springs.[49] The experiments with wooden springs also directly led to the development of a stool in plywood, using the same application of technology as the springs. (One might note here, perhaps in tribute to his drive to find wood replacements for metal, that in these years the students apparently affectionately referred to Moholy-Nagy as "Holy Mahogany."[50])

While individuals such as Charles and Ray Eames were conducting similar wartime experiments in the use of plywood, veneers, and glues for leg splints, airplane nose cones, and stabilizers that would directly contribute to the war effort, comparable schools of art and design, such as Cranbrook, neither assisted so assiduously in wartime design efforts, nor did they tend to attempt such direct cooperation with industry.[51] War-related activities at Black Mountain College were limited mainly to participation in the Enlisted Reserve Corps program, which was intended to provide officers with "leadership qualities" for the military by allowing enlisted students to defer service in order to complete their education first; the school was also approved by the US Relocation Authority to accept American-born Japanese transfer students from the Pacific coast.[52] Likewise, schools of architecture, which did offer some war-related courses (for example, camouflage courses were taught at the architecture school of the University of

Pennsylvania, and troops were offered camouflage instruction under the auspices of the Landscape Architecture Department at Harvard), did not dramatically reorient themselves to the war in the same manner as the School of Design, nor did they pursue wartime collaborations with industry in the same way.

For the duration of the war, the Chicago school's design activities were also undertaken with an eye toward design transformations to come once the war was over. The school sought to engage in industrial research and development for war-fettered companies that could not spare their own designers or engineers for new product studies – an effort that effectively positioned the school and its students for the postwar period, giving it the opportunity to offer well-trained potential employees and expertise, as well as possible design prototypes.[53] Already having established itself and its work, the school was called on for design solutions by outside manufacturers. Beyond the wooden springs, the school, as steel and other metals were withdrawn from civilian use, sought to design other consumer goods with possible lasting applications. A large mail-order company asked the school to experiment with a metal-less design for a chair for infants that had formerly been made of a canvas back and seat and metal frame.[54] Tackling the problem, students devised wood substitutes – a painted, easy-to-assemble, inexpensive version for lower-income homes and a streamlined, bent-and-polished plywood example. They also experimented with substitutions for wooden dowels, alternatively testing the combination of resin with paper and cotton. Other materials that had been essential to the functioning of the workshops – such as rubber, paper, and plastics – were also rationed, necessitating further innovations.[55]

As a result of these investigations and new designs, Walter Paepcke, the Chicago businessman and key benefactor of the school, wrote on its behalf to the War Production Board: "Dr. Moholy-Nagy has recently had a conversation with Capt. Benjamin Gelb of the Consumer Product Branch of the WPB [War Production Board]. The School is most anxious to be recommended for a research contract on new types of household goods and domestic appliances.... It trains and educates young men and women to become practical industrial designers of all war and postwar products.... I am convinced that the School could do an excellent job on research assignments for the Consumer Product Branch. I am recommending it most highly for favorable consideration in this connection."[56] Here was an attempt to set the school up not only for more formal wartime commissions but also for postwar production.

Other furniture designs, similarly born out of wartime shortages, show the ways in which the school was thinking about the transition to postwar furniture needs. Prototypes developed in the early 1940s illustrate the degree to which designers were already engaged in work that featured low-cost materials, mass production, and the ability to be packed flatly (in order to save shipping costs initially, but also allowing the user to easily store items of furniture). These prototypes include an inventive series of fiberboard chairs; some designs were entirely made of fiberboard, whereas others used a tubular steel support structure (fig. 4.3). Other examples include the plywood Knock-Down Chair by Robert Zinns in 1942, in which flat pieces of plywood were slotted into each other in lieu of fixed joints. Other experiments with plywood joints indicated

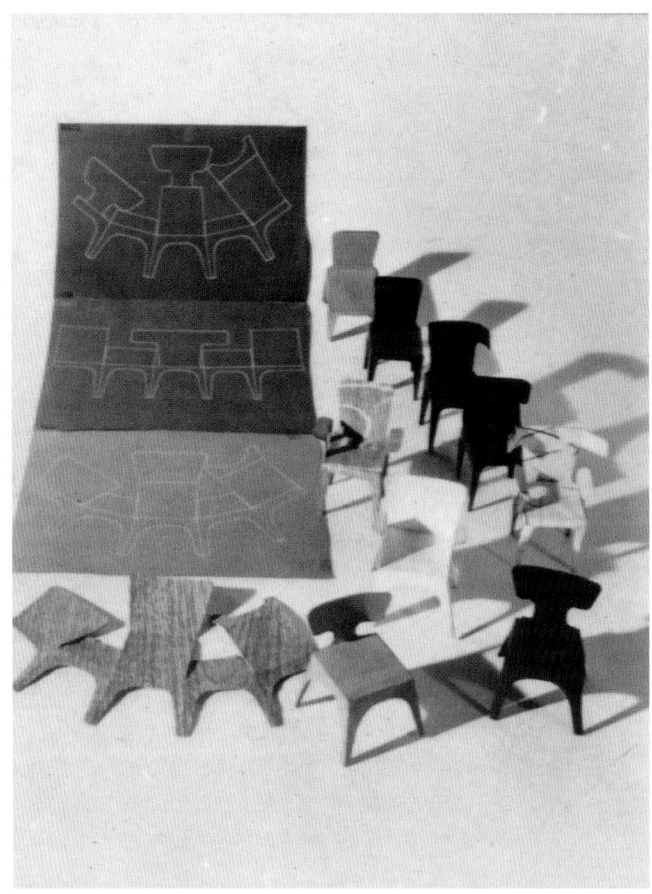

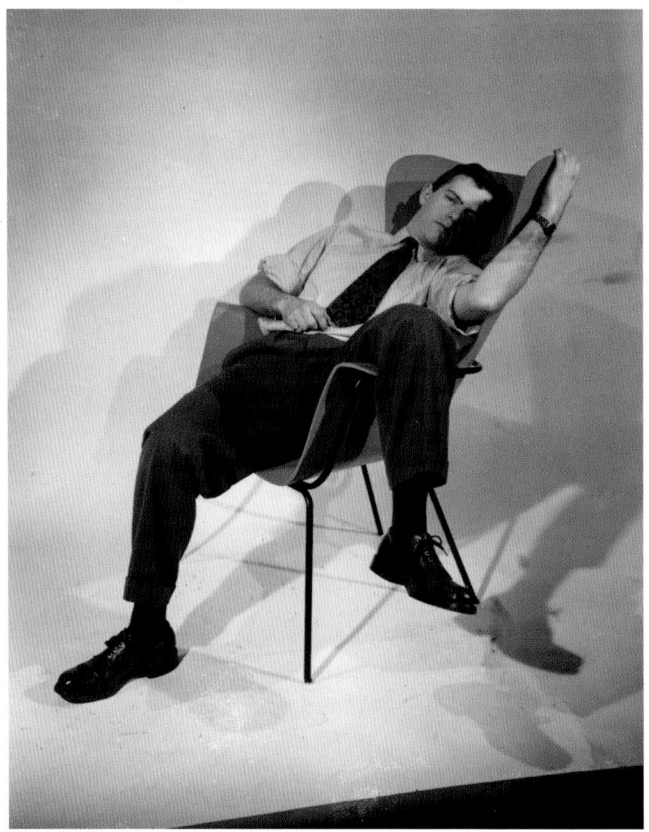

Fig. 4.3 *Top*, Fiberboard chairs, student work, School of Design, early 1940s. *Bottom*, Fiberboard chair, student work, School of Design, 1940–45.

that they could be strengthened by enlarging the gluing surface of the plywood edges.[57] Jack Waldheim's Z-Chair used thin, laminated wood instead of solid wood or thick plywood and featured a single, continuous Z-shaped wooden support to form the base, legs, and armrests. In the immediate postwar period, wartime problematics and aesthetics continued to influence furniture designs such as Robert Beard's 1947 Collapsible Chair, which could fold down completely flat, and Allan Johnson's design for a cot that compressed to a small size.

Like many other designers and companies in this period, the design school anticipated the factory retooling that would follow the war, and many prototypes coming from the school in the postwar period were specifically designed to be manufactured on the same machines that had been producing ammunition parts.[58] Military production and use of plywood, Moholy-Nagy envisioned, would lead to veneer or plywood furniture manufactured using the same type of blanking dies used in airplane factories for wings and in fuselage construction.[59] Therefore, the school devoted much design focus to lightweight, easily manufactured, laminated veneer and plywood furniture prototypes to be shaped on automatic molds that would require only several minutes per piece.

Amid these innovations, Moholy-Nagy was quick to assert that this ingenuity struck a long-established, particularly American note. As he told a newspaper interviewer, "The old American spirit of patent furniture has been reawakened in the students. Between 1830 and 1880 thousands of new ideas for furniture were submitted to the [United States] patent office. It was an ingenious American development.... Now we have taken it up again. And by being trained in the understanding of motion, joints, the transition of forces by lever, and the role of pivots and folds, and by combining this knowledge with new materials and new machines such as the infra-red oven for plastics and the electrical bending machine for plywood, the students have made a number of astonishing designs."[60]

This mannered assertion of a link to a particular aspect of American heritage, one that the United States had always used to distinguish itself from the traditions of Europe — that of American ingenuity — could be seen as one more important way to keep the school situated in its context, despite its foreign director and the many émigré members of its staff. The conditions under which they were working, the continuing precariousness of their personal situations, were likely never far from their minds.

The "War Courses" at the School of Design in Chicago

Beyond designing around wartime shortages and addressing war-related needs (and with an eye toward the period to follow), the school also offered an assortment of other "war courses" during these years. The majority of these were designed to take up immediate wartime training needs (although the survey art lecture course was retained and transformed to cover the "Social Usefulness of Twentieth Century Art and Its Relation to a Nation at War").[61] As the school's summer session brochure of 1942 intoned, "In a country at war education and vocational training are faced with the problem of achieving maximum results in minimum time without sacrificing the objectives of general education. The School of Design in Chicago—because of its past educational policy—has readily adapted its program to the requirements of the present emergency."[62] At a time when America's entry into the war quickly drained students from schools across the country, the School of Design's war courses significantly boosted the school's enrollment; as Moholy-Nagy reported, "The year 1942 was more positive for the School than we had the right to expect. Through the preparation of war courses—camouflage, war designs and experimentation with substitutes—we had our highest enrollment counting the day and night students together—over 230 students in the last semester."[63]

In accordance with the recommendations of the Wartime Commission for Higher Education, students could use summer session credit toward regular semester work, speeding up the timetable to graduation.[64] (In a nod to wartime privations, students attending the summer session held in the countryside outside of Chicago were instructed that it was "absolutely essential" to "bring all their ration cards, marked towels and one woolen blanket."[65]) The school's intensified program sought to keep "constant pace with war-time . . . requirements" while also making provisions for those "engaged in the war effort [by day] to pursue their education" through evening classes.[66] It also came to terms with the fact that it was losing students to military recruitment but did not lose the opportunity to publicize the fact that it was supplying the military with well-trained recruits who were especially suited to meeting new situations with resourcefulness and inventiveness.[67] Later on, war veterans were directly served, as the school, working closely with the Veterans' Administration, designed a special course of study specifically for those attending under the terms of the GI Bill, allowing veterans to condense two-year courses into one year of study.[68] At times, veterans outnumbered regular students by a ratio of four to one.

War-related classes offered by the school were much more practical and results-orientated than the earlier curriculum and included classes like "Model Airplane Building," which taught the principles of aeronautics, including experiments in plane design; "Design in Plastics Research," which investigated the potentials of thermo-setting and thermo-plastics; and a course called "Mechanical and Architectural Drafting Training for the War Industries."[69] Other wartime offerings included a general course on "Mechanical Drawing and Architectural Drafting," "Blue Print Reading," and "Photography for War Services."[70] In "Production Illustration," students learned explosion, X-ray, and cut-away techniques, axonometric projection, photomontage, superimposition, and single and stroboscopic motion projections. The school quickly reorganized, and in some cases, re-staffed, in order to provide these valuable wartime technical skills.

Notably, it also sought to use its particular expertise in visual design to aid in the war effort. A "Visual Propaganda in Wartime" class, also called "War Displays," working in cooperation with the army, focused on silkscreen poster design, display, and mobile exhibition design, with the goal of educating civilians on topics such as air-raid precautions, accident prevention, and first aid. The posters produced in this course had unsubtle slogans, common for the period, such as "The People Are on the March," "Wipe Out the Enemy," "War Loan for the Future," and "Smash Anti-Semitism."[71] Posters designed by student Richard

Filipowski, *Care Saves Wear* and *Deliver Us from Evil* (both from 1943), won prizes in Chicago and New York, respectively. For his graphic design contributions toward the war effort, Gyorgy Kepes, an instructor at the school, was awarded a "War Committee citation for extraordinary service rendered our Government."[72] Faculty, such as Kepes; former Bauhaus members in the close-knit circle of émigrés surrounding the school, such as Herbert Bayer; as well as students also created designs for the Container Corporation of America in support of the war effort. Sponsored by the company's president and benefactor of the school, Walter Paepcke, they and other European modern artists designed ads – for example, one by Herbert Bayer informed citizens that "Paperboard that goes to war is paper that wasn't burned. Save waste paper! Sell or give to local collections," as well as informational booklets, such as Kepes's *Paperboard Goes to War* (fig. 4.4). By providing crucial information to citizens in a graphically compelling – and thus memorable – manner, these designers were able to aid the war effort on a wide scale.

Forays in Other Directions: Rehabilitation at the School of Design

The "Occupational Therapy" course, designed to rehabilitate disabled servicemen returning from the war, was another cornerstone of the school's wartime effort and provided the opportunity to give its ideas about holistic design education a very public and social application. Sponsored by the deputy director of the Mental Hygiene Service of the Illinois State Department of Public Welfare, the school planned the training course in conjunction with veterans' hospitals, working closely with various officials. Moholy-Nagy envisaged that the war and the postwar period would need a large number of personnel for the rehabilitation of disabled veterans.[73] He identified groups in immediate need of rehabilitation such as army and navy aviators suffering from operational stress, soldiers experiencing breakdowns during training, and injured industrial workers. Moholy-Nagy was prescient in this regard – between 1940 and 1956 psychiatric hospital admissions doubled.[74] To this end, the school was able to develop its foundational teaching strategies in a very productive and outcome-orientated manner to serve the projected onslaught of postwar recuperative needs. But it also shows the degree to which Moholy-Nagy was thinking not just in a pragmatic vein, but also about how the design school might address postwar social needs and societal changes.

In what it viewed as a "constructive problem of education," the school broke with traditional therapies and applied contemporary ideas and practices in education, psychological research, psychoanalysis, and even scientific motion studies to its program of rehabilitation.[75] Ultimately, Moholy-Nagy envisioned a larger-scaled project with new types of hospitals designed for what he termed "constructive rehabilitation" – as opposed to "sentimental rehabilitation" – which would feature general workshops where the patients could work from six months to a year, as well as special workshops and laboratories for more advanced recovery work that would take from one to three years.[76]

At the time, the school offered two courses aimed at training rehabilitation personnel. "Rehabilitation I" focused on sensory experiences, especially visual expression, and workshop exercises.[77] "Rehabilitation II" tackled serious issues

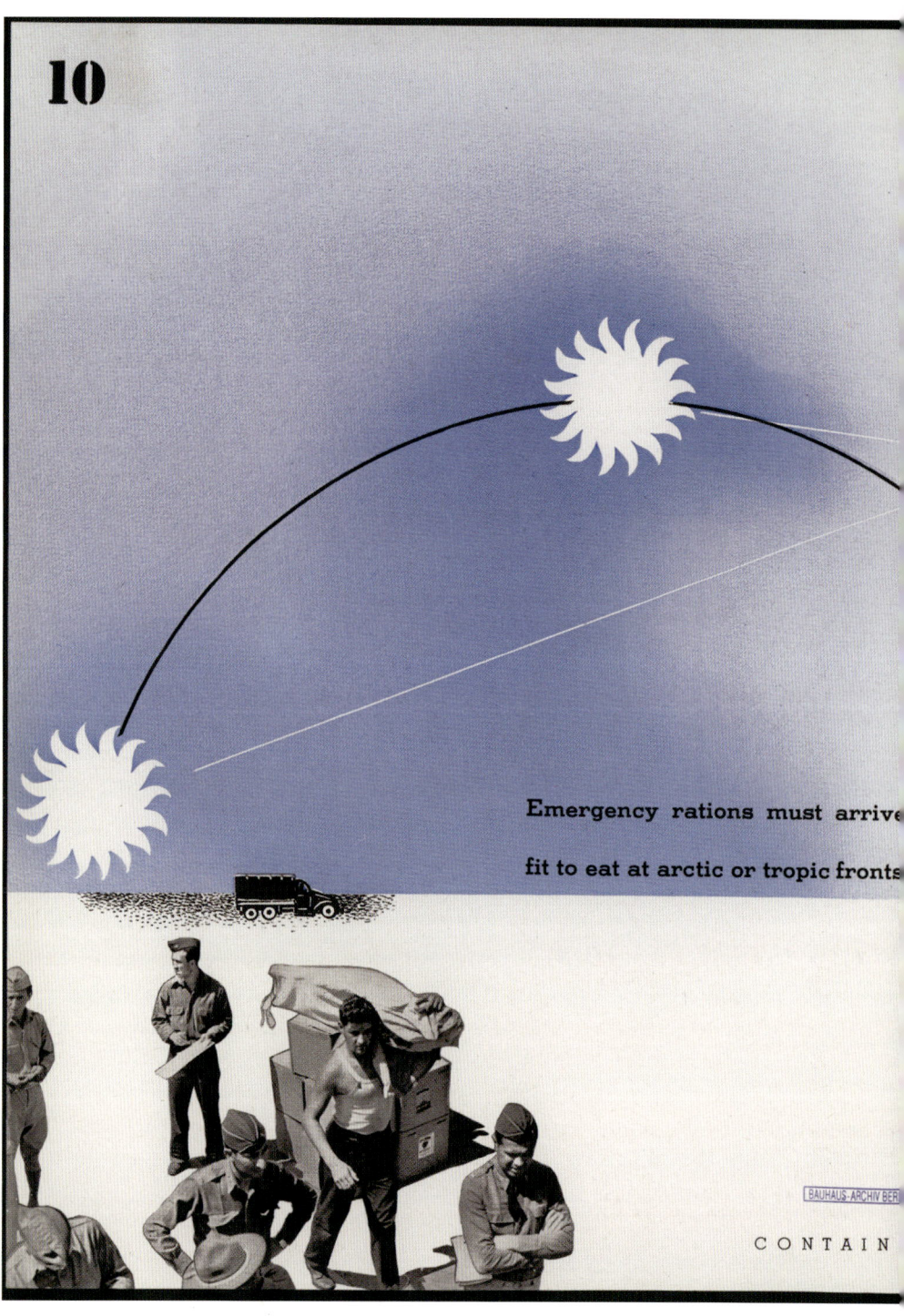

Fig. 4.4 Gyorgy Kepes, *Paperboard Goes to War*, booklet for the Container Corporation of America.

for a design school: occupational, physio- and psychotherapy, psychiatric integration, mental hygiene, scientific motion studies, family counseling, and problems of industrial workers, namely, fatigue and monotony.⁷⁸ Proposed rehabilitative activities for patients were similar to those already taking place at the school — photography, basket weaving, leather work, plastics, and other crafts, as well as writing, poetry, and drama. Students in the course produced sample pieces to simulate the work of bedridden patients.⁷⁹ The head of the Illinois Neuropsychiatric Institute, and Franz Alexander (a fellow Hungarian, whom Moholy-Nagy had

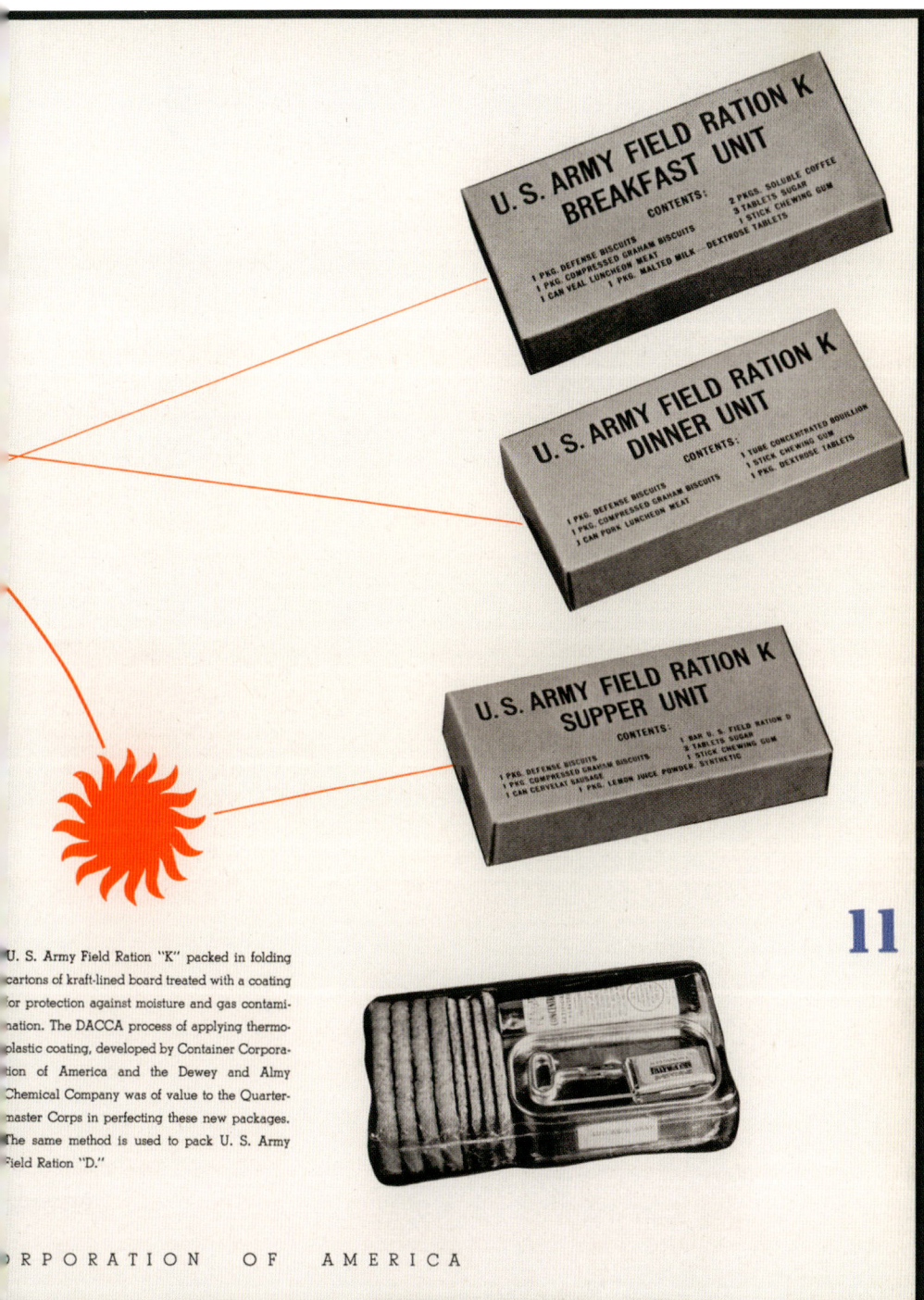

U. S. Army Field Ration "K" packed in folding cartons of kraft-lined board treated with a coating for protection against moisture and gas contamination. The DACCA process of applying thermoplastic coating, developed by Container Corporation of America and the Dewey and Almy Chemical Company was of value to the Quartermaster Corps in perfecting these new packages. The same method is used to pack U. S. Army Field Ration "D."

known at the University of Budapest, and who had worked previously in Berlin), a notable psychoanalyst and physician at the Chicago Institute for Psychoanalysis, supported the program, sending students, nurses, and social workers to attend classes as well as arranging for Moholy-Nagy's appearance before several medical conventions.[80] The school also offered a related evening lecture series on the topic of "rehabilitation," which featured twenty-seven experts in the fields of psychoanalysis, occupational and recreational therapy, "psycho-drama," and other areas focused on the issue of serving returning disabled men.[81]

Assimilating Unease

The courses sought to serve a wider population using key Bauhaus ideas and classroom exercises. To this end, the school was able to reach a different variety of pupil—distinctively not the artist, but rather the rehabilitation facilitator and injured alike. Furthermore, the courses offered an opportunity to use the Bauhaus method toward new ends, part of a long-standing Bauhaus belief, held particularly strongly by Moholy-Nagy himself, in the creative potential of every individual. To that end, therapists, aides, nurses, and laymen were trained in rehabilitation through a method designed to restore confidence in the disabled servicemen's own creative abilities.[82] As Moholy-Nagy determined, "Rehabilitation has different facets, but its main direction is at present to restore the patient physically and psychologically to the previous level of his normal status, by reestablishing his self-confidence and giving him opportunity to participate in purposeful production."[83]

Concerned with both cultivation of psychological well-being and a productive end result, the rehabilitation courses, termed "constructive occupational therapy" by Moholy-Nagy, represented another innovative application of Bauhaus ideas to American circumstances. Occupational therapy seems an odd choice for a design school, but it was much in keeping with Moholy-Nagy's pedagogical methodologies, as well as previous teaching practices developed at the German Bauhaus. Many Bauhaus instructional methods and core ideas dovetailed nicely with Moholy-Nagy's new concepts of a modern manner of rehabilitation. What he termed "the Bauhaus approach" in occupational therapy was intended to "awaken hidden capacities, increase self-confidence, leading to inventiveness and resourcefulness" through exercises aimed at self-discovery and "the awakening of consciousness about personal creative abilities."[84] Particularly evident in these rehabilitation courses would have been the sensory-based, process-oriented pedagogic practice that Jeffrey Saletnik has described, in reference to the original Bauhaus, as "design-as-process," an approach that was continued by Moholy-Nagy at the School of Design, as well as by other *Bauhäusler* at other institutions in America, especially the notion of art objects as connected to the *process* of their conceptualization and making.[85] Moholy-Nagy sought to use methods of art-making developed at the Bauhaus, methods that remained at the core of his school in Chicago, to aid in the recovery of war-related disabilities, an outcome that, again during the war years, represents a pragmatic use of art toward constructive ends designed to fulfill a crucial need. These courses also embodied a new application of the school's focus: here the pedagogical methods, combined with the fields of science and technology, were not in pursuit of a well-designed, useful *object*, but rather the aim was to turn the *individual* from an unproductive to a potentially productive entity within postwar American society.

The Art of Camouflage

The second "National Defense Course" devised by the School of Design during the war years was the "Principles of Camouflage" course, offered alternately as the "Industrial Camouflage Course," given under the auspices of the Office of Civilian Defense in Washington.[86] It offered an opportunity to test out the

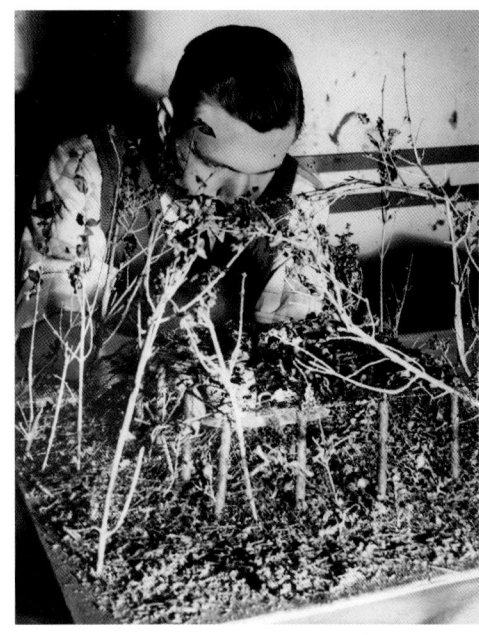

Fig. 4.5 Camouflage course, student work, School of Design, 1942–43.

school's ideas about the integration of practices and knowledge across varied fields in a new mode of "design." Following Pearl Harbor and his subsequent appointment to the Chicago Metropolitan Area camouflage section, Moholy-Nagy devised the course for the 1942 spring semester and then reached out to government officials to obtain official sponsorship for it, although he had been in discussion with various military and government representatives about introducing camouflage training into the school's workshops as early as the spring of 1941 (fig. 4.5). The development of the course so early in the war brought inquiries to the school on behalf of other institutions interested in offering such classes; Moholy-Nagy sought to organize a camouflage instructors' conference in Chicago that would bring together those teaching camouflage courses from around the country with the goal of creating a common policy.

However, this proposal was superseded by national plans under the auspices of the Office of Civilian Defense (OCD) in Washington to organize camouflage instruction, and an ensuing invitation to send a member of the school to Fort Belvoir, Virginia, for training followed shortly thereafter.[87] Gyorgy Kepes, after leading the school's initial "Principles of Camouflage" course in the spring of 1942, was made head of the newly created Camouflage Department at the school after being certified at the engineering school at Fort Belvoir.[88] The students included current pupils at the school; members of the pre-inducting class, which was also open to high school seniors; and professionals such as architects and engineers working in their respective fields.[89] The Office of Civilian Defense especially encouraged architects and engineers to participate in the training as "the ones to whom protective concealment problems will best be referred when such decisions are made by the War Production Board"; upon completion of the course, they would be qualified to "prepare plans, in accordance with principles established by the OCD in Washington, D.C."[90] The class was a War Services Project, and the work produced by the students was considered official government documentation. Several of the school's students went on to work for the army's Camouflage Research Department or to active camouflage battalions in Europe.[91]

At the School of Design, the course graduated over one hundred students and went beyond teaching the expected basic skills of military and industrial camouflaging of tanks, trucks, airplanes, and factories. Kepes led the students in designing a wide range of camouflage options that would conceal targets from both ground observation — including protection from snipers, low-altitude observation balloons, tanks, and submarine periscopes — and aerial attack methods — from area bombing to timed, precision bombing, dive bombing, and low-flying hedgehopping.[92] To aid the design process, students were trained in the fundamentals of aerial bombardment and the obstacles, including current modes of camouflage, that were typically faced by bombers.[93] From expert lecturers, they were instructed in infrared and night photography, the physiology of the eye and optics, atmospheric conditions, and certain landscape problems. In seeking new modes of camouflage, the students studied nature and animal camouflage, visual illusions, geometrical optics, techniques of basic photography, photo-topography, and stereoscopic photography, as well as practical skills such as cost estimating in order to submit bids to the military.[94] The course's content, as shown in the school's films *Design Workshops* (1944) and *Exhibition Work of Camouflage Class* (1943), demonstrates many elements of this wide-ranging instruction and also shows the students actively at work on camouflage problems, for example, utilizing aerial photographs to identify potential targets or using principles of abstraction to conceal regular forms and patterns (fig. 4.6). This kind of large-scale thinking and application of various types of skills — both very concrete and also more conceptual — was different from the crafts-based Bauhaus training of an earlier, perhaps more innocent era, but it does continue the technological legacy of the school, adding to its American iteration a greater urgency and application of science.

The school was in the unique position to combine science, technology, and art to aid the war effort, and the potential contribution of the visual artist was continually stressed. As Kepes pointed out in his introductory lecture, "The present emergency demands a reorientation into new fields of activity. . . . Camouflage requires the combined knowledge of people with a great variety of training — architects, engineers, painters, sculptors, graphic artists. They are finding a synchronization of their divergent knowledge in the fulfillment of this urgent task. This synchronization may be achieved only through . . . a mutual exchange of knowledge in each particular field. Thus the aim of this course is to acquaint the participants with all the factors involved in camouflage, enabling them to utilize their expert knowledge efficiently."[95]

According to the course outline, the school consciously tried to avoid what it saw as "economic waste . . . caused by the inertia of professional isolation" whereby "the painter saw only painting problems, the architect only architecture, [and] the engineer only engineering."[96] This was true of the school's entire larger design effort, generally. Instead, the goal was to engender "the necessary flexibility which emerges from a mutual grasp of each others' problems." The course was a serious undertaking that strove to combine the skills of several different professions and improve on past methods by merging specialties and

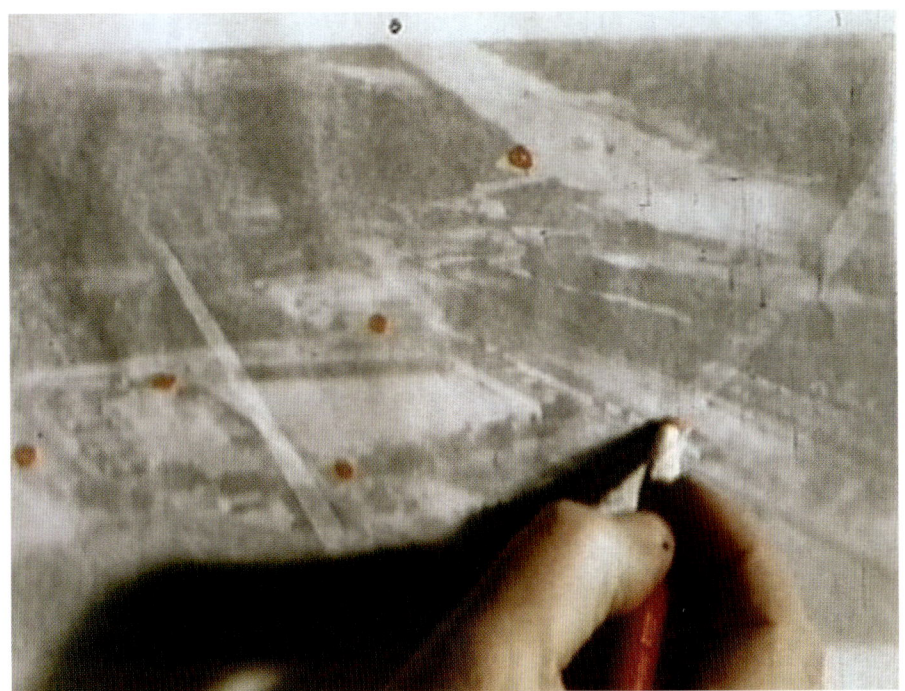

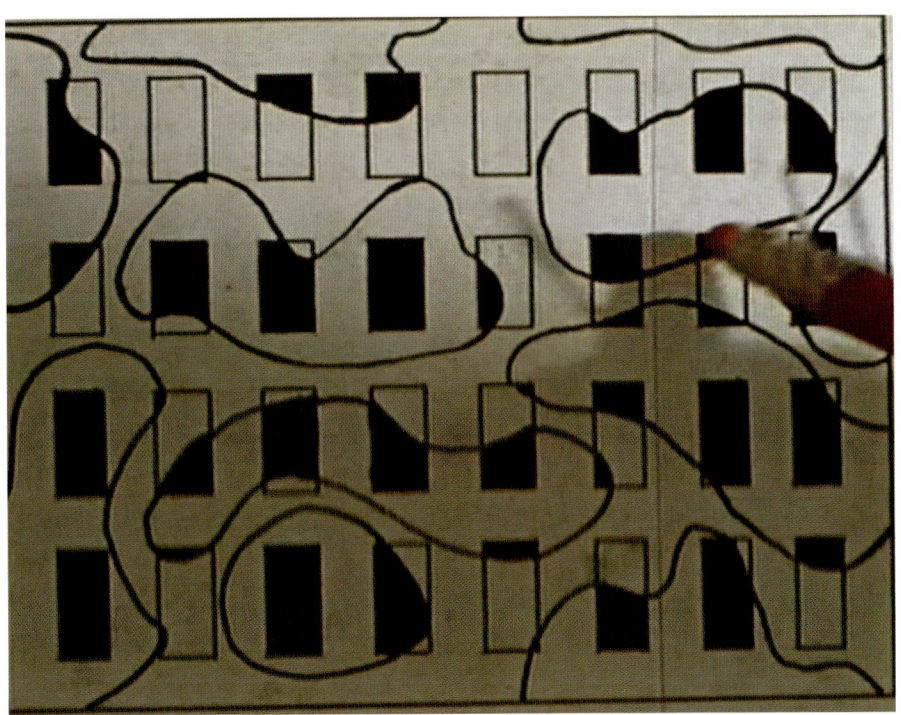

Fig. 4.6 Camouflage course, student work, School of Design, 1942–43. Film stills, *Design Workshops*, 1944, 16mm, color, silent.

disciplines—something the Bauhaus had always striven to achieve—toward practical and productive ends, namely, the war effort.

Beyond its collaboration with the Office of Civilian Defense for the camouflage course, the school proposed itself as the site of an entire camouflage "research laboratory," which would prepare volunteers for civilian and military camouflage tasks and also train teachers who could in turn train others. While the school was never fully expanded into this laboratory, it did conduct research and development work. This research was not just hypothetical but also situational. For example, specialists and students worked on potential methods of changing the appearance of the city of Chicago in order to camouflage it enough to confuse the enemy. The city presented unique difficulties because of its large lake and rivers; since it was supposed that general bombing could not be avoided, the idea was for precision bombing to be rendered inaccurate via large-scale camouflage.[97] Moving beyond standard blackout techniques, which interrupted travel and were ineffective for bodies of water, the group proposed a "moving-light" plan using "halation units"—large systems of lamps placed in patterns that would cast strong, confusing glows over or near target areas, rendering potential targets—such as workers' homes, factory sites, and airfields—invisible under a blinding light system that would fill the sky with luminous haze; extending this lighting out over the lake would distort the true contour of Chicago's lakefront.[98] Students studied color combinations, geometrical optics, lights and shadows, fog and smoke, and other undisclosed means of pockmarking the city so that a bomber would have difficulties finding a target.[99] Faculty were hard at work as well; Kepes took on the problem of the nightly flares at the steel mills, which were easy beacons for bombers, by conducting laboratory experiments, the results of which proposed turning green flood lights on the steel mills to render their red flames nearly invisible.[100]

Moholy-Nagy was himself a key player: he was appointed a member of the mayor's personal staff under the auspices of the city of Chicago's Civil Defense Commission, a group in charge of camouflaging Chicago against air attack, especially the Lake Michigan waterfront. After completing a survey of the area in small planes and patrol boats, he worked on a number of potential methods of disguising distinctive elements of the city, such as camouflaging the oil storage tanks along the city's south shoreline.[101] "The whole city could be camouflaged, if that were necessary," Moholy-Nagy told the *Chicago Daily News* in 1942. "It depends on how much money could be spent on such a project. . . . Dummy buildings could be built on barges in the lake to change the contour of the city. In this way the Loop could be projected a mile or two into the water. The drives could be covered over with painted burlap. Or scaffoldings could be built to resemble street intersections, or landscaped, to break up the length of the drives."[102] He also proposed obliterating the steel mills from aerial observation through the use of smoke and suggested a signal in response to which janitors in every city building would throw a chemical in the boiler resulting in an instant blanket of blackness, blotting out the entire area. The role of artificial light and light manipulation in obscuring targets drew on one of Moholy-Nagy's own long-standing, primary artistic interests, giving him an opportunity to capitalize on his previous experiments.

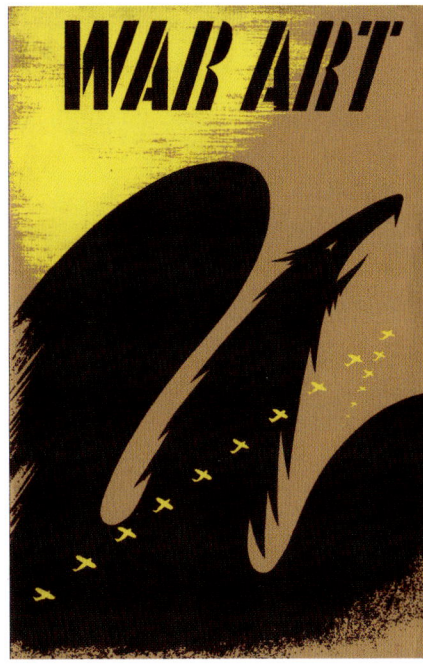
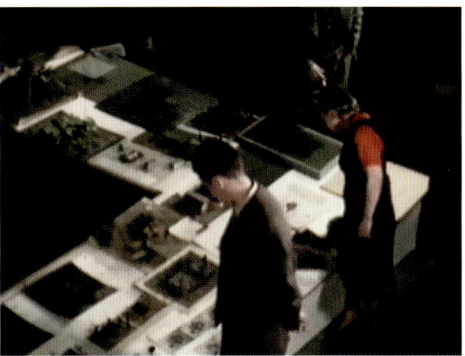

Fig. 4.7 *Left*, Gyorgy Kepes or Ralph Graham, *War Art*, catalog cover for exhibition at the Renaissance Society, Chicago, 1942. *Right*, Exhibition of the Camouflage Workshop, School of Design, 1943. Film still, *Exhibition Work of Camouflage Class*, 1943, 16mm, color, silent.

A June 1942 article in the journal *Civilian Defense* labeled Moholy-Nagy and Kepes "among the best informed men in America on camouflage techniques," both in terms of theory and practical application.[103] It noted also, centrally, that camouflage should not be undertaken by individual organizations, industrial plants, or agencies, but must be deployed on a community scale. Camouflage thus entailed in an uncanny way an almost seamless merging of important, originary Bauhaus ideals – the joining of the arts in work on a common goal, one that had aspects of both artistry and technology, and which could be undertaken only through working *as* a community and *within* a larger community.[104]

War Art: An Exhibition

Important portions of the school's research and new inventions were presented to the public in a wartime exhibition titled *War Art* (fig. 4.7).[105] This show represents an effort that reflected the school's expansion of its activities out into society, its interest in improving the means of visual communication, and the acute need to substantiate its accomplishments. Organized by Moholy-Nagy and featuring work by students from the School of Design and the Illinois WPA Arts and Crafts Project, the exhibition ran from April to May 1942 at the Renaissance Society of the University of Chicago. A related exhibition, under the auspices of Gyorgy Kepes's Camouflage Workshop, featuring much of the same work, was mounted at the school in 1943.[106] This exhibition was captured in a twenty-one-minute color film made at the school, *Exhibition Work of Camouflage Class*. The *War Art* exhibition at the Renaissance Society was conceived to demonstrate "new developments in art in their application to war activities."[107] Moholy-Nagy pointed out, "We are aware that many individual artists have contributed to the war objectives by their work, ideas and suggestions. These contributions, however, have not been generally publicized."[108] Before Pearl Harbor, he noted, his school had already begun to reorganize its work to meet perceived needs, and following that event, a much greater emphasis was placed on actual war requirements, particularly domestic defense. The exhibition was intended to illustrate the "contribution of the creative artist and the craftsman as he adapts himself to the urgent needs of today."[109]

A relatively simple one-room exhibition, most of the designs on display were mounted posters on walls or small-scale models. In addition to elucidating typical camouflage problems, it included a demonstration using two light boxes to show how light and shadow could conceal the character of forms. Also on display were designs featuring new materials, such as a cellophane and cheesecloth plastic "skin," and existing materials utilized in novel ways, such as the rubberized cloth units, mentioned previously. By the exhibition's opening, some of the designs were already in active use at army, navy, and air training bases.[110] A great number of designs were not allowed to be exhibited, however, as they were subject to censorship in the name of national security.[111] Curatorial files note that some of the restricted work included scale models of operations for landing and loading ordnance, and diagrammatic charts of airplane motors, ammunition components, and safety and production methods.[112]

In the catalog accompanying the show, Moholy-Nagy laid out the circumstances of his wartime educational program: "In a country at war, education and vocational training are faced with the problem of achieving maximum results in minimum time." He then connected them with the school's unique pedagogic vision and practices. The School of Design, he observed, "because of its educational policy – has readily adapted its program to the present emergency. Its classroom and workshop training, the coordination of hand and brain, helps to make the individual resourceful and inventive. He knows from direct experience how to handle the tools of the craftsman, the basic machines of industry, and the problems of contemporary science and art. With such an integrated training of art, science and technology the students of the school were able to attack civilian and military tasks with courage, achieving surprising results, many of which have good possibilities."[113]

Moholy-Nagy also noted how, within the wartime context, he was directing his school to a broader conception of the kinds of needs to which design, both through its products and its practices, could respond. He saw the economic and technical needs that the war had brought to the fore and that would persist in altered form once the war was over, not in isolation, but rather in the context of the larger "human" side of need, of which the war and its effects formed powerful evidence. It was in the context of this perception and its implications for design praxis that the school's contributions to the present war effort could be understood: "The creative and inventive mind of the artist has always been alert to human needs. So today, the arts, the applied or practical arts in particular, are serving to meet the urgent needs of the present, and new techniques and development are utilized to aid in the national effort."[114]

This exhibition, then, demonstrated the tangible results of the school's successful merging of the technology and science emphasized by its educational program with the creative problem-solving abilities of the trained artist. Calling into service the basic artistic skills that had always been taught at the school, including exercises in understanding and manipulating light, research into color and surface effects, the scientific testing of differing materials, and the visualization of form in three-dimensional space or other views, such as aerial perspectives, the school could demonstrate that it had the capabilities to carry out the practical and productive designs that it espoused.[115] Or, as the original catalog for the school proclaimed in 1937, its purpose was the development of "a new type of designer, able to face all kinds of requirements, not because he is a prodigy but because he has the right method of approach."[116]

In showing its contributions to the war effort at this exhibition, the school was able to very visibly legitimate itself on several levels; it demonstrated that its unconventional teaching practices – newly being introduced across America by *Bauhäusler* working in various institutions but systematically put into practice at the New Bauhaus, School of Design, and Institute of Design, under difficult and uncertain circumstances – could produce distinctively useful, practical results. This institution, led nearly exclusively by foreigners who had moved to the United States from Germany, was ready to make serious contributions to a new homeland's war effort (rather than merely taking shelter in it). In doing so, it was working to address more general problems at stake for design that were brought forward by the war exhibition format – such as the relationship between the visual and practical qualities of design products and the relationship between individual designers and a broader community.

In presenting new ideas via new objects to a nation at war, the school and its protagonists were able to show that they at the school, and its design more generally, were in the process of pragmatically facing the nation's challenges, both in a time of crisis, when the shock of the quick success of the Japanese at Pearl Harbor led many Americans to question their country's defensibility and readiness for war, and for the envisioned peacetime to follow. It was not enough to simply design for war and for peace in a pedagogical vacuum; the school had to successfully *communicate* its design practice, largely through objects, to a broader public. Indeed, this communicative element was integral to the expanded conception of pedagogy that the Chicago iteration of the Bauhaus was struggling to put into practice. The *War Art* exhibition, as well as other exhibitions didactically demonstrating the products of the school's workshops, were concrete examples of the school's members adapting their uneasy status, and that of the school, to a wartime and postwar audience, as part of its broader attempt to forge a new relationship between design and its audiences.

Creative Violence: Conciliatory Postwar Visions

This chapter has sought to underscore the novel pragmatism of Moholy-Nagy's version of the Bauhaus in Chicago – the degree to which the school in its American iteration was able to quickly adapt to the changed circumstances of a nation at war and to instigate a varied array of concrete solutions to wartime problems, rather than wait out the war in order to introduce its design in the peacetime to follow. Under Moholy-Nagy the New Bauhaus/School of Design addressed the war by offering specific programs and courses, forging key alliances with offices of the military, and using the school as a laboratory for solutions for the war effort. This pragmatism manifested itself in the extent to which, under his leadership, the school managed to offer real design solutions to a nation at war – from useful objects made of non-rationed materials to visual design to innovative teaching practices. But it also reflected a significant and radical attempt to pursue, to a new degree, in changed forms, and under different circumstances, a holistic, integrated reconception of design as a social and pedagogical practice with links to diverse forms of knowledge and artistic and industrial production.

Under Moholy's direction, this project, which had begun at the German Bauhaus, received a charged, bold new formulation under the pressure of events and acute circumstances in wartime Chicago. The combination of the broad anxiety produced by the war and the narrower anxiety felt by immigrants such as Moholy-Nagy, positioned precariously in the society that had received them and seeking to contribute skills and pedagogical practices that they had brought with them to fight against the state they had fled, seemingly provided the impetus to effectively redirect their efforts toward the kind of social transformation that the German Bauhaus of which Moholy-Nagy had been a part had previously proclaimed but largely failed to usher into being. The result was a successful melding of art and technology with science to devise technically advanced objects and educational models for the war effort – a melding that arguably represented a realization to a new degree of the Bauhaus's originary ideals.

While in Germany Bauhaus members often wondered why industry did not embrace their designs. In the United States, Moholy-Nagy quickly and successfully cooperated with complex American bureaucracies, such as the Office of Civilian Defense, and private investors alike. Although there were many Bauhaus members working in the United States in different capacities, furthering various aspects of the original school's methods and ideals, Moholy-Nagy particularly saw his work in America as a strong continuation of the German Bauhaus's organization and pedagogical methodologies, ones that he also viewed as potentially very useful to the war effort. A letter he wrote to the Wartime Commission of the US Education Department a few months after America's entry into the war captures what he saw as his school's contribution: "Our educational method, the coordination of hand and brain, the integration of workshop and intellectual training, may offer a good approach to your present problems, especially if the training in dexterity includes the basic machines of industry. . . . Continuing the educational work of the Bauhaus, the integration of art, science and technology, we have found that the youth of this country is very receptive to this type of training. It helps to make the individual resourceful and inventive, quick in decisions, courageous in approaching civilian and military tasks."[117]

The war indeed formed an urgently compelling new challenge for the reconception of design and design training that the "Bauhaus method" had embarked on. The pragmatic approach that Moholy-Nagy frequently trumpeted to those he had to win over was joined by a philosophical one, itself bearing some congenial affinities with American philosophical Pragmatism, one in which Moholy-Nagy and his fellow instructors and students used their particular areas of expertise to address problems of war, simultaneously cultivating a postwar role for modern design in America as a form of process-oriented, social problem-solving to be cultivated through new practices of pedagogy.[118] As the United States had

Chapter 5

Domesticating the Grid

Ludwig Hilberseimer's Housing

without costs for the social design vision that the wartime Chicago design school under Moholy-Nagy had sought to put into practice. Moholy-Nagy had looked forward to the possibility of a vibrant postwar future, one in which the possibilities in a new country must have seemed expansive – but he presumably did so with an acute awareness of the challenges of living together as human beings.

the fundamentals and building up from there a new knowledge of the social and technological implications of design. The new generation of designers, who have such a training, will be invulnerable against the temptations of fads, the easy way out of economic and social responsibilities."[124] Moholy-Nagy's iteration of the Bauhaus in Chicago gave this conception a new urgency, making its case for the future value of the results of its instruction for the country: designers who would assume social, technological, and economic responsibility in the postwar period — following in the footsteps of those who had designed for the war — and beyond the war — during the war.

Moholy-Nagy looked to the restorative power of art in the postwar period, putting a fragmented civilization back together again. In 1940, he had still expressed his broad conception of design in terms of peacetime life: "A designer trained to think with both penetration and scope will find solutions, not alone for problems arising in daily routine, or for development of better ways of production, but also for all problems of *living and working together*. There is design in family life, in labor relations, in city planning, in living together as *civilized human beings*."[125] Once at war, the school continued to look ahead to future peacetime design needs, framed not to consumer ends, but rather — in terms of production as benefiting of society: "After the war a great conversion from war to peace production will take place. Such inventiveness and resourcefulness are the qualities of the educational method of the School of Design in Chicago, these qualities will help the individual to find his right place in peacetime production. This should be to the mutual benefit of himself and the community."[126]

Two years later, in his graduation speech to the small class of 1942, Moholy-Nagy contended that in a time of war, it was a great privilege to be allowed the exercise of one's skill in design — a privilege granted by society, made for its future benefit, bringing with it an obligation to use one's creative skills for the "productive and harmonious existence of a new generation."[127] It was this obligation that the New Bauhaus had sought to assume through its wide-ranging participation in the war effort, but more important, in the service of a more peaceful future in the postwar period, in which design would continue to play a socially beneficial role. This participation necessarily entailed collaboration and compromises, through which Bauhaus émigrés such as Moholy-Nagy, who had arrived under tenuous circumstances, managed to contribute much in several short, but crucial years. In Moholy-Nagy's characterization of these contributions, and of the school's functioning during the war years, as "a great privilege to be allowed the exercise of one's skill in design," one continues to hear, perhaps, the conciliatory outlook that underscores the school's anxious beginnings. The task of the present generation, he declared in 1944, to which the New Bauhaus and School of Design had sought to contribute the resource of an invigorated design process and pedagogy, was the "preservation and refinement" of the "*individual* within a harmonious *social* existence, the value of which will be measured in terms of cooperation and social usefulness."[128]

When Moholy-Nagy died in November 1946, he was denied the further privilege, as he presumably would have seen it, of seeking to address design to the new and different social challenges of the boom period following the war, in which modern design was poised for far greater popular acceptance, though not watched the events unfolding in Europe with mounting alarm, Moholy-Nagy had not ceased to envision the potential social benefits of this design philosophy, as he proclaimed in 1940, with an eye toward the role of design in war and beyond: "Training in design is training in [the] appreciation of [the] essence of things. It is penetrating, comprehensive. It includes development of various skills in using materials, but goes much beyond that. It involves development of attitudes of flexibility and adaptability to meet all sorts of problems as they arise."[119] In the face of war, he and his school had stood self-consciously at the ready, practically and ideologically. Moholy-Nagy was keenly aware of the circumstances when he made this statement – as a foreigner in a nation on the eve of war leading a school without particularly stable financial or social backing – and he did not shy away from using wartime contributions to both mitigate his own uneasy status and, at the same time, assimilate the school and its design practices.

Even before the war broke out, perhaps channeling what he had seen in Europe as he fled, Moholy-Nagy cautioned, according to the *New York Times*, that no artist may "dodge his epoch. He may be crushed by it, or he can become bitterly aggressive, or can make use of it in various creative ways. The Bauhaus would make use of it in a creative way."[120] The wartime experience to follow further influenced this insistence that crises were to be met creatively and that design had a crucial role to play in this response. Moholy-Nagy framed his position sharply, emphasizing the parallels between the war effort and the design effort: "We have to use creative violence to redesign our life, just as we are using a scientific-technological violence to win the war."[121] But as he explained in 1944, he saw art as a tool also, or ultimately, for harnessing aggression, suggesting that war could not but be detrimental to creativity, that the object of design in war – even when it was working directly on the war effort – was to design beyond war: "Art as [an] expression of the individual can be a remedy by sublimation of aggressive impulses. Art educates the receptive faculties as well as revitalizes the creative abilities. In this way art is rehabilitation therapy through which confidence in one's creative power can be restored."[122]

In the midst of such a devastating war, a wariness about human potential abounded, and Moholy-Nagy saw the possibilities of education, including design education, as guarding against future violence: "We have to have a staff ready whose members have had time and concentration to watch closely the symptoms of war in our youth and to map a course for the future."[123] Moholy-Nagy's version of the Bauhaus in America during the war years took up the mantle of social responsibility with great vigor. Whereas the earlier Bauhaus had also conceived of art as standing at the center of a certain social mission, it was during the war that art found a guiding productive purpose in the institution's activities – even if in a necessary association with a certain violence – whether employed to help veterans recover, to aid civilian instruction, or to design equipment or camouflage for use in the war. The "creative violence" Moholy-Nagy spoke of was to be applied also to the practices of design itself, as an antidote to aggression and violence, in the name of cultivating a new generation that would not lead the world back into war like those preceding it had. This reformatory conception of design training was tidily summed up by Moholy-Nagy in 1943, describing his school as one that educates "by going back to

Was the North American grid the site that Ludwig Mies van der Rohe and Ludwig Hilberseimer had been waiting their entire career for?[1] Mies had arrived in Chicago in 1938, shortly followed by Hilberseimer, the planner and architect. They worked closely together, collaborating on many projects both formally and informally; in addition to unrealized plans and projects in and around Chicago, they designed what is often regarded as one of the most successful postwar housing developments, Lafayette Park, located in Detroit. This chapter examines architecture and plans that arose, and were impacted by, the conditions and contingencies on the ground – that is, when Hilberseimer was able to immigrate to Chicago and found himself working closely with Mies on the South Side, the Loop, and elsewhere, designing for, within, and against its grid. In the move from Berlin to Chicago, the conditions of design would need to respond to local circumstances, both practical, such as zoning regulations and calculating the duration of winter sunlight, and sociopolitical. In this context, Chicago plays a unique role as both an earlier inspiration for a generation of German architects and an eventual landing place for them, where they influenced the teaching practices and design environment there, in both built and unbuilt work. While their sketches, models, and plans may appear to visually align, their points of departure, working methods, and underlying belief systems of how the city should be designed differed greatly. Mies viewed urban design as a branch of architecture and was drawn to creating an organic unity dependent on architectural form, composition, and construction using street patterning, blocks, and squares as the means to create visual coherence.[2] Hilberseimer, an urban planner, designed using systematic units, constructed on a grid (fig. 5.1).

They had been close friends and colleagues in Germany, working together at the Bauhaus in Dessau, where Hannes Meyer had first hired Hilberseimer, who, in turn, had been instrumental in recruiting Mies as the school's third and final director (fig. 5.2). They shared an arrangement in which each commuted from Berlin and lived in Dessau on alternate teaching days so that one of them was at the school while the other was in the capital.[3] As designers in Berlin, Mies and Hilberseimer had each put forward radical visions for the future. Mies envisioned high-rises ahead of the technology that would facilitate their actual construction, such as his 1923 Friedrichstrasse Skyscraper projects, as well as later designs, that for economic and political reasons were not to be built, as was the case of his striking 1933 office buildings for the Reichsbank (fig. 5.3).

Hilberseimer, also a preeminent critic, theorist, and prolific writer, presented startling ideas of mass-produced towers as an urban workplace and living solution for the core of historic Berlin (figs. 5.4, 5.5). Workers would live – and shop – adjacent to their places of employment, alleviating congestion and daily commutes to the workplace. This was a practical and expedient solution, if uncompromising and unrelenting in its form and formalism. Life, it seemed, in this vision, could be contained within – if not embodied by – the superblock structure. Yet, as Hilberseimer himself would frame it in his important book *Metropolisarchitecture*, "Like every building, the high-rise is but a cell, a component of the urban organism, and it must be systematically connected to the latter."[4] These two components as a solution for modern housing – cell and grid – are the focus of this chapter. It

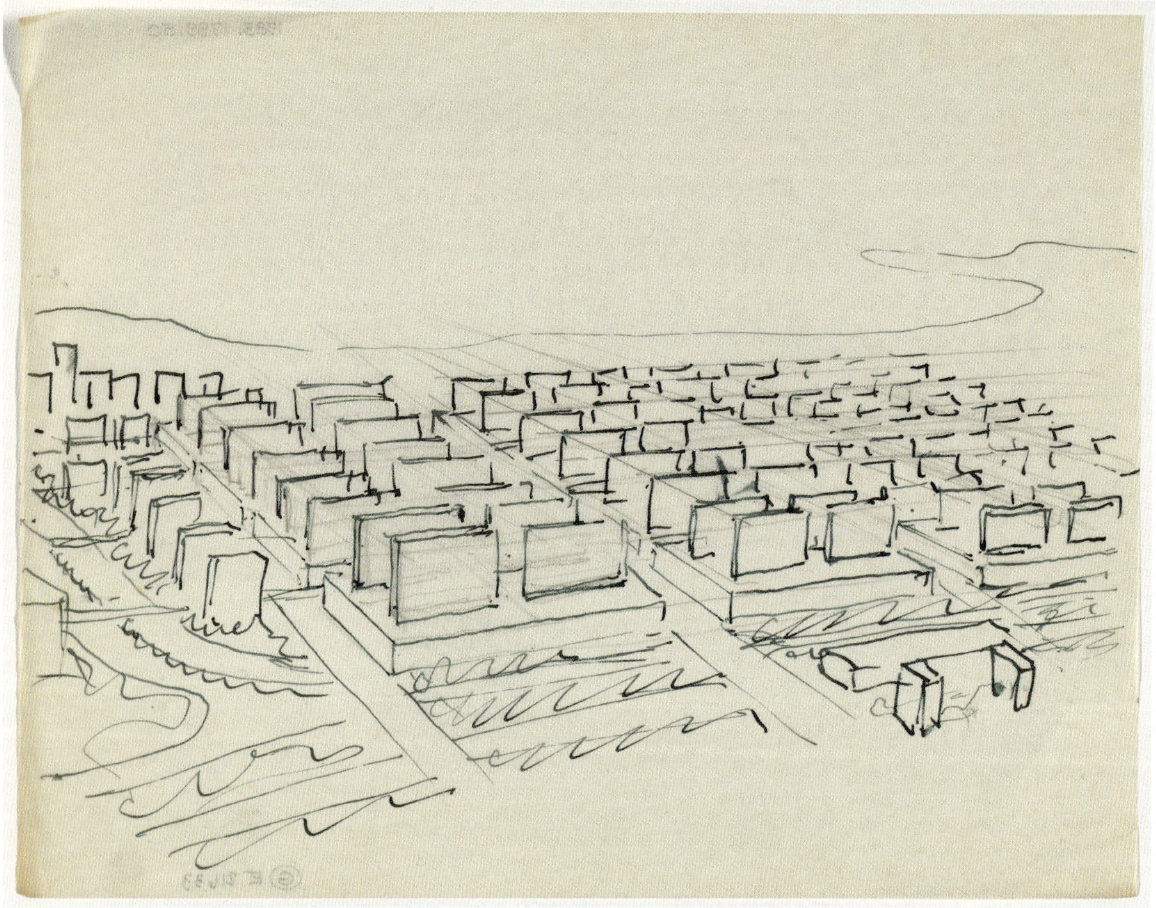

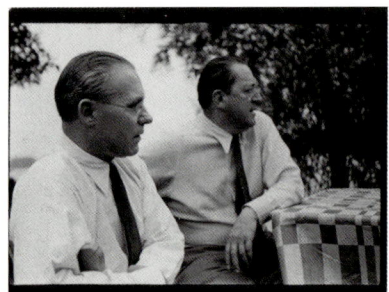

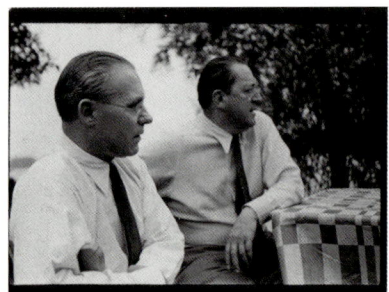 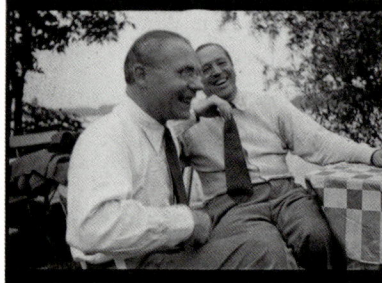 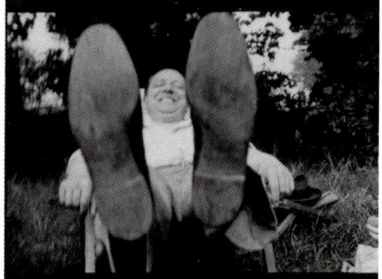

Fig. 5.1 Ludwig Hilberseimer (architect), sketches of Chicago downtown loop development project, aerial perspective, looking east. Art Institute of Chicago.

Fig. 5.2 Ludwig Karl Hilberseimer (*left*) and Ludwig Mies van der Rohe (*right*), ca. 1935, Germany. Art Institute of Chicago.

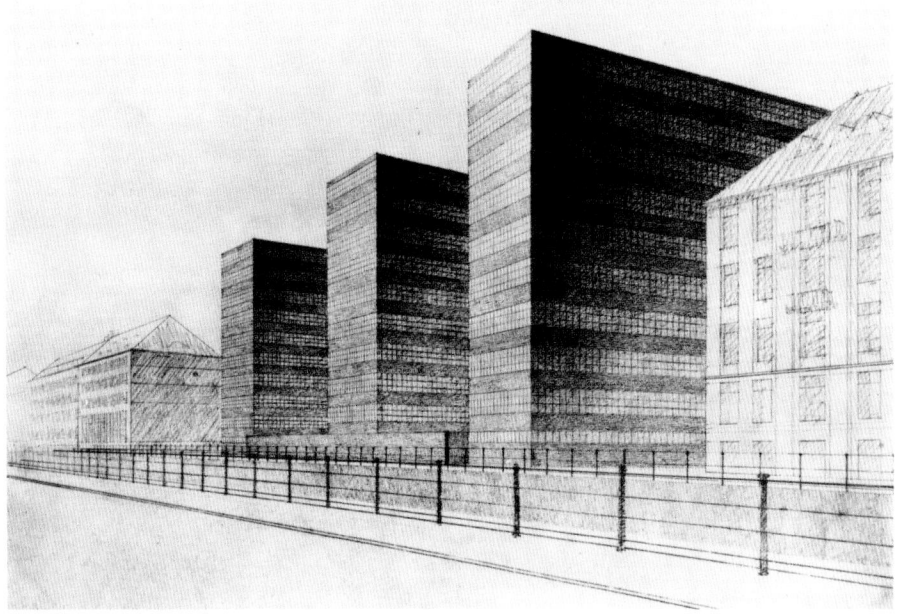

Fig. 5.3 Ludwig Mies van der Rohe, Reichsbank project (perspective drawing from the Spree Canal), 1933.

examines the complementary relationships, as theorized by Hilberseimer, between dwelling units, housing typologies, urban patterning, infrastructural systems, and the institutional, economic, and political frameworks of the period. I argue that from the individual cell of habitation to the large-scale metropolis, Hilberseimer's scalable unit and the grid onto which it was projected provided a template in which citizens could dwell individually and thrive collectively and urbanistically. It is a vision that Hilberseimer developed while still in Germany, honed in his final years there, and then adapted and developed further for the US context of wartime defense and planning for the postwar period. The cell and the grid represent, then, both a continuity of concept and a period of innovation — between Europe and America, between the pre– and post–World War II eras.

Hilberseimer, as this chapter contends, was interested in multiple types of grids and the cells that would populate them.[5] At times he proposed new ones, with blocks of towers lining up in dominating rows that demand a systematic street order, from which the skyscraper rises in orthographic projection as a vertical grid — the whole creating a lattice overlaid on a messy urban condition, with the previous chaos tamed by rational architecture. Like many German modernists, he was also interested in American grids: the so-called Jefferson Grid, dating to the Land Ordinance of 1785 that ordered the Northwest Territory, notably including what would become the state of Illinois, into nesting squares sized from six miles down to sixty feet per side, as well as the distinctive nineteenth-century American street grids found from New York to Chicago to San Francisco. These latter grids especially were defined by the surveyor's tools of the late Age of Discovery and the early Industrial Revolution, the rational ordering lines of the Enlightenment emboldened by the pressure of capitalism's vectors.[6] In Chicago, Hilberseimer sometimes worked within this overlay of American grids; in other instances he erased their contents, applying gridded measures and modules that structured spatial relations in the absence

Domesticating the Grid

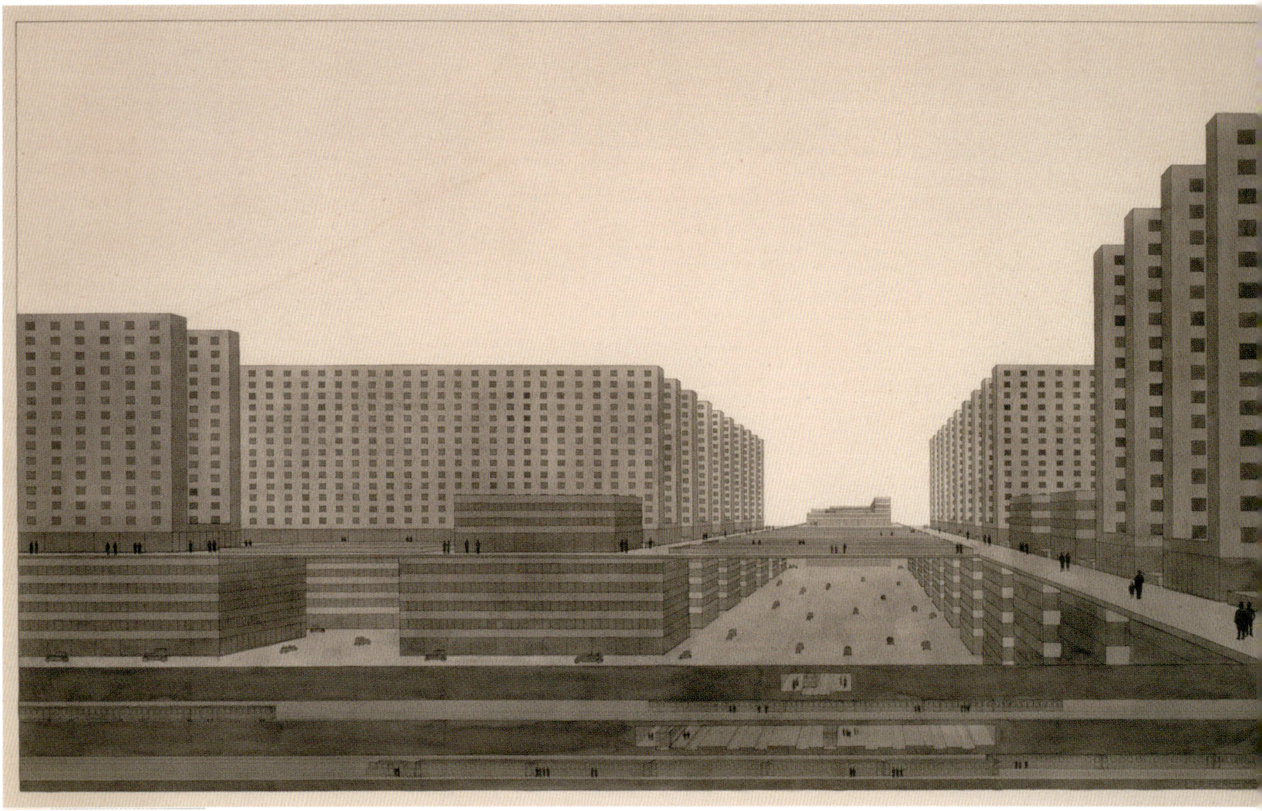

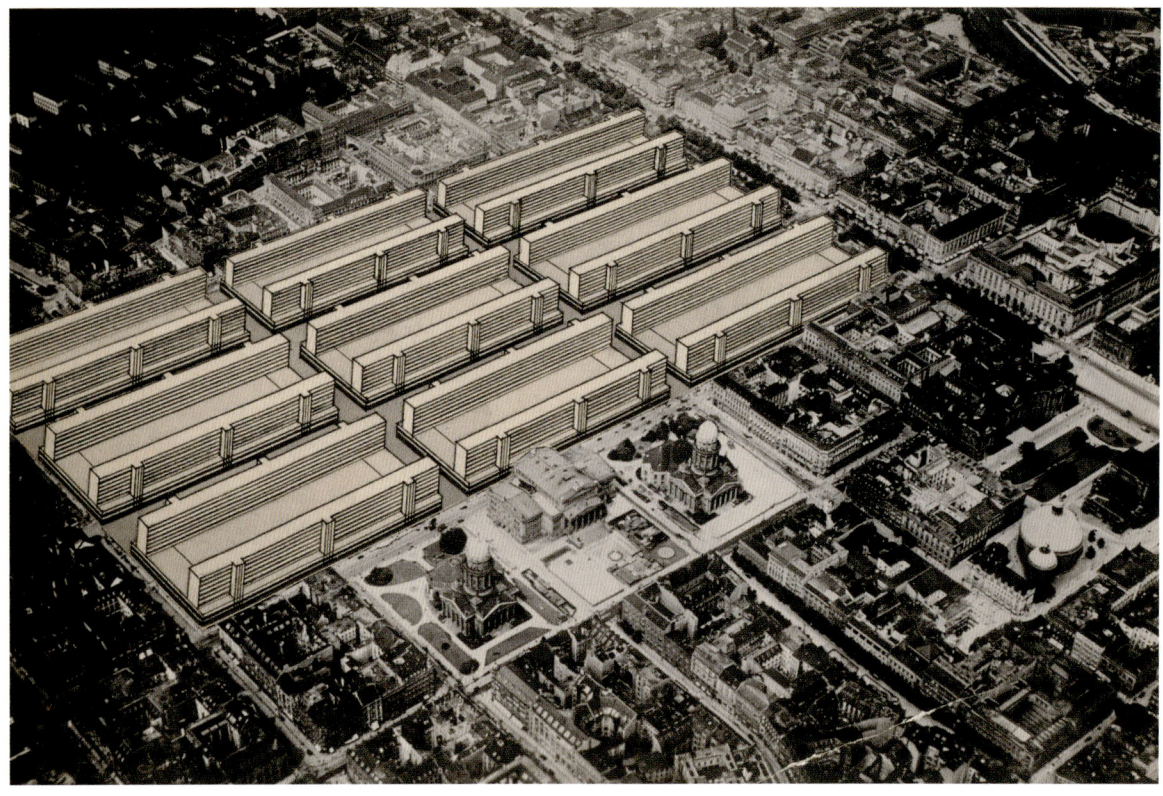

Chapter 5

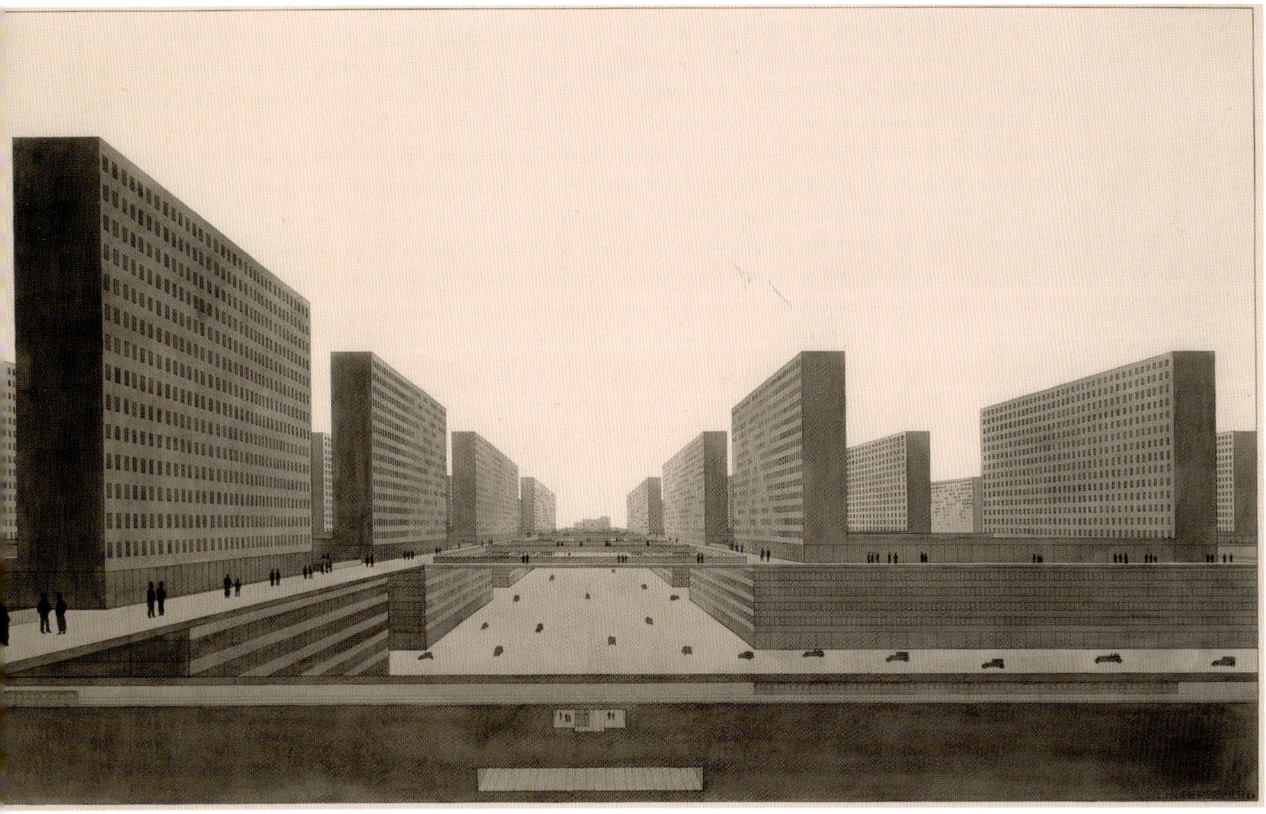

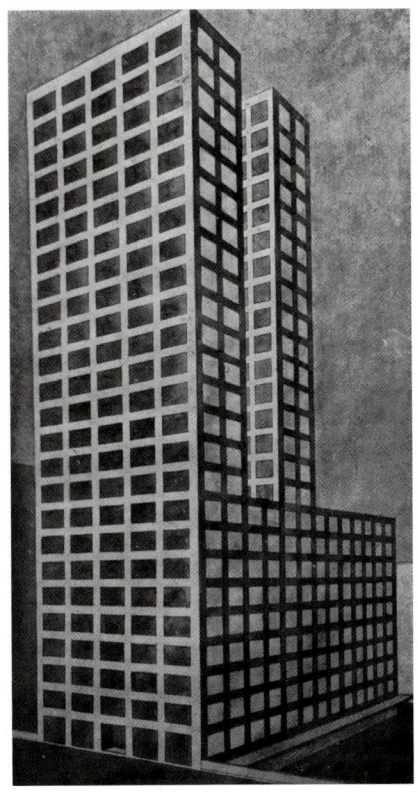

Fig. 5.4 *Opposite top*, Ludwig Hilberseimer, Highrise City, perspective view, 1924, ink and watercolor on paper. Art Institute of Chicago. *Above*, Hilberseimer, Highrise City, perspective view: north-south street, 1924, ink and watercolor on paper. Art Institute of Chicago.

Fig. 5.5 *Opposite bottom*, Ludwig Hilberseimer, Berlin development project, 1928, photocollage of ink on paper mounted on aerial photograph. Art Institute of Chicago.

Fig. 5.6 *Left*, Ludwig Hilberseimer, Chicago Tribune project, 1922. From Hilberseimer, *Grosstadtbauten*, 1925.

Domesticating the Grid 159

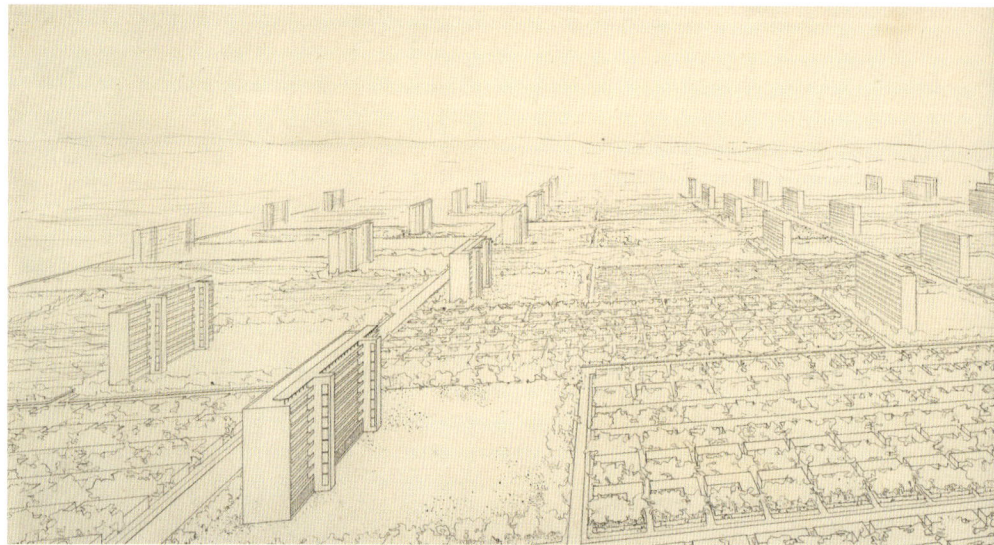

of the elided previous street grid. And in still other instances, his grid would arise merely from pencil and graph paper, a vision of some Platonic order yet to be applied, from the settlement to the minute workings of the dwellings, rooms, and furnishings in ever more diminutive cells.

Thus, Hilberseimer's large, repetitive, totalitarian-looking urban interventions, such as his proposal for Berlin's city center or his 1922 entry for the Chicago Tribune tower competition, seem more ready-made for the North American grid, where, unlike in Europe, a historic medieval or nineteenth-century core would not be in the way of "progress" (fig. 5.6; see also fig. 5.5). Soon thereafter, however, in his final years in Berlin prior to his emigration, Hilberseimer moved away from the urban tower to the row house and then to the single-family home, as an ideal living arrangement (fig. 5.7). The grid, so crucial to this vision of outgrowth, remained an integral part of this new way of housing the masses. A few towers, too, remained, in his domestic proposals for America.

In 1920s Germany, the question of how to plan cities for the present and the future, how the most vulnerable might be employed and housed, was an urgent one. Housing was the key economic, social, and political issue for architects at the time, as cities suffered from overwhelmingly crowded dwelling conditions because of the population shift from rural farm labor to factory work. The tenements that sprung up to alleviate the onslaught of new urban dwellers were overcrowded, resulting in subdivided, damp and dark spaces, often several courtyards deep into the block, with many informal arrangements in which the kitchen floor might be rented out to boarders. Bathrooms were often shared among many apartments, located off the common central staircase; an unhygienic solution.

One shift was represented by an interest in new economic formulations and technological solutions, that is, how new building techniques, at new scales, and in new configurations, might alleviate painfully crowded conditions and the ill health that often accompanied them. As Hilberseimer himself pointed out in the period, "the problem of housing cannot be solved in isolation, rather only in conjunction with today's economic and social relations" while "a reduction in

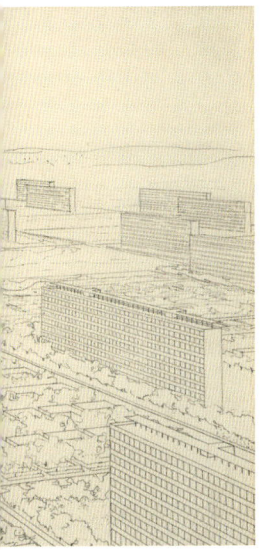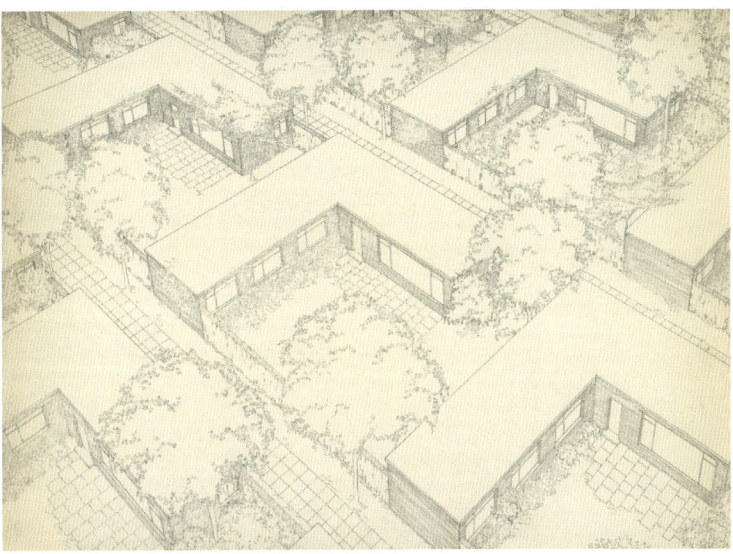

costs can only come via an adjustment in the production processes and methods of their financing."[7] Indeed, a key mode of inquiry falls at the intersection of urban form with social structures, through shifts in frameworks of knowledge and configurations of power. As Hilberseimer theorized in his early book *Grosstadtbauten* (*Metropolis Building*), published in 1925, two years before his expanded, much more widely known text, *Groszstadtarchitektur* (*Metropolisarchitecture*, 1927), "Architecture cannot be considered in isolation. It always relates to the surrounding matrix of contemporary social, economic, and psychological conditions and indeed is the means by which these are articulated in art."[8]

Mies's housing solutions in this same period were distinct from those of Hilberseimer. As I examine in detail, Hilberseimer moved from designing chiefly blocks of apartments to single-family homes arrayed on an ever-expanding grid, in a career-long, concentrated effort to address social and environmental problems. The contingent conditions — engendered by the shift in location and local circumstances — necessitated that his plans and designs be adjusted in response, but his core approach would not. It is essentially a question of houses versus housing; Mies's late German period can be characterized by single-family commissions, reserving his visions of skyscrapers for commercial offices, not habitation. Mies's houses are not modest proposals: though sometimes only a single story, they are expansive, feature rich materiality, and include amenities such as a garage for an automobile, still a luxury in this period, serving an elite clientele. His courtyard house, along with his earlier concrete country house, is thought to be one of the few designs he worked on with his own residence in mind. In the 1930s, Mies had already designed houses such as the L-shaped Lemke House in Berlin (1932–33) and given much thought to the problem of the courtyard house, found in such projects as his 1934 studies for a Mountain House.[9] They were often placed in settings of natural beauty, on large plots of land. He also regularly set the task of designing a courtyard house to his students at the Bauhaus and, subsequently, at IIT. Mies approached the design, as his sketches show, through a loose, expansive drawing style. His sketches

Fig. 5.7 *Left*, Ludwig Hilberseimer, Berlin mixed-height housing development: apartment blocks with L-shaped single-family houses, ca. 1930, ink on paper. Art Institute of Chicago. *Right*, Hilberseimer, settlement units, density studies, view of L-shaped houses, ca. 1943, ink on illustration board. Art Institute of Chicago.

Domesticating the Grid

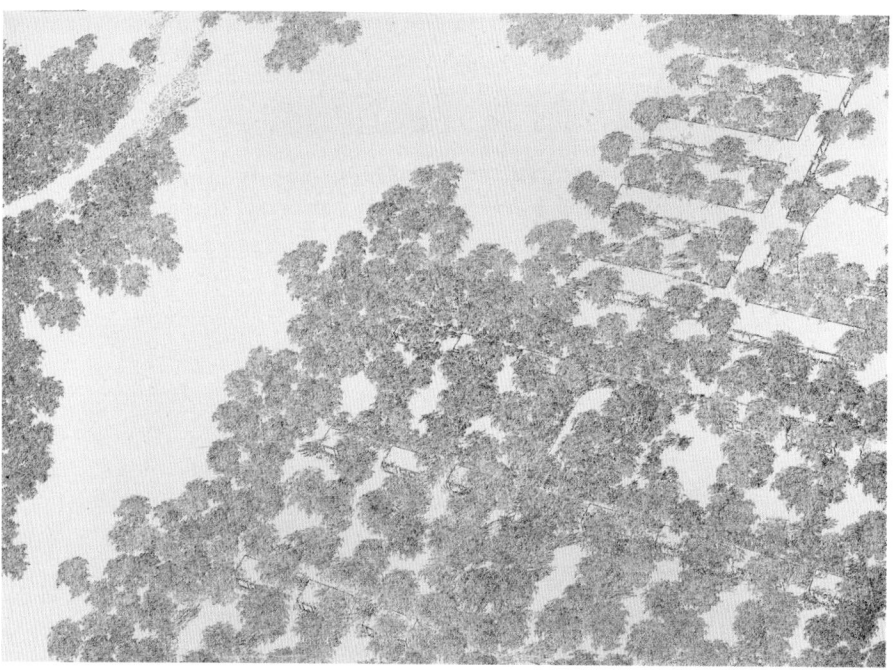

Fig. 5.8 Ludwig Hilberseimer, Chicago settlement units, 1940s, ("View of a Settlement Unit showing how the pattern of buildings and streets can be broken by trees and merged into the landscape resulting in natural concealment"). From Hilberseimer, *The New City*, 1944.

suggest ideas of open-ended space and free-floating walls and feature rich wooden room dividers. This represents a manner entirely different from Hilberseimer's constrained and delineated designs, carefully set out to be reproduced (and, he hoped, built). Although compact in floor plan, Mies's were elite designs; for example his 1934 "Court-house with garage" depicted a large motor car parked in the garage. His early Chicago courtyard houses continued his general penchant for modern but individualized housing solutions and his ongoing use of rich materials. Mies was eventually able to build luxury high-rises in Chicago and elsewhere, taking a very different direction than his colleague Hilberseimer in his move from individual modern homes to multi-unit towers. Mies's focus was on architectural solutions to specific architectural problems.

Hilberseimer chose the inverse: over the course of exactly the same period he moved from the proposed design of housing blocks and towers to disaggregated dwelling. These homes were envisioned in repetition and intended to be mass produced. His single-family houses are less well known, but folding as they do into a radical vision of future living, this chapter trains a spotlight on them, revealing their under-studied importance. It was a significant shift, and Hilberseimer's visions for single-family dwellings might seem at odds with this period of architecture, in which, for his fellow modernists, the tower block in the garden took on new urgency as a potential solution to a housing crisis across Europe and subsequently in the United States. Hilberseimer would always retain a few high-rise apartment buildings in his plans, but the real place of mass production and economies of scale lay, he believed, in his L-shaped houses, and their seemingly infinite reproducibility (see fig. 5.7).

Notions of home, then, as now, were decentered by mass movements of people made up of, on the one hand, economic migrants in search of a more stable existence, and on the other, a mobile, affluent elite. These spaces of habitation, at two economic extremes, were of heightened, critical importance to modern architects in this period. At one end of the spectrum, elite modern homes with interiors replete with zebrawood finishes, travertine floors, and nickel-plated cruciform columns served as objects of desire, whetting appetites for alluring modernism.[10] At the other end, architects strove to address a genuine, urgent need for adequate housing for the masses. Hilberseimer's designs are explicated in their larger social and economic context – that of their theoretical and architectural formulation and for their potential to serve the poor and the middle classes. Intended to uplift and improve the lives of their dwellers and to form and support a highly functioning community, his projects must be understood as political and also connected to the technical framework of the working city.

Much of the earlier housing discussed in this chapter was designed in the context of the Weimar Republic's accelerating technological advances as well as the social upheavals wrought by them, by the factory work and output of firms such as the AEG. This era closed with the final emigration in 1938 of Mies and Hilberseimer, among the last of the 1920s avant-garde architects to depart Germany. They arrived in Chicago with little knowledge of English and faced the uncertainty of exile during the ramp-up to World War II; this period was followed by the postwar boom, albeit accompanied by a deep questioning of the future of housing and the organization of urban contexts.

This chapter begins with the pre–World War II designs that formed the foundation for the North American postwar work that followed, a period that saw built as well as unbuilt projects. As the German grid traveled on Mies and Hilberseimer's graph paper, it encountered the American grid, which had been evolving on its own since the Enlightenment. It underwent vertiginous extremes of scale, from the domestic cell to the sky-high plumes of the atomic bomb. If today we live in a moment of new and correct skepticism toward formalism and standardization in housing, let us return to what appears to be ground zero of that hyper-formalization, in order to observe its origins and motivations.

With the help of a trove of archival documents and rare, unpublished images, this chapter presents some counternarratives to which history has thus far paid little attention. With Hilberseimer's houses with gardens, rather than a tower in the garden, I examine what in the first instance looks like formalism but in fact is more akin to a matte or field condition, to rhizomatic form with the potential for growth, especially across America's flat Midwest (fig. 5.8). The totalizing vision of Hilberseimer's proposal for Berlin's city center did not entirely disappear in the United States; indeed, his plans include projects for tall buildings, dominant and repetitive in the urban grid (see fig. 5.1). But I want to relate his Berlin towers to my examination of the US single-family homes because the same totalizing impulse is there, too – a vision for mass-produced housing. Hilberseimer's basic design tools are also his *theoretical* tools – that is, the unit and the grid – and they remain consistent.

Unit Dwelling: Macro to Micro and the Smallest Common Denominator

Hilberseimer believed that only when urban planning was conceived together with a building plan could the city function well as an organism.[11] Therefore,

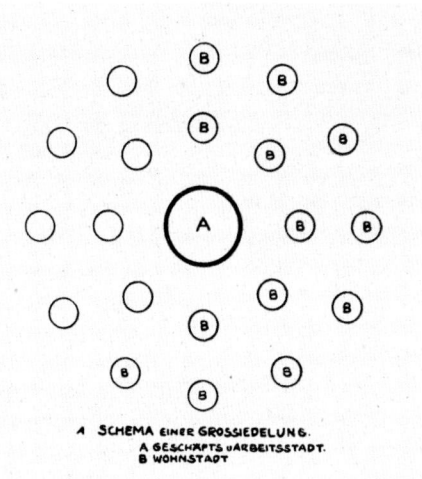

Fig. 5.9 Ludwig Hilberseimer, urban planning scheme, 1925. From Hilberseimer, "Über die Typisierung des Mietshauses," *Die Form* 1 (1926).

the specific designs of the buildings were not his primary concern, especially not in terms of their materials and details (in contrast to peers such as Mies or Erich Mendelsohn), nor was creating an enticing marketable object important to Hilberseimer, nor were larger ruminations about space and what it might mean to dwell in a modern manner, formulations of which his fellow architects of the period preoccupied themselves. Rather, Hilberseimer was concerned with large-scale planning for the city, in which dwelling space was calculated as modular units. His early live-and-work high-rise proposals soon gave way to a separation of the functions of working and living.

Hilberseimer formulated his urban theory as a relationship between an elementary cell and an urban whole. His 1925 urban planning scheme, based on Ernst May's satellite scheme, explicates these principles, with different types of cells making up the urban organism (fig. 5.9). In the scheme, "A" represents the centrally located place of commercial business and factory work, while the many surrounding "B"s designate the residential cities, each with rows of rental apartment blocks, tied to local amenities—schools, shops, a hospital, and the rail lines.[12] Illustrated in the round, a vestige of Ebenezer Howard's garden city movement, which inspired Hilberseimer, these cells are essentially units on a grid. Hilberseimer put into dialectic the parts to the whole, which he conceived in both social and human, as well as practical terms. He cared deeply about the living conditions of his potential dwellers—that their homes would receive enough sunlight, that interior spaces would be well-planned (if condensed), and that they could expediently and safely reach their places of education, work, and leisure. Hilberseimer's parts-to-whole ratios also represent carefully measured units, increments mapped on a grid—scaled ratios that accounted for relationships from the individual brick to the window frame to the door, from the terrace to the house plots, to the overall community grid and to the transportation network.

In the residential area that followed, Hilberseimer designed streets for local traffic and shops, with apartment blocks encircling green courtyards (fig. 5.10). Yet he was most concerned with the macro and micro—with the large-scale planning of the metropolis's overall functioning, and with the single room. His

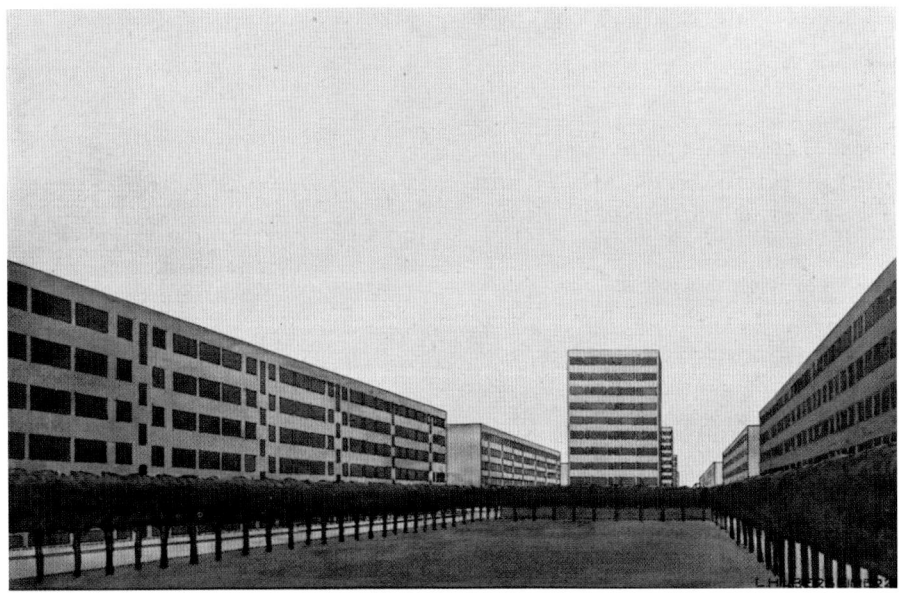

Fig. 5.10 Ludwig Hilberseimer, small apartments, 1929. From Hilberseimer, "Kleinstwohnungen," *Bauhaus* 3, no. 2 (April–June 1929).

so-called smallest apartments (*Kleinstwohnungen*) were indeed diminutive; in an article on the topic, he notes that the Berlin Wohnungsfürsorgegesellschaft (public housing authority) had determined that 48 square meters (ca. 500 sq. ft.) was adequate for a one-and-a-half room apartment, that 54 square meters (ca. 580 sq. ft.) was specified for a two-room apartment, and 62 square meters (ca. 670 sq. ft.) for a two-and-a-half room apartment.[13] Hilberseimer also argued that the counting of rooms or the total size of an apartment did not address the actual spatial needs of the occupants. He proposed, instead, that apartments be calculated and sized according to the potential number of beds needed for family members, also taking into consideration the gender of the siblings. This would then be set in the absolute minimal terms with regard to size: where four or fewer individual beds were required (calculated as two beds for the parents and two for the children), a minimum of 48 square meters (ca. 500 sq. ft.) was needed, for six beds he found that 58 square meters (ca. 620 sq. ft.) was required, and 70 square meters (ca. 750 sq. ft.) for eight beds.[14] In his smallest housing unit, a studio apartment for a single dweller (*alleinstehenden*), he proposed space-saving measures such as introducing a folding Murphy bed, or *Klappbett*, and he changed the delineation of the kitchen from *Küche* (kitchen) to *Kochraum* (cooking space/area)."[15]

At the heart of this vision for accommodating dwelling needs is an object – the room – which can be understood as both a dwelling space and a calculated unit of measurement (fig. 5.11). Built-in furniture made the calculation more precise, and, in fact, depended on it. Beginning with permutations of beds – often four- and six-bed units for the smallest dwelling – Hilberseimer worked outward to determine the number of rooms. His floor plans were thus often very detailed and included the furniture layout that he envisioned would allow so many family members to dwell in a compact space (fig. 5.12).

An overlooked aspect of Hilberseimer's theory of housing is his articulation of, and distinction between, "schematization" and "typification" in design.

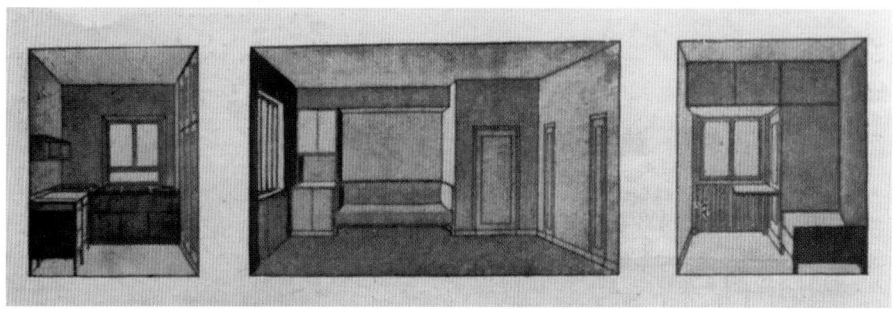

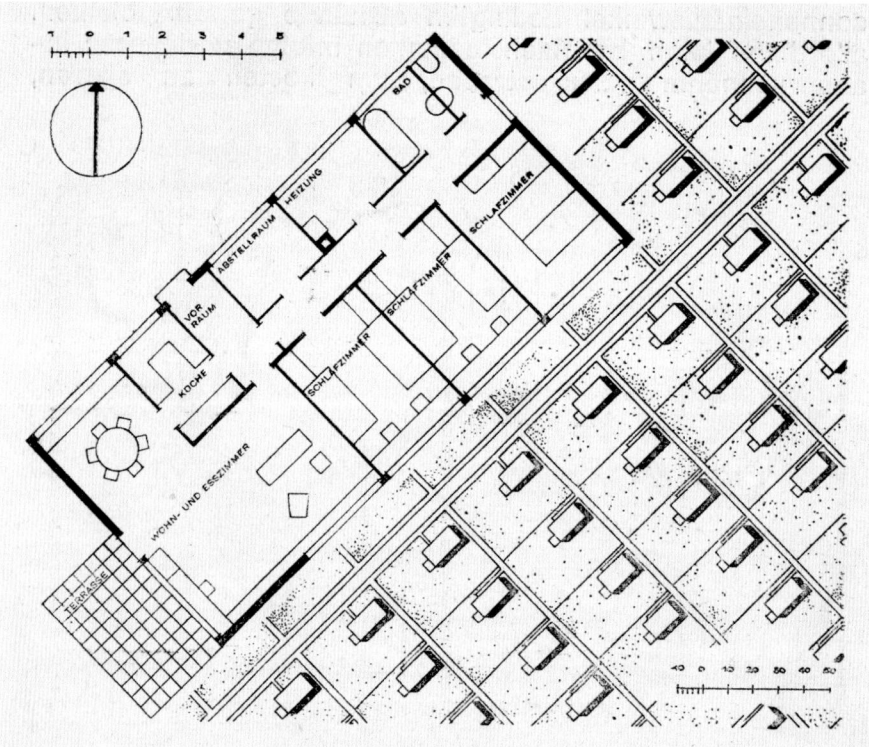

Fig. 5.11 Ludwig Hilberseimer, housing elements (kitchen, living–dining room, sleeping cabin), 1925. From Hilberseimer, *Grosstadtbauten*, 1925.

Fig. 5.12 Ludwig Hilberseimer, freestanding house plan and settlement, 1931. From *Bauhaus* 1 (January 1931).

In a key 1926 article, he argued against building speculators' "schematization" (*Schematismus*) of fixed floor plans that maximized profit, instead calling for "typification" (*Typisierung*).[16] *Typisierung* was a term popular in the period for the conception of a thoughtfully conceived and carefully tested prototype that would lead to the mass production of well-designed, standardized goods (usually discussed in relation to the development of furniture). Here, as applied to architecture, Hilberseimer meant identifying basic dwelling needs and devising the floor plans based on optimizing those functions – eating, sleeping, hygiene – while also allowing for a multitude of adaptable apartment configurations to accommodate a range of family sizes, from a single dweller to a seven-member household.[17] Typification in the future, he writes, "will have to extend beyond individual construction details to embrace spatial units."[18]

Using unit measurements, Hilberseimer sought an incrementalized solution that could scale up in size, while the main components of kitchen, bathroom, and living-dining room remained the same. However, his insight – and part of my larger argument – is that this unit could as easily be deployed as a single,

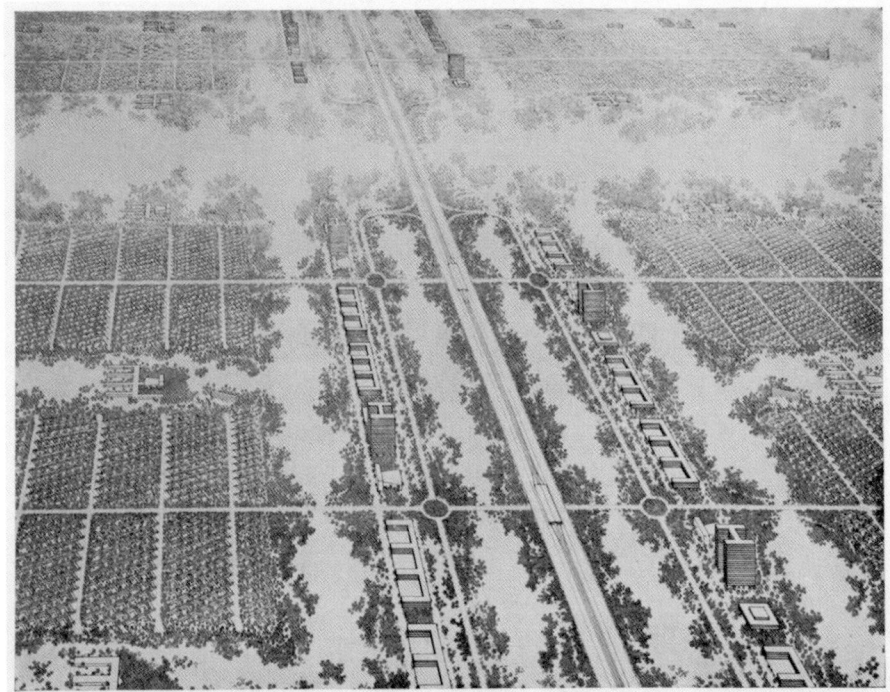

Fig. 5.13 Ludwig Hilberseimer, commercial area with surrounding settlement areas, 1944. From Hilberseimer, *The New City*, 1944.

stand-alone house as a multistory, high-rise tower. This eventually led him to the design of row houses and then individual small homes, which were – at least theoretically – also readily scalable in terms of the mass production of units.

Hilberseimer's houses were just one part of a larger vision for the design of future urban communities (fig. 5.13). With the room as the smallest unit, moving exponentially outward, multiple rooms (each hardly differentiated) made up the house; houses were aggregated to form a community adjoined to schools and leisure centers. This dwelling community was then situated within an infrastructure network comprising rail lines and roads, as well as places of work, including light industry, with heavy industry and agricultural work in the greater distance. The concept of the unit allowed him to further scale up to small, walkable, planned cities by creating "community units" encompassing housing, shopping and commercial activities, and industry. If placed in the landscape, Hilberseimer argued (in a lecture penned with his colleague, the landscape architect Alfred Caldwell), "future city growth takes place simply by the addition of more units. Thus our city could grow to any size and never be crowded."[19]

Pre-landing: Looking to America

From the early 1920s while based in Berlin, Hilberseimer, like many architects of his period, had a long-enduring enthusiasm for the built environment of North America, and especially the urban infrastructure and the architecture of the Chicago school. As early as 1920, Hilberseimer weighed in with an article titled "American Architecture," coauthored with Udo Rukser, in which he discusses noteworthy US buildings, but the article is littered with misattributions, indicating that he had not yet traveled there. He discusses Frank Lloyd Wright and the prairie, but he places Wright's Larkin Building in Chicago rather than Buffalo, New

Domesticating the Grid

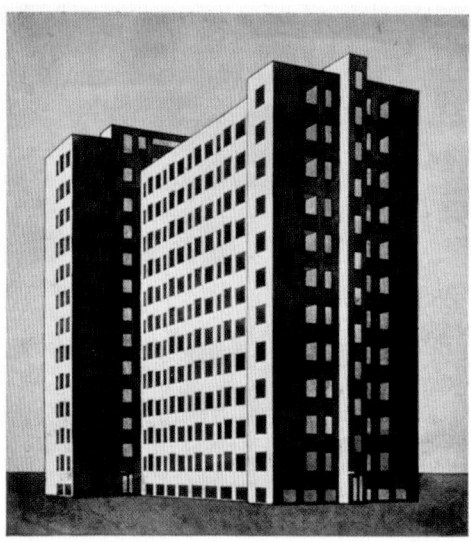

Fig. 5.14 Ludwig Hilberseimer, boardinghouse, ca. 1927. From Hilberseimer, *Großstadtarchitektur*, 1927.

York; he mistakenly notes that Louis Sullivan's Merchants' National Bank was located in Chicago, not Grinnell, Iowa; and he erroneously credits the American shingle-style architect H. H. Richardson as the designer of the Brooklyn Bridge rather than John Augustus Roebling.[20] It is especially prescient that he primarily looks to Chicago for remarkable architecture, even if he is conflating buildings actually located elsewhere.

Hilberseimer was inspired by, and conversant with, Chicago's commercial architecture, and he included Richardson's Marshall Field Store and Sullivan's Carson, Pirie, Scott Building in his important 1927 book, *Metropolisarchitecture*. He was especially taken by John Root's 1891 Monadnock Building. Not having yet traveled to Chicago, from the long-distance vantage point of 1927 Berlin, he praises sight unseen its "inner consistency and logical form" and claims that the "new that has arisen . . . has nothing to do with banal functionality; rather it is simultaneously the greatest coherence and concentration."[21]

Even before the move of so many modernists – Mies, Hilberseimer, László Moholy-Nagy, and Walter Peterhans – to Chicago, Berlin had enjoyed a special relationship to Chicago. Walter Rathenau, politician and heir to the AEG industrial empire, wrote that "Berlin was transforming from 'Athens on the Spree' to 'Chicago on the Spree.'"[22] While Weimar Republic Germany looked to the ideal of ordered, gridded North American cities such as Chicago, it would only be after emigration that these architects might truly engage with a grid, as well as the steel and economic infrastructure that allowed them to finally build at the skyscraper-scale they desired. Both Hilberseimer and Mies, thus, were already very much primed for their American experience, when they were still in 1920s and '30s Berlin. Both were interested in using the techniques of mass production for housing – in high-rises and for smaller homes. Especially at the Bauhaus, with its experiments with a steel house prototype, mass production was seen as a solution for future housing.

Although tall residential and commercial buildings were already common in the United States, especially by the early 1880s in Chicago and New York, they were unknown in Europe, where buildings tended to top out at six stories.

In *Metropolisarchitecture* Hilberseimer predicts in 1927, "High-rises will also become a possibility for the new way of life." Although he was yet to make his first visit to America, he continues authoritatively,

> In America buildings of ten to fifteen stories already exist, the so-called apartment houses. They combine every imaginable service and supply every comfort in the smallest amount of space. American apartment houses are furnished practically and are occupied especially by single people and couples without children where both members of the couple are employed. In general they comprise a living room that is equipped with a bed that folds away into a ventilated storage space, making it possible to use the space as a bedroom at night, a dressing room, a bathroom, and a small dining room with an attached cooking alcove. This cooking alcove is furnished meticulously. It has a gas stove with an oven and a range, counter space for washing dishes, an icebox, a garbage chute, and all of the labor-saving domestic appliances.[23]

He also expresses his deep admiration for Frank Lloyd Wright's "rental house" and his larger apartment complex, the Lexington Terraces, which Hilberseimer notes were very economical while still offering courtyards for light and air, well-ventilated apartments with extensive built-in furniture, and a range of sizes.[24]

He was particularly enthusiastic about the scale of American hotels, which were massive, block-long and deep edifices, designed at the turn of the century for both short- and long-term stays, and conceived as alternatives to apartment living. If well-serviced, Hilberseimer reasoned, the hotel room was the perfected single cell for habitation. These large-scale structures endeavored to serve all of the needs of their guests in terms of dwelling, eating, work facilities, and recreational amenities. It would be over a decade before Hilberseimer first visited the United States, but in his 1927 book, he reproduces McKim, Mead & White's Hotel Pennsylvania in New York City, a floor plan of Chicago's Surf Apartment Hotel,[25] and the Palmer House Hotel by Holabird & Roche, which could hold four thousand guests on twenty-four floors. Hilberseimer writes glowingly of the hotel as a future form of mass housing in that it "is adapted to provide all conveniences and the utmost comfort."[26]

Adjacent to the images and description of these American living hotels, Hilberseimer published a projection and plan of his own "Boardinghouse" (his term, written in English, eschewing the German *Privatpension*), inserting his own architectural design into the debate on high-rise dwellings of the future (fig. 5.14).[27] For his boardinghouse, Hilberseimer proposed two differently sized units — a living room, bath, and narrow, trainlike "sleeping cabin," and a larger variant with living room, bath, and regular-size bedroom with double bed. For this dwelling typology, he envisioned common facilities and services for all the residents, including cleaning and a central kitchen that would have the same quality food as a good restaurant.[28] Hilberseimer was writing in an extremely unstable economic climate of boom-and-bust cycles of severe recession, followed by inflation and then restabilization through economic recovery, only to be again subjected to a series of stock market crashes and global recessions.

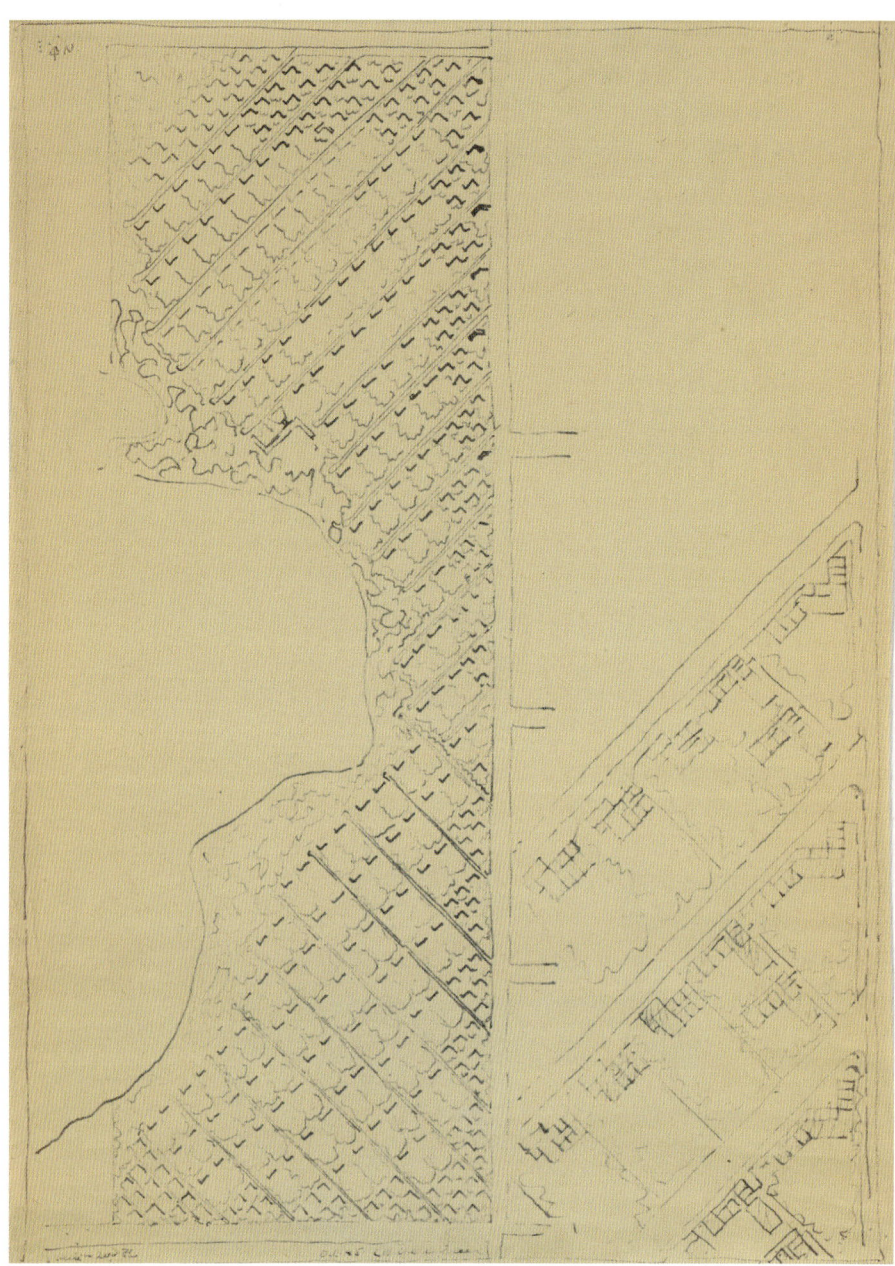

Fig. 5.15 Ludwig Hilberseimer, Chicago lake settlement, 1940s. Art Institute of Chicago.

His research, therefore, into the minimum unit size needed to house people was useful in terms of conceptualizing its ability to minimize the domestic requirements of working people and, perhaps, provide the most pared-down, inexpensive space for single people, the working poor, or the elderly, without necessitating sharing space with others.

The High-Rise: Hopes for Architecture's Reproducibility and Mass Production

Observing the death of the aura in Hilberseimer's highly reproducible architecture, K. Michael Hays notes that "the auratic architectural object is systematically and utterly defeated by techniques of reproduction now radically

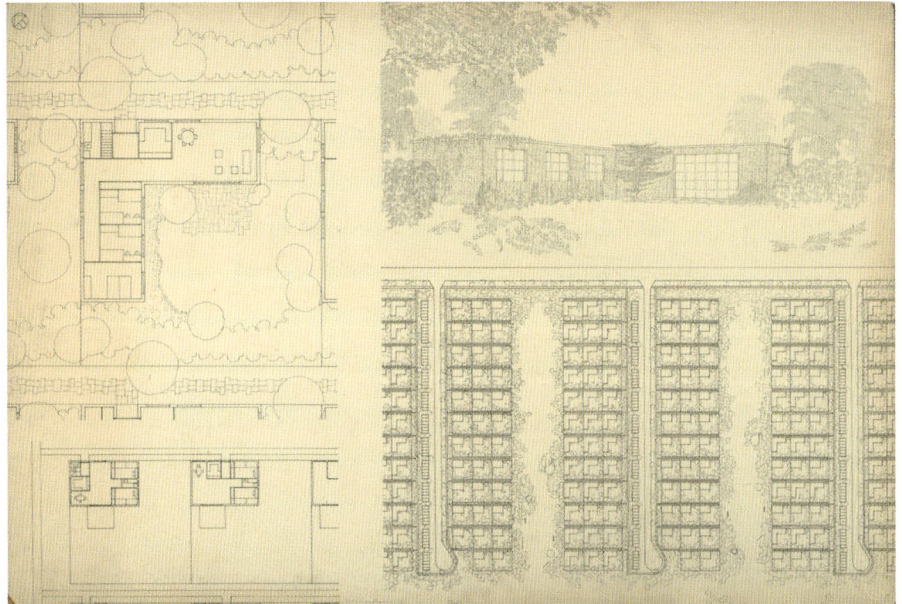

Fig. 5.16 Ludwig Hilberseimer (with Alfred Caldwell), Chicago L-shaped and rectangular houses in settlement units, multiple views, ca. 1940, ink on illustration board. Art Institute of Chicago.

rationalized and expanded."[29] This was key in booming Weimar-era Germany—both in the material concerns for the effects of mass production on architecture and in cultural and theoretical critical discourse. This is why Hilberseimer's Berlin-era entry for the Chicago Tribune building competition, although offices, not housing, is compelling (see fig. 5.6). Likewise, other designs from the mid-1920s, conceived before there was the technical or economic infrastructure to allow for their construction, are significant. Even in his sketches, Hilberseimer aestheticizes a deeply rational thought process and puts it on display as seemingly endlessly combined units (figs. 5.15, 5.16). The aura of these designs is one not attached to the unique object, as Walter Benjamin would desire; but rather, I would argue, their allure is their enticing sameness, their visualizations of reproducibility, and their aestheticization of rationality. Hilberseimer's projects' radical rationalization and repetition have, in fact, been aestheticized, even as they make claims to the contrary.

Hilberseimer's designs appeared at a time when architects, especially those in the circle of the Werkbund, were considering the uses of mass production to reproduce well-designed, well-made, tasteful goods, in order to meet—and to some extent tame—consumption. I would like to amplify the connection between reproducing buildings and the production of goods. Hilberseimer was not alone in taking on the rationalization of the dwelling unit, considering the ways it might be infinitely reproduced and consumed—consumed by being dwelled in—a packaged house, no different than a packaged cookie or an AEG light bulb. The logic of capitalism, the remove from the origins of production and the death of the unique object, puts both goods and housing into alignment—connecting the mass production of consumable goods to the mass production of consumable dwelling units. Hilberseimer, by negating the aura of uniqueness seems to be simultaneously addressing the totalizing effects of capital head on; offering, in spatial terms, the potential benefits of the industrial economy in improving housing availability while insulating populations from capitalism's

Domesticating the Grid

worst aspects. While other architects proposed tall buildings, none were as rationalized, as stark, as powerful in their relentlessness, nor so aligned with factorylike precision and sameness, as Hilberseimer's. One of his particular contributions is displayed in his Berlin-era High-Rise City project, in that it was intended to house workers and function as their place of work—thereby aligning the two (reproducible buildings intended for the reproducers of objects) in key ways that he continued, in different registers, for the rest of his career (see figs. 5.4, 5.5).

In interwar and postwar Chicago, with its building boom and influx of workers coming north to toil in its factories, a further alignment can be discerned between objects being mass produced (Sears refrigerators, Schwinn bicycles) and the desire for the production of housing units for the human producers of those goods. The scalable, reproducible housing unit connects especially well with Chicago's industrial and population growth in this period (see figs. 5.15, 5.16). Processes of reproduction can be found in both the production of the objects and the spaces those objects might be consumed in—and how the producers of those objects might be mirrored in the spaces; housing units that were, likewise, mass produced. The mass-production of goods is mirrored in the mass-production of dwelling cells. Hilberseimer's drawings of houses, like goods coming off an assembly line, are undifferentiated. Goods can be broken down into *single product units* and the metropolis can be broken down into *single dwelling units*. Neither the mass-produced object, infinitely reproduced, has any particular aura, nor does the individual dwelling unit. The sixteen buildings of the Robert Taylor homes (a typical housing project in Chicago built to address the post–World War II housing shortage), each twenty-eight stories high, are divisible into cells in a vertical grid; the building is utterly aura-less. Between producers, their habitations, and what they produce, there is no dialectical tension; there is just an alignment between producers and consumers; and between reproduced objects and reproduced dwelling cells. Applied to a cleared-out section in the center of Berlin, and thus constrained by the surrounding urban fabric, Hilberseimer's housing seems more folly than urban planning (see fig. 5.5). It begins to make sense, however, in his Chicago-era projects that reappropriate this idea of reproduction in housing; dwellings conceived in multiplicity but nestled within ample community and green space, as well as links to transport lines.

Hilberseimer believed in a future in which units of housing and functional furniture, both efficiently replicated, would be the norm. Already in 1927, years before he arrived in Chicago, Hilberseimer was investigating the automobile industry as a model to mass produce residential buildings intended for a large number of inhabitants. "Due to its production methods, the entire construction industry is calling for typification," he writes. "In contrast to the unique product delivered by handwork, industry produces serially and is therefore oriented toward standardization and the benefits this process provides. . . . industrial housing construction will achieve ever more refined forms and more perfect designs as a result of standardization and its application."[30] For his large buildings and his small, L-shaped houses alike, Hilberseimer was not looking for individualized solutions for individual lives but rather to replicate a single, standard well-designed exemplar (typification). This is the aura of Hilberseimer's architecture, where reproduction is appreciated not as material end results but as an aestheticized process. If aura can thus be understood as the visualization of reproduction, in its aestheticization, then Hilberseimer's repetitive plans, drawings, and photocollages are reinscribed with aura, rather than representative of its death. With Hilberseimer, the logic of the replication allows his housing plans to transcend the utilitarian, the instrumental, the capitalist, becoming auratic. Rather than any qualities associated with the individual object itself, the aura lies within the visualization of the *reproduction*, the aesthetics of such radical rationalization.

At Home in the Residential City

In 1923, Hilberseimer introduced his earliest residential city, which focused on urban housing (rather than places of work), conceived for a population of about 125,000 inhabitants. He presented a series of scaled plans for between three and seven family members; each apartment had an entryway, kitchen, bathroom, bedroom, sleeping alcove, and balcony (*Loggia*), which were roughly the same dimensions in all apartments, with only the largest room, the living-dining room changing in size according to the number of inhabitants.[31] Hilberseimer's blocks were designed to ensure sunlight and cross-ventilation in every room, which, unlike Berlin's typical "rental barracks" that they were meant to replace, had dark interior rooms several courtyards deep. To serve the inhabitants, rows of stores were placed at the southern ends of each block. Hilberseimer purposefully contrasts his residential city with what he describes in 1925 as "chaotic American cities" whose structure he sees as having evolved through "arbitrariness." Although he is inspired by their forms, he instead wishes to develop a high-rise city through careful planning, with skyscrapers "consolidated into blocks, uniform in organization and design."[32]

For this 1923 Residential City, Hilberseimer derived his "residential minimum," to be just 70 square meters (or 750 sq. ft.), for a family of six. This design utilized "the minimum amount of space," necessitating that it be "meticulously designed" in that it was "the most common form of dwelling in the metropolis," because families with children had the least financial means at their disposal.[33] However, envisioning nearly fully furnished units, with his built-ins, and a service staff for each floor, it is clear that Hilberseimer is considering a spatial minimum rather than an economic minimum.

Hilberseimer sees the apartment as "increasingly akin to a hotel outfitted with all modern conveniences, which embodies the most comfortable and freest way of living in today's world." But in order for the dwelling to achieve such efficiency, Hilberseimer notes,

> all cabinets and closets for clothes, linens, luggage, dishes, etc., as well as all of the kitchen's furnishings must be built-in. When even the smallest surface area matters, then things can no longer be left to chance. . . . For the cost of the space that furniture requires, one can comfortably build everything necessary in, so that in the future beds, chairs, and tables will be the only movable furniture to be dealt with.

Domesticating the Grid

> The simplification and adaptation of interior furnishings to their proper uses and the elimination of everything will simplify and ease domestic labor....
>
> The best apartment is without a doubt one that contains all that is necessary, fulfills all needs, and at the same time requires the least amount of labor. The comfort of living depends less on the size than on the functionality of the rooms in an apartment. [It] can and must be designed in such a way ... so as to become a perfect organism combining the greatest comfort with the smallest expenditure of energy.[34]

These tidy, spare spaces with built-in elements can be seen in his proposed rooms of the period (see fig. 5.11).

A consideration of the relationship of the cell to the urban organism is to be found in one of Hilberseimer's earliest essays, "The Will to Architecture," from 1923. He writes of architecture's being dependent on "solving two factors: the individual cell of the room and the collective urban organism" in which the room forms the building, which in turn creates the street block, which shapes the city structure, which "is the actual objective of architecture" (showing his cards as a true urban planner).[35] "Inversely," he writes, "the constructive design of the urban plan will gain considerable influence on the constructive formation of the room and the building."[36]

Hilberseimer cites the usual problem that his generation of architects lamented: that the room and its contents consisted of "pretentious luxury furniture and decorative works of art," which tried to conceal the essential elements, namely, the walls, floors, ceilings, doors, and windows.[37] Instead, "the design of the room can only proceed using the components of the room.... The room and furniture are to be defined by their functions as basic commodities. Their systematic construction and design will lead to that simplification which distinguishes every strictly and objectively executed object."[38] He envisions that his units would provide, as built-ins, all of the necessary cabinets and closets that, in Europe, were usually brought along in the form of stand-alone wardrobes and cupboards. His dwellers, by contrast, would need to supply themselves with only beds, chairs, and tables.[39] He opines, "By eliminating decorative furniture, which piles up in our present dwelling as if they were junk shops, space will suddenly be created in the smallest rooms, so that, in spite of its diminished size, the new apartment will have much more usable space than a larger standard apartment, which is however stuffed like a furniture storehouse."[40] With only a few remaining types of furniture to be designed, the architect, according to Hilberseimer, would be able to "devote full attention" to them, making them "meaningful once more, and their full value and purpose will again be acknowledged. After all, furnishings should not be useless decorations but perfect, functional objects."[41] With fewer, more thoughtfully designed objects reproduced as type-forms, the resulting furniture is infused with purposeful value rather than any exceptional exchange value. Once again Hilberseimer's objects are auratic not in their individualized character but in the fact that their replication itself is a foundational quality of their design.

This strict, pared-down approach to form, from the design of a chair to the plan of the metropolis, recalls German architect Hermann Muthesius, who proposed that architects should be involved in all levels of design, from "sofa cushion to urban plan." As Hilberseimer asserts, "The necessity of creating a law of form that is equally valid for every element, for an often monstrous and heterogeneous mass of material, requires that architectural form be reduced to the most concise, most necessary, and most general characteristics and restricted to the geometric cubic forms, the fundamental elements of all architecture."[42]

"A Feeling for Space": Architecture as Transition from Idea to Spatial Form

A key aspect of Hilberseimer's conception of architecture, which spanned his Berlin and his Chicago years, encompassing both the planning of centralized urban towers and individual houses grouped in the landscape — was his articulation of architecture as the "creation of space" (Raumschöpfung). This "creation of space" (Raumschöpfung) was grounded in "a feeling for space" (Raumgefühl) made manifest via architecture, a process of making material form from an idea. Hilberseimer writes, "Architecture is space creation. Its basis is the sense of space. Through material objectification the sense of space is made perceptible — material substance is shaped according to an idea. The formation of material substance according to an idea also entails the formation of ideal substance according to the laws of matter. *By combining both moments into a single form, architecture emerges. Architecture is therefore just as dependent on a spatial idea as on the space-enclosing material.*"[43] Buildings are the end result of the combination of ideas and material form, from which emerges an architecture that would be characterized as enclosed space. For Hilberseimer, however, architecture is the articulation of both the material enclosing of space and the space enclosed. In one of his earliest essays, "The Will to Architecture" (1923), he already sets this out: "The room and its constitutive elements of floors, walls, ceilings, openings in the walls, material and color, furniture and its arrangement, and the connection to neighboring rooms produce a large complex of creative-constructive possibilities. Constructivism generates a new conception of space, creates new spatial relationships, new forms and proportions. By organizing individual rooms in the floor plan, the functional building that encompasses an entire street block is born. In doing so, extensive relationships of form are produced. A comprehensive synthesis of form is made possible."[44]

Hilberseimer, writing in 1929, posits that elements, such as a pass-through hatch from the kitchen to the main living space, which was also used for dining, extended the functionality of rooms. He notes that judicious use of certain materials also aid efficient room use, such as glass panels between the kitchen and the living-dining room, which allow the woman of the house to simultaneously cook in the efficient but minuscule kitchen and watch her children playing in the next room.[45] However, Hilberseimer does not fetishize materiality, stating, "As important as they are, the material means of a building are never decisive. It is, as it was and always will be, the spirit in which they are used, the creative ability and the quality of work which make a building into a work of architecture and eventually into a work of art."[46]

Form, like material, is dependent on its dialectical relationship with space. Hilberseimer writes, "External form and internal space are mutually dependent. The organization of the interior determines the design of the exterior, just as, vice versa, interior space depends on essential features of exterior design. Exterior form and interior space share a common border in the external surface of a structure. These surfaces, as a concentration of both spatial conditions, constitute the actual architectonic form."[47]

These more theoretical aspects of Hilberseimer's work connect directly to his thinking about the single-family house. He writes, in 1949 (in the context of living in Chicago), of the house's importance for architecture, that the house "should be as perfect as possible.... The house itself, based on a new spatial concept and new structural elements, became the real object and carrier of creative architecture."[48] His formulation of the aims of architecture, namely, an architecture "without superimposed forms, an architecture in which structure and form are identical (the aim of our age), where the structure is expressed architecturally, where not the architect but the object finds its self expression."[49]

This is a key concept that melds well with the idea of the mass-produced house, or the house as imagined in the repetitive numbers that Hilberseimer projects in his drawings. In his view, the object is at the center of thought and form, and not the uniqueness of the architect or the specificity of materials. As opposed to the dazzle of the materiality of Mies's architecture, as found in the glass curtain wall envisioned for his Friedrichstrasse projects, the rich wood room dividers of his courtyard houses, or the steel frame and travertine flooring of the Farnsworth House, Hilberseimer's architecture can be characterized as having almost an aesthetic blankness. And yet, once again, Hilberseimer's designs are auratic and should be viewed precisely on equally aestheticized grounds — of reproducibility and intended to support a theory of housing.

The Grid Opens: Mixed-Type Developments and a Plurality of Housing

In the mid-1920s, Hilberseimer began to deviate from his design of centrally located apartment unit housing combined with places of work. A more nuanced mixture of housing solutions began to crystalize in his plans, with his High-Rise City giving way to a variety of building heights and sizes, systematically arrayed, from his 1930s proposal for a mixed-height housing development in Berlin to his US-era settlement areas (see figs. 5.4, 5.7, 5.13). An important early design and intermediate step in this direction was his 1926 Welfare City project (*Wohlfahrtsstadt*), which epitomizes Hilberseimer's vision of mass-produced housing laid out on a grid, with a range of unit sizes (fig. 5.17).[50] Envisioned as a central collection of fifteen-story, "comblike" high-rises; four-story horizontal slab buildings; and smaller, stand-alone buildings, the density decreased from center to periphery.[51] Again, however, the emphasis was on form and an unrelenting vision for the multiplication of housing, not material or design specificity. The large-scale model of Hilberseimer's Welfare City, intended as a schema for a midsize city of a half million inhabitants, was fabricated for an exhibition of "free welfare care," which showcased welfare organizations.[52] This exhibition opened in 1926 in Düsseldorf and subsequently traveled to Stuttgart.[53]

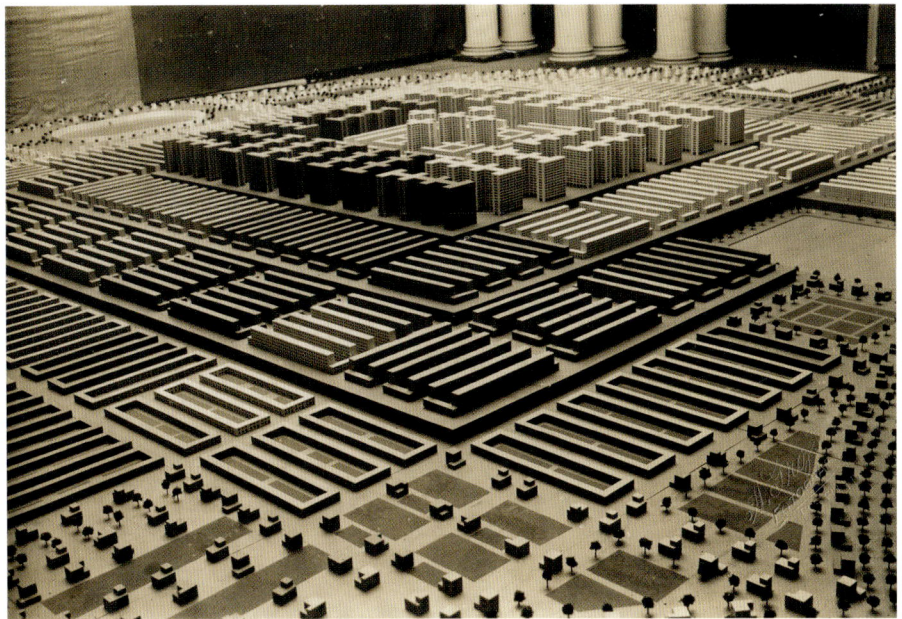

Fig. 5.17 Ludwig Hilberseimer, Welfare City model, exhibit, Stuttgart, Germany, 1927.

Many of his early high-rise city proposals had depended on massive apartment blocks as the only housing typology, while his treatise on urban architecture, *Metropolisarchitecture*, had charted the unsatisfactory history of individual houses: "The detached house, which transformed the metropolis into chaos, will vanish."[54] He writes, "The urban house's small scale seldom permits its construction as a freestanding building. For economic reasons, they are often built in pairs, groups, or in rows as local site conditions and the need for garden space permit.... [They] display a certain completeness and uniformity."[55] The earliest examples, he laments, were "bare, long, dingy rows of houses" in industrial centers such as London, later alleviated by Ebenezer Howard's garden city designs.[56] More promising, he felt, were the row houses designed by his German compatriots Heinrich de Fries and Peter Behrens, which reduced costs by grouping houses behind one another to minimize wasted street frontage and avoid running long stretches of urban infrastructure (sewers, utility lines, streets).[57]

Moving away from his high-rise city, and advancing the ideas of his Welfare City schema, in the 1930s Hilberseimer began to experiment with what he called a "mixed-type development," which included his L-shaped houses (see fig. 5.7). He terms the base living unit a *Wohnzelle* (dwelling cell), whether an apartment inserted into a high-rise or a single-family house, which he similarly considers a stand-alone unit (Hilberseimer terms these very small, flat-roofed houses *Flachbau* (flat houses), distinguishing them from a *Hochhaus*, or high-rise).[58] He draws and writes in great detail about his plans, specifying, for example, ten-story buildings with one- to four-bed apartments, roof gardens, and common ground floor facilities; and individual L-shaped houses with six beds – a master bedroom, two children's rooms with two beds each, plus a small garden.[59]

In another article, the January 1931 issue of the *Bauhaus* magazine, Hilberseimer discusses the ideal new settlement as a *Mischbebauung* or *Mischsiedlung*,

Domesticating the Grid

a "mixed-type development"; here he envisions a plan that has stand-alone, four- to six-bed houses with private gardens, as well as four- to five-story apartment buildings, for those, he explains, who don't want or need an individual garden but still want to live amidst a green environment (see fig. 5.12).[60] Hilberseimer's evocative sketches of these ideas, especially his balcony views, with the inclusion of potted plants on a side table and figures enjoying their outdoor space, underscore the quality of life he envisioned for his inhabitants (fig. 5.18). Although the apartment blocks of the mixed-height housing development loom large in all of the images, Hilberseimer refines his vision of the landscape in three successive balcony drawings. The view from the balcony first coalesces into one looking on clearly delineated L-shaped single-family homes, but, in the final drawing, the inclusion of the finely rendered potted balcony plants of the inhabitants and their view dominated by the greenery below become the predominant elements of his verdant vision. Although he doesn't directly reference mass-production techniques, an economy of scale would have clearly been utilized to execute these designs.

Hilberseimer credited the innovative approach of his mixed-type developments of the late 1920s and early 1930s to framing the problem in a new way, placing his tall apartment buildings only on two long sides, never with closed corners nor a completely closed block on all four sides (see figs. 5.7, 5.10).[61] In doing so, he left the block open while giving all of the rows of apartments the same orientation, ensuring views, ventilation, and ample daylight.[62] Attached to the apartment rows along the main street are low-lying, two-story commercial buildings that were envisioned for stores, workshops, and other necessities.[63] The real innovation, according to Hilberseimer himself, was giving up the apartment building as the "only practical solution for housing problems." He asked, "Why should we not plan housing developments which take cognizance of the composition of the population and thus more fully satisfy the needs of people? Some people, especially families with children, prefer houses with gardens. Others – childless couples and single persons, for instance – like to live in apartments. Why not provide both forms of housing? Each family and individual could then choose the kind of home best suited to his needs."[64] Importantly, and in contradistinction from his peers, many architectural variations were possible under Hilberseimer's scheme, especially because the multistoried apartment buildings could be dispersed or grouped together.[65] The result, declared the architect, was that this "mixed type of settlement combines privacy with spaciousness; it also provides architectural freedom."[66]

From their roots in 1930s Germany, these mixed development plans preoccupied Hilberseimer throughout his time in Chicago. As he wrote in 1944,

> The apartment house could, however, offer many advantages. It could be the ideal home for single persons and childless couples because it offers certain communal facilities impossible in other kinds of dwelling. The apartment house can be built with proper regard for its purpose. It can be free-standing so that those who live in it may enjoy the benefits of sunlight and fresh air. Though the apartment dweller has no garden, he can have a view over gardens. In a mixed type of settlement,

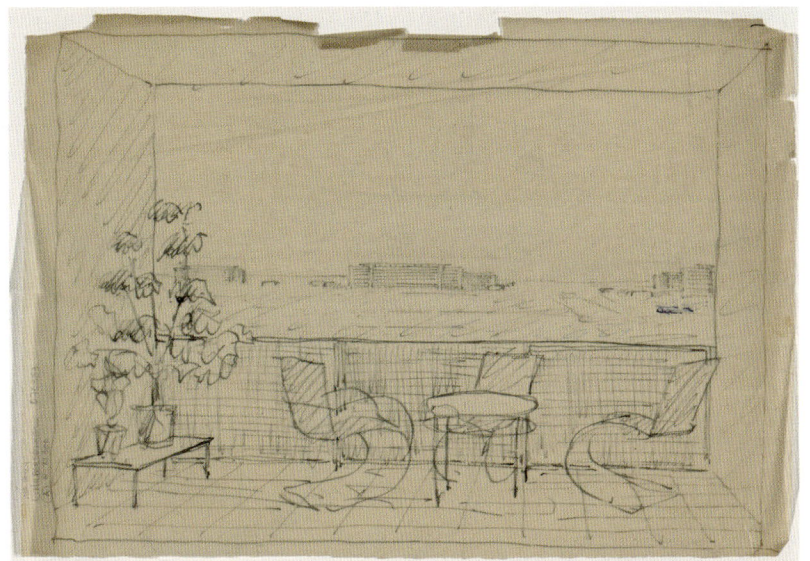
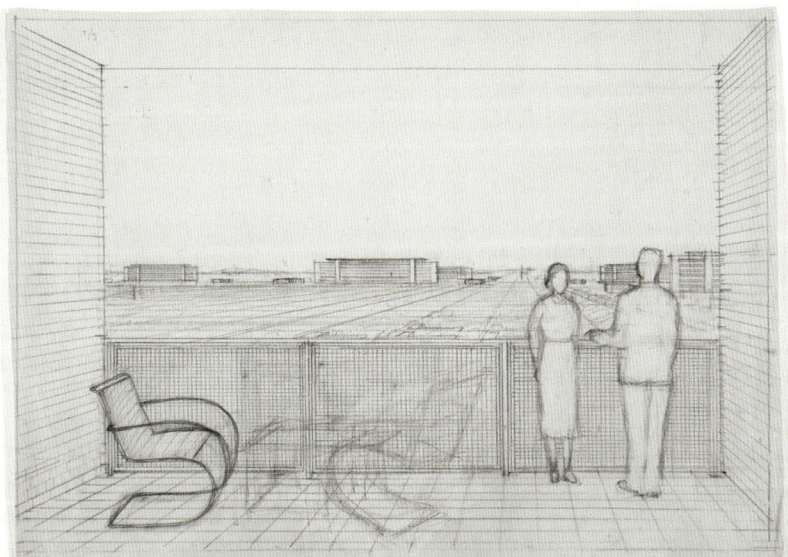
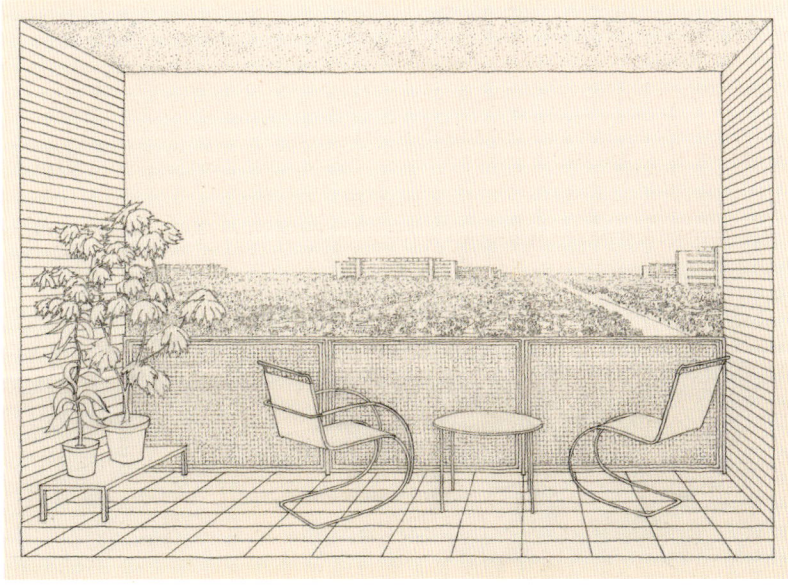

Fig. 5.18 Ludwig Hilberseimer, mixed-height housing development, views from balcony, ca. 1930.

where one-family houses are placed in the vicinity of apartment buildings, leaving open spaces between, such garden outlooks are easy to arrange. By building such mixed settlements, it is possible to meet the requirements both of single tenants and of families.[67]

While he had been experimenting in combining both single-family homes and apartment towers, by the time he reached America, he had, for the most part, given up his 1920s-era visions of tower after tower as an urban dwelling solution. In the United States, Hilberseimer disavowed his earlier block designs as a path forward. He does contextualize and justify these earlier projects, mentioning in his 1944 book, *The New City*, the "street and block system which was used in Egyptian cities four thousand years ago" and pointing out that the "function of the block has been the same at all times. It serves to group houses together, to connect them by means of streets, and to connect these with the entire street system," which until his present day, "functioned admirably."[68] Yet, continuing, he characterizes this "once perfect system" as questionable and even dangerous, writing, "We are beginning to consider and try out modifications of, and even departure from, the block system. We are trying especially to solve the problem created by the speeding automobile – the dangerous intersection."[69] Instead he suggests that two to eight – or even more – blocks could be put together, reducing streets and limiting a given area's intersections to four, cut down from fifteen.[70] He proposes creating a large park area in the center (with a school and a playground), surrounded by the blocks, each of which, uninhibited by the street patterns, could be optimally orientated to the sun (see fig. 5.13).[71] Hilberseimer's grid remains key, inhabited at various scales.

Hilberseimer was against expanding the density of the city core. Instead, he envisioned new settlements, especially in and around Chicago, laying out his ideas in a series of books on urban planning. He penned his first major treatise in English, *The New City*, in 1944, just six years after he arrived in the United States. It was followed five years later by *The New Regional Pattern* (1949) and six years after that by *The Nature of Cities* (1955), thereby completing a trio of meaningful volumes in just over a decade. A major focus of these books is the future of cities and how to distribute them, concentrating on what he terms "the settlement unit" (see figs. 5.8, 5.13). As Hilberseimer explains in 1944, "We can never arrive at an organic city structure by merely multiplying city blocks. Such a procedure only increases the traffic moving toward the city center. We need a new city element to replace the archaic block or gridiron system. The structure of this new settlement unit should permit, not only a general solution of all the different parts of the city and their relation to each other, but also free and unhindered urban growth."[72] This book, *The New City*, is key in that it lays out Hilberseimer's teaching and also his plans for future city rehabilitation and development, using Chicago as the base. Therein, he reconciles the idea of the city and without doing away with the grid, proposes a decentralized city that helps protect against aerial bombardment, an urban grid set in the landscape. He himself acknowledges this turn, noting, "It has taken time to arrive at the basic principles of City Planning, and many years of thought and work to evolve a solution in accordance with them. The first diagrams I made, some 20 years ago, dealt over-much with the metropolis and its traffic problems. In those days I made plans for skyscraper cities. Later I became interested in the considerably more important problems of sunlight, prevailing winds, small houses and gardens, and the human aspects of planning. I studied all the different problems involved, and developed planning principles out of the needs of life and the nature of things, and arrived at the solution presented in this book."[73]

In "Chicago – Urbs in Horto," an unpublished manuscript, he elaborates, "Chicago grew without a plan. The gridiron system, very convenient for selling land in advance of growth, determined the street pattern and was, because it made no discrimination, a guide to chaos. Of Chicago's 212 square mile city area approximately more than a quarter is streets and alleys. What a waste of space, what a waste of money, and in addition, what a danger for the people. Since the advent of motor vehicles, every corner is a death trap."[74] He proposes a solution: "The streets within such a unit would be closed-end streets. Through traffic is thus avoided. It would be, however, possible to drive to each house. The central street would lead to a main traffic street connecting the unit with others, as well as with the whole city."[75]

The unit remained a key, overarching organizational tool:

> Residential, working and recreation areas are the main elements of any city. The problem is to relate these different areas to each other so that each one fulfills its function best and is within walking distance of the others, in order to eliminate local means of mechanical transportation. Such a part we shall call a unit. A unit would be surrounded by a park, its natural recreation area, accessible without crossing streets, and in which schools and other public buildings would be located. The size of such a unit would be determined by walking distance, which nowhere would exceed fifteen to twenty minutes. The number of people living within such a unit would depend on the density of population which could vary, and would be determined by the factories, offices, etc., which belong to it. But there are other factors which will have a determining influence. As a unit would contain all the essentials of a community, its population should be large enough to meet the requirements of the individual as well as of the community life, to provide for variety and diversity and to make possible the maintenance of the necessary communal, cultural and hygienic institutions, as well as to furnish proper arrangements for the distribution of goods. But it should also be small enough in population to maintain an organic community life, so that democracy could prevail, and each individual could be a participant in community activities.[76]

Room to Grow: From the Row House to Stand-Alone Single-Family House

Row houses were Hilberseimer's point of entry into low-density housing and represent a key design transition for him between his dense high-rises and the individual houses with outdoor space. He worked on a series of row house designs

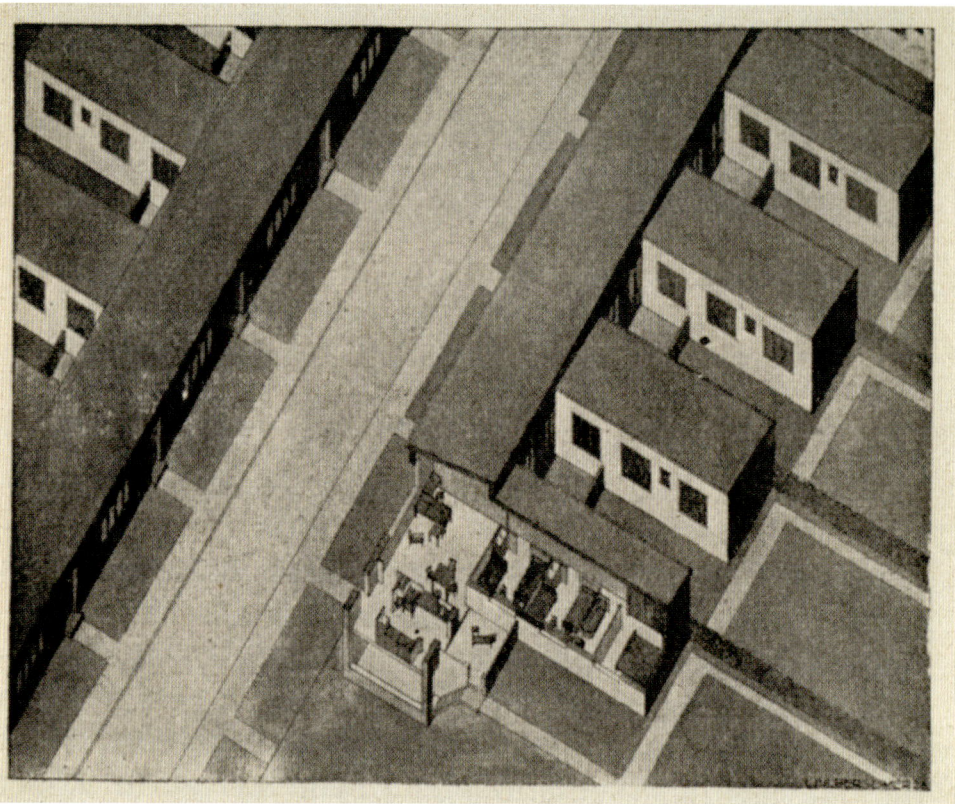

Fig. 5.19 Ludwig Hilberseimer, single-family row house design for Biesenhorst Siedlung, 1928, Berlin.

throughout the 1920s, with their carefully, and minimally, laid out rooms and furnishings. His earliest row houses date from around 1924, published in *Grosstadtbauten* (*Metropolis Building*) of 1925 and *Groszstadtarchitektur* (*Metropolisarchitecture*) of 1927. Most of his designs had the same provisions and a similar layout; an example from 1928, a single-family row house design for the Biesenhorst estate in Berlin, shows his typical planning, featuring a double-height living room, connected to a small kitchen, with sleeping accommodations for six individuals (two bedrooms with two single beds and a master bedroom), a terrace, and a grassy yard (fig. 5.19).

Hilberseimer, in his own row house designs, sought to move away from what he viewed as an "amorphous," "flat" character of earlier row houses, to which decorative elements were often affixed in an effort ameliorate their monotonous design; instead he proposed that by "gathering individual houses into groups, a three-dimensional arrangement of masses emerges as a result of the projection and recession of the houses themselves; that is, a powerfully accentuated corporeality becomes possible."[77] This can be seen in a design from 1924 that he featured in his book, *Metropolisarchitecture*, in which each row house featured an open, double-height living room, separate study/office, dining room and kitchen; and on the upper floor, a rooftop terrace, a family bathroom, and four bedrooms, three of which could hold no more than a single bed.[78] Hilberseimer termed these spaces not "bedrooms," but "sleeping cabins," a key indicator of how he was conceiving of the spatial layout and efficiency of this housing type (see fig. 5.11). These row houses could then be aggregated for an economy of scale.

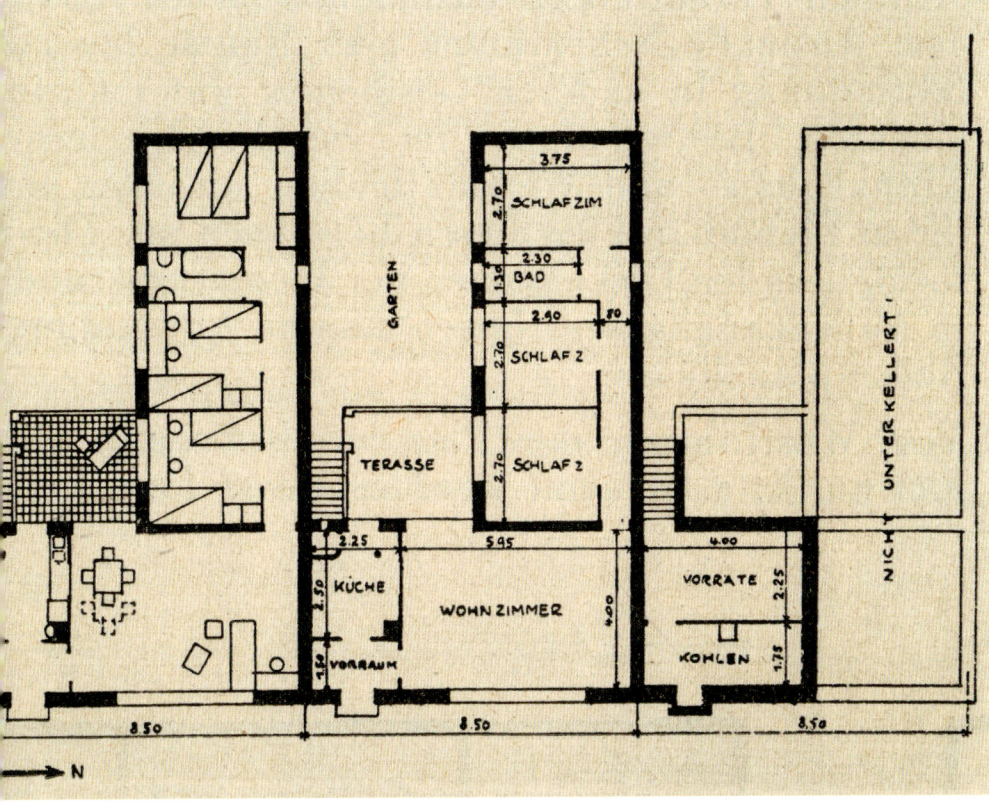

By being attuned to opportunities for economic savings, Hilberseimer, through these designs utilizing projection and recession, not only eliminates the need (in his view) for applied decorative motifs but allows the design to represent "systematically executed typification," resulting in a form that is the embodiment of an organism.[79] Again, this concept of "typification" is important for understanding Hilberseimer's thinking about systematizing units of housing. Here, in the context of row housing, like elsewhere in Hilberseimer's designs, what at first might appear as schematization or a fixed, repetitive solution with little variation, should be understood, instead, as "typification." Typification, in this instance, was an economically sensitive solution that offered visual variation on the exterior and flexibility on the interior. Rather than employing a monotonous linear perspective for row houses, Hilberseimer saw the groupings of housing as an organism, structured around the concept of typification.[80]

One unusual deviation from Hilberseimer's vision for row houses in a dense urban area, or as part of a larger settlement in which the row houses are offset with larger apartment buildings, are his designs for Evanston in the 1940s.[81] Here, in the context of a small suburban city just north of Chicago, he presents a series of connected double houses. Rather than understanding them as less dense than his propositions for more urban settings, presumably envisioned for a single land plot, they may be viewed as a *more dense* solution than the predominant housing typology found in Evanston: the single-family home.

After moving away from exclusively high-rise housing proposals to the decreased density of the row house, it was a short next step, albeit unusual in modern architectural circles of the period, for Hilberseimer to propose single-family

Domesticating the Grid 183

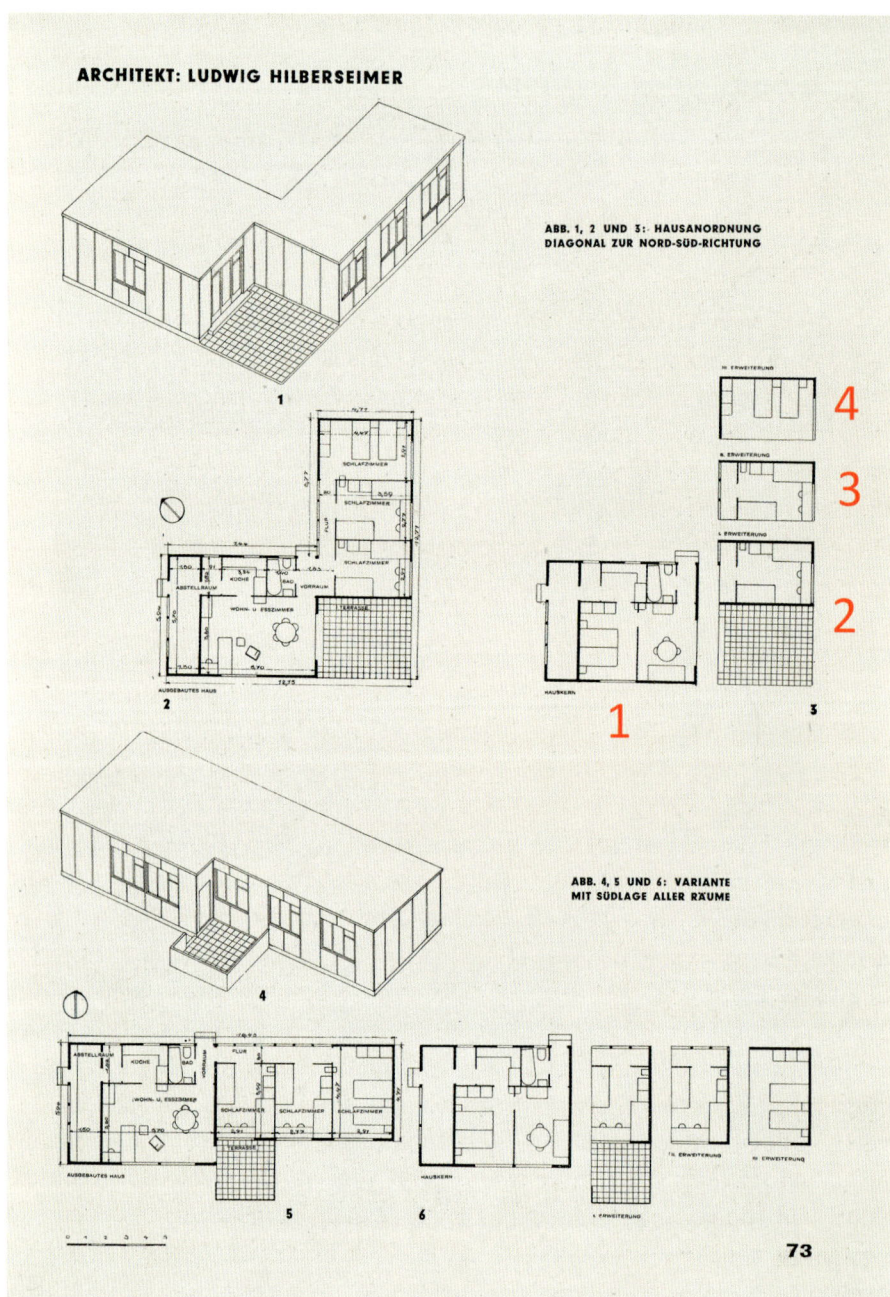

Fig. 5.20 Ludwig Hilberseimer, growing house, 1930–31 (red numbers added to show growth stages). From Martin Wagner and Otto Bartning, *Das wachsende Haus*, 1932.

housing. His small house's debut comes from an unlikely publication — his 1927 *Metropolisarchitecture* — underscoring the ways in which the single-family home was very much conceived by Hilberseimer as an *urban* — not *suburban* — solution. As Hilberseimer writes, "The conditions of the metropolis have given rise to the small urban house as well as the tenement."[82] Proposals for orderly yet seemingly infinitely sprawling layouts of small single-family homes ensued. Much in the same manner that he designed his high-rises, hotel, and boardinghouse prototypes, in keeping with the idea of typification, Hilberseimer envisioned an undifferentiated, scalable typology. His renderings included the overall site plan with the houses set in a repeating pattern, often accompanied with detailed floor plans, and a perspective drawing (see figs. 5.7, 5.16). Each L-shaped prototype

184   Chapter 5

seems infinitely reproducible – in both material form and also ideologically. "The house as commodity" was the motto Hilberseimer applied to the single-family dwelling he showcased at the 1927 Weissenhof Estate.[83]

Importantly, Hilberseimer differentiates between his typologies: "row houses," "L-shaped houses," and what he calls a "freestanding house" (*freistehendes Haus*), the latter being a house that would cost more in land allocation, infrastructure, and materials, and thus, he proposes, would benefit from incorporating Ford's techniques of mass production into the building industry (see fig. 5.12).[84] While each of the three housing types is roughly the same size in terms of number of bedrooms and overall square meters/feet, each typology offers a different amount of direct light, sound insulation (owing to distance from neighbors), and outdoor space.[85] One example in the "freestanding house" category was a small residence Hilberseimer designed in 1931 while teaching at the Bauhaus in Dessau, which he called "Die Kleinstwohnung im Treppenlosen Hause," published in the Bauhaus's own journal.[86] Another early, stand-alone, small house variant was a grouping of narrow, one-story houses with rounded roofs, from about 1922–23, for which only drawings exist.[87]

In 1932, just prior to his emigration to the United States, Hilberseimer further developed his small house concept as part of his participation in a group exhibition and book centered on the idea of the "growing house" (*wachsende Haus*), organized by the urban planner Martin Wagner (fig. 5.20).[88] All of the participants, among whom was Walter Gropius, designed houses with a small core that were accompanied by additional plans, so that each house could "grow," that is, it could expand in size as the family expanded in number. Set on generous plots of land, not only was there ample space for the house to grow, but also for the dwellers to put in a sizable garden, akin to Gropius's Törten Housing Estate (1926–28, Dessau) with its long garden plots, and other working-class settlements of the period.

Hilberseimer's "growing house" entry began with a simple, rectangular core consisting of a master bedroom, living/dining room, bathroom, and kitchen (see fig. 5.20, no. 1). The first growth spurt extended from this core, yielding a terrace and a second bedroom with two single beds (see no. 2). In the next expansion, the house began to take on Hilberseimer's L-shape, adding another room with two single beds while removing the partition wall between the original master bedroom and the living-dining room, thereby doubling the communal space but yielding no net gain in terms of bedrooms (see no. 3). The final extension added yet another bedroom with two single beds (see no. 4).[89] The house was made of wood and heated by a coal oven, although Hilberseimer indicates that he would have preferred modern central heating. Two reasonable prices were offered to the public, envisioned if it was put into serial production: 2,500M for the starter size, rising to 4,500M for the house at its fullest expansion, about a year's wages for a white-collar worker.[90]

The growing house connects to a larger point regarding Hilberseimer's work, and the received notion of it. Although he at times seems to be the master of monotony, and his drawings and renderings are replete with what appears to be, mind-numbingly, the same house repeated ad nauseam, formalism does not have to be fixed, and for Hilberseimer it was not. Modernism as a larger

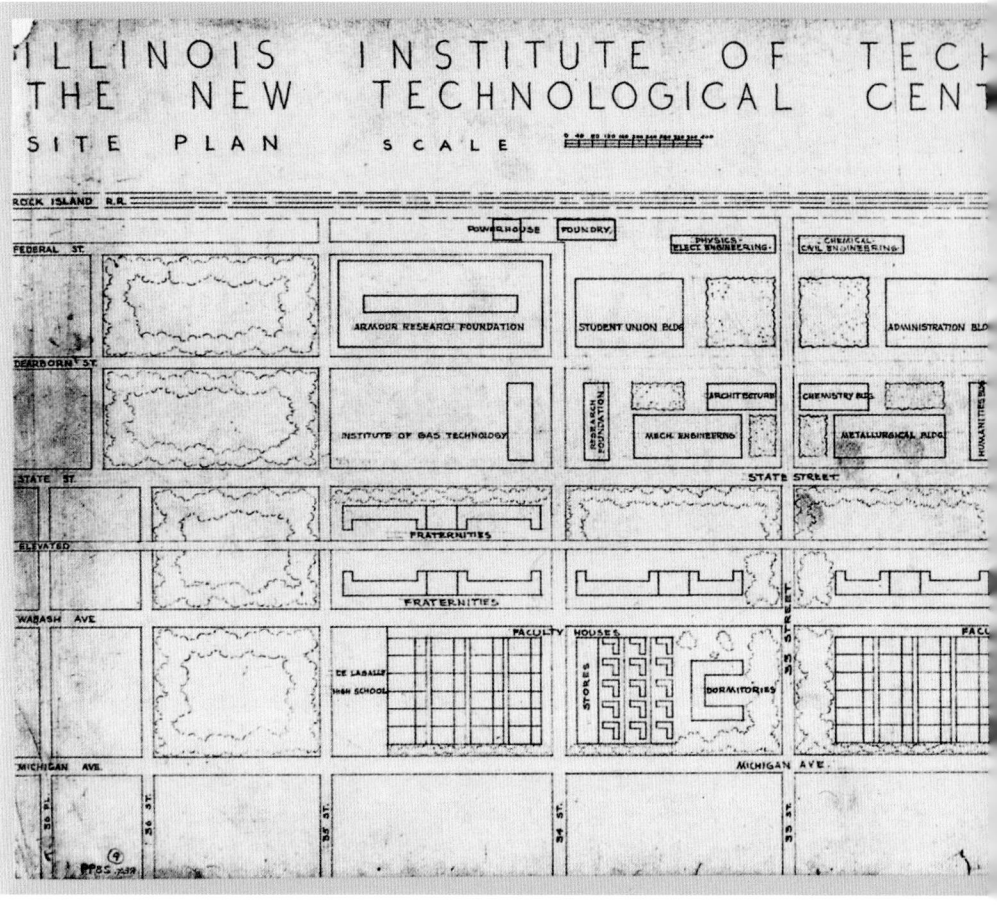

Fig. 5.21. Ludwig Mies van der Rohe and Ludwig Hilberseimer, IIT Master Plan, Chicago, site plan, ca. 1944, showing Hilberseimer's and students' plans for south of State Street student dormitories, apartments, faculty row houses, individual houses, and amenities.

movement, in housing and urbanism, as originally intended by its protagonists, was less fixed and more anticipatory of growth and change, than modernism's subsequent chroniclers have acknowledged. His dwelling unit — whether taking the form of an apartment slotted into a multistory apartment block, an L-shaped stand-alone house, or a "growing house" — each represents an anticipatory flexibility in his work, addressing dwellers' diverse needs, growing or shrinking families, and differing life stages. His oeuvre might even be viewed as a kind of formalized informality.

These examples also allow us to return to the notion of typification, and its importance for Hilberseimer's theoretical constructs as well as his concrete house plans. Typification, in Hilberseimer's articulation, did not mean a cookie-cutter, one-size-fits-all solution but rather flexibility within a given set of constraints and ideals. He was interested, as both theory and practice, in issues of seriality, scalability, multiplicity, and mutability, organized around what he called *Typisierung*. Hilberseimer's own differentiation between "schematization" and "typification" further provides a lens into his theorization of his architecture. As he formulated it, the "purely schematic approach to design ignores the needs of the users," and therefore typification, or standardization must take users' needs "as its starting point."[91]

The growing house is an example of this in practice: it bestows growing space — and along with it, economic breathing room — to its inhabitants. It thus

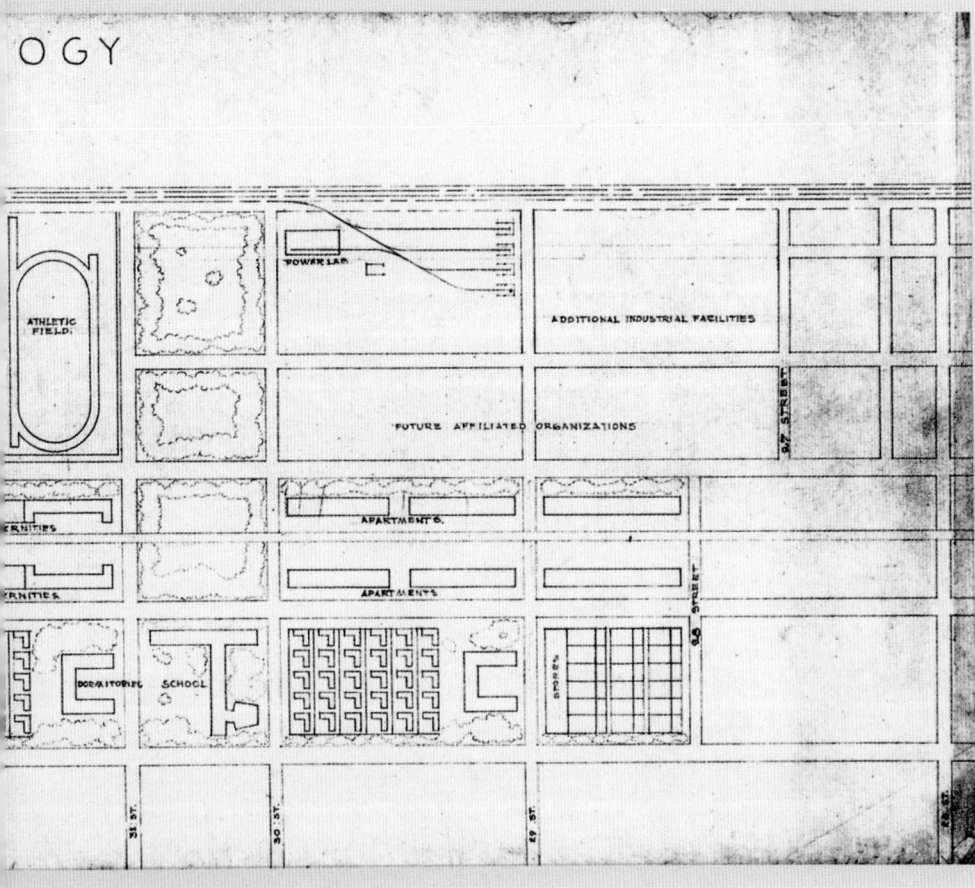

gives them agency and autonomy. It shows a deep respect for the dwellers and their changing needs, as did his inclusion of a few high-rises in every settlement project, to cater to childless couples or the elderly, or those who did not want a garden. Although it sometimes appears that he planned from 10,000 feet above, in reality, he planned from the field. And he did so sensitively, with the potential dweller in mind. He was, above all, a humanist. It was these ideas that he brought with him to America.

At Home in America

When they reached Chicago in 1938, both Mies and Hilberseimer began translating their architectural ideas for the local environment; the campus of IIT provided an early opportunity. Although ultimately built largely according to Mies's designs, the proposed institutional buildings and early campus plans they devised together were early statements, and reflections on, the relationship of the IIT campus to the city of Chicago, the urban policy of the period, as well as the political and economic aspects of race relations in that era.[92] However, it was their proposed solutions for housing — student dormitories and stand-alone, L-shaped faculty houses that were never realized — that serve as important points of connection between their European ideas and the new, North American situation in which they found themselves (fig. 5.21). In 1947, Hilberseimer made

Domesticating the Grid

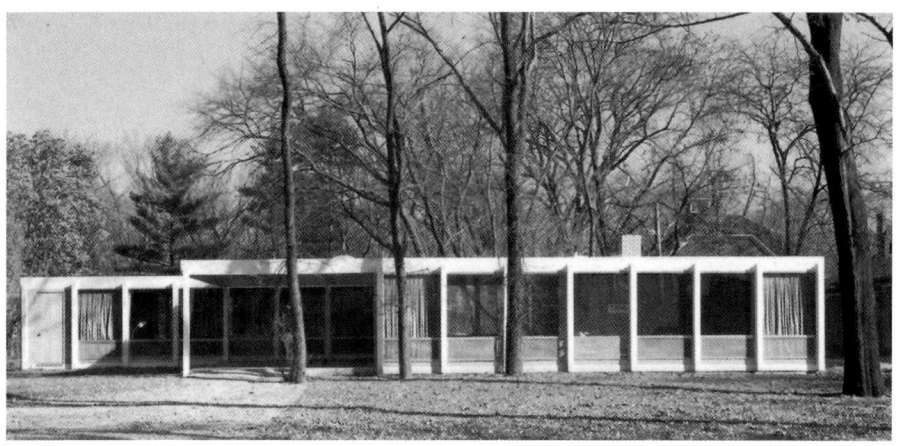

Fig. 5.22 Ludwig Mies van der Rohe, McCormick House, 1951, Elmhurst, Illinois.

significant renderings of IIT housing for students and faculty, a composition with buildings that were two, four, and eight stories in height.[93] He envisioned two dormitories, designed for a location on Thirty-Second Street between Michigan Avenue and Wabash Avenue, that had a capacity for 152 men (sixty-eight double rooms and sixteen single rooms) with attached entrances, two lounges, a dining room, and kitchen.[94] The need for postwar housing was acute, especially among returning veterans, eager to use the GI Bill to fund their education. Another 1947 IIT plan, by SOM, and published in IIT's alumni journal, *Technometer*, notes plans for a ten-story apartment building, two three-story apartment units, and two student dormitories to be built immediately; also shown on the plan were other buildings intended for a later building phase: several fraternity houses, additional dormitories and apartment houses, row houses, and a community store.[95] Apartment units, for students with families, and dormitory rooms, for individual students, were to be prioritized for veterans.

In many ways, Hilberseimer's work in America—both his teaching alongside Mies at IIT and his architectural practice—was a continuation of his ideas from Europe, set in a new context. His projects in partnership with Mies, for the IIT campus and elsewhere, helped both architects smooth their transition to Chicago, each building on the strengths of the other. However, they never formed a partnership in an official capacity, and at times their focus and projects diverged. Both were interested in scalable, modular housing and the concept of prototyping a design that could be repeated in great number, either utilizing the techniques of mass production to produce building elements that could be quickly assembled on site (the direction in which Mies pointed his creative energies) or, in the case of Hilberseimer, in greater planning, with small units of housing organized within a large scheme, but whose construction and material specificity was left vague.

In his first book published in the United States following his emigration, Hilberseimer continued to identify the single-family house as the urban ideal for those with children, writing in *The New City: Principles of Planning* in 1944, "The one-family house is generally regarded as the type which best fulfills the social, psychological, and hygienic requirements of life. It will always be the ideal type of dwelling for families because it connects the house with a garden, a

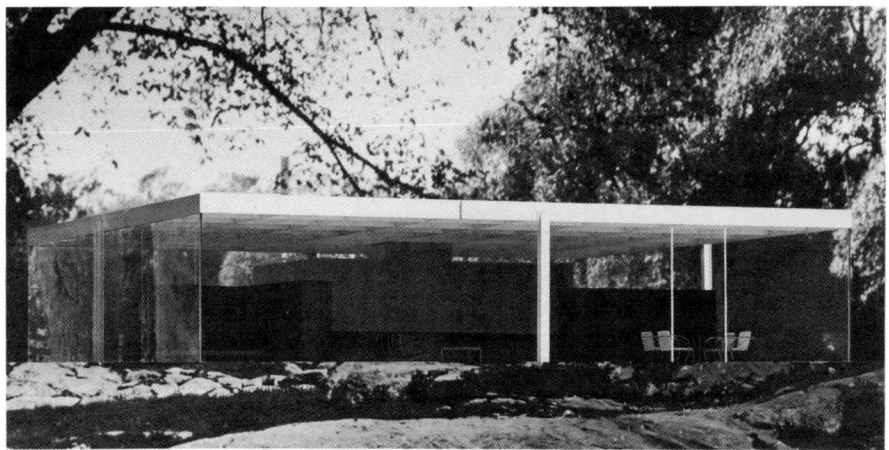

Fig. 5.23 Ludwig Mies van der Rohe, 50 × 50 House for Mass Production, 1951.

playground for children, and provides the privacy necessary for relaxation and recreation. The row house may achieve a considerable amount of privacy also if it is planned carefully and adequately. It can, however, never be quite as satisfactory as the free-standing house."[96] Even as late as 1944, Hilberseimer is planning for an imaginary six-member nuclear family, with each dwelling divided into three bedrooms: a master bedroom and two children's bedrooms, one for each gender. He mentions the importance of a living room "larger than actual necessity dictates" because a "feeling of spaciousness is important."[97] He sought to achieve this spaciousness not only through the floor area size but via windows, furnishings, and their placement in the room, as well as the use of light colors, which, he notes, make rooms look larger.

Several of Mies's early 1950s projects explored small-scale housing needs, and their distinct difference from the direction of Hilberseimer's proposals is instructive. For example, Mies's 1951 design of the steel-framed, modest McCormick House in the Chicago suburb of Elmhurst is a vital early step in the manufactured production of housing in the United States (fig. 5.22).[98] His earlier, likewise steel-frame and glass Farnsworth House, of 1950, was a singular design, and some of its solutions led to significant cost savings in the construction of the subsequent McCormick House. The McCormick House, designed for Robert McCormick and his family, was also a one-off building, whose structure and wall components were ordered from a factory, transported to Elmhurst, and, remarkably, constructed on-site in two days.[99] That potential spurred Mies's consideration of one-story houses for mass production – in conjunction with a second prototype Mies built in Weston, Connecticut, for Morris Greenwald. He also sought to build on his experience in systematizing the construction of the apartment units of the just-completed Lake Shore Drive apartments.

Mies's first genuine foray into designing for mass production is the 50 × 50 House for Mass Production, also known as the Square House or Core House, of 1951 (fig. 5.23).[100] Mies published detailed floor plans of this 50-square-foot house (he also considered the alternative dimensions of 40 × 40 feet and 60 × 60 feet). With four steel columns in the center of each side's glass wall, full open glass corners visually extend the diminutive internal space. The structure was to be capped with steel egg-crating welded to a steel sheet above, and

Domesticating the Grid

services were to be located centrally in the core. Mies eschewed ceiling panels and opted instead to leave the structure visible, with the steel egg-crate itself creating a rich, coffered ceiling, thus simplifying, articulating, and giving artistic expression to the structural system, as one period critic noted about the plan.[101] Mies originally designed the 50 × 50 House for the Chicago developer Herbert Greenwald, with whom he had worked on the Lake Shore Drive apartments.

As forward-thinking as Greenwald was, it is unclear how this design would have worked in practice. An expansive, and thus potentially expensive, lot size would have been needed in order to maintain privacy, given the large spans of glass. However, it is a mass reproducible design – the components could be factory manufactured, with the steel-frame walls and glass then easily and swiftly installed on site. Like Hilberseimer's L-shaped houses, Mies's design has been sited in nature – here its ephemerality is rendered concretely, using photographic montage to imagine it in a natural setting. It is clear Mies was thinking of both natural landscaping and fencing as solutions, as some sketches show a perimeter wall or fence. Most important for Mies, it is a potentially mass-reproducible design – and he put a great deal of effort into envisioning the minimum number of components needed, which were to be manufactured and delivered directly to the site.

Another related design in this period is Mies's Row House prototype, also of 1951.[102] The row houses were meant to have columns welded to the steel fascia of the floor slab and the roof fascia, with prefabricated steel wall frames and brick walls shoring up the ends.[103] Mies eschewed the custom aluminum frames that he had designed for the Lake Shore Drive apartments and utilized commercially available, less expensive, standard window frames, which opened only at the bottom; the top windows remaining fixed. The row house was composed of three units, with the same square footage arranged into three flexible dwelling options, depending on the number of inhabitants and their needs. Plans show the row house units configured into several options: one bedroom plus a study/guest room and a very large, open living-dining space; another shows two bedrooms and open living-dining areas; and a third design depicts a smaller living-dining space but provision for three small bedrooms. It was advertised in Chicago newspapers priced at $12,000, not including the site, a not inconsiderable sum in the period. Levittown houses, by comparison, sold for $6,900.

With the backing of Greenwald and McCormick, Mies developed yet another prototype for a prefabricated steel house in 1954. No longer a three-unit row house, this time the design was for a large, stand-alone house with carport. Designed as a seven-room house with two baths, it was above the mean in size and amenities for the period. Advertisements in the *Chicago Sun Times* proposed sites in nearby Bensenville, as well as Lake Forest, and list the price at $35,000, quite a steep sum for 1955.[104]

While neither Mies's prototypes nor Hilberseimer's full-scale community projects were ever built, and though they share commonalities, a key difference is in approach. Mies carefully focused on structural systems and methods of construction for eventual mass production, whereas Hilberseimer's attentiveness was to floor plan and an overall image of how a future settlement of small structures might be dispersed in a community and how it might function as a whole.

From the Cell to the Urban Plan

Although Hilberseimer's vision for tower blocks and repetitive L-shaped houses might be described as massive and totalizing, he placed enormous importance on the room, as its smallest unit. Furthermore, he described the importance of units, generally, as an architectural form-giving concept. (It is striking that none of his peers appear concerned with this kind of thinking or visualization, although one might have expected it—not Mies, Gropius, Taut, or Mendelsohn, for example—even though there was a significant housing crisis, in both pre–World War II Germany and postwar America and Germany, that architects strove to address.) This connection between the room unit and the urban scale was present in Hilberseimer's earliest thinking. "What the room represents on a small scale," Hilberseimer writes in 1923, "the urban structure is on a large one: an all-encompassing organization of reciprocal needs and relationships. A number of factors must be taken into account, some of which extend far beyond the spatial nature of the city. These are dependent on the economic and sociological structure of the state. The distinctiveness of an urban organism can be seen in its individual organs, which embody this distinction. The general law, in its universality, is represented in the entire organism; the individual building demonstrates one particular case."[105] From this 1923 text, he continued to articulate the room cell's relationship to the organization of the city in his 1925 *Metropolis Building* and the 1927 *Metropolisarchitecture*.[106]

While Hilberseimer had been experimenting in combining both single-family homes and apartment buildings, by the time he reached America, he had given up his visions of a city of towers. He was against expanding the density of the city core by multiplying city blocks or housing density, which he argued would only increase traffic moving toward the city center. Instead, he envisioned leafy, new satellite settlements with a mixture of housing but predominantly single-family homes, especially around Chicagoland (see figs. 5.8, 5.15, 5.16). In entirely discarding his previous metropolis with its inhuman aspects, he was trying to find, in his words, "a more human urban environment and a human scale for the community."[107]

As early as 1944, in his book *The New City*, Hilberseimer states, "We are beginning to consider and try out modifications of, and even departure from, the block system. We are trying especially to solve the problem created by the speeding automobile–the dangerous intersection."[108] He proposed that two to eight—or even more—blocks could be put together, reducing streets and limiting intersections to four instead of fifteen junctions. A large park area could be placed in the center of the development, along with a school and a playground, all of which could be reached by the area's children without ever crossing a street (see fig. 5.13).[109] He called this plan "City in the Landscape" (fig. 5.24). Although he remained committed to the grid and the units that populated it at varying scales, he utilized it as a means of giving rise to an urban community and to housing its denizens, while simultaneously addressing their social and practical needs. His grid and its replicable cells were a scalable means of responding to human needs; a humanist's vision, not the tools of a functionalist architect.

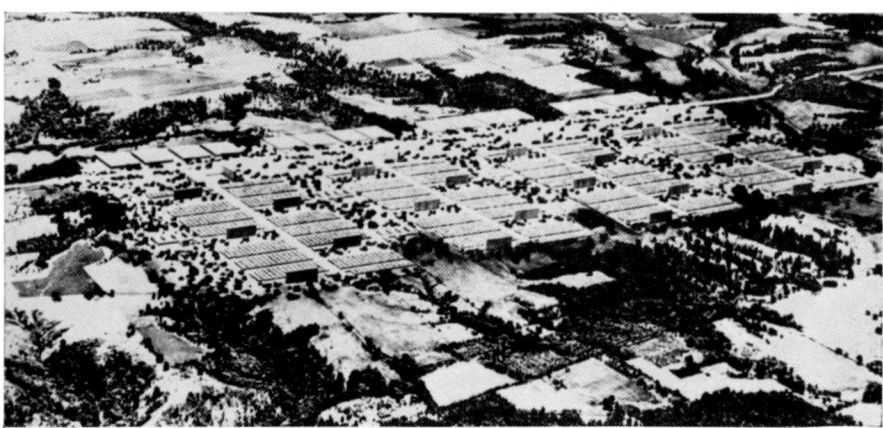

Fig. 5.24 Ludwig Hilberseimer, City in the Landscape, 1944. From Hilberseimer, *The New City*, 1944.

His renderings included the overall site plan with the houses set in a repeating pattern, often accompanied with well-considered, detailed floor plans, and perspective views. Thus, much in the same manner that he designed his earlier high-rises, for his houses, Hilberseimer envisioned an undifferentiated, scalable typology that implied serial production and its associated economies of scale. Yet, in contradistinction to Mies, he remains silent on specifics such as materials (whether wood frame, brick, or steel might be most cost-effective), construction methods, or finance structures.

Taking the design of the single-family house and replicating it outward, the house can be understood as a unit, one made up of rooms acting as expandable cells (and, in the case of the "growing house" designed to actually function in these practical terms). From Hilberseimer's earlier visions for the city to his last projects, these units can be understood in a consistent manner across his oeuvre, whether stacked in a high-rise, or evenly spread in the landscape. Again, akin to Hermann Muthesius's maxim that architects should be involved from "sofa cushion to urban plan," Hilberseimer is concerned with the relationship of the single cell to the urban plan, especially at large scales. In his written and design work alike, he addresses this range, from the placement of a bed to the design of the metropolis. The unit, with its infinite scalability, was reproduced by Hilberseimer in many different forms – cell, room, dwelling, block. He also terms his whole postwar urban community a "settlement unit" to indicate that these cities could be dropped down in multiple locations, effectively decentralizing the metropolis.

Decentralization and Dispersion: The Garden City in an Atomic Age

In the United States, Hilberseimer became increasingly interested in placing his settlements in the landscape, and increasingly that landscape was a rural one.[110] He remarked in a 1940 letter, "If I would not be too old I would like to do it [buy a farm] for myself. I think it is the only solution in this unsecure time."[111] And as early as that year Hilberseimer had proposed the decentralized, yet scalable city model; he asked, rhetorically, "Can this system for the planning of small cities be applied to greater settlements, let us say of several hundred thousand inhabitants, or even of some millions of inhabitants? Can such a huge center of metropolitan concentration be broken up, provided with small gardens and thus be connected with the landscape?"[112] As Alfred Caldwell noted, "Hilberseimer had the big view and wouldn't stop. He had an enormous sense of the thing, a garden city that would encompass the whole planet."[113]

Hilberseimer was influenced by Ebenezer Howard's garden city ideas of living in smaller communities away from heavy industry but with direct transportation links. Howard's book, *Garden City of To-morrow*, proposed dispersing the population into smaller groups (towns of thirty-two thousand inhabitants), set in an agricultural landscape, with ample gardens; these communities were to be linked by rail. Hilberseimer proposed, as Frank Lloyd Wright had done before him, that the American Midwest, especially the open, flat prairie that surrounded Chicago, reaching into Wisconsin, Indiana, and Ohio, could be used to create new, decentralized cities. Unlike Europe, the United States, with its vast tracts of potentially available land, opened up possibilities for stable employment for low-skilled workers in these new centers; Hilberseimer suggested that they could find jobs in local light and heavy industry and also be available for seasonal farm work, while enjoying lower housing and living costs. As Scott Colman has observed about Hilberseimer's ideas circa 1944, "By positing models for the potential (gradual) transformation of the *physical* environment, Hilberseimer strove to *reconstitute* society. He asserted the mutability of urban infrastructure and embraced the impermanence of extant settlements, designing new settlement patterns that accorded with desired political-economic principles and new and prevailing technologies. Invested with the tenets of anarcho-socialism, Hilberseimer's decentralist *New City* asserted the self-sustaining potential of a society reintegrated with landscape and agriculture while maintaining a newly distributed industrial capacity."[114] By around 1960, Hilberseimer had formalized his concept of the city such that, he writes, it would be "based on decentralization and communities with a low density. Architecturally its main feature is the mixed type of settlement, consisting of single-family houses with gardens attached to them and multi-story, freestanding apartment buildings."[115]

The looming menace of the atom bomb greatly influenced Hilberseimer's ideas for housing and cities.[116] He proposed a series of decentralized cities, an urban grid of settlement set in the landscape, which would help protect against aerial bombardment, owing to the dispersal of residential settlements and industrial plants (fig. 5.25). In his essay "Cities and Defense," penned around 1945, he outlined how city planning needed to decentralize to protect citizens from the atomic bomb, aligning regional urbanism with defense tactics:

> Today as always, military considerations in particular are affecting city planning profoundly; the need for protective measures against attacks from the air is leading to the dispersal of residential settlements and industrial plants as well as to the distribution of urban settlements over the entire country. A close connection between these urban settlements and the open countryside could be established. If we find a solution for our cities according to their needs, we may also have a solution according to defense demands. . . . With the advent of the airplane and in connection with the development of atomic weapons, the concentrated city becomes obsolete. Those highly concentrated

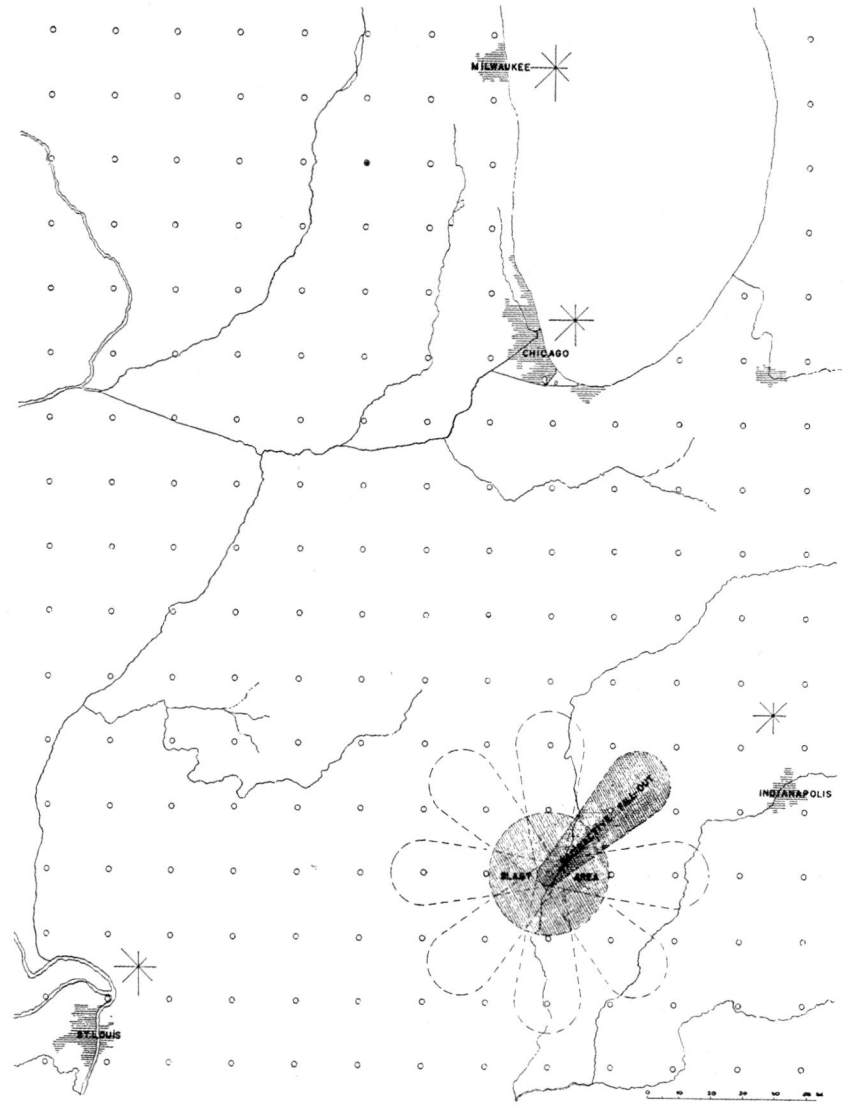

Fig. 5.25 Ludwig Hilberseimer, plan for decentralization, showing the effect of the atomic bomb on size and distribution of cities, 1955. From Hilberseimer, *Nature of Cities*, 1955.

centers of production, communication, and government are very vulnerable to destruction. If destroyed they would cripple not only production but also defense possibilities, and lower morale as well as resistance. Today, security, once provided behind walls, can only be found in the dispersion of cities and industries, and as new weapons become more and more destructive, only decentralization can provide the necessary security, especially when decentralization is combined with the integration of industry and agriculture and the creation of relatively self-sustaining regions that could provide a livelihood for their inhabitants in peace as well as in war.[117]

As landscape architect Alfred Caldwell, Hilberseimer's colleague and frequent design partner, summed up in a 1945 article about atomic bombs and city planning, "We could disperse our cities and decentralize our industries. Then the *city would be agrarian* and the *countryside would be industrial*. The *city would be everywhere and yet nowhere.* The enemy would have practically nothing to attack."[118] In a joint 1944 lecture, "Design to Fit the Human Spirit: The Evolution of City Plans," Hilberseimer and Caldwell noted that "aerial warfare dramatically demonstrates the piteous military vulnerability [of] massive cities and their centralized industries. Consequently, since the communal advantages of our large cities are vanishing, disintegration is inevitable."[119] In short, "Aerial warfare has made city concentrations dangerous. Future protection must be accomplished by disurbanization and dispersion."[120] Hilberseimer, in his designs of this period, proposed specifically to address this vulnerability.

In the mid-1950s, Hilberseimer drafted a proposal for a multipart microfilm (an analog storage medium able to hold a large quantity of scaled-down photographic reproductions of documents, stored on film reels) on the topic of city planning in Chicago, situating the present day in the context of Chicago's planning past and then projecting his ideas for its future development, while also addressing the looming threat of atomic warfare. Its impact, Hilberseimer points out, affected a city's layout more than its specific architecture: "The development of atomic weapons will effect [*sic*] the spacing of our communities but not their structure itself."[121] He outlined studies of damage resulting from a twenty-, forty-five- or one hundred-megaton bomb, predicting that such a bomb would demolish a radius from fifteen to twenty-five miles from the initial point of contact. The scattering of radioactive fallout, which usually occurs downwind, would result in a radioactive shadow extending "over an area fifty miles within the area of prevailing winds," he writes.[122] In considering the atomic impact on his own urban plan, Hilberseimer reasons that Chicago, Milwaukee, St. Louis, and Indianapolis could be destroyed entirely by the use of five H-bombs, but to destroy his proposed two hundred communities, many more would be required; he sets that number at two hundred bombs.[123] He further points out, "There is no absolute protection against atomic weapons, only a relative one. The smaller the communities, the larger the distances between them, the higher will be their relative safety. Decentralization, is so far as planning is concerned, the only effective means of defense."[124]

Hilberseimer was hardly alone in his calls for decentralization, a topic that also had political overtones. At a conference on decentralization in 1941, one speaker, Ralph Borsodi, argued, "Population and production, now centralized in great cities and giant factories, must be diffused. Ownership and control of property in land and homes and in means of production and distribution, now centralized in absentee corporations or being centralized in absentee government agencies, must be distributed among individuals and co-operatives. . . . Among the measures we believe necessary to achieve these ends are the institution of a just system of land tenure; the development of local resources and industries through locally owned and operated independent enterprises, co-operatives and credit unions."[125]

Hilberseimer understood the key parts he was working with – the building, the city that agglomerated the buildings, and the landscape in which they were sited – to be relational and interconnected. Yet the relationships were distinctive, he says: "Both architecture and city architecture are influenced by spatial concepts: the difference is not only in scale but also in the means. In city architecture it is the relationship between the buildings and the open spaces of a city, and eventually, between the built-up area and the landscape in which a city is located. The aim of city architecture is the ordering and sharing of space with the buildings that constitute a city."[126] For this reason, he, especially among his cohort of architects and urban planners, demonstrated a particular sensitivity to the nature that surrounded his buildings, a sensitivity that is delineated clearly in his plans and drawings (see figs. 5.16, 5.24).

Generally, in his postwar plans, Hilberseimer set his single-family houses in a natural landscape and also closely considered the individual plots allocated to each household. In a formulation reminiscent of, but on a larger scale than Gropius's Törten housing in Dessau, Germany (1926–28), with its long plots for individual productive vegetable gardens, Hilberseimer and his colleague Alfred Caldwell envisioned a new type of hybrid industrial-agrarian worker. They proposed in 1944:

> Industrial workers could till a garden and harvest the fruits of the year. Such part time work in the out of doors would help to offset the many disadvantages of industrial routine. It would bring release from indoor drudgery, and the soil and the sun would bring good health. A man deriving part of his living directly from the earth source would be individually more secure, less desperately dependent on wages, less bitterly penalized by unemployment. People following trades that require only seasonal employment, or a part of their time, could have much larger gardens – perhaps little farms of three or four acres with an orchard, chickens and a few pigs. They could depend on the land for most of their living.[127]

The natural setting could do more for the inhabitants. Hilberseimer articulated the use of gardens, parks, and greenswards as a means by which to break the pattern of buildings and streets. In his visions for the new city, he proposed to merge housing within the landscape – "concealing" and "camouflaging" it (his terms) (see fig. 5.8).[128] As he writes in 1944, "Settlement units such as we have been considering, with their gardens and surrounding parks and the adjoining agricultural areas, bring the city into close relation with the landscape – its natural recreation area. The city, in fact, becomes part of the landscape."[129] Hilberseimer is proposing a distinct alternative to urban sprawl. Mies, too, criticized the phenomenon, using the same terms but opposite in meaning, "There are, in fact, no cities anymore. It goes on like a forest."[130] Hilberseimer envisions nature as a tool for protecting, as well as breaking up, the urban condition.

Indeed, Hilberseimer meant to counter this ongoing and unchecked urban growth, the metaphorical forest, with something approximating a real woodlands. His proposed community, with a mix of structures, had higher buildings set in a parkland, contrasting with low, one-family houses, which would be used to "create a feeling of spaciousness and openness."[131] The narrow, confined streets of the city were meant to "give way to an entirely open and free city area," he writes prosaically. "Just as the house fuses with the landscape, the room with the garden, the interior with the exterior, so also the city itself can merge with the landscape and the landscape can come within the city."[132]

Hilberseimer's articulation of his architecture's relationship to the landscape was not just prosaic but key to his vision of a humane and humanly scaled housing solution:

> Architectural values may become possible and the feeling of spaciousness and openness may be achieved. This becomes possible because the single-family houses optically disappear behind the trees and bushes of their gardens and the communities' surrounding parks. What remains to be seen are the few, freestanding multi-story apartment buildings, which gain, through their disposition in space, a new architectural importance and also make possible the realization of a new space concept, based on openness. While the rooms of the houses had a view over their gardens, the rooms of the apartment buildings have a view of these gardens, over the park which surrounds the community and beyond it, over the landscape with its fields, meadows, and forests, its lakes, rivers, and mountains.[133]

He continues, writing in the third person, "This mixed type of settlement was conceived by Hilberseimer in the 1920s when he discarded his previous metropolis with its inhuman aspects and tried to find a more human urban environment and a human scale for the community."[134] He would later characterize his early 1920s work as a "sterile, restrictive, asphalt and concrete cityscape," more an inhuman "necropolis than a metropolis."[135]

A complex project that demonstrated these ideas was Evergreen I and Evergreen II, a leafy cooperative settlement planned for Chicago as a series of single-family houses mixed with several apartment buildings.[136] Again, the care that Hilberseimer took in laying out the projected house plans is noteworthy. Although it never came to fruition, the planning of this cooperative community was extensive, not only in its layout and intended dwellings but in terms of building economically and how the community was to function in a highly practicable manner. Hilberseimer had been approached to design the community in 1947, with the chairman of the Evergreen Cooperative hiring him for its planning and architecture in February 1948, along with the services of Alfred Caldwell.[137] By March, the chairman wrote to Hilberseimer that his "excellent" plans and models had been accepted by the Evergreen Cooperative, and noted with enthusiasm that their "eagerness to occupy the community you have presented is matched only by our determination to overcome every obstacle."[138]

The general planning concepts, as outlined by the Evergreen Cooperative's Planning and Architecture Committee, encompassed many of the items Hilberseimer had long been promoting. The group specified its general requirements and qualities such as "sunlight and greenery; clean air; space; safety; quiet; ease of maintenance; accessibility to rapid and efficient year-round transport; space for occupational use; farm area; . . . shade trees and verdure; community house – nursery, library, school, meeting hall, kitchen; commercial – grocery; community garages for most housing, not individual; community storage."[139] In order to construct affordably priced homes, Evergreen's Planning and Architecture Committee devised a concept for what they termed the "Basic House," accompanied by a plan to build a large number of smaller houses whose only design variation

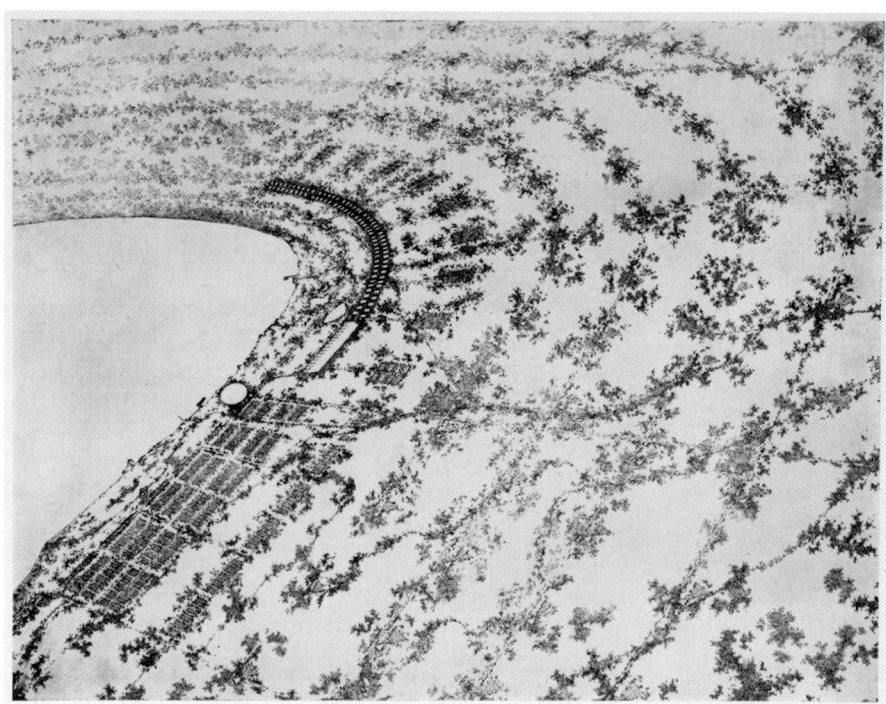

Fig. 5.26 Ludwig Hilberseimer, aerial view of the replanned city of Chicago, project, 1944. From Hilberseimer, *The New City*, 1944.

would be the number of bedrooms (initially only ranging from one to three bedrooms).[140] Beyond the Basic House, the committee intended Hilberseimer to design only two other options, presumably more expensive ones: a "finished and more spacious" house and "individually designed units."[141] It was envisioned that community members would exchange dwellings as their families grew and later diminished in size.[142]

Much thought was evidently given by the committee to the Basic House's design; the small footprint was to be mitigated by large windows overlooking the common green space and in order to remain affordable to working people there would be few variations of plan and shared amenities such as storage (for "goods, strollers, bicycles"), laundry, parking and garage space.[143] The house specifications are noteworthy for the bare-bones solutions aimed at reducing costs. Documents specify, for example, in the bathroom: "floor to be painted concrete if radiant heated," while leaving open the possibility for the future provision for "tile or later improvement" to the floor, and note that the bathroom was to have the "cheapest ventilation possible. (Window?)."[144] Other possible additions, intended for residents to add only at a later date, were for such objects as a medicine chest and linen storage. For the living room, it was specified that there was to be "no fireplace, nor provision for it," although the possibility for a "later addition of wall storage units" was indicated.[145] Yet for the bedroom, acoustic isolation from the rest of the house was considered an "essential requirement."[146] Ultimately, however, the Evergreen development did not materialize.

Another unbuilt project, designed from 1950 onward, was intended for Chicago's South Side, known as the State Street Project. It was perhaps Hilberseimer's most densely envisioned project, consisting of two-story family houses, five-story apartment buildings along the railroad, and ten-story apartment buildings. In spite of the high density, the row houses were each to have vegetable gardens

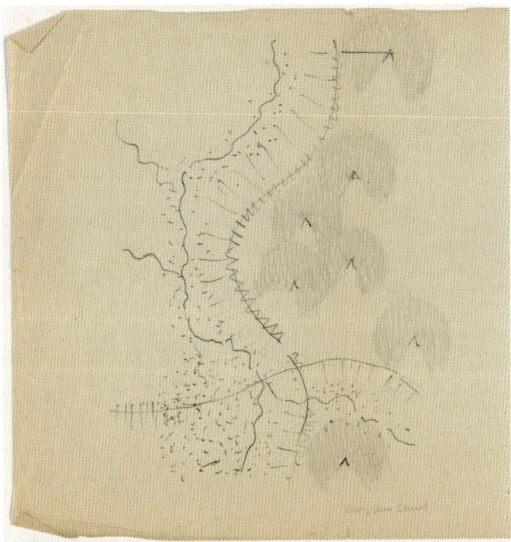

Fig. 5.27 Ludwig Hilberseimer, replanning diagram for Chicago, illustrating fumes, drawing, ca. 1940.

attached to them and preliminary drawings depict the rowhouses and towers rising from a lush landscape of mature trees and vegetation.[147]

However, Hilberseimer's scalar work, encompassing design for the family housing unit to entire planned communities, is perhaps best seen in his ambitious plans for the redesign of Chicago itself, conceived in 1944 (fig. 5.26; see also fig. I.8). He envisioned that the entire Chicago lakefront would become an unbroken park; within this large wooded area would be spacious residences, apartment houses, hotels, playgrounds, even gardens, farms, and camps.[148] Heavy industry was to be consolidated and moved to a canal inland, to the south, with a commercial area to the north, both with nearby residential districts, while a new system of highways and railway lines was to connect all of the parts.[149] The land between these scattered settlements was envisioned to be used for farms and woods.[150] Heavy industry, placed furthest away, was located according to the prevailing winds, so that smoke and fumes emitted by the factories would not reach citizens. Hilberseimer modeled the direction of pollution and translated the data into drawings (fig. 5.27). He placed light industry—which did not produce noxious fumes—parallel to the commercial area, also separated by a park strip. In a lecture, Alfred Caldwell and Hilberseimer presented a joint paper, introducing Hilberseimer's plans. "If the industries cause air pollution, then the location of residential and industrial areas to each other should be determined by prevailing winds. The distribution of all wind borne nuisances result in a diagram in which the sector of smoke is more or less extended within a circle," they explained. "To escape air pollution with its ill effect on the health of the people, the residential area should be placed outside the smoke sector. As prevailing winds are different in every part of the country, different forms and location of their respective areas to each other result."[151]

In explicating Hilberseimer's ideas, the two asked, "How could a city ever be changed in such a way?" They answered their own query with a response that has environmental currency today, but was decades ahead of its time: "Certainly not by destruction, by tearing down everything. On the contrary, by using everything until it becomes obsolete, and by building it new according to

Domesticating the Grid

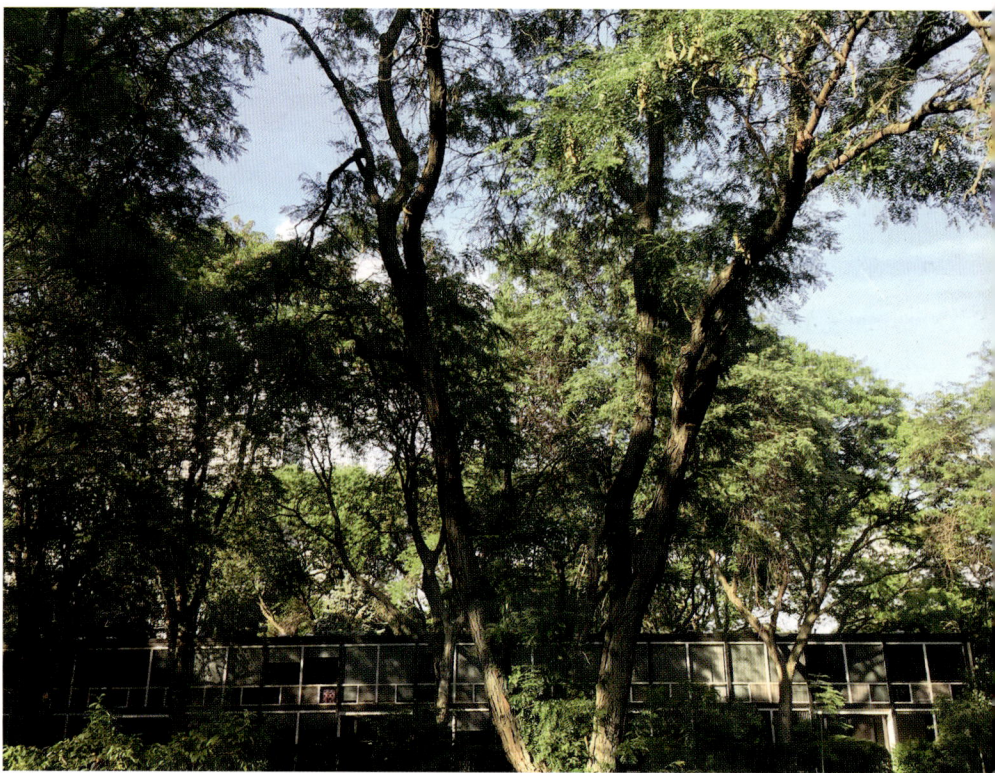

a plan in its proper place."¹⁵² They noted that the city "could be changed step by step, by a careful and patient following of such a plan. Then, the expenses incurred at each step would be a sound and constructive investment."¹⁵³ Furthermore, they declared, "It is not several little things that are wrong, but simply that the city exists without any valid structure, without any principle of being. Through the years it just got bigger and worse. It is idle to speak of parts by themselves, for it is clearly the whole which is wrong. In a word, to heal the city we must treat the disease and not the symptoms," and thus the plans were based on a "structural reorganization of the city as a whole. All the parts are related to one another. Industry, commercial area, administration, residential areas with schools and parks, have been planned and located according to needs and functions."¹⁵⁴

Hilberseimer and Caldwell mourned, "In building our crowded cities we have crowded out the sunlight, the trees and the green grass of meadows; we have sold out the earth, and cancelled out the sky, and made fresh air a luxury."¹⁵⁵ Instead, they asserted, Hilberseimer's plan proposed "to make the city smaller and to liberate space within the city for parks and gardens" via dispersal of small cities.¹⁵⁶ In writing about his plans, Hilberseimer proposed that such a city design would address the needs and demands of the modern day. Merged with the landscape, he concluded, "'Urbs in horto' – the city set in a garden – Chicago's old motto, could become reality again."¹⁵⁷ But, again, unlike Mies, Hilberseimer offers only studies and sketches, lacking concrete plans, perspectives, photomontages, or backing by which to bring this project to fruition.

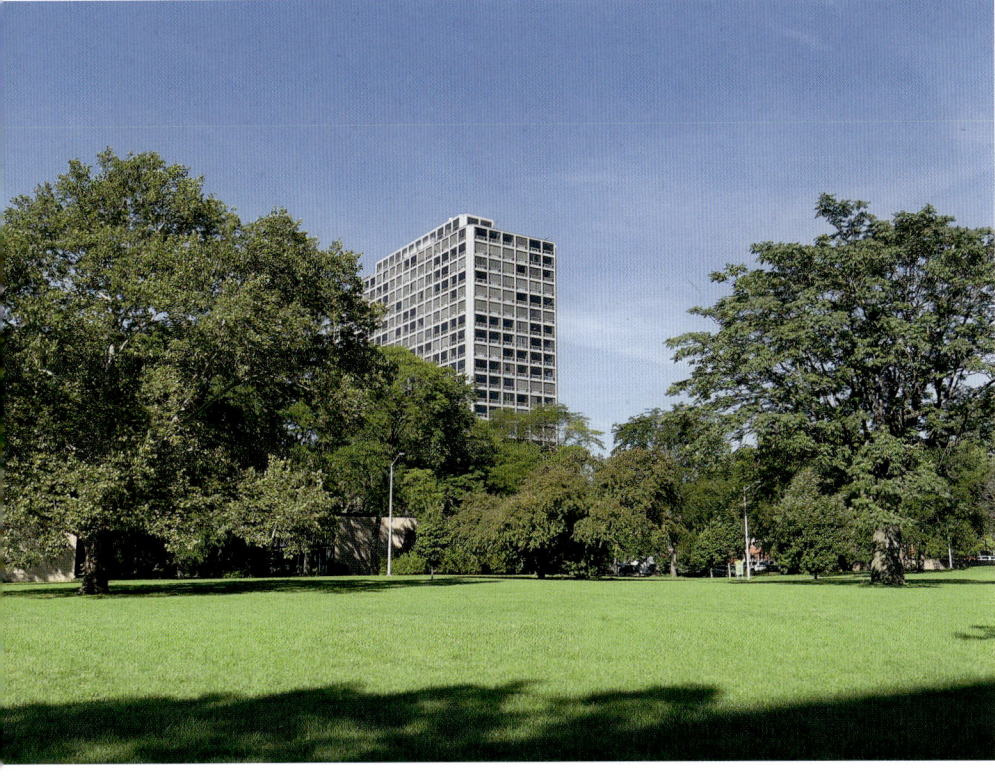

Lafayette Park—at Home in the Grid

Therefore, the project that best brings us full circle to the ideas of both Mies and Hilberseimer – with which I conclude – is that which, beginning in 1956, they designed and built together: Lafayette Park, located not in Chicago, but Detroit. Set just outside the downtown business district of Detroit's center, this mixed development is composed of a series of row houses and three apartment towers in a seventeen-acre landscape designed by Alfred Caldwell (fig. 5.28). Backed once again by the Chicago developer Herbert Greenwald, who was behind Chicago's Lake Shore Drive apartments and the mass produced housing designs by Mies, Lafayette Park merges the two projects – steel-framed high-rises and single-family homes.

An early "Statement of Principles" for the development noted that the community would be open to "groups representing as broad an economic range as possible," and on a variety of terms: rent, co-op ownership, or conventional purchase. Tenants were to be selected based on "character and responsibility," not "color [race]."[158] The statement also warned that the project should not be built too inexpensively, specifying that "every effort must be made to avoid designing dwelling units to minimum standards. It appears unfortunately true that minimum house standards have become maximum standards far too often." And it further stipulates, "The finest architectural talents should be utilized to plan the new community so as to avoid an institutional atmosphere of regimentation and standardization."[159]

Hilberseimer, in promoting the combination of larger apartment buildings set in green spaces and mixed among small, single-family L-shaped houses,

Fig. 5.28 *Opposite* and *above*, Ludwig Mies van der Rohe and Ludwig Hilberseimer, Lafayette Park, Detroit, with Alfred Caldwell landscape design.

had already in the 1930s previewed what was to be the successful outcome of Lafayette Park, which likewise began with a mixed set of typologies – small, one-story, L-shaped houses, two-story row houses, and apartment towers (although it was eventually reduced to just two typologies: row house and apartment tower) (fig. 5.29). Large scale, it was originally planned for 1,700 families, of which 1,390 were apartment units and 350 were two-story town houses. Although the row house ultimately prevailed, Hilberseimer's early designs included a series of L-shaped houses, accessed by car but without through roads, limiting traffic.

Mies's row houses, with their buff-colored brick ends and glass curtain walls running along a verdant landscape, connect well to the McCormick House and Mies's ideas for mass-produced housing. In a press release, Greenwald highlights that the "extraordinary advance of technology can be harnessed with sound architecture and sound planning to give a rebirth to our decaying cities. The city must be liberated from its confinement so that it may be linked to the open space of the landscape."[160] In place, as last, were standardized parts and reproducible forms, along with the economic structures necessary to build.

Verdant, yet situated within reach of the city, with its community facilities and walkable, non-through streets, Lafayette Park, too, takes much from Hilberseimer's plans for an ideal settlement, one that was engaged with infinite reproducibility, conceptually as much as materially, yet still concerned with creating a scalable, potentially mass-reproducible living situation for the postwar citizen.

■ ■ ■

We think of the grid as the ultimate neutral background: in North America, as an expedient economic tool to settle and create land plots that were, on the face of it, equal and available to all; in Europe, as a tool for rationalizing messy medieval, or earlier, city cores. At Lafayette Park and elsewhere, these two ostensibly neutral grids have met, and neither is neutral. Both are contingent. Likewise, mapping – from America's earliest surveys to the nineteenth-century plat to planning for the atomic age – was far from a neutral enterprise. Hilberseimer utilized the grid to offer his dwellers a house with a garden, and, he proposed to use it to protect the populace from atomic attack. Mies upended his grid, stacking units into the sky at Lake Shore Drive – unparalleled views at a moment of unparalleled capital; but many blocks to the south he also, simultaneously, radically displaced poor, urban Black residents for his IIT campus grid. The grid, despite its geometrical equivalence, is, in fact, full of slippages and misfits, displacements and misalignments, superimpositions, operations of subtraction and accretion.

Hilberseimer's constituent element of habitation, the unit – which, in his vision, ran from the brick to the single bed in the cell-like bedroom to a grid of the whole American Midwest – should also be understood as an exilic object, highly portable yet reliant on the contingencies of local conditions. His grids, and the cells that populated them at varying scales, were a means of establishing new systems of housing. His theory of housing, as human-centric "typification" (rather than developer-organized "schematization" of fixed floor plans and

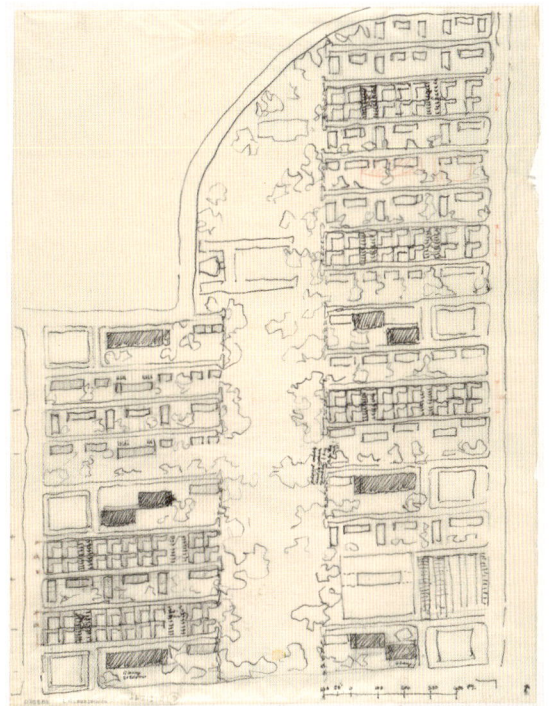

Fig. 5.29 Ludwig Hilberseimer, preliminary site plan, Lafayette Park, 1956. Art Institute of Chicago.

other modes of conventional profit maximization) and his means of design — cells, units, and grids, are inseparable from a discourse of exile and emigration, economics and flow. He offered a different type of spatial, social, and financial efficiency, in the service of his larger humanistic goals. Crucial, too, was the relationship of parts to the whole, both theoretical and architectural — or Hilberseimer's dwelling cell to the city organism. These questions hinged on concepts of controlled and thoughtful scalability. Subtle variations in a module layout may have cascading effects at urban scale, or perhaps vice versa. His work exists at a certain operational boundary between incremental development and sudden, sweeping transformation.

Hilberseimer's projects' radical rationalization and repetition had, in fact, been aestheticized, even as they made claims to the contrary. In his process-sketches, he aestheticized a deeply rational thought process, and put reproducibility on display. It is easy to assume, especially in his period of high modernism, that the rational is not meant to be aestheticized, but it is precisely this pristine aestheticization, not of *production* but *reproducibility*, that was deployed by Hilberseimer — an aesthetic meant to sell a theory of housing. Through the real and seeming efficiencies of repetition in mass housing, he takes us to a certain limit of a dream of reproducibility — one that was highly auratic.

If Hilberseimer's arc speaks to continuities and ruptures between his architectural theory and his architectural practice, and between prewar Europe and postwar America, his unchanged basic desire was to carefully plan for, and then build, sound dwellings that fulfilled timeless, basic human needs. The contingencies and continuously changing contexts of modernity brought new challenges. Ultimately, through the scalable unit — itself a design tool that could be used to produce, and reproduce, architecture — set in a larger grid, he believed citizens could make a modern home for themselves, wherever in the world they might be.

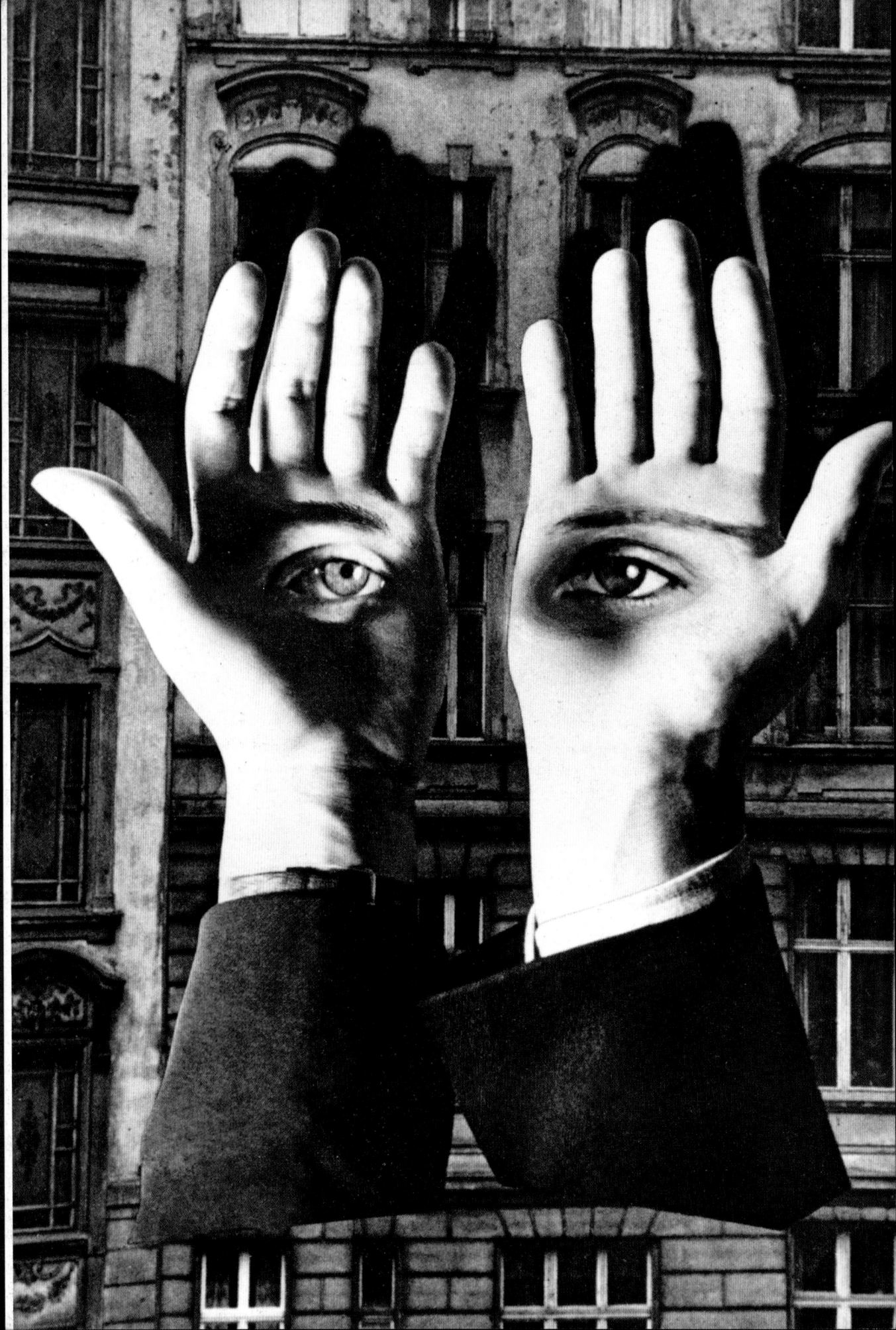

REMEDIATION

Chapter 6

Exigencies of Materializing Vision

Josef Albers's Glass Paintings to *Homage to the Square*

Describing Albers at work on a *Homage to the Square* painting, Elaine de Kooning in 1950 wrote, "Holding a tube of pigment in one hand and a palette-knife in the other, Josef Albers finished his *Homage to the Square* in five hours. Evenly painted in grey, black and white, the severe anonymous construction of this picture does not seem to demand a virtuoso touch. . . . The artist tends to describe his technique in terms of what he renounces: 'no smock, no skylight, no studio, no palette, no easel, no brushes, no medium, no canvas.' (He works on a table in any room handy, and can keep a white linen suit immaculate throughout a painting session.) . . . 'I want,' he concludes, 'to make my work as neutral as possible.'"[1] In the move from the Bauhaus in Germany to America (working and teaching first at Black Mountain College in North Carolina and then at Yale University in Connecticut), the diverse practice of Josef Albers can, at first glance, be seen as a shift from the patently material to the purely visual.[2] Albers did not begin to paint in earnest until he arrived in the United States, culminating in his decades-long *Homage to the Square* series (fig. 6.1; see also fig. I.2).

During the years at the German Bauhaus, his practice was dominated by artworks in glass, with some additional drawings and prints. Albers had also been deeply involved with making objects, such as furniture and domestic goods, especially those utilizing glass. For example, his nested stacking side tables (ca. 1927) achieved their bright colors via painted glass tops, the writing surface for his desk design consisted of an inlaid sheet of glass (ca. 1927, ash veneer, black lacquer, painted glass), and his tea table (ca. 1928) featured a white milk glass top. He also designed a by-now iconic modern tea glass with saucer and stirrer (1925) that was made of heat-resistant glass (with chrome-plated steel, ebony, and porcelain elements) (fig. 6.2). Albers designed lettering in glass as well (ca. 1928). Large-scale, stained glass windows were another key aspect of his late 1920s work: he created a series of major windows for the Bauhaus's architectural commission of the Sommerfeld House, for the Grassi Museum in Leipzig, and for the Ullstein publishing house's new headquarters in Berlin.[3]

His glass mixed media assemblage artworks and glass paintings of the early 1920s represent his most sustained and major artistic output prior to his emigration to America. Early works such as *Gitterbild* (*Grid Mounted*), circa 1921, and *Fensterbild* (*Window Picture*) of 1921 emerged as a response to the paucity of artistic materials available to him during the Weimar-era crisis of acute inflation that occurred from 1921 to 1923 (fig. 6.3). Albers writes about the works' origins, "with knapsack and hammer I went to the dumping grounds and broke glass bottles in order to find glass shards of all colors possible. Then, at my studio, I ordered and juxtaposed such shards to related size, shape, color, and arrived at various groupings, assemblages or compositions. Such works I mounted (beginning as a dilettante) on tin sheet or wire screens. . . . The glass assemblage is one of my very first trials towards some glass pictures."[4] In a 1921 letter in which Albers describes his process, the joy in his creation is evident, as well as his viewing of the resulting work as "paintings": "I am already doing a lot of painting in glass, all on my own. I look for the glass in the wine, liquor, and other old bottles in the Weimar inns. They are then mounted on metal sheets and wire. As wonderful as no other glasswork and studio glass."[5] At first glance, because they have a

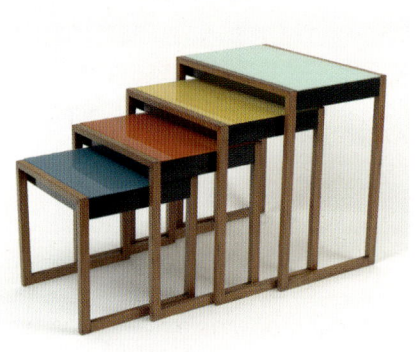 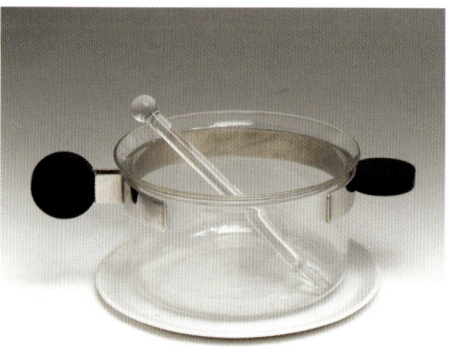

Fig. 6.1 Josef Albers, *Homage to the Square: Lone Whites*, 1963, oil on Masonite. The Josef and Anni Albers Foundation, 1976.1.629.

Fig. 6.2 *Left*, Josef Albers, stacking tables, ca. 1927, ash veneer, black lacquer, and painted glass. The Josef and Anni Albers Foundation, 2000.5.3a–d. *Right*, Josef Albers, tea glass with saucer and stirrer, 1925, heat-resistant glass, chrome-plated steel, ebony, and porcelain. The Josef and Anni Albers Foundation, 2006.17.1

deep materiality and object-ness, they may appear to connect to his domestic design work. However, these works were not meant to be read as small-scale stained glass windows related to his more architectural commissions. Rather, pieces such as *Fensterbild* and *Gitterbild*, which used the term *Bild* (picture, image; but also *sich ein Bild machen*, "to visualize") in their titles, clarified their status as artworks directly connected to the concept of visualization.

From the mid-1920s until his departure for the United States in 1933, his oeuvre was dominated by sandblasted flashed glass pieces. He created two different categories of glass works—those artworks that were opaque and meant to be hung on the wall he termed *Glas-Wandbilder* (glass wall-paintings),

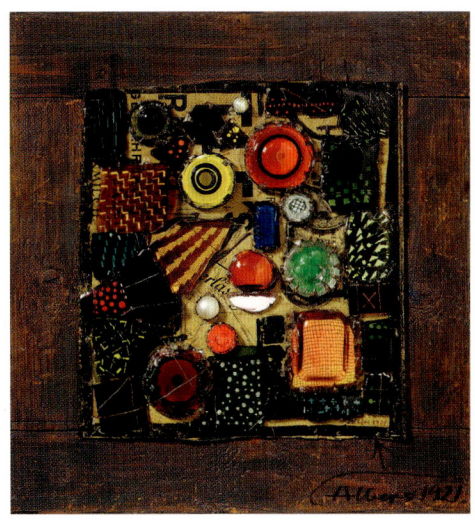

Fig. 6.3 Josef Albers, *Window Picture*, 1921, glass assemblage (glass, metal, wire, paint, nails, mesh, imitation pearls, and ink). Hirshhorn Museum and Sculpture Garden, Smithsonian Institution, Washington, DC.

while those meant to be seen against the light he called *Fensterbilder* (window paintings). However, for both types he carefully chose the word *Bild* (painting or image), which suggests a connection of the works to the high art status of paintings, as distinct from stained glass windows. When comparing his artwork *City*, a *Glas-Wandbild*, to a stained glass window, Albers explained that his glass painting "is made of opaque glass which is neither transparent nor translucent. We, therefore, do not look through it as is the case with stained glass but, because of this reflecting light, we look at it – on or in front of a wall, thus replacing a window in the opening of a wall."[6] In these works he experimented with manipulating the material surface of glass itself, creating layers through various processes of sandblasting and the application of paint.

He often took as his subject matter architectural motifs, especially skyscrapers, building designs that were rendered but unrealized in the period by European architects. These modernists often looked to the tall buildings of New York and Chicago – towering steel and curtain glass structures, strikingly illuminated at night. For example, Albers's *Skyscrapers on Transparent Yellow* (sandblasted glass with black paint, ca. 1929), features a prominent trio of vertical black line columns reminiscent of the modern movement's proposals for multifloor high-rises, while shorter stacks of lightly etched lines suggest buildings receding into the distance (fig. 6.4). The material ground is a translucent and richly bubbled yellow glass. As Albers reflected back on the Bauhaus years, he noted that it was the school's "way of approaching formal problems or material as such, that has made it famous. And the *emphasis on material*, especially its capacity, is my contribution."[7] This careful attention to material, especially its realization at the surface, is the focus of this chapter.

In the move to the United States a radical reduction in materiality and form seemingly took place, which I examine in Albers's most prodigious and prolonged artistic output on those new shores – that is, in the flat planes of his *Homage to the Square* series. Other works of his American years, his earliest paintings on Masonite in the period 1934–49 that led up to his more codified *Homages*, his works on laminate plastic and paper, as well as his architectural installations, are also investigated for their planar materiality. How might Albers's American

Exigencies of Materializing Vision

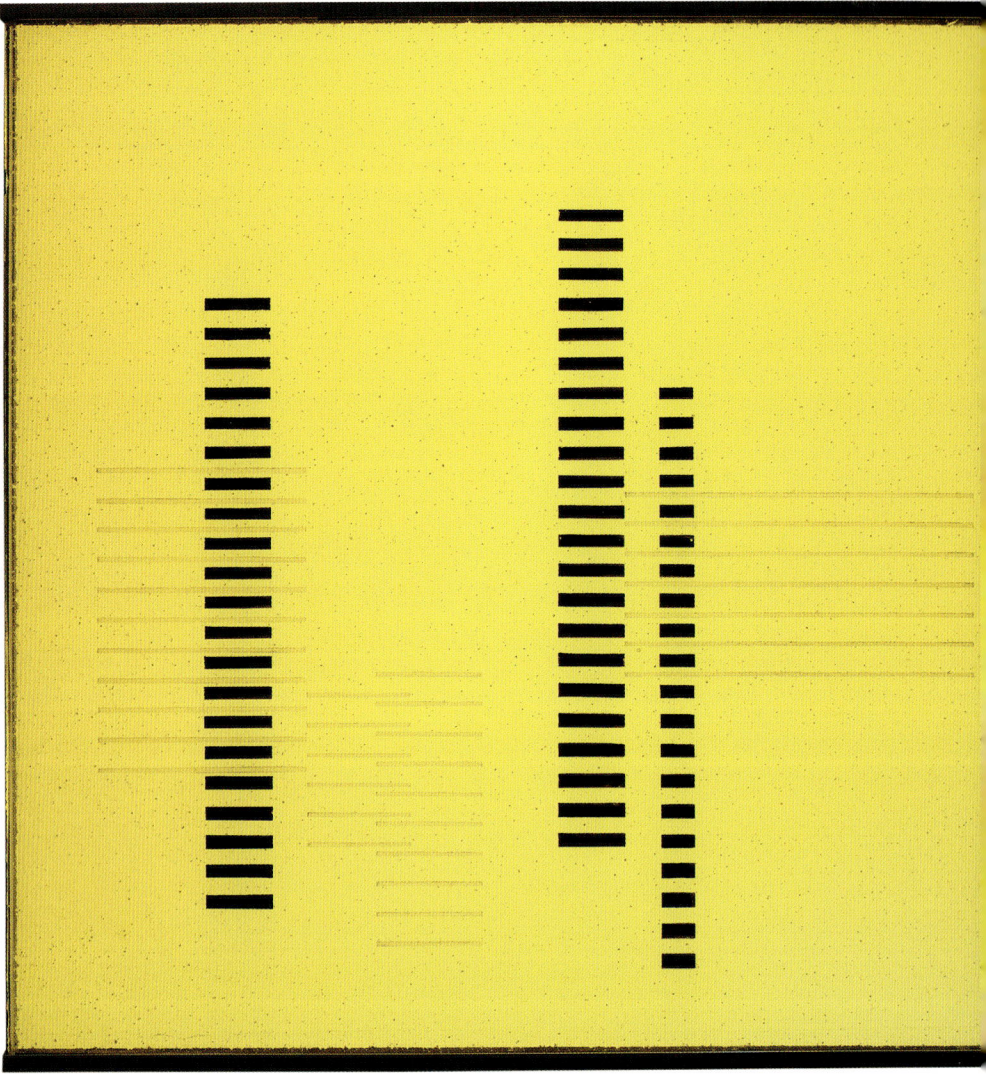

Fig. 6.4 Josef Albers, *Skyscrapers on Transparent Yellow* (and detail, *opposite*), ca. 1929, sandblasted glass with black paint. The Josef and Anni Albers Foundation, 1976.6.9.

oeuvre be understood in light of his German work, and how might the *Homage* series — his best-known works — be read anew, not only as a manifestation of his decades-long research into the interaction of color, but as works that are richly *material*, even if — or precisely because — that materiality, as with the subtle layers of the glass paintings, remains on a thin surface?

Albers's shift from the flat planes of the glass paintings to the equally planar *Homage to the Square* works can be understood, moreover, as a process of remediation. His works, despite significant shifts in scale, remain stable in remediation, from the double-height gold leaf and marble lobby installation to the doormat-sized plastic laminate works of his *Structural Constellations*. His is a productive transfer between media — glass, Masonite, plastic, paper — in which the attention to surface only enhances, in light of remediation, the continuity of his artistic goals and theories.

Furthermore, this chapter argues that Albers's practices related to visuality should be understood as directly connected to his conceptions of materiality and surface, and which ultimately give rise to key subject-object relationships.

From the *neues Sehen* — new vision — of 1920s Germany to conditions of visuality in the United States, this chapter traces an arc from his Bauhaus period to interwar and postwar America. In doing so, I theorize various strands of *visuality* in terms of *materiality* and find that Albers's surfaces should be understood as places of rich materiality and yet also embedded with ideas of visuality.

I employ the term "visuality" purposefully; as a concept, it can be understood in three concurrent modes: as the "quality or condition of being visible," as "visualness," and as "perceptibility." Under this rubric, this chapter seeks to encompass "new vision" and "perception" — both key period concepts in art movements and Gestalt psychology in Germany, along with Albers's own notions of "conscious seeing" and "visual perception."[8] These latter two concepts were very important in his classroom teaching, but they also present a useful means through which to understand how his works were intended to be actively encountered.

At the most fundamental level, *vision* is embedded into the three core aspects that preoccupied Albers throughout his entire life: his teaching, his art practice, and in his highly nuanced discourse *about* his practice. He framed it as an ongoing "search," versus "research" — the latter being a concept he opposed in art practice.[9] The notion of "vision" is inherent in his first utterances about what he hoped to achieve in America: "to open eyes."[10] This was an unwavering position; in an interview near the end of his life he stated, "although I was asked to come to Yale particularly to teach graduate painting students, I did not really teach painting but *seeing*."[11] Or again, in the important series of lectures, "Search versus Re-Search" that he gave in 1965, he expounded, "The content of art: Visual formulation of our reaction of life. . . . The aim of art: Revelation and evocation of vision."[12]

Crucially, this emphasis on visuality — and the destabilized visual relations between the viewing subject and the object perceived — had not always been the central thrust of scholarship surrounding Albers's work. Its importance in his teaching has been long accepted; indeed, Albers's most important contribution to modern art may be in his long and distinguished teaching career. Recently, art historians have delved more deeply into this seeing, especially in terms of Albers in the classroom, what Jeffrey Saletnik has highlighted as "pedagogic objects" and Eva Díaz has established as Albers's "ethics of perception."[13] This chapter builds on this research, but its primary focus is not on Albers's pedagogy. Rather it seeks to investigate conceptions of surface materiality, visuality, and subjectivity in his artworks. Designed to be an "evocation of vision" in Albers's terms, his artworks, especially their materiality, should be understood afresh as what this chapter frames as *materializing vision*.

In this chapter, I propose a reevaluation of the flat boards of Albers's *Homages*, namely, that they should be seen as whole artifacts, akin to icons, with the artist carefully controlling the surface-level effects. This surface materiality is one that is experienced by, and completed by, the perceiving, viewing subject in an open-ended manner. In the materializing of the surface in the *Homage* series — and other works on paper, on plastic — Albers's concerns about the surface and with visual perception are brought together. Albers draws our attention up to the surface of things; in doing so, he calls attention to both *surface* and *material* thing.

Teaching to See: Surface and Materiality from Germany to the United States

From the beginning, Albers was clear about his investigations of materiality and its intersection with light at the surface. He wanted to bring forth light's engagement with the materiality of the artwork itself. This was true of both his own artistic practice and his explorations with his students. As he articulated in an interview, he "wanted to work with direct light, the light which comes from behind the surface and filters through that surface plane. In this case, light is a volume, not a surface illusion."[14] In Albers's earliest period at the Bauhaus, it was initially suggested that he join the wall-painting workshop, but he was instead granted permission to open the glass workshop. Albers's teaching involved his students in a highly sophisticated and ongoing analysis of both materiality and vision. He taught at the Bauhaus from 1923 until its closure in 1933. His presence, and the

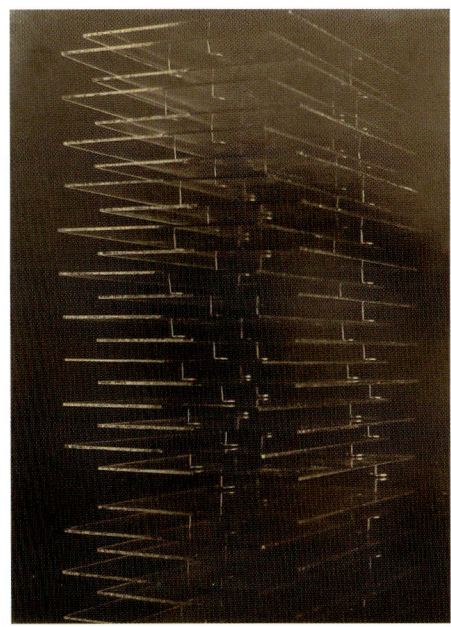

Fig. 6.5 Erich Consemüller, material exercise, Foundation Course taught by Josef Albers, undated. Bauhaus Student Work, 1919–33.

course he taught to first-year students in the Foundation sequence, was one of the few areas of continuity in the Bauhaus's short, but highly volatile, history. Many of the exercises that his Foundation Course yielded traveled with him to the United States and thus spanned not only his own teaching career but extended beyond it; many of his exercises, especially in folded paper, became standard first-year assignments in art and architecture programs alike throughout the postwar decades.

Overall, his teaching foregrounded investigations related to materials and seeing—exercises in tactility, surface materiality, and texture; experiments in the internal properties and structural possibilities of substances; and various types of spatial learning.[15] As Albers would state of his Bauhaus-era teaching, "*Material* is the beginning, not *matière* . . . that's the appearance. . . . I started with the material as *such*. . . . I turned the attitude towards the capacity of material."[16] One example, a "material exercise" (*Materialübung*) by Erich Consemüller, a Bauhaus student in Albers's Foundation Course, encompasses many of these ideas (fig. 6.5). Consemüller's piece features a careful construction of small glass plates, precisely stacked and—visually and structurally—balanced in a manner that simultaneously exploits the visual and material possibilities of glass. Here spatial and material learning are both in evidence; the small tower makes conspicuous its internal properties while simultaneously displaying a nuanced handling of the featured material: glass plates. The resulting piece celebrates modern ideas of transparency and clarity of structure, in a manner that is distinctly architectural, suggestive of a modern skyscraper.

Classroom exercises that focused on the intersection of visuality and materiality, sharpening the students' nuanced sensitivity to both, spanned the long arc of Albers's teaching. For Albers, a key goal was to develop in his students a sense for material and to address what he viewed as the problematic "longstanding practice of neglecting the natural surface of materials."[17] Thus his assignments attempted to inculcate an understanding for materials and surface

Exigencies of Materializing Vision

alike. To arrive at a common understanding with his pupils, Albers utilized three concepts, which he later succinctly summarized in a November 1938 telegram from Black Mountain College to MoMA's Alfred Barr:

> I use 3 terms, structure, facture, texture to describe surface appearances of materials as follows: firstly, structure concerns the inherent character of the raw material that is how it grew or was formed like the grain of wood or fiber of thread or crystalline structure of marble. Secondly, we speak of facture if the appearance is dominated by the effect of working the material; for example hammered metal twisted yarn or combed hair show the effect of treatment of the impression of tool used. Thirdly, we speak of texture if similar elements are combined in a constructive organ these elements may show both structure and facture for instance woven braided or knitted material and masonry.[18]

At the Bauhaus, Black Mountain, and Yale, Albers advanced his students' understanding of these terms in the curriculum he developed, one that allowed them to investigate the qualities of each, to "invent factures and textures and translate them into other materials, . . . or replace them with other effects, in some cases painted or drawn."[19] This is exemplified by Bauhaus student Monica Bella Broner-Ullmann's work—a drawing of fabric and nails to which she added collaged fabric pieces (fig. 6.6). It illustrates the virtuosity of her hand; it is difficult to ascertain which parts of the fabric have been collaged and which have been drawn. Her choice of objects—a frayed weaving sample and shiny metal nails—evinces careful attention to different types of materiality and their surface effects.

From his earliest Bauhaus years, Albers was especially interested in the skin of matter—in materials' appearance more than their substance. With students in his introductory *Vorkurs*, he alternated between exercises on *Material* (material), which was concerned with substance, properties of the material, and construction, and *Materie* (matter or *matière*), a term that denoted its surface appearance. *Matière* was an investigation into the visual effect of the material, not a study in deep materiality itself. As Albers scholar Frederick Horowitz explains, "A successful *matière* would make a smooth material look rough, a dry material look wet, or a brittle material look strong, and vice-versa."[20] As Albers noted, "The exercises with matter are concerned less with the inner qualities of the material than with its external appearance [*äußere erscheinung*], with its skin [*haut*], or epidermis, which is explored in terms of its relatedness or contrast to the skin of other materials."[21] As student John Urbain recalled about *matière*, "I have heard students use the word at the dinner table when a not too appetizing plate of food is placed before them. A pile of trash in one of the studies [atelier] is almost sure to provoke someone to exclaim, 'Oh! a *matière!*' Then, there is the retort, 'You name it and I'll make a *matière* out of it.' These remarks are, of course, entirely unharmful and not without humor."[22] He continued, "In paintings we find an arrangement of lines, spaces, and colors. The planning of these elements, according to the various principles in art, involves a matter of selection—the selection of lines, spaces, and colors. In creating a *matière* we are concerned with appearances of surfaces and materials. As in painting, one color

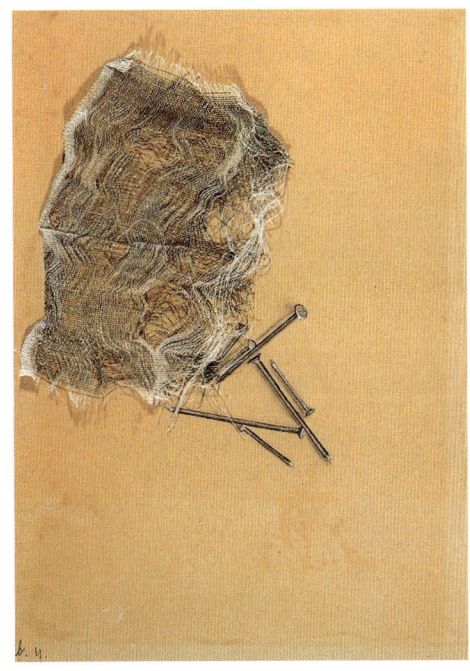

Fig. 6.6 Monica Bella Broner-Ullmann, drawing of fabric and nails with collaged fabric, Bauhaus, Foundation Course, 1929–30.

affects another, one value affects another, or one space affects another, so surface qualities influence other surface qualities. The visual arts involve the optical senses. With *matière*, there is involved an additional factor, that of the tactile senses. We desire to touch and feel the *matière* studies."[23] And he concluded, "Through the combination of materials we become sensitive to the subtle transitions and transformation of surface qualities. Hard, soft, smooth, and rough characteristics begin to take on more emphasis and meaning.... Through these experiments with *matière* studies we develop sensitivity in observing and attain new vision which has a stimulating influence in all our visual experiences."[24]

Similarly, an exercise known as "typofacture," which Albers made use of at all three schools, emphasized the optic and surface effects of objects. Students imitated a sheet of newspaper, not by miniaturization but via densely packed drawn marks and spacing, with uncannily realistic results. In later exercises in Albers's courses at both Black Mountain and Yale, students would draw an object from multiple points of view, a practice that, as historian Eeva-Liisa Pelkonen has pointed out, "emphasized that both the subject and the object existed in space" and that "the constantly changing relationships between things... mattered," rather than "the object or the subject in isolation."[25]

In contradistinction to his Bauhaus period, where Albers's pedagogical practice envisioned an eventual productive object (the design of a desk or a lamp), at Black Mountain College he emphasized processes that developed and valued underlying skills over finished results. At Black Mountain, his courses in drawing and painting utilized everyday objects in the rural environment, such as autumn leaves, eggshells, and wire. Not viewed as material objects in their own right, they were employed as materials in the service of various artistic and pedagogical processes, particularly seeing and surface investigations. Departing from the rich tactility that had constituted many of the classroom exercises of his German Bauhaus years, Albers's teaching at Yale, especially, focused on the

Exigencies of Materializing Vision

drawn line as well as the interaction of color, studied via colored papers placed flat against one another. "For the development of vision, all teaching which aims at art should be a training in observation," Albers stated in 1965.[26] As Robert Rauschenberg would reflect back on Albers as a teacher, "Years later . . . I'm still learning what he taught me, because what he taught had to do with the entire visual world."[27]

Materiality/Subjectivity: Albers and the Perceiving Subject

In his teaching and in his own artworks, Albers offered a new kind of visuality embodied by the practice of seeing. He recounted an early experience in his own development as an art student that is instrumental for thinking about surface materiality vis-à-vis subjectivity. As Albers recalled, "When I was in Berlin at the Königliche Kunstschule (1913–15), one morning Philipp Franck showed us Dutch photographs of van Gogh's charcoal drawings. He laid them out against the wall. I was so tempted to rub a little charcoal off; they were so marvelously reproduced. You know this marvelously powdery effect you get from charcoal stroke? Every morning I looked around to see if anyone was watching and I ran my finger across the surface. I knew they were photos, but I had to touch them to convince myself it was not charcoal."[28] Also relevant, and at an even more formative stage, is that Albers's father, a professional house painter, taught him to imitate wood and marble with a comb and a sponge.[29] This interaction — between the perception of an object's surface (a charcoal line, wood grains) and the representation of its surface through a different media (a photograph, a trompe l'oeil painting technique) — is foundational for understanding Albers's own keen attention to surface planes and the subtle exterior materiality of his own artistic practice. Moreover, his own subjectivity and that of his work's potential viewer (who might puzzle over the delicate surface layers of an Albers glass painting or his obtuse geometric forms) were also key factors in the processes of making and the subsequent reception of his works.

By interacting with the subjective viewer's eye and distorting perceptions through line — or in the *Homage* series, via color — his objects further projected their own agency and called into question the beholder's ability to understand them in stable, objective, and purely visual terms. Read this way, these precise and circumscribed art objects are contemplations on the subjective nature of vision itself. Albers made clear and acknowledged — even played with — the fallibility of perception. As the French critic Hubert Damisch has noted, Albers "set himself the program of working . . . on the development of a veritable, but strictly experimental, culture of the eye."[30] It was up to the subject to take on the manifold possibilities involved in viewing the object. *Steps*, a work in glass, presents what appears to be two sets of steps outlined in white — a large set of three steps faces the viewer while in the upper left a smaller trio of steps appears to be facing backward or, depending on how one reads the lines, unfolding upward. About *Steps*, Albers noted that he was teaching the subject to shift "away from an 'only-one-way' reading of visual form to a 'multiple' reading of the same image."[31] He wanted to impart "training in observation."[32] Albers invites the viewer to read it in multiple ways; it is up to the viewer to perform

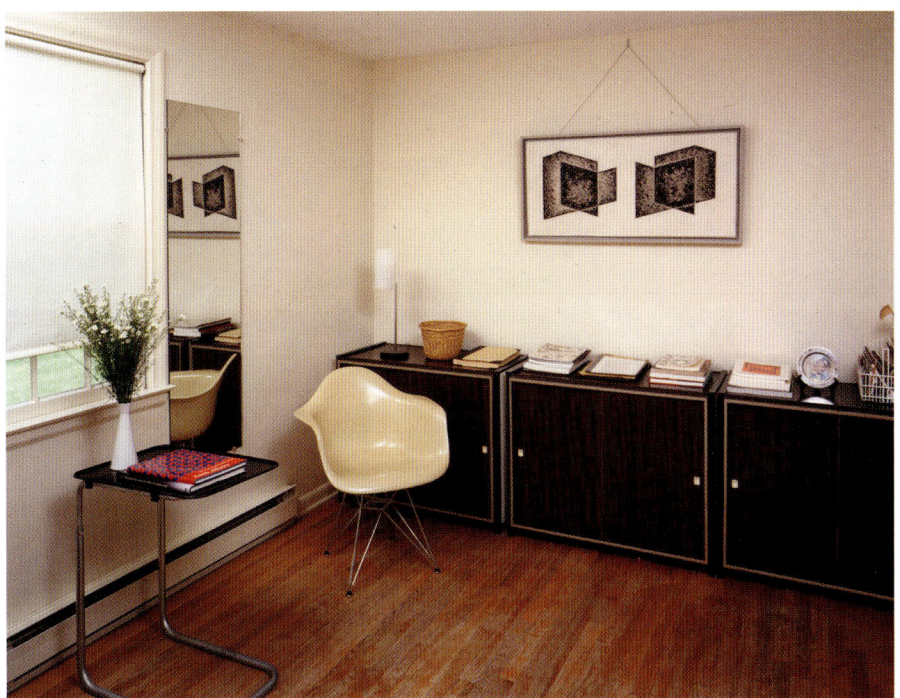

the simultaneous, multiple readings. The subject undertakes the visual task of decoding, rather than the art object presenting that information to the viewer. Famously, even Anni Albers puzzled for decades over a pair of forms that hung in her bedroom, a gift from her husband (fig. 6.7). The visual representations that Albers offered up were destabilized objects to the perceiving subject; this relationship represented a different mode of visuality. It obligated the viewer to focus not on the object depicted, but the object's representations.

Fig. 6.7 Josef Albers, *Equal and Unequal*, 1939, oil on Masonite, as hung in Anni Albers's bedroom, 808 Birchwood Drive, Orange, Connecticut. The Josef and Anni Albers Foundation, 1976.1.80.

Architecture in Glass

The glass paintings by Albers, on the other hand, tended to be less about multiple points of view than about layered flatness and the materials used to achieve it. The paintings' forms often only snap into tangible view upon the viewer's being informed of their title — with the works *City* (1928), for example, or, in *Interior a* and *Interior b* (1929), the objects become clearer as a series of, perhaps, windows and bookcases (figs. 6.8, 6.9). The glass paintings gave heightened status to nonobjective form while fixing abstraction into confident materiality.[33] They represent key early forays in pure color and pure materiality, concerns that connect to — even eventually directly gave rise to — the *Homage to the Square* paintings of the postwar period. They were flat but offered up a thick materiality in glass, their multiple layers and bubbles visible (see fig. 6.4).[34] Albers would make over seventy glass paintings in his lifetime.[35] He viewed them as paintings, akin to those of his Bauhaus colleagues Paul Klee or Wassily Kandinsky. He wrote of them, "Glass paintings ordinarily are transparent and therefore window pictures. They are composed from differently colored pieces of glass usually held together with lead. With my wall glass paintings I have developed a new type of glass picture. By using opaque glass and only one pane for a picture I

Exigencies of Materializing Vision   217

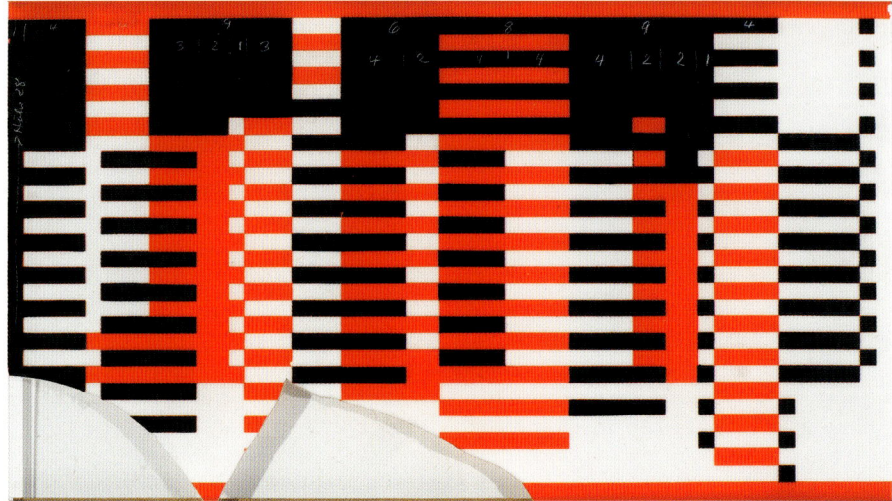

Fig. 6.8 Josef Albers, *City*, 1928, sandblasted opaque flashed glass with black paint (damaged). The Josef and Anni Albers Foundation, 1976.6.14.

achieved the movability of a small easel painting permitting [it] to be hung on a wall, as well as to be mounted into the wall as a fixed architectural part, both indoors and outdoors."[36]

Although he took complete authorship over the works, after creating a few assemblage glass works by hand in 1920–22, thereafter Albers designed, but did not himself execute, his glass artworks. Instead, he relied on two professional firms – predominantly the glass manufactory of Puhl und Wagner (located in the Treptow section of Berlin) but also Rudolph Sandbläserei, which was contracted to do any needed sandblasting. As gleaned from correspondence, he communicated his intentions via drawings and letters, but personal visits to the manufactories to clarify and oversee the work were also necessary. Albers wrote to Gottfried Heinersdorff, his fabricator at the firm Puhl und Wagner, "I kindly ask that you send me posthaste the drawings of my last small glass pictures (b/w on gray paper). Within a few days you will receive from Rudolph Sandbläserei three additional pieces of glass (with drawings), which I would like to have completed soon. I believe that the drawings and the notes on them will require a meeting before they are executed."[37] Albers carefully managed and oversaw the production work, writing to Heinersdorff, "Perhaps I'll drop by next Monday, as I once again would like to make some small pictures for which I seek specific colors. In the meantime, I have also had a number of them done using the sandblasting treatment, which are especially beautiful. I have also sold several."[38]

This fabrication procedure contrasts sharply with László Moholy-Nagy's process for the so-called *Telephone Pictures* (*Construction in Enamel 1, 2, and 3*, 1923), in which he sought to convey over the telephone, with graph paper and a color chart, artworks to be produced by a sign manufactory. Moholy-Nagy endeavored to minimize the artist's hand and presence, both practically and theoretically, in favor of showcasing new ideas about how modern art might be produced. Albers, on the other hand, sought to be directly involved in each step of the process; even if he did not have the advanced technical skills in glassmaking to produce the resulting works, they evidence his careful consideration regarding the types of glass and treatments that built up the fine layers, resulting in the final work.

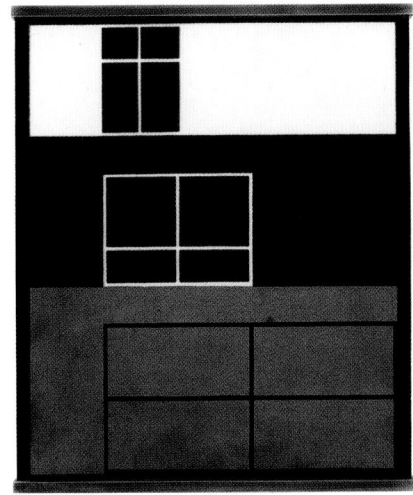

Fig. 6.9 Josef Albers, *Interior a*, 1929, sandblasted opaque flashed glass. The Josef and Anni Albers Foundation, 1976.6.17.

Albers's exacting focus was on a given glass painting's materiality and what could be achieved through a precise crafting process (albeit not executed by his own hand), as much as the work's subject matter. He offers a lengthy explanation of the intricate and multistage production process for *City* (see fig. 6.8):

> The picture (1928) was executed in orange-red flashed glass which was first treated by sand-blasting and thereupon was partially covered with black color – color for stained glass painting which only becomes lasting in the kiln.
>
> As for the flashed glass, the flashed front color (in this case red) is not painted on and then baked in, but is melted on by blowing the glass a second time. As a result a hair thin layer of color covers (flashes) a thicker core. In the case of stained glass, the latter usually consists of clear window glass. In opaque wall paintings, however, the flashed color usually covers a core of milk glass which is of the purest white – a white that is non-existent when looking through stained glass windows.
>
> The white, however, is visible only after the covering flashed glass has been removed. In this case this was done by sand-blasting (using a compressed air blower) instead of biting with liquid acid. While acids produce a smooth surface, sand-blasting creates sharper edges and above all sharper corners.
>
> Before sand-blasting the whole glass area is hermetically sealed with specially prepared stenciling paper or with a smooth rubber membrane to protect the remaining flashed glass.
>
> In the case of *City*, the stenciling paper which was glued on, was cut in straight lines from edge to edge: the height was equally divided into 29 horizontals, the width was divided into 20 verticals of varying width, but measured with the horizontal unit.
>
> Despite this rectangular, frontal and, therefore, distinctly flat subdivision, there is a feeling of a many-sided spaciousness.[39]

Exigencies of Materializing Vision

Albers was well-versed in the sequencing and each technically sophisticated step needed to achieve the desired final result. In discussing his processes for the 1931 glass work *Im Wasser* (*In the Water*), he highlighted its materiality and economy in design, which permitted "the most simple stencil cut possible. (The stencil is necessary since this glass painting is made in opaque glass and executed with sandblasting only.) So the composition is appropriate to material and technique."[40] In the fabrication method, each intricate treatment had to do with manipulating the surface while keeping it flat, working the materials, paradoxically, to keep materiality at bay in the service of a smooth planar surface. The three colors of *In the Water* — white, black, gray — are, he explains, "actually two colors, namely, white and glossy and dulled black. All color areas are without modulation, therefore flat."[41] For the opaque works, he often specified a layer of white milk glass covered with a hair-thin glass film — the flashing coat — of another color, which he then overlayed with a stencil and sandblasted off the remaining (uncovered) top coat, resulting in a relief being ground into the glass wherever it was uncovered, as can be observed in *Interior a* and *Interior b* (see fig. 6.9).[42] Also exemplified in the pair, a shorter sandblasting dulled the glossy surface, achieving a dull dark gray on a shiny deep black.[43] Glass painters' colors were also used, becoming permanent after a kiln firing. The overall result, Albers proclaimed, was "unusual color intensity, the purest white and deepest black and the necessary preciseness as well as the flatness of the design elements offer an unusual and particular material and form effect."[44]

It is nearly impossible to adequately capture in photography Albers's attention to surface, but *Stufen* (*Steps*), as Albers scholar Nicholas Fox Weber observes, is "remarkable in its textural variations: the sheen of the jet black plays against the slightly pebbled surface of the more matte, grayer black; that lighter black, while carefully machined and constant when viewed close up, is full of atmosphere and takes on a white bloom when seen at a distance. The gray is altered ad-infinitum as a result of its adjacency to the white."[45] This effect was noted in the period. In a review of a major exhibition of Albers's glass paintings at the Dessau Bauhaus (Josef Albers, *Glasbilder*, May 1–12, 1932), an art critic observed that "these pictures have a strong sense of tectonic contemporaneity about them. Indeed they possess the strongest sense of materiality."[46]

The materiality also gives the works luminance. As Weber points out, "Albers was able to achieve light of a striking quality with the opaque milk-glass. It is, in fact, a light reflected off an opaque surface that gives the illusion of being light shining through a translucent medium. We feel as if the main light source is behind the object, whereas in reality it comes from the side that we are on." Importantly, "Albers outdid nature in these flashed-glass pieces. He used opaque glass to create an apparent translucency more powerful than actual translucency, and he made reflected light appear to be light coming from a direct source."[47] Similarly, Albers himself noted in 1928 about his work *City*, "Apart from straight and mixed reds there even appear gradations within the hard poles of the color scale, that is within white and black. And the three colors, although in reality opaque, are perceived as being – transparent."[48] Through his processes, Albers was able to make the paintings more visible, seem more illuminated, than they were. Visuality revolved around the conditions of the visible, the degree of

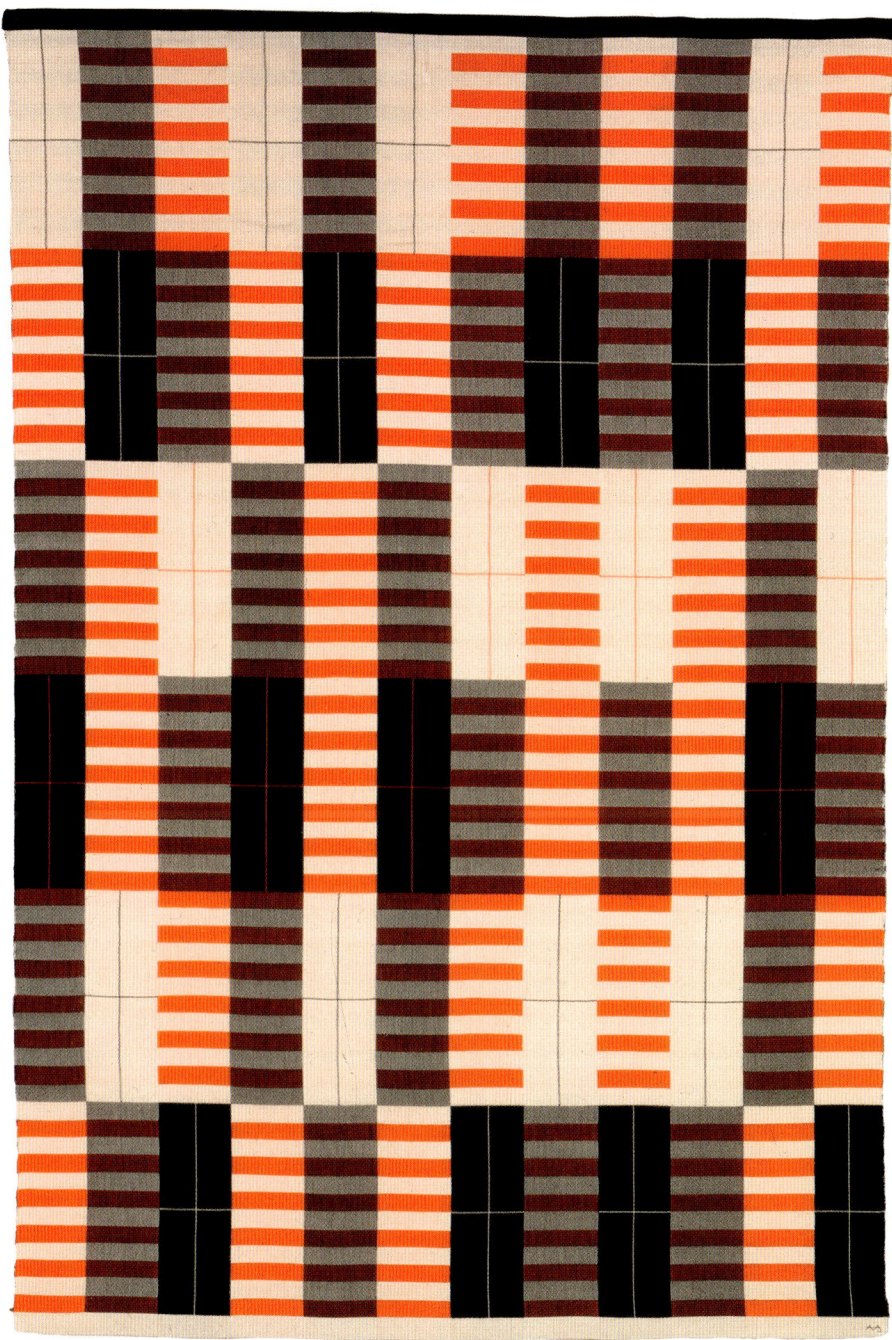

visibility, perceptibility. But it was also imbued with — and gave rise from — the materiality of the glass itself.

The glass paintings also connect to the flat, yet subtly textured, wall hangings made by his wife, renowned Bauhaus weaver, Anni Albers, from the same period. For example, her *Black White Red* weaving of 1927 aligns closely with *City* (fig. 6.10, see also fig. 6.8). Although *City* was made in 1928, Josef Albers had been creating similar abstracted patterns beginning in 1926 (see, for example, his *Fuge* [*Fugue*]), suggesting that husband and wife were likely influencing each other, using distinctly different materials, carefully constructed and

Fig. 6.10 Anni Albers, *Black White Red*, 1927/1965 (original 1927 [lost], re-woven by Gunta Stölzl in 1965), cotton and silk. Bauhaus-Archiv, Berlin.

Exigencies of Materializing Vision

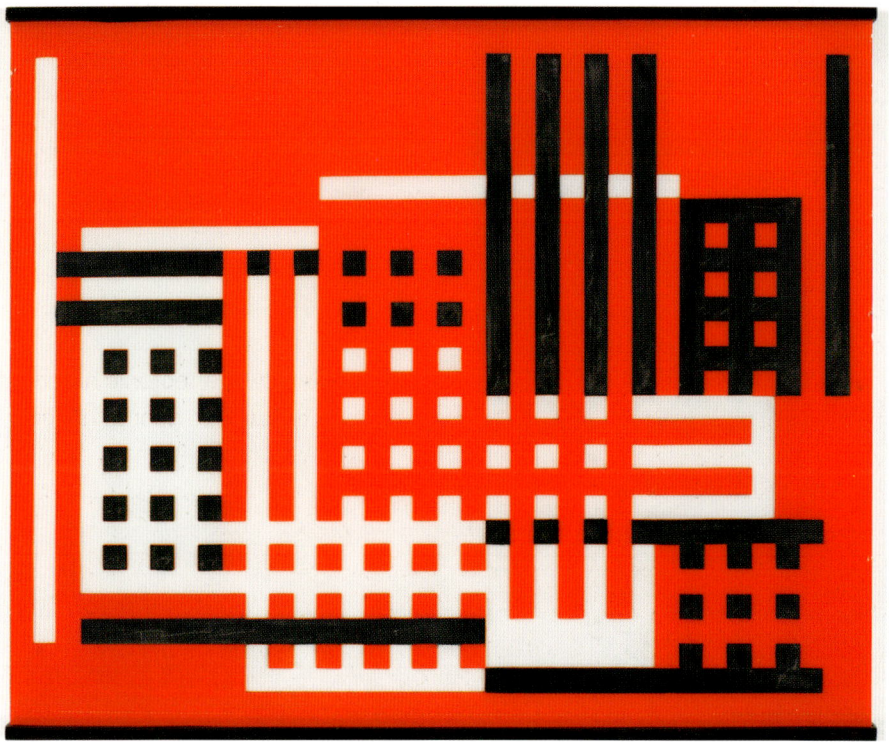

Fig. 6.11 Josef Albers, *Factory*, 1925, sandblasted flashed glass with black paint. The Joseph and Anni Albers Foundation, 1976.6.4.

layered. In dialogue with one another, each achieves a similar, flat effect through the careful selection and working of their chosen materials. Both wall hanging and glass painting appear to be flat, modern abstractions while evincing subtle materiality on close inspection of their surfaces. Yet this subtle surface materiality does not conflict with the flat, abstract geometric forms applied to – or woven on – that surface.

Although Albers's glass paintings were laboriously handmade by skilled glassworkers, the hand is downplayed; they are clearly meant to be understood as paintings, not as objects or handicraft. These works keep their distance – the glass is hard, cold, exceedingly flat, very fragile, yet rich in materiality. And they are about light – its luminance in glass – and the dark materiality of flat, opaque blackness, and about seeing. The importance of materiality is particularly perceptible in the more translucent works where the bubbles within the glass are visible, such as *Skyscrapers on Transparent Yellow*; that work utilizes a type of glass made intentionally with highly visible bubbles (see fig. 6.4). About the glass paintings, Albers wrote "the necessary preciseness as well as the flatness of the design elements offer an unusual and particular material and form effect."[49] This underscores the demarcation of boundaries between the subject and the artwork while the works heighten the viewer's awareness of vision itself. The glass paintings are about drawing attention to – and seeing – surface (not depth). In their very materiality (glass), they are about transparent and opaque surfaces, and layers in-between. And they are about light and glass's natural luminance and translucence. Glass, which the viewing subject is accustomed to seeing *through*, as when looking out a window, now becomes the *material object seen*, heightening the viewer's awareness of seeing and surface alike, materializing vision.

The paintings are also distinctly architectural, made in one of modern architecture's signature materials – glass – and often taking up architectural motifs, from windows to multistory skyscrapers. As titled, the works depict, in abstracted form, factories, skyscrapers, pergolas, and architectural objects such as steps, screens, and other patently manmade objects (see figs. 6.8, 6.9). They remind the viewer of our material world, its three-dimensional objects rendered flat and abstracted out. (Glass was just one material with which Albers worked on these architectural elements; the same motif of *Steps* was taken up by Albers in at least five other media: in casein on Masonite; baked enamel paint on Alumelite; gouache; oil on paper; and silkscreen).[50]

In works such as *Fabrik* (*Factory*) (fig. 6.11) and *City*, the tectonic nature of the subject matter is underscored by the strong rectilinear and geometric thrust of their composition. While *Factory* was originally titled in German (*Fabrik*), for his *City*, Albers rejected the German terms *Metropolis* or *Stadt* and gave the work a title in English, thereby linking the work to the advanced state of contemporary US building construction that so fascinated German modernists in this period. Albers's glass skyscraper works aligned closely with the actual visual effect of skyscrapers' glass windows. In *Hochbauten A & B* (*Skyscrapers A & B*), he reversed his color patterns to feature a city skyline of buildings illuminated in white light against a black night sky (*Skyscrapers A*) (fig. 6.12) and the same buildings in broad daylight (*Skyscrapers B*), now with their windows (and floor plates) silhouetted in black on a white ground. These works closely align with built and unbuilt modern architectural designs of the period – multistory buildings that featured glass curtain walls such as Ludwig Mies van der Rohe's Friedrichstrasse skyscraper designs or a project from 1922, Walter Gropius's Chicago Tribune Tower Competition Entry (fig. 6.13) – to which Albers's skyscraper works, for example *Dissolved* from 1927, as well as *Skyscrapers A & B*, bear a close resemblance.

An Exile in Shards: The Glass Paintings and Emigration

Albers worked on his glass paintings series for more than a decade, from 1921 until 1932, shortly before his emigration in the fall of 1933. He and Anni Albers arrived in New York City on November 25 and enjoyed several art-filled days in the city's museums before leaving for Black Mountain College. Beyond the closure of the Bauhaus at its final site in Berlin and the antimodern sentiments of the Nazis, which meant declining opportunities, Anni Albers's Jewish heritage also put the couple in danger. Of their precarious situation during his final period in Berlin, Albers reported to his friend Franz Perdekamp, "Shortly before Easter the B.H. [Bauhaus] was surrounded; a lot of police searched the premises, performed body searches, took many away and let them go after being given proof of identification. The building is closed because, according to the newspapers, a lot of incriminating material and illegal tracts were found.... Hence [the] Bauhaus closed, without money and without furnishings. The faculty reduced as well. I had to show [an] ancestry chart.... Worked for naught till now; now without money. No prospects.... Can't pay the rent. But we can still eat thanks to our in-laws, who aren't doing well either."[51] He also notes that making glass pictures has

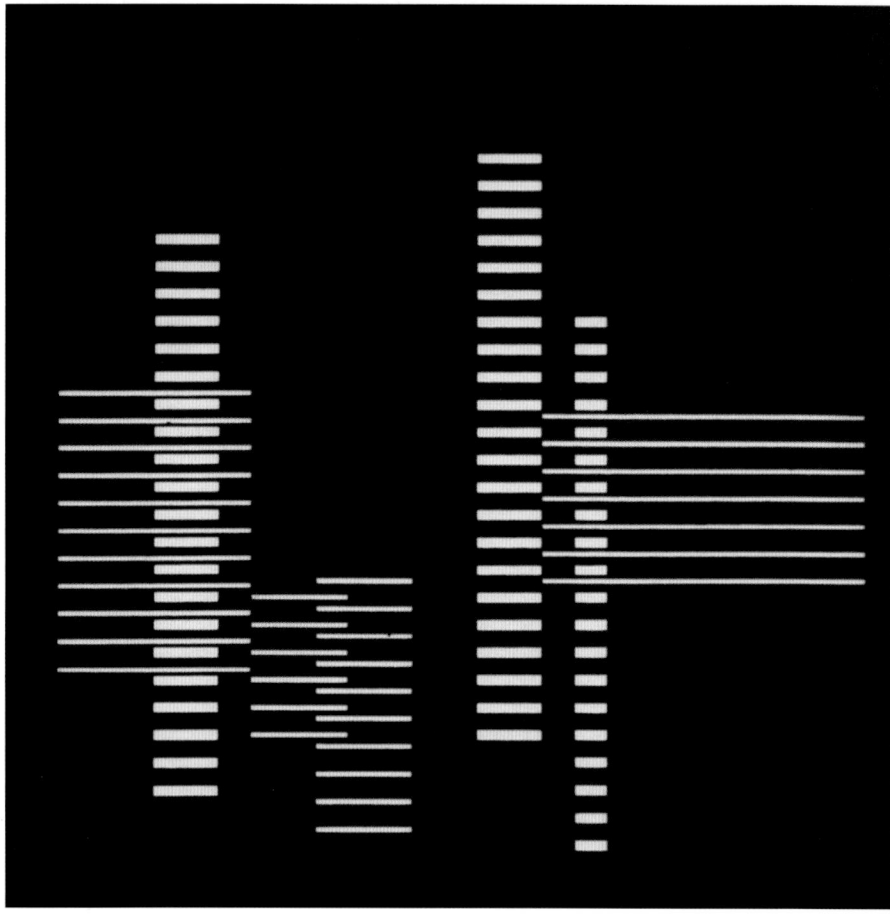

Fig. 6.12 Josef Albers, *Skyscrapers A*, 1929, sandblasted flashed glass. Yale University Art Gallery, New Haven, Connecticut.

become "too expensive since summer." The invitation to Black Mountain College was timely, giving the couple a place to settle and dual teaching positions. In preparation for their American emigration, by September 1933 both Josef and Anni were taking English lessons.[52] In contrast to later waves of people who left under extreme duress, if they were able to get out at all, the Alberses were able to pack and depart Germany in a measured and well-considered manner.

Their landing in New York City, arriving as they did into the company of friends and a network of other exiled Germans, was comfortable. The transfer of their worldly belongings, by contrast, ended in tragedy. They had been fortunate enough to ship nine large wooden boxes containing household goods, an entire weaving loom, weaving material, pictures, and painting equipment. The shipment of their goods resulted in the poignant loss of one-third of Albers's carefully packed glass paintings at the hands of Customs House officials in New York – at least ten glass paintings had arrived safely but were subsequently reduced to shards or permanently damaged during the customs inspection process, including one of his two versions of *City* (see fig. 6.8).[53] This experience of loss underscores the fragility of the glass artworks, which Albers had carefully crated with thick cartons between them.[54] Evidently they had survived the passage, along with his other meticulously packed items. When he had arrived in New York and identified his belongings at the Custom House, the works were still intact: "Upon our arrival on Nov. 24 all the boxes and trunks were examined. Some pictures

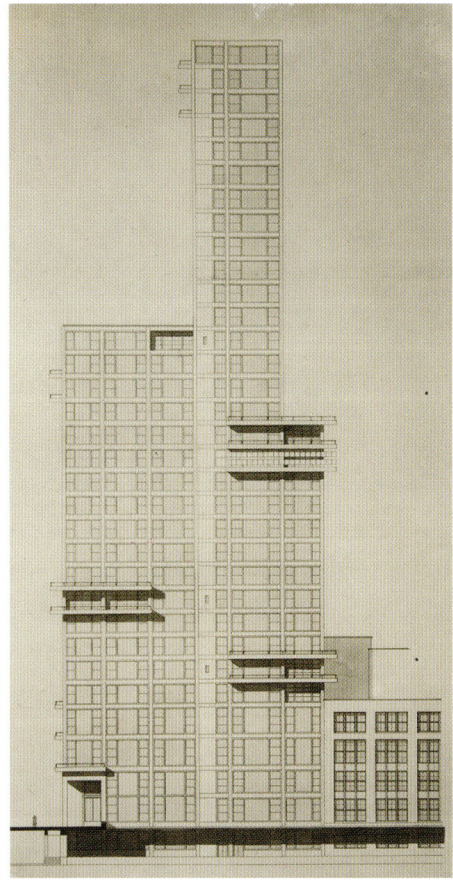

Fig. 6.13 Walter Gropius and Adolf Meyer, drawing, Chicago Tribune Tower competition entry (project), 1922.

were taken out of each box and we discovered not one damaged or broken one. Several friends who met us at the steamer can bear witness to this statement."[55] The belongings subsequently went through a process of appraisal and clearing of customs, emerging on the other side greatly damaged from the roughshod handling, not only of the artworks but almost all of their goods – "a glass measuring cup (used for photographic work) into which wood-carving instruments had been pressed in the most senseless manner" and "glass plate in a photo camera is entirely splintered in spite of the fact that the camera was placed in a heavy leather case and securely wrapped in goods."[56] A compilation, dated January 25, 1934, and now held at the Albers Foundation, lists the titles of thirty-two glass paintings, noting which works were broken.[57]

In a letter of complaint to the director of customs at the Treasury Department in Washington, DC, on February 12, 1934 (in fluent English, which Nicholas Fox Weber notes would have had to have been written for him), Albers reports about the first group of items that he was permitted to collect, "We found all our boxes except one, broken open without keys. Our things were carelessly thrown around on the floors and tables. On the dirty floor between shavings, paper and mess, we saw our linen, our personal belongings, our pillows and the weaving yarns. On the tables, our flat silver among painting utensils and our goods and cloth samples in disorderly piles strewn around. It was a disgusting sight, showing the entire ruthlessness and inefficiency of those who had handled the articles."[58]

Exigencies of Materializing Vision

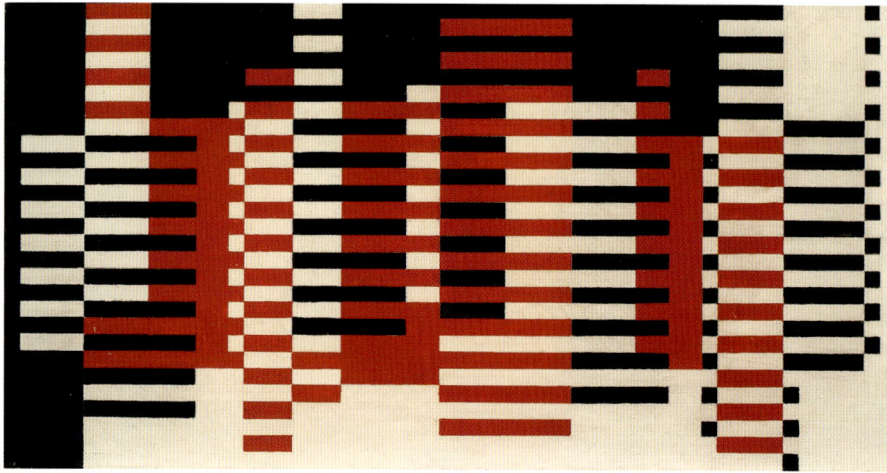

Fig. 6.14 Josef Albers, *City*, 1936 (after a 1928 glass work of same design), tempera on Masonite. The Josef and Anni Albers Foundation, 1976.1.1365.

The remaining boxes, which included the glass paintings, were subsequently released to the Alberses in February, arriving at Black Mountain in a similar state of disarray. "Dirt, dust, and ashes had penetrated the boxes during the train transportation. Most of the things are soiled, the weaving yarns in confusion and tangle. The books, mostly costly art books of which each single one had been carefully wrapped in paper, arrived without their covering, dirty, scratched or ruined. The wrappings were removed and torn.... Ten of my thirty-two Glass Pictures were broken or cracked.... They had been ruthlessly and carelessly stacked against each other without the least consideration of their fragility, size, or weight."[59]

The poignancy of the loss — the couple would never return to Germany to live; the entirety of their lives was contained in this shipment — comes to the fore in small details, such as an instance where Albers lists as "entirely missing" one of two similar horsehair pillows with a yellow satin cover and monogrammed A.F. "You can see by this description how we felt," he writes in his letter of complaint about the Customs House authority.[60] Despite letters and the institutional support of Ted Dreier, one of Black Mountain's well-connected founders, and John Andrew Rice, the rector of Black Mountain College, demands for compensation were denied by customs and immigration officers and the relevant US senators, as was the claim of mishandling. As the commissioner of customs wrote, "from the facts developed by the investigation it would appear that the merchandise was handled in a careful manner and I must conclude that the Customs Service was in no way responsible for the damage complained of in this case."[61] Owing to the fused, planar, and seamless nature of their design, his glass paintings — unlike traditional stained glass windows, whose individual leaded color panes could be replaced — satisfactory repair was not possible.

While the glass paintings had made up almost the entirety of his output in the previous years, his move to the United States led to an important shift in the material basis of Albers's work thereafter. As he would explain to his old friend, Franz Perdekamp, "Here in the States I have not created any new glass pictures.... Thus, I am doing oil paintings again. In addition, I did a lot of woodcuts, litho[graph]s and some dry-point engravings."[62] At least one key work, *City*, was re-made by Albers in 1936, but in tempera paint on a Masonite panel (fig. 6.14).

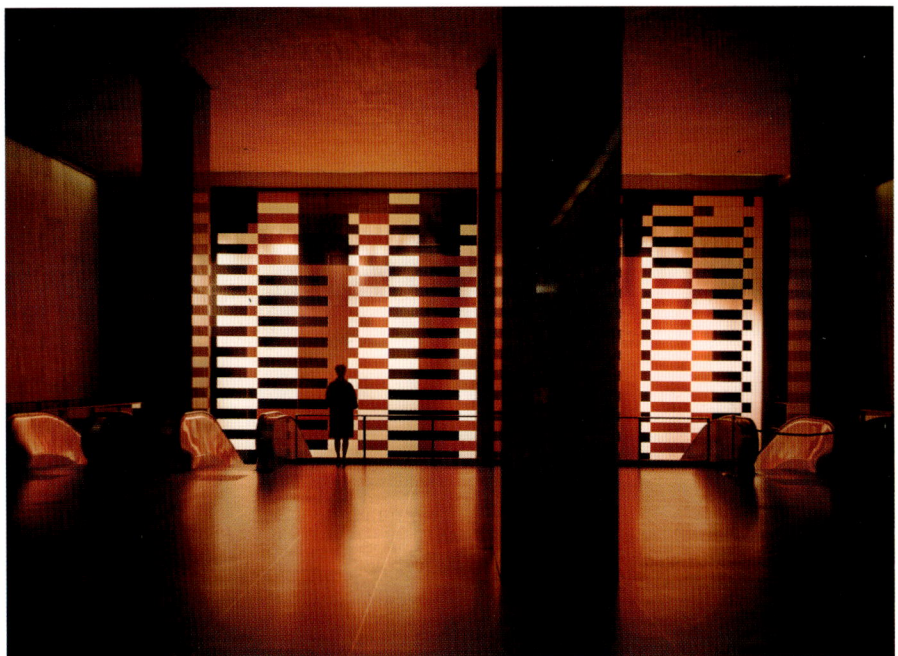

Fig. 6.15 Josef Albers, *Manhattan*, 1963, Formica panels. Lobby, Pan Am Building (today, MetLife Building), New York City.

It replaced the damaged glass original *City*, which is still held in the Albers Foundation collection (see fig. 6.8). He made versions of other early glassworks through a process similar to that of the original glass paintings – sandblasting surfaces – but used polished and painted aluminum panels in place of glass.[63] But these creations were exceptions, and in any event, the glass seemingly could not be satisfactorily re-created in other media. In the United States, after the breakage of an extensive portion his oeuvre of glass paintings, and because of his remote location at Black Mountain College without ready access to the technicians and glass manufactories that had executed his works in Germany, as well as the lack of an art market for glassworks, his investigations in surface materiality and architecture would take a different path. He turned to paintings on Masonite and other flat substrates, works on plastic and paper, and to several large-scale architectural commissions in varying media.

Architectural commissions, especially, provided an opportunity to scale up his earlier investigations, while experimenting in other materials. As Albers realized designs at a new architectural scale, his compositions and underlying objectives remained consistent. Retaining his early works' city skylines of skyscrapers in vertical banded blocks, he translated the materiality of his 1920s glass paintings to substances more stable and more permanent, and also more appropriate to architecture, renaming the works as well for this new US context. This is evidenced in his glass *City*, which was reconceived in large-scale Formica panels. Titled *Manhattan* (1963), this mural for the lobby of the Pan Am Building, designed by Walter Gropius, directly related to Albers's 1928 *City*, bridging his 1920s output to 1960s New York City (fig. 6.15; see also fig. 6.8).

Likewise, in his brick skyline *America* (1950), a sculptural relief installed in the Graduate Commons, commissioned for the Harvard University Graduate Center, the city is reimagined in brick (fig. 6.16).[64] Instead of contrasting colors representing the illuminated windows and dark silhouetted floorplates, for the

Exigencies of Materializing Vision

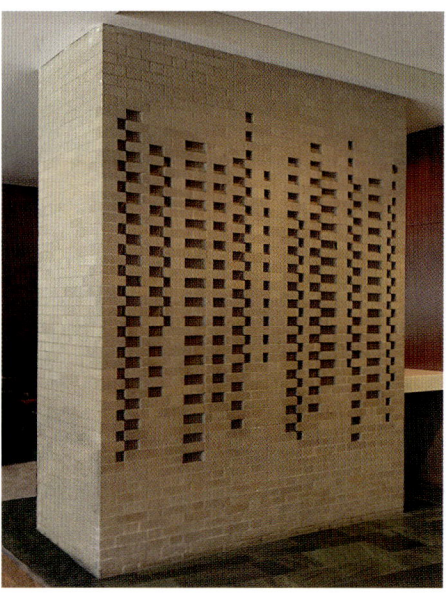

Fig. 6.16 Josef Albers, *America*, 1950, brick. Harkness Commons Graduate Center, Harvard University.

by-now familiar skyline of vertical skyscraper forms, he used recesses in the brickwork to create voids that can be read either as the windows or the steel structure. The work is integrated into a freestanding wall, which had a fireplace on the other side, seemingly following Albers's belief that "any design organically connected with an architectural structure should be related to that structure, no matter whether this design is to emphasize or to complete, to change or to correct, the appearance or function of the building or space concerned."[65] To articulate the city, he explained, he elected not to use different colors or shades of brick, or a pattern of protruding and receding bricks. Rather, he developed a composition utilizing the shadows produced by the bricks that receded by about two and a half inches, preserving the flatness present in his other *City* works in glass and other media.[66] Albers wrote to Gropius about the way in which he understood the skyscrapers symbolically, their vital movement upward "emphasizing the tendency of dematerialization" of modern structures.[67] As Jeffrey Saletnik has argued, this work, composed of voids, should be read through this interest of dematerialization and directly corresponding to Gropius's architecture, especially in dialogue with the spatial dynamics engendered by open massing of the Harvard complex buildings and the surrounding spaces.[68]

In other installation works, the relationship between the viewing subject and the art object is destabilized as a result of the visual distortion of the thing being perceived. This effect is enhanced fourfold in Albers's *Two Structural Constellations* in gold leaf on marble, his 1959 installation in the lobby of the Corning Glass Building in New York City, a twenty-eight-story glass skyscraper by Wallace K. Harrison and Max Abramovitz (fig. 6.17). Here, large boxes float indeterminately, dematerialized forms held in tension between projection and void. The geometry of *Two Structural Constellations* also relates to Albers's 1920s projective architectural designs – two small shops for the selling of the Ullstein publishing house's sewing patterns (fig. 6.18). With the Corning Lobby installation, the viewer is confronted with an overwhelming scale and an arresting materiality of marble and gold leaf. Even as he scaled up his work and adapted it to a

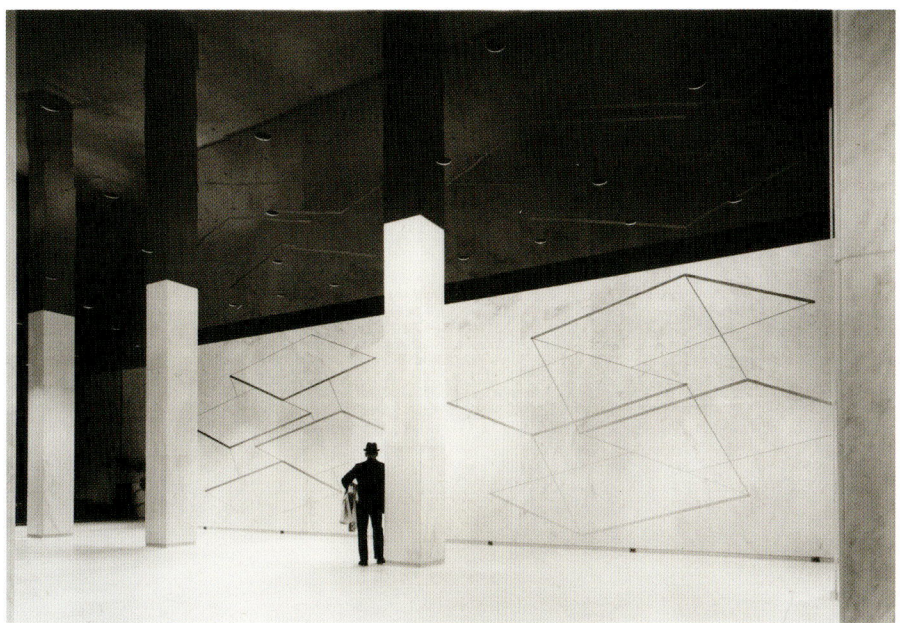

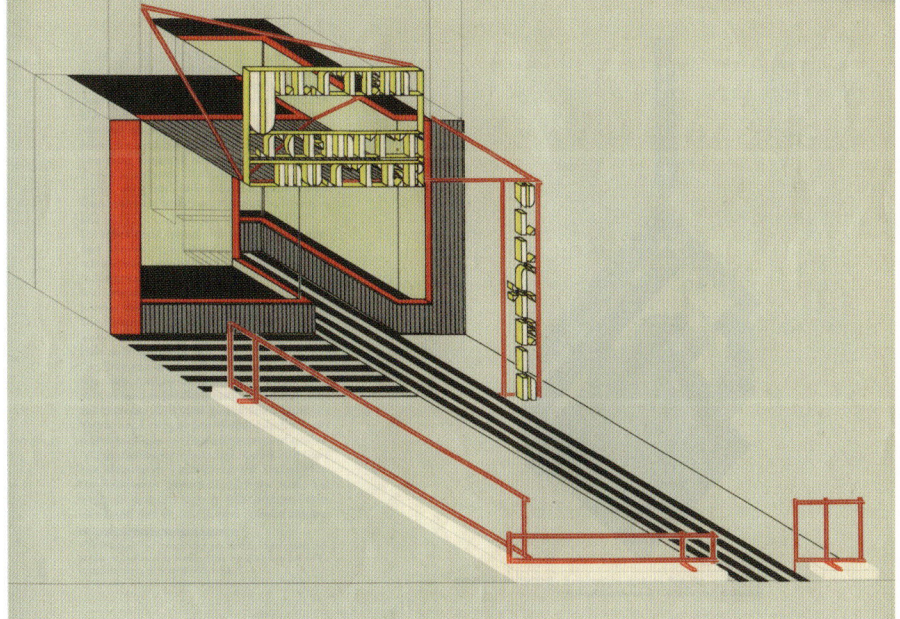

new architectural context, the commonality between these postwar installations in America and Albers's prewar work includes an ongoing investigation of a flat surface materiality (from Formica to marble), geometry and its destabilization, and a key relationship between subject and object as the eye meets the surface of a given work. The *Homage to the Square* series should be considered with these ideas in mind.

Homage to the Square: Materiality in Context

The compositions of squares on flat, square-shaped boards, titled *Homage to the Square*, of which there are more than two thousand works, was a series

Fig. 6.17 Josef Albers, *Two Structural Constellations*, 1959, Vermont marble and gold leaf. Lobby, Corning Glass Building, 717 Fifth Avenue, New York City.

Fig. 6.18 Josef Albers, design for a remodeled storefront selling Ullstein sewing patterns, Berlin, 1926.

Exigencies of Materializing Vision

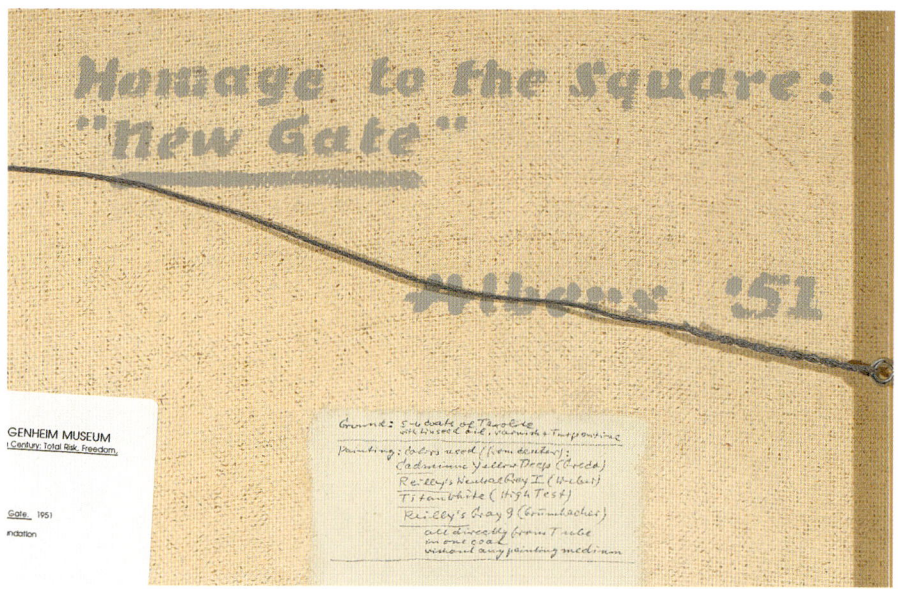

Fig. 6.19 Josef Albers, verso, *Homage to the Square: New Gate*, 1951, Masonite with list of colors used, in Josef Albers's hand. The Josef and Anni Albers Foundation, 1976.1.702.

Albers worked on from 1950 until his death in 1976 (see figs. I.2, 6.1).[69] They represent his predominant US output, an extended project whose individual pieces should be viewed in terms of their surface materiality and as a continuum (albeit with intermediate experimentations) – in relation to the glass works Albers created prior to his emigration. *Homage to the Square* works are on fixed format compressed wood fiberboard, usually the Masonite brand, which Albers took care to prepare with four to eight coats of gesso before painting his circumscribed squares by applying pure color from the paint tube with a palette knife. The width of the edges of the squares determined how they appeared to be receding or moving toward the viewer. They were predominantly painted under the controlled conditions of fluorescent light and using factory-mixed colors, the details of which Albers neatly charted on the paintings' versos (fig. 6.19).

These were not his first foray into artworks dependent on wood fiberboard supports. Before arriving at the *Homage* in 1950, honing in on the square as his composition and as subject matter, in the 1930s and 1940s he experimented with a range of related subjects and formats, on both generic wood fiberboards and Masonite.[70] Paintings in this early US period, like those that followed, featured a rich range and variety of colors. Some of the works were pure abstractions, their evocative subject matter only identified through titles such as *Evening (an Improvisation)* (1935) or *December* (1940). But many paintings presage the geometrical focus of the *Homage* series and feature abstracted geometric shapes, not only squares, but rectangles and other quadrilaterals, as well as circles and ovals. In works such as *Angular* (1935), *Proto Form A* (1937), or *Gate* (1936), there is a tension between the flatness of the picture plane and the rendering of architectural forms and elements.

Architecture comes to the fore in a series of works from the period 1947–58, many of them, but not all, titled *Variant/Adobe*. These oil paintings arose from the art and architecture he and Anni discovered during multiple transformative trips the couple took to Mexico.[71] Similar to the careful color decisions for the subsequent *Homage* works, these paintings of adobe structures featured a

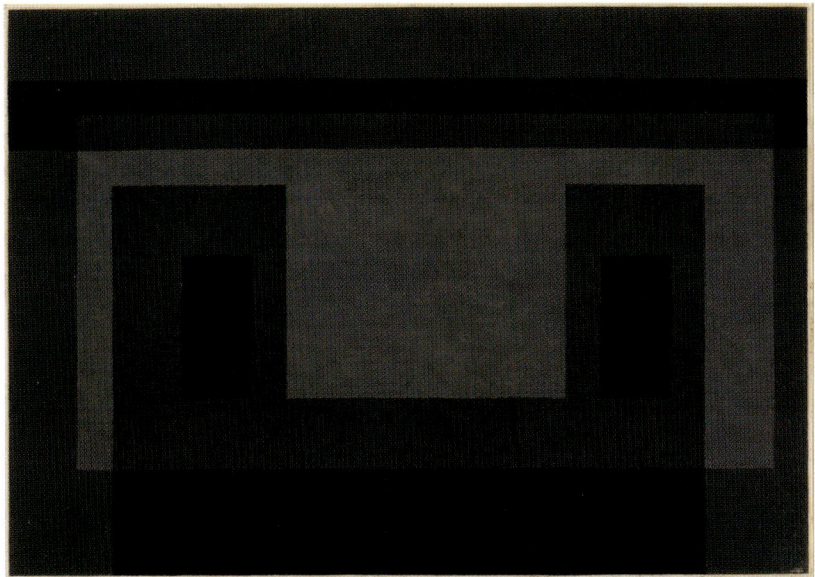

Fig. 6.20 Josef Albers, *Dark*, 1947, oil on Masonite. The Josef and Anni Albers Foundation, 2020.1.1.

circumscribed choice of colors in lively contrasting pigments, or in monochrome, such as *Dark* from 1947 (fig. 6.20). A small but important 1949 exhibition at the Cincinnati Art Museum featured *Variants*. For the publication that accompanied the show, Albers took pains to explain his process; he began with an underlying structure that provided a "definite relationship of all parts and therefore unification of form" upon which the colors were applied, unmixed, "with a palette knife directly from the tube to the panel, in one primary coat without under or over painting, without any correction."[72] Not as distilled as the *Homage* series would eventually cohere to — the *Adobe* works conform to a basic graphic composition. They show his experiments in the preparation of the substrate, as well as his early interest in Masonite and fiberboards, readily available in the United States. Finally, they also display a range of finished surfaces that can be understood as an interim stage in his experiments, some of which are more opaque in terms of the surface underneath the paint, while in others the speckle of white base is left visible through the top colors.

By the time that he began his *Homage to the Square* series, a flat substrate was essential for Albers. He preferred the smooth side of the wood fiberboard during his earliest *Homage* period, from around 1950 to 1953; thereafter he mostly used the textured side. Whereas Albers felt canvas was too soft and absorbent, the fiberboard offered the rigidity he desired.[73] As Albers scholar Jeannette Redensek has pointed out, "The firmness and flatness of the panels provided a surface especially amenable to applying paint with a palette knife."[74] As conservator Patricia Sherwin Garland notes, "These panels were carefully selected by Albers for their regularity," and early on "Albers painted on the smooth side of the panels, priming them ... on both sides, to reduce warpage."[75] Later, he discovered that priming the reverse led to the possible development of dry rot and thus, instead of in effect "sealing" the panel, he rubbed linseed oil into the reverse to prevent warping.[76] The building up of the layers of gesso was executed with care. As Garland describes the panels' preparation, an assistant "would first brush away loose particles and then apply the first coat of ground,

Exigencies of Materializing Vision

which would be left to dry overnight. It then was sanded and the second coat was brushed on, which would also dry overnight. The panels would generally take five or six coats of the gesso, but some took up to eight, in order to achieve the supremely smooth surface Albers required."[77] He felt that the paint adhered better to the rough side of the boards and that he could ultimately achieve a flatter, smoother surface. Although Albers sometimes tinted his grounds, more often the gesso grounds were strikingly white, allowing for the *most* luminous and pure painted surface.[78] This smooth, sealed, semigloss result can be compared to the surface of his glass works.

Once the base was ready, Albers would use a palette knife to apply pure oil color, usually straight from the tube. His process allowed for a very thin layering up of the material surface — he kept the surface thin and flat so that he could achieve intense color within a context of flatness. The final painting was very much dependent on the substrate material, its hardness, and its priming. As he reiterated in his published treatise *Interaction of Color*, in his classroom exercises, and the *Homage* series, color was a stabilizing element. Although placing one color next to another one might alter the appearance of each to the

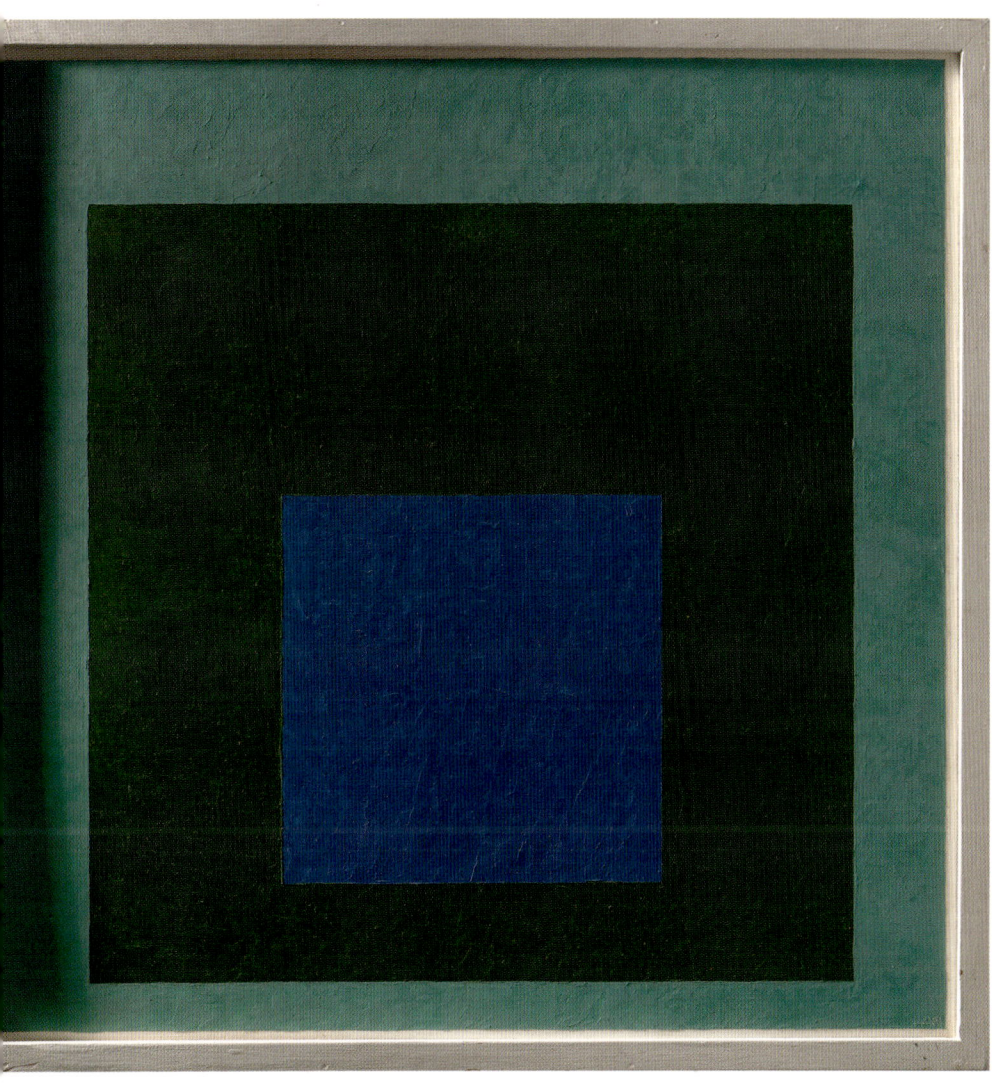

viewer – despite appearances, the material fact remained that the color itself had not changed. The surface of a painting became a key site, both in terms of how it appeared and its actual materiality. This surface materiality also served as the work's content. Unlike a *Variant/Adobe*, where a connection remained to adobe architecture as the work's point of reference, the shape of the square itself was practically meaningless in a *Homage*. And if all the meaning for Albers, and thus the content, was condensed to this materializing surface, then one could keep on making works in the series indefinitely, because the content was never – and never could be – exhausted. Each *Homage* is different, not just in its coloration and size of square, but in its surface materiality.

These works might be viewed as the flattened summation of an unwavering artistic praxis. And yet they are marked by a rich materiality at the surface plane, aided by the palette knife, which has been thickly loaded with color, rather than a brush smoothly applying thinned paint. This can be observed in paintings at close distance, for practically any *Homage*, for example, *Homage to the Square: Renewed Hope* from 1951 (fig. 6.21). Additionally, the application of a single layer of paint to the board's surface also marks Albers's *Homage* project as one

Fig. 6.21 Josef Albers, *Homage to the Square: Renewed Hope* (detail, *opposite*, and full work, *above*), 1951, oil on Masonite. The Josef and Anni Albers Foundation, 1976.1.1343.

Exigencies of Materializing Vision

Fig. 6.22 Josef Albers, *Homage to the Square: Embedded* (detail, *above*, and full work, *opposite*), 1963, oil on Masonite. The Josef and Anni Albers Foundation, 1976.1.909.

concerned with surface. The board's white substrate often shows through, purposefully giving the paintings a slightly mottled surface when examined closely, rather than a perfected solid finish gained by multiple coats (fig. 6.22). As art historian Eva Díaz observes about a 1958 *Homage*, "In the seemingly elementary demonstration of concentric squares and rectangles, the complicated language of vision is built up so that the illusions of representation are confronted by the materiality and inherent flatness of paint."[79]

Far from an image-laden Jasper Johns, Andy Warhol, or Roy Lichtenstein, removed from a paint-laden Jackson Pollock, or an object-laden Robert Rauschenberg – the *Homage* works seem somewhat detached, yet still subtly evince the artist's hand. Albers elected not to use tape for meticulously edged squares, so the line wavers slightly. There is a subtle but pronounced painterliness to the surface. He could have achieved absolutely flat surfaces, with spray paint, for example, or by using plastic or other kinds of support for the squares, yet they were hand-painted, and that materiality – a product of Albers's (albeit steady and precise) hand – is manifestly present. About an Albers painting he owned, artist Donald Judd described the many treatments and resultant

differing surface effects and opacities: "The outer band of ultramarine green is scraped to middling transparency. The white ground is clearly evident. The band in between, the cobalt green light, is almost solid and is not scraped. The central square of cobalt green is in between the other areas in transparency. . . . The identity of the color is not separable from the expanse of the areas or from the texture or transparency."[80]

Albers sought to make the viewer aware of the picture plane and his intervention in it. As Jeannette Redensek explains, "Because, as he put it, he wanted people 'to know where the painting begins,' Albers always left a thin white edge of primed ground around the finished work, and made sure that this unpainted margin remained visible in the framed picture."[81] This is most apparent when works are unframed, and it can be seen, for example, in *Homage to the Square: Lone Whites* and *Homage to the Square* (see figs. 6.1, I.2, respectively). Seemingly undifferentiated and mechanical when beheld from a distance, the paintings require the viewer to draw near and look carefully to see all that is subtly occurring on the surfaces. As art theorist Hubert Damisch has incisively observed about the *Homage* series, "The essential thing is that the controlled oscillation

Exigencies of Materializing Vision   235 between the surface effects and three-dimensional effects, as between those of relief and of depth, is played out only in the two dimensions of the plane."[82]

Beyond this subtle, surface materiality, the overarching effect of the *Homages* is one that represents the purely visual; emptied of content and heavy impasto alike, the overall impact is that of meticulously painted planes of color. The surface of these artworks represent as much "form" as Albers seemed to need. Form was embedded in color and related, for Albers, to visual perception. As he remarked, the *Homage* series intended "to proclaim color autonomy as a means of plastic organization." Importantly, he leaves the task open-ended for the viewer and his or her own perceptions of the color, repeatedly pronouncing his foundational belief that we all see color differently. With color, Albers dazzles; the surface of the painting is where the action is and where effects — visual and material — are taking place. As Albers explained, "I like to take a very weak color and make it rich and beautiful by working on its neighbors. What's gloomier than raw sienna? Now look at what I've done to it there: it's gold. It's shining and alive, like an actor on the stage. Turning sand into gold, that's my life and aim."[83] The work proclaims its materiality on — and with — this gleaming surface, which also becomes its content. When discussing the *Homage* works many years after Josef's death, Anni Albers pointed out that an eternal quality was part of Josef's goal for the paintings, contrasting his work to what she viewed as the ephemerality of the works produced by his neo-expressionist peers such as Frank Stella, seeing them as mere "decoration." She noted that Albers strove to create "lasting things" and that "he said he was making icons."[84] Indeed, Albers's works can be understood in the context of those earlier artforms, such as Byzantine icons, with their rich surface materiality of applied gold and shimmering paint, reflecting light back such that it appears to radiate from the objects.

The play of light also functions in a remarkable manner in Albers's paintings. "The effect of light is so direct as to appear to be coming through the canvas," critic Margit Rowell observes in *Artforum*. "We are as in the presence of real light, not the kind of illusionism through which light is artificially projected from an outside source onto the support of the canvas. . . . Albers's light emanates from within, it emerges from the surface like a gas and hovers over the colored field. The whole surface is animated and articulated by lambent incandescence."[85] This effect of light connects the *Homages* to his earlier glass paintings, such as the amber *Skyscrapers on Transparent Yellow* (see fig. 6.4). In the glass paintings — although he had yet to sever the subject matter entirely (they still clearly depict pergolas, steps, and factories) — content and meaning was to be found in the subtle sandblasted surfaces that simultaneously harvested light and reflected it back at viewers. After completing a *Homage* painting — whether it had been painted in a thickly applied color impasto or a thin glaze — Albers added a topcoat in either a matte or glossy varnish.[86] This top layer represents a final decision about surface, akin to his careful decisions about the surface layers and registers of luminosity — shiny or matte — of his glass works.

For Albers, viewing was not a manner of dogmatic, essentialized seeing; rather, he was interested in what he termed "conscious seeing."[87] It is this fusing of visual perception with the concentration of materiality at the surface that this chapter terms the *materializing vision* of Albers's *Homage* series. This is a dynamic viewing that strives to bring together an active surface and an engaged viewing subject. As with his fused glass paintings, with the complex materiality of their thin layers, the end effect of the *Homages* is one of flat surface imbibed with the concerns of materiality. They are, above all, like the glass paintings that preceded them, sites of materialized vision. This was understood by his viewers in the period. An art critic for the *Frankfurter Allgemeine Zeitung* wrote in a 1957 review of the "objectness" (*objectivierung*) of the *Homage* works and how one "experiences a sublime cleansing of vision. On leaving the exhibition one senses a heightened visual sensitivity and sees the world in a completely new way."[88]

The *Homages* are perceptual objects, bracketed by notions of color interaction and Gestalt theory, and they depend on subjective viewers. Albers demonstrated to his students, and – once his *Interaction of Color* was published, to a wider audience – that the perception of color is not, in fact, stable. A color can appear very different, depending on the color it is adjacent to. Thus, it is at a *Homage*'s surface that visuality is materialized, and simultaneously destabilized, for the viewer. As Eva Díaz has noted about a *Variant* (relevant in that it was a direct forerunner to the *Homage* series): "The viewer vacillates between two roles that Albers himself occupies as creator: acting as subject of the experiment in vision and as organizer of the mutable effects transpiring in the visual field as the image's components are scanned. Experiencing the basic units of perception, his audience is invited to work through sections of the picture plane, to weigh imbalances and test dynamic relations."[89] However, no matter how complex these paintings actually are, Albers keeps us, the viewers, on (and *at*) the surface of his paintings.

The *Homages* function at the surface in part because they do not intend to go beyond the surface, not the literal, flat, painted surface, nor beyond the surface in terms of greater meaning or content. If there is no content within the painting, then *the surface can become* that content. As a critic at *Artforum* noted in 1972, "it would be closer to the truth to argue that Albers chose the square not as a form but as a non-form, a neutral matrix for color. The square, because of its symmetry, stability, repetitive structure and identity of parts, is a weak form. This is especially true when it exists in a unified visual field, where no intercourse with differential configurations or spatial situations is provided. Moreover, the square is a relatively nonallusive form."[90] We experience the materializing surface in a manner initiated by Albers, and yet he allows the subject to perceive the work – as object – in a nonallusive, nonprescriptive manner. Trapped as we are by Albers on the surface, we can bridge the gap between us and it – subject and object held in tension – and then settle in and respond to the painting on its own terms, or on ours.

Trajectory of a Line: Confounding Geometries, Modern Surfaces

Albers's investigations into both surface and thing can be seen in a final set of examples that exploited a range of modern materials, especially taking advantage of newly available substances. He used laminated plastic, with its absolutely flat surface, for a series of about thirty-five engravings he called *Transformation of a Scheme* (1949–52), and a related series known as *Struc-*

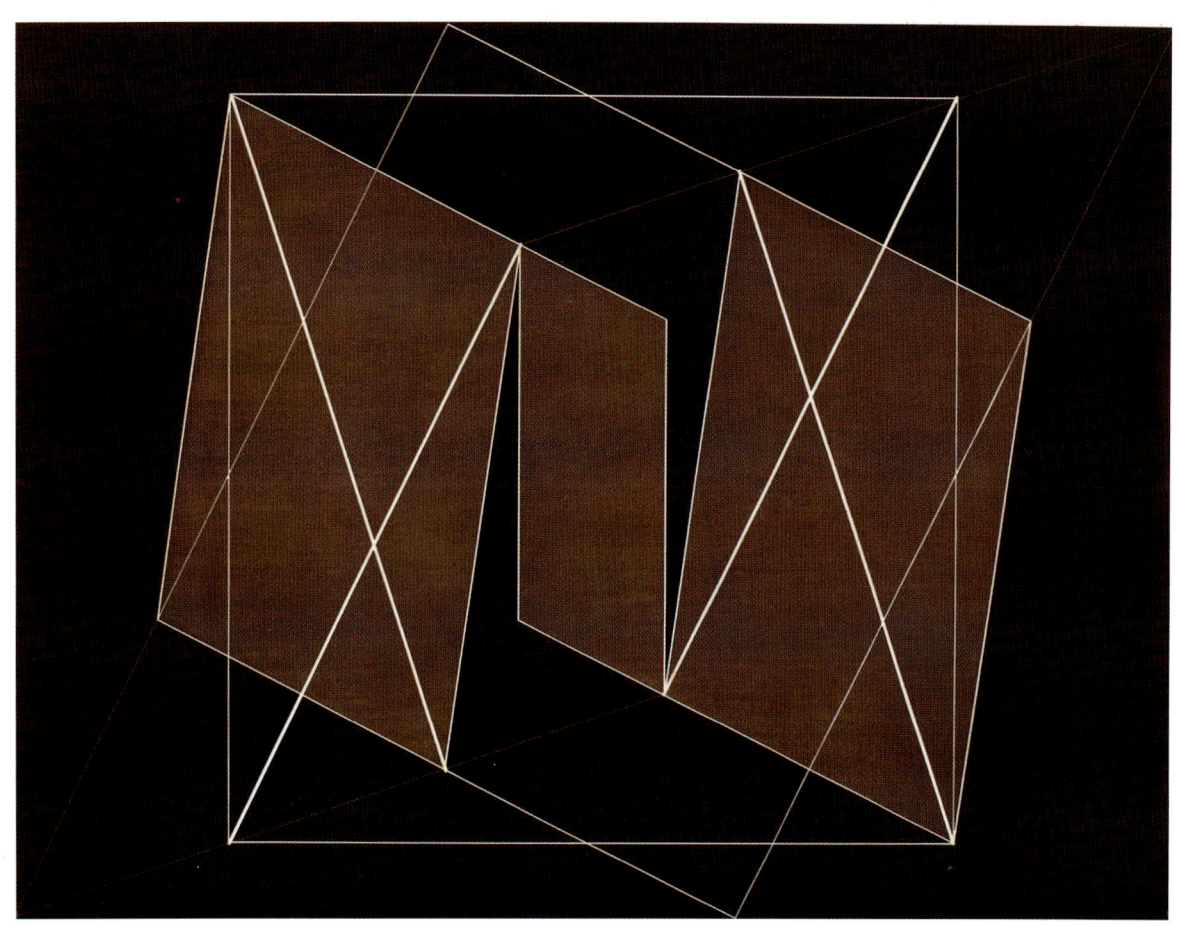

Fig. 6.23 Josef Albers, *Structural Constellation: Transformation of a Scheme No. 19*, 1950, machine-engraved plastic laminate mounted on wood. The Josef and Anni Albers Foundation, 1976.8.1725.

tural Constellations (through the mid-1960s), for which there are another hundred works.[91] In these series, Albers showcased, and played with, notions of surface and unconvincing, artificial depth — not through color but with geometric lines. For his *Structural Constellation: Transformation of a Scheme No. 19*, in contrast to the hand-painted *Homage* works, Albers had his forms professionally machine-engraved on laminated sheets (fig. 6.23).[92] He reported to Anni Albers in 1949, "On Friday I received my first engraving on laminated plastic. Pretty good, and much less expensive than in New York. Tomorrow I want to go to a factory which makes laminated plastics."[93] The machine-engraved lines were incised into two-layered laminated plastic to reveal the white layer below, similar to his Bauhaus-era sandblasted flashed glass paintings.[94] In their attention to surface and their dependence on exacting external fabricators, these laminated plastic and Vinylite works are analogous to his earlier glass paintings. As Albers wrote to his old friend Franz Perdekamp, "I merrily continue to exhibit. And more constructions are growing, which are engraved into laminated plastic with a machine. The result is similar to my sand-blown glass pictures. Just even more neutral and even less 'expression.'"[95]

On the flatness of the *Structural Constellation* series Brenda Danilowitz has observed, "Line by its very nature affirms the two-dimensionality, the flatness of the medium and continually reminds us that three-dimensional volume on a flat surface is illusion, artifice — at least one remove from reality. Albers's drawings make this assertion most eloquently and dazzle with their restrained yet spectacular ability to create a shifting and fugitive space. Simultaneously we see and read surface and depth and are held by the tension at the very heart of 'picture making.'"[96] If the *Homages* were organized around the surface relationships of color, then the *Structural Constellations* are centered around the instability of lines — presented as unresolvable, confounding geometries. Both series, in varying media and surfaces, occupied Albers acutely for decades and were about both the surface and our perceptions of it. As Albers exhorted, "Look at those lines. They are not tricks. They are real and they work and they make you think."[97] Here again, Albers celebrates the material surface; he manipulates the flat plastic laminate through the engraving process, and in doing so, engages the visual perceptions of the viewer at the surface of the work.

In works on paper, Albers once more exploited these ideas. In a series of prints made from plywood woodcuts, the striking wood grain is emphasized (fig. 6.24). In this plywood series, he brings to the fore a materiality that is, once again, rich and yet restricted to the flat, planar surface. Even more pared down, his inkless intaglio works were made using brass plates on an etching press. They eschew ink or paint; instead, they rely solely on the visible raised surface of the paper itself for their legibility (fig. 6.25). As Brenda Danilowitz has noted, "Albers was particularly sensitive to the inherent nature of the material: the finely textured linoleum of the linocut, the natural grain of the wood-cuts and the sleek, impersonal, machined surface of the engravings from brass plates are as visible and present as the lines incised into them. In an essentially symbiotic relationship the quality of the line is predicated by the nature of its host material."[98] The material surfaces were the site of content; the place at which lines reverberated, colors shifted uncertainly, and thus where the works resonated. Whether setting

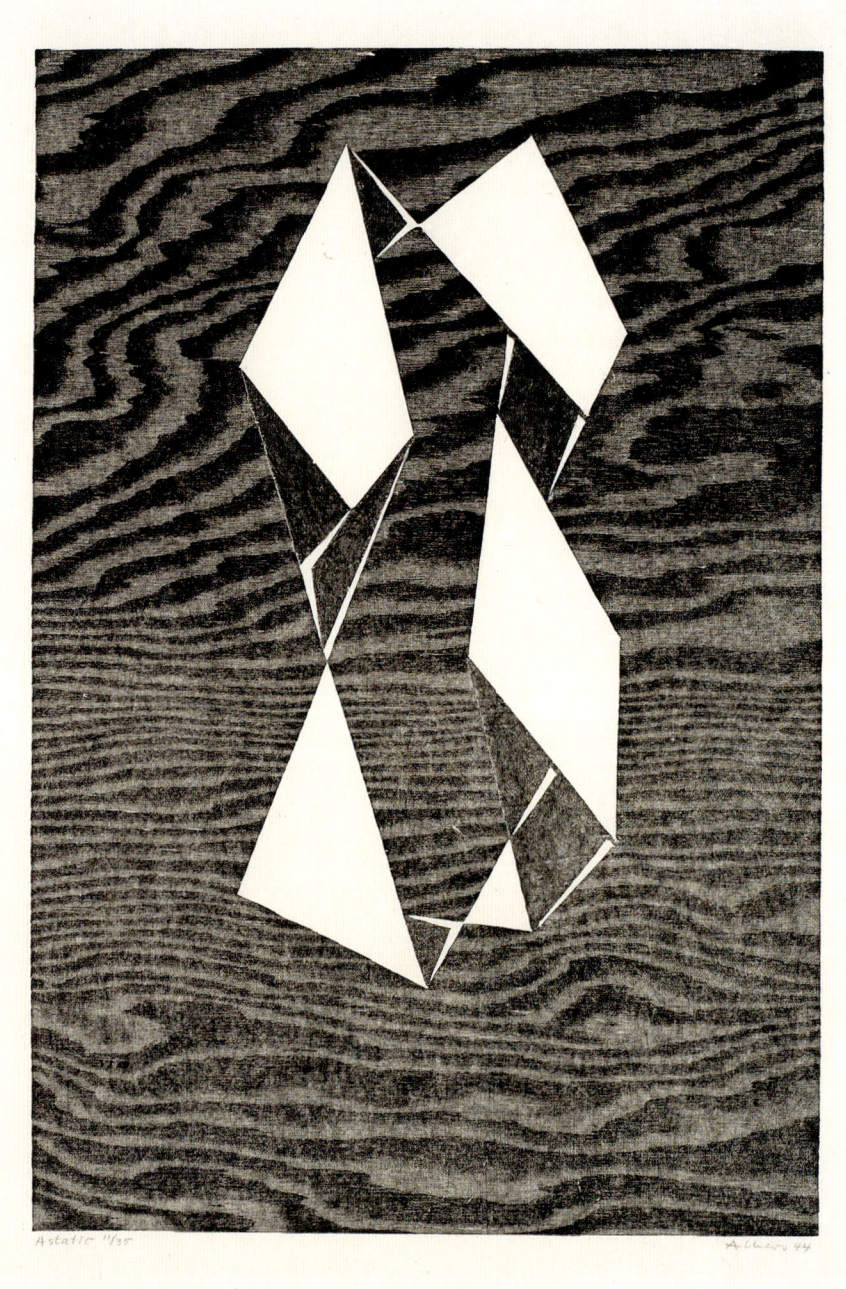

Fig. 6.24 Josef Albers, *Astatic*, 1944, woodcut from plywood: sheet. The Josef and Anni Albers Foundation, 1976.4.116.

into motion interacting colors or interacting lines, the material surface was, as ever, a place of heightened, even perplexing vision.

∎ ∎ ∎

For Albers, a painted square, an incised line on plastic, or a print on paper did not strive to depict reality or even represent what he saw, but rather, the surface of the board, plastic, or paper was the site of connection, where the subject met and visually interacted with the object, heightening awareness. Taken together, Albers's works do not have much depth nor even subject matter, because he

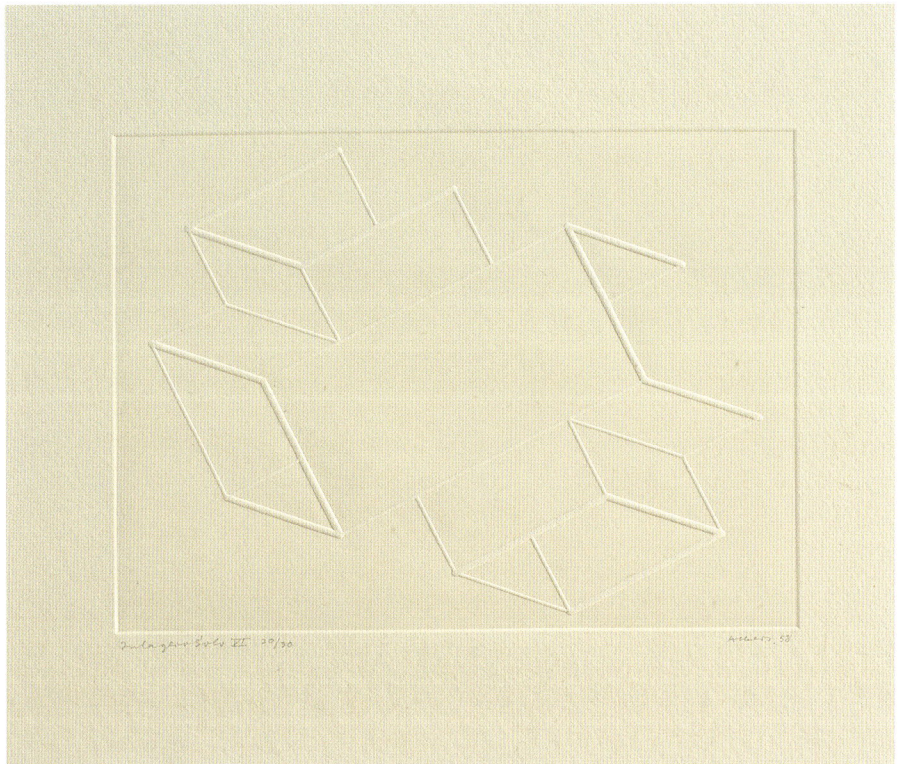

Fig. 6.25 Josef Albers, *Intaglio Solo VI*, 1958, inkless intaglio from brass plate sheet. The Josef and Anni Albers Foundation, 1976.4.141.

was interested in highlighting this interaction more than what was drawn or painted or raised on that surface. Surface was a visualized point of mediation between people and things, an interaction between subjects and objects; and it illuminated perception in the visible world. To that end, through its flattened materiality, surface itself becomes content and can be understood as being abstracted out. What is on display in the paintings, prints, and other works that have been discussed is an abstraction of surface itself.

Albers imparted an almost endless permutation of ways of seeing and shifting perceptual relationships. Beginning in Germany and from his earliest days and onward in America, the aim of art for Albers was the "revelation and evocation of vision."[99] It was his preoccupation with visuality that manifested itself in his teaching and art praxis – vision that was made resonate by differing materialities, remediated relationships, surfaces, planes, and spaces. His architectural installations in America, whether in brick, marble, or Formica, both connect to earlier works and make bold new material statements.

In his fused glass paintings, despite the differing sandblasted layers and the hand-applied paint, the end effect was one of flat surface but imbibed with the concerns of materiality. Likewise, his *Homage* series on Masonite, his works on plastic, and his prints use flatness to heighten an awareness of material, and of surface. From the material to the visual in Albers's art practice, from Germany to the United States, the varying strands of visuality in his oeuvre seemed to flatten, to require more perception on the part of the viewer, to be less dependent on material itself and more dependent on the viewing subject. The importance of this turn lies in the emphasis on the materiality of surface itself, ultimately as an evocation of materializing vision.

Exigencies of Materializing Vision

Chapter 7

Anni Albers's Design Theory and Its Objects

Typewriter Studies to Architecture's Pliable Plane

Anni Albers focused on materiality toward ends that were both more theoretical and more object-oriented than those of Josef Albers. As a weaver, materiality was critical to — and at the forefront of — her work, but this chapter focuses on the ways in which weaving's materiality was a springboard for other output, especially when put into dialogue with her theoretical writing on design. Crucial, in this context, are the objects she used in conjunction with the teaching and production of weaving — such as typewriter patterning, samples from the natural world, jewelry composed from elements purchased from a hardware store, and woven room dividers that were architectural in nature — each embodying different types of materiality (fig. 7.1). I examine the range of materials she uses and how she harnesses them to unique ends in order to better understand her theory of weaving as one entwined in — and arising from — productive processes of remediation.

Interested in art from a young age, Albers had undertaken some training in painting when she entered the Bauhaus in 1922; the weaving workshop was far from her first choice.[1] As she noted, "I wanted to go into the glass workshop, where Josef had already started, but was told they wouldn't admit anyone anymore." The other possibilities were wall-painting (but she didn't want to climb tall ladders); the metal workshop (too many sharp edges); carpentry (the blocks of wood were too heavy and too large); thus, as she summed up, "only weaving was left" (see fig. 6.10).[2] She married Josef in 1925, and they remained at the Bauhaus together through its moves to Dessau and Berlin, where it closed. In 1933 they were invited to teach at Black Mountain College, permanently emigrating from Germany. Her years in America were remarkably fruitful in terms of pedagogy and creative output, beginning with her position as an assistant professor at Black Mountain. This represents an important step up from her roles in the weaving workshop at the Bauhaus, where, apart from an interim short-term position — in 1930 Albers briefly headed the weaving department during the absence of its director — she did not have a leadership role. Already by 1949, she had established herself enough to be presented with the opportunity to have a solo exhibition devoted to her work at the Museum of Modern Art (MoMA) in New York. But it is her writing that brings to the fore her theoretical thinking while elucidating her material output. Albers also used writing as a means through which to obliquely address the underlying conditions of war.

Starting From Zero: Immigration

"Starting from zero" was a phrase Albers used in her teaching, building from the ground up the skills students needed to learn to weave, as well as to design for weaving. But it was also the approach she took when embarking on any new project — initial careful study of the conditions, decisions regarding the materials, a consideration of technique, followed by precise and flawless execution. Although the Alberses were fortunate to take the threat posed by Hitler seriously and to depart from Germany in 1933 with job offers and a place to land, "starting from zero" in many ways also describes their arrival in the United States. It did not begin auspiciously — their ship, the SS *Europa*, arrived in New

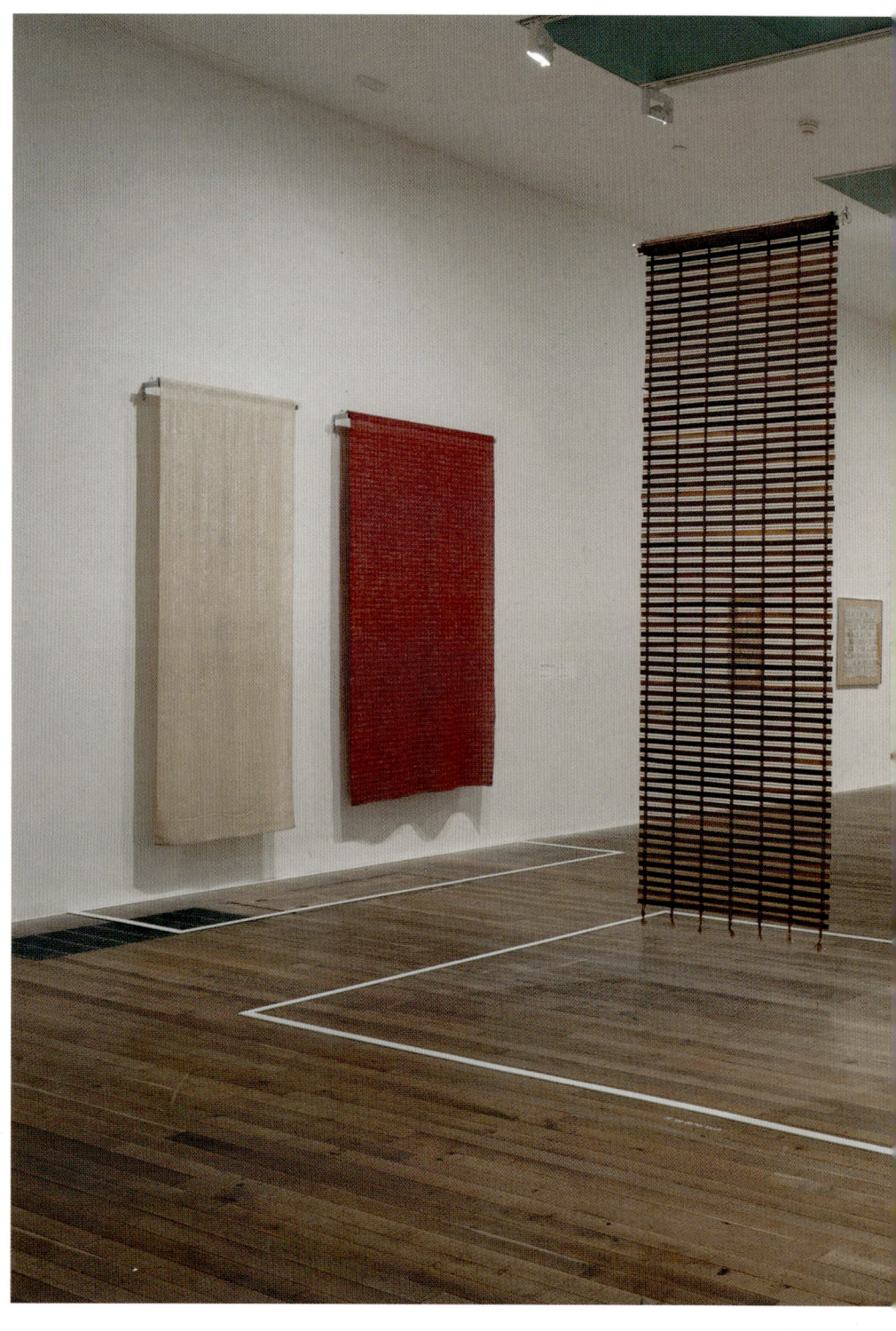

Fig. 7.1 Anni Albers, room dividers. Installation view of exhibition *Anni Albers*, Tate Modern, London, 2018.

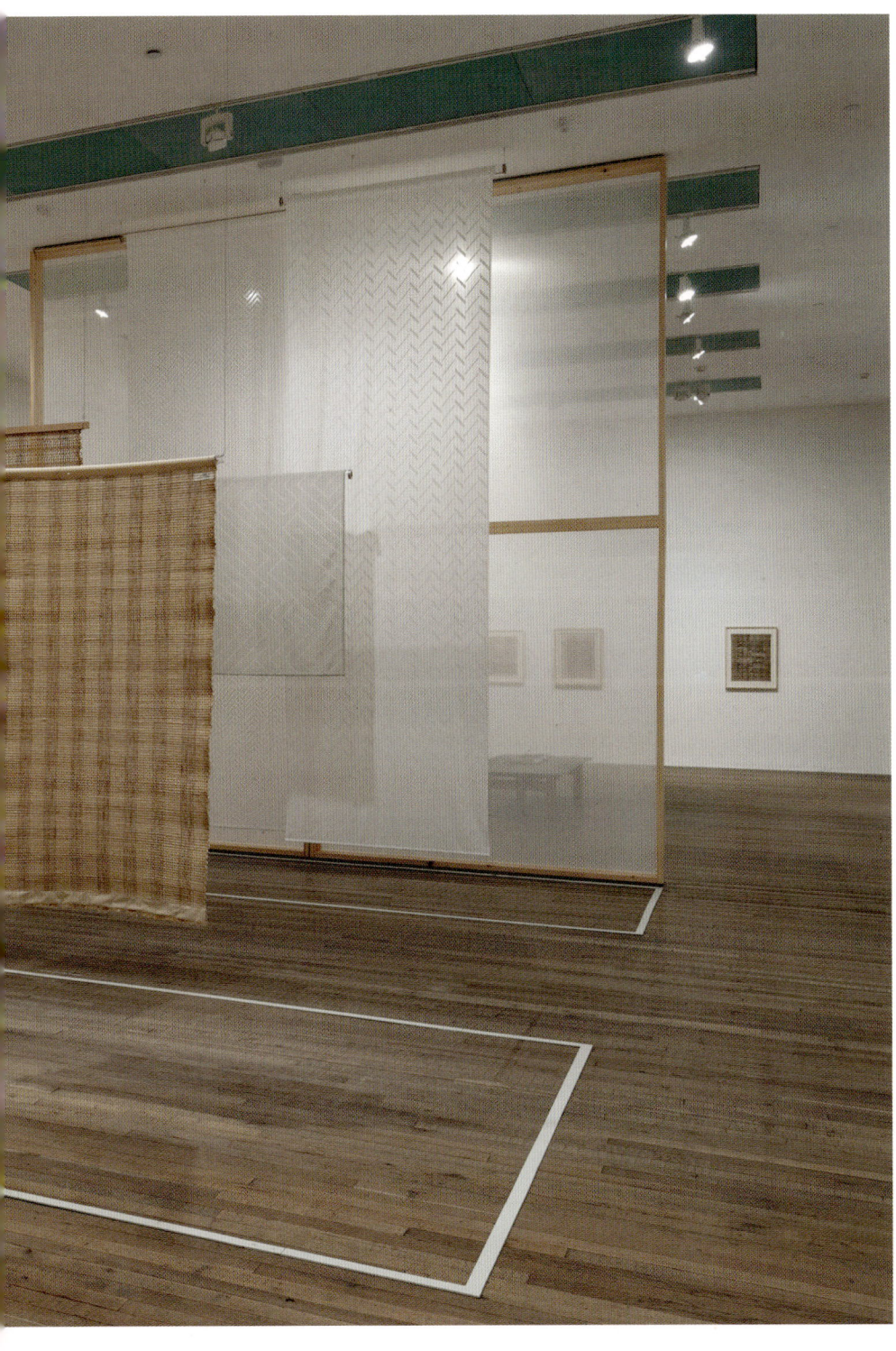

Anni Albers's Theory and Objects

York City on November 24, 1933, docking after nightfall because it had encountered a storm. For this reason, they would not experience the Statue of Liberty until a subsequent voyage, nearly thirty years later, in 1960. They maintained an affinity to the statue, and as committed as they were to modern art, when they first saw it, they were very much moved by it and as Anni would later recount, they realized "there are times in life when abstract art is *not* the solution."[3] They made their way by train from New York to Black Mountain, North Carolina, the college's rural location. Anni remembered their arrival: "We got there and after three or four days . . . there was a big festival at the college which had only fifty or sixty students all dressed up for a great event that was the holiday, Thanksgiving. And we thought it was really a day to be thankful for and we celebrated it."[4] Thanksgiving remained particularly special to the couple thereafter.

In many ways, the circumstances of their exit from Nazi Germany was marked by both fortune and happenstance, in addition to the talents the two possessed. Although she was nonpracticing, Anni's Jewish heritage put the couple in danger. By chance, Anni happened upon Philip Johnson at the door of Mies van der Rohe's apartment while Johnson was on a trip to Berlin and invited him to tea at the Alberses. For Johnson's visit, Albers put out her wall hangings, and as she described her selection, "they all had to do with practical ideas, strawlike material that could be brushed off or cleaned in some specific way and with various transparencies and so on."[5] Johnson was very impressed with the work, and when he was leaving, remarked, "Would you like to come to America?" As Anni recalled, "And it was just the high time for us to leave. For instance, the Bauhaus was closed. I had the wrong kind of background in Hitler's ideas and so on and we said, 'Well, of course.' And it was after six weeks we got a letter asking us to come to this newly founded college. . . . [The letter] said that we are quite an experimental place, not a safe place in that sense, but an experimental place with new ideas. When we came to that point Josef and I said 'that is our place.'"[6]

Because they left Germany so early in the 1930s, visas were still relatively easy to obtain; a situation that would drastically change shortly thereafter. Although many notable former Bauhaus members were able to emigrate to the United States and elsewhere, many remained trapped in Europe, languishing or perishing, even though they had job offers and support from former colleagues who had earlier relocated. As Albers remembered, the visa official asked Josef, "'Do you want a visiting visa or a more permanent one?' And he said, 'Oh no, only visiting.' And [the immigration officer] said, 'I think we ought to give you a permanent one.' Thank heavens, just think of it. . . . And when we came to America I always for years said, 'I still don't understand it, we must have a little gold star on our visa.' And only after endless years we discovered who it was, and amongst them [Edward] Warburg, Philip Johnson, Mrs. [Abby Aldrich] Rockefeller, big names and meaningless to us, saved our lives. And that of our families—we had to get parents out, our sisters and nephews out and so on. Very hard to do without money."[7]

Anni's uncle and his brothers owned the Ullstein publishing house, then Germany's biggest publisher of magazines and newspapers. Hermann Ullstein, in a 1940 article for the *Saturday Evening Post*, a clipping of which is in Anni

Albers's archive, looked back to the hair-raising event of the national boycott of Jewish businesses on April 1, 1933, and how pro-Hitler demonstrators, many of them the company's own employees, marched through the halls of the Ullstein Berlin offices on that day.[8] The company would be expropriated and Aryanized by the Nazis in 1934; members of the Ullstein family remained in Berlin and eventually fled under much more fraught circumstances than the Alberses had faced.

Albers stated that whenever Josef was asked, "What do you admire about America?" he said, "To be given a chance."[9] It was this sense of opportunity that both Alberses seized, feeling fortunate while working hard in their new environment. In an interview Anni was asked, "Would you say now, looking back, that it was lucky to get to America?" She replied, "Josef's whole life started here, mine too. And America is wonderful."[10] Nevertheless, the early years were challenging. Josef spoke little English upon arrival, while Anni could speak some basic English, having had an English governess as a child, but she noted the limited practicality of her vocabulary in those early days, "I knew words like guinea pig. But nothing abstract."[11] When asked whether it was hard to start out in a new country, Albers acknowledged, "It was difficult because I . . . had to build up a workshop . . . and had looms built, and had to try to find material."[12] However, unlike many others who would make the passage, the Alberses were able to carefully pack and ship a large portion of their domestic and artistic goods to the United States. As well as weaving material, Anni shipped over her own loom, carefully crated by a carpenter.[13] The outcome, however, was a disaster for the pair — US customs officials opened and searched their meticulously packed crates and then repacked them in a slipshod manner, resulting in the destruction and loss of many personal items, including a large number of Anni's weaving fibers which emerged tangled and dirty.[14]

Although their emigration was a major move, and one with exceptional travails, in many ways, from the beginning of their relationship, circumstances meant that the Albers had always been mobile, even nomadic. They had met when the Bauhaus was still in Weimar, moving with the school to Dessau, living in rented accommodations and then in the student dormitories there, before being given the opportunity — upon the resignation and departure of László Moholy-Nagy — to move into one of the masters' houses designed by Walter Gropius for his faculty. They then followed the Bauhaus to Berlin, remaining at the school until it was dissolved. In the United States, they went first to Black Mountain, staying until 1949, and then lived for a short period in New York, before Josef's taking up of his faculty position at Yale, living in two subsequent locations in Connecticut. They also took long sojourns to Central America as well as accepted short visiting teaching positions in the States.[15] When asked about the term "nomadic" in an interview in 1965, Albers stated, "Nomadic is my word, really, in regard to textiles. . . . We see it cropping up in so many places. For instance, in air travel we no longer use big trunks; we turn more and more to lightweight containers. Those zipper bags that you put over your arm with your suit, these are illustrations of the nomadic character of textiles. And I think that in regard to art, pictorial weaving, that is, a kind of portable mural, has a new future."[16] In many ways, Albers's peripatetic life connected well to the terms in which she viewed textiles.

War Effects—War Efforts

The couple regularly acknowledged their good fortune to be in America during a darkening period for Europe. Anni noted that they emigrated "just when the Chancellery in Germany was burned and everything [in Germany] was in ruins — going into ruins."[17] It would be some years later before the United States entered World War II, and even then the Alberses were particularly insulated from it owing to their rural location in North Carolina. There was a sense on campus that the school was too far away to be of much practical help. Unlike other institutions, which sprang into action during the war, the Alberses and other faculty at Black Mountain College seemingly made few concrete plans.

As World War II bore down on Black Mountain College, the faculty appeared at a loss in terms of how it might help the war effort. Unlike their colleagues in design and architecture schools along the Northeast corridor, or in major cities of the Midwest and on the West Coast, they felt that their remote location hampered any direct aid. And in contradistinction to schools of design, such as the New Bauhaus in Chicago, or architecture schools, such as Pratt in New York or the Graduate School of Design at Harvard, Black Mountain College focused on art within an overarching program in the humanities. Therefore its curriculum was devoid of technical training as well as the equipment and materials such training would require, so it could not easily ramp up as war commenced.

It is clear, however, that at the start of the war, extensive discussions took place at Black Mountain College. A short, typewritten document projecting wartime needs and ways the school could address them, proposed a three-pronged solution: a "change of age requirements," a "farm plan," and a "soldier education plan."[18] By proposing to lower the minimum age requirement for matriculation, the college sought to address the impending absence of both male and female college-age students who would either soon be called for active military duty or would leave of their own volition to aid the war effort through taking up practical training in other fields, such as nursing. In their stead, the college proposed maintaining the same curriculum but opening their institution to sixteen- and seventeen-year-olds, those in the final one or two years of high school, in order to retain "a nucleus of students" and keep the college going.[19] If it turned out that the educational standards could not be maintained in these younger students, it was suggested that the college could revert to its normal age group in the postwar period, having survived as an institution. The "farm plan" called for more intensive farming, citing the issue of potential food shortages — not only for the duration of the war but also in the immediate postwar period (an issue that had plagued the nascent Bauhaus following World War I in Germany). And it revealed a concern regarding the potential for a sharp rise in food prices that would, in turn, impact the college's financial situation. The plan also reflected a desire by members of the college "to be doing something immediate and concrete," through a direct contribution to the war effort, one that was also — the document notes — "humanitarian" in nature.[20]

The pacifist outlook of the faculty and their belief in a curriculum based on independent decision making and learning, and against the rote acquisition of set content, is evident in the proposals. They did not recommend new wartime courses addressing tactical, medical, or other types of training, as the Chicago Bauhaus had; rather they concentrated on postwar educational offerings. The section proposing a "soldier education plan" recommended that Black Mountain College serve as an experimental site for returning veterans, envisioned as a place where soldiers could be given "an opportunity for genuine convalescence, both physical and mental"; the plan suggested that the college's unique curriculum could allow them to learn "how to choose and how to lead," eschewing the "particular doctrines and interests" they felt other educational institutions displayed.[21]

Once war broke out, the college still looked to the postwar period – rather than the wartime present – in terms of what its members could contribute to society. In an untitled typescript addressing the problems confronting American colleges and universities, written in December 1941 or early 1942, the uncertain future and consequences of war were considered: "At the end of this war – whatever the outcome may be – America will find itself, together with the rest of the world, in an economic, social, and political crisis of gigantic dimensions.... Victory also would mean the defeat of Germany; this would necessarily be followed by strong symptoms of dissolution in that country, and like all epidemics, such a plague will not respect political frontiers.... One thing is sure; at the end of the war we will not return to the same shore from which we departed."[22] The document identifies the education of returning veterans as the most important objective of peacetime efforts, and as an immediate task for universities and colleges, even while still immersed in wartime: "When and how the war may end, what stipulations the treaties will contain, what conditions of civilian life will flow therefrom, nobody can predict in detail. Nevertheless it is possible at this moment to anticipate in outline the major great problems that will arise after the peace, and to foresee them with such certainty that plans for practical action" could be put into effect in the present.[23] Following wartime, the document advocated that education be used as a force to tackle an uncertain future and its as-of-yet unknown problems, and to ensure that the "intelligent and judicious rather than the vociferous and ignorant" would become the leaders of the generation forming a new world, leaders who could "provide a stabilizing force" during the difficult postwar period ahead.[24]

Similarly, the *Black Mountain College Bulletin* from January 1943, in an article titled "Liberal Education Today as a Tool of War," queried the US government's priority of technological training, while foregrounding the college's emphasis on the humanities and made the case for its use-value in wartime:

> Realizing the necessity of speed in the war effort, the College yet must question the narrow technical training the government is instituting. It asks whether some knowledge of – and more important, an enormous interest in – the social, psychological, historical, and economic background to the war; its possible outcomes, the civilizations and cultures out of which it grew, and the people who are fighting it, is not as necessary to a democratic army in a people's war as engineering and mathematical training. Intentionally or otherwise, the army training plan becomes a regimentation of thinking, a mass-production molding of

ideas and personalities, a way of making functional soldier-mechanics instead of thinking men.[25]

The article continues, laying out the college's core belief system as it intersected with educational policy, worth quoting at length:

> Black Mountain believes, and has for ten years attempted to realize its beliefs, that only through a truly liberal education can a young person come to any understanding of the complex and chaotic world in which he lives; that only by coming to see the world as a world of people, and by coming to know some of the reasons people agree or disagree, the ways in which they live and work side by side, can a student approach the ideal of a better society. A college must be concerned with scrutinizing the values of modern society and the frameworks through which people see themselves and their world; it must question convention and tradition, be unafraid to condemn or to criticize, be continually in search of the basic, the fundamental, and the real. In time of war, when meaningless verbal symbols are multiplied a hundredfold, when emotionalism tends to replace analysis, when propaganda takes the place of information, and when unconsidered judgments make a thousand intermediate greys black or white, such education is of tremendous importance.[26]

It does not seem that Black Mountain College – whether for reasons of location, logistics, or political outlook – was able to directly contribute much to the war effort itself. In 1942, the institution responded to a questionnaire on higher education and wartime. In it, the school was asked, "Does the interest in industrial arts education increase with the program for National Defense?" to which it replied, "Our work program (construction of buildings, interiors, farm work) is recognized as education for national defense"; to the question "Are special courses offered with regard to the present situation?," the response was, perhaps not surprising given the school's ambivalence, "So far, only First Aid, but there are several plans for new courses"; and finally, "How do fine arts and industrial arts education cooperate with community needs?" to which the college responded, "So far, no activities. We are too far from the nearest towns."[27] It is not clear that any new courses were added to the curriculum, and ultimately the school was only able to hobble through the war. Neither Josef nor Anni addressed World War II in a particularly public manner nor did their teaching change to reflect the situation. It would appear that their thinking and actions were aligned with the position of the college generally.

War Writing: A Theory of Consumption

Importantly, though, Anni Albers's writing during the war years can be examined and understood as highly political, albeit nuanced, responses to the war. She began haltingly. For example, a 1942 lecture by Albers, predominantly about her work in jewelry, took place just a few months after the US entry into the war but acknowledges the growing weight of the conflict. It also shows how her own reaction to the war was very similar to that of the Black Mountain College's community. She stated, "When I was asked to speak here about some work I had been doing... I was asked too, if I could refer in some way to defense work, in the mind of so many of us the most urgent work of the moment.... It is obvious that the urge we feel for doing our part in a catastrophe of such huge proportions as this war, stands in the foreground of all of our thoughts. But I think we have found that for many of us our part can not be that of going into a munitions factory or that of helping those who suffer in this way in a direct way. Many of us are tied to our homes, to our normal circle of action, to our work continuing as usual."[28] She went on, "But in all of us, I believe, the need to take some part is accelerating. The work we are doing may have no immediate effect on the outcome of the war, as also the work I am going to speak about here, will have no influence on it now. But as every action transmits its sense or nonsense beyond its actual radius, whatever we do has its effect. To give our actions the meaning we want them to have implies questioning them anew and becoming conscious of their implications."[29] This philosophical outlook of personal engagement and efficacy, this underlying consideration of individual action, resonates with the approach the school took toward the war more generally, supported by the fundamental objectives of the college's curriculum.

Albers concluded her lecture with this antiwar appeal, "If we can more and more free ourselves from values other than spiritual, I believe we are going in a direction that will help prevent wars. Every general movement is carried by small parts, by single people forming their way of believing and subordinating everything to this belief. We have to work from where we are. But just as you can go everywhere from any given point, so too the idea of any work, however small, can flow into an idea of true momentum."[30] This statement seems to indicate that Albers believed in the power of harnessing small elements, atomized individuals, into a larger collective movement of peace; and that she held a nuanced position on her part, and that of others, in taking personal responsibility. The war effort could be bolstered by small but powerful gestures, rather than large effects.

Albers also manifestly laid the blame for war on consumerism, viewing the constant acquisition of goods as an inherent source of strife. Her articles obliquely addressing war often appeared under innocuous titles, such as "Designing," an essay published midway through World War II, in May 1943. Here she clarifies the negative role she believed consumerism played, explaining, "Our urge for possessing is constantly nourished and is again and again a cause of war. We will have to be more sensitive to the effect of things on us and be aware of the implications that come with possessions. For things such as tools call for action; objects of art, for meditation."[31] Objects, Albers implies, are not neutral in how they resonate outward and reverberate in society, nor are they passive; rather, they can be activated or can spur thoughtful contemplation. In this essay she puts forth an argument that acquiring unnecessary, especially novel, things is detrimental to one's sense of self. She writes, "We shall have to choose between those [objects] bringing distraction and those accentuating anonymous service or self-centered individualism; between the emphasis *on being or on having*. Very few of us can own things without being corrupted by them, without having pride involved in possessing them, gaining thereby a false security. Very few of us can resist being distracted by things."[32]

As an alternative to individualism, she endorses a sense of inclusivity that suffuses both the object itself and the people who encounter it:

> We need to learn to choose the simple and lasting *instead of the new and individual*; the *objective and inclusive form in things*, in place of the *extravagantly individualistic*. This means reducing instead of adding, the reversal of our habitual thinking. Our households are overburdened with objects of only occasional usefulness.... But they cling to us as we cling to them and thus *they hamper our freedom*. Possessing can degrade us.... Having fewer things sets for the designer, or craftsman, a fundamentally new task as it implies designing things for more *inclusive use*. His attitude will have to be changed from exhibiting personal taste and the exaggeration of personal inclinations in designing to *being quietly helpful*.[33]

While rejecting frenetic change for its own sake, Albers nevertheless qualifies her bid for simplification: "Giving up continuous change does not necessarily mean that we reach a state of stagnation or boredom; it does mean overlooking moods and modes. This stabilization need not be equivalent to limitation, nor need it mean scantiness. It is designing in a manner to hold our interest beyond the moment.... It is easy to invent the extravagant, the pretentious and the exciting; but these are passing, leaving in us only neurotic aimlessness."[34] The fact that she is writing prior to the end of the war, and well before the postwar boom of domestic consumption, shows the forward-thinking nature of her design writing. Her reference to a "neurotic aimlessness" seems to anticipate the atomization and isolation felt by so many that would come to characterize — despite material plenty — the upcoming peacetime years.

Another war-era piece of design theory is an article from 1944 titled "We Need the Crafts for Their Contact with Materials." In this essay, Albers pleads for materiality as a mode of repair and urgently needed point of reconnection, a possible salve for a war-damaged world. She writes, "Our world goes to pieces, we have to rebuild our world. We investigate and worry and analyze and forget that the new comes about through exuberance and not through a defined deficiency. We have to find our strength rather than our weakness. Out of the chaos of collapse we can save the lasting: we still have our 'right' and 'wrong,' the absolute of our inner voice.... We have to gather our constructive energies and concentrate on the little we know, the few remaining constants."[35] The depth of her thinking and concern for humanity is particularly evident in her wartime writing about design. She sees design as a set of possibilities, as a way out of a dark period: "We have to learn to respond to conditions productively. We cannot master them but we can be guided by them. Limitation from the outside can stimulate our inventiveness rather than confine it. We need such flexibility of reaction in times of crisis."[36]

Less than a year and a half after the war, in February 1947, Albers continued to write presciently about the society that would follow — raising warning flags about atomization and discontentedness in her essay "Design: Anonymous and

Timeless": "Deeply concerned as we are with form and with the shape of objects surrounding us — that is, with design — it is time to look at the things we have made, to pause, think, wonder, and maybe even worry. . . . The evidence of our work is before us; we cannot escape its verdict. Today it tells us of separateness, of segregation and fragmentation." Albers identifies two distinct points of departure for design problems: the scientific/technological and the artistic. Her concern is that the approaches arrive at separate results rather than a "single, all-inclusive form that embodies the whole of our needs." She highlights the "need for the functioning of a thing" and the "need for an appearance that responds to our sense of form."[37] The anomie of the postwar period is a real risk, she portends, and yet Albers offers readers a method by which to avert disaster: through a fully embodied design process that considers users' rational needs as well as addressing their visceral senses with an artistic response.

Theory: Writing—Materiality—Weaving

Albers's antiwar writing, framed in a language of anti-consumption, materiality, and connectedness, also aligns with her design theory more broadly. "I want to make things for the contemplative mind, for those moments when you sink back into yourself," she wrote.[38] Her design praxis and her theoretical writing come together in her unique pursuit of objects that resonate cerebrally as well as artistically. Her theoretical framings are a means for understanding her sophisticated critical stance, while also offering a through line from her writing to her working processes — from her type-writing, to her typewriter studies, to her predominant artistic output: her weaving praxis. The strong link between Albers's writing and her artistic practice is key to understanding each. In bringing together her words and her weaving, T'ai Smith perceptively argues, "Writing (or typing) would become another medium through which she understood her woven practice — this becoming perfectly metaphorized in her studies for fabric patterns on a typewriter. It was in the back-and-forth (the mediation) between these two media — the two languages as they touched on one another — that she grappled with the problems of translation, or the complicated relationship between communication and materiality within her practice."[39]

As Brenda Danilowitz notes, the connection between Albers's writing and her weaving can also be seen in the titles she gave her pictorial weaving works, such as *Ancient Writing*, *Code*, *Haiku*, and *Open Letter*.[40] After her arrival in the United States, Albers penned a number of short essays in the late 1930s and 1940s that were published in journals of craft, art, and design. Thereafter, she coalesced her thought into two major books, *On Designing* (1961) and *On Weaving* (1965).[41] Her writing processes might be understood as reflecting the same qualities as her weaving praxis — both are marked by a careful build up and a line-by-line crafting, they are precise yet experimental in execution, and the results reveal insight into the medium. Her prose did not come easily but only after studied effort. Albers noted, in an interview, that she found the writing of her books enjoyable but also admitted that the precision of her formulations represented strenuous effort on her part and that the sentences were "really carefully thought out" and that it was "hard labor to be precise."[42] Albers herself would note the parallels: "All forming takes place within a framework — self-imposed or/and — imposed by the working material and the work process. We always build a structure within which to function. Think of music, think of poetry, think of social structures, think of grammar."[43] Albers's framework, which conjoined working processes with thoughtful analysis of materiality is key to understanding her systematic artistic investigations more broadly. Alongside this materials research sits her writing.

This attention to the task of producing meaningful prose is not only evident in the writing itself but can be understood as laying the groundwork for understanding her weaving at a deeper level. Beyond its form and its materiality, beyond its surface texture and complex construction, weaving can be understood as an embodiment of Albers's larger theory and outlook, and vice-versa. Both display a contemplative, reflective side, which, in turn, activates their making and reception. Her 1946 essay "Constructing Textiles" is an example of this. She begins, "Retrospection, though suspected of being the preoccupation of conservators, can also serve as an active agent. As an antidote for an elated sense of progress that seizes us from time to time, it shows our achievements in proper proportion and makes it possible to observe where we have advanced, where not, and where, perhaps, we have even retrogressed. It thus can suggest new areas for experimentation."[44]

Her writing clarifies her understanding of her weaving work and pedagogical processes as ones of active experimentation, as an evolving process of arriving at a completed piece, and also the myriad qualities — some of them phenomenological in nature — that the final work should encompass. Her writing also explains her larger outlook and the studied nuance of her design work more generally. She writes, "The form of an object which has been dictated solely by fitness is often beautiful, but in a quiet and reticent way. The engaging quality we ask for may be independent of this form, something given to it. Proportion or color or surface treatment can be such an extra quality, bearing this happy sensation we are looking for."[45] Weaving is as much a framework for making textiles emerge from thread, as it is a literal framework for dividing the space of a room, as it is a framework for contemplating the nature and varying effects of materials, surface tensions, and form itself (see fig. 7.1). Her writing allows us to see this more clearly. The restrained nature of her postwar weaving is reflected in her championing of those subtle terms ("reticent," "quiet," "retrospection") in her design criticism. She writes with a precise exactitude, while simultaneously expressing the amorphous, understated qualities of what she attributes to successful design.

Other issues that Albers touches on in her writing reflect long-standing debates in art and architectural circles. She joins in the earlier critique of the division of labor and workers' estrangement from the full cycle of production, lamenting that often the process of making goods "is so divided into separate steps that one person is rarely involved in the whole course of manufacture, often knowing only the finished product."[46] Likewise, she reiterates the prevailing anti-ornament design ethos, put forth since the nineteenth century by William Morris and the arts and crafts movement in England, by Adolf Loos in Austria, and extended into German modern circles of the interwar period. Albers writes: "Through decorating we have also learned the trick of hiding a poor material under a rich pattern. Moreover through ornament we give modest things undue emphasis. Since we have far more things than people had in former times, the rivalry among these objects becomes great. No common rhythm of design can tie them together: our chairs cry 'hey' and our ashtrays 'ho'! We esthetically overcharge our surroundings."[47] Ultimately, she seems to suggest, beauty in design is individual and impressionistic, "Rightly or wrongly, we strive for beauty by adding qualities like color, texture, proportions or ornamentation; yet beauty is not an appendage.... In works of art our characteristic uniformity, obviousness and regularity are lost in the search for a synonym, in terms of form, for an inner relation. It is easy to detect the human mind behind it, but like nature, it remains in the end impenetrable."[48] In Albers's conceptualization, the relationship between form and external, surface qualities — as well as the search for beauty in design — was a sometimes halting, even obtuse, path.

In contrast to this process, observing and working with materiality, according to Albers, ought to be approached in a straightforward manner. From the late 1930s onward, she wrote (and spoke) in a sustained manner about solid interactions with material. In her 1937 essay (published in 1938), "Work with Material," she exhorts her readers: "We must come down to earth from the clouds where we live in vagueness, and experience the most real thing there is: material."[49] She declares, "Civilization seems in general to estrange men from materials, that is, from materials in their original form.... But if we want to get from materials the sense of directness, the adventure of being close to the stuff the world is made of, we have to go back to the material itself, to its original state, and from there partake in its stages of change."[50] In a 1939 essay, Albers articulates the importance of the careful study and useful drawing out of the properties of materials as a way to release art from subjectivity and representation — as a method to solidly center artistic output.[51] She posits, "Recognizing in matter its potentialities and its limitations may also help us clarify the ideas of the medium in art when it is immaterial. This idea of the medium in art is often misunderstood. A distinction is necessary, to any artistic end, between the medium serving a purpose outside itself and the medium in its own right as for instance words used for reporting vs. words used in poetry. Some media have to be released from their representative meaning to make them fit for purpose."[52] Albers, in considering notions of subjectivity, saw materiality as a mode to ground oneself more objectively.

Albers theorized materiality as a linchpin in terms of subjective (which she deplored) versus objective output. She identified certain designs as problematically subjective — using a unique, handwoven tablecloth that was not suited for industrial production as an example. As she explained, such a tablecloth "wasn't satisfying because it was an over-subjectifying of something that wasn't worth it. When you have a tablecloth that is so active you can't put a plate on that tablecloth, you can't put a vase with flowers on it, it was far too dominating."[53] Albers sought to counteract the subjective and the representative in objects with a concrete valorization of materiality; a search for the right form for the material. In a 1968 interview, she articulated how materials should be used in order to produce objective, rather than subjective, work:

Albers: When a painter or weaver or someone has to prepare the material you learn what the material tells you and what the technique tells you. While today —
Interviewer interjects: There's a sort of dialogue between you and the material.
Albers: And that frees you from this too-conscious searching of your soul which very often turns just into this kind of intestinal painting. It frees you and gets you away from a too-subjective way of work.
Interviewer: Yes, I understand. But although, as you said, that it frees you from the subjective —
Albers: From the too-subjective. You can't avoid being subjective. But a kind of objectifying happens when you have to concentrate on the demands of the materials and the technique. . . . And I find that healthy and not limiting. And I still think that it really might be the salvation for many of those who dabble so easily in the too-readily-available materials.[54]

Elsewhere, she advocated for "direct work with a material," as "one way that might give us back a greater sense of balance, of perspective and proportion in regard to our perhaps too highly rated subjectiveness, projected so often as the theme in those areas of art that are not operating under a resistant material."[55] She championed breaking out of the mold in artistic practice — by truly engaging and pushing the boundaries of a material itself. In doing so, the goal was to create strong, new work that was objective in nature, less disposed to individual subjectivity.

Albers believed that the materiality should define a work, rather than personal authorship. As she stated in a 1947 article, "The less we, as designers, exhibit in our work our personal traits, our likes and dislikes, our peculiarities and idiosyncrasies, in short, our individuality, the more balanced the form we arrive at will be. *It is better that the material speaks than that we speak ourselves*. The design that shouts, 'I am a product of Mr. X' is a bad design."[56] She suggests that the material itself be given agency: "The good designer is the anonymous designer, so I believe, the one who does not stand in the way of the material; who sends his products on their way to a useful life without an ambitious appearance."[57] In the same vein, she argued two years later, in 1949, one should not "esthetically overcharge our surroundings — it is better that the material speak than that we speak ourselves."[58]

In order to find a successful and truly creative design outcome, Albers would also look to the push and pull of materiality, and the need to sometimes transcend the potential limitations of a material. She noted, "the stuff the world is made of, the inherent discipline of matter acts as a regulative force: not everything 'goes.' To circumvent the NO of the material with the YES of an inventive solution, that is the way new things come about — in a contest with the material. It is this knowledge that rules are the nature of nature, that chaos is senseless, that is thus transmitted to and through a work that is art."[59] The rules and limitations of materiality — either self-defined or external — pushed the mind and creativity of the artist, Albers believed. As she stated, "The process from the

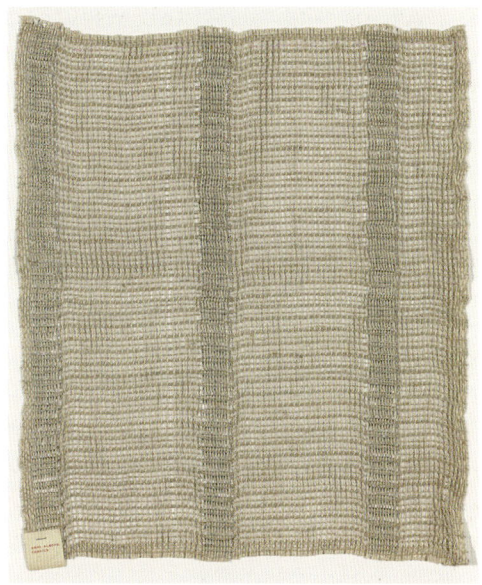

Fig. 7.2 Anni Albers, fabric sample, ca. 1949, linen and metallic thread.

vague impulse to make something to the final condensation is not served best by limitless freedom but by limitation, by the compelling rules of matter or by self-imposed rules."[60]

In her own weaving, Albers's use of materials was highly experimental, both stretching the limits of traditional materials and folding in new substances. She held materiality in the highest regard, asserting, "Little is gained when nothing can be learned about the inherent tidy behavior of matter."[61] Her inventive use of a range of materials was singled out for praise by critics throughout her life. First in Germany she experimented with jute, cellophane, rayon, and other synthetic goods, often mixing them with more traditional fibers for added structure, texture, or other qualities, such as sound-absorption or light reflectivity (culminating in her innovative wall coverings for a trade school auditorium by Hannes Meyer in 1930).[62] In the United States, she kept abreast of technological changes and was highly interested in what the chemical industry could offer in terms of new materials and their special properties, resulting in works in, for example, a combination of linen and metallic thread (fig. 7.2). In her essay "Constructing Textiles," she makes the point that the basic process and techniques of weaving had not changed for centuries but that the momentous development was in the modern materials with which one could weave. She cites noteworthy materials that were "glazed or water-repellent, crease-resistant, permanent-pleated, or flame-retarding, mothproof, or shrinkage-controlled, and those made fluorescent."[63] It was this experimentation and studied pushing of creative boundaries in her carefully selected materials, coupled with a substantial theoretical body of writing elucidating her practice, that allowed Albers to flourish from the time she arrived in America.

The MoMA Exhibitions

Albers's recognition and success in America was nearly immediate, and sustained. It can be measured by her rapid entry into established design circles, especially her continuous presence in exhibitions at the Museum of Modern Art. During her lifetime, her work was included in no fewer than twelve exhibitions there, beginning with the groundbreaking *Bauhaus, 1919-1928* (winter 1938–39), which introduced the school, its pedagogies, and output to an American audience. She was shown in the group exhibition *Textile Design* (1945), and her jewelry designs, created in collaboration with Alex Reed, were exhibited as part of the show *Modern Handmade Jewelry* (1946). Other celebrations of modernism at MoMA encompassed her work, such as *Modern Art in Your Life* (1949) and *Three Modern Styles* (1950). Albers's exemplars were also present in *Good Design* (1951–52) and *New Design Trends* (1952). The *Good Design* series, like its predecessor, the *Useful Objects* series, was a multiyear run of exhibitions in the 1950s, developed in collaboration with Chicago's Merchandise Mart, in which a jury committee annually selected and displayed objects of excellent design that were readily available on the commercial market. For example, the Albers piece selected was a gray-and-white textured cotton, manufactured by the Original Textile Company and priced at $6.90 a yard (quite expensive for 1950). In a nod to its potentially elite clientele, the brochure accompanying *Good Design* noted that the fabric was available through decorators and architects, as well as at the store Patterson Fabrics.[64]

Her most important show, however, was the major monographic exhibition, *Anni Albers Textiles*, which was installed by Philip Johnson and ran from September 14 to November 6, 1949 (fig. 7.3).[65] It was one of the first exhibitions of a female artist at MoMA, the first solo exhibition there by a weaver, and the first female monographic exhibition in the Department of Architecture. After debuting in New York, it then traveled extensively in the years 1950–53 as part of MoMA's program of circulating shows. In all, the tour consisted of twenty-six venues – museums, galleries, and universities – in the United States and Canada including, among others, the Newark Museum, MIT, Harvard, Northwestern University, the Baltimore Museum of Art, Newcomb Art School of Tulane University, the Albright Art Gallery, Indiana University, and the University of Manitoba.[66] A MoMA press release hailed Albers as "one of the most imaginative and daring of modern weavers working in the United States. . . . The show will be a selection from her enormous creative output covering a wide range of expression including educational experiments using paper, corn, grass and string to produce textile effects; her famous drapery, upholstery and dress materials, and pictorial tapestries."[67] The exhibition received good feedback from the venues and institutions that subsequently showed it. The gallery of Newcomb Art School, at Tulane University, reported back to MoMA that "the exhibition was one of the best we have had this year. Anni Albers textiles are some of the best and most imaginative textiles of today."[68]

Albers had long known Philip Johnson from her days in Berlin; he had been instrumental in the Alberses' invitation to America. But it was Edgar Kaufmann, head of the Department of Industrial Design at MoMA, who during a visit to Black Mountain College to give a guest lecture, saw Albers's work and offered her the opportunity to exhibit at MoMA.[69] The exhibition planning correspondence is predominantly between Kaufmann and Albers. Organized in groupings, the first section of the show was pedagogical in nature and included her

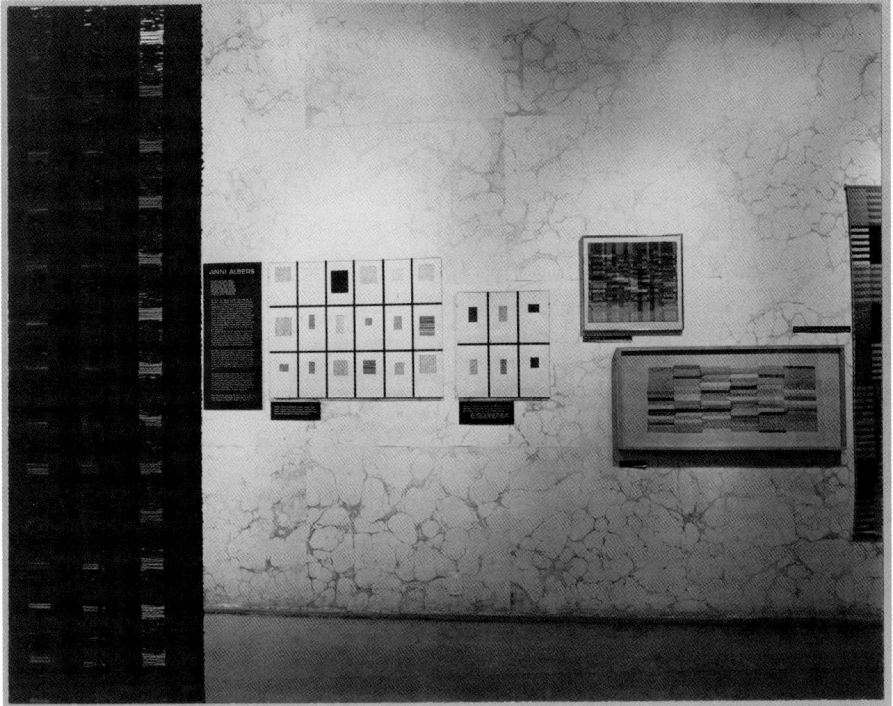

Fig. 7.3 Anni Albers, room divider (*left, foreground*), typewriter studies (*center, framed*), weavings (*right*) in exhibition *Anni Albers Textiles*, Museum of Modern Art, September 14–November 6, 1949, gelatin silver print. Photograph by Soichi Sunami.

Bauhaus-era fabric samples, sketches, and tapestries; pre-weaving texture samples made at Black Mountain College; and materials illustrating the steps from the pre-weaving studies to the actual weaving of fabric. The remainder of the show comprised sections demonstrating her weavings' material qualities and usage, including areas devoted to "Partition Material," "Drapery Material," and "Stiff Material."[70] On display were tapestries, as well as samples of Albers's designs for wall coverings, cellophane mats, partitions, and drapery.

The pre-weaving studies represent a core part of Albers's design process and pedagogy. She used them to explore the visual effects possible through differing materiality – they were mainly composed from a range of materials gleaned from the natural world – before advancing to the stage in which actual fibers or threads would be employed. As Albers articulated, "These textile illusions deal, of course, only with the appearance of textiles and not with their actual and practical characteristics, like being soft or stiff, heavy or light, porous or dense, warming, etc. the long list of qualities we expect of textiles."[71] In labeling the studies for display at MoMA, she gave precise descriptions indicating the patterning by orientation or type, which signaled the purpose of each exercise: "dried grass – vertical lines," "sections of twigs cut open – vertical design," "dried grass flowers and sections of stems – stripe arrangements," and "bark twists – checker board pattern."[72] Checklists from the exhibition and installation photographs show that twenty-four studies were exhibited in all, framed in clusters of eighteen "appearance" studies using natural materials and six "weave construction" studies.[73]

As evidenced by the exhibition, the materiality of Albers's praxis was paramount. In the carefully detailed lists of materials Albers shipped to MoMA, her varied choice – and creative use of – threads was evident. This included natural threads such as cotton, raffia, and hemp; those traditionally used in textile production, such as gold thread, chenille, and copper thread; as well as newer, synthetic materials, including rayon and cellophane.[74] Often she mixed the two — traditional and new — in woven works, combining jute and aluminum, hemp and cellophane, or linen and metallic thread (see fig. 7.2). She noted that the choice of the raw material and the construction of the weave could "support each other or counteract each other. Soft threads can be used to make a stiff material and vice versa. Silk threads are soft in a satin construction and stiff in a plain weave, or taffeta weave."[75] In weaving, she might be understood to be putting *structure* into a dialogue — or sometimes a dialectic — with *materiality*.

Lessons in Materiality

In the classroom, Albers strove to use materials and materiality as a mode of creative thinking. Her teaching praxis was another area where she sought to impart clarity in thought and in the design of objects alike, as with her writing and exhibitions. Though she had taught at the Bauhaus, for a period leading the weaving workshop, it was only after emigrating to the United States and taking up the position of assistant professor of art at Black Mountain College that her pedagogical skills were formally rewarded. She and Josef both taught there for sixteen years, from 1933 to 1949.

Josef's skill at teaching has been well-documented, but Anni was also an inspiring teacher. "Today my fourth day of teaching with mounting enthusiasm, in fact they applauded today after my lecturing session," she reported in a letter to Josef in June 1955 when she was away teaching a summer session at Haystack Mountain School of Crafts, on Deer Isle, Maine.[76] Careful and detailed notes on Albers's classroom teachings have been preserved by Lore Kadden-Lindenfeld, a student in Albers's course at Black Mountain from 1944 to 1948.[77] They record notes on the ideal fibers for a variety of weaving outcomes, careful graph paper charts of patterns for weaving, as well as drawings of weaving knots and designs (fig. 7.4).

Upon Albers's arrival at Black Mountain College, a functioning weaving workshop was not immediately available; it took some time for the school to acquire and set up looms. She used the intervening period to develop a curriculum that readied students for their eventual loom work. It proved so successful that she retained components of these pre-weaving exercises, even after the workshop was fully equipped. During another period without access to the weaving workshop's looms, when the new buildings at Lake Eden were being constructed, she developed further assignments. In an interview, she recalled "I had to teach a class without any roof over my head, or looms — no looms were available. And we had to do something that could be done by just sitting down together, and we started by selecting grasses and seeds, and so on, and putting them together in specific orders, which are textile orders."[78] These texture designs, predominantly in natural materials, included the use of ears of wheat, melon seeds, and wood and metal shavings (fig. 7.5). In Albers's pedagogical practice, crafting encompassed a mode of deliberate thought with regard to form, entwined with a hands-on experimental relationship to materials. This

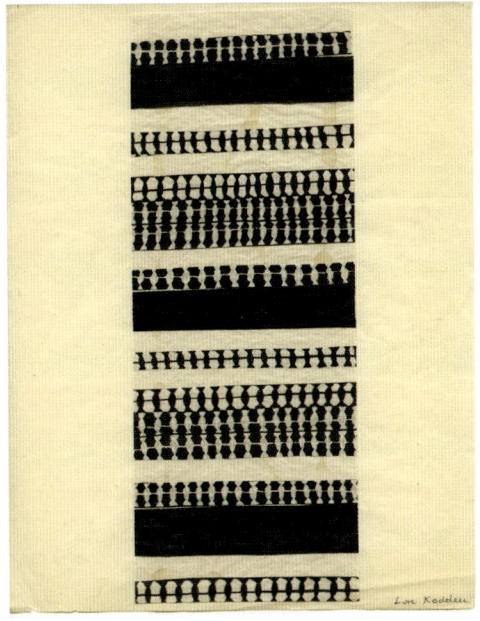
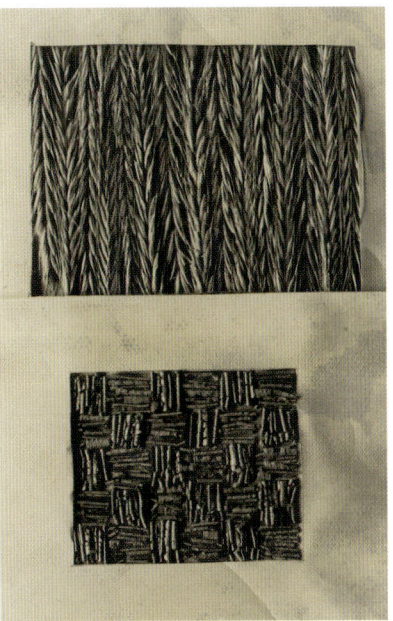

Fig. 7.4 Lore Kadden-Lindenfeld, weaving study from Anni Albers's weaving class at Black Mountain College, ca. 1945, ink and pencil on cut paper mounted on paper. The Josef and Anni Albers Foundation.

Fig. 7.5 Studies made with grass seed heads (*top*) and wood shavings and twigs (*bottom*), Black Mountain College, 1940–41. Photograph by Claude Stoller.

outlook is summarized well in her 1944 article "We Need the Crafts for Their Contact with Materials," in which she states, "Education in general means to us academic education, which become[s] synonymous with an unproductive one. If we want to learn to do, to form, we have to turn to art work and specifically to craft work as part of it. Here learning and teaching are directed toward the development of our general capacity to form. They are directed toward the training of our sense of organization, our constructive thinking, our inventiveness and imagination, our sense of balance in form — toward the apprehension of principles such as tension and dynamic . . . the long list of faculties which finally culminate in a creative act."[79]

Training in vision and form-making, via a careful analysis of materiality, was the pedagogical process by which she led her students into increasingly specific tasks. Yet her regard for the simple, the clear, and the basic was often the end objective of the design process, arrived at via a set of steps or creative operations. As she explained, "Learning to form makes us understand all forming. . . . This is fundamental knowing. The difficult problems are the fundamental problems; simplicity stands at the end, not at the beginning of a work. If education can lead us to elementary seeing, away from too much and too complex information, to the quietness of vision, and discipline of forming, it again may prepare us for the task ahead, working for today and tomorrow."[80] This was the mode by which she taught her students to analyze the world and to create within it. A 1949 article observed about Albers's teaching, "In her educational work she tries to restore the tactile and visional sensibilities of her students to their fullest usefulness. To achieve this she initiated a series of texture and pattern studies using any material, from string through newspaper to ears of corn, and from meticulously perforated sheets of cardboard to typewritten doodles on slips of colored paper."[81] More than imparting intricate weaving techniques, Albers grounded her pedagogy in the exploration and analysis of materiality, to build up skills and sensitivity in her students.

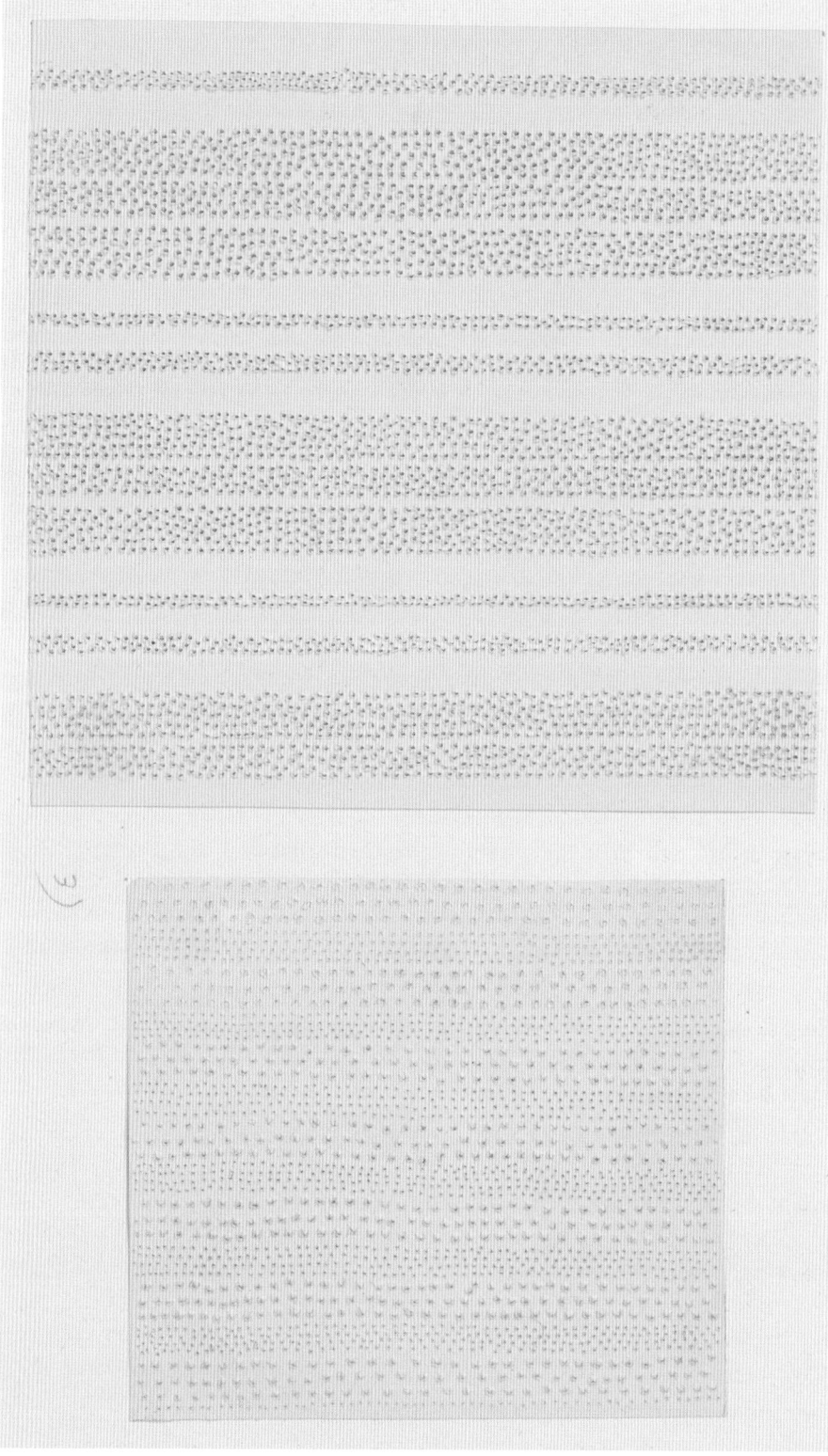

Fig. 7.6 Anni Albers, studies made by puncturing paper, n.d. (ca. 1940s), pinpricks on paper mounted on board. The Josef and Anni Albers Foundation, 1994.18.9.

The surface materiality—or its *appearance* as material—was also key. Albers taught this in the form of *matière* studies. To the same degree that it was for Josef, *matière* was an essential teaching tool and concept in Albers's classroom. As she defined it, *matière* was a term used to indicate the surface appearance of a material, for example, roughness or smoothness, dullness or gloss, or an articulation of the grain. "*Matière*," wrote Albers, "being mainly a quality of appearance, is an aesthetic quality and therefore a medium of the artist; while quality of inner structure is, above all, a matter of function and therefore the concern of the scientist and the engineer."[82]

Besides surface appearance, other central components in the educational trajectory of her students were investigations of texture, touch, and working with the varying tactility of materials. Albers strove to impart "sensitivity toward textile surfaces" via her exercises in texture.[83] She recognized receptiveness to tactility as a receding skill; consequently, students were in need of training. In her important book *On Weaving*, one of the most fundamental chapters is "Tactile Sensibility," where she makes the point that we are out of touch with touch. "All progress, so it seems, is coupled to regression elsewhere. . . . We certainly have grown increasingly insensitive in our perception by touch, the tactile sense. . . . [There is] little chance—to handle materials, to test their consistency, their density, their lightness, their smoothness."[84]

As Albers recalled in an interview about her teaching in this period, "I have developed some new ways of developing this tactile sense, which has been lost to a large degree because of our always using ready-made materials: cellophane-wrapped bread, instead of the dough."[85] In order to revitalize their sense of tactility, she asked her students to explore the inherent surface quality of materials by gathering moss, bark, paper, flower stems, shavings of wood and metal and affixing them to paper.[86] Albers further instructed the students to go out and find "any kind of material they wanted to use" and then array it to produce textile arrangements, within a rectangular structure, which, she observed, went back to the earliest weaving (see fig. 7.5). About these works she noted, "By preserving an underlying textile structure which is horizontal-vertical, it looks almost like a textile and helps clarify a concept of the appearances of textiles. In that respect this is a Black Mountain development of mine."[87] These skills in "tactile effects," she points out, are as important for weavers as volume is to a sculptor, space to an architect, color to a painter.[88]

Paper, with its unique surface and structural possibilities, as well as its ready availability, played as significant a role in Albers's exercises, as it did for Josef. Paper surface experiments resulted in a variety of manipulations, including "scaly" patterning, paper fringes, thin paper strips laid over corrugated surfaces, and arrangements of horizontal and vertical paper twists.[89] Another exercise was to make a smooth piece of paper appear fibrous by scratching its surface, perforating it, tearing it, or twisting it.[90] Students also used paper to imitate the appearance of textiles—these included explorations in corrugated paper, in pinprick patterning, and in other types of perforations (fig. 7.6). The pinprick results were described by Albers using textile terminology as works in "stripes," "herringbone pattern," "wide stripes," "vertical stripes," "all over small

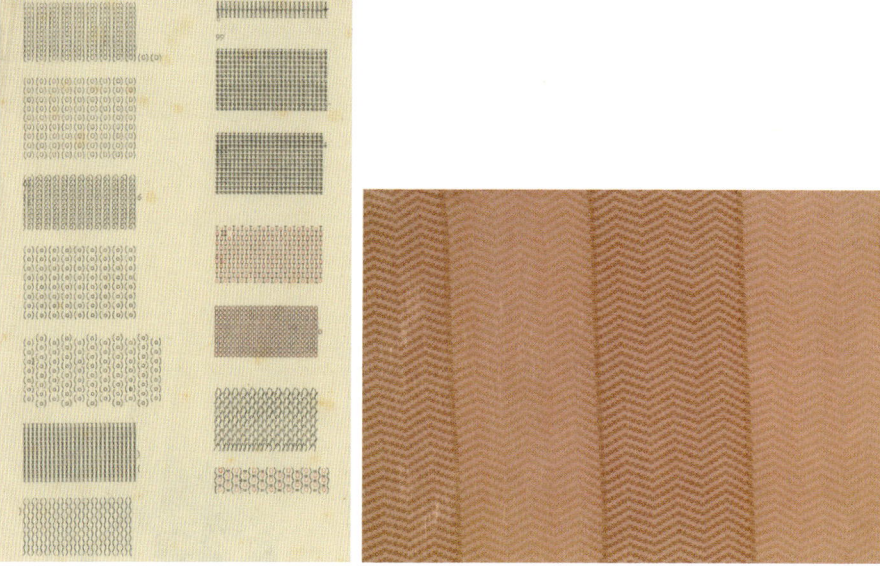

Fig. 7.7 *Left*, Katja Rose, designs for fabric using patterns made from typewriter printing, 1932. *Right*, Hajo Rose, fabric using typewriter patterning, 1932, linen and artificial silk. Bauhaus-Archiv, Berlin.

pin-pricks," and "all over large pin-pricks."[91] Students also made simple paper weavings in brown and white paper.

Finally, Albers brought all of her exercises together in the act of weaving itself. In moving on to the final form and structure of an actual weaving, materiality – as surface tactility and as substance – remained at the core. As she asserted, in weaving, or, at a larger scale, in works of architecture, the "material surface together with material structure" represented the main components of a work.[92] From the basic studies with simple materials gleaned from the natural world surrounding Black Mountain College, to more complex exercises, leading up to weaving on the loom, Albers strove to give her students a fundamental education that would serve them well in a rapidly changing world. Instead of training them in the latest techniques, she believed in a path of discovery that led to a core understanding of weaving's properties, and thus its potentialities. As she noted, she, "tried to develop a rather basic approach to the problem of construction of weaves, emphasizing the structure, rather than what is so easily done in handweaving, the decorative side."[93] Even as her students organized ears of wheat or lined up twists of paper, her goal was always a serious one – to give them a foundational education that would prepare them for employment as designers in industry or for careers in teaching.

The Typewriter Studies: Typing as Textile Thinking

Beyond the close study and experimentation with materials such paper and objects from nature, Albers looked to the potential of other media – and thus other ways of seeing and pattern-making – for educating weavers. Her use of typewriter studies represent just such a mode of alternative investigation.[94] The typewriter as a design tool was not a new concept; it directly connects to earlier work at the Bauhaus in Germany. In the 1930s, students at the school had experimented with typewriting and textiles. They conceived of fabric designs using typewriter characters, some of which were made into textiles. For example,

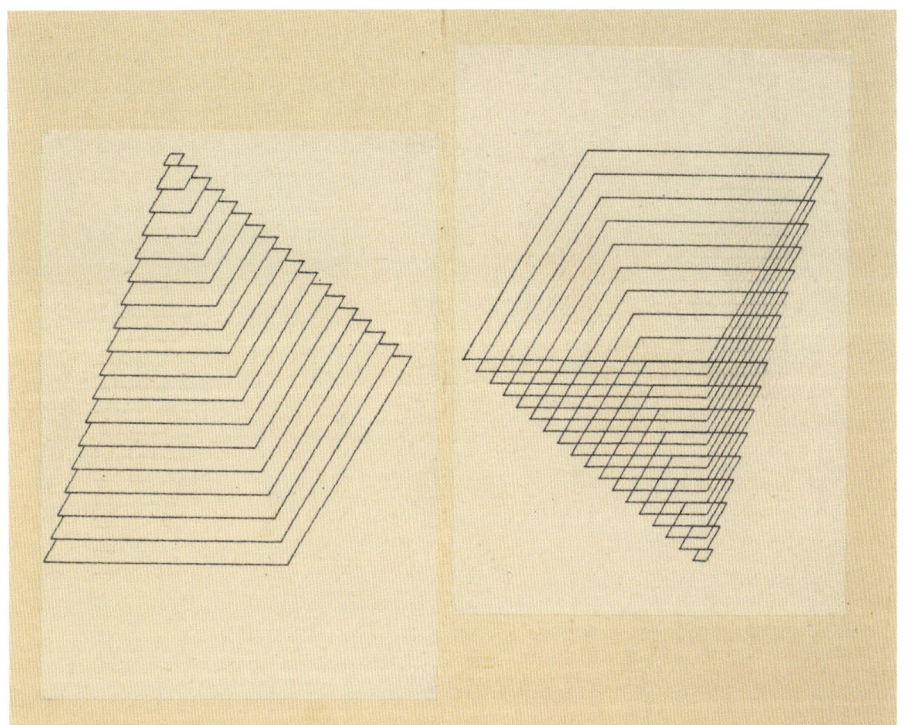

Fig. 7.8 Student typewriter study, Bauhaus, ca. 1923–33, typewriter ink on paper mounted on board. The Josef and Anni Albers Foundation, 1976.26.10.

Bauhaus students Katja Rose and Hajo Rose used a typewriter to make red-and-black typed text patterning designs on paper, with some exemplars converted into typewriter character patterning on linen and rayon fabric (fig. 7.7).[95] However, these works seem to be investigations into modern print patterns, with the potential for mass production as fabric.

As part of their lessons, both Josef and Anni Albers assigned their students creative tasks to be accomplished using a typewriter but with different objectives in mind. Josef, deploying the exercise in his Bauhaus Foundation Course in the late 1920s and early 1930s, termed his assignments "construction exercises," and they were intended to help students understand two- and three-dimensional relationships. Utilizing a limited number of characters on a typewriter, the resulting student works were two-dimensional images, but they suggested three-dimensionality. For example, the typewriter study of "pyramids created from two keys," made from horizontal and oblique key strokes, create the illusion of positive, solid and negative, empty three-dimensional volumes (fig. 7.8). Other Bauhaus-era typewriter works depicted two-dimensional intersecting planes, made from differing key patterns and appearing to be three-dimensional, while another exercise focused on the task of creating the illusion of opaque and transparent forms by using the typewritten characters.[96] Josef Albers also used guilloche patterns for teaching – these were ornamental, machine-made design patterns featuring intricate connecting circles and curves; the patterns are more elegant and complex than typewriter marks, yet the repetition of a machined mark clearly connects the two.[97]

While Josef Albers's assignments emphasized using a modern machine with the goal of projecting three-dimensional forms on a flat paper surface, Anni Albers's objective was very different. As part of her curriculum at Black Mountain

Anni Albers's Theory and Objects   265

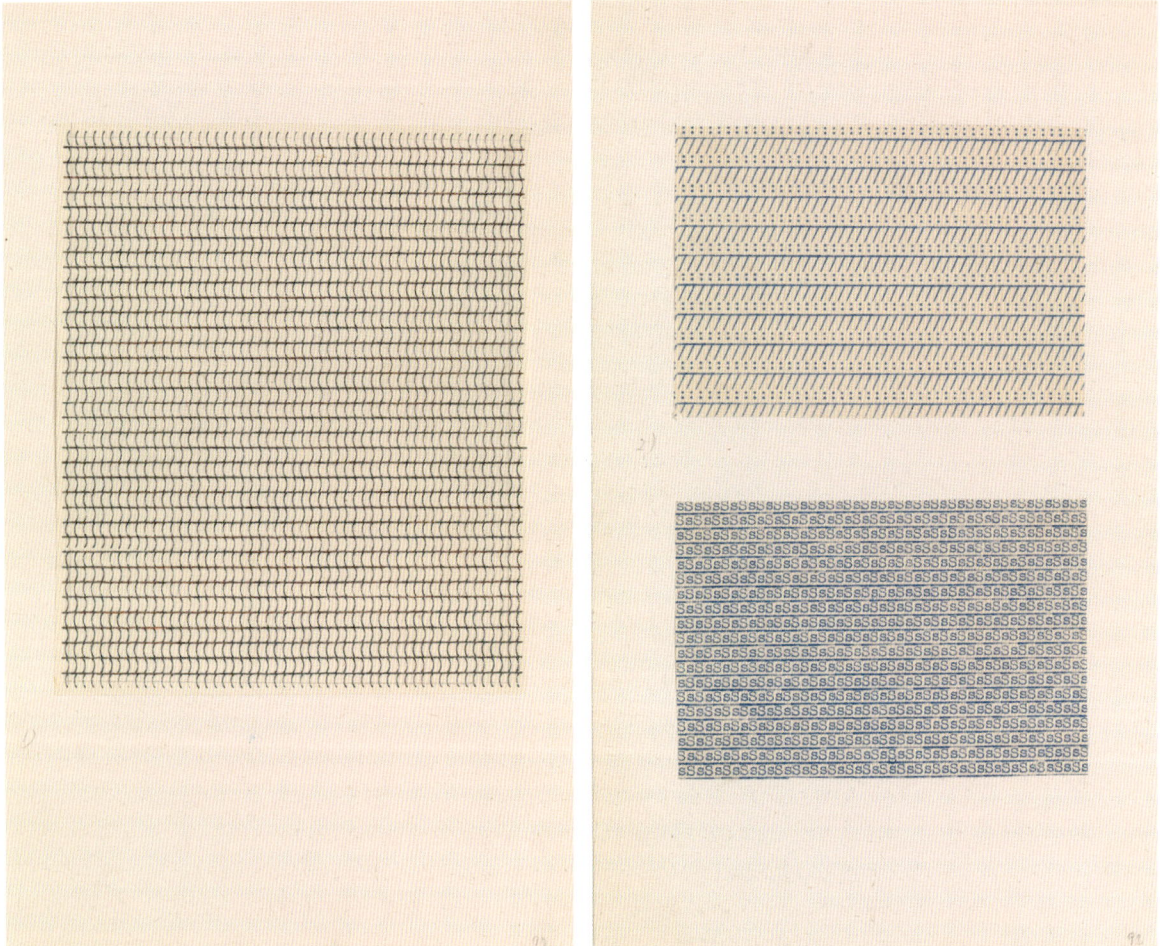

Fig. 7.9 *Left*, Anni Albers, study made on the typewriter, n.d., typewriter printing in black ink on paper mounted on board. The Josef and Anni Albers Foundation, 1994.18.7. *Right*, Anni Albers, studies made on the typewriter, n.d., typewriter printing in blue ink on paper mounted on board. The Josef and Anni Albers Foundation, 1994.18.4.

College, though still having the students work in two dimensions in order to understand three dimensions, she directed them to use the typewriter keys to create the illusion of three-dimensional texture. Her goal was to foster an awareness of surface and of the tactile nature of weaving itself, as a "pre-weaving" step in the training for woven textile design.

Albers called her typewriter exercises "training in textile thinking" and wanted her pupils to be able to isolate the "textile qualities" in their work. The aim was to give an illusion of weaving, without yet deploying weaving techniques, by using typed marks to focus on what she termed the "form-characteristics of weavings."[98] She began with two different typewriter assignments; the first required students to concentrate on the horizontal and the vertical, a key aspect of weaving. The next, in which students needed to simulate three-dimensional textures using only the two-dimensional output of the typewriter keys, enhanced that kind of thinking (fig. 7.9). Thus, as Albers explained, in the first typewriter exercise, the objective was to create an "illusion of the horizontal-vertical interlacing of the line as elements – threads," while the second exercise used horizontal rows to give a textured effect, such as one might see in a woven twill.[99]

The use of a typewriter and typewriting was far from incidental. As part of her pedagogical program, Albers sought to develop in her students a new "vocabulary" and "language" of tactility. In *On Weaving*, she explains that the "tactile-textile" works produced on the typewriter are "varied experiments in articulation . . . to be understood not as an end in themselves but merely as a help to us in gaining new terms in vocabulary of tactile language." She elaborates, "Our experience of gaining a representational means through the use of different surface qualities leads us to the use of illusions of such qualities graphically produced, though not by the means of representational graphic – that is, the modulated line. Drawing or print that shows hatching or stippling, rippled or curled lines, etc., and thus has a structural appearance, can be used to produce, if not actual tactile surfaces, the illusion of them."[100] She includes, within the illustrations of this chapter, reproductions of three typewriter studies (see fig. 7.9).[101]

Typewriter studies were deemed critical enough for understanding her praxis that thirteen of her own typewriter works, some in blue, others in black ink, were included in the 1949 MoMA exhibition, *Anni Albers Textiles*. Albers's checklist that accompanied the shipment specified each work by typewriter key or keys used to create it – percent signs, bracket stripes, "L" pattern, dots and quotes, paragraph marks and brackets, etc.[102] The choice of the individual keys was ancillary yet significant in that together they formed a vocabulary of marks in pursuit of a language of tactility. Textile represented through text. It was this tactility of the marks aggregated together via the repetitive hammering of typewriter keys that suggested the materiality of a woven surface.

Jewelry: The Materiality of the Five-and-Dime Store

Another output that utilized the materiality of the technical realm for artistic ends is a collection of jewelry made from hardware and other small parts sourced from five-and-dime stores, which Albers designed with Alex Reed (who was a student and then later a teacher at Black Mountain).[103] Just as the typewriter studies illustrate how a machine intended for one purpose was activated for very different, artistic means – the industrial nature of the jewelry, too, expresses the creative potential of the production line, celebrating both its processes (machined parts) and its modern materials (aluminum, steel, rubber, and more). By using everyday elements of little commercial value – in place of costly gems and precious metals normally used in jewelry-making – Albers and Reed were also rejecting the patterns of consumption of the period. Consumption, she had warned in her writings in these years, was an underlying cause for war. Most of the jewelry pieces were, in fact, made around 1940 (and through the early 1940s), when Europe was already at war and the United States was sending military supplies and other assistance, before it eventually entered World War II itself. Especially because of the negligible value of their constituent parts and the timing of their creation, they can be understood as a subtle political statement.

The materiality of the factory floor is showcased in the jewelry: necklaces were constructed from bobby pins arrayed on a ball-link chain; perforated aluminum drain strainers were hung with paperclips; and aluminum washers and brass grommets were strung on grosgrain or chamois ribbons (fig. 7.10). Albers and Reed restricted themselves to common, everyday objects, underscoring an interest in existing mass-produced, factory-made goods as the solution to modern living. This had been a basic principle – if not always a reality – of German Bauhaus design.[104] Albers noted how the mode of creation gave rise to greater inventiveness: "We found that having to work with given elements or units brought about new ways of construction, new ways of linking parts together, new catches, new ways of suspending parts."[105]

In addition to the materiality of industry, inspiration also came from antiquity. The first stimulus to make jewelry from hardware came from the precious jewels of ancient Mexico – the treasure of Monte Alban. As Albers explained, "These objects of gold and pearls, of jade, rock-crystal, and shells, made about 1,000 years ago, are of such surprising beauty in unusual combinations of materials that we became aware of the strange limitations in materials commonly used for jewels today. . . . Later, back in the States, we looked for new materials to use. In the 5 & 10 cents stores we discovered the beauty of washers and bobby-pins. Enchanted we stood before kitchen-sink stoppers and glass insulators, picture books and erasers. The art of Monte Alban had given us the freedom to *see things detached from their use, as pure materials*, worth being turned into precious objects."[106] Just as the jewelry constructed in ancient Mexico put together the materials of the environment – shells and rock crystals, Albers and Reed sought to subvert consumer culture by assembling jewelry from common, nearly worthless elements from their own twentieth-century environment.

In line with Albers's theoretical writing on design, to make the jewelry, the pair was activating the materiality of the industrial pieces themselves – to further ingenious experimentation that strove to be more objective than subjective. They worked with the simplicity and limitations imposed by the parts, enhancing them through the use of repetition, ingenious methods of attaching the elements, and pattern-making. The duo can be understood as releasing machined

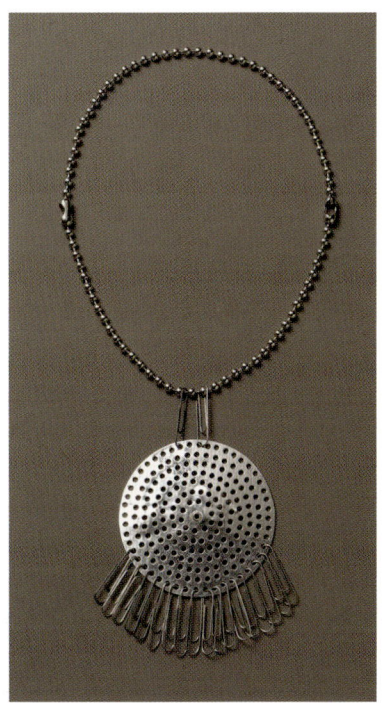 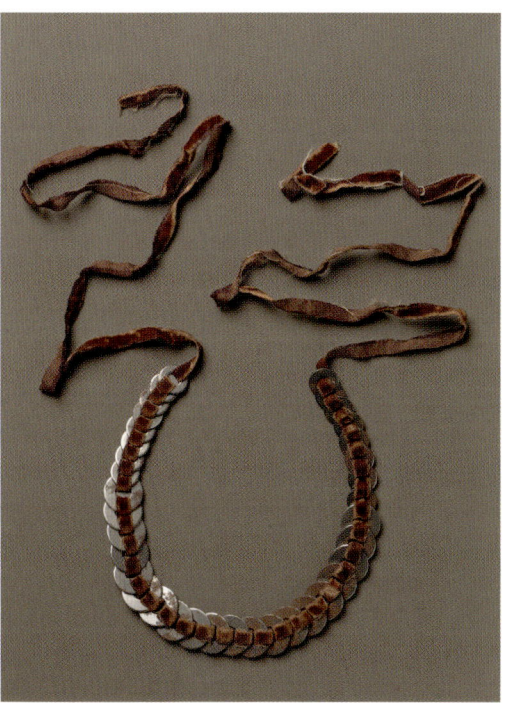

Fig. 7.10 *Left*, Anni Albers and Alexander Reed, necklace, ca. 1940, aluminum strainer, paper clips, and chain. The Josef and Anni Albers Foundation, 1994.14.16. *Right*, Anni Albers and Alexander Reed, necklace, ca. 1940, washers and dark brown velvet ribbon. The Josef and Anni Albers Foundation, 2006.14.3.

parts from individual uses (as bobby pins, faucet washers, grommets), and their associated representative meanings, toward new inventive ends as jewelry — jewelry understood as beautiful adornment, not as showy signifiers of wealth. Albers's idea that the medium had to be freed from its representative meaning to make it fit for another purpose can be mapped onto the outcome. As she noted,

> our greatest surprise was that others, like ourselves, did not care about the value or lack of value of the materials we used, but enjoyed, instead of material value, that of surprise and inventiveness — a spiritual value. . . . From the beginning we were quite conscious of our attempt not to discriminate between materials, not to attach to them the conventional values of preciousness or commonness. In breaking through the traditional valuation we felt this to be an attempt to rehabilitate materials. We felt that our experiments perhaps could help to point out the merely transient value we attach to things, though we believe them to be permanent. . . . We thought that our work suggested that jewels no longer were the reserved privilege of the few, but property of everyone who cared to look about and was open to the beauty of the simple things around us.[107]

The jewelry should also be seen in the larger context of a period of growing interest in the aesthetic of modern factory-produced goods in the United States (a fascination with the machine was already well-established in Europe in these years). For example, the 1934 MoMA exhibition *Machine Art* featured highly polished industrial objects — an aluminum plane propeller, enormous steel springs — which were mounted on the gallery wall like paintings, or carefully displayed on pedestals, while the smallest items, such as tiny screws were lit, jewel-like, in velvet-lined vitrines.[108] Albers would have been very familiar with the show, curated by Philip Johnson, because Josef Albers advised extensively on the graphic design of the *Machine Art* exhibition catalog cover, which featured a photograph of ball bearings.[109] Albers and Reed's jewelry was also showcased at MoMA, in the exhibition *Modern Handmade Jewelry*, which ran from mid-September to mid-November 1946, and included four necklaces by the pair. The exhibition featured jewelry by other modern artists and designers such as Harry Bertoia and Alexander Calder, in addition to craftsmen who worked predominantly in jewelry.[110] Many of the others in the show made their wares modern by giving them a contemporary form while still using the rarified materials expected of jewelry — the exhibition checklist is replete with pieces in silver, gold, and brass and with emeralds, tourmaline, and rubies.[111] The Black Mountain College duo's entries stood out from the others owing to their use of common objects in industrial materials; featured in the exhibition was the necklace with strainer and clips, one with screws and coral beads, a necklace of colored jacks, and one with "L" braces.[112] The MoMA press release for the exhibition singled out the "hardware jewelry" by Albers and Reed, noting that its composition of "washers, screws, angles, curtain rings, with a necklace combing a sieve, paperclips and a key chain, have the elegance of good design."[113]

This critical output by Albers and Reed is significant on many levels. Their lighthearted, inexpensive jewelry subverted conspicuous consumption and ostentatious displays of wealth during wartime, while celebrating a desired industrial future, one constructed from mass-produced parts and materials. It also functioned at the intersection of everyday materiality and the highest echelons of the country's design vanguard, namely, through its inclusion in the MoMA exhibition. Finally, the jewelry ties in with Albers's theoretical writing at the time, which was focused on materiality and urged designers and artists to move away from the standard representative properties of an object to instead focus on creating new meaning and relationships. A necklace made of a strainer and paper clips certainly fills that mandate.

In Conclusion: A Flexible Architecture

Albers's theory, with which this chapter begins, was a means by which she could articulate the terms of her far-reaching practice, informed by the experience of immigration and the subsequent adjusting of her creative work and her teaching to the US context. Within that framework, the through line is a continual investigation and reconceptualization of materiality. Remediation and the changes wrought in her practice and pedagogy arose from a productive transfer between media forms and the resulting highly original outcomes. Encounters with — and pushing the bounds of — materiality shaped her pedagogical exercises, especially her pre-weaving assignments; it took pride of place in her weaving in natural and modern, man-made fibers. Fundamental was various materials' emergence from, and engagement with, industry. One last area in which Albers engaged materiality for especially constructive ends is where her work may be understood as architectural.[114]

A recognition of the complex relationship between the two-dimensional view and the three-dimensional structural experience of Albers's weaving is important for understanding her work in an architectural light. In 1959, Buckminster Fuller insightfully described this aspect of her work: "From aeronautical altitudes, the crisscross grids of Earth's cities seem to be two-dimensional planar arrangements, as do woven fabric surfaces, seen from a distance. Seen from inside the city streets or within the loom, both cities and fabrics disclose multi-dimensional structuring of great complexity. Anni Albers, more than any other weaver, has succeeded in exciting mass realization of the complex structuring of fabrics. She has brought the artist's intuitive sculpturing faculties and the age-long weaver's arts into historically successful marriage."[115]

Albers herself carefully articulated the connection between her weaving and its spatiality in architecture. Writing in the journal *Arts and Architecture* in 1948, she states, "textiles for interior use can be regarded as architectural elements. In contrast to other elements their special characteristic is their dynamic quality. Fabrics above all else are pliable, and being pliable they can change their position. We draw a curtain to let in light or to shut it out; to close off a section of space or to open it up; we spread out a cover or fold it.... Where the unique characteristic of pliability is the primary consideration, as in drapery materials, there is no substitute for textiles."[116] Albers gave much consideration to the ideal functioning of drapes and their materiality, as an important structural component in the home, one that also required flexibility, mobility, and durability. She continues, "If we recognize the function of drapery textile in the house as the function of being flexible, of changing positions, we have already established an attitude toward the problem of designing them. We will avoid bulkiness or great weight, for instance, which would make the change of position difficult. We will further analyze the many-faceted problem of designing a curtain for translucency or opaqueness, cleaning, fading, warmth and maintenance."[117] In 1949, for the Walter Gropius–designed Harvard Graduate Center, she was able to put her theory to the test, especially her use of textiles to create self-enclosed space. For the men's dormitory rooms, Albers produced innovative room dividers – a series of hard-wearing hanging dividers on runners, as well as many fabrics for the commission, such as plaid bedspreads. For a communal space within the building, Harkness Commons, she designed additional drapery material. And for her MoMA exhibition in the same year, she showed a number of free-hanging room dividers using such diverse materials as cellophane, jute, Lurex, and cord (fig. 7.11; see also fig. 7.1).

One of her most important articles, "The Pliable Plane: Textiles in Architecture," for Yale's architectural journal, *Perspecta* (1957), charts the importance of textiles for architecture throughout the ages and concludes: "The essentially structural principles that relate the work of building and weaving could form the basis of a new understanding between the architect and the inventive weaver."[118] Albers also taught architecture students from time to time, giving a few seminars to students at Yale's School of Architecture.[119]

Intellectual and material pliability was paramount in Albers's expansive notion of "textile" – whether a plane forming an architectural element, a two-dimensional sheet with repetitive, typewritten patterning to suggest three-dimensional weaving texture, or texture studies to heighten the sensitivities of students toward tactility. Albers connected a theoretical concept of making

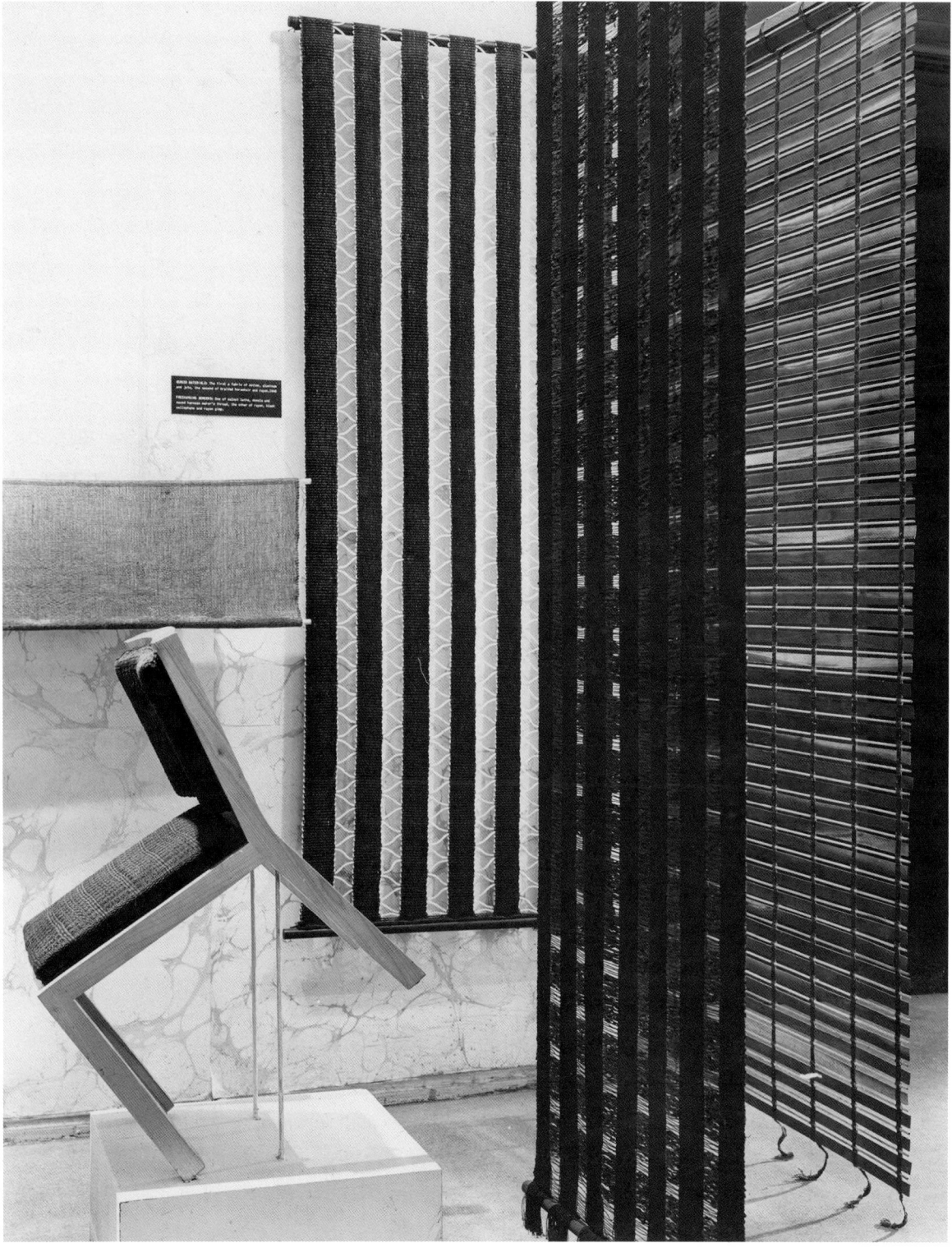

Fig. 7.11 Anni Albers, installation view of room dividers and chair upholstery in exhibition *Anni Albers Textiles*, Museum of Modern Art, September 14–November 6, 1949. Photograph by Soichi Sunami.

and materiality to her final products, whether that outcome was pedagogical, museological, or a woven room divider. To reprise her statement, so apt in her day, and today, "We have to work from where we are. But just as you can go everywhere from any given point, so too the idea of any work, however small, can flow into an idea of true momentum."[120]

Chapter 8

Herbert Bayer's Expanded Vision and the Instrumentalizing of Design

The intensified turn toward the social usefulness of art by Bauhaus member Herbert Bayer can be traced as an arc from his initial research in Germany to its materialization in the United States.[1] Émigrés brought with them to America the sophisticated graphic design of the European modern movement and a bold manner of conceiving of and laying out exhibitions – Bayer was among the most innovative of these designers departing Germany to land on US shores. He was deeply invested in reaching viewers; he experimented with techniques of display and graphic design, using remediation as a means of communicating visually in new ways. "My aim is the total design process," is how Bayer would frame it, "because it is a vision which I am pursuing, not perfection nor specialization in a technique."[2] His work and vision would become ever more imperative as the country entered World War II (fig. 8.1).

Bayer cycled from one media form into another, a process of remediation that strengthened his message, as it allowed him to reach a wider audience through that individual's direct experience of a given media – some would encounter his didactic exhibitions, others his mass-media magazine covers for *Fortune*. This concluding chapter argues that Bayer's designs, especially those related to his "expanded vision" – read via a range of media: magazine covers, posters, paintings, exhibition design, and didactic drawings – can be understood as a totality of vision, one created out of the unique circumstances of the exilic wartime condition and the imperative of social design in this period. In doing so, this chapter brings together three overarching arguments of this book: that the experience of exile informed the modernism subsequently produced by the émigrés; that rather than being ruptured, the modernist strands stretched across the prewar, wartime, and postwar period, connecting the output from places left behind with that produced in new locales; and that never far from the core of this modernism was a genuine concern for society and lived experience.

A critical moment in Bayer's trajectory from continental Europe to America occurred at the 1930 Paris exhibition of the Société des artistes décorateurs, where he joined Walter Gropius, László Moholy-Nagy, and Marcel Breuer in creating a striking series of exhibition rooms representing Germany. Here Bayer advanced a visually immersive new method of exhibition display and bold modern graphic design for the accompanying catalog, and he began to develop his theories about vision, all of which he would elaborate and refine in the United States. In Paris, Bayer installed large-scale photographs of modern buildings suspended at tilted angles from floor to ceiling; in this sweeping new mode of exhibition display, he sought to activate the full range of optical angles of the viewer's eye, which he termed "expanded vision" (fig. 8.2). The exhibition catalog's illustration of a large, all-seeing eye that replaces the head of a man in a three-piece suit and tie depicted how this radical exhibition design could alter the very basic act of seeing.

Upon arrival in the United States, Bayer continued to deploy innovative techniques that forged new kinds of connections between viewers and the objects under examination. In a series of exhibitions he designed for the Museum of Modern Art, beginning with the 1938 Bauhaus show, which introduced the school and its protagonists to an American audience, Bayer was able to develop his ideas on the viewer's experience, capturing the museum-goer's

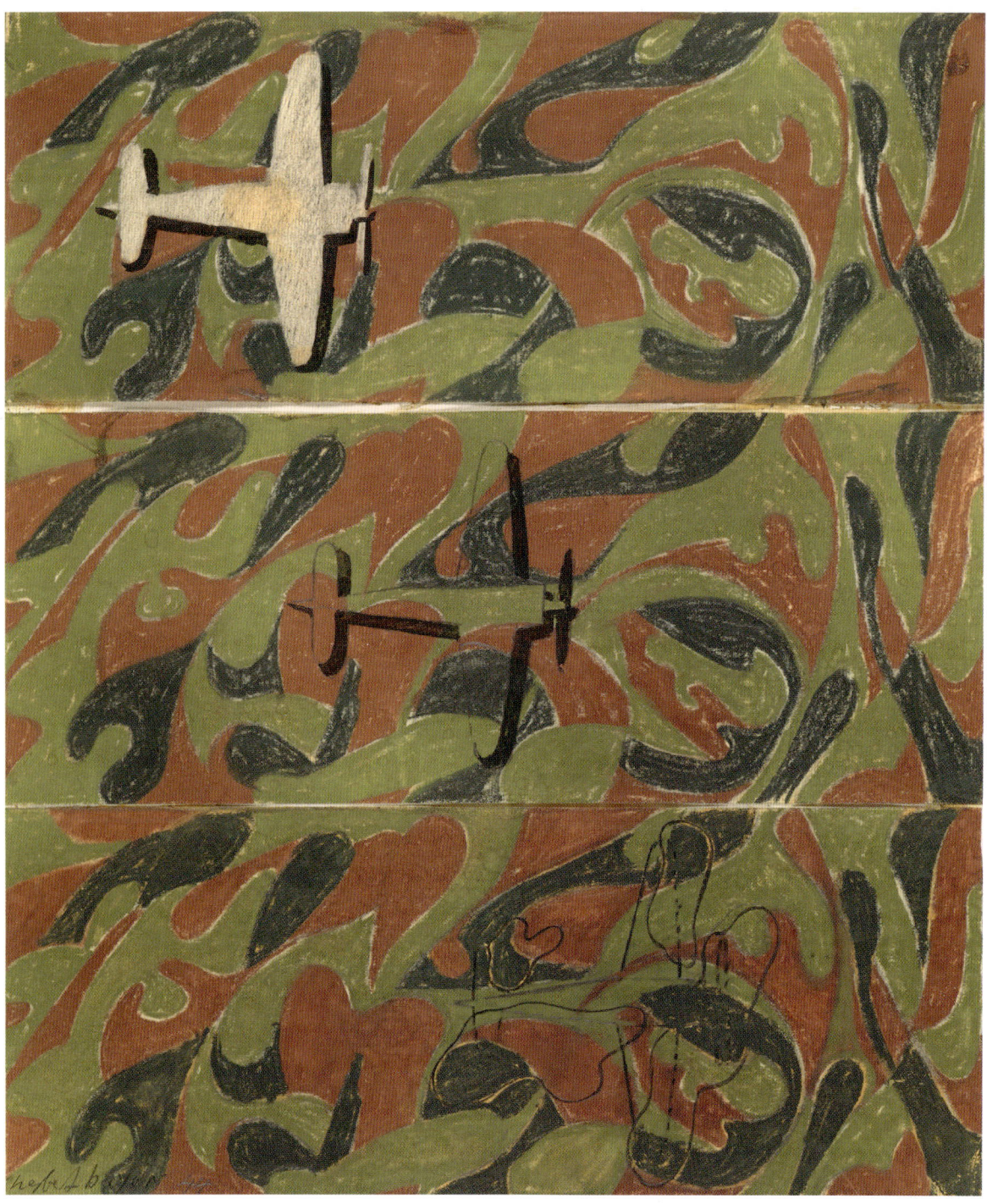

Fig. 8.1 Herbert Bayer, magazine cover design (camouflage), 1944, pastel, ink, graphite, paper. Denver Art Museum, Gift of the Estate of Joella Bayer, 1986.1222.

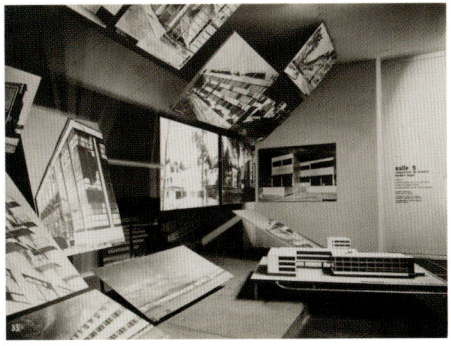 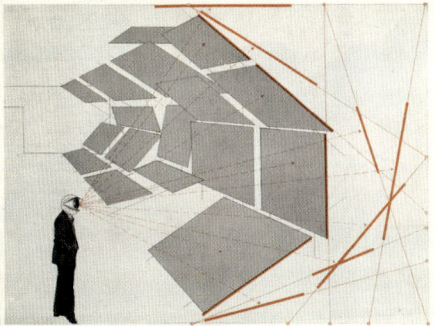

Fig. 8.2 *Left*, Herbert Bayer, Room 5, German section of the *Société des artistes décorateurs* exhibition, 1930, Paris. *Right*, Bayer, diagram of field of vision, 1929. Page from *Section allemande: Exposition de la Société des artistes décorateurs*, Paris, 1930.

eye with his arresting installations. This led to further commissions for Bayer, which addressed the nation now at war. For example, in collaboration with the US government's Office of War Information, he designed the museum's 1942 *Road to Victory* exhibition and, with the Red Cross, developed MoMA's 1943 exhibition on *The Arts in Therapy*. For these exhibitions, Bayer brought wartime messages to a general audience through a process of continual remediation—he used large-scale photographs, photomontage, oversize text, floor patterning, ramps, and other structures that framed the content, or sometimes even the visitors themselves.

Bayer's Bauhaus-era graphic design was also deployed for the American war effort and its public information campaigns, through posters for the WPA War Services and the Civil Aeronautics Administration. Also key were his contributions to corporate initiatives in support of the war effort, posters and messaging for *Fortune* magazine and the Container Corporation of America (known as the CCA).[3] The CCA was a paperboard company that supported an international roster of artists who brought striking modern design to the broader public in the form of moving wartime informational and public service messages. These initiatives, discussed in depth here, simultaneously brought the Bauhaus's typography and graphic design to a widespread American audience, thus reaching the masses to an extent that the Bauhaus had always sought but had never achieved. In wartime America, the stakes surrounding this new, dynamic viewing experience were higher because the design was intended to deploy critical wartime information.

Bayer had emigrated late, arriving in New York in August 1938. Walter Gropius had implored him to come earlier, but Bayer, although never a Nazi party member, was undeniably slow to leave Germany and had found some graphic design work for Nazi-era exhibitions. For several years, he assisted Gropius in settling affairs related to the Bauhaus and organized the exportation of objects from Europe for the major Bauhaus exhibition planned for the Museum of Modern Art, arriving just a few months prior to the show's opening in early December 1938 (the show ran through January 30, 1939). For MoMA's *Bauhaus, 1919–1928*, Bayer was responsible for the innovative exhibition design, laying out the major accompanying catalog, and editing it, with Ise and Walter Gropius. Bayer remained in New York City until 1946, when he relocated to Aspen, Colorado. His early activities in New York included important designs for the war effort, illustrations for magazines, advertising and packaging, exhibition design for MoMA, and his own painting practice. Pragmatically, design work was a necessary means of earning income in the United States. Bayer confronted significant economic hardships as a newcomer to New York in a constricting economy, arriving as he did on the brink of World War II, whereas those who had earlier reached US shores had benefited from some time to assimilate and integrate into their new circumstances.

But despite the hardships he faced personally as an émigré, Bayer put design at the forefront of a social mission, stating in 1940, "I feel that the artist of our time has no right to withdraw from the complexity of modern living to personal meditation. The artist of today must, like any other individual, live the life of our times in order to give form and meaning to the present."[4] Unlike other modernists who saw the United States chiefly as a place of refuge and as a means of continuing their lives and livelihoods, Bayer, like Moholy-Nagy, actively engaged with the war effort, using his multifaceted talents to support it in diverse ways. Moreover, the war era design contributions of Moholy-Nagy, Kepes, and Bayer are unique, and their participation should not be understood as a forgone conclusion. Other, equally talented former Bauhaus members, such as Walter Gropius, Ludwig Hilberseimer, Ludwig Mies van der Rohe, or Josef and Anni Albers, did not contribute to the war effort to any meaningful degree.

Modern Graphic Design in Wartime: A Nation at War with the Nation Left Behind

Bayer joined fellow émigrés, including Gyorgy Kepes, Xanti Schawinsky, Fernand Léger, and other European modern artists, in applying their skills to create innovative graphic design for the war effort, for example, in advertising campaigns for the Container Corporation of America (CCA). Hired by the company's president, Walter Paepcke, who was also a major private benefactor of the New Bauhaus school in Chicago, they created striking messaging to inform citizens about how they could contribute to the war effort. The artists designed informational booklets such as *Paperboard Goes to War* and advertisements that touted the benefits of paper products for wartime uses and urged their conservation (fig. 8.3; see also fig. 4.4). Using dynamic layouts, a pared-down color palette, and modern typography, Bayer produced advertisements for the CCA that enjoined the public to "save waste paper" and to appreciate its myriad uses in the war effort.

This campaign was designed by the CCA with corporate citizenship in mind and with an eye to cementing new uses for paper in the postwar economy to come. Bayer articulated a nuanced and assimilatory position with regard to what might be termed the "corporate war effort," later stating: "The enlightened company makes an important cultural contribution to the society from which it draws its income. This is an aspect of contemporary American culture perhaps not yet known to Europeans. Beneath the superficial confusions of the American scene, and the apparent preoccupation with profits, there is a cultural growth, a new receptivity to the arts, that challenges the artist to give his best."[5] There is a subtext to this statement, reflecting the different cultural sphere that many émigrés encountered in the United States, namely, an unease – one that sometimes

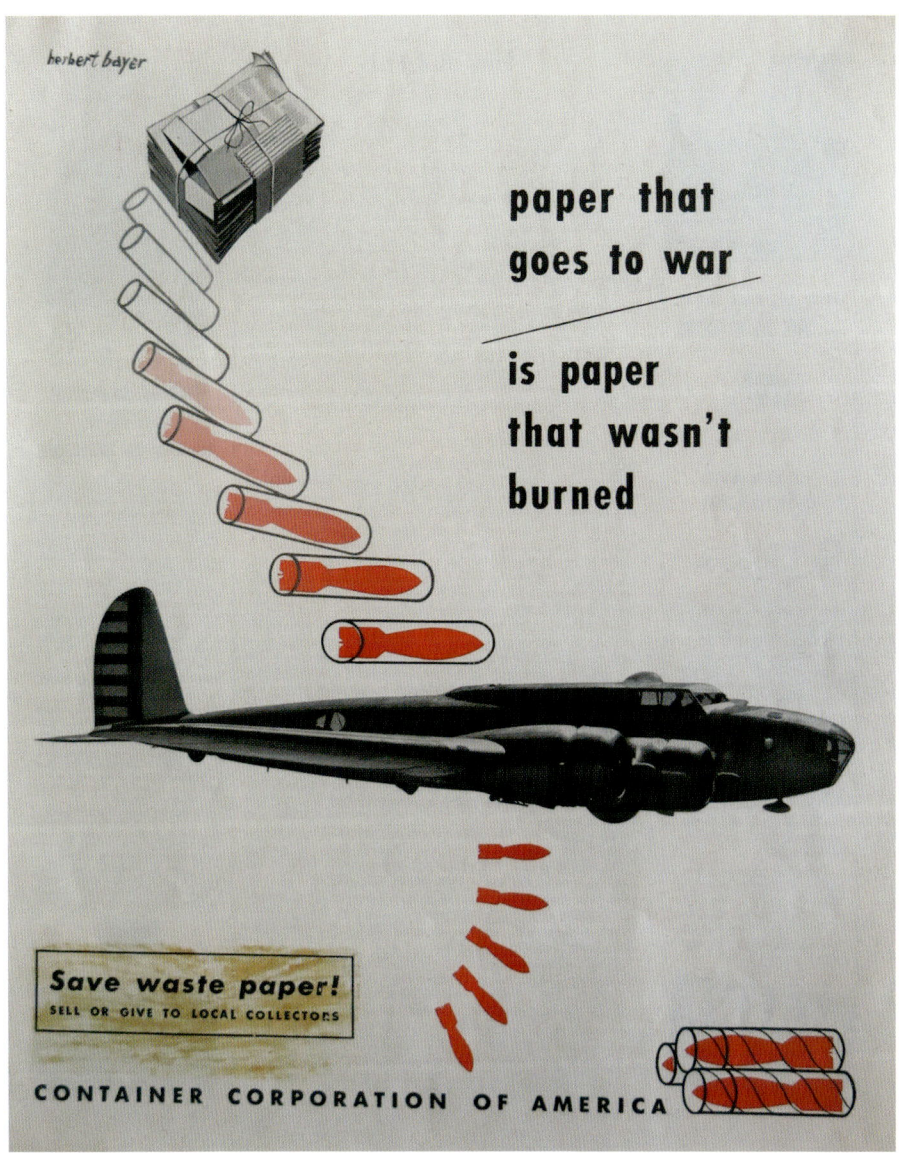

Fig. 8.3 Herbert Bayer, *Save Waste Paper!*, advertisement for Container Corporation of America, 1942, photomontage, opaque watercolor.

percolated to the surface—about the ways in which commerce and capitalism mixed with art in a manner that was unknown in the Europe they had left behind.

Other designs, such as a magazine cover that featured a camouflaged plane disappearing as it flies over the landscape, integrate graphic design with "war" design, in this case camouflage, in a straightforward and highly legible, but sophisticated, manner (see fig. 8.1). As was evident in his other public messaging campaigns and in his exhibition design alike, Bayer's graphic design practice was didactic, clear, and effective, and this was especially pronounced in his war-related designs. In the United States, the message, and the graphic design that supported it, became simpler, bolder, and more immediate, especially during wartime, when it was imperative that it reach its intended audience. For example, posters circulated by the Civil Aeronautics Administration—such as *Guidance in Flight: CAA Speeds the War*—illustrated how technology enhanced US capabilities, reassuring civilians during wartime (fig. 8.4). Bayer also noted occasions when his illustrations were not released to the general public. For example, in

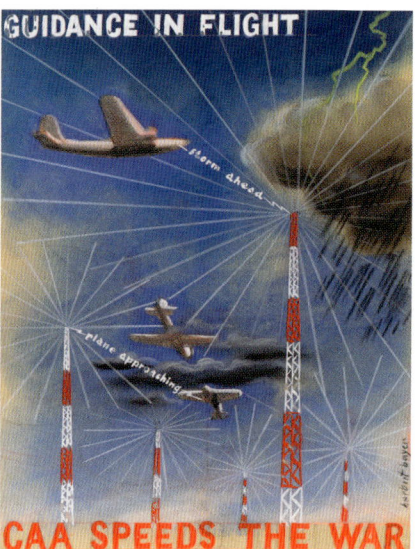 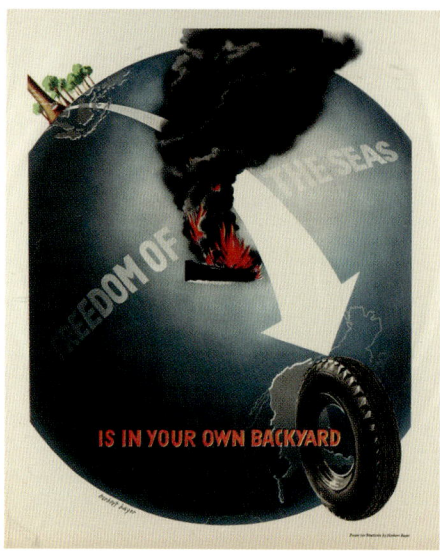

Fig. 8.4 Herbert Bayer, *Guidance in Flight*, poster for Civil Aeronautics Administration, 1942, pastel, colored pencil, tempera, paper. Denver Art Museum, Gift of the Estate of Joella Bayer, 1986.1220.

Fig. 8.5 Herbert Bayer, *Freedom of the Seas Is in Your Own Backyard*, poster, *Fortune* magazine, 1939.

1941 he did four full-page illustrations for *Life* magazine that included a radio beam detector that ultimately was not published because the army did not want the information released.[6]

His propaganda posters likewise aided the war effort. Bayer's *Freedom of the Seas* was part of a portfolio of defense posters commissioned and published by *Fortune* magazine, which were then offered to the US government for further production and distribution (fig. 8.5).[7] On the back of *Freedom of the Seas* was a note from the artist: "Men in industry cannot be told too often or in too many ways that 'Production will win the war,' and that on them, the producers, rests the final responsibility for the nation's safety. American workmen can tackle any job and do it well: don't let them forget it. Women also work and are equally deserving of a place in industrial posters of this general type.... Tied in here with the defense-bond sales campaign, this poster could be used as readily for the purposes of general morale."[8] Other *Fortune* commissions followed, including several magazine covers related to the wartime economy and its infrastructure, such as *Moving the Stuff of Production*, a February 1943 *Fortune* cover that depicted dynamic yellow and gray cranes lifting heavy industrial elements against a vibrant blue sky. Others featured gas mains and the grid delivery system (August 1940) and synthetic rubber (June 1942).

Aptly describing the émigrés' quandary in wartime America, especially the relationship with technology, which had just a few years earlier held such promise for designers, Bayer's colleague Gyorgy Kepes stated:

> The enormous expansion of human conflict in World War II and its consequences made so many ideas seem shallow that I was impelled, like many others, to search for values rather than tools. The social horizon, with its immense and seemingly insoluble problems, did not seem to contain the key to those values. The scientific revolution, with its menaces, benefactions, and promises, did seem to open an emotional window. Basically, I felt, the world made newly visible by science contained the essential symbols for our reconstruction of physical

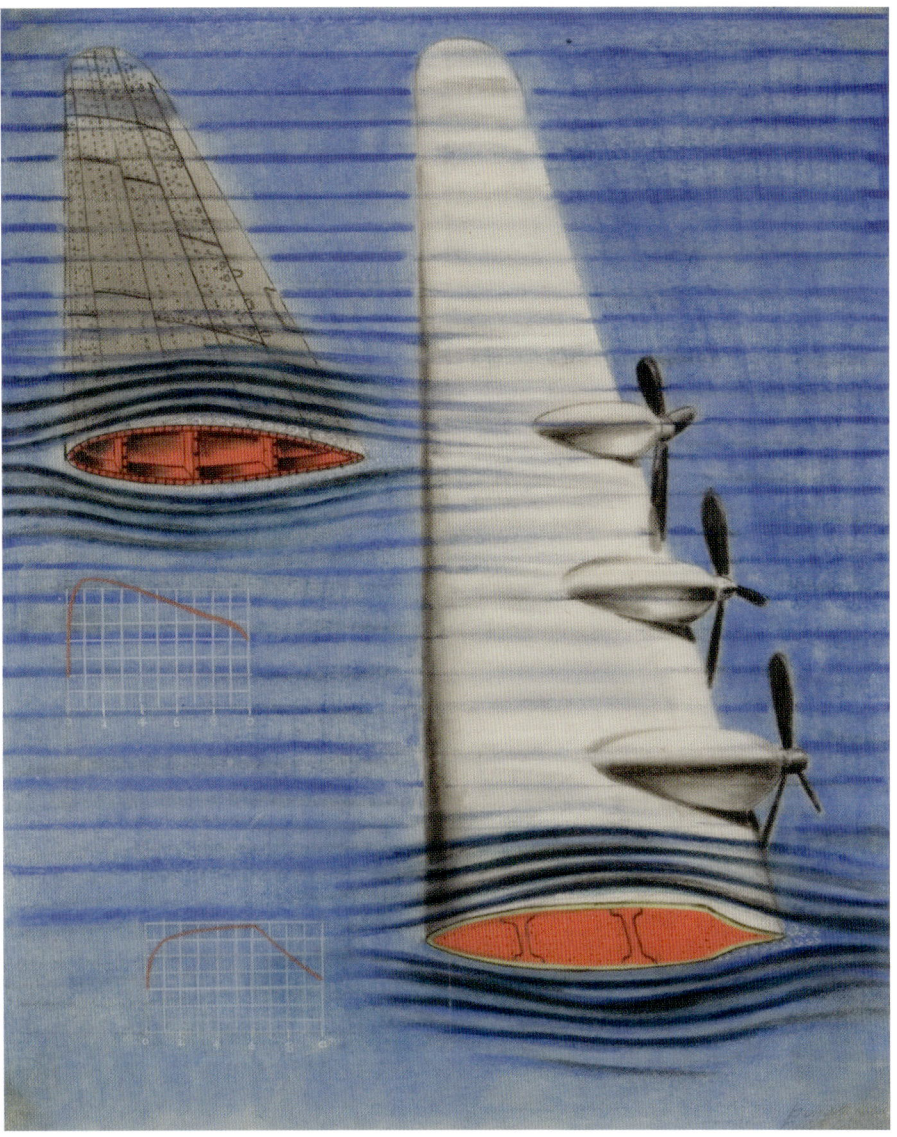

Fig. 8.6 Herbert Bayer, wing diagram, 1944, colored graphite on paper. Denver Art Museum, Gift of the Estate of Joella Bayer, 2006.46.

surrounding and for the restructuring of the world of sense, feeling, and thought within us. I was drawn to the converging contributions made by art and science, and to the distillation of the images common to our expanding inner and outer worlds.[9]

Kepes's articulation of the changing place of technology for artists during wartime finds a corollary in Bayer's striking preparation drawing of airplane wings from 1944 (fig. 8.6). The pathos engendered by the bold red of the wings' interiors, which make them look like severed limbs, was a reminder of the human lives at stake.

Bayer's style was well received in his new milieu. MoMA curator James Johnson Sweeney, writing in 1943, astutely highlighted Bayer's "curiously personal combination of formal clarity and an unfamiliar, provocative juxtaposition of visual elements. This clarity, on the one hand, offers a ready readability which arrests and entertains the eye; and on the other, the play of associations

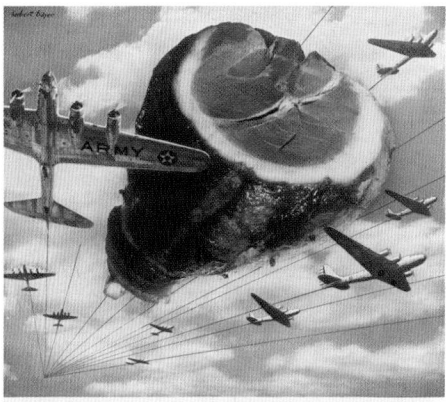

A Victory Recipe: Pork and Planes Cooked by Gas!

Fig. 8.7 Herbert Bayer, *A Victory Recipe: Pork and Planes Cooked by Gas!*, advertisement, ca. 1940. Denver Art Museum, Gift of the Estate of Joella Bayer, 1997.923.

Fig. 8.8 *Opposite top*, Herbert Bayer, *America Needs More Meat*, poster for Rural Electrification Administration, 1942, reproduced by NYC WPA War Services. Bauhaus-Archiv, Berlin. *Opposite bottom*, Bayer, *Home Grown Wheat*, poster for Rural Electrification Administration, 1942, gouache on paper. Denver Art Museum, Gift of the Estate of Herbert Bayer, 1986.1203.

stimulated by the unusual juxtaposition of visual details holds the observer's interest while the major message is being brought home."[10] An advertisement featuring an enormous flying ham accompanied by fighter planes provides just one example of this eye-catching visual clarity that juxtaposes striking elements for an instantly comprehensible message (fig. 8.7). Bayer's *A Victory Recipe: Pork and Planes Cooked by Gas!*, from around 1940, touts the utility value of gas for fighter plans and Sunday roasts alike, while also drawing on the contemporary art movements of surrealism and photomontage.

In a series of posters created for the Works Progress Administration under the aegis of the US War Services and the Rural Electrification Administration, Bayer brought Bauhaus typography and the clarity of rational, *sachlich* graphic design to a widespread American audience. Works such as *Our Allies Need Eggs* (see fig. I.3), *America Needs More Meat* (fig. 8.8 *top*), and *Home Grown Wheat* (fig. 8.8 *bottom*), all from 1942, directly link to avant-garde European poster design, employing a sans serif font, flat field backgrounds, and bold, simple objects. Moreover, by urging American farmers to supply "our allies" with eggs, the poster also signals a material connection to the European war effort. In posters such as *America Needs More Meat*, which pictures bacon and an American rifle, and *Grow It Yourself*, depicting a row of planted vegetables, their roots vibrantly sinking into rich soil, his designs seek to directly engage distinctively American viewers and their capacity for self-sufficiency. Strands of modernism were already flourishing in the United States in this period, and Bayer's designs from the late 1930s and early 1940s should be viewed in the context of influence operating in two directions.[11]

Posters that encouraged citizens to grow products for their own domestic use, thereby allowing more food to be shipped out for the war effort, such as those celebrating homegrown wheat and exhortations to "grow it yourself," were clear in language and image alike, speaking directly to rural citizens and their potential to contribute materially. The Rural Electrification Administration (REA) was a newly formed agency under Franklin D. Roosevelt's "New Deal" that sought to connect rural farms to the electric grid through the help of local cooperative groups. The REA promoted the use of electric power over other energy sources, such as kerosene or gas, and encouraged the acquisition of new farm

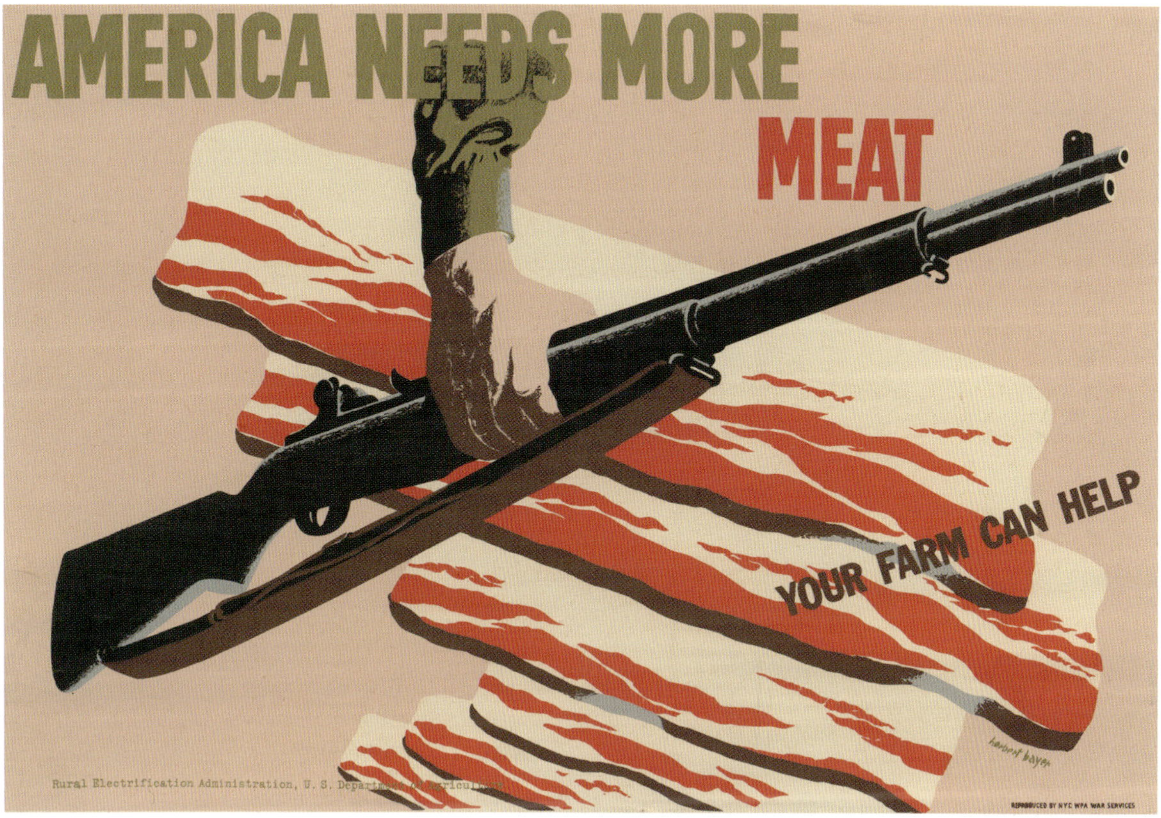

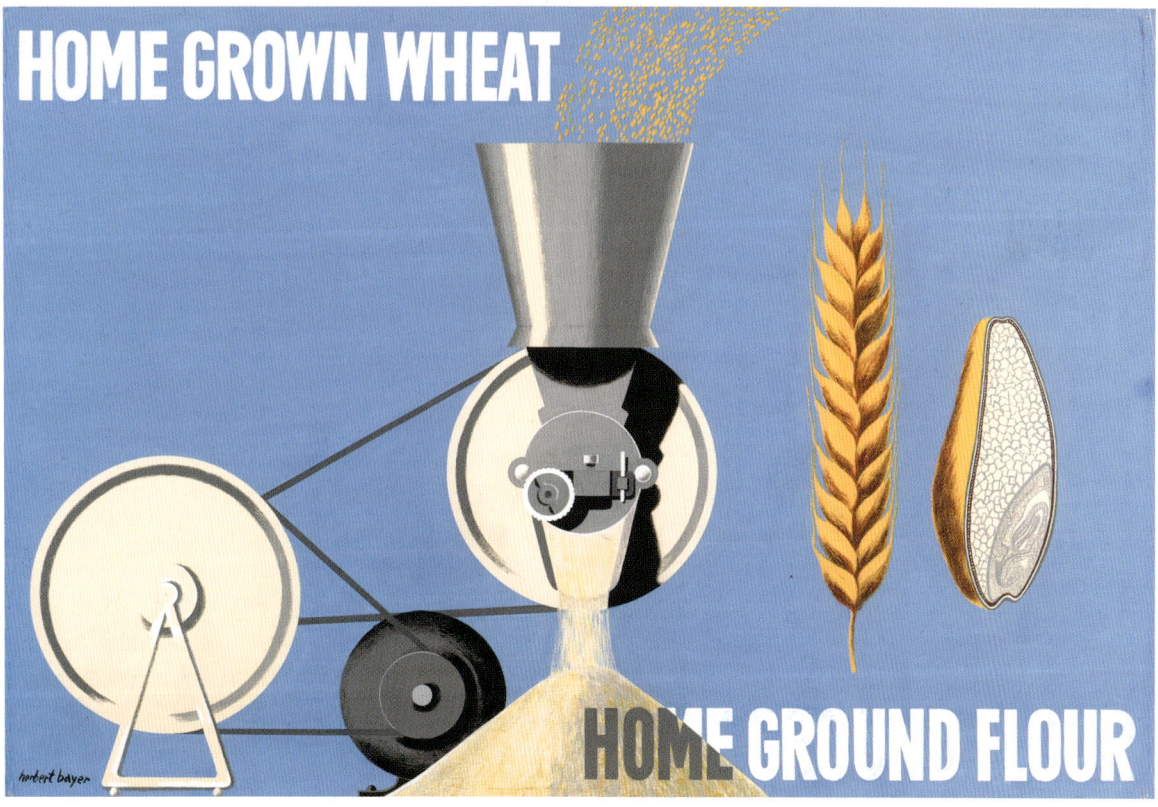

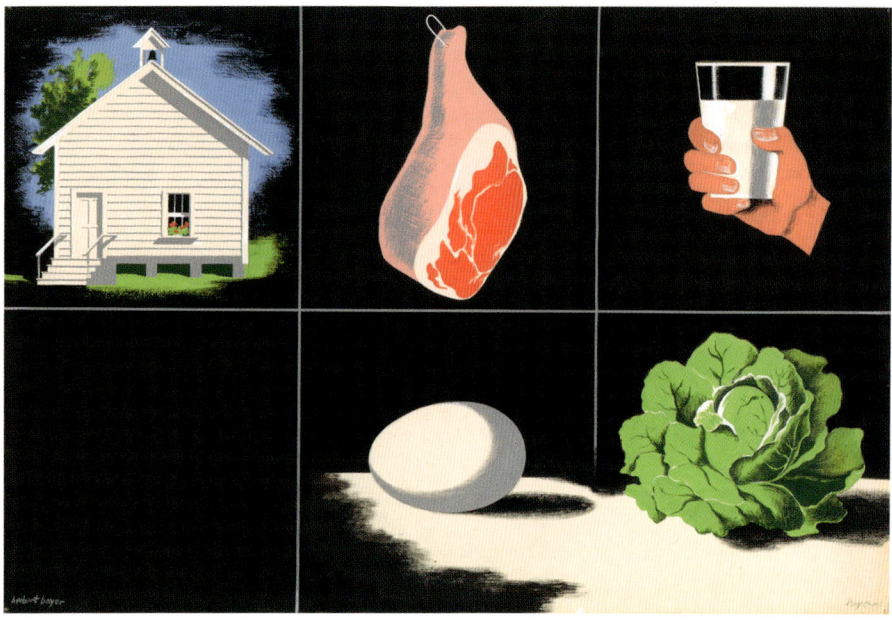

Fig. 8.9 Herbert Bayer, poster design (incomplete), for Rural Electrification Administration, 1942. Denver Art Museum, Gift of the Estate of Herbert Bayer, 1986.1204.

and domestic appliances that utilized electricity. The REA posters encouraged technical progress on the home front in aid of the war effort abroad.

On his underlying aims and methods in poster design, Bayer observed, "In our time where it is so important to tell something quickly, clearly, impressively and even beautifully, where our ways of life are so complicated and many-sided, it is necessary to have a more direct language. In our posters it can only be achieved by the picture. The poster must head toward a more visual interpretation."[12] Works such as *More Milk* and an untitled poster with five rural objects (single-room schoolhouse, hunk of meat, glass of milk, egg, head of lettuce), found in Bayer's archive, presumably intended to tout rural self-sufficiency, use this direct visual language of clear imagery to communicate with viewers (fig. 8.9). Particular to wartime, visuality is deployed here in design for urgent, war-related public service messages. And in Bayer's work of this period, this visuality is more immediate, more forthright, and more imperative than what had come before.

Simultaneously, for Bayer this period was also one of unprecedented, formal artistic productivity that was directly connected to the experience of war. His oil paintings, like his diaries, divulge difficulties in coping with wartime strife. In a series of paintings made during those years, he represents World War II's geopolitical conflicts, utilizing the seemingly straightforward graphical arrow symbol, possibly meteorological weather arrows (a now bygone graphical relict of the weather map; they indicated the direction of wind flowing around air pressure isobars). In paintings such as *Antipodes* (1942), directional arrows indicate opposing sides locked in battle around a globe, and in *Clashing Forces* (1942) (fig. 8.10), he paints Europe blotted with red, bloody puddles, using arrows, again, to indicate antagonistic sides and sites of conflict. In *Atmospheric Conditions* (1942), a battle of arrows swirls around loose, deep-red flames and ominous, dark smoke that curls upward, while *Celestial Spaces* (1942–45) likewise features directional arrows and dark, unfurling smoke.

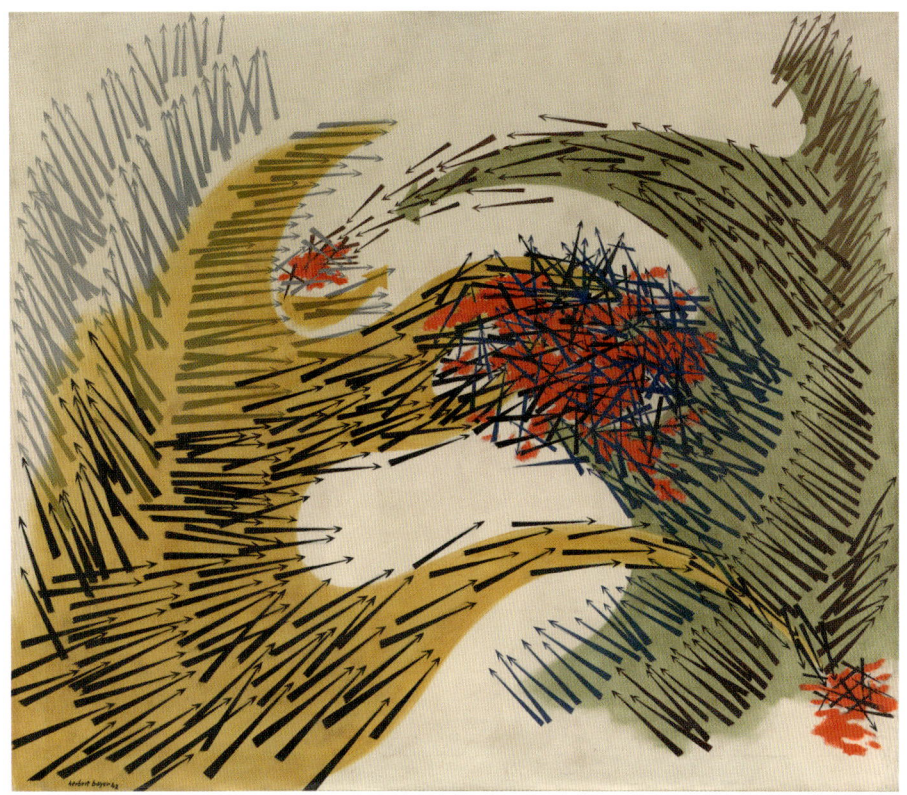

Fig. 8.10 Herbert Bayer, *Clashing Forces*, 1942, oil on canvas. Denver Art Museum, Gift of the Estate of Joella Bayer, 2003.65.

Bayer would remain in New York City through the war, leaving a year after its conclusion. In 1946, he relocated to Aspen at the invitation of Walter Paepcke, owner of the Container Corporation of America.[13] An avid skier, Bayer helped develop Aspen's ski resort and, more generally, popularize skiing as an activity, nationally. His multifaceted career continued to thrive in peacetime, despite his departure from New York's hub of urban creative activity. In Aspen, he designed logos, advertising, and product packaging for corporations and acted in an advisory capacity in other areas of design, including for the US government's peacetime international initiatives, which included cultural diplomacy. In his 1958 report to the United States Information Agency on "Culture in the US Government," Bayer recommended that the government back cultural initiatives and exhibitions outside the United States.[14] He was involved in other activities, even inventions, such as a textile-generating device for the printing of fabric patterns.[15] With Paepcke he built up the Aspen Institute for Humanistic Studies, an international nonprofit think tank; Bayer worked on the architectural design of its campus and also its programming, especially the International Design Conference. Additionally, in the postwar period, he lectured widely on visual communication and graphic design.

War Efforts and Expanding Vision in Exhibition Design

To New York, Bayer brought many new elements that he would deploy in his American exhibitions, foremost fomenting a new, direct engagement between the viewing subject and the object viewed. But that relationship between viewer

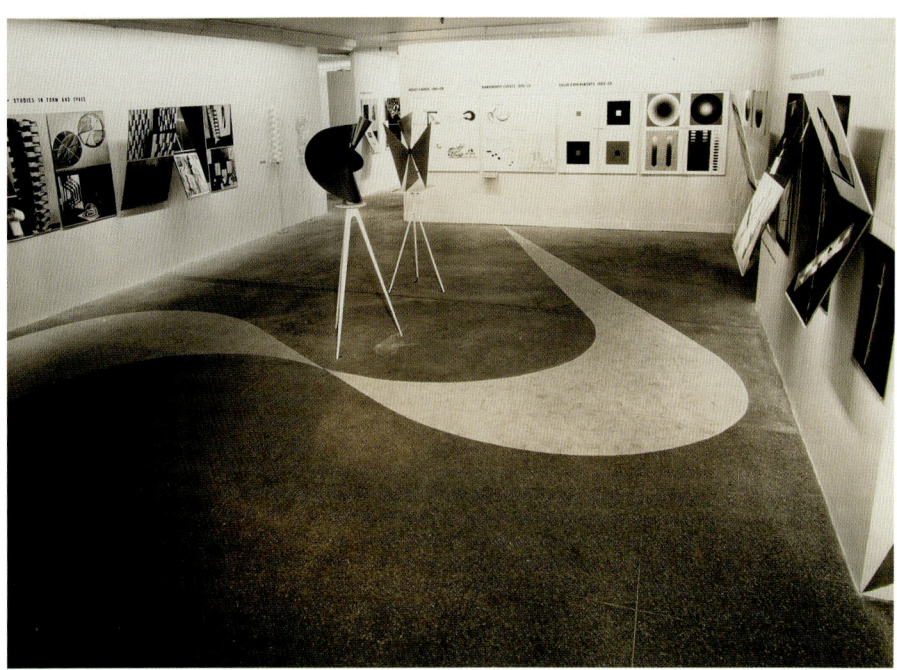

Fig. 8.11 Herbert Bayer, exhibition design for *Bauhaus, 1919–1928*, Museum of Modern Art, 1938, gelatin silver print. Photograph by Soichi Sunami. Harvard Art Museums/Busch-Reisinger Museum, Gift of Lydia Dorner.

and object was rarely stable; rather, Bayer deployed shifting physical elements and a continuous cycle of changing media in a process of remediation that gave rise to a dynamic viewing environment. In his 1938 Bauhaus show at MoMA, abstract floor markings directed visitors through the exhibition, while panels were mounted from the wall at varying heights and angles (fig. 8.11). This "active" viewing experience built on the exhibitions he — and others such as Moholy-Nagy, El Lissitzky, and Alexander Dorner — had conceived in late 1920s and early 1930s Germany.[16] Shortly after the MoMA Bauhaus show opened, in an important article published in 1939 titled "Fundamentals of Exhibition Design," Bayer explained his position on exhibition viewers and meeting their increasingly sophisticated needs. "As a result of the dynamic quality in man, a dynamic and purposeful construction is reached," he wrote, one that seeks to produce a "new, open, and seemingly variable ground plan."[17] He strove to analyze and dissect museum-goers' movements, to capture their attention, and create a dynamic pathway through a given show. To accompany "Fundamentals of Exhibition Design," he made drawings outlining his exhibition theories, such as "curved wall," "reading direction," and "disordered" versus "organized" exhibition viewer traffic (fig. 8.12). The illustrations that accompanied the article underscore Bayer's concerns for activating viewers phenomenologically in the space while simultaneously deeply engaging them in the exhibition's content.

These ideas took on heightened importance during the war years and found fruition in a series of successful MoMA exhibitions that engaged topics directly related to the war. In 1942, to raise spirits, MoMA prepared the *Road to Victory* exhibition for the US Office of War Information, commissioning Bayer for the exhibition design (fig. 8.13). *Road to Victory* was composed of enlarged photographs selected by the photographer Edward Steichen; it loosely narrated a stirring story of triumph conceived by Carl Sandburg. Echoing his 1930 Paris

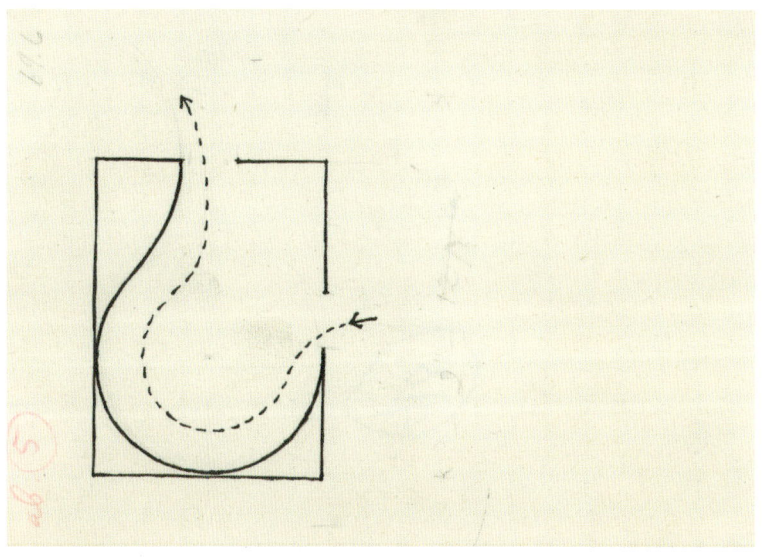
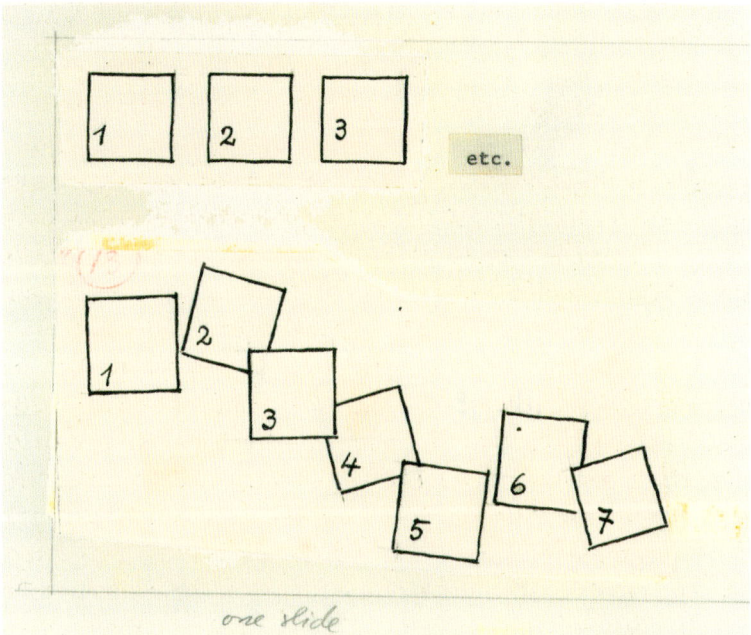
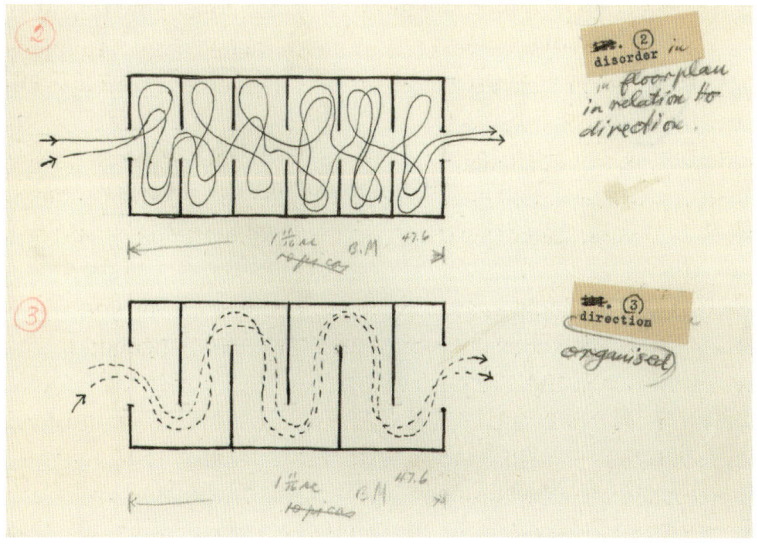

Fig. 8.12 Herbert Bayer, illustrations for "curved wall," "reading direction," "disorder in floor plan in relation to organized direction," and "organized direction," for "Fundamentals of Exhibition Design," *PM*, 1939. Herbert Bayer Papers, Denver Public Library.

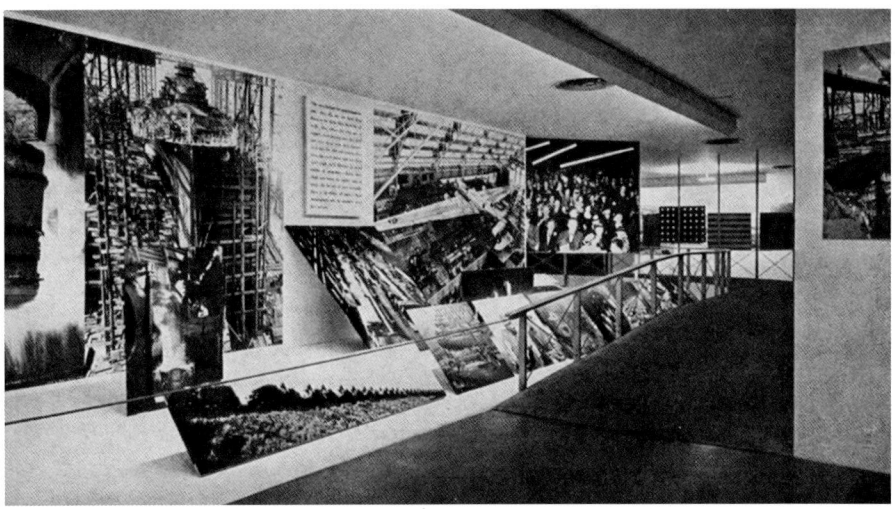

Fig. 8.13 Herbert Bayer, *Road to Victory* exhibition, 1942, Museum of Modern Art. From *Bulletin of the Museum of Modern Art* 9, nos. 5–6 (June 1942).

conception and ideas of "expanded vision," and building on viewing devices that he had utilized in the *Bauhaus* show, Bayer installed the large-scale photographs at varying tilted-up angles from the floor, as freestanding vertical elements, and affixed flat to the walls. The pathway for viewers – tracing a metaphoric "road to victory" – took them over raised ramps in some sections, creating an immersive and shifting visual experience. The exhibition was the result of a close collaboration with the government; as a 1942 issue of the MoMA *Bulletin* noted, various US government departments and agencies supplied 90 percent of the images used.[18] Steichen had enlisted in the US Navy Reserve and was already "Lieutenant Commander Steichen" when he worked on the exhibition. MoMA carefully referred to him throughout its publicity materials surrounding the show as "Commander Steichen."[19] The installation was a popular success, attested to by a critic for the *New York Times* who enthused, "Breathtaking and poignantly memorable. I think it would be no exaggeration to say that the Museum of Modern Art has not, since its career began, performed a more valuable service to the public. *Road to Victory* is a genuine contribution to the war effort."[20]

For a second MoMA wartime exhibition, *Airways to Peace* (1943), Bayer took his ideas of expanded vision to 360 degrees by creating a large "inside-out globe" that visitors could enter (fig. 8.14).[21] This provided an even more three-dimensional and immersive experience than the tilted wall displays of *Road to Victory*. His design for *Airways to Peace* also featured large-scale photographs and air-related graphic cutouts, huge spherical globes, objects, and other three-dimensional displays. The exhibition space was dynamically cut through by cords strung at angles, affixed to the ceiling and the floor. In collaboration with the Red Cross's "arts and skills" unit, Bayer also designed display tables for MoMA's 1943 *Arts in Therapy*, an exhibition that showcased the restorative potential of art for returning soldiers, through an engagement with therapeutic art-making (fig. 8.15).

By February 1943, MoMA had inaugurated an extensive "Armed Services Program" that included the circulation of films, entertainment for GIs, as well as traveling exhibitions in the service of the war effort.[22] Both *Road to Victory* and *Airways to Peace* traveled to other major US cities; exhibitions proved to be a

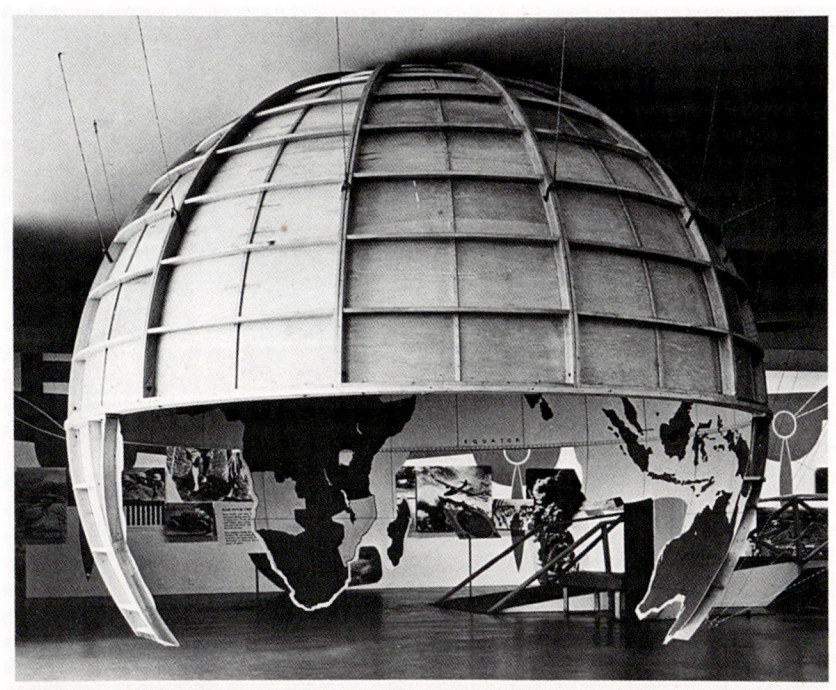

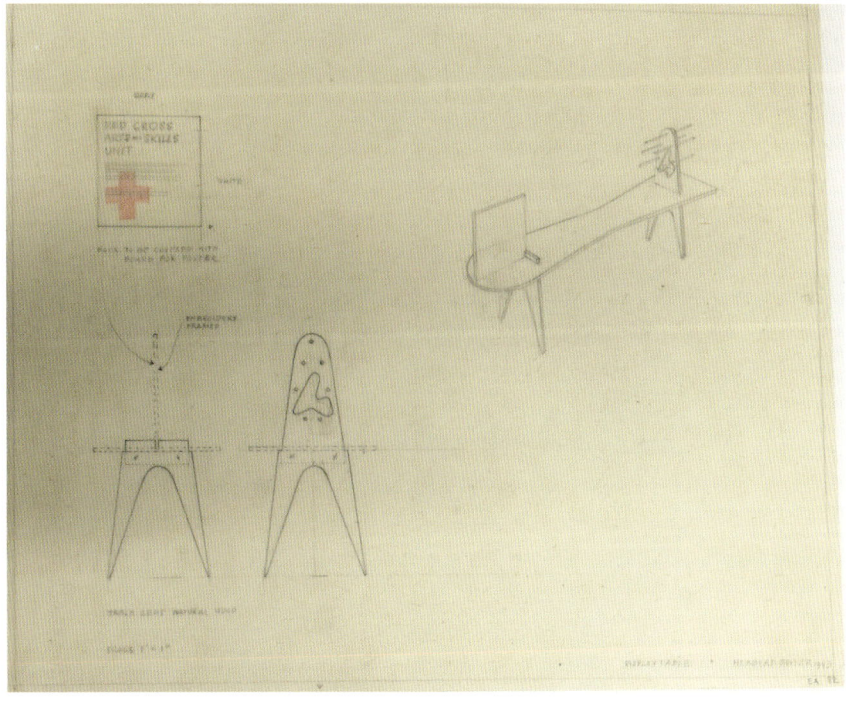

Fig. 8.14 Herbert Bayer, *Airways to Peace* exhibition, 1943, Museum of Modern Art.

Fig. 8.15 Herbert Bayer, design for display table for *The Arts in Therapy* exhibition, 1943, Museum of Modern Art. Denver Art Museum.

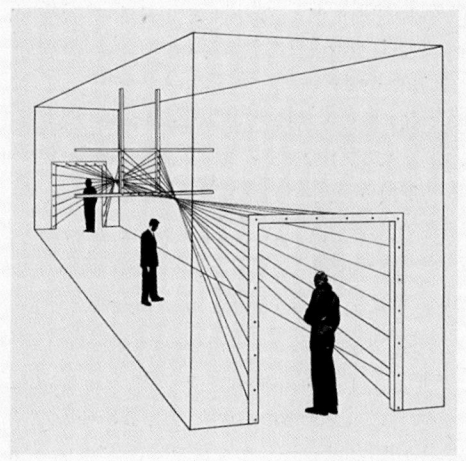

Fig. 8.16 Herbert Bayer, entrance design for *Modern Art in Advertising* exhibition, 1945, Art Institute of Chicago.

social tool that reached viewers and could positively impact morale. Via these and other exhibitions, the social usefulness of design comes to the fore through wartime didactic display.[23]

The All-Perceiving Eye: Remediation in an Expanding Field of Vision

Bayer continued to investigate differing formats and structures in order to bring innovative exhibition design to fruition, while also testing how varying vantage points and materials impacted the viewer's experience. He did so in a range media forms, depending on processes of remediation to transfer content and meaning into new formats, and thus new understanding. In his exhibition design, this translated into presenting museum-goers with unexpected and immersive encounters with the content. For example, his designs for *Modern Art in Advertising*, held at the Art Institute of Chicago in 1945, utilized a highly structured layout, which was unusual for Bayer.[24] This exhibition, which showcased the work that the Container Corporation of America had commissioned from Bayer and a large circle of international, mostly émigré, artists, depended on a modular framework. This format allowed Bayer to mount images at varying heights, including those that stretched to the ceiling, creating a montage effect and challenging the visitor's expected visual planes. However, his illustration for the entrance of this exhibition does something different. While many of Bayer's illustrations show a figure looking outward with an expanded point of view, his entrance plan shows lines converging into one-point perspective, for a narrowing viewpoint (fig. 8.16). Bayer oscillated between ever-widening viewpoints in order to coax museum-goers into taking in many images at once, and alternately, converging views that prompted them to focus on more specific aspects. He described the visual displays in his exhibitions in terms of a series of cuts, and as montage: "The idea of the panoramic point of view has disappeared because we dissect and put together again. Thus we have conceived a new view which is super-dimensional: the montage."[25] This concept of a montage is important because in the United States, in an ever-expanding manner, Bayer was thinking about – and working with – multiple means of communication and display formats, subjecting them to a constant process of remediation.

Bayer synthesized many of these concepts into what he called a "fundamental analysis of the field of visualization," presenting them as a lecture titled "Presentation and Display," which took place at New York University in 1940.[26] There he put forward "a genealogy of presentation" against an axis of "communication" (these are his terms), with his period's media organized according to perception by the eye, the ear, and the hand.[27] In a diagram, which itself relies on several formats – text, pictograms, and lines, he plots out a range of media, including braille, sound signs, flag signals, typewriter, shorthand, symbols, radio, film, photography, and street signs (fig. 8.17). From it, one can see how Bayer conceptualized different media, such as print or television, as intended for different receptive organs – eye, ear, and hand. In other drawings for the lecture, he experimented with purposefully labeling objects with false identifying text (a flower is labeled "mountain"; a leaf is labeled "leaf" in one instance and "horse" in another) to note the effects (fig. 8.18). This friction was productive as it engaged viewers, encouraged them to think actively and question their assumptions and perceptions – particularly useful in the context of exhibition design. Bayer described his multivalent praxis thus: "Exhibition design has evolved as a new discipline, as an apex of all media and powers of communication and of collective efforts and effects. The combined means of visual communication constitutes a remarkable complexity: language as visible printing or as sound, pictures as symbols, paintings and photographs, sculptural media, materials and surfaces, color, light, movement (of the display as well as the visitor), films, diagrams and charts. The total application of all plastic and psychological means (more than anything else) makes exhibition design an intensified and new language."[28]

Remediation is key in this formulation. In harnessing all available media to express and communicate, the end result could – and did – produce a multiplicity of new forms and formats; Bayer indicates as much in his description of language taking shape as printing or as sound, and his use of plastic and psychological means. This continuous process of remediation resulted in a productive transfer of ideas as much as in new and ever-shifting media forms within exhibitions.

Already in 1930, at the German section of the Société des artistes décorateurs exhibition in Paris, Bayer had demonstrated a new relationship between the viewer and the exhibition material on display.[29] Bayer mounted large photographs of architecture at angles so that the viewer encountered the works at several heights and degrees. Accompanying the installation was an illustration by Bayer that explicated his thinking; a cool figure, hands in pockets, whose head consists simply of an enormous eye, gazes out at the exhibit (see fig. 8.2 *right*). The figure takes in eleven images at once, as demonstrated by orange arrows emanating from his eye and landing on eleven thick, orange lines that represent the edges of the mounted photographs in the installation. Bayer termed this an "expanded field of vision." Leaving the focus to the eye alone, he designated the objects affixed to the walls as "bodiless displays."[30]

In the late 1930s in the United States, he would renew his investigations of these concepts. Kristie La has noted the continuities and changes in Bayer's exhibition design from Germany, including his work during the Nazi period, to his emigration to the United States, using the MoMA's exhibition *The Road to Victory*

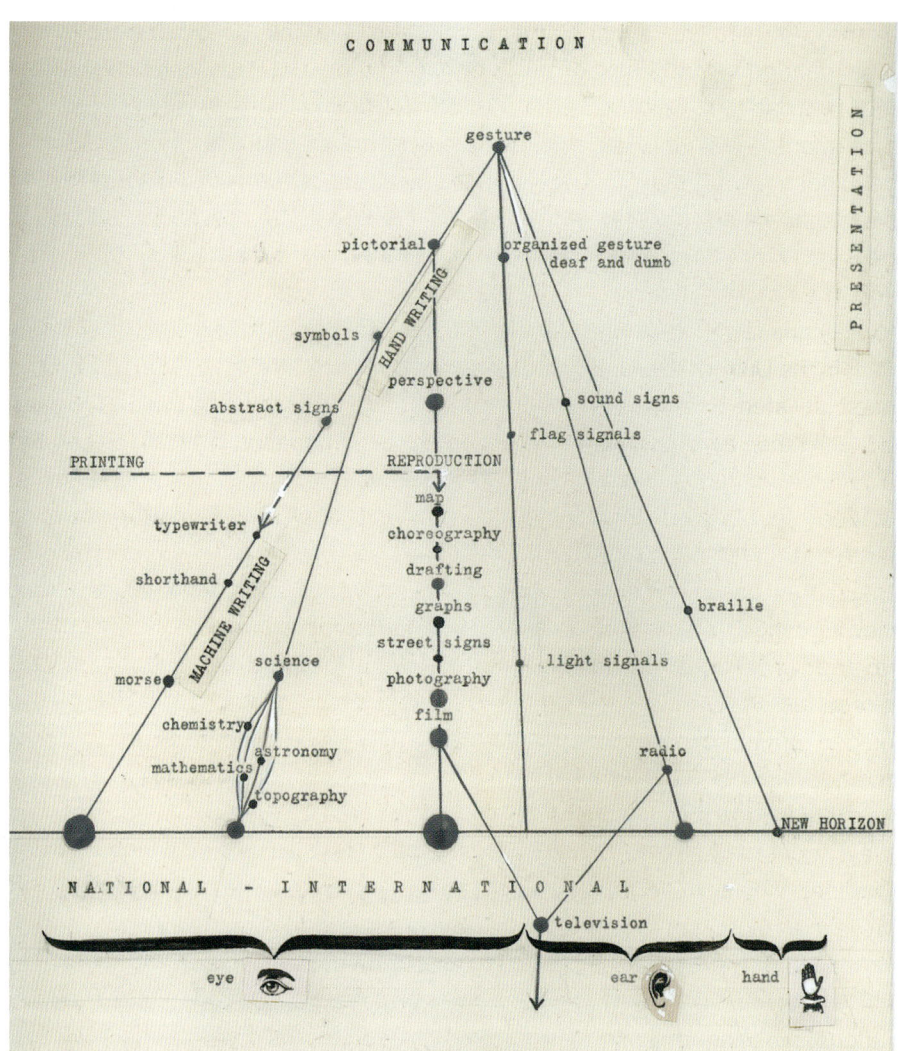

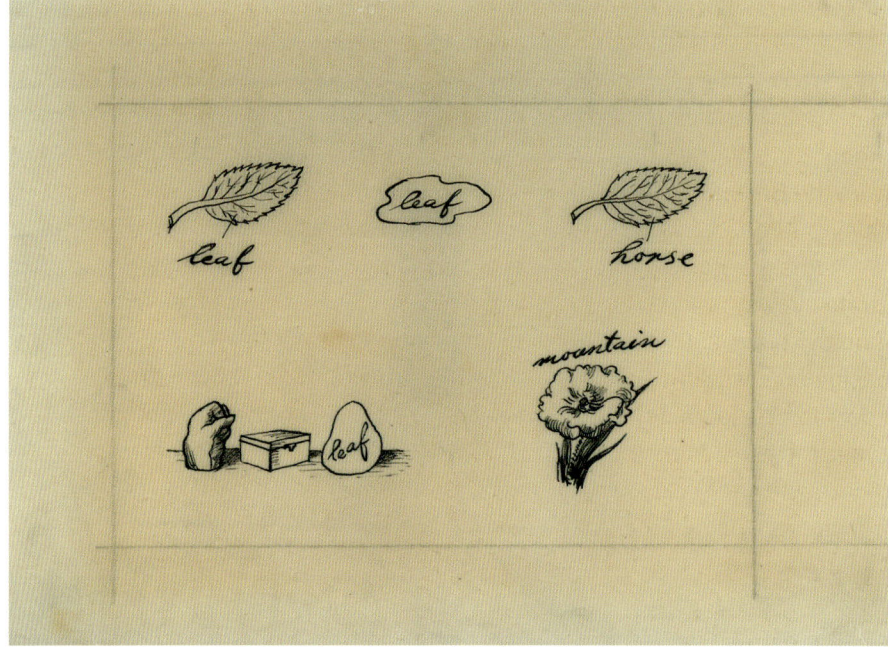

Fig. 8.17 Herbert Bayer, "Presentation and Display" lecture diagram, New York University, December 5, 1940. Herbert Bayer Papers, Denver Public Library.

Fig. 8.18 Herbert Bayer, "Presentation and Display" lecture illustration, New York University, December 5, 1940. Herbert Bayer Papers, Denver Public Library.

as the central focus.[31] Among other points, she connects Bayer's formulation of an expanded field of vision, from its origins in the 1930 Paris installation to the MoMA exhibition. She argues for his careful orchestrating of museum-goers' movements within this expanded field. I want to expand this notion further, to consider the way in which Bayer might have thought about – and implemented – his ideas related to the expanded field of vision not just as a tool of exhibition design in three-dimensional spaces but more broadly, for visual communication and in a process of remediation. Moreover, his ideas of "expanded vision" in a totality can illuminate the exilic condition and social design alike.

In the United States, Bayer built on the concepts of expanded vision that he had cultivated circa 1929 in Germany and had first tested at the Paris 1930 exhibition. In the years 1937–39 (thus spanning his immigration in 1938), he created a series of remarkable drawings related to exhibition layouts and his articulation of ideas about vision that engaged the viewing figure's attention – depicted by a large eyeball, sometimes also with eyelashes and eyebrow (fig. 8.19). He labeled these drawings in two slightly different ways: "field of vision" indicated a normal viewing range, whereas "expanded vision" goes beyond it, many degrees further up or down, even, as he suggests in one diagram, as much as 360 degrees in all directions. His German-era 1929 drawing of a viewer took in images that were placed roughly into three zones – elevated, in the center, and at a low angle near the floor; for his 1939 diagram, he sets the viewer on a slightly raised platform and then suggests an expansion of the possibilities of vision to encompass displays located in all 360 degrees, including on the ceiling and below the viewer's feet. Viewed collectively, these drawings illustrate a wide range of points of visual connection that he hoped his new displays would engender.

Expanded vision should not necessarily be thought about phenomenologically in terms of the visitor moving through an exhibition, but rather in stasis. Indeed, "expanded vision man" is always depicted as fixed, even transfixed, and not about to immediately stroll onward. He is coolly contemplative, taking in many objects from his vantage point, perhaps not even simultaneously, but sequentially. His are not fragmented, overstimulated metropolitan nerves, which the German sociologist Georg Simmel famously charted in the essay "The Metropolis and Mental Life" (1903), but rather he has developed the necessary organ – an enlarged eye – to master his new surroundings.[32] In these drawings from the Bayer archive, some of which he published in 1939, some of which he never published, Bayer considers a range of possibilities for his field of vision.

Other exemplars of graphic illustration by Bayer more concretely demonstrate the way in which he understood the eye as perceiving an object, imprinting it on the brain, and then actualizing a human response. One of the last graphic design commissions that Bayer did before leaving Germany for America was a cover for the journal *Gebrauchsgraphik / International Advertising Art* that illustrates the immediate relationship between the eye and an object – a connection that Bayer vividly visualizes for the cover.[33] In the illustration, a red line is traced from a grouping of three tall trees, to a window, into a blackened interior space, and drawn in through the cornea of an eye. The red line then makes a small loop through the back of the eye and descends to a hand with pencil, emerging out of its tip. Bayer was especially keen to project how advertising might benefit

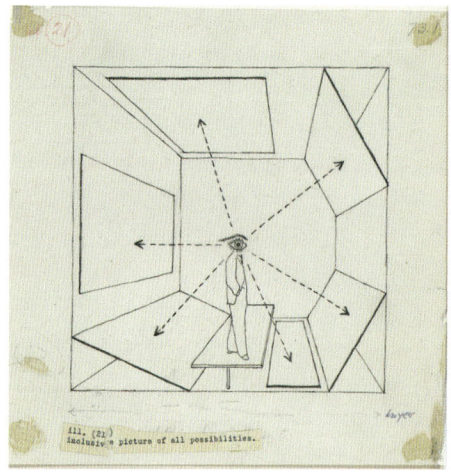
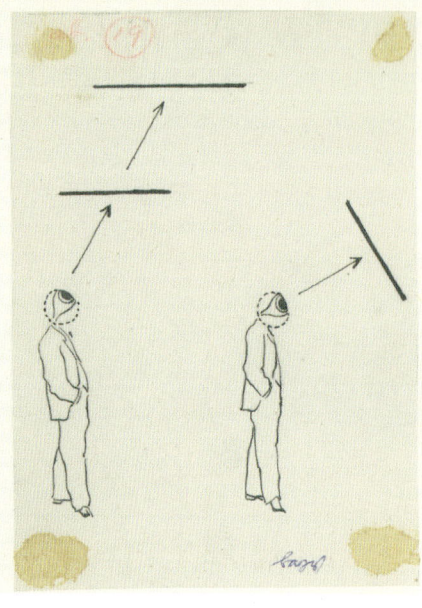
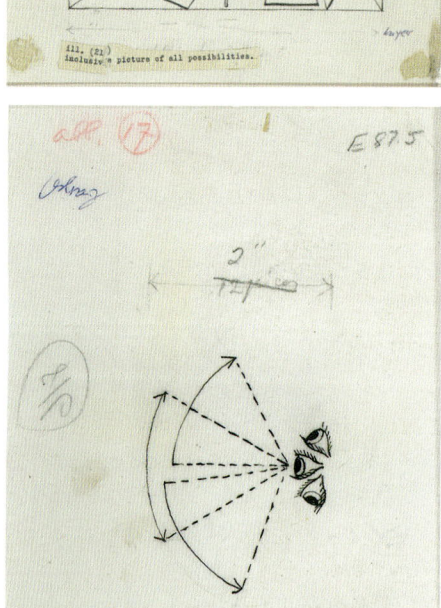
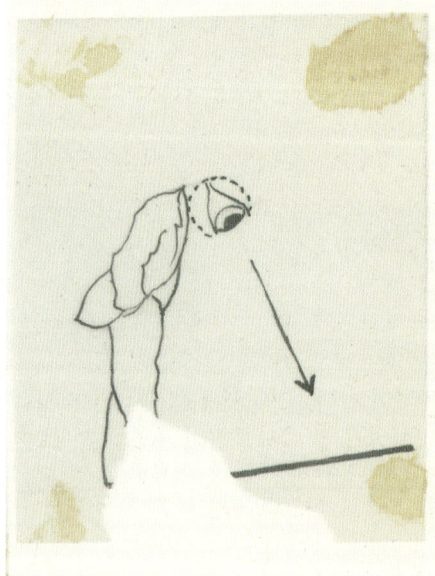
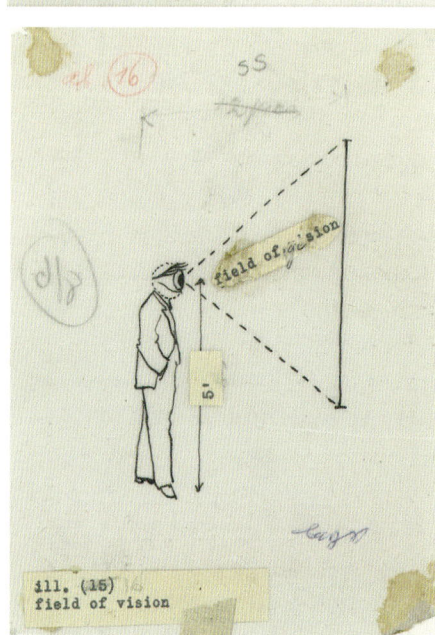

Fig. 8.19 Herbert Bayer, drawings depicting field of vision and expanded vision, 1937–39. Herbert Bayer Papers, Denver Public Library.

Left, top: Diagram of 360-degree field of vision, 1939, ink drawing; final version published in Bayer, "Fundamentals of Exhibition Design," *PM*, 1939.

Left, middle: Expanded vision, 1937–39, ink drawing; final version published in Bayer, "Fundamentals of Exhibition Design," *PM*, 1939.

Left, bottom: Field of vision, 1937–39, ink drawing; final version published in Bayer, "Fundamentals of Exhibition Design," *PM*, 1939.

Right, top and bottom: Expanded vision, 1937–39, ink drawings.

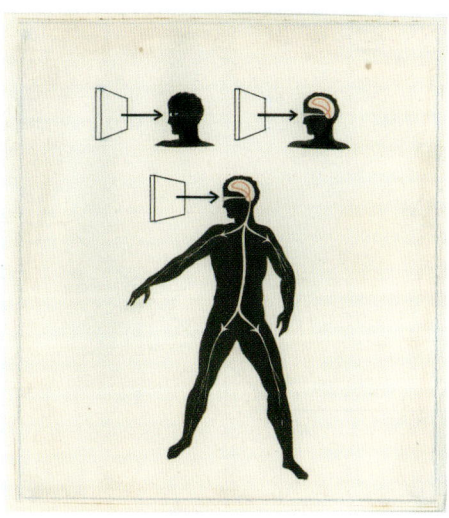

Fig. 8.20 Herbert Bayer, "Presentation and Display" lecture illustration, New York University, December 5, 1940. Herbert Bayer Papers, Denver Public Library.

from the science of optics, making his case in an illustration for his 1940 "Presentation and Display" lecture at New York University, in which a figure takes in content from a white rectangle, it is inscribed in the brain, and then travels through the nervous system (fig. 8.20).[34]

He further illustrates this concept in a "sample subway car advertisement," which depicts an external object, which is perceived and seemingly enters the eye, followed by the brain's response. Similar to the magazine cover, for the subway advertisement, Bayer draws vibrantly colored objects connected to lines that are drawn into a gray-shaded head in profile; they bypass the retina (where they ought to appear, upside down) in favor of being projected to the back of the brain, where the visual cortex is located. The sample advertisement diagram suggests that images of products (under which Bayer has written the text "selling...selling...selling..."), if viewed often enough, can be inscribed on the back of the brain, and ultimately result in "sold" objects. Bayer, however, was very familiar with the actual scientific principles of vision, which he illustrated to accompany a 1939 article, "The Human Eye – a Living Camera," published not long after his arrival in the United States; for a lay audience, it vividly and accurately laid out how the eye and vision functioned.[35] Although advertising, then, as now, was engaged in convincing an audience to buy goods, Bayer took his role as a designer seriously, as one with potential for social usefulness and social good. As he formulated it in another 1940 lecture, "'public' taste is more a question of psychology than art. The public is somehow helpless. It has to take what it gets. It is up to us to give the public the best not the lowest because the public wants it. It's just as if one gave nothing but foolish books to a child because that was what he liked. We all should realize that the influence of advertising on education and morals is tremendous. We should fully sense the responsibility which lies on us and the great possibilities for the culture of our time."[36]

Whether in support of the war effort (graphic design for the WPA, the Container Corporation of America, and the Civil Aeronautics Administration), exhibition theory and design, or in postwar advertising, Bayer was deeply concerned with reaching viewers. As he would frame it, "Design is a fundamental outlook at the service of the visual improvement of life."[37] In America, the preponderance of objects to be sold, the need for selling through new visual connections, and against a backdrop of the vibrant visual scene where work needed to stand out—all necessitated a new approach to design. For this, a new visuality was needed, too. Out of a fragmented, dispersed set of images, products, messages, and futures, in these years, Bayer created a totality that offered containment, organization, and focus.

Estrangement: The Designer in Exile

For Bayer, the eye functioned as an essential tool for encountering the world and encoding the findings onto the brain; it was a symbolic element that allowed him to explore concepts of expanded vision in his exhibition designs; and he vividly engaged the eye in his striking graphic design, underscoring urgent messages such as "Our Allies Need Eggs." On a more prosaic level, his view of design's role in "the visual improvement of life" was heartfelt, as was his ardent belief in the social usefulness of art. In Bayer's work, the eye is remediated—from its usefulness in exhibition design and display, with its wider range of vision allowing the viewer take in more exhibition content—into a new form of advertising that drives home a sale. But the eye is also implicated in a condition of estrangement when it is again remediated into another form: photomontage.

In *Einsamer Großstädter* (*Lonely Metropolitan*), a 1932 photomontage, the eye appears as a disembodied trope into an interior condition, recalling the uncanny, and also urban processes of estrangement (fig. 8.21). Fellow German émigré to America, art historian, and progressive museum director Alexander Dorner, writing in his 1947 book *The Way beyond "Art,"* which showcases Bayer's work and ideas, describes the hands depicted in *Lonely Metropolitan* as "everyday hands" and the setting as the "everyday walls" of Berlin's courtyard apartments. Dorner writes poignantly about this work and the untethered nature of modern life, from the perspective of 1947: "The hands have lost their identity . . . they are invaded by eyes, which appear miraculous like stigmata. . . . We have lost our habitual static formation. Our old world was one fixed state of Being. This world is the very act of Becoming. Its self-changeability makes new minds of our minds."[38] Dorner continues about the work, "There is no identity of subject matter, either, to erect the absolute geometry of traditional logic on. The 'this' and 'not this,' the 'here' and 'not here' are overruled. They are only the traditional platform from which we jump off into the water of the new reality of creative self-changeability. Small wonder, then, that this composition attacks us with the power of a new language, understandable to everyone and yet endowed with a new, stirring intensity."[39] Dorner also references Bayer's "new vision of autonomous change."[40] Although writing about a 1932 work of art, Dorner is doing so in 1947, in the context of the aftermath of a major relocation by both men and a destructive, global war. The eye is a hinge between a heightened outer awareness and inner introspection.

"Autonomous change" and "acts of becoming"—these phrases were written by a German émigré about a fellow émigré in the time frame of both individuals' recent emigration. About exhibition design, Dorner explicitly mentions estranged realities. Representing any number of examples that could be brought

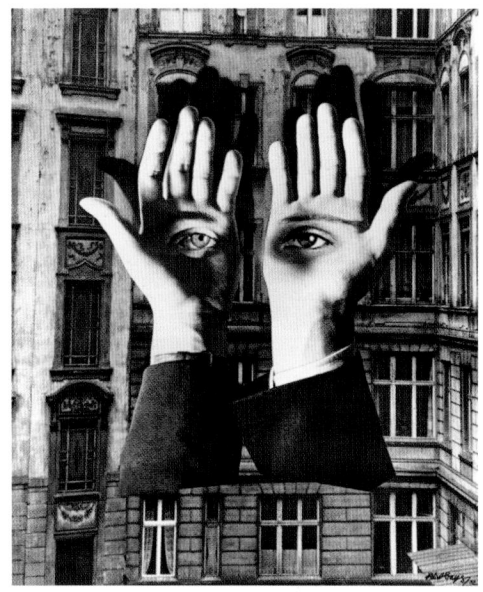

Fig. 8.21 Herbert Bayer, *Lonely Metropolitan*, 1932, photomontage. Berlin.

to the fore, these are just a few ways to think about defamiliarization in the context of a process of finding one's way, of assimilating to new circumstances, of overcoming estrangement, for what could be termed Bayer's "new visuality" in design. The pragmatism that the exiles adopted in order to assimilate to America undoubtedly pushed their work forward, to some degree resulting in success out of sheer necessity. Viewed in another light, paradoxically, possible uneasy conditions of estrangement in America, as exiles, created the circumstances in which they assiduously strove to assimilate into their new context.

The notion of estrangement (*Verfremdungseffekt*, "alienation effect," "estrangement effect") is useful for further thinking about the exilic situation, more widely, of Bauhaus members in America. "Defamiliarization" had already been at the core of Bauhaus practice, a mode of presenting known objects in new ways (cantilevered chairs instead of four legged-chairs), or via new materials (use of metal or glass instead of wood), or with enhanced emphasis (large-scale curtain window walls instead of small windows punctuating a facade). Likewise, Bauhaus Foundation Course exercises involving *Faktur* and *matière* were also processes of remediation from one material into another – or at least the appearance of doing so – while also heightening defamiliarization with regard to the materials used.

In graphic design, defamiliarization can be seen in the form of an all lowercase, sans serif alphabet, especially jarring to Germans, who utilize capital letters for a higher proportion of their words than do other languages. In collages or photomontages such as *Lonely Metropolitan*, it is the reassembly of known images into a new context, giving rise to new meanings. And in exhibition design, Bayer's expanded field of vision offers content all at once – it overwhelms – leaving the observer to take in only as much as the eye can manage. Bayer asks his viewer to contemplate if all of the content in the "field of vision" is ever even graspable. He presents an aloof figure, one that at best remains at a dispassionate distance, coolly taking it all in. Through remediation Bayer presents his design vision and its message through new modes and representations.

∎ ∎ ∎

Estrangement presented the opportunity for new criticism and objectivity, even a new form of modernism, which, this book has argued, occurred when Bauhaus members arrived in America. This literal and figurative distance from their "source" of European avant-garde art and design allowed them the capacity to work in America with fresh eyes; the defamiliarization causing them to reevaluate and reorient toward productive, as well as hopeful, new ends. The challenges they faced from an American public at best unfamiliar with modernism, and at worst alienated by it, presented another clarifying moment of estrangement – one they strove to overcome by bringing their ideas and forms into new settings and materials through processes of transposition, by meeting and addressing contingent conditions, and through remediation.

Architecture, too, is – broadly speaking – very contextual, whether the context is in relationship to a place, to the materials chosen, to the design elements, to the economic context, or the fulfillment of a perceived program or social agenda. That is why the possibility for architectural estrangement can be so potentially productive. Architectural estrangement is the lens that allows for critical distance, confrontations between self and place, confrontations between architecture and place. Estrangement shapes and sharpens ideas through the effects of defamiliarization.

Artistic emancipation occurs through displacement, through the unfamiliar. It allows for unique architecture, such as Mies's Seagram Building on Park Avenue: set back from the plaza, its facade of liquor-colored bronze decorative elements confronts a sea of stone buildings. But quickly that estrangement, that difference, if successful, can turn into the everyday, into contextual assimilation – such as that which took place a couple of avenues over, on Sixth Avenue, in which multistory building after building was erected down the block in a similar fashion. In case after case, modernism, this book has argued, became a coherent object only after it passed through conditions of exile and was assimilated in a more localized context. Something, however, was always changed in the process – transposed, contingent on another factor, remediated.

Avant-garde ideas came together and emerged as mainstream modernism in the vibrant postwar period, thereby securing a future for modern objects and their originators alike. Raw, open possibilities in the United States gave the émigrés unique opportunities to build and design in a new manner that had merely been the seeds of ideas in Europe. Bayer's bold, clear graphic design and his exhibition layouts are just one example of how this was achieved.

The combination of the variety of needs produced by the war and the anxiety felt by immigrants such as Moholy-Nagy or Bayer, who were positioned precariously in the society that had received them, compelled them to action. Both sought to contribute the skills and pedagogical practices that each had brought with him in order to aid this new country of residence. Putting into action the pliable Bauhaus problem-solving methods, protagonists such as Gropius, Josef and Anni Albers, and Hilberseimer, too, were also able to effectively redirect efforts toward the kind of social transformation that the German-era Bauhaus had advocated. Although not all of their proposals were taken up,

Bauhaus émigrés in America were remarkable in the degree to which they were able to offer direct solutions.

The wartime situation in the United States presented problems that needed immediate attention. The pragmatism of these émigrés in America was noteworthy—particularly the degree to which they were able to quickly adapt to the changed circumstances of a nation at war and to address wartime problems through a varied array of striking poster designs, exhibition installations, and other designs. The result was a successful melding of art and technology with science to devise advanced visual design for the war effort—an assimilation that arguably represented a realization to a new degree of the Bauhaus's originary ideals. Although when they were in Germany, Bauhaus members often wondered why industry did not embrace their designs, in the United States they quickly and successfully cooperated with complex American bureaucracies, such as the Department of Defense and the WPA, and with private investors alike, to bring their ideas to fruition. Bauhaus modernism, one could say, only congealed and cohered after it passed through these conditions of exile.

Beyond their practical successes, the demands of the war and living in exile gave the émigrés the opportunity to attempt to make good on an expansive philosophy. In a lecture titled "Total Design," Bayer noted, "In living and practicing the integration of art and life through design I have recognized that no strict divisions should be drawn and that it is all of common citizenship. For this reason I am above all concerned with the total shape and content of the human scene, although one must necessarily deal with the individual fragments which add up to a totality."[41] He continued, "Visual enrichment of life becomes a fundamental outlook because it encompasses all of man's activities and aspirations. But the artist must be firmly anchored in the organization of his society. Only then can we say that he is not a luxury."[42]

Just a few years following the close of the devastating second world war, in 1949 the Aspen Institute hosted the Goethe Bicentennial Convocation, an event bringing together different humanistic disciplines for positive cultural renewal. In a lecture titled "Goethe and Art Today," Bayer specified his stance: "A creative person must be drawn into the problems of his time. Why should an artist be spared and separated from realities and be made escapist? Would not art end as pure self-expression if it does not participate in our life on common grounds?"[43] Bayer argued in favor of the "exploration of all visual potentialities"—toward their fusion and synthesis—so that a "meaningful totality" could evolve.[44]

In foregrounding this social basis, with an emphasis on citizenship, the fragmented individual and the praxis of design come together in a totality, serving sets of needs from wartime activities to peacetime contributions of visual culture. This was the achievement of these émigrés to the postwar modernism to follow. In our present period, the fraught migration and movement of peoples has again come to the fore. This book has trained a lens on an earlier period of the sometimes forced, sometimes elective, movement of an exceptional group of artists and designers. It has shown how, catalyzed by the tragedy of war, the ideas and objects of exile impacted, and furthered, modernism. It illustrates how once a crisis has passed, and the project of rebuilding begins, intense periods of change can positively impact our longer-term visual and built environment.

Acknowledgments

Across a decade and two continents, I have benefited from the generosity of many. From large conference lectures where my ideas have been challenged and shaped, to convivial discussions over dinners that led down new paths of inquiry, to the willingness of conservators to bring out one-hundred-year-old, exceedingly fragile glass plate negatives, this book about exile and dislocation was shaped by its opposite – intellectual welcomings and a sense of shared belonging, of being at home in modernism.

Curators, archivists, and librarians have shared their holdings and collections while giving generously of their time and expertise. At the Bauhaus Archive in Berlin, for what is now decades-long support, I would like to especially thank Annemarie Jaeggi, Sabine Hartmann, Wencke Clausnitzer-Paschold, Nina Schönig, Erika Babatz, and Berthold Eberhard. Stretching even further back, at Harvard University's Busch-Reisinger Museum I am very grateful for the ongoing generosity of Laura Muir and Lynette Roth. Over the course of many visits to the Bauhaus Stiftung, Dessau I am grateful for the collegiality of Regina Bittner, Barbara Steiner, Torsten Blume, Florian Strob, and Wolfgang Thöner. I would like to thank Gwen Chanzit for sharing Herbert Bayer materials in the archives and collections of the Denver Museum of Art. At the Art Institute of Chicago, across many research trips, I am thankful for the assistance of Autumn Lorraine Mather of the Ryerson and Burnham Archives and the expertise and friendship of Alison Fisher of the Architecture and Design Department. I thank Catherine Bruck at the University Archives, Illinois Institute of Technology, and Valerie Harris at the Special Collections, University of Illinois at Chicago. For enabling a deep dive into the Isokon archival materials of the Pritchard Papers, I am indebted to Bridget Gillies at the Archives and Special Collections of the University of East Anglia Library. I am also thankful for the reference staff at the Dessau Stadtarchiv, the Kunstbibliothek der Staatlichen Museen zu Berlin, and the Manuscripts Division at the Library of Congress. An especially warm welcome accompanied my protracted research time at the Josef and Anni Albers Foundation – I am as thankful to Brenda Danilowitz, Nicholas Weber, Amy Jean Porter, Fritz Horstman, and Jeannette Redensek for the time spent discussing the Alberses on the archive's terrace as for the generous sharing of fragile artworks and documents. And I am especially indebted to Hattula Moholy-Nagy at the Moholy-Nagy Foundation for her convivial research hosting and sustained intellectual support and rapid reply to any query, large or trivial, over a long period of friendship.

As this book has taken shape, it has benefited enormously along the way from invitations to present work in progress and for ensuing discussions and insights among scholars, students, and members of the audience at the Bard Graduate Center; Bauhaus Stiftung, Dessau; Bauhaus University Weimar; the Clark Art Institute; John H. Daniels Faculty of Architecture, Landscape, and Design, University of Toronto; German Center for Art History, Paris; Harvard Art

Museums; HTC Forum, Massachusetts Institute of Technology; the Newberry Library; Papanek Foundation, University of Applied Arts, Vienna; Radcliffe Institute for Advanced Study, Harvard University; Terra Foundation for American Art; V&A/Royal College of Art; and Yale School of Art. Research and publication of this book was assisted by a grant from the Graham Foundation for Advanced Studies in the Fine Arts. A year-long fellowship from the Gerda Henkel Foundation enabled critical time to dedicate to the project. I am grateful for the ongoing support from Nicolai and Katja Tangen and the AKO Foundation.

I am indebted to exceptional scholars who took the time to carefully read and respond to sections of the book in progress: Zeynep Celik Alexander, Oliver Botar, Scott Colman, Brenda Danilowitz, Noam Elcott, Hattula Moholy-Nagy, Thomas de Monchaux, Elizabeth Otto, Jeannette Redensek, Jeffrey Saletnik, and Charles Waldheim. I am especially thankful for the careful reading of the entire manuscript and insight provided by Kathleen James-Chakraborty and Frederic J. Schwartz, for whose expertise, guidance, and friendship I am especially grateful. The Courtauld Institute of Art provided intellectual conviviality and resources that supported this work. I would especially like to thank Jo Applin, Rebecca Arnold, Sussan Babaie, Alixe Bovey, Lucy Bradnock, Esther Chadwick, Klara Kemp-Welch, Caroline Levitt, Maria Mileeva, Gavin Parkinson, Dorothy Price, Wenny Teo, Stephen Whiteman, and Sarah Wilson.

Discussions with colleagues and friends have helped the shape this book's broad contours as well as its smallest asides. I am indebted to Annie Bourneuf, Thomas Dyja, Philipp Ekardt, Magnus Englund, Clemens Finkelstein, Laura Frahm, Eliza Garrison, Alanna Gedgaudas, Amy Hamlin, Freyja Hartzell, Charles W. Haxthausen, Timothy Hyde, Kristie La, Ana Miljacki, Dietrich Neumann, Julie Park, Bill Rankin, Patrick Rössler, Sasha Rossmann, Rolf Sachsse, Jan Tichy, Jordan Troeller, Joyce Tsai, Ines Weizman, and Claire Zimmerman. Two collectives coalesced during the writing of this book, providing an intellectual framework for my thinking. I would like to thank members of Care Collective: Christina Crawford, Brian Goldstein, Jennifer Hock, Min Kyung Lee, Catalina Mejía Moreno, Olga Touloumi; and Unsettled Subjects: Nick Beech, Ana Betancour, Shumi Bose, Derin Fadina, Emily Mann, Buhle Mathole, Kavitha Ravikumar, Shahed Saleem, Dubravka Sekulic, and Tania Sengupta. In the weeks and months in which I sought to draw this book to a close, the full-scale invasion of Ukraine by Russia created the greatest mass dislocation that Europe has seen since World War II. For joining forces with me on initiatives in support of Ukrainian art and architectural historians, preservationists, and architects – activities that gave this book an urgency and a new context – I am thankful for working alongside Christina Crawford, Katia Denysova, Sofia Dyak, Simon Evans, Francis Farrell, Maria Mileeva, Michał Murawski, Bill Sherman, Uta Staiger, and Ada Wordsworth. Subsequently, I am grateful for new colleagues and friends, especially Dmytro,

Tymofii, Arseniy, and Mariana Bukhanevych; Kateryna Kublytska; Antonina Palahniuk; Vira Tsypuk; and Anastasiia and Polina Yurusova.

At Princeton University Press, I am very grateful for the expertise of Michelle Komie and the support of the editorial, production, and design team: Beth Gianfagna, Mark Bellis, Steve Sears, Annie Miller, Jess Massabrook, and Jeff Wincapaw.

My deepest gratitude goes to my family circle, John Ackerman; Eric Schuldenfrei and Marisa Yiu; Emily, Dylan, and Lawrence Davey; John Neville; and my mother, Elaine Eskesen. And most of all to Henry and Theo, who, in their own quest for good German baked goods, have gamely accompanied me in crossing many borders in my pursuit of modernism.

Notes

Introduction

1. This book builds on broader studies of exile, art, and design, such as Stephanie Barron's groundbreaking exhibition and catalog, *Exiles + Émigrés: The Flight of European Artists from Hitler* (New York: Abrams, 1997); Richard A. Etlin, ed., *Art, Culture, and Media under the Third Reich* (Chicago: University of Chicago Press, 2002); Bernd Nicolai, ed., *Architektur und Exil: Kulturtransfer und architektonische Emigration 1930 bis 1950* (Trier: Porta Alba, 2003); Peter Rose, ed., *The Dispossessed: An Anatomy of Exile* (Amherst: University of Massachusetts Press, 2005); Sabine Eckmann and Lutz P. Koepnick, eds., *Caught by Politics: Hitler Exiles and American Visual Culture* (London: Palgrave Macmillan, 2007); Burcu Dogramaci and Karin Wimmer, eds., *Netzwerke des Exils: Künstlerische Verflechtungen, Austausch und Patronage nach 1933* (Berlin: Gebr. Mann Verlag, 2011); Pamela Potter, *Art of Suppression: Confronting the Nazi Past in Histories of the Visual and Performing Arts* (Berkeley: University of California Press, 2016); and Alison J. Clarke and Elana Shapira, eds., *Émigré Cultures in Design and Architecture* (London: Bloomsbury, 2017).

    Objects in Exile also connects to studies on the impact of war on architecture, such as Donald Albrecht, ed., *World War II and the American Dream: How Wartime Building Changed a Nation* (Cambridge, MA: MIT Press, 1995); Jean-Louis Cohen, *Architecture in Uniform: Designing and Building for the Second World War* (New Haven, CT: Yale University Press, 2011); and Robert V. Sharp and Elizabeth Stepina, eds., *1945: Creativity and Crisis: Chicago Architecture and Design of the World War II Era* (Chicago: Art Institute of Chicago, 2005).

2. The glass plate is in the collection of Hattula Moholy-Nagy. The only flower photogram represented on the glass negative that has not been lost is *Untitled* (fgm 151), 1925–26, which is now in the Musée National d'Art Moderne, Centre Georges Pompidou, Paris.

3. While most of the protagonists examined here taught at the Bauhaus, this is not a project on the Bauhaus in diaspora; this book seeks to engage critically the ways in which exile itself impacted the trajectory of modernism in my protagonists' works. In doing so, it builds on the crucial work by scholars in Kathleen James-Chakraborty's excellent edited volume, *Bauhaus Culture: From Weimar to the Cold War* (Minneapolis: University of Minnesota Press, 2006), as well as my own coedited volume, with Jeffrey Saletnik, *Bauhaus Construct: Fashioning Identity, Discourse, and Modernism* (London: Routledge, 2009); Barry Bergdoll and Leah Dickerman, eds., *Bauhaus 1919–1933: Workshops for Modernity* (New York: Museum of Modern Art, 2009); Bauhaus-Archiv Berlin et al., eds., *Bauhaus: A Conceptual Model* (Ostfildern: Hatje Cantz, 2009); and Margret Kentgens-Craig, *The Bauhaus and America: First Contacts, 1919-1936* (Cambridge, MA: MIT Press, 1999). Moreover, monographs on individuals have significantly contributed to our knowledge of the period and its artworks, such as Achim Borchardt-Hume, *Albers and Moholy-Nagy: From the Bauhaus to the New World* (London: Tate, 2006).

4. A significant aspect is Britain's role in the development of these Bauhaus protagonists' modernism, with important stays in London as a key site before their emigration to the United States, the ramifications of which have been downplayed to date. *Objects in Exile* builds on texts such as Charlotte Benton, *A Different World: Émigré Architects in Britain 1928-1958* (London: RIBA Heinz Gallery, 1995); James Peto and Donna Loveday, eds., *Modern Britain 1929-1939* (London: Design Museum, 1999); Andreas Schätzke, *German Architects in Great Britain: Planning and Building in Exile 1933-1945* (Stuttgart: Menges, 2013); Alan Powers, *Bauhaus Goes West: Modern Art and Design in Britain and America* (London: Thames & Hudson, 2019); and Valeria Carullo, *Moholy-Nagy in Britain, 1935-1937* (London: Lund Humphries, 2019).

5. See, for example, Jennifer L. Roberts, *Transporting Visions: The Movement of Images in Early America* (Berkeley: University of California Press, 2014). See also the history and theory of failure and unreliability, as discussed in the context of paperwork, in Ben Kafka, *The Demon of Writing: Powers and Failures of Paperwork* (New York: Zone Books, 2012).

Chapter 1: Architecture's Material Abstraction

1. László Moholy-Nagy, *Vision in Motion* (Chicago: Paul Theobald, 1947), 13. Text written in 1946, published posthumously.
2. Ibid., 15.
3. For a discussion of *Traffic (City Lights Eastgate Hotel)*, see Jeannine Fiedler and Hattula Moholy-Nagy, eds., *Laszlo Moholy-Nagy: Color in Transparency, Photographic Experiments in Color, 1934-1946* (Göttingen: Steidl, 2006), 76.
4. Although Moholy-Nagy never trained as an architect, he worked closely with key modern architects, even traveling from Marseille to Athens on the ship journey of the 1933 Congrès internationaux d'architecture moderne (C.I.A.M.), making a film of the meeting. There are just three instances in which he attempted to act as an architect in the traditional sense. As Lloyd C. Engelbrecht charts, in the United States, he entered an architectural competition for a new art center for Wheaton College (1938); in collaboration with established architect George Fred Keck, he worked on a theater and fine arts building for the College of William and Mary (1939); and he approached Hilla Rebay, putting himself forward as a possible architect for the Solomon R. Guggenheim

Museum (1943). See Engelbrecht, *Moholy-Nagy: Mentor to Modernism* (Cincinnati, OH: Flying Trapeze Press, 2009), 2:641–51.

5 Emphasis in the original. James Merle Thomas, "The Human Factor: Applied Abstraction and Habitable Space," in Joyce Tsai, *The Paintings of Moholy-Nagy: The Shape of Things to Come* (New Haven, CT: Yale University Press, 2015), 115–16.

6 Ernő Kállai, "Ladislaus Moholy-Nagy," *Jahrbuch der Jungen Kunst* (1924), trans. in Krisztina Passuth, *Moholy-Nagy* (New York: Thames and Hudson, 1985), 416.

7 László Moholy-Nagy, "Isms or Art," *Vivos Voco* 8–9 (1926), reprinted in Richard Kostelanetz, *Moholy-Nagy* (New York: Praeger, 1970), 35.

8 Sigfried Giedion, Foreword, *Telehor* 1–2 (February 1936): 27–28.

9 Péter Mátyás (Ernő Kállai), "Moholy-Nagy," *MA* 6, no. 9 (1921): 119, trans. in Passuth, *Moholy-Nagy*, 412. Oliver Botar identifies the painting Kállai is describing as *Telegraf und Eisenbahnlandschaft*, n.d. (ca. 1921). Botar, *Technical Detours: The Early Moholy-Nagy Reconsidered* (New York: Art Gallery of the Graduate Center, the City University of New York, 2006), 117–18.

10 Kállai continues, "Although still not with the centralism of the self-containing architectonic structures, the pieces are coalescing into cohesive units, replacing the exploded conglomerate forms. Structures, still open, but set into motion from sharper defined and closer interrelated centers, emerge." Mátyás (Kállai), "Moholy-Nagy," trans. in Passuth, *Moholy-Nagy*, 412.

11 László Moholy-Nagy, *Malerei, Fotografie, Film* [*Painting, Photography, Film*] (Munich: Albert Langen Verlag, 1925; 2nd ed., 1927); trans. Janet Seligman (London: Lund Humphries, 1969), 18. In a footnote related to this statement, Moholy-Nagy makes a rare direct comment on color and architecture:

> Color in architecture helps to create a sense of comfort to suit the room and its occupant. It thus becomes a coequal means of spatial composition which can be further supplemented by furniture and materials. The origin of contemporary experiments in painting the walls of rooms in different colors is as follows: The effect of rooms painted homogeneously is hard. There is too much self-emphasis in their uniform color. In such a room the presence of the single color, whatever it may be, is constantly with us. When, however, the various walls are painted in various harmonizing colors it is only the relationships of the colors which operate. A resonance arises which displaces color as a self-accentuated material and creates instead an effect in which color relationships alone play a part. This gives the whole room a sublimated, atmospheric quality: comfortable, festive, diverting, concentrating, etc. Some system in the choice and distribution of color is determined by the room and its function (hygiene, lighting technique, communication, etc.). It follows that the habit of painting walls in different colors cannot be indulged everywhere indiscriminately. (18–19)

12 László Moholy-Nagy, "On the Problem of New Content and New Form," *Akasztott Ember* 3–4 (1922): 3, trans. in Passuth, *Moholy-Nagy*, 287.

13 Emphasis added. Kállai, "Ladislaus Moholy-Nagy," trans. in Passuth, *Moholy-Nagy*, 417.

14 On the *Book of New Artists*, see Oliver A. I. Botar, *Sensing the Future: Moholy-Nagy, Media and the Arts* (Zurich: Lars Müller Publishers, 2014), 62–66; and Passuth, *Moholy-Nagy*, 33–34. Although the 1922 *Buch neuer Künstler* preceded the 1923 *Toward a New Architecture*, Le Corbusier had previously published most of his essays in the magazine *L'Esprit Nouveau* from 1921, where the authors could have seen them.

15 See Moholy-Nagy, *Painting, Photography, Film*, trans. Seligman; *Von Material zu Architektur* [*From Material to Architecture*] (1929; repr., Mainz: Klorian Kupferberg Verlag, 1968), trans. Katrin Schamun and Jillian DeStone (Zurich: Lars Müller Publishers, 2021); *The New Vision: Fundamentals of Bauhaus Design, Painting, Sculpture, and Architecture with Abstract of an Artist* (1947; repr., Mineola, NY: Dover, 2005); *Vision in Motion*.

16 László Moholy-Nagy, *Dynamic of the Metropolis*, in *Painting, Photography, Film*, trans. Seligman, 124–37.

17 *Dynamic of the Metropolis* is introduced on pp. 122–24 and occupies pp. 124–37 in *Painting, Photography, Film*. On the place of the book *Painting, Photography, Film* and the script *Dynamic of the Metropolis* in Moholy-Nagy's oeuvre, see Joyce Tsai, *László Moholy-Nagy: Painting after Photography* (Berkeley: University of California Press, 2018), 32–41; and Botar, *Sensing the Future*, 68–77.

18 Moholy-Nagy, *From Material to Architecture*, trans. Schamun and DeStone, 236, fig. 209.

19 Moholy-Nagy, "Abstract of an Artist" (1944) in *The New Vision* (2005 reprint), 216.

20 See Elizabeth Otto, "A 'Schooling of the Senses': Post-Dada Visual Experiments in the Bauhaus Photomontages of László Moholy-Nagy and Marianne Brandt," *New German Critique* 107, vol. 36, no. 2 (Summer 2009): 92. Moholy-Nagy publishes an image of *merzbild 425* (1922) by Schwitters in *From Material to Architecture*, trans. Schamun and DeStone, 67.

21 Moholy-Nagy, caption under image of *Relief S*, in *From Material to Architecture*, trans. Schamun and DeStone, 124.

22 Kállai, "Ladislaus Moholy-Nagy," trans. in Passuth, *Moholy-Nagy*, 418.

23 Tschichold cited by Frederic J. Schwartz, *Blind Spots: Critical Theory and the History of Art in Twentieth-Century Germany* (New Haven, CT: Yale University Press, 2005), 55.

24 On the *Reliefs*, see Moholy-Nagy, *From Material to Architecture*, trans. Schamun and DeStone, 124; and *The New Vision* (2005 reprint), 72. See also Botar, *Technical Detours*, 130–32.

25 Ludwig Hilberseimer, "Moholy-Nagy," review of exhibition at Galerie Der Sturm, February 1922, *Sozialistische Monatshefte* 28, no. 58 (1922): 242–43. Citation and trans. in Botar, *Technical Detours*, 132.

26 It should be noted that Moholy-Nagy was highly aware of—and influenced by—the work of the Russian constructivists, which was being regularly shown in Berlin in the years he was active there. To cite just one instance, see his discussion of "neoplasticism, suprematism and constructivism," especially mentioning Kazimir Malevich, in his book *From*

Material to Architecture, trans. Schamun and DeStone, 88, 89; see also Moholy-Nagy, *The New Vision with Abstract of an Artist* (New York: Wittenborn, Schultz, 1947), 38, 39. In the same book, he also publishes images of the work of Russian constructivists Alexander Rodchenko and Karlis Johansson, and includes an installation image from the Russian constructivist show that took place in 1921 in Moscow (see pp. 122, 132, 133). On Moholy-Nagy's work of this period, in addition to the Russian constructivists, Oliver Botar has noted the influence of other artists such as van Doesburg, Puni, and Archipenko. See Botar, *Technical Detours*, 132.

27 Ise Gropius, Diary, December 22, 1926, Bauhaus-Archiv Berlin.

28 Moholy-Nagy, *The New Vision* (2005 reprint), 84 (figs. 69, 70).

29 Sibyl Moholy-Nagy, interview by Studs Terkel, May 26, 1969, audiocassette, Chicago Historical Society, transcribed by Hattula Moholy-Nagy, transcript p. 13, Moholy-Nagy Foundation, Ann Arbor, MI.

30 The Tate gallery notes that Moholy-Nagy's first wife, Lucia Moholy, stated that "the 'K' in the title stands for the German equivalent of 'Construction' (*Konstruktion*), not for Canvas, which in those days was more likely to be represented by 'L' (*Leinwand*)" (Lucia Moholy to unknown recipient, July 6, 1962). The Tate catalog entry furthermore notes, "That the 'K' stands for 'Konstruktion' is supported by the fact that a picture by Moholy-Nagy, probably this one, was exhibited at the Juryfreie Kunstschau in Berlin in 1924 as 'Konstruktion KVII,' and that several paintings of a similar kind were reproduced in the *Jahrbuch der jungen Kunst* in 1924, pp. 183–4, 187 as 'Konstruktion V^{10}' 1923, 'Konstruktion IIc' 1922, etc." Tate website, accessed March 10, 2021, https://www.tate.org.uk/art/artworks/moholy-nagy-k-vii-t00432.

31 Sibyl Moholy-Nagy to unknown recipient, October 8, 1969. Tate website, accessed March 10, 2021, https://www.tate.org.uk/art/artworks/moholy-nagy-k-vii-t00432.

32 Kállai, "Ladislaus Moholy-Nagy," trans. in Passuth, *Moholy-Nagy*, 417.

33 Moholy-Nagy, "Abstract of an Artist" (1944) in *The New Vision* (2005 reprint), 219.

34 For an extended discussion on Moholy-Nagy's projection of light, including many of the works discussed here, see "Projection Spaces," in Botar, *Sensing the Future*, 101–28.

35 Moholy-Nagy, *From Material to Architecture*, trans. Schamun and DeStone, 173–74.

36 A similar construction is found in another photomontage titled *Joseph and Potiphar's Family* (ca. 1926), a gelatin silver print of which is at the Getty Museum (object number: 84.XM.997.22); in the Getty print, the right-angled transparent object is suggestive of panes of glass, on either side of which Moholy-Nagy has placed photomontaged figures. A further photomontage from the same period (ca. 1926–28) also used the construction, this time beaming downward, a gelatin silver print of which is at the Getty (object number 84.XM.997.35). For a description of the figures depicted in *City Lights*, see Irene-Charlotte Lusk, *Montagen ins Blaue: Laszlo Moholy-Nagy Fotomontagen und–collegen 1922–43* (Gießen: Anabas, 1980), 92. For a discussion of gender relations as depicted in the photomontages, see Otto, "A 'Schooling of the Senses,'" 118–20.

37 *Human Mechanics (Variety)*, 1925, was an illustration Moholy-Nagy published to accompany his 1925 essay, "Theater, Circus, Variety," in Oskar Schlemmer, László Moholy-Nagy, and Farkas Molnár, *The Theater of the Bauhaus*, ed. Walter Gropius and Arthur S. Wensinger, trans. Arthur S. Wensinger (1925; repr., Middletown, CT: Wesleyan University Press, 1961), 65.

38 László Moholy-Nagy, "Subject without Art," contribution to "Art without Subject, Subject without Art," *Studio* 112 (November 1936): 259.

39 László Moholy-Nagy to Jane Heap, September 12, 1926, editorial files of the *Little Review*, special collections of the Golda Meir Library, University of Wisconsin-Milwaukee, translated in Dennis Read, "Laszlo Moholy-Nagy's Letters to Jane Heap: Promises Made and Broken," unpublished paper, 10, Moholy-Nagy Foundation.

40 László Moholy-Nagy to Jane Heap, December 23, 1926, trans. Read, "Laszlo Moholy-Nagy's Letters to Jane Heap," unpublished paper, 16, Moholy-Nagy Foundation.

41 László Moholy-Nagy to Franz Roh, March 23, 1934, Franz Roh Papers, Getty Special Collections, Getty Research Center, Los Angeles. Cited by Tsai, *László Moholy-Nagy: Painting after Photography*, 133–34.

42 Moholy-Nagy, *Painting, Photography, Film*, 25n.

43 On Moholy-Nagy's contributions to the 1930 Paris exhibition, see the official exhibition catalog, *Section allemande: Exposition de la Société des artistes décorateurs* (Berlin: Verlag Hermann Reckendorf, 1930), n.p. See also Robin Schuldenfrei, *Luxury and Modernism: Architecture and the Object in Germany 1900-1933* (Princeton, NJ: Princeton University Press, 2018), 255–69. Moholy-Nagy's Paris exhibition design and its contents fed into his subsequent plans for the unrealized *Raum der Gegenwart* (Room of our time) developed for museum director Alexander Dorner's Hanover Provincial Museum. See Noam M. Elcott, "Rooms of Our Time: László Moholy-Nagy and the Stillbirth of Multi-media Museums," in *Screen/Space: The Projected Image in Contemporary Art*, ed. Tamara Trodd (Manchester: Manchester University Press, 2011), 25–52; and Jennifer King, "Back to the Present: Moholy-Nagy's Exhibition Designs," in *Moholy-Nagy: Future Present*, ed. Matthew S. Witkovsky, Carol S. Eliel, and Karole P. B. Vail (Chicago: Art Institute of Chicago, 2016), 139–50.

44 "Trolitauszug," March 3, 1930, Marcel Breuer Papers, Syracuse University Library, Syracuse, NY.

45 László Moholy-Nagy, "Produktion–Reproduktion," *De Stijl* 5, no. 7 (July 1922): 98–100, trans. in Passuth, *Moholy-Nagy*, 289. See also Moholy-Nagy, "Production Reproduction," in *Painting, Photography, Film*, trans. Seligman, 30–31.

46 For extended discussions on modern production and reproduction technologies as the conceptual and artistic basis of Moholy-Nagy's multivalent practice, see Robin Schuldenfrei, "Iteration of the Non-iterative: Revaluation and the Case of László Moholy-Nagy's Photograms," in *Iteration: Episodes in the Mediation of Art and Architecture*, ed. Robin Schuldenfrei (London: Routledge / Taylor & Francis, 2020), 71–104; Botar, *Sensing the Future*, 41–58; and Tsai, *László Moholy-Nagy: Painting after Photography*, 48–51. On the *Telephone Paintings*, see also Botar, *Sensing the Future*, 150–54; Brigid

Doherty, "László Moholy-Nagy: Constructions in Enamel, 1923," in *Bauhaus 1919–1933: Workshops for Modernity*, ed. Barry Bergdoll and Leah Dickerman (New York: Museum of Modern Art, 2009), 130–33; Stephanie D'Alessandro, "Through the Eye and the Hand: Constructing Space, Constructing Vision in the Work of Moholy-Nagy," in *Moholy-Nagy: Future Present*, 62–63; and Tsai, *László Moholy-Nagy: Painting after Photography*, 12–15, 30–32, 50–54.

47 Moholy-Nagy, *The New Vision with Abstract of an Artist* (1947 ed.), 79. Oliver Botar notes that the enamel works were produced for Moholy-Nagy by the enamel sign manufacturer Stark & Riese, based in Tannroda, a village south of Weimar. Botar, *Sensing the Future*, 153.

48 See Frederic J. Schwartz, *The Werkbund: Design Theory and Mass Culture before the First World War* (New Haven, CT: Yale University Press, 1996).

49 Moholy-Nagy to Jane Heap, December 23, 1926, trans. Read, "Laszlo Moholy-Nagy's Letters to Jane Heap," unpublished paper, 16, Moholy-Nagy Foundation.

50 Moholy-Nagy, *The New Vision with Abstract of an Artist* (1947 ed.), 40.

51 Moholy-Nagy's photograms have been the focus of sustained attention, see especially Moholy-Nagy, *Painting, Photography, Film*; Andreas Haus, *Moholy-Nagy: Photographs and Photograms*, trans. Frederic Samson (New York: Pantheon Books, 1980); Passuth, *Moholy-Nagy*, 35–36; Floris M. Neusüss, "Laszlo Moholy-Nagy: Fotogramme," in *Das Fotogramm in der Kunst des 20. Jahrhunderts: Die andere Seite der Bilder, Fotografie ohne Kamera*, ed. Floris M. Neusüss and Renate Heyne (Cologne: DuMont, 1990), 128–34; Renate Heyne, Floris M. Neusüss, and Herbert Molderings, eds., *Laszlo Moholy-Nagy: Fotogramme 1922–1943* (Munich: Schirmer-Mosel, 1995); Herbert Molderings, "Laszlo Moholy-Nagy und die Neuerfindung des Fotogramms," in *Kunst und Fotographie*, ed. Renate Heyne (Marburg: Jonas Verlag, 2003), 117–37; Renate Heyne and Floris M. Neusüss, with Hattula Moholy-Nagy, eds., *Moholy-Nagy: The Photograms: Catalogue Raisonné* (Ostfildern: Hatje Cantz, 2009); Michael W. Jennings, "László Moholy-Nagy Photograms," in *Bauhaus 1919–1933: Workshops for Modernity*, ed. Barry Bergdoll and Leah Dickerman (New York: Museum of Modern Art, 2009), 216–19; Witkovsky et al., *Moholy-Nagy: Future Present*, esp. 29, 188–91, 228; Éva Forgács, "'This Is the Century of Light': László Moholy-Nagy's Painting and Photography Debate in *i 10*, 1927," *Leonardo* 50, no. 3 (2017): 274–77; Sylvie Pénichon, Krista Lough, and Paul Messier, "An Objective Revaluation of Photograms by László Moholy-Nagy," *Leonardo* 50, no. 3 (2017): 292–96.

52 Moholy-Nagy, "Light Display, Black and White and Gray" (1925–30), in *Vision in Motion*, 289. This phrase was the concluding line of a film synopsis he wrote that was intended to demonstrate "the refined values of the black-white-gray gradations of the photogram (the cameraless photography) in continuous motion" (288). Only one portion of the film was realized, *Light Display: Black-White-Gray*.

53 Written 1932, published as László Moholy-Nagy, "A New Instrument of Vision," *Telehor* 1–2 (February 1936): 35.

54 Ibid.

55 László Moholy-Nagy, "Space-Time and the Photographer," *American Annual of Photography* (1942), reprinted in Kostelanetz, *Moholy-Nagy*, 61.

56 László Moholy-Nagy to D. Rhodes Johnson, October 13, 1941, Moholy-Nagy Foundation.

57 Moholy-Nagy, *Von Material zu Architektur* (1929 ed.), 88–89; see also trans. in Moholy-Nagy, *The New Vision with Abstract of an Artist* (1947 ed.), 38–39.

58 An in-depth discussion of the *Light Prop* is beyond the scope of this chapter. For its artistic, cultural, and theoretical significance, see especially Alex Potts, "*The Light Prop for an Electric Stage*," in *Bauhaus 1919–1933: Workshops for Modernity*, ed. Barry Bergdoll and Leah Dickerman (New York: Museum of Modern Art, 2009), 274–77; Hannah Weitemeier, *Licht-Visionen: Ein Experiment von Moholy-Nagy* (Berlin: Bauhaus Archive, 1972); Botar, *Sensing the Future*, 112–27; Tsai, *The Paintings of Moholy-Nagy*, 34–45; Tsai, *László Moholy-Nagy: Painting after Photography*, 85–112. On the ramifications of Moholy-Nagy's work across media and the importance of its realization in several platforms and formats, including a discussion of the *Light Prop*, see also Noam M. Elcott, "Laszlo Moholy-Nagy: Solomon R. Guggenheim Museum," *Art Forum* 55, no. 2 (October 2016): 260–61, 294; and Elcott, "Rooms of Our Time," 25–52.

59 Moholy-Nagy, *Vision in Motion*, 288.

60 Sibyl Moholy-Nagy, interview by Studs Terkel, transcript p. 12. The painting owned by Mrs. Paepcke that she references in the interview, which took place to mark the occasion of a large Moholy-Nagy retrospective exhibition held at the Guggenheim in New York and the Museum of Contemporary Art in Chicago, is *Leu #1*, 1945, oil on canvas, reproduced in *László Moholy-Nagy: An Exhibition* (Chicago: Museum of Contemporary Art, 1969), p. 47, cat. no. 68. Note that the exhibition catalog date is incorrect; the verso of the painting, which is signed by Moholy-Nagy, includes its title and a date of 1945. Correspondence, including image of verso, between author and Hattula Moholy-Nagy, March 10, 2021.

61 Moholy-Nagy to D. Rhodes Johnson, October 13, 1941.

62 For more on the stagings of the *Light Prop* and the "Room of Our Time" (alternatively known as the "Room of the Present") see Elcott, "Rooms of Our Time," 25–52; King, "Back to the Present."

63 Emphasis in original. Jack W. Burnham, "On Moholy's Light-Display Machine," *Beyond Modern Sculpture* (New York: George Braziller, 1968), 290–92, reprinted in Kostelanetz, *Moholy-Nagy*, 160.

64 Valeria Carullo, *Moholy-Nagy in Britain, 1935–1937* (London: Lund Humphries, 2019), 41.

65 Martin Heidegger, "Building, Dwelling, Thinking," in *Poetry, Language, Thought*, trans. Albert Hofstadter (New York: Harper Colophon Books, 1971), 151.

66 Moholy-Nagy, *The New Vision* (2005 reprint), 86.

67 Moholy-Nagy to D. Rhodes Johnson, October 13, 1941.

68 Moholy-Nagy to Jane Heap, December 23, 1926, trans. Read, "Laszlo Moholy-Nagy's Letters to Jane Heap," unpublished paper, 16, Moholy-Nagy Foundation.

69 Moholy-Nagy, *Painting, Photography, Film*, trans. Seligman, 9.

70 Emphasis added. Written in June 1934, published as László Moholy-Nagy, "Letter to Fra. Kalivoda," *Telehor* 1–2 (February 1936): 30.

71 Sibyl Moholy-Nagy, *Moholy-Nagy: Experiment in Totality* (New York: Harper & Brothers, 1950), 59. Hattula Moholy-Nagy perceptively points out that Moholy-Nagy was likely inspired by, and then built on, the idea of a day in the life of the city from Walter Ruttmann's 1927 *Berlin: Die Sinfonie der Großstadt* (*Berlin: Symphony of a Metropolis*). Correspondence with author, August 9, 2022.

72 Sibyl Moholy-Nagy, *Moholy-Nagy: Experiment in Totality*, 69.

73 Moholy-Nagy attempted to realize *Reflected Image* but could not, because a permit would have been required from the Bureau of Public Safety in order to shoot the street scenes from a truck. Sibyl Moholy-Nagy reports that the Nazi gangs already roaming the streets had "terrorized the authorities to a point where they dreaded any demonstration that might provoke curiosity" and that the "project was rejected as dangerous to public security." Sibyl Moholy-Nagy, *Moholy-Nagy: Experiment in Totality*, 74. Moholy-Nagy would realize three films grounded in the urban experience: *Impressionen vom alten Marseiller Hafen (Vieux Port)* (Impressions of the old harbor of Marseille, 1929–30), *Berliner Stilleben* (Berlin still life, 1931–32), and *Grossstadt-Zigeuner* (Metropolitan gypsies, 1932–33).

74 See, for example: Moholy-Nagy, "Letter to Fra. Kalivoda," 30–32; "Light Architecture," *Industrial Arts* 1, no. 1 (Spring 1936), reprinted in Kostelanetz, *Moholy-Nagy*, 155–56; "From Pigment to Light," *Telehor* 1–2 (February 1936): 32–34.

75 Moholy-Nagy, "Letter to Fra. Kalivoda," 30.

76 Ibid.

77 Ibid.

78 Moholy-Nagy, *Von Material zu Architektur* (1929 ed.), 89; see also trans. in Moholy-Nagy, *The New Vision with Abstract of an Artist* (1947 ed.), 39.

79 Moholy-Nagy, "Letter to Fra. Kalivoda," 30.

80 Moholy-Nagy, *Painting, Photography, Film*, trans. Seligman, 26.

81 Moholy-Nagy, "Letter to Fra. Kalivoda," 30. For a discussion of the "Letter to Fra. Kalivoda," see Oliver A. I. Botar, "Editorial Note: Melancholy for the Future," in the *Commentary and Translations* volume accompanying the facsimile reprint László Moholy-Nagy, *Telehor*, ed. Oliver A. I. Botar and Klemens Gruber (Zurich: Lars Müller Publishers, 2013), especially pp. 15–19. Moholy-Nagy rearticulated these ideas in a very similar essay published in 1936, where he writes:

> Since the invention of photography the direction of development for painting has been "from pigment to light." That is to say that just as one paints with brush and pigment, in recent times one could have "painted" directly with light, transforming two-dimensional painted surfaces into *light architecture*.
>
> I dreamed of a light-apparatus, which might be controlled either by hand or by an automatic mechanism by means of which it would be possible to produce visions of light, in the air, in large rooms, on screens of unusual nature, on fog, vapor and clouds. I made numberless projects, but found no architect who was prepared to commission a light-fresco, a light architecture, consisting of straight or arched walls, covered with a material such as galalith, trolite, chromium or nickel, which by turning a switch, could be flooded with radiant light, fluctuating light-symphonies, while the surfaces slowly changed and dissolved into an infinite number of controlled details. I wanted a bare room with twelve projection devices, so that the white void would come to life and action under crossing sheaves of colored light. (Moholy-Nagy, "Light Architecture," *Industrial Arts* 1, no. 1 [Spring 1936], reprinted in Kostelanetz, *Moholy-Nagy*, 155–56).

82 Written 1923–26, published as Moholy-Nagy, "From Pigment to Light," *Telehor* 1–2 (February 1936): 34.

83 Written 1928–30, published as Moholy-Nagy, "Problems of the Modern Film," *Telehor* 1–2 (February 1936): 40. He rounds off these ideas with the statement "Finally the abstract morphosis of light and objective film reportage will gain by the emergence of plastic projection which is promised by the development of stereoscopic photography." In combining abstract light with objective film reportage, presumably his interest lies in achieving for modern motion pictures – or rather, for the newsreels that preceded feature films – the same three-dimensional effects of depth and realism that stereoscopic cards achieved for the illusion of three dimensions in photographic scenes. Moholy-Nagy published an earlier version of this essay as "The Problems of the Modern Film" (written 1928–30), in *Cahiers d'Art* 8, nos. 6–7 (1932), trans. in Kostelanetz, *Moholy-Nagy*, 131–38.

84 M. Seklemian, "A Study of the Principles of Camouflage Conducted at the School of Design Chicago," September 1942–January 1943, Institute of Design Records, Illinois Institute of Technology, Chicago.

85 "Kelly and Army Plan Hiding of City from Foe," *Chicago Daily News*, May 8, 1942.

86 Capitalization in the original. Moholy-Nagy, "Theater, Circus, Variety," in *The Theater of the Bauhaus*, 67.

87 On Moholy-Nagy's set design for *Der Kaufmann von Berlin* (*The Merchant of Berlin*), see also Erwin Piscator, *Das politische Theater* (Berlin: Schultz, 1929); Sibyl Moholy-Nagy, *Moholy-Nagy: Experiment in Totality*, 50–55; Lusk, *Montagen ins Blaue*, 160–61; Otto, "A 'Schooling of the Senses,'" 125–26; Ingrid Pfeiffer and Max Hollein, *Moholy-Nagy: Retrospektive* (Munich: Prestel, 2009), 108–9; Botar, *Sensing the Future*, 104, 112; Tsai, *László Moholy-Nagy: Painting after Photography*, 103; and Elcott, "Rooms of Our Time," 37–38. For a discussion of Moholy-Nagy's early interest in the theater as well as his 1920 set designs for *Die Menschen* by Walter Hasenclever (not staged) and Upton Sinclair's *Prince Hagen* (staged in December 1920 by Erwin Piscator in Berlin), see Botar, *Technical Detours*, 100–107.

88 Moholy-Nagy, "Problems of the Modern Film," 40.

89 For more on *Tales of Hoffmann*, see Moholy-Nagy, *From Material to Architecture*, trans. Schamun and DeStone, 219; Sibyl Moholy-Nagy, *Moholy-Nagy: Experiment in Totality*, 49; Elcott, "Rooms of Our Time," 35–37; Tsai, *László Moholy-Nagy: Painting after Photography*, 101.

90 Moholy-Nagy, *The New Vision* (2005 reprint), 197. See also Hans Curjel, "Moholy-Nagy and the Theater," *Du* (November 1964): 11–15, trans. Sibyl Moholy-Nagy, reprinted in Kostelanetz, *Moholy-Nagy*, 95.

91 *Things to Come* was written by H. G. Wells, directed by William Cameron Menzies, and produced by Alexander Korda. The sets in the commercial release were predominantly

designed by Vincent Korda; although glimpses remain, much of Moholy-Nagy's work was cut from the final version.

92 Sibyl Moholy-Nagy, *Moholy-Nagy: Experiment in Totality*, 129.

93 Emphasis in the original. Moholy-Nagy, "Man and His House," *Korunk* 4 (1929): 298–99, trans. in Passuth, *Moholy-Nagy*, 309.

94 Moholy-Nagy, *The New Vision* (2005 reprint), 178.

95 Written 1932, published as Moholy-Nagy, "A New Instrument of Vision," *Telehor* 1–2 (February 1936): 36.

96 For more on Moholy-Nagy's teaching at the Bauhaus, especially his *Vorkurs*, or Foundation Course, and its output, see Robin Schuldenfrei, "Preliminary Objects for Modern Subjects: László Moholy-Nagy's Bauhaus Theory and Lucia Moholy's Photographic Representation," in *Object Lessons: The Bauhaus and Harvard*, ed. Laura Muir (New Haven, CT: Yale University Press, 2021), 96–114. The importance of materiality, material qualities, and surface for Moholy-Nagy was made clear by the Chicago Bauhaus curriculum. At the New Bauhaus, for autumn 1937, the curriculum brochure set out the following objectives and materials: "Emphasis on materials, use of wood, plywood, paper, plastics, rubber, cork, metal, glass, plasticine, in terms of their: tactile values; structure; texture; surface effect and the use of their values; in plane; in volume; and in space . . . subjective and objective qualities, the scientific testing of materials. Under supplementary section, included Light as an instrument of visual notes, using light as a new medium of expression, and also visits to factories, newly constructed buildings, museums, exhibitions, theatres." See Bauhaus curriculum, New Bauhaus, Chicago, Fall 1937, reprinted in Kostelanetz, *Moholy-Nagy*, 173.

97 As scholars have shown, however, the distinctions between the optic and the haptic were not always discrete. For a discussion of Moholy-Nagy's complex notion of tactility and associated exercises, see Zeynep Çelik Alexander, "Designing: Discipline and Introspection at the Bauhaus," in *Kinaesthetic Knowing: Aesthetics, Epistemology, Modern Design* (Chicago: University of Chicago Press, 2017), 167–201; Rainer K. Wick, *Teaching at the Bauhaus* (Ostfildern-Ruit: Hatje Cantz, 2000), 149–54; T'ai Smith, "The Haptics of Optics: Weaving and Photography," in *Bauhaus Weaving Theory: From Feminine Craft to Mode of Design* (Minneapolis: University of Minnesota Press, 2014), 79–110; Botar, *Sensing the Future*, 21–27; D'Alessandro, "Through the Eye and the Hand," 66–67; Jeffrey Saletnik, "Pedagogy, Modernism, and Medium Specificity: The Bauhaus and John Cage" (PhD diss., University of Chicago, 2009). As Saletnik writes, "The purpose of these varied exercises was to increase students' awareness of the intrinsic properties of the materials of design through a process of experimentation and sensory refinement. One must first explore the physical and sensory properties of matter prior to contemplating their possible application to a design problem" (38–39).

98 See Wick, *Teaching at the Bauhaus*, 156, where he cites Moholy-Nagy. See also Moholy-Nagy, *From Material to Architecture*, trans. Schamun and DeStone, esp. 134–47; Moholy-Nagy, *New Vision*, esp. 113–21; and Herbert Bayer, Walter Gropius, and Ise Gropius, eds., *Bauhaus: 1919–1928* (New York: Museum of Modern Art, [1938] 1975), 91.

99 Rainer Wick aptly terms the works in the *Vorkurs* "studies of spatial experience"; see Wick, *Teaching at the Bauhaus*, 154. Wick cites (p. 156) the spatial constructions of the Russian constructivists, as well as Moholy-Nagy's own sculpture, as important predecessors to the student works.

100 Walter Gropius, "László Moholy-Nagy," *Korunk* (1937): 244–46, reproduced in Passuth, *Moholy-Nagy*, 431.

101 Moholy-Nagy, "Modern Art and Architecture," speech, informal general meeting of the RIBA, December 9, 1936, published in the *Journal of the Royal Institute of British Architects* 44, no. 5 (January 1937), reproduced in Passuth, *Moholy-Nagy*, 340.

102 Moholy-Nagy, *The New Vision with Abstract of an Artist* (1947 ed.), 76.

Chapter 2: Minimal Dwelling

1 Ise and Walter Gropius arrived in London on October 18, 1934; PP/15/4/2/3, Pritchard Papers, Archives and Special Collections, University of East Anglia, Norwich, England (hereafter only the "PP/" reference code will be cited). On Bauhaus members in the United Kingdom, Isokon, its founder Jack Pritchard, and Lawn Road Flats, see Jack Pritchard, *View from a Long Chair: The Memoirs of Jack Pritchard* (London: Routledge & Kegan Paul, 1984); Charlotte Benton, ed., *A Different World: Emigre Architects in Britain 1928-1958* (London: RIBA Heinz Gallery, 1995); Alastair Grieve, *Isokon* (London: Isokon Plus, 2004); Elizabeth Darling, "Modern Dwellings for Modern Needs," in *Re-forming Britain: Narratives of Modernity before Reconstruction* (London: Routledge, 2007), 81–107; David Burke, *The Lawn Road Flats: Spies, Writers and Artists* (Woodbridge, UK: Boydell Press, 2014); Leyla Daybelge and Magnus Englund, *Isokon and the Bauhaus in Britain* (London: Batsford, 2019); Alan Powers, *Bauhaus Goes West: Modern Art and Design in Britain and America* (London: Thames & Hudson, 2019); and Valeria Carullo, *Moholy-Nagy in Britain, 1935–1937* (London: Lund Humphries, 2019). On émigrés to the United Kingdom more generally, see Lucy Wasensteiner, ed., *Sites of Interchange: Modernism, Politics and Culture between Britain and Germany, 1919-1955* (Bern, Switzerland: Peter Lang, 2022); Cheryl Buckley and Tobias Hochscherf, "Introduction: From German 'Invasion' to Transnationalism; Continental European Émigrés and Visual Culture in Britain, 1933–56," *Visual Culture in Britain* 13, no. 2 (2012): 157–68; Marian Malet and Anthony Grenville, eds., *Changing Countries: The Experience and Achievement of German-Speaking Exiles from Hitler in Britain from 1933 to Today* (London: Libris, 2002); Daniel Snowman, *The Hitler Émigrés: The Cultural Impact on Britain of Refugees from Nazism* (London: Chatto & Windus, 2002); and Anthony Grenville, ed., *Refugees from the Third Reich in Britain*, vol. 4, *Exilforschung: Ein internationales Jahrbuch* (Amsterdam: Rodopi, 2002).

2 Gropius to Pritchard, April 7, 1935, Bauhaus-Archiv, Berlin (hereafter BHA).

3 Pritchard to Gropius, October 22, 1935, BHA.

4 See, for example, Gropius's dealings with – and overtures to – the Nazi authorities in pursuit of work: Winfried Nerdinger, "Bauhaus Architecture in the Third Reich," in

Bauhaus Culture: From Weimar to the Cold War, ed. Kathleen James-Chakraborty (Minneapolis: University of Minnesota Press, 2006), 139–52; Winfried Nerdinger, ed., in collaboration with the Bauhaus-Archiv, Berlin, *Bauhaus-Moderne im Nationalsozialismus: Zwischen Anbiederung und Verfolgung* (Munich: Prestel, 1993); and Barbara Miller Lane, *Architecture and Politics in Germany 1918-1945* (Cambridge, MA: Harvard University Press, 1968).

5 Moholy-Nagy to Herbert Read, January 24, 1934, reprinted in Richard Kostelanetz, *Moholy-Nagy* (New York: Praeger, 1970), 19.

6 Beyond his work for Isokon, Moholy-Nagy would find many commissions during his years in England – in film (*Lobsters*) and set design (*Things to Come*), photography for journals and photobooks (such as the *Architectural Review* and *The Street Markets of London*), book and other graphic design (London Underground), advertising (Imperial Airways), and store displays (Simpson's), as well as gallery exhibitions of his artworks. See Terence Senter, "Moholy-Nagy: The Transitional Years," in *Albers and Moholy-Nagy: From the Bauhaus to the New World* (London: Tate Publishing, 2006), 85–91; Carullo, *Moholy-Nagy in Britain*; and Leah Hsiao, "The Dislocation of Amateurism: Moholy-Nagy in England, 1935–1937," in *Sites of Interchange: Modernism, Politics and Culture between Britain and Germany, 1919–1955*, ed. Lucy Wasensteiner (Bern, Switzerland: Peter Lang, 2022), 91–111.

7 My references to the *Gesamtkunstwerk* are exclusively in the sense of the architectural notion of the term. On luxury and modernism, see Robin Schuldenfrei, *Luxury and Modernism: Architecture and the Object in Germany 1900-1933* (Princeton, NJ: Princeton University Press, 2018).

8 Walter Gropius to Morton Shand, June 7, 1934, PP/24/2/2.

9 Prichard to Gropius, June 20, 1934, BHA.

10 Gropius to Prichard, June 23, 1934, BHA.

11 Moholy-Nagy resided at Lawn Road Flats for only a few months. He moved into a house at 7 Farm Walk with his family, in an nearby area, Chalk Farm, in September 1935. Daybelge and Englund, *Isokon and the Bauhaus in Britain*, 230n11.

12 Christopher Wilk, *Marcel Breuer: Furniture and Interiors* (New York: Museum of Modern Art, 1981), 127.

13 J. M. Richards, "Wells Coates 1893–1958," *Architectural Review* 124, no. 743 (December 1, 1958): 360.

14 See Schuldenfrei, *Luxury and Modernism*, chap. 3, "Capital: The Haus am Horn and the Early Bauhaus," 116–37.

15 Ludwig Hilberseimer, *Groszstadtarchitektur* (Stuttgart: Julius Hoffmann, 1927), 23. Translated as "the residential minimum," in Ludwig Hilberseimer, *Metropolisarchitecture and Selected Essays*, ed. and trans. Richard Anderson (New York: GSAPP Books, 2012), 142.

16 Hilberseimer, *Groszstadtarchitektur*, 100; trans. Anderson, 270.

17 Ibid., 19; trans. Anderson, 128.

18 In the original "sorgfältig durchgebildet" and "wird stets besondere Sorgfalt gewidmet." Hilberseimer, *Groszstadtarchitektur*, 23, 38; trans. Anderson, 142, 167.

19 Hannes Meyer, "Über die kapitalistische Wohnungsarchitektur der Nachkriegszeit (1919–1934)" [The architecture of capitalist housing in the postwar period (1919–1934)], 1935, manuscript, in Hannes Meyer, *Bauen und Gesellschaft: Schriften, Briefe, Projekte*, ed. Lena Meyer-Bergner (Dresden: Verlag der Kunst, 1980), 180.

20 Hannes Meyer, "On Marxist Architecture," 1931, manuscript, reprinted and translated in Claude Schnaidt, ed., *Hannes Meyer: Buildings, Projects and Writings* (Stuttgart: Verlag Gerd Hatje, 1965), 31. Meyer sees this transformation, or building up of elements to a total architecture as one that provides possibilities for a distinctly *socialist* way of life.

21 Meyer, "On Marxist Architecture," 31.

22 See K. Michael Hays, "Hannes Meyer's 'Co-op Interior,'" *GSD News* (Winter–Spring 1993): 20–21; and Hays, *Modernism and the Posthumanist Subject: The Architecture of Hannes Meyer and Ludwig Hilberseimer* (Cambridge, MA: MIT Press, 1992), especially "Co-Op Vitrine and the Representation of Mass Production" (24–53) and "Contra the Bourgeois Interior: Co-Op Zimmer" (54–81).

23 Hannes Meyer, "Die neue Welt," *Das Werk* 13, no. 7 (July 1926): 223; reprinted and translated as "The New World" (1926) in *Architecture and Design: 1890-1939*, ed. Tim and Charlotte Benton with Dennis Sharp (New York: Whitney Library of Design, 1975), 108.

24 Ibid., 109.

25 Ibid.

26 Hannes Meyer, "Bauhaus und Gesellschaft," *Bauhaus* 3, no. 1 (1929): 2; reprinted and translated as "Bauhaus and Society," in Schnaidt, ed. *Hannes Meyer*, 101. Translation amended.

27 Meyer, "On Marxist Architecture," 31.

28 Meyer, "Die neue Welt," 223; trans. Benton, 108.

29 Karel Teige, *The Minimum Dwelling* (1932), trans. Eric Dluhosch (Cambridge, MA: MIT Press, 2002), 1.

30 Ibid., 4.

31 The congress's proceedings, illustrated with many floor plans, were published as *Die Wohnung für das Existenzminimum*, ed. Internationale Kongresse für Neues Bauen und Städtisches Hochbauamt in Frankfurt am Main (Frankfurt am Main: Englert & Schlosser, 1930).

32 Le Corbusier and Pierre Jeanneret, "Analysis of the Fundamental Elements of the 'Minimum House' Problem" (p. 2) and Ernst May, "The Dwelling for the Living Income Earner" (p. 7) in *Die Wohnung für das Existenzminimum*, "English Summaries" section.

33 Walter Gropius, "Sociological Foundations of the Minimum Dwelling," in *Die Wohnung für das Existenzminimum*, "English Summaries" section, p. 14. See also Tanya Poppelreuter, "Social Individualism: Walter Gropius and His Appropriation of Franz Müller-Lyer's Idea of a New Man," *Journal of Design History* 24, no. 1 (2011): 37–58.

34 Gropius, "Sociological Foundations of the Minimum Dwelling," 15.

35 Franz Möller and Carl Fieger in Gropius's office assisted with the plans and drawings. See Winfried Nerdinger, *Der Architekt Walter Gropius: Zeichnungen, Pläne und Fotos aus dem Busch-Reisinger-Museum der Harvard University Art Museums, Cambridge/Mass. und dem Bauhaus-Archiv Berlin* (Berlin: Gebr. Mann Verlag, 1985), 176–77.

36 Walter Gropius, "Minimalwohnung und Hochhaus," typescript, August 1934, p. 2, BHA. "Standard" was a term frequently used by architects in this period to represent their search for norms. The Aaltos, likewise, utilized the term

37 Pritchard, *View from a Long Chair*, 79–80.
38 Wells Coates to Jack Pritchard, July 13, 1930, quoted by Fiona MacCarthy, "Introduction," in Pritchard, *View from a Long Chair*, 12.
39 Wells Coates, interview with Geoffrey Boumphrey, "Modern Dwellings for Modern Needs," *Listener* 9, no. 219 (May 24, 1933): 819.
40 Dr. Rosemary Pritchard, Opening Speech, July 9, 1934, PP/16/2/23/3, cited in Daybelge and Englund, *Isokon and the Bauhaus in Britain*, 74.
41 Pritchard, *View from a Long Chair*, 80.
42 The exhibition ran from June 20 to July 12 at Dorland Hall, Lower Regent Street, London. For correspondence and information about Isokon's participation, including the furnishings, fittings, and external suppliers of the model flat, see PP/15/1/17.
43 "Historic Pioneers: Architects and Clients," *Architects' Journal* (March 11, 1970): 595.
44 Pritchard, *View from a Long Chair*, 85. The building consisted of twenty-two flats (25 square meters) known as "minimum flats," three flats (32 square meters) known as "studio flats," and four (33 square meters) flats. See Florentina-Aventura Freise, *Asketischer Komfort: Das Londoner Servicehaus Isokon* (Oberhausen: Athena, 2009), 45.
45 Pritchard, *View from a Long Chair*, 85.
46 Charlotte Benton, "The 'Minimum' Flat," in *Thirties: British Art and Design before the War* (London: Arts Council of Great Britain, 1979), 267; Daybelge and Englund, *Isokon and the Bauhaus in Britain*, 69.
47 Wells Coates, "Furniture Today – Furniture Tomorrow," *Architectural Review* 72, no. 428 (July 1932): 34.
48 Gropius to Pritchard, October 29, 1935, BHA.
49 Pritchard to Gropius, April 12, 1935, BHA.
50 Gropius to Pritchard, April 14, 1935, BHA.
51 For Breuer's detailed plan of the restaurant and club room (dated July 8, 1937), see PP/35/2/1.
52 "Isobar Club, Lawn Road, Hampstead: Marcel Breuer and F.R.S. Yorke, Architects," *Architectural Review*, 83, no. 499, Decoration supplement (June 1, 1938): 313.
53 See PP/17/1/2/9; PP/17/1/2/16; PP/17/2/3/11; PP/17/1/1/2.
54 MacCarthy, "Introduction," 22.
55 Ibid.
56 Jack Pritchard, memorandum, July 3, 1933, reprinted in Alastair Grieve, "Isokon," in *Modern Britain 1929–1939*, ed. James Peto and Donna Loveday (London: Design Museum, 1999), 80.
57 Pritchard to Gropius, March 12, 1936, PP/24/4/12.
58 Pritchard to Gropius, March 16, 1936, PP/24/4/14. See also correspondence between Gropius and Pritchard regarding the site plan for a restaurant building and small cottages, Gropius to Pritchard, April 2, 1936, PP/15/1/16/2/11.
59 See correspondence between Isokon and various landowners and stake-holders, April–July1935, PP/15/1/16/2/1–8.
60 As Gropius would write to Fry, September 18, 1934: "Would you do me the favor to write me what I have to do at the British authorities to get allowance to work over there?" To which Fry kindly responded, on September 26, "You will like to know that I am taking steps to get the necessary permit which as soon as it is in order we will send over to you." See PP/32/1/11; PP/32/1/12.i.
61 E. Maxwell Fry to Gropius, June 15, 1934, PP/32/1/1. Shand would give a similar report to Gropius in a letter dated the following day, "Unofficially, the situation seems best summarized as follows. As soon as all the Lawn Road flats are let (at present just under half are gone) the capital used there will be released to start the next block of flats (i.e. yours)." Shand to Gropius, June 16, 1934, PP/24/2/5.
62 PP/15/4/3.
63 E. Maxwell Fry to Gropius, July 3, 1934, Manchester, PP/32/1/5.
64 "Report on Manchester Possibilities," November 1, 1934, PP/15/4/1/8.
65 Ibid., p. 5.
66 Prichard to Prof. and Mrs. Florence [landowners], December 9, 1935, PP/15/5/1/3.
67 For a site plan, see "Isokon Nr. 4 Lageplan," in folder "Wohnanlage Birmingham," 1935, BHA.
68 Gropius to Pritchard, December 4, 1935, PP/15/5/2/1.
69 Pritchard to Gropius, July 31, 1935, BHA.
70 Calculations on the total expenditure and income of the Birmingham scheme, March 2, 1936, 2/3/36PP/15/5/3/1.
71 Pritchard to Gropius, February 5, 1936, PP/15/5/2/4.
72 Ibid.
73 Rees-Reynolds & Hunt to Pritchard, March 31, 1936, PP/15/5/4/5.
74 "Cry Stop to Havoc or Preservation by Concentrated Development," *Architectural Review* 77, no. 462 (May 1, 1935): 189.
75 Henry-Russell Hitchcock Jr., "Modern Architecture in England" in *Modern Architecture in England* (New York: Museum of Modern Art, 1937), 33. See also Anthony Jackson, "The Politics of Architecture: English Architecture 1929–1951," *Journal of the Society of Architectural Historians* 24, no. 1 (March 1965): 97–107.
76 Keeper of the Privy Purse to Pritchard, April 25, 1935, PP/15/3/1/21.
77 Two blocks are featured in Walter Gropius and E. Maxwell Fry, "Where Life Is Living," prospectus for St. Leonard's Hill Windsor, Isokon Control Company, ca. 1934–35, n.p. (p. 2), BHA. However, three apartment blocks and the figure of 110 units are cited in "Cry Stop to Havoc," 191–92.
78 "Cry Stop to Havoc," 191.
79 Gropius and Fry, "Where Life Is Living," n.p. (p. 5).
80 Ibid.
81 Isokon Control Company, Code, St. Leonard's Hill Windsor, 1935, n.p., BHA.
82 Isokon Limited, Prospectus, St. Leonard's Hill Windsor, 1935, n.p., BHA.
83 Ibid.
84 Pritchard to Harrods (attn. C. E. Wiles Esq.), May 21, 1935, PP/15/3/1/35.

85 Ibid.
86 Flyer, Hampton's, 20 St James's Square, London, June 28–July 31, 1935, PP/15/3/1/66.
87 Pritchard to Gropius, July 31, 1935, BHA.
88 See also his project for the "Packaged House," with Konrad Wachsmann, of 1942–52. See Nerdinger, *Der Architekt Walter Gropius*, 204.
89 On the Benn Levy House, see "Sixty-Six, Church Street: Benn Levy at Home in Chelsea," *Bystander* (July 28, 1937): 145; on the Wood House, see "A Timber House in Kent," *Architectural Review* 83, no. 495 (February 1, 1938): 61–63. See also Alan Powers, "A Popular Modernism? Timber Architecture in Britain 1936–1939," *Architectural Theory Review* 25, nos. 1–2 (2021): 245–66.
90 "A Timber House in Kent," 61–63. For a photograph of Donaldson family members in front of their house, see Haus J.G.S. Donaldson, Shipbourne, Kent, 1936–37, BHA or Nerdinger, *Der Architekt Walter Gropius*, 266, fig. 98.
91 In a planning meeting held in 1936, it was agreed that Gropius would design the exhibition and that Kendal Milne's in-house "display department" would construct it, with Venesta supplying the plywood. Report on Meeting held at Manchester, October 29, 1936, PP/18/5/8/1.
92 Brochure, *The Flat of '37: An Explanation by the Designer* (Manchester: Kendal Milne & Co., 1937): n.p.
93 Ibid.
94 "Manchester Sees German Idea," *Manchester Evening News*, February 8, 1937.
95 Brochure, *The Flat of '37*.
96 Ibid.
97 John Gloag, Speech at opening of Gropius's Flat of '37, February 8, 1937, p. 2, PP/24/4/30.
98 Ibid., p. 1.
99 "The Minimum: The Interior for Living," *Architectural Review* 82, no. 493 (December 1, 1937): 245–60.
100 Ibid., 246.
101 Walter Gropius, "The Formal and Technical Problems of Modern Architecture and Planning," *Royal Institute of British Architects Journal* 41 (May 19, 1934): 691.
102 Ibid.
103 Ibid.
104 Christopher Wilk, *Plywood: A Material Story* (London: Thames & Hudson, 2017), 151; Daybelge and Englund, *Isokon and the Bauhaus in Britain*, 101.
105 For a comprehensive history of the work of the Aaltos, see Stritzler-Levine, *Artek and the Aaltos*, especially therein Harry Charrington, "Retailing Aalto in London before Artek," 101–41.
106 See "Standard Wooden, Furniture at the Finnish Exhibition: Alvar Aalto, Designer," *Architectural Review* 74, no. 445 (1933): 220–21; Kevin Davies, "Finmar and the Furniture of the Future: The Sale of Alvar Aalto's Plywood Furniture in the UK, 1934–1939," *Journal of Design History* 11, no. 2 (1998): 145–56; Charrington, "Retailing Aalto in London before Artek," 103; Wilk, *Plywood*, 149–51; Daybelge and Englund, *Isokon and the Bauhaus in Britain*, 96. For another typical period article popularizing the Aaltos' furniture in the United Kingdom, see "Bent Construction Furniture," *Architectural Review* 74, no. 441 (August 1933): 69–70.
107 Stritzler-Levine, "Artek and the Aaltos," 45; Carullo, *Moholy-Nagy in Britain*, 14.
108 Charrington, "Retailing Aalto in London before Artek," 127.
109 Stritzler-Levine, "Artek and the Aaltos," 45.
110 Charrington, "Retailing Aalto in London before Artek," 125.
111 Hitchcock, *Modern Architecture in England*, 36. The exhibition, consisting of enlarged photographs of buildings and Moholy-Nagy's twenty-five-minute film *New Architecture for the London Zoo*, was held at the Museum of Modern Art, February 10–March 7, 1937.
112 Daybelge and Englund, *Isokon and the Bauhaus in Britain*, 100.
113 Wilk, *Plywood*, 152.
114 Hitchcock, *Modern Architecture in England*, 36n2.
115 Charrington, "Retailing Aalto in London before Artek," 115.
116 Ibid., 125.
117 "My negotiations for starting a Furniture Company are progressing, and I would like to ask you to act as a Consultant to the company for a year; to assist in selecting a designer and to help guide him along the right lines. I should also very much like you to do some designing, if necessary. May I suggest that as a basis the fee should be somewhat the equivalent of the rent of your flat?" Pritchard to Gropius, October 25, 1935, BHA. For the terms of Gropius's agreement with Pritchard to design for Isokon furniture, dated November 25, 1935, see PP/18/7/2.
118 Nerdinger, *Der Architekt Walter Gropius*, 306.
119 See Pritchard to Gropius, December 4, 1936, BHA. The waste can was also sold through the retailer Gordon Russell Ltd. for £3.10, a hefty price for the period; for details and a photograph, see "Waste-Paper Basket Designed by Walter Gropius," *Architectural Review* 80, no. 476 (July 1, 1936): 48.
120 Pritchard to Gropius, December 1, 1936, BHA.
121 See correspondence regarding development of Isokon furniture, PP/18/7/2. For the proposed manufacture of plywood furniture to Gropius's designs, see correspondence between Pritchard, representing Isokon, and W. Irschick, for the plywood firm Luther Ltd., over the course of autumn 1936, PP/18/8/26/4–6.
122 Pritchard wrote to Gropius, seeking his commitment to complete these pieces before Gropius left England for the United States. Pritchard to Gropius, December 1, 1936, BHA.
123 See pencil drawings and letter, Gropius to Pritchard, December 12, 1935 and March 31, 1936, PP/18/7/2/1; PP/18/7/2/8.
124 Prichard to Moholy-Nagy, January 22, 1936, BHA.
125 For Breuer's agreement with Pritchard and his terms at Isokon, see PP/18/7/4. The arrangement was also remunerative, a rare occurrence in this period. For example, for the year 1936, Breuer received royalties of £150, a large sum at the time (PP/18/7/4/42). According to Kevin Davies, in the interwar period, three-quarters of all households received an annual salary of less than £250 per year, a figure that represents the rough dividing line between a middle-class and a working-class salary (Davies, "Finmar and the Furniture of the Future," 153).
126 For blueprints and plans, especially of remarkable designs not put into production, see PP/35/1, PP/35/2, and PP/35/.
127 The London Aluminum Company was asked to construct an exemplar of Breuer's aluminum nesting chair; see Breuer to Pritchard, April 26, 1937, PP/18/7/8/15.

128 For patent documents related to the aluminum nesting chair and other "chairs, tables, stools and like pieces of furniture," see specifications filed July 16, 1937, PP/18/3/8, PP/18/3/10, and PP/18/3/10/5.

129 Isokon Furniture Company, *The New Isokon Chair*, sales brochure, 1936. For patent documents related to Breuer's Long Chair, see PP/18/3/6.

130 See Dunlop Rubber Co. to Isokon Furniture Co., October 7, 1936, PP/18/8/10/1, PP/18/8/10/6; and correspondence between Isokon and Hairlok Ltd., January–April 1937, PP/18/8/18.

131 Isokon, *The New Isokon Chair*.

132 Ibid.

133 Wilk, *Marcel Breuer*, 132–33.

134 Marcel Breuer, "Architecture and Material," in *Circle: International Survey of Constructive Art*, ed. J. L. Martin, Ben Nicholson, and Naum Gabo (London: Faber & Faber, 1937; repr., 1971), 199.

135 Gill, Jennings & Every-Clayton, Chartered Patent Agents, Draft specifications for proposed British provisional patent application to be filed in the name of Marcel Breuer, Nesting Furniture: "Improvements in Furniture," n.d. (1936), BHA.

136 Ibid.

137 The nesting plywood chair patent was awarded on August 6, 1937, as "Nesting Furniture," PP/18/3/8. For a figure of the chair for the patent, see PP/18/3/8/18.

138 Gropius to Pritchard, February 23, 1937, letter suggesting Breuer as successor, PP/18/7/1/8.

139 Meyer, "Die neue Welt," trans. Benton, 109.

140 Ibid.

141 Robin Evans, "Translations from Drawing to Building," in *Translations from Drawing to Building and Other Essays* (Cambridge, MA, MIT Press, 1997), 154. For diverse modes of understanding translation in architecture see also Esra Akcan, *Architecture in Translation: Germany, Turkey, and the Modern House* (Durham, NC: Duke University Press, 2012); Mark Wigley, "The Translation of Architecture, the Production of Babel," *Assemblage* 8 (February 1989): 7–21; Karen Koehler and Jeffrey Saletnik, eds., "Translation and Architecture," special issue, *Art in Translation* 10, no. 1 (March 2018), especially therein Saletnik, "Introduction: Objects of Architectural Translation," 4–10.

142 David Elliott, *Gropius in England, A Documentation 1934–37* (1974), reprinted in *A Different World: Emigre Architects in Britain 1928-1958*, ed. Charlotte Benton (London: RIBA Heinz Gallery, 1995), 107 and 226n3.

143 Maxwell Fry, *Autobiographical Sketches* (London: Elek, 1975), 146–47.

144 Gropius, "The Formal and Technical Problems of Modern Architecture and Planning," typescript (heavily annotated), May 16, 1934, BHA.

145 Gropius to Shand (in German), June 8, 1934, PP/24/2/3.

146 Gropius to Shand (in German), July 2, 1934, PP/24/2/14.

147 Shand to Gropius, July 15, 1934, PP/24/2/15.

148 Gropius, speech at farewell dinner, Trocadero, London, March 9, 1937, typescript, n.p. (p. 2), BHA. And as Gropius framed it, "the English expedition" was "rather a bold enterprise" (p. 2).

149 See Jill Pearlman, *American Modernism: Joseph Hudnut, Walter Gropius, and the Bauhaus Legacy at Harvard* (Charlottesville: University of Virginia Press, 2007).

150 Walter Gropius, *The New Architecture and the Bauhaus*, trans. Morton Shand (London: Faber and Faber, 1935). On the importance of translation in this text and more widely, see Karen Koehler, "Walter Gropius and Herbert Read: Architecture, Industry, Transitions and Translations," in *Sites of Interchange: Modernism, Politics and Culture between Britain and Germany, 1919-1955*, ed. Lucy Wasensteiner (Bern, Switzerland: Peter Lang, 2022), 155–76.

151 Albert Mayer, "Modern Architecture: What It Is and Where It Is Going, Two Books by Walter Curt Behrendt and Walter Gropius That Clarify the Entire Field," *New York Times Book Review*, June 6, 1937.

152 "Televising Architecture," *Radio Times Television Supplement* (March 5, 1937): 6. The program featuring Gropius was broadcast on March 8, 1937.

153 Walter Benjamin, "The Task of the Translator" (1923), in *Walter Benjamin: Selected Writings*, ed. Marcus Bullock and Michael W. Jennings, vol. 1, *1913-1926* (Cambridge, MA: Belknap Press of Harvard University Press, 1996), 260.

154 Ibid., 255.

155 Ibid., 254.

156 Laura Cohn, *The Door to a Secret Room: A Portrait of Wells Coates* (Aldershot: Scholar Press, 1999), 184–85.

157 Ibid., 186.

158 See Peter Cook et al., eds., *Archigram* (Basel, Switzerland: Birkhäuser, 1972; repr., New York: Princeton Architectural Press, 1999); Reyner Banham, "A House Is Not a Home," *Art in America* 2 (April 1965): 70–79.

159 Banham, "A House Is Not a Home," 75.

160 Cook et al., *Archigram*, 64.

161 Ibid., 80.

162 Ibid., 52–53, 82.

Chapter 3: Images in Exile

1 This chapter was previously published as "Images in Exile: Lucia Moholy's Bauhaus Negatives and the Construction of the Bauhaus Legacy," *History of Photography* 37, no. 2 (May 2013): 182–203. In German: "Lucia Moholys Bauhaus-Negative und die Konstruktion eines modernistischen Erbes," in *Lucia Moholy: Das Bild der Moderne*, ed. Tobias Hoffmann, Thomas Derda, and Fabian Reifferscheidt (Cologne: Wienand, 2022), 114–41. A shorter version appeared in German as "Bilder im Exil: Lucia Moholys Bauhaus-Negative und die Konstruktion des Bauhaus-Erbes," in *Entfernt: Frauen des Bauhauses während der NS-Zeit—Verfolgung und Exil*, ed. Inge Hansen-Schaberg, Wolfgang Thöner, and Adriane Feustel (Munich: Richard Boorberg Verlag, Edition Text + Kritik, 2012), 251–73. I would like to acknowledge the collaboration with Jeffrey Saletnik on the initial research of this chapter's subject matter, beginning in 2008 for the conference "Bauhaus Palimpsest: The Object of Discourse" held at Harvard University Art Museums (March 14–15) and published subsequently in the introduction to our edited volume, *Bauhaus Construct: Fashioning Identity, Discourse, and Modernism* (London: Routledge, 2009).

Rolf Sachsse's two books on the photography of Lucia

Moholy remain the most authoritative and significant: Sachsse, *Lucia Moholy* (Düsseldorf: Marzona, 1985); and *Lucia Moholy: Bauhaus Fotografin* (Berlin: Museumspädagogischer Dienst Berlin/Bauhaus-Archiv Berlin, 1995). On Lucia Moholy's Bauhaus photography, see also Lucia Moholy, "Das Bauhaus-Bild," *Werk* 6, no. 55 (1968): 397–402; Lucia Moholy, *Marginalien zu Moholy-Nagy: Dokumentarische Ungereimtheiten / Moholy-Nagy, Marginal Notes: Documentary Absurdities* (Krefeld: Scherpe Verlag, 1972); Rolf Sachsse, "Notes on Lucia Moholy" and "Architectural and Product Photography," in *Photography at the Bauhaus*, ed. Jeannine Fiedler (London: Dirk Nishen, 1990), 24–33, 184–203; Sachsse, "Lucia Moholy, oder: Vom Wert der Reproduktion," in *Das Neue Sehen: Von der Fotografie am Bauhaus zur Subjektiven Fotografie*, ed. Rainer K. Wick (Munich: Klinkhardt & Biermann, 1991), 91–105; Sachsse, "Die Frau an seiner Seite: Irene Bayer und Lucia Moholy als Fotografinnen," in *Fotografieren hiess teilnehmen: Fotografinnen der Weimarer Republik*, ed. Ute Eskildsen (Düsseldorf: Richter, 1994), 67–75; Anja Baumhoff, "Zwischen Kunst und Technik: Lucia Moholy und die Entwicklung der modernen Produktfotografie," in *Klassik und Avantgarde: Das Bauhaus in Weimar 1919-1925*, ed. Hellmut Th. Seemann and Thorsten Valk (Göttingen: Wallstein-Verlag, 2009), 169–84; Ulrike Müller, with the collaboration of Ingrid Radewaldt and Sandra Kemker, "Lucia Moholy," in *Bauhaus Women: Art, Handicraft, Design* (London: Thames & Hudson, 2009), 142–49; and Claire Zimmerman, "Lucia Moholy," public lecture, Museum of Modern Art, "Women and the Bauhaus Lecture Series," January 6, 2010, http://www.moma.org/explore/multimedia/audios/188/1953. Subsequently published work on Lucia Moholy includes Angela Madesani and Nicoletta Ossanna Cavadini, *Lucia Moholy: Between Photography and Life 1894-1989* (Milan: Silvana Editorale, 2012); Claire Zimmerman, "Aura Deferred: *Bauhausbauten Dessau*," in *Photographic Architecture in the Twentieth Centry* (Minneapolis: University of Minnesota Press, 2014), 149–77; Rose-Carol Washton Long, "Lucia Moholy's Bauhaus Photography and the Issue of the Hidden Jew," *Woman's Art Journal* 35, no. 2 (Fall–Winter 2014): 37–46; Lucia Moholy, Thomas Derda, and Oliver A. I. Botar, *Material und Architektur: Lucia Moholy und die Fotografie am Bauhaus, Nachlass László Moholy Nagy* (Berlin: Derda, 2016); Meghan Forbes, "'What I Could Lose': The Fate of Lucia Moholy," *Michigan Quarterly Review* 55, no. 1 (Winter 2016): 24–42; Miriam Szwast, ed., *Lucia Moholy: Fotogeschichte schreiben* (Cologne: Museum Ludwig, 2020); Jordan Troeller, "Lucia Moholy's Idle Hands," *October* 172 (Spring 2020): 68–108; Michelle Henning, "Lucia Moholy and German Photography History in Britain," in *Sites of Interchange: Modernism, Politics and Culture between Britain and Germany, 1919-1955*, ed. Lucy Wasensteiner (Bern, Switzerland: Peter Lang, 2022), 113–33; and Tobias Hoffmann, Thomas Derda, and Fabian Reifferscheidt, eds., *Lucia Moholy: Das Bild der Moderne;* and Jordan Troeller, ed., *Lucia Moholy: Exposures* (Prague: Kunsthalle Praha, forthcoming 2024).

2 The building can no longer be experienced in this way because various restorations and renovations have replaced the original glass curtain wall, which was destroyed during World War II, with more modern variants. The original polished plate glass (Kristallspiegelglas) was an expensive, new glass developed in the 1920s that featured exceptional transparency and prevented visual distortions. For more on the glass of the Bauhaus Building, see Monika Markgraf, "The Glass Facades of the Bauhaus Dessau Building," in *Glass in the 20th Century Architecture: Preservation and Restoration*, ed. Franz Graf and Francesca Albani (Mendrisio, Switzerland: Mendrisio Academy Press, 2011), 19–39.

3 Claire Zimmerman's meticulous work on the visual implications for modernism of the architectural photograph, chiefly in the work of Mies van der Rohe, is especially helpful in light of the images under discussion here. See "Photographic Modern Architecture: Inside 'the New Deep,'" *Journal of Architecture* 9, no. 3 (Autumn 2004): 331–54. Through the famous photographs of the Tugendhat House, she traces various developments and distortions of its architecture (including what she terms the "spatiality of photographic architecture") and convincingly argues that the postwar historical writing of architectural history was heavily influenced by photographic presentations of modern architecture, pointing out that "architectural photographs continued throughout the 1920s, with little critical discussion. In architectural circles, to be understood as metonyms of the buildings they depicted" (331–32, 347). See also Zimmerman, "Tugendhat Frames," *Harvard Design Magazine* 15 (Fall 2001): 24–31; and Zimmerman, "Modernism, Media, Abstraction: Mies van der Rohe's Photographic Architecture in Barcelona and Brno (1927–1931)" (PhD diss., City University of New York, 2005).

4 Lucia Moholy, *Marginalien zu Moholy-Nagy*, 61.

5 Moholy's darkroom was created within the guest room on the ground floor, and when the pair moved out, Josef and Anni Albers moved in. Before they did so, both they and the Bauhaus's director, Hannes Meyer, requested, in a formal letter to Dessau mayor Fritz Hesse, that the room be returned to its full former use as a guest room: that the dividing wall that had been inserted to enclose the darkroom be removed, that repairs be made to the wall owing to the removal of a sink, and to the linoleum floor, and that a hole that had been opened for ventilation be closed. Letters, Josef Albers to Fritz Hesse, June 14, 1928 and Hannes Meyer to Hesse, July 23, 1926, Dessau Stadt Archiv, SB / S3–402.

6 Moholy, *Marginalien zu Moholy-Nagy*, 55. She goes on to lament that they had kept quiet about the extent and manner of their collaboration.

7 The role that Lucia played in helping compose texts published under László's name alone, as well as her collaboration on his photographic oeuvre, is only being slowly acknowledged. For a discussion of the working relationship between László and Lucia, including the lack of attribution for her contributions, including her photography, see Moholy, *Marginalien zu Moholy-Nagy*; and Mercedes Valdivieso, "Eine 'symbiotische Arbeitsgemeinschaft': Lucia und László Moholy-Nagy," in *Liebe Macht Kunst: Künstlerpaare in 20. Jahrhundert*, ed. Renate Berges (Cologne: Böhlau Verlag, 2000), 65–85.

8 Moholy-Nagy's ability to capture extreme views was aided by his use of a light, flexible Leica camera, purchased in the spring of 1925; in particular, the Leica newly allowed for the

separation of the camera from the photographer's body, resulting in a new flexibility of viewpoint and the quick capture of images. See Rolf Sachsse, "Telephon, Reproduktion und Erzeugerabfüllung: Zum Begriff des Originals bei László Moholy-Nagy," in *Über Moholy-Nagy, Ergebnisse aus dem internationalen László Moholy-Nagy Symposium Bielefeld, 1995, zum 100: Geburtstag des Künstlers und Bauhauslehrers*, ed. Gottfried Jäger and Gudrun Wessing (Bielefeld: Kerber Verlag, 1997), 78–82; and Andreas Haus, *Moholy-Nagy: Fotos und Fotogramme* (Munich: Schirmer-Mosel, 1978), 85–86. This was in contradistinction to the painstaking images produced by Lucia's cumbersome, large-format camera on a tripod.

9 For the move away from this earlier kind of straightforward descriptive photographing of whole objects in architectural space and the later interest, from 1928 onward, in using photography to convey the tactility as well as the optical elements in pictorial reproductions of Bauhaus products, see T'ai Smith, "Limits of the Tactile and the Optical: Bauhaus Fabric in the Frame of Photography," *Grey Room* 25 (Fall 2006): 6–31.

10 As she later reminds Herbert Bayer about her Bauhaus-era photographs, "I took those photographs on my own account and my own responsibility, and have been entitled, in all cases, to claim fees for publication and other uses." Moholy to Bayer, April 2, 1955, Lucia Moholy Archive, Bauhaus-Archiv, Berlin (hereafter BHA; unless otherwise specified, materials are from the Lucia Moholy Archive within the BHA). This enormous, time-consuming task executed by a Bauhaus wife was in keeping with the hard work, mostly unacknowledged and always unpaid, of many other Bauhaus wives in dedication to their husbands' pursuits and the school's causes. See, for example, Lucia Moholy's contributions to László Moholy-Nagy's oeuvre in Moholy, *Marginalien zu Moholy-Nagy*, and the documentation of Ise Gropius's, and other wives', tireless assistance in Müller, *Bauhaus Women*, especially the entry "Ise Gropius," 136–41.

11 Baumhoff, "Zwischen Kunst und Technik," 179. For more on product photography at the Bauhaus, see Sachsse, "Architectural and Product Photography," in *Photography at the Bauhaus*, 184–203.

12 See Robin Schuldenfrei, "Production: The Bauhaus Object and Its Irreproducibility," in *Luxury and Modernism: Architecture and the Object in Germany 1900–1933* (Princeton, NJ: Princeton University Press, 2018), 138–56.

13 Notable exceptions are Marianne Brandt's 1928 photomontage *me (Metal Workshop)*, which prominently features a photograph, by Brandt, of a towering stack of metal lampshades, and in later photographs, when the school was under the directorship of Hannes Meyer, which depict vitrines filled with rows of the same Bauhaus object, such as for the 1930 Bauhaus traveling exhibition.

14 See, for example, industrial products photographed in Renger-Patzsch's masterwork of *Neue Sachlichkeit* photography, *Die Welt ist schön: Einhundert Photographische Aufnahmen von Albert Renger-Patzsch* (Munich: Kurt Wolff Verlag, 1928). For a discussion of how straightforward, *sachlich* photographs by Renger-Patzsch and others were used by early-twentieth-century German educational photographic archives for use in teaching and academic study and ways in which it led to the development of *Neue Sachlichkeit* as a style, see Pepper Stetler, "The Object, the Archive and the Origins of *Neue Sachlichkeit* Photography," *History of Photography* 35, no. 2 (August 2011): 281–95.

15 Lucia Moholy, "The Missing Negatives," *British Journal of Photography* 130 (January 7, 1983): 6. She also utilized 9 × 12 cm photographic film stock in this period.

16 Sibyl Moholy-Nagy, *Moholy-Nagy: Experiment in Totality* (New York: Harper Brothers, 1950), 133.

17 Ibid., 67.

18 Lucia Moholy forged links to important British academic figures, as well as titled nobility. She was likely a key figure in getting British patrons interested in Neubauer's case, who then exerted external pressure on his behalf. For example, on April 21, 1934, the London Times published a letter by Princess Elizabeth Bibesco, daughter of former Prime Minister Herbert Asquith and wife of a Romanian prince, calling for an international press campaign to save his life; likewise, signers were sought among professors at Oxford and Cambridge for a petition asking for Neubauer's release. Peter Crane, *Wir leben nun mal auf einem Vulkan*, trans. Rolf Bulang (Bonn: Weidle Verlag, 2005), 227–28. Elizabeth Fox Howard, an English Quaker, became involved with the effort to free several key political prisoners and traveled to Germany on several occasions, including flying from England to Berlin to plead on behalf of Neubauer (whom she refers to as Dr. T). See Howard, *Across Barriers* (Essex: Chigwell Press, 1941), 65, 71–78. For more on the circumstances of Theodor Neubauer's captivity and the intervention of patrons in his behalf, see Crane, Howard, and Sonja Müller, *Theodor Neubauer: Lebensbilder großer Pädagogen* (Berlin: Volk und Wissen, 1971). I would like to acknowledge and thank Peter Crane for his generous sharing of information pertaining to Neubauer.

19 Moholy to Heinrich Jacoby, October 1, 1947, BHA. The letter is in German. Reprinted in Sachsse, *Lucia Moholy: Bauhaus Fotografin*, 81.

20 Lucia Moholy, "Summary of Events," February 1956, p. 2, BHA.

21 She did not, as was common in this period, receive any financial support from her former husband.

22 Elizabeth Otto, "Designing Men: New Visions of Masculinity in the Photomontages of Herbert Bayer, Marcel Breuer, and László Moholy-Nagy," in *Bauhaus Construct: Fashioning Identity, Discourse, and Modernism*, ed. Jeffrey Saletnik and Robin Schuldenfrei (London: Routledge, 2009), 183–204, especially 188–90. On Moholy's portraits, see Matthew S. Witkovsky, "Lucia Moholy Photograph of Georg Muche," in *Bauhaus 1919-1933: Workshops for Modernity*, ed. Barry Bergdoll and Leah Dickerman (New York: Museum of Modern Art, 2009), 236–41. While it does not affect the image Moholy-Nagy wanted to project, according to Lucia Moholy, the garment was in actuality not a machinist's suit but a dark orange fishermen's coverall from northern France, as noted by Sachsse, "Telephon, Reproduktion und Erzeugerabfüllung."

23 In May 1936 Moholy was given official permission to reside in England for a year and to open a private studio for

photographic work on private commission, but she was not allowed to open a "shop or business premises." See letter from K. G. Davies, private secretary, Home Office, to Herbert Samuel, May 23, 1936, BHA.

24 Margot Oxford and Asquith to Moholy, March 6, 1936, BHA.

25 Lucia Moholy, *A Hundred Years of Photography: 1839–1939* (Harmondsworth: Penguin Books, 1939).

26 See "Konzept einer Kulturgeschichte der Fotografie," ca. 1930, and "Exposé zu einer geplanten Kulturgeschichte der Fotografie," 1932, BHA. Excerpts are reprinted in Sachsse, *Lucia Moholy: Bauhaus Fotografin*, 76–77.

27 "Foto-buch," n.d., typescript, BHA.

28 By Moholy's own representation, see BHA.

29 Moholy, *A Hundred Years of Photography*, 164.

30 Ibid., 165–66.

31 For a contextual synopsis of these discussions via an analysis of texts by authors such as Josef Maria Eder, Helmut Gernsheim, Lucia Moholy, László Moholy-Nagy, Beaumont Newhall, and Erich Stenger, see Claude W. Sui, "Helmut Gernsheim: Pioneer Collector and Historian of Photography," in *Helmut Gernsheim: Pioneer of Photo History*, ed. Alfried Wieczorek and Claude W. Sui (Ostfildern-Ruit: Hatje Cantz, 2003), 27–34. See also Martin Gasser, "Histories of Photography 1839–1939," *History of Photography* 16, no. 1 (Spring 1992): 50–60; and Matthew S. Witkovsky, "Circa 1930: Art History and the New Photography," *études Photographiques* 23 (May 2009): 139–49. For a discussion of Moholy's *A Hundred Years of Photography* within the context of contemporaneous histories of photography, see the relevant sections of Miriam Halwani, "Marginalien zur Geschichtsschreibung der Fotografie 1839–1939" (PhD diss., University of Hamburg, 2010); and Halwani, *Geschichte der Fotogeschichte, 1839–1939* (Berlin: Reimer, 2012).

32 Moholy, *Marginalien zu Moholy-Nagy*, 55–56.

33 Gernsheim knew Moholy in London; he met her in the late 1930s, when she attended an exhibition of his photographs and came to know her work during subsequent visits to her studio. He cites her book as "probably the first book on the history of photography" that he read. Helmut Gernsheim interviewed by Val Williams, 1995, "An Oral History of British Photography," © British Library, catalog reference C459/66.

34 BHA. She was made an "Associate" of the Royal Society of Photography in May 1938.

35 Moholy to Mrs. Cavendish Bentinck, February 23, 1937, BHA.

36 Letter, Lucia Moholy to László Moholy-Nagy, November 16, 1940, BHA.

37 Franz Schulz, affidavit of support for Lucia Moholy, October 7, 1940, BHA.

38 Sibyl Moholy-Nagy to Moholy, July 7, 1940, BHA. It is notable that almost all of the correspondence between members of the Bauhaus circle after leaving Germany was written in English. Although this was sometimes the result of a letter being dictated to a secretary, in most instances this was not the case. Writing exclusively in English, perhaps, reveals one of the ways in which Bauhaus members attempted to quickly assimilate in their new host countries. They may have also written in English to avoid the suspicion that they were enemy spies or to not draw attention to themselves as German-speakers, generally, by those encountering their mail. (Where correspondence was originally in German, this will be noted.)

39 Eventually Moholy conceded defeat and remained in England. In 1959, she moved permanently to Switzerland, where she lived until her death in 1989 at the age of ninety-five.

40 In this period in Britain, many photographers would not publicly affirm their ties to Judaism or would outright negate their Jewish heritage, yet the role that Jews played in photography is significant. See Michael Berkowitz, "Beaumont Newhall and Helmut Gernsheim: Collaboration, Friendship, and Tension amidst the "Jewishness" of Photography," *Perspectives, Journal of the Woolf Institute* (Spring 2010): 17–21; and Berkowitz, "Photography as a Jewish Business: From High Theory, to Studio, to Snapshot," *Eastern European Jewish Affairs* 39, no. 3 (2009): 389–400.

41 Rolf Sachsse's dates indicate that Moholy was twenty when she left for Wiesbaden, yet she states in the short biographical paragraph of *A Hundred Years of Photography* that she was eighteen. See Sachsse, *Lucia Moholy: Bauhaus Fotografin*, 12; and Moholy, *A Hundred Years of Photography*, back flap of dust jacket.

42 Sachsse, *Lucia Moholy: Bauhaus Fotografin*, 11.

43 Donald Kuspit, "Meyer Schapiro's Jewish Unconscious," *Prospects* 21 (October 1996): 491–508.

44 See correspondence spanning the period from March 9, 1936 to June 13, 1947 in BHA. She resided in England without a valid passport. See Moholy to Herbert Samuel, October 19, 1946, BHA. Moholy's application for naturalization was submitted on September 12, 1939; she was awarded British citizenship in June 1947, expedited through the intervention of Samuel, a powerful friend with connections to the British Home Office.

45 See BHA, Sammlung Briefe Moholy-Karsten.

46 On the negatives generally, see Moholy, "The Missing Negatives," 6–8, 18; Sabine Hartmann, "Anmerkungen zum fotografischen Nachlaß," in Sachsse, *Lucia Moholy: Bauhaus Fotografin*, 113–16. Regarding the appropriation of the negatives by Gropius, see Saletnik and Schuldenfrei, "Introduction," in *Bauhaus Construct*, 1–9; Mercedes Valdivieso, "Lucia Moholy, el ojo anónimo que retrató la Bauhaus," *La Balsa de la Medusa* 40 (1996): 85–87; Valdivieso, "Eine 'symbiotische Arbeitsgemeinschaft,'" 84n40; and Müller, *Bauhaus Women*, 146–48. On the acquisition of the negatives by the Bauhaus Archive, Berlin in 1992, see Sibylle Hoiman, "Lucia Moholy: Zur Geschichte ihres Nachlasses im Bauhaus-Archiv Berlin," in *Special Delivery: Von Künstlernachlässen und ihren Verwaltern*, ed. Volkmar Hansen, Ulrike Horstenkamp, and Gabriele Weidle (Bonn: Arbeitskreis selbständiger Kultur-Institute, 2011), 170–81.

47 Gropius's shipment reached him on October 20, 1937. Letter from Gropius to Alfred Barr, October 21, 1937, Walter Gropius Papers (MS Ger 208), Houghton Library, Harvard University.

48 Lucia Moholy to László Moholy-Nagy, July 19, 1946, BHA.

49 As Moholy recalls in a letter to Gropius: "When I left, all my things i.e. books, pictures, household goods and negatives were in one place, and I know nothing about subsequent arrangements. When Moholy and Sybil [*sic*] came to London, some of my furniture and a few other odd things came

along in their lift—but not unfortunately the negatives. I presume they were left behind on account of their weight, being glass.... It was of course impossible to do anything about it during the war years. When, later, I wrote to Moholy asking him about the circumstances, he was too ill to reply. When Sybil [sic] came to London on her way to Germany, I brought the subject up, and it was then that she said (I had never heard it before) that the negatives were moved to your place. And, she continued, as the house was bombed, the negatives, no doubt, have been destroyed." Moholy to Gropius, January 21, 1954, BHA.

50 Moholy to Gropius, June 1, 1950, BHA. The Moholy-Gropius correspondence all occurred in English.

51 Ibid.

52 Cable, Gropius to Moholy, BHA.

53 Gropius to Moholy, June 20, 1950, BHA.

54 Moholy to Gropius, June 12, 1950, BHA. The typescript for the lecture notes, telegraphically, at the conclusion: "Slides — few — difficult to come by." "Lecture for the London School of Printing and Graphic Arts," 8, Typescript with handwritten corrections, BHA.

55 Moholy, "The Missing Negatives," 7.

56 Moholy to Gropius, January 21, 1954, BHA.

57 Ibid.

58 Gropius to Moholy, February 25, 1954, BHA. Gropius had, in fact, already deposited the negatives with the museum by March 1950, as the curator writes to Gropius: "I wish to take this opportunity to thank you for your very generous gift of some two hundred negatives of Bauhaus material. These will prove of enormous value to us and I shall proceed with having the prints made in the near future. I understand you would like to have prints for your own record and I shall be very happy to send these to you." Charles L. Kuhn to Gropius, March 9, 1950, Walter Gropius Papers (MS Ger 208), Houghton Library, Harvard University. Evidently, the prints were not promptly delivered, and Gropius, eager for the material, made the following request to the museum a year later: "I wonder whether I could get copies of the negatives on Bauhaus production which you promised me when I handed all the negatives out to be stored in the Museum. I would highly appreciate having a set of these copies in my personal file." Gropius to Kuhn, January 23, 1951, Walter Gropius Archive, BHA. The museum did make copies, which remain in the collection today; see, for example, figs. 3.6, 3.7, 3.8, 3.10.

59 Moholy to Gropius, March 20, 1954, BHA.

60 Moholy consulted both international and copyright lawyers for assistance in first getting her negatives back from Gropius—before he would release them he wanted her to sign a legal document negating her claims to any compensation in the years he held the negatives—and attempting to obtain compensation for her loss of their use. Gropius maintained that storing them and shipping them back would be compensation enough (although they are ultimately shipped back at Moholy's expense).

61 Charles Aukin (Moholy's lawyer) to Gropius, May 3, 1957, Walter Gropius Archive, BHA.

62 Hartmann, "Anmerkungen zum fotografischen Nachlaß," 113.

63 Moholy to Gropius, October 30, 1954, BHA. The letter is excerpted here as it appears in the original, in English with the German parenthetical "zu treuen Händen," a precise phrase for the safekeeping of objects in trust, added here in German as if to underscore to Gropius, by invoking his mother tongue, his responsibility to her.

64 Charles Aukin to Gropius, October 17, 1956, BHA.

65 Sibyl Moholy-Nagy to Lucia Moholy, August 7, 1947, BHA.

66 Moholy to Gropius, October 30, 1954, BHA.

67 Moholy, "Summary of Events," February 1956, p. 8, BHA.

68 Moholy also maintained a meticulous card catalog of her images, with each one identified by number, size, and subject. Despite its bulk, the card catalog was of enough importance to her that it was among the few possessions she brought with her into flight. It is available as part of the Lucia Moholy collection at the Bauhaus Archive, Berlin.

69 After protest over the omission of her name in the photo credits of *Bauhaus, 1919-1928*, for the 1955 reprint translated into German, Moholy was credited, but only for thirteen images of the forty used.

70 For an examination of the ways in which the exhibition neutralized the school's social and political history, in light of period political events and Gropius's own status as an exile, see Karen Koehler, "*The Bauhaus, 1919-1928*: Gropius in Exile and the Museum of Modern Art, N.Y., 1938," in *Art, Culture, and Media under the Third Reich*, ed. Richard A. Etlin (Chicago: University of Chicago Press, 2002), 287–315. Koehler points out the importance of recognizing "the extent to which the decisions made in 1938 by the organizers of the MoMA exhibition have had a lasting effect on the Bauhaus legacy" (309). See also Koehler, "Angels of History Carrying Bricks: Gropius in Exile," in *The Dispossessed: An Anatomy of Exile*, ed. Peter I. Rose (Amherst: University of Massachusetts Press, 2005), 257–80.

71 Although the organizers, including Gropius himself, wanted the exhibition to cover the entirety of the school's history, they had to limit it to Gropius's tenure, as Ludwig Mies van der Rohe, despite multiple entreaties, refused to participate because of what Gropius, in a letter to Alfred H. Barr Jr., cites as "the difficulties in Germany." As Gropius continues in the letter, "We were eager to avoid any difficulties and to make the show as objective as possible. If we show anything of the period following my departure from the Bauhaus, there might result disagreeable situations which I do not want to face; and, without their [the other former directors'] cooperation, I do not feel entitled to describe their own intentions." Gropius to Barr, September 8, 1938, Walter Gropius Archive, BHA.

72 "Notes on the Reception of the Bauhaus Exhibition," MoMA, by Alfred H. Barr Jr., January 19, 1939, Walter Gropius Archive, BHA. However, Mary Anne Staniszewski argues that the show was perceived by the public, critics, and the museum itself as a failure. See "The *Bauhaus* Debacle," in Staniszewski, *The Power of Display: A History of Exhibition Installations at the Museum of Modern Art* (Cambridge, MA: MIT Press, 1998), 142–52. In terms of popularizing the school in the United States, helping its former members establish themselves in exile, and allowing certain protagonists such as Gropius, Bayer, Moholy-Nagy, and Breuer to forge close ties to key people within MoMA, relationships that would serve them well for the rest of their careers, the exhibition should be viewed as a success.

73 Gropius to Bayer, November 14, 1937, Walter Gropius Archive, BHA. Letter in German. Unless otherwise noted, translations are the author's own.

74 Gropius to Dorothy H. Dudley, MoMA, January 4, 1939, p. 2, Walter Gropius Archive, BHA.

75 Press release, *Bauhaus 1919–1928*, p. 3, Walter Gropius Archive, BHA. Despite this statement, the same press release announced that "about 700 individual items in wood, metal, canvas and paint, textiles, paper, glass and many other substances" were on exhibit (p. 1).

76 Henry McBride, "Attractions in the Galleries," *New York Sun*, December 10, 1938, 11, cited in Staniszewski, *The Power of Display*, 151.

77 Moholy also intended to author a book on the Bauhaus, taking pains to note that she had at her disposal ample material to richly illustrate it. For several variations of proposals sent to English and German publishers over a period of years between 1958 and 1963, see BHA.

78 Moholy to Sigfried Giedion, February 11, 1955, BHA.

79 Marcel Breuer to Moholy, September 16, 1958, BHA. This is in reference to Breuer's book, *Sun and Shadow: The Philosophy of an Architect*.

80 Marcel Breuer to S. Phelps Platt Jr., Dodd, Mead & Company, September 16, 1958, BHA.

81 See Magdalena Droste, "The Bauhaus Object between Authorship and Anonymity," in *Bauhaus Construct: Fashioning Identity, Discourse, and Modernism*, ed. Jeffrey Saletnik and Robin Schuldenfrei (London: Routledge, 2009), 205–25; and Ise Gropius, Diary, BHA.

82 There were, for example, vintage Moholy Bauhaus photographic prints stamped by Stoedtner, imported and mounted on cardboard by a New York service (Rudolf Lesch Fine Arts, Inc.) which were part of a large set of general art and architectural images circulated in the United States for instructional use in art schools and in art history departments. I am grateful to Elizabeth Otto for bringing the holdings of such prints at the State University of New York at Buffalo to my attention.

83 When Moholy discovered that the Stoedtner Archive was reproducing and selling her images and investigated further, she learned that prints and negatives in Stoedtner's collection not previously destroyed by bomb, fire, and water damage during the war had been removed from Berlin to Düsseldorf in July 1948 in a British airlift, but that all business documents and correspondence (which would have definitively clarified how her images entered the archive) remained inaccessible in the Russian sector of Berlin. See Ottilie Stoedtner to Moholy, July 28, 1958, BHA.

84 Ludwig Hirschfeld-Mack to Moholy, October 20, 1964, BHA. (Hirschfeld-Mack is quoting a letter, from Gropius to Hirschfeld-Mack, dated December 14, 1962.)

85 See Annemarie Jaeggi, *Fagus: Industrial Culture from Werkbund to Bauhaus*, trans. Elizabeth M. Schwaiger (New York: Princeton Architectural Press, 2000), 107, and, more generally, the chapter titled "Fagus and Photography," 105–22. See also Jaeggi, *Die Moderne im Blick: Albert Renger-Patzsch fotografiert das Fagus Werk* (Berlin: Bauhaus-Archiv/Museum für Gestaltung, 2011).

86 Gropius had already been circumspect about images in 1923, as he noted in a letter to Adolf Behne "that he could not give photographs of the Bauhaus to Behne [who was preparing his important history of architecture, *The Modern Functional Building*] because he was already planning a 'special publication' [his own Bauhaus series book *Internationale Architektur*] that 'obligated' him not to release illustrations beforehand." Rosemarie Haag Bletter, introduction to Adolf Behne, *The Modern Functional Building* (Santa Monica, CA: Getty Research Institute for the History of Art and the Humanities, 1996), 32.

87 For a consideration of the inverse, the examination of an archival photograph as a modernist object, specifically its role as a generator of multiple meanings and narratives of the Bauhaus, and more broadly in representing modernist visuality itself, see Paul Paret, "Picturing Sculpture: Object, Image, Archive," in *Bauhaus Construct: Fashioning Identity, Discourse, and Modernism*, ed. Jeffrey Saletnik and Robin Schuldenfrei (London: Routledge, 2009), 163–80.

88 Herbert Bayer to Moholy, March 23, 1955, BHA.

89 Moholy, *A Hundred Years of Photography*, 164.

Chapter 4: Assimilating Unease

1 This chapter has been previously published in *Atomic Dwelling: Anxiety, Domesticity, and Postwar Architecture*, ed. Robin Schuldenfrei (London: Routledge, 2012), 87–126. Simultaneous or subsequently published work related to this topic includes Maggie Taft, "Better Than Before: László Moholy-Nagy and the New Bauhaus in Chicago," in *Chicago Makes Modern: How Creative Minds Changed Society*, ed. Mary Jane Jacob and Jacquelynn Baas (Chicago: University of Chicago Press, 2012), 31–43; Anna Vallye, "Vision's Value for Democracy: Kepes and Moholy-Nagy in Chicago," in *Émigré Cultures in Design and Architecture*, ed. Alison J. Clarke and Elana Shapira (London: Bloomsbury, 2017), 175–91; and John R. Blakinger, *Gyorgy Kepes: Undreaming the Bauhaus* (Cambridge, MA: MIT Press, 2019).

2 "America Imports Genius," *New York Times*, September 12, 1937, sec. 4.

3 László Moholy-Nagy, "Relating the Parts to the Whole," *Millar's Chicago Letter* 2, no. 23 (August 5, 1940): 6.

4 On the recommendation of Walter Gropius, who had initially been offered the position, the organizing representatives of the Association of Arts and Industries invited Moholy-Nagy to be the school's director. He arrived in Chicago in July 1937 to meet with the association's board, agreeing to lead the newly established institution, which opened in October. The school changed names and iterations frequently in its initial years of operation: it began as "The New Bauhaus: The American School of Design" in 1937 but was closed in 1938 by the Association of Arts and Industries. In 1939, it became independent from its original benefactors and was reopened and renamed the "School of Design in Chicago." In the spring of 1944 it became the "Institute of Design"; it persisted in this form, despite Moholy-Nagy's death in 1946, until 1949, when it retained its name but became a school within the Illinois Institute of Technology, as it remains today.

5 For a detailed analysis of the reception of European modern architecture in the United States, including a nuanced

discussion of the tenuous position of Bauhaus émigrés, of attempts at assimilation vis-à-vis the contemporary culture of the United States, and of the many myths surrounding their success, see Kathleen James-Chakraborty, "From Isolationism to Internationalism: American Acceptance of the Bauhaus," in *Bauhaus Culture: From Weimar to the Cold War*, ed. Kathleen James-Chakraborty (Minneapolis: University of Minnesota Press, 2006), 153–70. See also James-Chakraborty, "Changing the Agenda: From German Bauhaus Modernism to U.S. Internationalism," 235–52, and Franz Schulze, "The Bauhaus Architects and the Rise of Modernism in the United States," 224–34, in *Exiles and Emigrés: The Flight of European Artists from Hitler*, ed. Stephanie Barron (New York: Harry N. Abrams, 1997). In *Domesticity at War* (Cambridge, MA: MIT Press, 2007), Beatriz Colomina examines the architectural context in the immediate postwar years, viewing the engagement with World War II as the event that finally created the conditions for the development of modern architecture in the United States (12). She argues that there was a shift from war to domesticity to product design that resulted in a milieu that she terms an "obsessive, embattled domesticity" (19).

6   László Moholy-Nagy, transcript of "Conference on Industrial Design, A New Profession" held at the Museum of Modern Art for the Society of Industrial Designers (November 11–14, 1946), 54, 60, Institute of Design Records, University Archives, Paul V. Gavin Library, Illinois Institute of Technology, Chicago (hereafter Institute of Design Records, IIT). Moholy-Nagy's expertise on design education was held in high regard by 1946. He was introduced at the conference by Joseph Hudnut, dean of the architecture school at Harvard, as "the most able and vigorous and successful pioneer in educational discipline based upon objective analysis of the modern scene. We imitate him at Harvard, and he is imitated all over the world, chiefly because he has been able to see a role for the architect and the designer in the kind of training which he is developing which, I think, is going to be a keystone in the education of this new profession" (59–60).

7   Helping to smooth this transition would have been the post-Depression circumstances during Moholy-Nagy's initial years in the United States, when many government officials had participated in the administering of New Deal and WPA (Works Progress Administration) projects and thus would have been sympathetic to leftist ideals. The decision to let certain émigrés into the United States was sometimes predicated on how the government viewed their potential contribution to the country.

8   Gropius, in *Three Addresses at the Blackstone Hotel on the Occasion of the Celebration of the Addition of the Institute of Design to Illinois Institute of Technology*, April 17, 1950, 11, offprint, Institute of Design Records, IIT.

9   School of Design, *1942–43 Course Catalogue* (Chicago: School of Design, 1943), Institute of Design Collection, Special Collections, Daley Library, University of Illinois Chicago, Chicago (hereafter Institute of Design Collection, UIC).

10 While there were key members of the former German Bauhaus spreading Bauhaus ideas and pedagogical practices through their teaching at institutions across America, from Black Mountain College to IIT to Harvard, as well as at smaller institutions, the New Bauhaus (and its later iterations) under Moholy-Nagy remained the institution most closely linked to the original Bauhaus's structure, program, and desired end results. Copious correspondence demonstrates that Gropius remained closely affiliated and invested in the school's future throughout its stormy history, beginning by nominating Moholy-Nagy as its first leader, then, over the years advising Moholy-Nagy on how to structure the institution, lending his name to its initiatives, and stepping in periodically to reassure the school's administration and benefactors.

11 For sources that examine connections in design from wartime to postwar boom time, see especially Donald Albrecht, ed., *World War II and the American Dream: How Wartime Building Changed a Nation* (Cambridge, MA: MIT Press, 1995); Andrew M. Shanken, *194X: Architecture, Planning, and Consumer Culture on the American Home Front* (Minneapolis: University of Minnesota Press, 2009); and Jean-Louis Cohen, *Architecture in Uniform: Designing and Building for the Second World War* (New Haven, CT: Yale University Press, 2011). Although my focus here is primarily on Moholy-Nagy, many other émigrés with key skills in art, architecture, and design, some of whom had been affiliated with the Bauhaus and some not, also contributed to the war effort in many ways, large and small. For example, former *Bauhäusler* Herbert Bayer, working closely with Edward Steichen as curator, designed the 1942 *Road to Victory* exhibition at the Museum of Modern Art, which drew on powerful visual narrative, intended to have maximum impact on the audience, to celebrate America and its resolute strength in entering the war. Bayer also designed the installation for MoMA's 1943 *Airways to Peace: An Exhibition of Geography for the Future* and devised a series of flexible display units for posters and war propaganda that was used for traveling exhibitions put on by the US government, both of which are discussed further in chapter 8. Following the war, Bayer continued to aid US government efforts, for example, by contributing the design for the 1957 United States Information Agency exhibition *Volk aus Vielen Völkern* (*Nation of Nations*) in Berlin. See Arthur A. Cohen, *Herbert Bayer: The Complete Work* (Cambridge, MA: MIT Press, 1984), 300–308. Modern German architects Erich Mendelsohn and Konrad Wachsmann advised the US government about traditional German building techniques and materials (and their relative combustibility), aiding the 1943 construction of a full-scale "German village" on the Dugway Proving Grounds in Utah. Fellow German émigrés Paul Zucker, Hans Knoll, and George Hartmueller oversaw the construction of authentic interior furnishings, and Antonin Raymond, a Czech émigré, advised on a companion "Japanese village." The two villages were repeatedly bombarded and rebuilt, in order to ascertain the most effective means of their destruction. Mendelsohn also advised on typical German factory construction, especially their roofs' susceptibility to incendiary bombs. See Cohen, *Herbert Bayer*, 231–39.

12 For a contextualized discussion of the extent to which the exile experience of Walter Gropius was characterized by his efforts to circumvent political controversy and separate art from politics, as manifested in his avoidance of historical

specificity in the design and contents of the 1938 Museum of Modern Art exhibition and accompanying catalog, *The Bauhaus, 1919-1928*, see Karen Koehler, "The Bauhaus, 1919-1928: Gropius in Exile and the Museum of Modern Art, N.Y., 1938," in *Art, Culture, and Media under the Third Reich*, ed. Richard A. Etlin (Chicago: University of Chicago Press, 2002), 287–315. Koehler notes the fear of—and hostility toward—new immigrants in 1938, the year that the exhibition opened. Anti-German and anti-Bolshevist propaganda was commonplace (Bauhaus artists had the potential to be identified pejoratively as either Germans or Bolsheviks), and in a period of continued unemployment in the United States, the new émigrés were also regarded as a threat as potential labor competition (296–300). See also Koehler, "Angels of History Carrying Bricks: Gropius in Exile" in *The Dispossessed: An Anatomy of Exile*, ed. Peter I. Rose (Amherst: University of Massachusetts Press, 2005), 257–80. For a wide-ranging study on exiled artists and architects of this period, see Barron, *Exiles and Emigrés*.

13 Herbert Bayer is said to have arrived in New York with less than twenty dollars in his pocket. Sibyl Moholy-Nagy claimed that Moholy-Nagy, by insisting on speaking German, "lost most of his English vocabulary" en route from Chicago to Mills College in Oakland, where he had been invited to conduct a summer school in 1940. Sibyl Moholy-Nagy, *Moholy-Nagy: Experiment in Totality* (New York: Harper Brothers, 1950), 180. William H. Jordy has noted that Mies relied on others to translate for him during his initial four years in the United States before making an effort to speak English. Jordy, "The Aftermath of the Bauhaus in America: Gropius, Mies, and Breuer," in *The Intellectual Migration: Europe and America, 1930-1960*, ed. Donald Fleming and Bernard Bailyn (Cambridge, MA: Belknap Press of Harvard University Press, 1969), 516.

14 Hal Foster, "The Bauhaus Idea in America," in *Albers and Moholy-Nagy: From the Bauhaus to the New World*, ed. Achim Borchardt-Hume (London: Tate Publishing, 2006), 97.

15 The original Bauhaus, especially under Gropius, as well as its predecessor led by Henry van de Velde, had always sought to minimize reliance on government support through commercial work and with the stated goal of forging an alliance with industry, yet it was unable to substantially achieve this; Moholy-Nagy in America did not have the luxury of direct financial support from the government, although he actively sought it as a sponsor of the school's wartime activities. He also spent a great deal of energy courting companies, large and small, for funding, materials, and technical equipment. Without a stable source of income, his school was perpetually in crisis. After its original board of directors dissolved the school within its first year, Moholy-Nagy reopened without a board that would fund the school, but rather with a "sponsors committee" of prominent cultural figures. Later, benefactor Walter Paepcke formed a board to support the school, a body to which Moholy-Nagy was not always deferential, having a strong personal vision for the institution. Paepcke also tried to interest local institutions of higher learning in annexing the school and called in Gropius, Bayer, and Breuer to assess whether Moholy-Nagy could be advised in the direction the school should take to become more stable (see Alain Findeli's description of the "Moholy affair" in "Design Education and Industry: The Laborious Beginnings of the Institute of Design in Chicago in 1944," *Journal of Design History* 4, no. 2 [1991]: 97–113). Gropius, ensconced in the stability of Harvard, and Mies at IIT were not forced to face general financial difficulties, nor were they responsible for contending with declines in student enrollment, both greatly exacerbated by the war. (Harvard's Graduate School of Design dropped to twenty-six students and began admitting women to take up the places of absent male students. See Jill Pearlman, *American Modernism: Joseph Hudnut, Walter Gropius, and the Bauhaus Legacy at Harvard* [Charlottesville: University of Virginia Press, 2007], 200–201. At the School of Design, which had always admitted women, it was only during the war that it had more female than male students.)

16 Letter, Moholy-Nagy to Sibyl Moholy-Nagy, April 26, 1944, reprinted in Sibyl Moholy-Nagy, *Moholy-Nagy*, 216.

17 Although, at the same time, she expresses relief at no longer having to regularly write to her own and Moholy-Nagy's families, a "tormenting correspondence" that was "terminated by a power beyond our personal decision." Sibyl Moholy-Nagy, "Domestic Diary of America's Participation in the Second World War," December 11, 1941, 5, Sibyl and Laszlo Moholy-Nagy Papers, Archives of American Art, Smithsonian Institution, Washington, DC.

18 She then goes on to report the momentous event that had just taken place: "So the European victory, the defeat and death of the greatest objective enemy we have known in our life-time, the end of twelve incredibly strenuous years, was mentioned between us only in passing." Sibyl Moholy-Nagy, Diary, May 13, 1945, Sibyl and Laszlo Moholy-Nagy Papers, Archives of American Art, Smithsonian Institution.

19 The difficult realities of wartime and especially postwar Europe highlights another reason (beyond the discussion below) why Moholy-Nagy and others would stay in the United States. Letters between Lilly Reich and Mies show that he supplied his extended family, Reich and her family, and former clients such as Carl Crous with CARE (Cooperative for American Remittances to Europe) packages—prepackaged staples that could be purchased for delivery to Europe. Reich repeatedly wrote to Mies, asking for goods such as coffee, tea, rice, and eggs, and thanking him for the packages as they arrived safely. Reich especially pleaded for goods to be sent to her brother, who was unemployed and had numerous children at home. Once installed at Harvard, Walter and Ise Gropius began a tireless campaign assisting friends and colleagues out of Germany, and they, like Mies, also sent provisions. They began a "Bauhaus Fund," which sent parcels to former Bauhaus members remaining in Germany. At one point in 1947, worried about provisions for the upcoming winter months and unable to raise adequate monies from *Bauhäusler* working in America, Ise Gropius wrote to Philip Johnson at the Museum of Modern Art, asking if he would put her in touch with potential American donors. A letter from Herbert Bayer to Ise Gropius, in response to her appeal for money for the Bauhaus Fund, demonstrates the typical level of émigré support of those remaining in Europe: "A few days ago we counted the number of people to whom we send more or less regularly and we arrived at a figure

of fifty." Ise Gropius to Philip Johnson, September 1947, and Herbert Bayer to Ise Gropius, August 18, 1947, Walter Gropius Papers, Houghton Library, Harvard University, Cambridge, MA (hereafter Walter Gropius Papers, Harvard).

The Moholy-Nagys, with little disposable personal income, positions that were continuously unstable, and a future uncertain owing to grappling with a woefully underfunded school chronically on the brink of collapse, sent a tremendous amount back to Europe. Sibyl's sister, in a letter thanking Sibyl for the latest food package, writes of the relief it gave, and reports a darkening situation, compared with the previous January, in which the hitherto lack of food and clothing was made worse by the newer shortages in electricity, gas, and at times, water. Eva Pietzsch to Sibyl Moholy-Nagy, January 3, 1947, Sibyl and Laszlo Moholy-Nagy Papers, Archives of American Art, Smithsonian Institution, Washington, DC. Subsequent letters detail their "fight to feed themselves" ("Kampf ums fressen"). The Moholy-Nagys also sent CARE packages, funds, and other assistance to friends, including the contemporary dancer Gret Palucca and artists Paul Citroen, Raoul Hausmann, and Kurt Schwitters. Lloyd C. Engelbrecht, *Moholy-Nagy: Mentor to Modernism*, 2 vols. (Cincinnati: Flying Trapeze Press, 2009), 1:272, 2:673–77.

20 Harold J. Coolidge, American Defense, Harvard Group, to Gropius, January 10, 1941, Walter Gropius Papers, Harvard.

21 For discussion and reproduction of key FBI documents, see Margret Kentgens-Craig, *The Bauhaus and America: First Contacts, 1919-1936* (Cambridge, MA: MIT Press, 1999), 238–40 and appendix.

22 A letter of explanation was sent to Moholy-Nagy from Joseph Edelman, an attorney retained by Moholy-Nagy to expedite his case. The letter also pointed out that other Hungarians had been naturalized within a period of six months to a year and a half, whereas at this point in the process Moholy-Nagy had already been in the United States for eight years. Part of the FBI investigation seems to have been due to Moholy-Nagy's involvement, while in America, with the Hungarian Democratic Council, which sought to foster democracy in Hungary. See Edelman to Moholy-Nagy, March 23, 1945, and Moholy-Nagy to Andrew Jordan, district director, US Department of Justice, November 12, 1945, Sibyl and Laszlo Moholy-Nagy Papers, Archives of American Art, Smithsonian Institution, Washington, DC. Moholy-Nagy, after much effort and outreach in many directions, finally obtained his naturalization papers on April 10, 1946 (seven months before his death).

23 Karen Koehler, "The Bauhaus Manifesto Postwar to Postwar: From the Street to the Wall to the Radio to the Memoir," in *Bauhaus Construct: Fashioning Identity, Discourse and Modernism*, ed. Jeffrey Saletnik and Robin Schuldenfrei (London: Routledge, 2009), 28. See also a copy of the 1942 US Department of Justice "Regulations Controlling Travel and Other Conduct of Aliens of Enemy Nationalities" in the Walter Gropius Papers, Harvard.

24 For an extended discussion of this fictional radio play and its significance see Koehler, "The Bauhaus Manifesto Postwar to Postwar," 24–28.

25 Ibid., 26.

26 Ibid., 25.

27 Sibyl Moholy-Nagy to Robert Tague, June 9, 1945, Bauhaus Archive, Berlin (hereafter BHA).

28 Moholy-Nagy to Robert Tague, July 14, 1945, BHA. Moholy-Nagy seemed determined to stay from the very beginning, writing from Chicago, not long after his arrival, to Sibyl, who was still in London, "You ask whether I want to remain here? Yes, Darling, I want to remain in America. There's something incomplete about this city and its people that fascinates me; it seems to urge one on to completion. Everything seems still possible. The paralyzing finality of the European disaster is far away. I love the air of newness, of expectation around me. Yes, I want to stay." Moholy-Nagy letter to Sibyl Moholy-Nagy, August 8, 1937, reprinted in Sibyl Moholy-Nagy, *Moholy-Nagy: Experiment in Totality*, 145.

29 Moholy-Nagy to Dr. P. P. Keppel, Carnegie Corporation of New York, January 7, 1943, Institute of Design Collection, UIC.

30 Emphasis in the original. László Moholy-Nagy, *Vision in Motion* (Chicago: Paul Theobald, 1947), 64.

31 This technological anxiety was compounded by the development of far-more-devastating, atomic weapons (a key local role was played by Enrico Fermi's laboratory at the University of Chicago) and their deployment at Hiroshima and Nagasaki; Moholy-Nagy reacted by painting *Nuclear I* and *Nuclear II* in early 1946. See Timothy J. Garvey, "László Moholy-Nagy and Atomic Ambivalence in Postwar Chicago," *American Art* 14, no. 3 (Autumn 2000): 22–39.

32 A.B.D., "School of Design on Threshold of Fourth Year," *Chicago Sun*, January 3, 1942.

33 Moholy-Nagy, *Vision in Motion*, 10. *Vision in Motion* was largely written in 1944, as the war still raged on, although it was not published until 1947, after the war's conclusion and also posthumously.

34 Moholy-Nagy, *The New Bauhaus Catalogue* (Chicago: School of Design, 1937), 4, Institute of Design Collection, UIC.

35 See Robin Schuldenfrei, "The Irreproducibility of the Bauhaus Object," in *Bauhaus Construct: Fashioning Identity, Discourse, and Modernism*, ed. Jeffrey Saletnik and Robin Schuldenfrei (London: Routledge, 2009), 37–60. Exceptions are mainly objects produced in the years that Hannes Meyer led the school, after the departure of Moholy-Nagy: several textiles from the weaving workshop and the Bauhaus wallpapers were mass produced, not the iconic objects usually associated with the original Bauhaus today.

36 Moholy's "naive" use of this term (largely) preceded the advent of today's vast, for-profit military-industrial complex. See, for example, Moholy-Nagy to George Kepes, November 19, 1942, BHA. The Hungarian Kepes was born with the first name "György," but (presumably as an act of assimilation) he used the German form of his name, "Georg," for the period of his Berlin years, then "George" during his initial years in America, later reverting back to "Gyorgy" but without the umlaut. His name is cited throughout this chapter in accordance with how it appears in the original source quoted.

37 For images and short descriptions of these projects, see box 23, vol. 7, Institute of Design Records, IIT.

38 Moholy-Nagy to Walter B. Kirner, National Defense Research Committee, January 7, 1944, BHA.

39 Betty Prosser, "Design for Wartime Living and When Peace Comes," 1943, newspaper clipping of unidentified source, Institute of Design Collection, UIC.

40 László Moholy-Nagy, "Modern Designs from Chicago," *Modern Plastics*, December 1942; reprinted in *Timber of Canada*, February 1943, 19.

41 "New Slant on New Product Planning: How Outside Help, from Private Research Groups and Schools, Can Ease War Plant Job of Finding Products for Tomorrow, Give Designers a New 'Lift,'" *Modern Industry*, June 15, 1943, 46–47. War Production Board (WPB) Limitations Order L-49 set severe limits on the total amount of iron and steel available for the manufacture of furniture springs, see *Official Weekly Bulletin of the Office of War Information, Washington, D.C.* 3, no. 41 (October 13, 1942). Illustrating the seriousness with which the government viewed metal from beds for the war effort, the next *Bulletin* reported that used metal beds and bedsprings were being sold at inflated prices and ordered a review of all cases in which jobbers, manufacturers, and distributors might be violating the provisions of the general maximum price regulations for such items; *Bulletin* 3, no. 42 (October 20, 1942). On November 1, the production of metal springs for civilian use was banned altogether, and by December policies had been put in place to encourage the use of wooden springs, with the provision that furniture with wooden springs could not be approved for sale without demonstrable laboratory test reports showing that the new springs met standards prepared by the Office of Price Administration in cooperation with the National Bureau of Standards, *Bulletin* 3, no. 49 (December 8, 1942). The school's experiments with wooden springs began well in advance of these directives, putting it at a distinct advantage.

Similarly, the Museum of Modern Art in New York adapted its popular *Useful Objects* annual exhibition series to contend with wartime restrictions, opening *Useful Objects in Wartime* in 1942. On display were household objects featuring nonpriority materials with the Conservation and Substitution Branch of the War Production Board making recommendations to the museum about possible inclusions and omissions. No metal objects were selected for display, which relied heavily on glass and ceramic objects, while featuring some unusual materials, such as a cornhusk doormat. The museum's *Bulletin* featured images of common household objects such as steel ladles and Bakelite dishes with a large "X" struck through them, noting for which sectors of war production such materials were being reserved—for example, Lucite and Plexiglas for airplane construction and nylon for parachutes. Also included in the exhibition were objects designed in response to requests by men and women in the army and navy and supplies necessary for civilian defense. See "Useful Objects in Wartime," *Bulletin of the Museum of Modern Art* 10, no. 2 (December 1942–January 1943): 1–21. See also Mary Anne Staniszewski, *The Power of Display: A History of Exhibition Installations at the Museum of Modern Art* (Cambridge, MA: MIT Press, 1998), especially 209–35.

42 "New Slant on New Product Planning," 46–47.

43 "'Sleep like a Log' on New Wood Springs," *Bruce Magazine*, May–June 1943, Institute of Design Records, IIT.

44 Moholy-Nagy, "Modern Designs from Chicago," reprinted in *Timber of Canada*, February 1943, 20.

45 "Wooden Springs," *Business Week*, October 31, 1942.

46 "New Slant on New Product Planning," 46–47.

47 Moholy-Nagy to Nikolaus Pevsner, March 18, 1943, BHA. The by-now long-standing idea of promoting modern materials for furniture to replace stuffed upholstered furniture—a concept that modern architects had promoted vigorously in 1920s Europe—got renewed currency in Moholy-Nagy's Chicago context, where the modern plywood, Lucite, and metal chairs being designed at the school were introduced to a midwestern audience, many of whom would not have been familiar with the earlier European developments.

48 "Wooden Springs."

49 Moholy-Nagy to Kepes, November 19, 1942, BHA.

50 "The New Springs," 34–35, undated, unidentified article, Institute of Design Records, IIT.

51 Moholy-Nagy's ideas may have directly influenced Charles Eames; according to R. Craig Miller, during the time that Eames was teaching design at Cranbrook (September 1939–June 1941) and simultaneously working in the Saarinen office, he often went to Chicago on weekends to consult with Moholy-Nagy. See Miller, "Interior Design and Furniture," in *Design in America: The Cranbrook Vision, 1925–1950* (New York: Abrams, in association with the Detroit Institute of Arts and the Metropolitan Museum of Art, 1983), 109. In comparison to the School of Design, Cranbrook did not offer comprehensive work in industrial design and in the late 1930s and early war years had considerable difficulty in maintaining a design department; for a period during the war, the department was closed (1943–44). Likewise, the Metalcraft Department was suspended for most of the duration of the war, because of shortages.

52 "The College in a World at War," *Black Mountain College Newsletter* (November 1942): 4–5.

53 "New Slant on New Product Planning," 46–47.

54 "Design for Wartime Living and When Peace Comes."

55 Findeli, "Design Education and Industry," 100.

56 Walter Paepcke to Donald M. Nelson, War Production Board, February 3, 1944, Institute of Design Collection, UIC.

57 Moholy-Nagy, "Modern Designs from Chicago," 20.

58 See, for example, "Industrial Design: New Forms for Postwar Hardware," 51–53, unidentified journal, Institute of Design Records, IIT. The article, which features prototypes being developed at the school, notes, "War production already hums twenty-four hours a day in many plants, and we are scheduled to reach total conversion next June. This means that re-tooling will follow when the war ends, bringing with it sweeping changes in the accustomed forms of all our manufactured products" (51).

59 Al Bernsohn, "The New Wood That Bends," April 1941, 23, unidentified journal, Institute of Design Records, IIT.

60 Emery Hutchison, "Stories of the Day," *Chicago Daily News*, June 28, 1944.

61 School of Design, brochure, *National Defense Courses* (Chicago: School of Design, 1942), Institute of Design Collection, UIC.

62 School of Design, brochure, *Summer Session 1942* (Chicago: School of Design, 1942), Institute of Design Collection, UIC.

63 Moholy-Nagy to P. P. Keppel, Carnegie Corporation of New York, January 7, 1943, Institute of Design Collection, UIC. In the fall of 1942, Moholy-Nagy could report that the school had 206 students, of which 134 were in the camouflage course. Moholy-Nagy to Robert J. Wolff, October 6, 1942, BHA.

64 Ibid.

65 School of Design, brochure, *Summer Session 1943* (Chicago: School of Design, 1943), Institute of Design Collection, UIC.

66 School of Design, brochure, *Day and Evening Classes 1943–1944* (Chicago: School of Design, 1943), Institute of Design Collection, UIC.

67 As Moholy-Nagy explained in a letter to P. P. Keppel, Carnegie Corporation of New York, January 7, 1943, Institute of Design Collection, UIC.

68 School of Design, *Report on Public Relations Activities* (Chicago: School of Design, February 6, 1945), 1–2, Institute of Design Collection, UIC.

69 School of Design, brochure, *Academic Year 1942-1943* (Chicago: School of Design, 1942), Institute of Design Collection, UIC.

70 School of Design, brochures, *Summer Session 1943* and *Photo Classes 1943* (Chicago: School of Design, 1943), Institute of Design Collection, UIC.

71 For these posters and others, see box 25, vol. 9, tab D, Institute of Design Records, IIT.

72 This was awarded by the Society of Typographic Arts. Raymond Heer, secretary, Society of Typographic Arts to George Kepes, December 22, 1942, Gyorgy Kepes Papers, Archives of American Art, Smithsonian Institution, Washington, DC.

73 Paper given by Moholy-Nagy at the 1943 annual meeting of the American Psychiatric Association. Moholy-Nagy, "New Approach to Occupational Therapy," 1943, 1–9, Institute of Design Collection, UIC. Organizations across the United States, including other art-related cultural institutions, also began to address this need—specifically the potential for artists, the arts generally, and museums to aid in the recovery process. For example, an exhibition at the Museum of Modern Art in New York, *The Arts in Therapy* (1943), looked to the potential role of the crafts in occupational therapy and the psychiatric use of media such as painting, sculpture, and drawing in therapy. The museum sponsored a contest for objects and projects of therapeutic and recreational value; second prize was awarded to School of Design members Juliet Kepes (wife of Gyorgy Kepes) and Marli Ehrman (head of the textile workshop) for a multitextured, multisensory cloth children's book. See "The Arts in Therapy," *Bulletin of the Museum of Modern Art* 10, no. 3 (February 1943): 1–24.

74 See William Leuchtenberg, *A Troubled Feast* (Boston: Little, Brown, 1973), 104; cited by Cohen.

75 Moholy-Nagy, "Orientation Course in Occupational Therapy," 1, Institute of Design Collection, UIC.

76 Moholy-Nagy, "New Approach to Occupational Therapy," 3.

77 Moholy-Nagy, "Orientation Course in Occupational Therapy," 3.

78 Ibid., 4.

79 John Craig, "Stories of the Day," *Chicago Daily News*, February 26, 1943.

80 Sibyl Moholy-Nagy, *Moholy-Nagy: Experiment in Totality*, 185.

81 The school offered its supporters, the "Friends of the School of Design" free entrance to this lecture series. Letter from Moholy-Nagy to Friends of the School of Design, 27 September 1943, Walter Gropius Papers, Harvard.

82 School of Design, *Summer Session 1943* Brochure.

83 Moholy-Nagy, "New Approach to Occupational Therapy," 1.

84 Ibid., 4.

85 See especially chapters 1 and 2 of Jeffrey Saletnik, "Pedagogy, Modernism, and Medium Specificity: The Bauhaus and John Cage" (PhD diss., University of Chicago, 2009), 18–121.

86 School of Design, brochure, *National Defense Courses 1942* (Chicago: School of Design, 1942), Institute of Design Collection, UIC. Another example of the school's work with local officials and government bodies was an informational booklet on camouflage that was produced by the course as a WPA (Works Progress Administration) activity, sponsored by the Chicago Metropolitan Area Office of Civilian Defense. See "Selected List of References on Camouflage," November 1942, Institute of Design Records, IIT. The School of Design was not the only school to offer such a course; during the war years, institutions of higher education offered courses of instruction on camouflage from Paris to Burma as well as across the United States. See chap. 6, "Camouflage, or the Temptation of the Invisible," in Jean-Louis Cohen, *Architecture in Uniform,* 187–219, especially therein "Didactics of Camouflage, from Chicago to Brooklyn," 195–201.

87 Moholy-Nagy to Walter Paepcke, March 18, 1942, Institute of Design Collection, UIC; and Moholy-Nagy to George Kepes, November 19, 1942, BHA. During this period, Moholy-Nagy noted that he was also being apprised by officials of the structure of similar courses being organized at Pratt Institute in New York.

88 Kepes underwent eighty-five hours of specialized training from June 22 to July 4, 1942. See Certificate, Engineer School, Fort Belvoir, Virginia, Gyorgy Kepes Papers, Archives of American Art, Smithsonian Institution, Washington, DC.

89 School of Design, brochures, *Summer Session 1943* and *Principles of Camouflage* (Chicago: School of Design, 1943), Institute of Design Collection, UIC.

90 School of Design, *Principles of Camouflage*.

91 Including Myron Kozman, Robert Preusser, and Jesse Reichek. John L. Scott, with László Moholy-Nagy and Gyorgy Kepes, "A Bird's-Eye View of Camouflage," *Civilian Defense* (July–August 1942): 10.

92 George Kepes, "Introductory Lecture for the Camouflage Course" (lecture summary, School of Design in Chicago, September 16, 1942), 1–4, Institute of Design Collection, UIC.

93 Thus the students were apprised of the most up-to-date aspects of camouflage concealment vis-à-vis aerial bombardment—the relationship of altitude, speed, distance, and angle to the time of bomb release, and, especially, the role of visibility of target—and the various means of obscurement that had come into use: namely, artificial light patterns, blink lights, mercury vapor, false fires, mirror devices, and other forms of light projection. "Outline of the Camouflage Course at the School of Design in Chicago, 1941–1942," 3–4, Institute of Design Collection, UIC.

94 Ibid.

95 Kepes, "Introductory Lecture for the Camouflage Course," 1.

96 "Outline of the Camouflage Course at the School of Design in Chicago, 1941–1942," 1.

97 M. Seklemian, "A Study of the Principles of Camouflage Conducted at the School of Design Chicago," September 1942–January 1943, Institute of Design Records, IIT.

98 Ibid.

99 "Kelly and Army Plan Hiding of City from Foe," *Chicago Daily News*, May 8, 1942.

100 Ibid.

101 Donald S. Vogel to George J. Mavigliano, September 2, 1983, in Mavigliano, "The Chicago Design Workshop: 1939–1943," *Journal of Decorative and Propaganda Arts* 6 (Autumn 1987): 42.

102 "Kelly and Army Plan Hiding of City from Foe." Moholy-Nagy also noted, "Germany is reputed to have spent $1,000,000 in camouflaging the Fokker aircraft factory at Amsterdam alone. Chicago, of course, has some special problems of camouflage. There is the lake, which like a sore thumb sticks out and points to the city and to its largest industrial arm, the steel mills. Then there is the river, like a road sign. And the many beautiful parks, all good landmarks for fliers."

103 John L. Scott, with László Moholy-Nagy and Gyorgy Kepes, "Civilian Camouflage Goes into Action," *Civilian Defense* 1, no. 2 (June 1942): 8.

104 Prompted by precisely this wartime difficulty of camouflaging cities, fear of aerial bombardment, and later the atom bomb, the decentralization of the city became an important aspect in postwar planning, impacting the location and shape of communities, industrial dispersion, and centers of knowledge and science. See, for example, Peter Galison, "War against the Center," *Grey Room* 4 (Summer 2001): 5–33; David Monteyne, *Fallout Shelter: Designing for Civil Defense in the Cold War* (Minneapolis: University of Minnesota Press, 2011); Jennifer S. Light, *From Warfare to Welfare: Defense Intellectuals and Urban Problems in Cold War America* (Baltimore, MD: Johns Hopkins University Press, 2003); Matthew Farish, "Disaster and Decentralization: American Cities and the Cold War," *Cultural Geographies* 10, no. 3 (2003): 125–48; and Margaret Pugh O'Mara, *Cities of Knowledge: Cold War Science and the Search for the Next Silicon Valley* (Princeton, NJ: Princeton University Press, 2004).

105 Other war-focused exhibitions and art-related activities were mounted across wartime America; for example, the Museum of Modern Art in New York presented an extensive series of exhibitions including *Britain at War* (1941), *Art in War* (1942), *Road to Victory* (1942), and *Camouflage for Civilian Defense* (1942), for which a second version was also prepared for touring in 1942–43. The museum sponsored competitions, placing a selection of the entries on display, including the photography contest *Image of Freedom* (1941) and three poster competitions (former Bauhaus member Xanti Schawinsky's poster was among the winners): *National Defense Posters* (1941), *United Hemisphere Posters* (1942), and *National War Posters* (1942). A roster of circulating wartime exhibitions that traveled to ninety-three cities across America was also developed in this period; see "The Museum and the War," *Bulletin of the Museum of Modern Art* 10, no. 1 (October–November 1942): 3–19.

106 Sibyl Moholy-Nagy, *Moholy-Nagy: Experiment in Totality*, 184.

107 *War Art* press release, Renaissance Society at the University of Chicago Records, Archives of American Art, Smithsonian Institution, Washington DC (hereafter Renaissance Society Records, Smithsonian).

108 *War Art* (Chicago: Renaissance Society, 1942), n.p. An example of this small exhibition catalog is available in the Renaissance Society Records, Smithsonian; in the Institute of Design Collection, UIC; and Institute of Design Records, IIT.

109 *War Art* press release, Renaissance Society Records, Smithsonian.

110 For example, according to the *War Art* press release, the "visual education charts" for teaching camouflage and mechanical skills.

111 *War Art* press release, Renaissance Society Records, Smithsonian.

112 Also restricted was camouflage for ordnance operations; three-dimensional illuminated panels that showed radio and weather charts; and specially designed furniture such as designs for officers' lounges and a servicemen's recreation center. See curatorial files, Renaissance Society.

113 *War Art* (Chicago: Renaissance Society, 1942), n.p.

114 Ibid.

115 For a complete list of the skills taught as well as general aims, see the original 1937 school catalog, Moholy-Nagy, *The New Bauhaus Catalogue*, Institute of Design Collection, UIC.

116 Ibid., 4.

117 Moholy-Nagy to F. J. Kelly, executive director, Wartime Commission, US Office of Education, March 13, 1942, Institute of Design Collection, UIC.

118 Armed with a letter of introduction from mutual educator and colleague Charles Morris, Moholy-Nagy met with John Dewey in November 1938 in New York; at that meeting Dewey gave him his recently published book *Experience and Education*. Dewey was among the academics and intellectuals, such as Gropius and Alfred H. Barr, that Moholy-Nagy had enlisted to support his school. Dewey's 1934 *Art as Experience*, particularly his belief in the *process* of the development of a work of art as an *experience*, rather than simply that the resulting work of art itself was the main object, likely would have influenced, and dove-tailed with, Moholy-Nagy's own educational philosophies, particularly the first year Basic Course. *Art as Experience* was a required text of the Product Design workshop, and Moholy-Nagy refers to Dewey's practices directly in *Vision in Motion*. See Alain Findeli, "Moholy-Nagy's Design Pedagogy in Chicago (1937–46)," *Design Issues* 7, no. 1 (Autumn 1990): 4–19, especially 13–15.

119 Moholy-Nagy, "Relating the Parts to the Whole," 6.

120 Moholy-Nagy quoted by Ruth Green Harris, "The New Bauhaus: A Program for Art Education," *New York Times*, May 29, 1938.

121 Moholy-Nagy quoted by Reed Hynds, "Blueprint for the Post-War World," *St. Louis Star-Times*, January 22, 1942.

122 László Moholy-Nagy, "The Task of This Generation: Reintegration of Art into Daily Life," *Department of Art Education N.E.A. Bulletin*, 1944, n.p. (2), offprint, Institute of Design Records, IIT.

123 Moholy-Nagy to P. P. Keppel, Carnegie Corporation of New

York, January 7, 1943, Institute of Design Collection, UIC. Moholy-Nagy would continue to be disturbed by humans' injurious power. For example, for a discussion of Moholy-Nagy's concerns about the destructive power of nuclear energy following the dropping of the atom bomb on Hiroshima and his own 1945–46 radiation treatments for leukemia, including a thorough discussion of his 1946 paintings *Nuclear I* and *Nuclear II*, see Timothy J. Garvey, "László Moholy-Nagy and Atomic Ambivalence in Postwar Chicago," 22–39.

124 László Moholy-Nagy, "Design Potentialities" (1943), in *New Architecture and City Planning*, ed. Paul Zucker (New York: Philosophical Library, 1944), 686–87.

125 Moholy-Nagy, "Relating the Parts to the Whole," 6. For a discussion of Moholy-Nagy's pedagogical aims at the new Bauhaus – including the conviction that the school should offer an education combining the humanistic and technical spheres that would emphasize the integration of the designer into society – as well as his belief that the designer could bring an integrated, humanistic element (including a biologically necessary "organic design") into a technologically mediated new vision, see also Reinhold Martin, *The Organizational Complex: Architecture, Media, and Corporate Space* (Cambridge, MA: MIT Press, 2003), 53–58.

126 School of Design, brochure, *Day and Evening Classes 1943* (Chicago: School of Design, 1943), Institute of Design Collection, UIC.

127 Sibyl Moholy-Nagy, *Moholy-Nagy: Experiment in Totality*, 188.

128 Moholy-Nagy, "The Task of This Generation," n.p. (1). Emphasis in the original.

Chapter 5: Domesticating the Grid

1 On key German modern architects and connections between Berlin and Chicago, see Kathleen James-Chakraborty, "From Chicago to Berlin and Back Again," in *Chicago Makes Modern: How Creative Minds Changed Society*, ed. Mary Jane Jacob and Jacquelynn Baas (Chicago: University of Chicago Press, 2012), 91–109. On Hilberseimer, see K. Michael Hays, *Modernism and the Posthumanist Subject: The Architecture of Hannes Meyer and Ludwig Hilberseimer* (Cambridge, MA: MIT Press, 1992); Charles Waldheim, ed., *Case: Lafayette Park Detroit, Hilberseimer / Mies van der Rohe* (New York: Prestel Verlag, 2004); Waldheim, *Landscape as Urbanism: A General Theory* (Princeton, NJ: Princeton University Press, 2016); Scott Colman, "Organism and Artefact: The Ludwig Mies van der Rohe Circle and the Chicago School: Architecture, Planning, and Sociology circa 1944" (PhD diss., University of Sydney, 2006); Pier Vittorio Aureli, "Architecture for Barbarians: Ludwig Hilberseimer and the Rise of the Generic City," *AA Files* 63 (2011): 3–18; Ludwig Hilberseimer, *Metropolisarchitecture and Selected Essays*, ed. and trans. Richard Anderson (New York: GSAPP Books, 2012); Daniel Köhler, *The Mereological City: A Reading of the Works of Ludwig Hilberseimer* (Bielefeld: Transcript, 2016); Florian Strob, ed., *Architect of Letters: Reading Hilberseimer* (Basel: Birkhäuser Verlag, 2022); and Scott Colman, *Ludwig Hilberseimer: Reanimating Architecture and the City* (London: Bloomsbury, 2023).

2 Detlef Mertins, "Living in a Jungle: Mies, Organic Architecture, and the Art of City Building," in *Mies in America* ed. Phyllis Lambert (New York: Harry N. Abrams, 2001), 622.

3 Howard Dearstyne, "Mies van der Rohe's Teaching at the Bauhaus in Dessau," in *Our Bauhaus: Memories of Bauhaus People*, ed. Magdalena Droste and Boris Friedewald (Munich: Prestel, 2019), 80.

4 Ludwig Hilberseimer, *Groszstadtarchitektur* (Stuttgart: Hoffmann, 1927); in English, Hilberseimer, *Metropolisarchitecture*, trans. Anderson, 203.

5 My thinking on grids is indebted to a series of exchanges on the topic with Charles Waldheim and Thomas de Monchaux, whom I would like to thank.

6 I would argue that Hilberseimer was less interested in the economic potential of the grid than in its ordering principles to establish a system for architecture. Critics and historians have read Hilberseimer's work as engaging the economic wheels of modern urbanism, a confronting of the capitalist city, See for example Pier Vittorio Aureli, "In Hilberseimer's Footsteps," in Hilberseimer, *Metropolisarchitecture*, 334–63.

7 Ludwig Hilberseimer "Die Wohnung unserer Zeit," *Die Form* 6, no. 7 (July 15, 1931): 249–50.

8 Ludwig Hilberseimer, *Grosstadtbauten* (Hanover: Aposs-Verlag, 1925); trans. in *Metropolis Berlin: 1880–1940*, ed. Iain Boyd Whyte and David Frisby (Berkeley: University of California Press, 2012), 415.

9 See Terence Riley and Barry Bergdoll, *Mies in Berlin* (New York: Museum of Modern Art, 2001), 280–81.

10 See Robin Schuldenfrei, *Luxury and Modernism: Architecture and the Object in Germany 1900-1933* (Princeton, NJ: Princeton University Press, 2018).

11 Ludwig Hilberseimer, "Stadt- und Wohnungsbau," *Soziale Bauwirtschaft* 5, no. 14 (July 15, 1925): 188.

12 This often republished image was first published in 1925 in Hilberseimer, *Grosstadtbauten* (Aposs-Verlag), 11.

13 Ludwig Hilberseimer, "Kleinstwohnungen," *Bauhaus* 3, no. 2 (April–June 1929): 1.

14 Ibid., 2.

15 Ibid.

16 Ludwig Hilberseimer, "Über die Typisierung des Miethauses," *Die Form* 1 (1926): 338; trans. as Hilberseimer, "On Standardizing the Tenement Block" (1926), in *Metropolis Berlin*, 480. The translation of *Typisierung* into English as "standardizing" does not adequately capture the nuance and importance of the term in German, in which research and an iterative design process, including prototyping, would precede the production of the "standardized" design. The term "typification" is closer to the original German.

17 Ibid., 338–39; trans. in *Metropolis Berlin*, 480–81.

18 Ibid., 339; trans. in *Metropolis Berlin*, 481.

19 Ludwig Hilberseimer and Alfred Caldwell, typescript, "Design to Fit the Human Spirit: The Evolution of City Plans," November 7–8, 1944, p. 17, as part of a lecture series, The City: Organism and Artifact, Ludwig Karl Hilberseimer Papers, Ryerson and Burnham Archives, Art Institute of Chicago (hereafter AIC; unless otherwise specified, materials are from the Hilberseimer Papers, Ryerson and Burnham Archives, within AIC).

20 Ludwig Hilberseimer and Udo Rukser, "Amerikanische Architektur," *Kunst und Künstler* 18, no. 12 (1920): 537–45.

21 Hilberseimer, *Groszstadtarchitektur*; trans. in Hilberseimer, *Metropolisarchitecture*, trans. Anderson, 209–11.

22 Walther Rathenau, "Die schönste Stadt der Welt," *Die Zukunft* 26, no. 1 (1899); cited by Anderson, "Introduction," in Hilberseimer, *Metropolisarchitecture*, 64. Anderson notes that Rathenau uses "City" in English as shorthand for financial city, like City of London, to distinguish it from the rest of the city, *Stadt*.

23 Hilberseimer, *Groszstadtarchitektur*; trans. in Hilberseimer, *Metropolisarchitecture*, 167.

24 Ibid., 152.

25 Ibid., 39, fig. 75.

26 Ibid., 128.

27 Hilberseimer published a version of his boardinghouse, initially labeled "Hochhaus," in Hilberseimer, *Grosstadtbauten* (Aposs-Verlag), p. 21, fig. 18 and p. 27, fig. 30; and later, as "Boardinghouse" in Hilberseimer, *Groszstadtarchitektur* (Hoffmann ed.), p. 39, fig. 76 and p. 40, fig. 77.

28 Hilberseimer, *Grosstadtbauten* (Aposs-Verlag), 28.

29 K. Michael Hays, *Modernism and the Posthumanist Subject: The Architecture of Hannes Meyer and Ludwig Hilberseimer* (Cambridge, MA: MIT Press, 1992), 173.

30 Hilberseimer, *Groszstadtarchitektur*; trans. in Hilberseimer, *Metropolisarchitecture*, 149.

31 Ibid., 158.

32 Hilberseimer, *Grosstadtbauten* (Aposs-Verlag), 28.

33 Hilberseimer, *Groszstadtarchitektur*; trans. in Hilberseimer, *Metropolisarchitecture*, 142–43.

34 Ibid., 144–45.

35 Hilberseimer, "Der Wille zur Architektur," *Das Kunstblatt* 7 (1923): 133–40; trans. in Hilberseimer, *Metropolisarchitecture*, 287.

36 Ibid.

37 Hilberseimer, *Groszstadtarchitektur*; trans. in Hilberseimer, *Metropolisarchitecture*, 145.

38 Ibid.

39 Ibid., 146.

40 Ibid.

41 Ibid.

42 Ibid., 279.

43 Emphasis added. Translation amended. First published in Hilberseimer, *Grosstadtbauten* (Aposs-Verlag), 2, and subsequently republished in Hilberseimer, *Groszstadtarchitektur*; trans. in Hilberseimer, *Metropolisarchitecture*, 265.

44 Hilberseimer, "Der Wille zur Architektur," 133–40; trans. in Hilberseimer, *Metropolisarchitecture*, 287–88.

45 Ludwig Hilberseimer, "Grossstädtliche Kleinwohnungen," *Zentralblatt der Bauverwaltung* 32 (1929): 5.

46 Ludwig Hilberseimer, "The Art of Architecture" (1949), repr. in *In the Shadow of Mies: Ludwig Hilberseimer, Architect, Educator, and Urban Planner*, ed. Richard Pommer, David Spaeth, and Kevin Harrington (New York: Rizzoli, 1988), 99.

47 Hilberseimer, *Groszstadtarchitektur*; trans. in Hilberseimer, *Metropolisarchitecture*, 265.

48 Hilberseimer, "The Art of Architecture," 96.

49 Ibid., 99.

50 The model was begun in spring 1926 and first exhibited in May–October 1926 at the *Ausstellung der freie Wohlfahrtspflege* in Düsseldorf, subsequently in Stuttgart in May–June 1927. See Richard Pommer, "'More a Necropolis Than a Metropolis': Ludwig Hilberseimer's Highrise City and Modern City Planning," in *In the Shadow of Mies: Ludwig Hilberseimer, Architect, Educator, and Urban Planner*, ed. Richard Pommer, David Spaeth, and Kevin Harrington (New York: Rizzoli, 1988), 52n116.

51 Köhler, *The Mereological City*, 124.

52 Ibid., 123.

53 Pommer, "'More a Necropolis than a Metropolis,'" 39.

54 Hilberseimer, *Groszstadtarchitektur*; trans. in Hilberseimer, *Metropolisarchitecture*, 124.

55 Ibid., 169.

56 Ibid., 169–71.

57 Ibid.

58 Hilberseimer, "Die Wohnung unserer Zeit," 251.

59 See "10 geschossige laubenganghäuser mit wohnungen für 1, 2, und 4 betten, dachgarten und gemeinschaftsräumen und erdgeschoss – einfamilien – L – häuser mit 6 betten und kleinem garten," ca. early 1930s, photograph, AIC. See also Ludwig Hilberseimer, "Flachbau und Stadtraum," *Zentralblatt für Bauverwaltung* 51 (December 23, 1931): 773–78. He makes a similar assertion, but formulated more simply, in another 1931 article, noting that for a childless couple or single person a high-rise unit with a view is ideal, whereas for children the unit as a simple house with a gardern is preferable; see Hilberseimer, "Die Wohnung unserer Zeit," 251. See also Ludwig Hilberseimer, *Entfaltung einer Planungsidee* (Berlin: Ullstein, 1963), 24–26.

60 Hilberseimer, "Die kleinstwohnung im treppenlosen hause," *Bauhaus* 1 (January 1931): 2.

61 Hilberseimer explains his thinking about his mixed development proposals of the 1920s and 1930s in a later book, *Contemporary Architecture: Its Roots and Trends* (Chicago: Theobald, 1964), 152.

62 Ibid.

63 Ibid.

64 Ibid., 152–53.

65 Ibid., 153.

66 Ibid.

67 Although writing in 1940s Chicago, in this text, Hilberseimer is referring to his Mixed-Height Housing Development from around 1930. Ludwig Hilberseimer, *The New City: Principles of Planning* (Chicago: Theobald, 1944), 75.

68 Ibid., 100.

69 Ibid.

70 Ibid.

71 Ibid.

72 Ibid., 104.

73 Ibid., 192.

74 Ludwig Hilberseimer, "Chicago – Urbs in Horto," typescript, n.d., p. 5, AIC. This essay was written after 1949 because it cites Hilberseimer's *New Regional Pattern*, published in that year. An earlier version of this essay, titled simply "Urbs in Horto," was published in 1944 in Hilberseimer's *The New City*.

75 Hilberseimer, "Chicago – Urbs in Horto," 15.

76 Ibid., 14.

77 Hilberseimer, *Groszstadtarchitektur*; trans. in Hilberseimer, *Metropolisarchitecture*, 172.
78 Ibid., 175–76.
79 Ibid., 172.
80 Hilberseimer does not take individual credit for these designs; he situates his own designs as relating to the work of many of his contemporaries, such as Jan Wils, Victor Bourgeois, and J.J.P. Oud, among others. See Hilberseimer, *Groszstadtarchitektur*; trans. in Hilberseimer, *Metropolisarchitecture*, 173–76.
81 For a sketch of Hilberseimer's 1940s row house design project for Evanston, Illinois, see Christian Wolsdorff, ed., *Der vorbildliche Architekt: Mies van der Rohes Architekturunterricht 1930–1958 am Bauhaus u. in Chicago* (Berlin: Nicolai, 1986), 144.
82 Hilberseimer, *Groszstadtarchitektur*; trans. in Hilberseimer, *Metropolisarchitecture*, 169.
83 Noted by Anderson in Hilberseimer, *Metropolisarchitecture*, 314–15.
84 Hilberseimer, "Die kleinstwohnung im treppenlosen hause," 1–2.
85 Ibid., 1.
86 Ibid., 1–2. Original drawings, dated December 1930, are located in the collection of the Art Institute of Chicago.
87 See perspective, plan, and section drawings of the rounded roof house design in the collection of the Art Institute of Chicago.
88 Martin Wagner, *Das wachsende Haus: Ein Beitrag zur Lösung der städtischen Wohnungsfrage* (Berlin: Dt. Verl.-Haus Bong, 1932). A detailed section of Hilberseimer's Growing House, dated January 1932, is in the drawing collection of the Art Institute of Chicago.
89 Wagner, *Das wachsende Haus*, 72–75.
90 Ibid., 72.
91 Hilberseimer, "Über die Typisierung des Mietshauses," 338; trans. as Hilberseimer, "On Standardizing the Tenement Block," in *Metropolis Berlin*, 480.
92 For an in-depth examination of South Side planning and the complexities of Mies's plans for IIT vis-à-vis the urban subject and the urban fabric, the grid, canonical modernism, and postwar economics, see Sarah Whiting, "Bas-Relief Urbanism: Chicago's Figured Field," in *Mies in America*, ed. Phyllis Lambert (New York: Harry N. Abrams, 2001), 642–91.
93 See Hilberseimer, *Entfaltung einer Planungsidee*, 127, figs. 108, 109.
94 IIT proposed dormitory plans, July 9, 1947, AIC.
95 "Proposed $22,000,000 Campus with Student and Staff Housing Units," *Technometer*, April 1947, 1.
96 Hilberseimer, *The New City*, 74–75.
97 Ibid., 74–76.
98 On the McCormick House, see Barry Bergdoll, "Mies's McCormick House Revealed: New Views," in *Mies van der Rohe McCormick House*, ed. John McKinnon and Barry Bergdoll (Elmhurst, IL: Elmhurst Art Museum, 2018).
99 Detlef Mertins, *Mies* (New York: Phaidon, 2014), 367.
100 On the 50 × 50 House, see also Phyllis Lambert, "Space and Structure," in *Mies in America*, ed. Phyllis Lambert (New York: Harry N. Abrams, 2001), 455–61.
101 Philip Johnson, *Mies van der Rohe* (New York: Museum of Modern Art, 1947; rev. ed., 1978), 170.
102 Ibid., 178–79, and illustration pp. 180–81.
103 Ibid., 169.
104 "4 Glass-Steel Homes Planned near Elmhurst," *Chicago Sun Times*, May 22, 1955.
105 Hilberseimer, "Der Wille zur Architektur," 133–40; trans. in Hilberseimer, *Metropolisarchitecture*, 288.
106 *Grosstadtbauten* (Aposs-Verlag), 4; Hilberseimer, *Groszstadtarchitektur*; trans. in Hilberseimer, *Metropolisarchitecture*, 270.
107 Ludwig Hilberseimer, "City Architecture: The Trend toward Openness" (ca. 1960) repr. in Pommer et al., *In the Shadow of Mies*, 112.
108 Hilberseimer, *The New City*, 100.
109 Ibid.
110 For key insights into Hilberseimer's ideas on the urban in relation to landscape (agrarian urbanism), see Waldheim, *Landscape as Urbanism*.
111 Hilberseimer to Alfred Caldwell, November 27, 1940. Cited by Dennis Domer, "The Life of Alfred Caldwell," in *Alfred Caldwell: The Life and Work of a Prairie School Landscape Architect*, ed. Dennis Domer (Baltimore, MD: Johns Hopkins University Press, 1997), 35.
112 Ludwig Hilberseimer, "The Elements of City Planning," *Armour Engineering and Alumnus* (repr., Dec. 1940): 12.
113 Alfred Caldwell, interviewed in film *Creating Coummunity*, cited by Mertins, *Mies*, 416.
114 Emphasis in the original. Scott Colman, "Promoting the New City: Ludwig Hilberseimer at the Art Institute of Chicago, 1944," in *Exhibitions and the Development of Modern Planning Culture*, ed. Robert Freestone and Marco Amati (Farnham, UK: Ashgate, 2014), 123.
115 Hilberseimer, "City Architecture," 112.
116 As Charles Waldheim notes, Hilberseimer's "interest in adapting modern urbanism in the service of decentralized industry was fueled after 1945 by the equally compelling civil defense imperative toward decentralization in the atomic age." Waldheim, "Introduction: Landscape, Urban Order, and Structural Change," in *Case: Lafayette Park Detroit*, 24.
117 Hilberseimer, "Cities and Defense" (ca. 1945); repr. in Pommer et al., *In the Shadow of Mies*, 93.
118 Emphasis added. Alfred Caldwell, "Atomic Bombs and City Planning," *Journal of the American Institute of Architects* 4 (December 1945): 298–99; repr. in Domer, *Alfred Caldwell*, 178.
119 Ludwig Hilberseimer and Alfred Caldwell, typescript, "Design to Fit the Human Spirit: The Evolution of City Plans," November 7–8, 1944, p. 1, AIC. This was as part of lecture series titled "The City: Organism and Artifact."
120 Ibid., 2.
121 Hilberseimer, "Suggestions for a Microfilm of Planning in Chicago," typescript, n.d. (ca. 1950s), n.p. (p. 2), AIC.
122 Ibid.
123 Ibid., n.p. (p. 3).
124 Ibid.
125 Ralph Borsodi, "A Plan for the Decentralization of Chicago and Its Industries," typescript, lecture at the Congress on Decentralization, May 16–17, 1941, Chicago, p. 6, AIC.

126 Hilberseimer, "City Architecture," 102.
127 Hilberseimer and Caldwell, "Design to Fit the Human Spirit," 18.
128 Hilberseimer, *The New City*, 126–27.
129 Ibid.
130 Mies, transcript of interview with John Peter, 1955, Library of Congress, 14–15, cited by Waldheim, *Landscape as Urbanism*, 2.
131 Hilberseimer, *The New City*, 191.
132 Ibid.
133 Hilberseimer, "City Architecture," 112.
134 Ibid.
135 Ludwig Hilberseimer, "Denisity and Traffic," in *Planning and Architecture*, ed. Dennis Sharp (New York: George Wittenborn, 1967), 33.
136 On Evergreen, see AIC and Hilberseimer, *Entfaltung einer Planungsidee*, 120–21.
137 Robert E. Lewis, chairman, Evergreen Cooperative, to Hilberseimer, February 20, 1948, AIC.
138 Lewis to Hilberseimer, March 22, 1948, AIC.
139 Lewis to Hilberseimer, November 23, 1947, AIC.
140 Lewis to Hilberseimer, November 15, 1947, AIC.
141 Ibid.
142 Basic House specifications, p. 1, enclosed in Lewis to Hilberseimer, November 15, 1947, AIC.
143 Ibid.
144 Ibid., 2.
145 Ibid., 3.
146 Ibid., 2.
147 State Street Project, ca. 1950, AIC.
148 Hilberseimer, *The New City*, 147.
149 Ibid.
150 Ibid.
151 Hilberseimer and Caldwell, "Design to Fit the Human Spirit" (p. 4), AIC.
152 Ibid.
153 Ibid.
154 Ibid., 11.
155 Ibid.
156 Ibid.
157 Hilberseimer, *The New City*, 149.
158 Gratiot press release, February 1, 1956, AIC.
159 Ibid.
160 Ibid.

Chapter 6: Exigencies of Materializing Vision

1 Elaine de Kooning, "Albers Paints a Picture," *Art News* (November 1950): 40. The painting de Kooning describes, *Homage to the Square "A,"* is now in the collection of Mickey Cartin. See Jeannette Redensek, "*Farbenfabeln*: On the Origins and Development of the *Homage to the Square*," in *Josef Albers: Interaction*, ed. Heinz Liesbrock in collaboration with Ulrike Growe (New Haven, CT: Yale University Press, 2018), 180–81.
2 The centrality of vision (alternatively, "visual expression," or "direct seeing") in Albers's work and pedagogy has been discussed in detail by scholars to date. See, for example, Hal Foster, "The Bauhaus Idea in America," in *Albers and Moholy-Nagy: From the Bauhaus to the New World*, ed. Achim Borchardt-Hume (London: Tate Publishing, 2006), 92–110; Eva Díaz, "The Ethics of Perception: Josef Albers in the United States," *Art Bulletin* 90, no. 2 (2008): 260–85; and Jeffrey Saletnik, *Josef Albers, Late Modernism, and Pedagogic Form* (Chicago: University of Chicago Press, 2022).
3 On the Sommerfeld and Ullstein glass commissions, see chap. 2 of Jordan Troeller, "Scenes from the Archive: Photography, Objecthood, and the Bauhaus" (PhD diss., Harvard University, 2018), 133–202.
4 Josef Albers, "Zu meinen Glas-wandbildern," *A bis Z: Organ der Gruppe progressiver Künstler* 3 (February 1933): 117; trans. as "On My Glass Pictures," in *Josef Albers: Interaction*, ed. Heinz Liesbrock in collaboration with Ulrike Growe (New Haven, CT: Yale University Press, 2018), 67.
5 Josef Albers to Franz Perdekamp, Weimar [ca. March–April] 1921, Perdekamp Correspondence USA 1933–1951, Josef and Anni Albers Foundation, Bethany, CT (hereafter JAAF).
6 Josef Albers, Statement on *City* (1928), translation in *Jahresbericht 1960* of Zürcher Kunstgesellschaft, typescript, 1960, n.p. (p. 1), JAAF (unless otherwise specified, materials are from the Josef Albers Papers, within the JAAF).
7 Emphasis added. Albers, 1968, cited in *Josef Albers: Interaction*, ed. Heinz Liesbrock in collaboration with Ulrike Growe (New Haven, CT: Yale University Press, 2018), 78.
8 Josef Albers, "General Education and Art Education: Possessive or Productive," in *Search versus Re-Search: Three Lectures by Josef Albers at Trinity College, April 1965* (Hartford, CT, Trinity College Press, 1969), 9. Albers spoke of the commencement of a new era in teaching in which "visual perception" was defined as two distinct components – seeing and vision – which "will achieve proper recognition." Albers wrote about "conscious seeing," in an undated typescript, "Art Courses," for 1948–49 courses at Black Mountain College. Cited by Jeffrey Saletnik, "Pedagogic Objects: Josef Albers, Greenbergian Modernism, and the Bauhaus in America," in *Bauhaus Construct: Fashioning Identity, Discourse, and Modernism*, ed. Jeffrey Saletnik and Robin Schuldenfrei (London: Routledge, 2009), 96.
9 In his emphasis on "search" as opposed to "research" Albers sought to put the physical practice of seeing and other learning-by-doing before "research" or theoretical, received knowledge. See *Search versus Re-Search*.
10 Albers, "General Education and Art Education," 11.
11 Albers, emphasis in the original, in John H. Holloway, John A. Weil, and Josef Albers, "A Conversation with Josef Albers," *Leonardo* 3, no. 4 (October 1970): 459.
12 Albers, "General Education and Art Education," 10.
13 See Saletnik, "Pedagogic Objects," 83–102 and Díaz, "The Ethics of Perception," 260–85. See also Saletnik, *Josef Albers, Late Modernism, and Pedagogic Form*.
14 Josef Albers, interview with Margit Rowell, June 25, 1970, as quoted in Rowell, "On Albers's Color," *Artforum* 10, no. 5 (January 1972): 36.
15 As outlined in his key 1928 essay, "Teaching Form through Practice." See Josef Albers, "Werklicher Formunterricht," *Bauhaus*, nos. 2–3 (1928): 3–7, facsimile ed. and trans. as "Teaching Form through Practice," *Bauhaus Journal 1926–1931* (Zurich: Lars Müller Publishers in collaboration with

Bauhaus-Archive/Museum für Gestaltung, Berlin, 2019), 38–39.

16 Josef Albers, BBC interview, June 21, 1968, transcript, pp. 4–5, copy at JAAF.

17 Albers, "Teaching Form through Practice," 39.

18 Albers to Alfred Barr, MoMA, telegram, Black Mountain, NC to NYC, November 26, 1938, JAAF.

19 Albers, lecture version of "Teaching Form through Practice," 1928, published in *VI. Internationaler Kongress für Zeichnen, Kunstunterricht und Angewandte Kunst in Prag, 1928* (Prague, 1931) repr. and trans. in *AA Files* 67 (2013): 131. This version is slightly different from the earlier "Werklicher Formunterricht," published in the *Bauhaus* journal. In his sessions of the *Vorkurs*, László Moholy-Nagy also taught similar concepts, terming them *Faktur*, often transliterated as "facture"; structure (*Struktur*); and texture (*Textur*). See Robin Schuldenfrei, "Preliminary Objects for Modern Subjects: László Moholy-Nagy's Bauhaus Theory and Lucia Moholy's Photographic Representation," in *Object Lessons: The Bauhaus and Harvard*, ed. Laura Muir (New Haven, CT: Yale University Press, 2021), 96–114.

20 Frederick A. Horowitz, "Design," in Horowitz and Brenda Danilowitz, *Josef Albers: To Open Eyes; The Bauhaus, Black Mountain College, and Yale* (London: Phaidon, 2006), 130. As Horowitz writes, "By the mid-1940s, the exercise had pervaded the culture of the school.... Any unusual substance came to be labeled a '*matière*' – an unpalatable dinner, moldy leftovers, a pile of trash, or a chip of cow dung. Students had fun with concept and ... along with the humor came a new way of seeing, one that engendered the habit of responding to absolutely everything in visual terms" (130).

21 Albers, lecture version of "Teaching Form through Practice," *AA Files*, 131.

22 John Urbain, "Matière Studies –1946," *Black Mountain College: Sprouted Seeds, An Anthology of Personal Accounts*, ed. Mervin Lane (Knoxville: University of Tennessee Press, 1990), 157.

23 Ibid.

24 Ibid.

25 Eeva-Liisa Pelkonen, "Interacting with Albers," *AA Files* 67 (2013): 124.

26 Albers, "General Education and Art Education," 10.

27 Cited by Mary Emma Harris, "Josef Albers: Art Education at Black Mountain College," in *Josef Albers: A Retrospective* (New York: Solomon R. Guggenheim Foundation, 1988), 55.

28 Albers, interview with Margit Rowell, April 14, 1971, in Rowell, "On Albers's Color," 30.

29 Albers, as quoted by Jean Clay, "Albers: Josef's Coat of Many Colours," *Réalitiés* (March 1968): 67.

30 Hubert Damisch, "The Theoretical Eye," trans. Anthony Auerbach, *Journal of Art Historiography* 5 (December 1, 2011): 2.

31 Albers, "Statements of Content," Portfolio I, *Josef Albers: Formulation—Articulation*, with text by T. G. Rosenthal (London: Thames & Hudson, 2006), 25.

32 Albers, "General Education and Art Education," 10.

33 Nicholas Fox Weber, "The Artist as Alchemist," in *Josef Albers: A Retrospective*, 23.

34 On Albers's glass paintings, see "Josef Albers: Glasbilder," *Volksblatt* (Dessau), May 4, 1932, exhibition review, trans. as "At the Bauhaus: Glass Pictures by Josef Albers," by Jeannette Redensek, JAAF; Albers, "Zu meinen Glaswandbildern," *A bis Z: Organ der Gruppe progressiver Künstler*, 117; repr. as Albers, "On My Glass Wall Paintings," trans. in Achim Borchardt-Hume, ed., *Albers and Moholy-Nagy*, 155, and in *Josef Albers: Interaction*, 67; Josef Albers, untitled statement on the glass pictures, n.d. (1955 or later), Josef Albers Papers, vol. 2, Sterling Memorial Library, Manuscripts and Archives, Yale University, repr. as Albers, "A New Type of Glass Picture," in *Josef Albers: Glass, Color, and Light* (New York: Guggenheim Museum, 1994), 141–42; Paul Overy, "Josef Albers: Painting in the Light of Glass," *Burlington Magazine* 149, no. 1254 (September 1, 2007): 597–606; Brenda Danilowitz, "From Symbolism to Modernism: The Evolution of Josef Albers's Architectural Glass Works," in *Josef Albers: Vitraux, dessins, gravures, typographie, meubles*, ed. Oliver Barker (Paris: Hazan, 2008), 168–81; Brenda Danilowitz, "'Quite Charming, if a Bit Brutal': Josef Albers's Glass Assemblage," in *Bauhaus: A Conceptual Model*, ed. Bauhaus-Archiv Berlin/Museum für Gestaltung, Stiftung Bauhaus Dessau, and Klassik Stiftung Weimar (Ostfildern: Hatje Cantz, 2009), 94–96; Peter Nisbet, "Josef Albers Lattice Picture 1921" in *Bauhaus 1919-1933: Workshops for Modernity*, ed. Barry Bergdoll, Leah Dickerman (New York: Museum of Modern Art, 2009), 92–95; and Troeller, "Scenes from the Archive," 133–202.

35 Brenda Danilowitz, "Josef Albers: Exile and Émigré," in *Josef Albers: Interaction*, ed. Heinz Liesbrock in collaboration with Ulrike Growe (New Haven, CT: Yale University Press, 2018), 21.

36 Josef Albers, untitled statement on the glass pictures, n.d. (1955 or later), repr. as "A New Type of Glass Picture," in *Josef Albers: Glass, Color, and Light*, 141.

37 Josef Albers to Gottfried Heinersdorff (of firm Puhl und Wagner), June 14, 1927, Puhl and Wagner files, JAAF.

38 Albers to Heinersdorff, February 9, 1928, Puhl and Wagner files, JAAF.

39 Josef Albers, statement on *City* (1928), trans. in *Jahresbericht 1960*, n.p. (p. 1).

40 Josef Albers, untitled typescript, n.d. [ca. 1931], 1 page, JAAF.

41 Ibid.

42 Albers, untitled statement on the glass pictures, n.d., repr. as "A New Type of Glass Picture," 141.

43 Ibid.

44 Ibid.

45 Weber, "The Artist as Alchemist," in *Josef Albers: A Retrospective*, 28.

46 "Josef Albers: Glasbilder," *Volksblatt* (Dessau), May 4, 1932, JAAF.

47 Weber, "The Artist as Alchemist," in *Josef Albers: A Retrospective*, 23.

48 Albers, statement on *City* (1928), trans. in *Jahresbericht 1960*, n.p. (p. 2).

49 Albers, untitled statement on the glass pictures, n.d., repr. as "A New Type of Glass Picture," 141.

50 *Josef Albers: Glass, Color, and Light*, cat. entry 43.

51 Josef Albers to Franz Perdekamp, June 10, 1933, Berlin, original letter, in German, with Perdekamp heirs in Reckling-

52 Edward M. M. Warburg to Theodor Dreier, September 26, 1933, Black Mountain College. Original letter in Western Regional Archives, Asheville, NC, Dreier BMC Collection; reproduced in *Josef Albers: Interaction*, ed. Heinz Liesbrock in collaboration with Ulrike Growe (New Haven, CT: Yale University Press, 2018), 106.

[Note 51 continued from previous page:] hausen; copy at the JAAF. Trans. and reproduced in *Josef Albers: Interaction*, ed. Heinz Liesbrock in collaboration with Ulrike Growe (New Haven, CT: Yale University Press, 2018), 105.

53 The two works varied slightly; one version of *City*, measuring 11 × 22⅛ inches, is in the collection of Kunsthaus Zürich (Inv. Nr. 1960/8); a slightly larger, damaged version, measuring 13 × 21¼ inches, is in the collection of the JAAF (Inv. Nr. GL-14).

54 Josef Albers to the director of customs, Treasury Department, Washington, DC, February 12, 1934, p. 2, JAAF.

55 Ibid, 1.

56 Ibid., 1–2.

57 List of damaged glass paintings, January 25, 1934, JAAF.

58 Albers to the director of customs, February 12, 1934, p. 2, JAAF.

59 Ibid. Also cited by Nicholas Fox Weber, "A New Light: Josef Albers's Work in Glass," in *Josef Albers: Glass, Color, and Light*, 13; and Danilowitz, "Josef Albers: Exile and Émigré," 19.

60 Josef Albers to the director of customs, February 12, 1934, p. 2, JAAF.

61 James H. Moyle to Thad Page, secretary to Honorable Josiah W. Bailey, US Senate, July 7, 1934, Black Mountain College Archives, Western Regional Archives, North Carolina State Archives, Asheville. Cited by Danilowitz, "Josef Albers: Exile and Émigré," 19.

62 Josef Albers to Franz Perdekamp, May 2, 1948, Perdekamp Correspondence USA 1933–1951, JAAF.

63 Jeannette Redensek, "On Josef Albers' Painting Materials and Techniques," in *Josef Albers: Minimal Means, Maximum Effect* (Madrid: Fundación Juan March, 2014), 27.

64 For an in-depth discussion of this work, see Jeffrey Saletnik, "*America*: Josef Albers's Brick Relief at Harvard," in *Object Lessons: The Bauhaus and Harvard*, ed. Laura Muir (New Haven, CT: Yale University Press, 2021), 173–88.

65 Josef Albers, in Eleanor Bittermann, *Art in Modern Architecture* (New York: Reinhold Publishing, 1952), 148.

66 Ibid., 148–49.

67 Albers to Walter Gropius, January 2, 1950, Architects Collaborative Collection, MIT Museum, Cambridge, MA, cited by Saletnik, "*America*," 179.

68 Saletnik, "*America*," 179.

69 For the *Homage to the Square* series, see especially Redensek, "*Farbenfabeln*," 172–91. As Redensek summarizes, "The *Homages* are about color, about the mutability of color relationships, and about the malleability of subjective perceptions of color. The *quantity* of *Homages* created is part of the meaning of the work; the careful *crafting* of the *Homages* is part of the meaning of the work. The *Homages* are not principally about squares, nested or otherwise, but the artist's decision to make squares is part of the meaning of the work" (173).

70 For a range of paintings from this period, see *Anni et Josef Albers: L'art et la vie* (Paris: Musée d'Art Moderne de Paris–Paris Musées, 2021), 101–13, 139–47. For an authoritative description of Albers's working methods and materials, see Redensek, "On Josef Albers' Painting Materials and Techniques," 21–41. According to Redensek, Masonite was "a trademark of one particular manufacturer. The process for producing Masonite boards was invented in 1924. Wet wood pulp was forced down onto a fine mesh screen under great pressure. The result was a panel with a 'smooth' side from the weight of the steel plate, and a 'rough' side from the impression of the screen. Wood fiberboards could be purchased in varying thicknesses and sizes from commercial lumberyards" (27).

71 On the influence of visits to Mexico on Albers's oeuvre, see, for example, Heinz Liesbrock, "The Promised Land of Abstract Art: Josef Albers in Mexico," in *Josef Albers: Interaction*, ed. Heinz Liesbrock in collaboration with Ulrike Growe (New Haven, CT: Yale University Press, 2018), 140–46.

72 Josef Albers, *Albers* (Cincinnati, OH: Cincinnati Art Museum, 1949), n.p.

73 Patricia Sherwin Garland, "Josef Albers: His Paintings, Their Materials, Technique, and Treatment," *Journal of the American Institute for Conservation* 22, no. 2 (Spring 1983): 63. Jeannette Redensek notes that Albers, in addition to Masonite, used Insulite, Scantex, and possibly Celotex, as well as TEK boards and aluminum panels from the Aluminum Canvas Corporation, which were primed with a white paint softly textured like canvas. See Redensek, "*Farbenfabeln*," 178.

74 Redensek, "On Josef Albers' Painting Materials and Techniques," 27.

75 Garland, "Josef Albers: His Paintings, Their Materials, Technique, and Treatment," 63.

76 Ibid.

77 Ibid., 63–64.

78 Ibid., 63.

79 Díaz, "The Ethics of Perception," 275.

80 Donald Judd, in *Josef Albers* (Cologne: Distel-Verlag, 1991), 23–24.

81 Redensek, "On Josef Albers' Painting Materials and Techniques," 38.

82 Damisch, "The Theoretical Eye," 5.

83 Albers quoted by Clay, "Albers: Josef's Coat of Many Colours," 64.

84 Anni Albers, interview by Richard Polsky (conducted for the American Craftspeople Oral History Project), January 11, 1985, pp. 49–51, JAAF.

85 Rowell, "On Albers's Color," 27.

86 Redensek, "*Farbenfabeln*," 187.

87 Albers, "Art Courses," undated typescript for 1948–49 courses at Black Mountain College, JAAF. Cited by Saletnik, "Pedagogic Objects," 96.

88 Lambert Einhaus [pseudonym for Albert Schulze Vellinghausen], "Hin zum 'abstrakten Expressionismus,'" *Frankfurter Allgemeine Zeitung*, February 11, 1957, 9. Cited and trans. in Danilowitz, "Josef Albers: Exile and Émigré," 27.

89 Díaz, "The Ethics of Perception," 273.

90 Rowell, "On Albers's Color," 27.

91 Jeannette Redensek, "Josef Albers: *Structural Constellation*

and *Variant of Related*," in *Bauhaus and America: Experiments in Light and Movement*, ed. Hermann Arnhold (Bielefeld: Kerber Verlag, 2018), 155. The plastic laminate used by Albers was manufactured under the trade name Vinylite in the United States and Resopal in Germany, and Albers's works "comprised a thin layer of white plastic sandwiched between two equally thin layers of black plastic. Vinylite was customarily used in signage, name plates, and machine panels" (155).

92 Redensek describes the fabrication process: "Albers supplied a master drawing to a machine shop, and the mechanics made a template from wood or Lucite. The template was placed on a pantograph connected to a flatbed drill press. As the pantograph traced the lines in the template, the drill bits cut shallow lines into the sheet of laminate on the flatbed, revealing the white inner layer beneath the black surface. The drill heads were changed out for varying widths, from hair-thin to about one sixteenth of an inch wide. When finished the incised laminate was mounted onto a slab of thick black-painted plywood, unframed and finished with an inverse beveled edge on the reverse so that the picture plane floated two to three centimeters in front of the wall." Redensek, "Josef Albers: *Structural Constellation* and *Variant of Related*," 155.

93 Josef Albers to Anni Albers, October 30, 1949, JAAF, cited by Horowitz and Danilowitz, *Josef Albers: To Open Eyes*, 45.

94 Brenda Danilowitz, *The Prints of Josef Albers: A Catalogue Raisonné, 1915–1976* (New York: Hudson Hills Press, 2001), 21.

95 Josef Albers to Franz Perdekamp, April 27, 1950, Perdekamp Correspondence USA 1933–1951, JAAF.

96 Brenda Danilowitz in *Josef Albers* (Cologne: Distel Verlag, 1991), 31.

97 Albers, quoted in Douglas Davis, "Man of a Thousand Squares," *Newsweek*, January 18, 1971, 77, 78, cited by Horowitz and Danilowitz, *Josef Albers: To Open Eyes*, 89.

98 Danilowitz in *Josef Albers* (Cologne: Distel Verlag, 1991), 32.

99 Albers, "General Education and Art Education," 10.

Chapter 7: Anni Albers's Design Theory and Its Objects

1 The seminal work situating the Bauhaus weaving workshop in the Bauhaus's larger discursive field of media and medium specificity, writing, and modern craft practice is T'ai Smith, *Bauhaus Weaving Theory: From Feminine Craft to Mode of Design* (Minneapolis: University of Minnesota Press, 2104). See especially her contextualization of Bauhaus weavers' writings on their craft—and the workshop's evolving modernist theory of weaving—in light of four other media: painting, architecture, photography, and patents.

2 Judith Pearlman, notes from interview with Anni Albers, May 22, 1982, p. 3, Anni Albers Papers, Josef and Anni Albers Foundation (hereafter JAAF; unless otherwise specified, materials are from the Anni Albers Papers, within the JAAF).

3 Albers quoted in Nicholas Fox Weber, *Anni and Josef Albers: Equal and Unequal* (London: Phaidon, 2020), 87. Josef Albers would also carefully photograph the Statue of Liberty from the boat; for a reproduction, see ibid., 188.

4 Anni Albers, interview by Maximilian Schell, December 16, 1989, tape 2, p. 5, JAAF.

5 Ibid., 4.

6 Ibid.

7 Ibid.

8 Hermann Ullstein, "We Blundered Hitler into Power," *Saturday Evening Post*, July 13, 1940. In exile in New York City, Ullstein would go on to write the history of the publishing house from its founding until its takeover by the Nazis, see Ullstein, *The Rise and Fall of the House of Ullstein* (New York: Simon and Schuster, 1943).

9 Anni Albers, interview by Richard Polsky (conducted for the American Craftspeople Oral History Project), January 11, 1985, pp. 35–36, JAAF.

10 Albers, interview by Maximilian Schell, 4.

11 Albers, interview by Richard Polsky, 34.

12 Ibid.

13 Josef Albers to the director of customs, Treasury Department, Washington, DC, February 12, 1934, p. 1, Josef Albers Papers, JAAF.

14 Ibid.

15 Anni and Josef Albers's travels to, and interest in, Latin America has been discussed in depth by scholars, including Virginia Gardner Troy, "L'art précolombien, transmetteur de sens," in *Anni et Josef Albers: L'art et la vie* (Paris: Éditions Paris Musées, 2021), 86–97; María Minera, "Discovering Monte Albán," in *Anni Albers*, ed. Ann Coxon, Briony Fer, and Maria Müller-Schareck (London: Tate, 2018), 74–85; Nicholas Fox Weber, ed., *A Beautiful Confluence: Anni and Josef Albers and the Latin American World* (Bethany, CT: Josef and Anni Albers Foundation, 2015); *Anni y Josef Albers: Viaje por Latinoamerica* (Madrid: Museo Nacional Centro de Arte Reina Sofía, 2006); and Virginia Gardner Troy, *Anni Albers and Ancient American Textiles: From Bauhaus to Black Mountain* (London: Ashgate, 2002).

16 Neil Welliver, "A Conversation with Anni Albers," *Craft Horizons* (July–August 1965), offprint, n.p. (p. 8).

17 Albers, interview by Maximilian Schell, 5.

18 "Tentative Proposals Regarding the College and Its Relation to the War," n.d., typescript, 2 pp., Josef Albers Papers, JAAF.

19 Ibid., 2.

20 Ibid., 1.

21 Ibid., 2.

22 Untitled typescript [The war confronts the American colleges and universities with tremendous problems], n.d., (ca. December 1941–early 1942), p. 2, Josef Albers Papers, JAAF.

23 Ibid.

24 Ibid., 5.

25 "Liberal Education Today as a Tool of War," *Black Mountain College Bulletin* 1, no. 2 (January 1943): n.p. (p. 1).

26 Ibid., n.p. (p. 2).

27 WWII defense questionnaire and response, Black Mountain College, 1942, Josef Albers Papers, JAAF.

28 Anni Albers, untitled lecture, Black Mountain College, annotated typescript, March 25, 1942, p. 1, JAAF.

29 Ibid.
30 Ibid., 4.
31 Anni Albers, "Designing," reprinted in *Anni Albers: Selected Writings on Design*, ed. Brenda Danilowitz (Middletown, CT: Wesleyan University Press, 2000), 20. Originally published in *Craft Horizons* 2, no. 2 (May 1943): 7–9.
32 Emphasis added. Ibid.
33 Emphasis added. Ibid., 20–21.
34 Ibid., 21.
35 Anni Albers, "We Need the Crafts for Their Contact with Materials," *Design* 46, no. 4 (1944): 21–22, here p. 21; repr. and retitled "One Aspect of Art Work," in Anni Albers, *On Designing* (Middletown, CT: Wesleyan University Press, 1959), 29–33; and in *Anni Albers: Selected Writings on Design*, 25–28.
36 Albers, "We Need the Crafts for Their Contact with Materials," 21.
37 Anni Albers, "Design: Anonymous and Timeless," *Magazine of Art* (February 1947): 51. Revised version in *Anni Albers: Selected Writings on Design*, 34–41.
38 Anni Albers, untitled statement, handwritten, JAAF.
39 Smith, *Bauhaus Weaving Theory*, 146. On Anni Albers's teaching and the renewal of her writing practice in the United States, see the final chapter: "Conclusion: On Weaving, On Writing," 141–74.
40 Brenda Danilowitz, introduction to *Anni Albers: Selected Writings on Design*, xiii.
41 For a nuanced introduction to Anni Albers's writing on design, see Danilowitz, *Anni Albers: Selected Writings on Design*, ix–xiii. For a germane consideration of Albers's conceptions for, and development of, *On Weaving*, as well as its place in her larger oeuvre, see T'ai Smith, "On Reading *On Weaving*," in Anni Albers, *On Weaving* (1965), new expanded ed. (Princeton, NJ: Princeton University Press, 2017), 234–46.
42 Albers, interview by Richard Polsky, 40–41.
43 Anni Albers, untitled lecture [Some considerations of designing], no date, p. 3, JAAF.
44 Anni Albers, "Constructing Textiles," *Black Mountain College*, special issue, *Design* 47, no. 8 (April 1946): 22, repr. in *Anni Albers: Selected Writings on Design*, 29.
45 Albers, "Designing," 18.
46 Anni Albers, "Work with Material," *Black Mountain College Bulletin* 5 (1938), repr. in *Anni Albers: Selected Writings on Design*, 6.
47 Albers, "Designing," 19.
48 Ibid.
49 Albers, "Work with Material," 6.
50 Ibid.
51 Anni Albers, "Art – a Constant" (1939), repr. in *Anni Albers: Selected Writings on Design*, 14.
52 Ibid.
53 Anni Albers, interview by Sevin Fesci, typescript, New Haven, CT, July 5, 1968, p. 6, Archives of American Art Oral Histories Project, JAAF.
54 Ibid., 3.
55 Anni Albers, "Conversations with Artists" (February 1961), repr. in *Anni Albers: Selected Writings on Design*, 52–54 (here p. 53).
56 Emphasis added. Anni Albers, "Design: Anonymous and Timeless," 52.
57 Ibid.
58 Albers, cited in "Handweaving for Modern Interiors," *Craft Horizons* 9, no. 4 (Winter 1949): 23.
59 Albers, "Conversations with Artists," in *Anni Albers: Selected Writings on Design*, 53.
60 Ibid., 54.
61 Ibid., 53.
62 As Martin Filler has noted, "One of her proudest accomplishments at the Bauhaus – and the scheme that won Albers her diploma in 1930 – was a sound-absorbent curtain for the echo-plagued auditorium of Hannes Meyer's ADGB Bundesschule in Bernau. Using cellophane that she unraveled from a cap she bought on holiday in Italy, she wove the new material with chenille to form a light-reflective wall hanging that effectively deadened the room's acoustic reverberation." Filler, "A Marriage of True Minds: The Designs of Josef and Anni Albers," in *Josef and Anni Albers: Designs for Living*, ed. Nicholas Fox Weber and Martin Filler (London: Merrell, 2004), 40.
63 Albers, "Constructing Textiles," 22.
64 Brochure, *Good Design* (New York: Museum of Modern Art, 1951), n.p.
65 On this exhibition, see also Priyesh Mistry, "Exhibiting Textiles: MoMA 1949," in *Anni Albers*, ed. Ann Coxon, Briony Fer, and Maria Müller-Schareck (London: Tate, 2018), 130–33.
66 *Anni Albers Textiles* exhibition, list of dates and institutions for the circulating version of the exhibition, Museum of Modern Art (hereafter MoMA) Archives.
67 *Anni Albers Textiles* exhibition, press release, MoMA Archives.
68 *Anni Albers Textiles* exhibition, publicity report returned by institution to MoMA, August 17, 1950, MoMA Archives.
69 Albers, interview by Richard Polsky, 28.
70 Memo to Mr. [Philip] Johnson from Miss Daniel, January 14, 1949, Museum of Modern Art, JAAF.
71 Albers, untitled lecture [Some considerations of designing], 7–8.
72 List of materials lent by Anni Albers to MoMA for *Anni Albers Textiles* exhibition, February 25, 1949, p. 3, JAAF.
73 *Anni Albers Textiles*, exhibition checklist; Photographic Archive, IN421.2, MoMA Archives.
74 Packing list, Anni Albers to Edgar Kaufmann, MoMA, 1948, JAAF.
75 Anni Albers, untitled lecture [Some considerations of designing], 7–8.
76 Anni to Josef Albers, June 30, 1955, Josef Albers Papers, JAAF.
77 Notes on Anni Albers's design course, Lore Kadden-Lindenfeld Papers, JAAF.
78 Anni Albers, interview, March 1965, published as "Teaching Weaving and Design," in *Black Mountain College: Sprouted Seeds, an Anthology of Personal Accounts*, ed. Mervin Lane (Knoxville: University of Tennessee Press, 1990), 43.
79 Albers, "We Need the Crafts for Their Contact with Materials," 21–22.
80 Ibid., 22.
81 "Handweaving for Modern Interiors," 24.
82 Albers, *On Weaving* (2017 ed.), 45.
83 Welliver, "A Conversation with Anni Albers," n.p. (p. 7).

84 Albers, *On Weaving* (2017 ed.), 44.
85 Anni Albers, interview, "Teaching Weaving and Design," 43.
86 Albers, *On Weaving* (2017 ed.), 46.
87 Welliver, "A Conversation with Anni Albers," n.p. (p. 7).
88 Albers, *On Weaving* (2017 ed.), 46.
89 List of materials lent by Anni Albers to MoMA for *Anni Albers Textiles* exhibition, February 25, 1949, p. 1, JAAF.
90 Albers, *On Weaving* (2017 ed.), 46.
91 These investigations were important enough to be included in the 1949 MoMA exhibition, *Anni Albers Textiles*. The checklist of works dispatched to MoMA by Albers serves as a useful record of the output from the pre-weaving exercises. See list of materials lent by Anni Albers to MoMA for *Anni Albers Textiles* exhibition, February 25, 1949, p. 1, JAAF.
92 Albers, *On Weaving* (2017 ed.), 45.
93 Albers, interview, "Teaching Weaving and Design," 41–42.
94 On typewriter works at the Bauhaus, and as an art genre more widely, see Hans M. Wingler, *The Bauhaus: Weimar, Dessau, Berlin, Chicago*, trans. Wolfgang Jabs and Basil Gilbert (Cambridge, MA: MIT Press, [1969] 1976), 504; Barrie Tullett, *Typewriter Art: A Modern Anthology* (London: Laurence King Publishing, 2014); and Alan Riddell, ed., *Typewriter Art* (London: London Magazine Edition, 1975). On Anni Albers, the typewriter works, and textiles, see also Igor Siddiqui, "Slashed Interiors: Text/Space," *Interiority* 3, no. 1 (January 2020): 5–20; Brenda Danilowitz, "Typewriter Study," in *Original Bauhaus Workbook*, ed. Friederike Holländer and Nina Wiedemeyer (Munich: Prestel, 2019), 112–15; and Maria Müller-Schareck, "Typewriters and Tactile Textiles: How Anni Albers Brought a Modernist Touch to the Ancient Art of Weaving," *Interwoven* (2018) http://kvadratinterwoven.com/typewriters-and-tactile-textiles, accessed November 25, 2022.
95 See, for example, the following at the Bauhaus-Archiv Berlin: Katja Rose, Design for a swatch with typewriter-characters, ink on paper, 29.5 × 20.9 cm, 1932, Inv.nr.: 5821/2 and 5821/2; Hajo Rose (Hans-Joachim Rose), Design for a fabric print pattern made from typewriter type, 29.7 × 21.8 cm, 1932, Inv.nr.: 3987/1–2; Hajo Rose, Design for a fabric print pattern made from typewriter type, 28.1 × 12.9 cm, 1932, Inv. nr.: 10251/1; and Hajo Rose, Fabrics with printed typewriting pattern, 1932, linen weave and rayon, Inv.nr.: 3986/1 and 3986/2.
96 Frederick A. Horowitz, "Design," in Horowitz and Brenda Danilowitz, *Josef Albers: To Open Eyes; The Bauhaus, Black Mountain College, and Yale* (London: Phaidon, 2006), 118.
97 See Josef Albers Papers, JAAF. The guilloche, popular from the 1770s onwards, was of renewed interest to designers in the 1920s. Josef Albers carefully collected and filed materials on the guilloche. Among the materials in his files are articles including "Die Guillochierung," *Deutsche Graveur-Zeitung* 15 (1927): 339–42; and "Versuche zur Belebung der Gehäusemacherei," *Die Uhrmacher-Woche* 38 (1927): 611–12. Albers also placed a number of guilloche illustrations in an envelope marked "Teaching Ideas: The Guilloche." See Horowitz, "Design," in *Josef Albers: To Open Eyes*, 165n35.
98 Anni Albers, untitled lecture [Some considerations of designing], 6.
99 Ibid.
100 Albers, *On Weaving* (2017 ed.), 47.
101 Ibid., see plates 41–42.
102 List of materials lent by Anni Albers to MoMA for *Anni Albers Textiles* exhibition, February 25, 1949, p. 2, JAAF.
103 "Five-and-dime" stores were a type of ubiquitous store that sold everyday general domestic necessities such as stationary, trinkets, household hardware, toiletry articles, and other general merchandise for ten cents or less – a store similar to a "dollar store" today. On Albers's jewelry, see also Clara Salomon, "'Réhabiliter' les matériaux: Les bijoux d'Anni Albers," in *Anni et Josef Albers: L'art et la vie*, 128–31; Brenda Danilowitz, "Working from Where We Are: Anni Albers' and Alex Reed's Jewelry Collection," http://www.bauhaus-imaginista.org/articles/3094/working-from-where-we-are, accessed November 25, 2022; and Filler, "A Marriage of True Minds," 49–50.
104 See Robin Schuldenfrei, *Luxury and Modernism: Architecture and the Object in Germany 1900–1933* (Princeton, NJ: Princeton University Press, 2018), 138–56.
105 Anni Albers, "On Jewelry," typescript of an untitled talk given at Black Mountain College, March 25, 1942, repr. in *Anni Albers: Selected Writings on Design*, 22–24 (here p. 23).
106 Emphasis added. Ibid., 22–23.
107 Ibid.
108 For more on the *Machine Art* exhibition, see Mary Anne Staniszewski, *The Power of Display: A History of Exhibition Installations at the Museum of Modern Art* (Cambridge, MA: MIT Press, 1998), 152–60.
109 See corresondence between Johnson and Albers: letter, Philip Johnson to J. Albers, January 30, 1934; notes for a telegram from Albers to Johnson, February 3, 1934; letters, Johnson to J. Albers, February 28 and March 8, 1934, Josef Albers Papers, JAAF.
110 Photographic Archive, IN330.10, MoMA Archives.
111 *Modern Handmade Jewelry*, exhibition checklist, MoMA Archives.
112 Ibid.
113 *Modern Handmade Jewelry*, press release, September 11, 1946, p. 2, MoMA Archives.
114 For an analysis of architecture and the weaving workshop in the earlier period of the Bauhaus in Germany, see T'ai Smith's tracing of architectural criticism's rhetorical strategies, its terminology and concepts that Bauhaus weavers (including Gunta Stölzl, Benita Koch-Otte, Otti Berger, and Anni Albers) deployed in creating a theoretical framework – as well as strategies of production and marketing – for understanding their practice. Smith, chap. 2, "Toward a Modernist Theory of Weaving: The Use of Textiles in Architectural Space," in *Bauhaus Weaving Theory*, 41–78.
115 Press release, Yale University News Bureau, New Haven, CT, December 6, 1959, pp. 2–3, JAAF.
116 Anni Albers, "Fabrics," *Arts and Architecture* (March 1948): 32.
117 Ibid.
118 Anni Albers, "The Pliable Plane: Textiles in Architecture," *Perspecta: The Yale Architectural Journal* 4 (1957): 36–41, repr. in *Anni Albers: Selected Writings on Design*, 44–51 (here p. 51).
119 Albers, interview by Richard Polsky, 17.

120 Albers, untitled lecture, Black Mountain College, annotated typescript, March 25, 1942, p. 4, JAAF.

Chapter 8: Herbert Bayer's Expanded Vision and the Instrumentalizing of Design

1 On Bayer, see Arthur A. Cohen, *Herbert Bayer: The Complete Work* (Cambridge, MA: MIT Press, 1984); Eckhard Neumann, ed., *Herbert Bayer: Kunst und Design in Amerika 1938–1985* (Berlin: Bauhaus-Archiv, Museum für Gestaltung, 1986); Gwen Chanzit, *Herbert Bayer: Collection and Archive at the Denver Art Museum* (Seattle: University of Washington Press, 1988); Gwen Chanzit, *From Bauhaus to Aspen: Herbert Bayer and Modernist Design in America* (Boulder, CO: Johnson Books, 2005); Patrick Rössler and Bauhaus-Archiv, Berlin, eds., *Herbert Bayer: Die Berliner Jahre—Werbegrafik 1928-1938* (Berlin: Vergangenheitsverlag, 2013); Patrick Rössler and Gwen Chanzit, *Der einsame Großstädter: Herbert Bayer, eine Kurzbiografie* (Berlin: Vergangenheitsverlag, 2014); and Patrick Rössler, *Herbert Bayer, Graphic Designer: From the Bauhaus to Berlin, 1921–1938* (London: Bloomsbury, 2023).

2 Herbert Bayer, "Design, Designer and Industry," *Magazine of Art* 44, no. 8 (December 1951): 325.

3 See *Art, Design, and the Modern Corporation: The Collection of Container Corporation of America* (Washington, DC: Smithsonian Institution Press, 1985); Container Corporation of America, *Modern Art in Advertising: Designs for Container Corporation of America* (Chicago: P. Theobald, 1946); and Justus Nieland, "Container Culture: Film, Packaging, and the Design of Corporate Humanism at the CCA," *Post45*, https://post45.org/2021/02/container-culture-film-packaging-and-the-design-of-corporate-humanism-at-the-cca, accessed November 25, 2022.

4 Herbert Bayer, "Lecture at the Art Directors Club," Philadelphia, PA, February 26, 1940, typescript, p. 1, Herbert Bayer Papers, Denver Public Library, Denver, CO (hereafter HBP).

5 Herbert Bayer, "Design as an Expression of Industry," *Gebrauchsgraphik* 23, no. 9 (1952): 57.

6 Herbert Bayer to Walter Gropius, November 28, 1941, Bauhaus-Archiv, Berlin (hereafter BHA).

7 "Posters for Defense," *Bulletin of the Museum of Modern Art* 8, no. 6 (September 1941): 6.

8 Herbert Bayer, verso of *Freedom of the Seas*, wartime poster for *Fortune* magazine, BHA.

9 Gyorgy Kepes, "Introduction," in "The Visual Arts Today," special issue, *Daedalus* (Winter 1960): 5.

10 James Johnson Sweeney, in *Herbert Bayer: Exhibition of Paintings, Posters, Montages, Advertising Design* (Denton: North Texas State Teachers College, 1943), 1.

11 See, for example, Wanda Corn, *The Great American Thing: Modern Art and National Identity, 1915–1935* (Berkeley: University of California Press, 1999).

12 Herbert Bayer, "Posters," speech delivered at the A-D Gallery, October 2, 1940, pp. 2–3, HBP.

13 In many ways, Bayer's move to Aspen brought him back to his roots. Originally from Austria, Bayer is said to have walked to the Bauhaus to begin his studies, sauntering in wearing traditional German lederhosen. Therefore, the archival documents of Bayer's exacting alpine sweater patterns, from 1947, and gray and purple wool slipper sock drawings, from 1948, created shortly after he moved to Aspen, are not surprising.

14 Herbert Bayer, "Culture in the US Government," report, April 21, 1958, typescript, HBP.

15 A textile-generating device by Bayer from 1953–54, made of glass, plastic, metal, and paint—presumably for making textile patterns—is held at the Denver Art Museum (see object 1986.2037–38).

16 See, for example, Sarah Ganz Blythe and Andrew Martinez, eds., *Why Art Museums? The Unfinished Work of Alexander Dorner* (Cambridge, MA: MIT Press, 2018), especially therein Rebecca Uchill, "Storehouse to Powerhouse: The Museum Perspectives of Alexander Dorner," 41–67. See also Rebecca Uchill, "Re-viewing *The Way beyond 'Art'*: Herbert Bayer, Alexander Dorner, and Practices of Viewership," *Architectural Theory Review* 23, no. 1 (2019): 114–45.

17 Herbert Bayer, "Fundamentals of Exhibition Design," *PM* (1939): 19.

18 Monroe Wheeler, "Road to Victory: A Procession of Photographs of the Nation at War," *Bulletin of the Museum of Modern Art* 9, nos. 5/6 (June 1942): 18–20.

19 Ibid.

20 Edward Alden Jewell, "Art in Review," *New York Times*, May 21, 1942, p. 22.

21 On *Airways to Peace*, see also Cohen, *Herbert Bayer*, 302–8; and Mary Anne Staniszewski, *The Power of Display: A History of Exhibition Installations at the Museum of Modern Art* (Cambridge, MA: MIT Press, 1998), 227–36.

22 James Thrall Soby, "The Arts in Therapy," *Bulletin of the Museum of Modern Art* 10, no. 3 (February 1943): 3. James Soby was the director of MoMA's Armed Services Program.

23 It is important to note that during the war MoMA did not completely reorient its focus but continued to maintain its normal museological functions, such as non-war-related exhibitions, gallery talks, and a steady pace of sales of color reproductions and postcards in the museum shop. Bayer continued to work on projects for MoMA, including the authoring of a 1943 proposal for a "Visual Communications" department to be formed at the museum. He made the case that MoMA should begin to collect and exhibit advertising and other examples of graphic design.

24 Herbert Bayer, *Modern Art in Advertising: Designs for Container Corporation of America* (Davenport, IA: Davenport Municipal Art Gallery, 1949).

25 Herbert Bayer, "Presentation and Display," lecture at New York University, December 5, 1940, p. 14, HBP. This lecture's roots can be found in a similar document in German, titled "Darstellung," from 1936.

26 Ibid., 1.

27 Ibid., 3.

28 Herbert Bayer, "Aspects of Design of Exhibitions and Museums," *Curator* 4, no. 3 (1961): 257–58.

29 Bayer also designed the German section's catalog; see *Section allemande: Exposition de la Société des artistes décorateurs* (Berlin: Verlag Hermann Reckendorf, 1930), n.p. See also Wallis Miller, "Points of View: Herbert Bayer's Exhibition

Catalogue for the 1930 *Section allemande*," *Architectural Histories* 5, no. 1 (2017): 1–22. Especially important is Miller's insight into the catalog, like the exhibition itself, as a spatial experience, and the modes by which both catalog and installation constructed the way in which visitors encountered, and thus understood, the new interiors and objects on display. About the exhibition, see Paul Overy, "Visions of the Future and the Immediate Past: The Werkbund Exhibition, Paris 1930," *Journal of Design History* 17, no. 4 (2004): 337–57; and Sandra Karina Löschke, "Communication Material: Experiments with German Culture in the 1930 Werkbund Exhibition," in *The Material Imagination: Reveries on Architecture and Matter*, ed. Matthew Mindrup (Farnham, UK: Ashgate, 2015), 215–35.

30 Cohen, *Herbert Bayer*, 294.

31 Kristie La, "'Enlightenment, Advertising, Education, Etc.': Herbert Bayer and the Museum of Modern Art's *Road to Victory*," *October* 150 (Fall 2014): 63–86. Bayer's work and politics in the years under the National Socialists before he finally departed Germany are controversal, as La charts (69–75). Patrick Rössler asserts, "Bayer repeatedly and clearly distanced himself from the racial ideology of the Nazis. This was chiefly demonstrated by his intense and lasting friendships with Jewish artists such as Marcel Breuer and Xanti Schawinsky. Willy B. Klar, his colleague at Dorland and close friend – himself classified as a 'half-Jew' according to the regime's definitions – noted in his memoirs that Bayer nurtured a deep hatred of both Hitler and Joseph Goebbels, and hinted that Bayer even joked about planning their assassinations. Such pranks, had they been reported to the authorities, would have resulted in instant Gestapo harassment." Rössler, *Herbert Bayer, Graphic Designer: From the Bauhaus to Berlin, 1921-1938* (London: Bloomsbury, 2023), 95; Rössler cites Willy B. Klar, . . . *ein bißchen Chuzpe und ein Haufen Glück: Mein Leben mit Texten und Textilien* (Oberaudorf: Verlag Willy B. Klar, 1981*)*, 79. See also Alexander Schug, "Herbert Bayer: Ein Konzeptkünstler in der Werbung der Zwischenkriegszeit," in *Ahoi Herbert! Bayer und die Moderne* (Linz, Austria: Lentos Kunstmuseum Linz, 2009), 173–85; and Rössler, *Herbert Bayer: Die Berliner Jahre*. For a key account of several Bauhaus members' work in relation to the National Socialist regime in the years before departing Germany see Michael Tymkiw, *Nazi Exhibition Design and Modernism* (Minneapolis: University of Minnesota Press, 2018). On *The Road to Victory*, beyond La's definitive account, see also Staniszewski, *The Power of Display*, 209–24.

32 See Georg Simmel, "The Metropolis and Mental Life" (1903), repr. in Richard Sennett, ed., *Classic Essays on the Culture of Cities* (Englewood Cliffs, NJ: Prentice-Hall, 1969), 47–60.

33 Herbert Bayer, cover of *Gebrauchsgraphik / International Advertising Art*, October 1938.

34 Bayer, "Presentation and Display" lecture illustration.

35 Herbert Bayer, "The Human Eye – a Living Camera," 1939, original publication unknown, tear sheet in BHA.

36 Bayer, "Lecture at the Art Directors Club," 1–2.

37 Bayer, "Design, Designer and Industry," 325.

38 Alexander Dorner, *The Way beyond "Art": The Work of Herbert Bayer* (New York: Wittenborn, Schultz, 1947), 147.

39 Ibid., 148.

40 Ibid., 158.

41 Herbert Bayer, "Total Design," lecture, University of Southern California, Santa Barbara, February 1969, p. 2a, typescript, HBP.

42 Ibid., pp. 2a–2b. He continues, "subsequently, the only valid truth is a concept in which the various arts are not isolated instances but become a welded unity. I am not, however, advocating the idea of multiple activity. It is only that I have chosen to live by it" (p. 3).

43 Herbert Bayer, lecture at the Goethe Bicentennial Convocation, Aspen, CO, June 23, 1949, typescript, p. 3, HBP. Published as Bayer, "Goethe and the Contemporary Artist," *College Art Journal* 11, no. 1 (Fall 1951): 39–40.

44 Bayer, "Total Design," p. 4.

Index

Note: Page numbers in *italic* type refer to illustrations.

Aalto, Alvar, 82–83, 309n36; Paimio Sanatorium, 82–83
Abramovitz, Max, Corning Glass Building (with Wallace K. Harrison), 228
abstraction: Albers (Josef) and, 217, 230; materials/materiality and, 9; Moholy-Nagy and, 8–9, 22, 53, 55; and space, 22, 36–37
acetate, 45
Adorno, Theodor, 129
advertising: Bayer and, 293, 295; in Berlin, 23; Moholy-Nagy and, 27, 33; standardization of, 39–40; use of light by, 33
AEG, 163, 168, 171
Airways to Peace (exhibition, 1943), 288, *289*, 318n11
Albers, Anni, 3, 243–73; and the architectural, 270–71; at the Bauhaus, 243, 247; at Black Mountain College, 131, 226, 243, 246–50, 260, 265, 267; critical reception of, 257–60, 271; emigration from Germany of, 223–26, 243, 246–47; exhibitions of work of, 243, *244–45*, 258–60, *259*, 267, 270, *272*; exile's effect on, 5, 7, 226; and jewelry, 243, 250, 258, 267–70; Jewish heritage of, 223, 246–47; and Josef Albers's paintings, 217, 236; marriage to Josef, 243; and materials/materiality, 15–16, 243, 252–57, 259–64, 267–73; objects ruined in transit, 247; pedagogy of, 5, 15, 254, 259–67, 270; and space, 271; theories and statements on art and design, 15, 243, 247, 250–57, 259, 261, 263–64, 267–68, 270–71, 273; in the United States, 223–24, 243, 246–48; and weaving, 5, 15–16, 243, 253–54, 257–61, 263–64, 270–71; and World War II, 250–53; at Yale University, 131, 271
Albers, Anni, works: *Ancient Writing*, 253; *Black White Red*, 221–22, *221*, 243; *Code*, 253; fabric sample, 257, *257*, 260; *Haiku*, 253; installation view of room dividers and chair upholstery, 271, *272*; necklaces (with Alex Reed), 268, *269*; *Open Letter*, 253; room dividers, 243, *244–45*, 271; studies made by puncturing paper, *262*, 263; studies made on the typewriter, *266*, 267; wall coverings for trade school auditorium, 257, 331n62
Albers, Anni, writing: "Constructing Textiles," 254, 257; "Designing," 251–52; *On Designing*, 253; *On Weaving*, 253, 263, 267; "The Pliable Plane," 271; "We Need the Crafts for Their Contact with Materials," 252, 261; "Work with Material," 255
Albers, Josef, 3, 207–41; and abstraction, 217, 230; and architecture, 209, 218, 223, 227–31; at the Bauhaus, 13, 22, 51, 207, 209, 212–14, 223, 247; at Black Mountain College, 131, 207, 215, 226–27, 260; and color, 232–33, 236–37; critical reception of, 220, 237, 239; emigration from Germany of, 223–26, 243, 246–47; exile's effect on, 5, 7, 226–27; and Gropius, 227–28; influence of, 212–13; and light, 212, 220, 222, 236; marriage to Anni, 243; and materials/materiality, 13, 15, 207–23, 226–27, 229–41, 329n73; and objects, 15, 207–8, 237; objects ruined in transit, 5, 15, 224–26; paintings of, 226, 229–37; pedagogy of, 13, 51, 211–16, 265; and space, 239; and subjectivity, 216–17, 222; and surface, 15, 209–16, 220, 230–41; theories and statements on art and design, 212, 214, 231–33, 239, 241; in the United States, 223–24, 246–48; and visuality, 13, 15, 207–17, 220–22, 236–37, 241; works in glass, 207–10, 217–27, 230, 232, 236–37, 239, 241; at Yale University, 13, 131, 207, 215, 247
Albers, Josef, works, 232–33; *America*, 227–28, *228*; *Angular*, 230; *Astatic*, 239, *240*; *City* (glass), 209, 217, *218*, 219, 220–21, 223, 224, 227; *City* (tempera), 226–27, *226*; conference table, *117*, 118; *Dark*, 231, *231*; *December*, 230; design for a remodeled storefront selling Ullstein sewing patterns, 228, *229*; desk, 207; *Dissolved*, 223; *Equal and Unequal*, 217, *217*; *Evening (an Improvisation)*, 230; *Factory*, 222, 223; *Fensterbild (Window Picture)*, 207, 208, *209*; *Fensterbilder* (window paintings), 207, 208; *Fuge (Fugue)*, 221; *Gate*, 230; *Gitterbild (Grid Mounted)*, 207, 208; *Glas-Wandbilder* (glass wall-paintings), 208–9; *Hochbauten A & B (Skyscrapers A & B)*, 223, *224*; *Homage to the Square: Embedded*, 234 (detail), *235*; *Homage to the Square: Lone Whites*, 208, 235; *Homage to the Square: New Gate*, 230 (verso); *Homage to the Square: Renewed Hope*, 232 (detail), *233*, 233; *Homage to the Square* series, 1, 2, 15, 207, 209–10, 212, 216–17, 229–37, 239, 241; *Im Wasser (In the Water)*, 220; *Intaglio Solo VI*, 239, *241*; *Interior a*, 217, *219*, 220, 223; *Interior b*, 217, 220; *Lattice Pictures (Gitterbilder)*, 15; *Manhattan*, 227, *227*; *Proto Form A*, 230; *Skyscrapers A*, *224*; *Skyscrapers on Transparent Yellow*, 209, *210*, *211* (detail), 222, 236; stacking tables, 207, *208*; stained-glass windows, 207; *Steps*, 216; *Structural Constellations*, 210, 237, 239; *Structural Constellation: Transformation of a Scheme No. 19*, *238*, 239; *Stufen (Steps)*, 220, 223; tea glass with saucer and stirrer, 207, *208*; tea table, 207; *Transformation of a Scheme*, 237; *Two Structural Constellations*, 228–29, *229*; *Variant/Adobe* series, 230–31, 233, 237
Albers, Josef, writings, *Interaction of Color*, 232
Albers Foundation, 225, 227
Alexander, Franz, 140–41
aluminum, 8, 83–84
America, the Haven (radio series), 129
American Bauhaus. *See* New Bauhaus, Chicago
American Defense Committee, Harvard Group, 128
A. M. Luther, 82
Anni Albers (exhibition, 2018), *244–45*
Anni Albers Textiles (exhibition, 1949), 258–59, *259*, 267, 271, *272*
anti-materiality/dematerialization: Albers (Josef) and, 228; art and design influenced by, 5–6; Bauhaus buildings and, 97; Moholy-Nagy and, 29, 31, 55; resulting from exilic conditions, 5. *See also* visuality
Archigram: Capsule Homes, 92; Cushicle, 92–93; Inflatable Suit-Home, 93; Living-Pod Dwelling Capsule, 93; Suitaloon, 92
Architectural Review (magazine), 80, 82, 112
architecture: Albers (Anni) and, 270–71; Albers (Josef) and, 209, 218, 223, 227–31; Bauhaus instruction and, 51–52; estrangement and, 298; *Gesamtkunstwerk* concept in, 10, 62, 65–66, 81, 88–89, 92–93; industry and, 24–27; landscape's relationship to, 76, 167, 178, 180–81, 191–97, 200; minimal existence concept, 10, 61, 63; Moholy-Nagy and, 6, 8, 21–31, 34, 47, 50–53, 303n4, 304n11; photography of, 313n3; and space, 26, 175–76. *See also* housing
"Architecture Today" (television show), 90
art and artists: authorship of, 39, 40, 121–23, 207, 218, 234–35, 256; desubjectivization of, 40, 65; industry linked to, 39–41; postwar role of, 151–52. *See also* social role of art and design
Artek, 82
Artforum (magazine), 237
Art Institute of Chicago, 290
art nouveau, 66, 88, 93
Arts and Architecture (journal), 271
arts and crafts movement, 91
Arts in Therapy, The (exhibition, 1943), 16, 277, 288, *289*, 322n73

335

Aspen, Colorado, 285, 333n13
Aspen Institute for Humanistic Studies, 285, 299
Association of Arts and Industries, 317n4
atomic bomb, 193–95, *194*, 202, 320n31, 324n123
aura, reproducibility and, 170–74, 176, 203

Banham, Reyner, The Environment Bubble (with François Dallegret), 92, *93*
Barr, Alfred H., Jr., 116, 214
Bauhaus: Albers (Anni) and, 243, 247; Albers (Josef) and, 13, 22, 51, 207, 209, 212–14, 223, 247; Bayer and, 122; closure of, 223; finances of, 319n15; furniture patents of, 5; Gropius and, 1, 5, 57, 90, 103, 116, 122, 131; Hilberseimer and, 155; influence in America, 16, 277; instruction in architecture, 51–52; legacy of, 1, 10, 12, 97, 103, 113, 115–16, 118–19, 121–23, 131; marketing and public relations for, 103; and mass production, 104, 122, 131, 168, 320n35; Mies van der Rohe and, 155, 161; and modernism, 51, 131; Moholy-Nagy and, 21, 51, 99, 103, 131; Moholy's photographs of, 1, 5, 10, 12, 97–106; New Bauhaus compared to, 130–32; pedagogy of, 51–53, 213–15, 264–65, 297; and social role of art and design, 52, 66; *Vorkurs* (Foundation Course), 51–53, *213*, 297; wives of faculty of, 314n10. *See also* New Bauhaus, Chicago
Bauhaus (magazine), 116, 177, 185
Bauhaus, 1919–1928 (exhibition and catalog, 1938–1939), 16, 113, 116, 118–19, 121, 258, 275, 277, 316n71, 316n72, 318n12; installation view, 116, *117*, 286, *286*
Bauhaus 1919-1933: Workshops for Modernity (exhibition and catalog, 2009–2010), 118
Bauhaus: A Conceptual Model (exhibition and catalog, 2009), 118
Bauhaus Archive, Berlin, 114
Bauhaus book series, 25, 26, 103, 118, 119
Bauhaus Fund, 115, 319n19
Bayer, Herbert, 3, 275–97; and the Bauhaus, 122; design for the war effort, *3*, 16, 139, 277–84, 318n11; emigration from Germany of, 277; estrangement in the work of, 296–97; exhibition designs by, 16, 116, 275, 277, *277*, 286, *286*, 288, *288–90*, 290–93, 318n11; expanded vision of, 16, 275, 288, 291, 293–97; in Germany, 277, 334n31; and the social role of design, 275, 278–90, 295–96, 299; theories and statements on art and design, 16, 275, 278, 284, 286, 291, 299; in the United States, 129, 277–78, 285, 319n13, 319n19; and World War II, 284
Bayer, Herbert, works: *America Needs More Meat*, 282, *283*; *Antipodes*, 284; *Atmospheric Conditions*, 284; *Celestial Spaces*, 284; *Clashing Forces*, 284, *285*; design for display table for *Arts in Therapy* exhibition, *289*; diagram of field of vision, 275, *277*, 291; drawings depicting field of vision and expanded vision, 293, *294*; entrance design for *Modern Art in Advertising* exhibition, 290, *290*; *Freedom of the Seas Is in Your Own Backyard*, 280, *280*; *Grow It Yourself*, 282; *Guidance in Flight*, 279, *280*; *Home Grown Wheat*, 282, *283*; illustrations for "curved wall," "reading direction," "disorder in floor plan in relation to organized direction," and "organized direction," in "Fundamentals of Exhibition Design," 286, *287*; *Lonely Metropolitan*, 296, 297, *297*; magazine cover design (camouflage), 275, *276*, 279; *More Milk*, 284; *Moving the Stuff of Production*, 280; *Our Allies Need Eggs*, 2, *3*, 17, 282; poster design (incomplete) for Rural Electrification Administration, 284, *284*; "Presentation and Display," lecture diagram, 291, *292*; "Presentation and Display," lecture illustration, 291, *292*, 295, *295*; *Save Waste Paper!* 139, 278, *279*; *A Victory Recipe: Pork and Planes Cooked by Gas!* 282, *282*; wing diagram, 281, *281*
Bayer, Herbert, writings: "Fundamentals of Exhibition Design," 286; "Goethe and Art Today," 299; "The Human Eye – a Living Camera," 295; "Presentation and Display," 291, *292*, 295, *295*; "Total Design," 299
Beard, Robert, Collapsible Chair, 137
Behrens, Peter, 177
Benjamin, Walter, 171; "The Task of the Translator," 91–92
Berlin, Germany, 21–27, 29, 33, 34, 47, 155, 160, 163, 165, 168, 172, 182
Bertoia, Harry, 270
Black Mountain College, 7, 15, 78, 131, 134, 207, 215, 223–24, 226–27, 243, 246–50, 260, 265, 267
Black Mountain College Bulletin, 249
Bogler, Theodor, storage jars, 103, *104*
Borsodi, Ralph, 195
Boumphrey, Geoffrey, 82
Brauneck, August, 51
Brecht, Bertolt, 129
Breton, André, 4
Breuer, Marcel, 3; emigration from Germany of, 59–63; in England, 59–63, 89; exhibition design by, 275; at Harvard University, 9, 131; and Isokon, 1, 9, 82–87; and Moholy, 119–20; partnership with F.R.S. Yorke, 59, *72–73*, 73, 81; use of plywood by, 5, 9, 73, 83–87
Breuer, Marcel, works: armchair (later titled TI 1a), *117*, 118; B9 Nesting Tables, 85, *87*; bent metal chairs, 83; blueprint for aluminum nesting chair, 84, *85*; blueprint for Isokon Short Chair, 84, *86*; blueprint for plywood nesting chair, *89*; blueprint for plywood nesting table, *88*; dining area of the Isobar, London (with F.R.S. Yorke), *72–73*, 73; Gropius Residence, Lincoln, Massachusetts (with Walter Gropius), 78, *79*, 91; Isokon Long Chair, 1, 5, *6*, *60–61*, 84–85, *86*, 91; Isokon Short Chair, 84–85; Isokon Stacking Tables, 85, *87*; London Theatre Studio (with F.R.S. Yorke), 83; Model 313 chaise longue, 84, *84–85*; molded plywood chairs, 83; show house for P. E. Gane (with Maxwell Fry), 83; tubular steel chairs, 104, *105*; tubular steel furniture, 85
Breuer, Marcel, writings, "Architecture and Material," 85
British Industrial Art in Relation to the Home (London, 1933), 69, *70*
Broner-Ullmann, Monica Bella, drawing of fabric and nails with collaged fabric, 214, *215*
Burnham, Jack W., 44
Buscher, Alma: changing table, *117*, 118; ship toy, *117*; toy cabinet, *117*, 118
Busch-Reisinger Museum, Harvard University, 112, 114, 122

Calder, Alexander, 270
Caldwell, Alfred, 167, 193–97, 199–201; Chicago L-shaped and rectangular houses in settlement units (with Ludwig Hilberseimer), 171, *171*; "Design to Fit the Human Spirit" (with Ludwig Hilberseimer), 195; landscape design for Lafayette Park, Detroit, *200*, 201, *201*
camouflage, 2, 12, 48, 128, 134–35, 142–48, 322n86; magazine cover design by Herbert Bayer, *276*; School of Design student work, *143*, *145*, *147*
capitalism, 21, 24, 128, 157, 171–73, 202, 279. *See also* industry
CARE (Cooperative for American Remittances to Europe) packages, 115, 319n19
CCA. *See* Container Corporation of America
cells: in housing, 13, 64, 69, 88, 91, 93, 172, 177; in urban design, 13, 64, 89, 155, 164, 174, 191–92. *See also* unit
Chagall, Marc, 4
Chermayeff, Serge, 59, 69, 81, 82; De La War Pavilion (with Erich Mendelsohn), 83
Chicago, Illinois: Berlin's relationship with, 168; camouflaging of, during World War II, 48, 146; Civil Defense Commission, 128, 146; German exiles in, 155; Hilberseimer and, 13, 155, 168, 180–81,

187–88, 198–99; mass production in, 21, 172; Mies van der Rohe in, 13, 155, 162, 187–89; Moholy-Nagy in, 21, 48; urban design of, 13, 181, 195, 199–200. See also New Bauhaus, Chicago
Chicago Daily News (newspaper), 146
Chicago Institute for Psychoanalysis, 141
Chicago school, 3
Chicago Sun (newspaper), 130
Chicago Sun Times (newspaper), 190
Christie, Agatha, 62
CIAM. See *Congrès internationaux d'architecture moderne*
Cincinnati Art Museum, 231
cities: grid plan for, 12–13; materials of, 26–27, 29, 34; modern, 23, 30, 34; Moholy-Nagy and, 8, 21–27, 29–30, 33, 34, 45, 47–50, 53; objects of, 41; unit module applied to, 12–13
Citroen, Paul, 320n19
city planning. See urban design
Civil Aeronautics Administration, 277, 279
Coates, Wells, 62, 69, 90; Lawn Road Flats / Isokon Flats, London, 58, 61, 63, 64, 68–69, 68, 69, 70, 71, 82; "Room Unit Production," 92
Cold War, 121–22
Colman, Scott, 193
Colomina, Beatriz, 318n5
color, Josef Albers and, 232–33, 236–37
Congrès internationaux d'architecture moderne (CIAM), 67, 82, 129, 303n4
Consemüller, Erich, 104; material exercise for Foundation Course taught by Josef Albers, 213, *213*
consumerism, 251–52, 268
Container Corporation of America (CCA), 16, 129, 139, 277, 278, 285, 290
contingency, 10, 12–13
Cranbrook Academy of Art, 134, 321n51
Customs House, New York, 224–26

Dada, 27
Dallegret, François, The Environment Bubble (with Reyner Banham), 92
Damisch, Hubert, 216, 235–36
Danilowitz, Brenda, 239, 253
decentralization, 180, 192–95, *194*, 200
decoration. See ornament and decoration
defamiliarization, 297–98
de Kooning, Elaine, 207
dematerialization. See anti-materiality/dematerialization
design, for the war effort and postwar society, 2, 12, 16, 48, 127, 130–53, 247–50, 252–53, 277–84, 318n11. See also furniture design; social role of art and design
Design Workshops (School of Design film), 144; film stills, *145*
desubjectivization, 40, 65
Dewey, John, 323n118
Díaz, Eva, 212, 234, 237
division of labor, 254
Dorner, Alexander, 286, 296
Dreier, Ted, 226
Dunlop Rubber Co., 84
Dwelling in Our Time, The (Berlin, 1931), 63

Eames, Charles and Ray, 134, 321n51
Ehrman, Marli, 322n73
Einstein, Albert, 125
Embru, 84
Emma, Countess of Oxford and Asquith, 107–8, *107*

enamel, 39–40
Engelbrecht, Lloyd C., 303n4
England: Bauhaus members in, 9–10; Breuer in, 59–63, 89; German exiles in, 7, 59–63, 89–92; Gropius in, 57, 59–63, *59*, 71–72, 74–81, 89; modernism in, 9–10, 80; Moholy in, 106–11, 314n18; Moholy-Nagy in, 59–63, 89, 309n6, 309n11; rules on employment of foreign nationals, 59, 107; as site of translation of design principles, 89–92
English language, 7, 57, 89–90, 127, 224, 247, 315n38, 319n13
Enlisted Reserve Corps, 134
Evans, Robin, 89
Evanston, Illinois, 183
Evergreen Cooperative, 197–98
Exhibition Work of Camouflage Class (School of Design film), 144, 147; film still, *147*
exile: conditions of, 7, 62, 74; contingencies of, 7; design in England affected by, 61–62; as estrangement, 297; Hilberseimer's housing design linked to, 202–3; modernism shaped by, 1–17, 298–99; and translation, 91
exiles: assimilation of, 12, 125, 127–29, 297, 315n38; assistance sent to Europe by, 115, 319n19; design for the war effort, 278; in England, 7, 59–63, 89–92; French, 3–4, 129; German, 1, 3–4, 57, 59–63, 89–92, 106, 109–10, 121, 125, 127–30, 149, 155, 246–47, 277–81, 296–99, 315n38, 318n11, 319n19; social networks of, 129; in the United States, 127–28, 277–81, 296–99, 319n12, 319n19
Existenzminimum. See minimal existence/dwelling
expanded vision, 16, 275, 288, 291, 293–97

Federal Bureau of Investigation (FBI), 128
fiberboard chairs, 135, *136*
Filipowski, Richard: *Care Saves Wear*, 139; *Deliver Us from Evil*, 139
film, Moholy-Nagy and, 25, 45, 47, 50, 307n83
Finmar, 82
Fordism, 3
Ford Motor Company, 26, 185
form: Albers (Anni) and, 252–56, 260–61; Albers (Josef) and, 236; anti-materiality and, 5; Hilberseimer and, 176, 185–86; Moholy-Nagy and, 30–31
Fortnum & Mason, 82
Fortune (magazine), 275, 277, 280
Foster, Hal, 127–28
France, exiles from, 3–4, 129
Franck, Philipp, 216
Fränkel, Rudolf, Lichtburg Kino, *32*
Frankfurter Allgemeine Zeitung (newspaper), 237
Frankfurt Kitchen, 63–64
Franz Stoedtner Archive, 120
freestanding houses, *166*, 177, 185, 188–89
Fries, Heinrich de, 177
Fry, Maxwell, 59, 62, 74–76, *76*, 78, 81, 90; Impington Village College (with Walter Gropius), 78, 83; show house for P. E. Gane (with Marcel Breuer), 83; Wood House, Kent (with Walter Gropius), 78, *79*, 91
Fuller, Buckminster, 92, 271
furniture design and furnishings: exile's effect on, 9; Hilberseimer and, 165, 173–74; and minimal dwelling, 81–89; New Bauhaus and, 135–37, 321n47; patents for, 5, 137; in plywood, 71, 79, 82

garden city concept, 164, 177, 193
Garland, Patricia Sherwin, 231–32
Gebrauchsgraphik / International Advertising Art (journal), 293
Gelb, Benjamin, 135

George V, King of England, 76

Germanic Museum. *See* Busch-Reisinger Museum, Harvard University

Germany: Bayer in, 277, 334n31; exiles from, 1, 3–4, 57, 59–63, 89–92, 106, 109–10, 121, 125, 127–30, 149, 155, 246–47, 277–81, 296–99, 315n38, 318n11, 319n19; the grid in, 163, 168; Hilberseimer in, 155, 157, 160–61; housing in, 160–61; Mies van der Rohe in, 12, 13, 155; modernism in, 1, 3, 7, 59–60; Moholy-Nagy in, 21–24. *See also* Berlin, Germany; Nazis

Gernsheim, Helmut, 109, 315n33

Gerson, Lotte, Architectural Construction with Sections of Glass, 51, *52*

Gesamtkunstwerk (total work of art), 10, 62, 65–66, 81, 88–89, 92–93. *See also* totalization

Gestalt psychology, 211, 237

GI Bill, 138, 188

Giedion, Sigfried, 22–23, 62; *Mechanization Takes Command*, 3; *Walter Gropius: Work and Teamwork*, 119

glass: Albers (Josef) and, 207–10, 217–27, 230, 232, 236–37, 239, 241; Consemüller's material exercise in, 213, *213*; Moholy-Nagy and, 8, 22, 26–27, 30, 34

glass architecture, 24, 26–27

Gloag, John, 80

Goethe Bicentennial Convocation (1949), 299

Gogh, Vincent van, 216

Good Design (exhibition, 1951–1952), 258

Graham, Ralph (or Gyorgy Kepes), *War Art* catalog cover, *147*

Grassi Museum, Leipzig, Germany, 207

Greenberg, Clement, 111

Greene, David: Inflatable Suit-Home, 93; Living-Pod Dwelling Capsule, 93

Greenwald, Herbert, 190, 201, 202

Greenwald, Morris, 189

grid: in Chicago, 13, 181; in Europe, 202; in Germany, 163, 168; Hilberseimer and, 6, 12–13, 155, 157, 160–61, 163, 176, 180, 191, 202; housing and, 155, 160–61; Mies van der Rohe and, 155, 202; as object of exile, 202–3; theoretical significance of, 13; in the United States, 155, 157, 160, 163, 168, 202; in urban design, 12–13, 155, 157, 176

Gropius, Ise, 29, 57, 62, 71, 106, 112–14, 277, 319n19

Gropius, Walter, 3; Albers (Josef) and, 227–28; apartment of, in Lawn Road Flats, 57, 59, *70*; and the Bauhaus, 1, 5, 57, 90, 103, 116, 122, 131 (*see also* and Moholy's Bauhaus photographs); and *Bauhaus, 1919-1928* catalog, 277; and *Bauhaus, 1919-1928* exhibition, 116; certificate of residence registration, *59*; critical reception of, 80, 90; emigration from Germany of, 59–63, 71; in England, 57, 59–63, *59*, 71, 71–72, 74–81, 89; and English language, 57, 89–90; exhibition design by, 275; FBI files on, 128; at Harvard University, 9, 89, 91, 122, 131, 319n15; housing designed by, 74–81, 93, 185; and Isokon, 9–10, 81–83, 87; and Le Corbusier, 4; on Moholy-Nagy, 55, 127; and Moholy's Bauhaus photographs, 1, 5, 10, 111–21, 316n58, 316n60; Moholy's personal relationship with, 103, 110, 114–15; and the New Bauhaus, 317n4, 318n10; objects taken into exile by, 106; partnership with Maxwell Fry, 59, 62, 74–76, 78, 81; and photography, 120–21; and standardization, 67, 81; success in exile, 12; theories and writings on art, 88; and the unit, 67; in the United States, 125, 128–29, 319n19; use of plywood by, 83

Gropius, Walter, works: apartment of, in Lawn Road Flats, 71–72; architectural models, 5; Bauhaus Building, *11*, 69, *70, 98, 100, 101*; *Baukasten*, 63; Benn Levy House, London, 78; Chicago Tribune Tower competition entry (with Adolf Meyer), 51, 223, *225*; dormitory plan, Black Mountain College, 78; dormitory plan, Christ's College, Cambridge University, 78; Flat of 1937, 79–80, *80*, 81; "The Formal and Technical Problems of Modern Architecture and Planning," 89; furniture design, 79, 83; Gropius Residence, Lincoln, Massachusetts (with Marcel Breuer), 78, *79*, 91; Gropius Standard, 67, *68*; Harvard Graduate Center, 271; housing proposals for England, 62, 74–81, *76, 77*; Impington Village College (with Maxwell Fry), 78, 83; masters' houses, Bauhaus, 57, *101*, 118, 247; memorial to workers killed in the Kapp Putsch, 51; *The New Architecture and the Bauhaus*, 90; Pan Am Building, 4, 227; Törten Housing Estate, 185, 196; Wood House, Kent (with Maxwell Fry), 78, *79*, 91

Gropius, Walter, writings: "The Formal and Technical Problems of Modern Architecture and Planning," 81; "Minimal Dwelling and Tower Block," 67; *The New Architecture and the Bauhaus*, 9–10, 116; "Sociological Foundations of the Minimum Dwelling," 67

Gropius Standard, 67, *68*

Grosz, George, 129

Grote, Toma, 52

growing house, 185–87, 192

Haines, Pat, 93

Hairlok, 84

Hampton's, 78

haptic sense. *See* touch/tactile sense

Harrison, Wallace K., Corning Glass Building (with Max Abramovitz), 228

Harrods, 77–78

Hartmueller, George, 318n11

Harvard University, 2, 78, 91, 131; Busch-Reisinger Museum, 112, 114, 122; Graduate Center, 227, 271; Graduate School of Design, 9, 89, 122, 319n15; Landscape Architecture Department, 135

Hausmann, Raoul, 320n19

Hays, K. Michael, 170

Haystack Mountain School of Crafts, 260

Heal's, 82

Heidegger, Martin, 45

Heinersdorff, Gottfried, 218

high-rise architecture and skyscrapers: Albers (Josef) and, 209, 223, 228; Gropius and, 10, 76; Hilberseimer and, 155, 157, 162, 164, 167–73, 177; Mies van der Rohe and, 50, 155, 161, 162, 168; modernism and, 209; Moholy-Nagy and, 45, 50; in the United States, 3, 168, 209

Hilberseimer, Ludwig, 3, 12–13; at the Bauhaus, 155; and Chicago, 13, 155, 168, 180–81, 187–88, 198–99; and furnishings, 165, 173–74; in Germany, 155, 157, 160–61; and the grid, 6, 12–13, 155, 157, 160–61, 163, 176, 180, 191, 202; housing designed by, 6, 64, 81, 155, 157, 160–67, 172–89, 191–93, 197–99, 201–2; and materials/materiality, 175–76; Mies van der Rohe's collaborations with, 155, *156*, 188; and minimal dwelling, 64; on Moholy-Nagy, 29; replanning diagram, Chicago, Illinois, 13, *14*; and space, 175–76; theories and statements on art and design, 13, 155, 161, 163–64, 169, 173–78, 180–89, 191–203; typification in the work of, 165–66, 172, 183–84, 186, 202–3, 324n16; and the unit, 6, 12–13, 64, 66, 155, 157, 163–67, 171–72, 176, 181, 191–92, 202; and urban design, 6, 155, 157, 160, 163–67, *164*, 173, 176–81, 191–203; and US design, 167–69

Hilberseimer, Ludwig, works: aerial view of the replanned city of Chicago, 198, *198*; Berlin development project, *158*, 160, 172; Berlin mixed-height housing development, *160–61*, 162, 176, 177, 178, 184; boardinghouse, *168*, 169; Chicago lake settlement, *170*, 171, 172, 191; Chicago L-shaped and rectangular houses in settlement units (with Alfred Caldwell), 171, *171*, 172, 184, 191, 196; Chicago settlement units, *162*, 163, 180, 196; Chicago Tribune project, *159*, 160, 171; City in the Landscape, 191, *192*, 196; commercial area with surrounding settlement areas, 167, *167*, 176, 180, 191; dwelling for Weissenhof Estate, 185; freestanding house plan and settlement, 165, *166*, 178, 185; growing house, *184*, 185–87; Highrise City, *158*, *159*, 172, 176; housing elements, 165, *166*, 174, 182; IIT Master Plan (with Ludwig Mies van der Rohe), *186–87*, 187–88, 202; Lafayette Park, Detroit (with Ludwig Mies van der Rohe), 13, 155, *200*, 201–2, *201*; mixed-height housing development, 178, *179*; plan for decentralization, showing the effect of the atomic bomb on size and distribution of cities, 193, *194*; preliminary site plan, Lafayette Park, 202, *203*; replanning diagram, Chicago, Illinois, 199; replanning diagram for Chicago, illustrating fumes, 199, *199*; settlement units, density study, 160, *161*, 162, 176, 177, 178, 180, 184, 191; single-family row house design for Biesenhorst Siedlung, 182, *182–83*; sketches of Chicago downtown loop development project, *156*, 163; small apartments, 164–65, *165*, 178; State Street Project, 198; urban planning scheme, 164, *164*; Welfare City, 176–77, *177*

Hilberseimer, Ludwig, writings: "American Architecture" (with Udo Rukser), 167–68; "Chicago–Urbs in Horto," 181; "Cities and Defense," 193; "Design to Fit the Human Spirit" (with Alfred Caldwell), 195; *Groszstadtarchitektur* (*Metropolisarchitecture*), 155, 161, 168–69, 177, 182, 184, 191; *Grosstadtbauten* (*Metropolis Building*), 161, 182, 191; *The Nature of Cities*, 180; *The New City*, 180, 188, 191; *The New Regional Pattern*, 180; "The Will to Architecture," 174, *175*

Hirschfeld-Mack, Ludwig, *The Bauhaus: An Introductory Survey*, 120

Hitchcock, Henry-Russell, 76, 82–83

Hitler, Adolf, 243, 246–47, 334n31

Höhlig, Martin: BVG-Wartehalle (waiting room, Berlin urban transit), 30, *31*; Lichtburg Kino (Lichtburg movie theater), *32*

Holabird & Roche, Palmer House Hotel, 169

Horkheimer, Max, 129

Horowitz, Frederick, 214

hotels, 169, 173

housing: in Germany, 160–61; and the grid, 155, 160–61; Gropius and, 62, 74–81; Hilberseimer and, 6, 64, 155, 157, 160–67, 172–89, 191–93, 197–99, 201–2; Isokon and, 74–81; luxury, 162–63; mass production of, 162–63, 167, 168, 171, 172, 176, 185, 188–90; Mies van der Rohe and, 13, 161–62, 189–90; minimal dwelling and, 63–74, 92–93; Moholy-Nagy and, 50–51; prefabrication and, 92, 189–90; reproducibility in, 170–73, 184–85, 192, 203; standardization in, 172; totalization and, 65, 67, 88, 92–93, 163, 171, 191; and the unit, 155. *See also* freestanding houses; L-shaped homes; row houses; single-family homes

Howard, Ebenezer, 164, 177, 193; *Garden City of To-morrow*, 193

Hudnut, Joseph, 318n6

Illinois Institute of Technology (IIT), 131, 161, *186–87*, 187–88, 317n4, 319n15

Illinois Neuropsychiatric Institute, 140

Illinois State Department of Public Welfare, 12, 139

Illinois WPA Arts and Crafts Project, 147

individualism: consumerism linked to, 252; modernist rejection of, 65, 67, 88–89

industry: architecture and, 24–27; art and, 39–41; materials of, 21, 24, 26–27, 29, 268–70; Moholy-Nagy and, 21–27, 34, 36–41; New Bauhaus's collaboration with, 134–35; standardization in, 40. *See also* capitalism

Institute of Design, Chicago. *See* New Bauhaus, Chicago

internationalism, 4–5

International Style, 5

Isobar, Lawn Road Flats, London, 72–74, *72–73*

Isokon Building, 81

Isokon Flats. *See* Lawn Road Flats / Isokon Flats, London

Isokon Furniture Company: Breuer and, 1, 9, 82–87; formation of, 69; German exiles in, 59; Gropius and, 9–10, 81–83, 87; and the housing market, 74–81; Moholy-Nagy and, 9, 82, 83, 87; and standardization, 74; and the unit, 74; use of plywood by, 57, 59, 69, 71, 73, 82–87

Isokon Long Chair (Breuer), 1, 5, *6*, *60–61*, 84–85, *86*, 91

Isokon Short Chair (Breuer), 84–85

Jaeggi, Annemarie, 120

Jeanneret, Pierre, 67

Jefferson Grid, 157

jewelry, of Anni Albers, 243, 250, 258, 267–70

Johansson, Karlis, 305n26

John Lewis (store), 83

Johns, Jasper, 234

Johnson, Allan, 137

Johnson, Philip, 129, 246, 258, 270, 319n19

Jucker, Carl J., table lamps (with Wilhelm Wagenfeld), *102*, 103

Judd, Donald, 234–35

Kadden-Lindenfeld, Lore, 260; weaving study from Anni Albers's weaving class at Black Mountain College, 260, *261*

Kállai, Ernő, 22, 24–25, 30–31

Kandinsky, Wassily, 120, 217

Kassák, Lajos, *Buch neuer Künstler* (*Book of New Artists*) [with László Moholy-Nagy], 25

Kaufmann, Edgar, 258

Keck, George Fred, 303n4

Kendal Milne Department Store, 79

Kepes, Gyorgy, 139, 143, 144, 146, 147, 278, 280–81, 320n36; *Paperboard Goes to War*, 139, *140–41*, 278; *War Art* catalog cover (possibly by Ralph Graham), *147*

Kepes, Juliet, 322n73

Klee, Paul, 120, 217

Knoll, Hans, 318n11

Koch, Carl, 25

Koehler, Karen, 128, 318n12

Krajewski, Max, tea glass holders, *102*, 103, 122

Kuspit, Donald, 111

La, Kristie, 291, 293

labor, 254

Lafayette Park, Detroit, 13, 155

laminated plastic, 237, 239, 330n91

Land Ordinance (United States, 1785), 157

landscape, architecture's relationship to, 76, 167, 178, 180–81, 191–97, 200

Lawn Road Flats / Isokon Flats, London, 9, 57, *58*, 62–63, *63*, 64, 66–74, *68–70*, 82, 91, 92

Le Corbusier, 4, 67, 304n14; *Toward a New Architecture*, 25

Léger, Fernand, 4, 278

Leibniz-Keks butter cookies, enamel sign, 40, *40*

Levittown houses, 190

Lichtenstein, Roy, 234

Life (magazine), 280

light: advertising's use of, *33*; Albers (Josef) and, 212, 220, 222, 236; Moholy-Nagy and, 8, 26–27, 29–31, 33–34, 41–45, 47–50; photograms and, 41–43; space and, 41–43

Lissitzky, El, 286

London Aluminum Company, 83

Loos, Adolf, 254

L-shaped homes, 13, *160–61*, 161–62, *171*, 172, 177–78, 184–87, 191, 201–2

Lubetkin and Tecton, 81
Lucite, 132

MA (*Today*) [magazine], 24
MacCarthy, Fiona, 74
Machine Art (exhibition, 1934), 269–70
Mackintosh, Charles Rennie, 90
Malevich, Kazimir, 304n26
Mann, Thomas, 125
Marcek, George, 132
Marsio-Aalto, Aino, 82–83, 309n36
Masonite, 1, 15, 209, 210, 223, 226–27, 230–31, 241, 329n70
mass production: the Bauhaus and, 104, 122, 131, 168, 320n35; in Chicago, 21, 172; Gropius and, 67, 79; Hilberseimer's housing proposals for, 162–63, 167, 172, 176, 185; and housing, 168, 171, 201, 202; industrialization and, 21; Isokon and, 62, 82; Mies van der Rohe and, 188–90, *189*, 201, 202; modern design and, 65; Werkbund and, 40, 171. *See also* reproduction/reproducibility; standardization
materials/materiality: abstraction and, 9; Albers (Anni) and, 15–16, 243, 252–57, 259–64, 267–73; Albers (Josef) and, 13, 15, 207–23, 226–27, 229–41, 329n73; of the city, 26–27, 29; Hilberseimer and, 175–76; industrial, 21, 24, 26–27, 29, 268–70; Mies van der Rohe and, 176; Moholy-Nagy and, 8–9, 21–24, 26–27, 29–30, 34, 36–41, 44–45, 53, 55; New Bauhaus curriculum and, 308n96; urban, 26–27, 29, 34; visuality in relation to, 210–15; weaving and, 243, 254, 257, 259–64, 267, 271. *See also* objects; surface of the work
May, Ernst, 67, 163–64
McCormick, Robert, 189, 190
McKim, Mead & White, Hotel Pennsylvania, New York City, 169
Mehring, Walter, *Der Kaufmann von Berlin* (*The Merchant of Berlin*), 49
Mendelsohn, Erich, 318n11; *Amerika*, 3; De La War Pavilion (with Serge Chermayeff), 83; partnership with Maxwell Fry, 81; partnership with Serge Chermayeff, 59
Merchandise Mart, Chicago, 258
metal, Moholy-Nagy and, 8, 22, 24, 26–27
Meyer, Adolf, Chicago Tribune Tower competition entry (with Walter Gropius), 51, 225
Meyer, Hannes, 64–67, 69, 81, 88, 93, 120, 155, 320n35; ADGB Bundesschule auditorium, Bernau, 257, 331n62; "Bauhaus and Society," 66; Co-op Interior, *65*, 93; "The New World," 65
Mies van der Rohe, Ludwig, 3, 4; at the Bauhaus, 155, 161; in Chicago, 13, 155, 162, 187–89; and English language, 90; FBI files on, 128; furniture patents of, 5; in Germany, 12, 13, 155; and the grid, 155, 202; Hilberseimer's collaborations with, 155, *156*, 188; housing designed by, 13, 161–62, 189–90, 201–2; at Illinois Institute of Technology, 131, 161, 319n15; and materials/materiality, 176; objects left behind by, 12; pedagogy of, 161; success in exile, 12; in the United States, 128, 319n13, 319n19; and urban design, 155, 196
Mies van der Rohe, Ludwig, works: 50 x 50 house for mass production, 189–90, *189*; "Court-house with garage," 162; Farnsworth House, 176, 189; Friedrichstrasse Skyscraper projects, 155, 176, 223; glass skyscraper designs, 50; Greenwald House, 189; IIT Master Plan (with Ludwig Hilberseimer), *186–87*, 187–88, 202; Lafayette Park, Detroit (with Ludwig Hilberseimer), 13, 155, *200*, 201–2, *201*; Lake Shore Drive apartments, 189–90, 201, 202; Lemke House, 161; McCormick House, *188*, 189, 202; Mountain House studies, 161; Reichsbank project, 155, *157*; Row House prototype, 190; Seagram Building, 4, 298
minimal existence/dwelling: concept of, 10, 61–67, 91; furnishings for, 81–89; as *Gesamtkunstwerk*, 65–66, 92–93; Gropius and, 81; Lawn Road Flats and, 67–74; social role of, 65–67

mixed-type developments, 178–81, 193
Modern Architecture in England (exhibition, 1937), 82, 311n111
Modern Art in Advertising (exhibition, 1945), 290, *290*
Modern Art in Your Life (exhibition, 1949), 258
Modern Handmade Jewelry (exhibition, 1946), 258, 270
modernism: attitudes toward, 80; Bauhaus and, 51, 131; contingent factors shaping, 10; in England, 9–10, 80; exile's shaping of, 1–17, 298–99; freedom associated with, 81; in Germany, 1, 3, 7, 59–60; and *Gesamtkunstwerk*, 88–89, 92–93; and internationalism, 4–5; key themes of, 7; Moholy-Nagy and, 22–23; pedagogy linked to, 52; production and reproduction in, 38–41; rejection of individualism by, 65, 67, 88–89; and skyscrapers, 209; social goals and role of, 6, 67; and transnationalism, 5; and the unit, 63; in the United States, 2, 3, 12, 89, 122, 127, 150, 223, 277, 298, 318n5; and universalism, 4–5
modernity: the city and, 23, 30, 34; communicative potential of, 8–9
Moholy, Lucia, 3; Bauhaus photographs taken by, 1, 5, 10, 12, 97–106, 111–21, 316n58, 316n60; compensation for Bauhaus photographs, 119–20, 316n60; critical reception of, 109; emigration from Germany, of, 60, 106; in England, 106–11, 314n18; exile's effect on, 106–7, 110–16; and Gropius, 103, 110–15; influence of, 109; Jewish background of, 111; and László Moholy-Nagy, 97, 99, 106–7, 109–12, 313n7; objects left behind by, 10, 97, 106, 110–15; and photograms, 99; photographic practice in exile, 107–9; photography of objects, 99, 103–4, 108–9; in Switzerland, 110, 315n39; theories and writings on photography, 108–9
Moholy, Lucia, works: armchair (later titled TI 1a) by Marcel Breuer, *117*, 118; Bauhaus Building by Walter Gropius, northwest corner of the workshop wing (print), 97, 99, *101*; Bauhaus Building by Walter Gropius, studio wing balcony (glass negative), 97, *98*; Bauhaus Building by Walter Gropius, studio wing balcony (print), *11*, 97; Bauhaus Building by Walter Gropius, view from northeast (print), 97, *100*; Bauhaus Building by Walter Gropius, view from southwest (glass negative), 97, *100*; Bauhaus director's office, *117*, 118; changing table by Alma Buscher, *117*, 118; conference table by Josef Albers, *117*, 118; five unattributed photographs featured on pages 108–9 of the exhibition catalog *Bauhaus, 1919–1928*, 118, *119*; kitchen containers by Theodor Bogler, 103, *104*; masters' houses by Walter Gropius, view from northwest (print), 97, *101*; *Portrait of Emma, Countess of Oxford and Asquith*, 107, *107*, 109; ship toy by Alma Buscher, *117*, 118; stands with tea infusers by Otto Rittweger, 104, *105*; tea glass holders by Max Krajewski, *102*, 103, 122; toy cabinet by Alma Buscher, *117*, 118; tubular steel chairs by Marcel Breuer, 104, *105*; two table lamps by Carl J. Jucker and Wilhelm Wagenfeld, *102*, 103; verso of photographic print, 103, *103*, 112–13
Moholy, Lucia, writings: *A Hundred Years of Photography*, 108–9, 123; "Kulturgeschichte der Fotografie" (A cultural history of photography), 108; "Production-Reproduction" (with László Moholy-Nagy), 38, 40–41
Moholy-Nagy, László, 3, 21–55; and Aalto, 82; and abstraction, 8–9, 22, 53, 55; and advertising, 27, *33*; and the architectural, 6, 8, 21–31, 34, 47, 50–53, 303n4, 304n11; at the Bauhaus, 21, 51, 99, 103; and camouflage, 146–47; in Chicago, 21; and the city, 8, 21–27, 29–30, 33, 34, 45, 47–50, 53; death of, 152; design for the war effort and postwar society, 127, 130–53, 278; emigration from Germany of, 59–63; in England, 59–63, 89, 309n6, 309n11; exhibition designs by, 275, 286; exile's effect on, 5; FBI investigation of, 128, 320n22; and film, 25, 45, 47, 50, 307n83; in Germany, 21–24; and industry, 21–27, 34, 36–41; influence of, 53; and Isokon, 9, 82, 83, 87; layers in work of, 29–31; and light, 8, 26–27, 29–31, 33–34, 41–45, 47–50; and Lucia Moholy, 97, 99, 106–7, 109–12, 313n7; and materials/materiality, 8–9, 21–24, 26–27, 29–30, 34, 36–41, 44–45, 53, 55; and modernism, 22–23;

at the New Bauhaus, 9, 12, 51, 125, 127, 130–53, 317n4, 319n15; and objects, 27, 53; objects left behind by, 5, 12, 106; objects taken into exile by, 106; paintings of, 23–24, 26, 29–36, 44, 55; pedagogy of, 26, 51–53, 130–32, 142, 148–52, 308n96, 318n6, 323n118, 324n125; photography of objects, 313n8; prints of, 23–24; and space, 8, 22, 26, 29–31, 34, 36–37, 41–45, 50–51, 53, 55; success in exile, 12; and surface, 8, 30, 36–41, 45, 53; and the theater, 49–50; theories and statements on art and design, 22, 24–27, 31, 34, 36–43, 47–51, 55, 129–30, 151–52; and transparency, 27, 29–31, 34, 36, 44–45; and transposition, 8–9, 21; in the United States, 125, 127–28, 319n13, 320n19, 320n22, 320n28; works in glass, 8, 22, 26–27, 30, 34

Moholy-Nagy, László, works: *A II* (*Construction A II*), 29; *A IX*, 29; *A 19*, *32*, 33, 44; *A XX*, *28*, 29; *Architecture* (*Eccentric Construction*), 23, 27; *Architecture* series, 34; *Architektur 1*, 23; *AXL II*, 33; *B-10 Space Modulator*, 45; *Bridges 1 K 33*, 23, *23*; brochure, *The New Isokon Chair*, 60–61, 84–85; *CH 1*, 45; *CH 7* (or *Chicago Space 7*), 53, *54*; *CH P Space Modulator* or *Iridescent Space Modulator*, 45; *City Lights*, 33–34, *35*, 305n36; *Construction*, 33, *35*; cover for Erwin Piscator's *Das Politische Theater*, 49; cover for Walter Gropius's *The New Architecture and the Bauhaus*, 9, 90; *EM 1*, 39–40, *39*, 218; *EM 2*, 39–40, *39*, 218; *EM 3*, 39–40, *39*, 218; *Glass Architecture III*, 24, *25*; *Glass Architecture* series, 27, 34; *Human Mechanics* (*Variety*), 34, *35*, 37; Isokon logo, 83, *84*; *Joseph and Potiphar's Family*, 305n36; *K VII*, 29–30, *30*, 34, 37, 305n30; *Light Prop for an Electric Stage* (*Light Space Modulator*), 4, 5, 8, 31, 41, 43–45, 47, 106; model city for film adaptation of H. G. Wells's *Things to Come*, 45; *Photograph* (*Light Prop*), 43, *43*; *Raum der Gegenwart* (*Room of the Present*), 44; *Reflected Image*, 47, 307n71, 307n73; *Relief S*, *26*, 27; *Reliefs* series, 26, 27, 34, 44; Room 2, 37, *38*; set design for H. G. Wells's *Things to Come*, 45, *50*, 307n91; set design for Jacques Offenbach's *The Tales of Hoffmann*, 49–50; set design for Walter Mehring's *Der Kaufmann von Berlin*, 49; *Sil 2*, 8, 9, 36, 38; *Six Flowers*, vi, 1; *Space III*, 45, *46*, *46* (detail); *Space Modulator*, 44, 45; *Space Modulator* (*Rhodoid*), 45; *Space Modulator CH for Y*, 44; *Space Modulator L3*, 44; *Telephone Paintings*, 39–40, *39*, 218; *Tp 2*, *36*, 37, *38*; *Two Circles with Beam*, 23; *Untitled*, 42, *42*; *Untitled* (*Glass Architecture Series*), 24; *Z II*, 33

Moholy-Nagy, László, writings: *Buch neuer Künstler* (*Book of New Artists*) [with Lajos Kassák], 25; *Dynamik der Gross-Stadt* (*Dynamic of the Metropolis*), 25–26; "Light Architecture," 47; *Malerei, Fotografie, Film* (*Painting, Photography, Film*), 24, 25, 36, 47, 109; "Man and His House," 50–52; Moholy-Nagy and, 33–34; *The New Vision*, 25, 41; "On the Problem of New Content and New Form," 24; "Production-Reproduction" (with Lucia Moholy), 38, 40–41; "Theater, Circus, Variety," 34; *Vision in Motion*, 25; *Von Material zu Architektur* (*From Material to Architecture*), 25–27, *26*, 33, *33*

Moholy-Nagy, Sibyl, 29, 30, 43–44, 47, 50, 74, 110–12, 115, 128, 320n19

MoMA. *See* Museum of Modern Art (MoMA), New York

MoMA Bulletin, 288

montage, 27, 290. *See also* photomontage

Monte Alban treasure, 268

Moore, Henry, 62

Morris, William, 90, 254

Muche, Georg, 22

Museum of Modern Art (MoMA), New York, 16, 82, 113, 121, 129, 243, 258–60, 267, 269–71, 275, 277, 281, 286, 288, 291, 293, 318n11, 321n41, 322n73, 323n105, 333n23

Muthesius, Hermann, 175, 192

nationalism, 5

Nazis, 5, 59, 61, 111, 223, 277, 291, 307n73, 334n31

Nekimken, Elic, life belt units, 132, *133*

Neubauer, Theodor, 106, 111, 314n18

Neue Arbeiten der Bauhauswerkstätten (*New Work of the Bauhaus Workshops*), 118

Neue Sachlichkeit (New Objectivity), 99, 104, 108–9, 123

New Bauhaus, Chicago (later called School of Design, then Institute of Design), *126*; Bauhaus compared to, 130–32; Bauhaus principles preserved in, 142, 144, 146–47, 150, 318n10; design for the war effort and postwar society, 127, 130–53; educational mission of, 130–32, 137–38, 142, 148–52, 308n96, 324n125; exiles' shaping of, 2; finances of, 129, 319n15; Foundation Course, 131; furniture design at, 135–37, 321n47; Moholy and, 110; Moholy-Nagy and, 9, 12, 48, 125, 127, 130–53, 317n4, 319n15; names of, 317n4; postwar role and influence of, 127

New Deal, 282

New Design Trends (exhibition, 1952), 258

"New Vision" (*Neues Sehen*), 99

New York Times (newspaper), 125, 151, 288

Northwest Territory, 157

objects: agency of, 5–6, 216; Albers (Josef) and, 15, 207–8, 237; left behind, 5, 10, 12, 97, 106, 110–15, 121; meaning of, 6; Moholy-Nagy and, 5, 12, 27, 53; Moholy's photographs of, 99, 103–4, 108–9; photograms and, 41–42; role of, in exilic modernism, 5; ruined in transit, 5, 15, 224–26, 247; urban, 41. *See also* materials/materiality

occupational therapy. *See* rehabilitation therapy

Offenbach, Jacques, *Les contes d'Hoffmann* / *Hoffmanns Erzählungen* (*The Tales of Hoffmann*), 49–50

Original Bauhaus (exhibition and catalog, 2019), 118

Original Textile Company, 258

ornament and decoration, 174, 182–83, 236, 254–55

Paepcke, Walter, 129, 135, 139, 278, 285, 319n15

Paimio Sanatorium, Finland, 82–83

Palucca, Gret, 320n19

paper, 139, 263–64, 278

patents: Bauhaus, 5; Breuer, 85, 87; for furniture design, 5, 137; Mies van der Rohe, 5

Patterson Fabrics, 258

pedagogy: Albers (Anni), 5, 15, 254, 259–67, 270; Albers (Josef), 13, 51, 211–16, 265; and architecture, 51–52; Bauhaus, 51–53, 213–15, 264–65, 297; Black Mountain College, 248–50; German exiles, 2; Mies van der Rohe, 161; and modernism, 52; Moholy-Nagy, 26, 51–53, 130–32, 142, 148–52, 308n96, 318n6, 323n118, 324n125; New Bauhaus, 130–32, 137–38, 142, 148–52, 324n125

P. E. Gane, 83

Pelkonen, Eeva-Liisa, 215

perception. *See* visuality

Perdekamp, Franz, 223, 226, 239

Perspecta (journal), 271

Peterhans, Walter, 120

Pevsner, Nikolaus, 134

photograms, 1, 41–43, 47–48, 99

photography: of architecture, 313n3; at the Bauhaus, 120; Gropius's use of, for Bauhaus's promotion and legacy, 1, 5, 10, 12, 97–106, 111–23; meaning of, 121; by Moholy, of the Bauhaus, 1, 5, 10, 12, 97–106, 111–23; Moholy's cultural history of, 108–9; *sachlich* (objective), 97, 99, 104, 108, 123; as substitute for the inaccessible/nonexistent, 12

photomontage, 13, 34, 49, 190, 200, 277, 282, 296. *See also* montage

Piscator, Erwin, 49

Plexiglas, 8, 39, 44–45, 47, 132

plywood: Aalto and, 82; Albers (Josef) and, 239; Breuer and, 5,

Index 341

plywood (*continued*)
9, 73, 83–87; furnishings made of, 71, 79, 82–87; Gropius and, 83; Isokon's use of, 57, 59, 69, 71, 73, 82–87; New Bauhaus's experimentation with, 135, 137; springs made from, 134
Pollock, Jackson, 13, 234
posters, 2, 16, 138–39, 277, 279–80, 282–84
Pragmatism, 150
prefabrication, 92, 189–90
Pritchard, Jack, 57, 59, 62, 68–69, 71–72, 74–75, 77–78, 82–83
Pritchard, Molly, 68–69, 73
Puhl und Wagner, 218

Quakers, 110

Rathenau, Walter, 168
Rauschenberg, Robert, 216, 234
Raymond, Antonin, 318n11
Rebay, Hilla, 303n4
Red Cross, 16, 277, 288
Redensek, Jeannette, 231, 235
Reed, Alex, 258, 267–70; necklaces (with Anni Albers), 268, *269*
rehabilitation therapy, 12, 139–42, 322n73
Reich, Lilly, 63, 319n19
remediation, 13, 15–16, 210, 243, 270, 275, 290–91, 293
Renaissance Society, University of Chicago, 147
Renger-Patzsch, Albert, 104
reproduction/reproducibility: aestheticization of, 203; anti-materiality and, 5; and aura, 170–74, 176, 203; and *Gesamtkunstwerk*, 88; Hilberseimer's housing proposals and, 170–73, 184–85, 192, 203; Mies van der Rohe's housing design and, 13; Moholy-Nagy and, 38–41; of objects and space, 13; photography and, 121–22; productive potential of, 38–41. *See also* mass production; scalability
Rhoades, Nolan, 132–33
Rhodoid, 44–45, 47
Rice, John Andrew, 226
Richardson, H. H., 168
Rittweger, Otto, stands with tea infusers, 104, *105*
Road to Victory (exhibition, 1942), 16, 277, 286, 288, *288*, 291, 293, 318n11
Rockefeller, Abby Aldrich, 246
Rodchenko, Alexander, 305n26
Roebling, John Augustus, 168
Roh, Franz, 36
Roosevelt, Franklin D., 282
Root, John, 168
Rose, Hajo, fabric using typewriter patterning, *264*, 265
Rose, Katja, designs for fabric using patterns made from typewriter printing, *264*, 265
Rosenberg, Harold, 111
Rowell, Margit, 236
row houses, 160, 167, 177, 181–83, *182*, 185, 189–90, 198–99, 201–2
Royal Institute of British Architects (RIBA), 55, 59, 89–90
Royal Photographic Society, 109
Rudolph Sandbläserei, 218
Rukser, Udo, "American Architecture" (with Ludwig Hilberseimer), 167
Rural Electrification Administration, 282, 284
Russell, Gordon, 82
Russian constructivism, 304n26

sachlich (objective) photography, 97
Saletnik, Jeffrey, 142, 212, 228

Sandburg, Carl, 286
Saturday Evening Post (magazine), 246
scalability, Hilberseimer and, 13, 157, 160, 162, 166–67, 172, 184, 186, 188, 191–92, 203
Schawinsky, Xanti, 278
Schlemmer, Oskar, 22; *The Theater of the Bauhaus* (with László Moholy-Nagy and Farkas Molnár), 34
School of Design, Chicago. *See* New Bauhaus, Chicago
Schütte-Lihotzky, Margarete, Frankfurt Kitchen, 63–64
Schwitters, Kurt, 27, 320n19
screens, 47–48
Seng Company, 134
set design. *See* theater
Shand, Morton, 62, 74, 82–83, 90
Sheeler, Charles, 26
silberit, 36–39, 47
Simmel, Georg, "The Metropolis and Mental Life," 293
single-family homes, 13, 76, 81, 160–63, *160-61*, 176–78, 180, 182–85, *182-83*, 188, 191–93, 196–97, 201–2
skyscrapers. *See* high-rise architecture and skyscrapers
Smith, T'ai, 253
social role of art and design: Albers (Anni) and, 252–53; Bauhaus and, 52, 66; Bayer and, 275, 278–90, 295–96, 299; Gropius and, 67; Hilberseimer and, 163, 193, 196; minimal existence/dwelling and, 65–67; modernism and, 6, 67, 88–89; Moholy-Nagy and, 34, 55, 137, 139–42, 151–53; New Bauhaus and, 130–53; post–World War II, 130–32, 149–53. *See also* design, for the war effort and postwar society
Société des artistes décorateurs, 1930 Paris exhibition, 37, 44, 275, *277*, 291
SOM, plan for Illinois Institute of Technology, 188
Sommerfeld House, 207
space: abstraction and, 22, 36–37; Albers (Anni) and, 271; Albers (Josef) and, 239; architecture and, 26, 175–76; Hilberseimer and, 175–76; light and, 41–43; Moholy-Nagy and, 8, 22, 26, 29–31, 34, 36–37, 41–45, 50–51, 53, 55; photograms and, 42–43
standardization: in advertising, 39–40; and *Gesamtkunstwerk*, 88; Gropius and, 67, 81, 309n36; in housing construction, 172; in industry, 40; Isokon and, 74; minimal dwelling and, 63–66; prefabrication and, 92; Werkbund and, 40. *See also* mass production; unit
Statue of Liberty, 246
Steichen, Edward, 286, 288, 318n11
Stella, Frank, 236
Stoedtner, Franz, 120
Stoedtner, Ottilie, 120
studies made with grass seed heads and wood shavings and twigs, Black Mountain College, 260, *261*, 263
subjectivity: Albers (Anni) and, 255–56; Albers (Josef) and, 216–17, 222, 237; Moholy-Nagy and, 40; role of, in experience and production of art, 13, 15, 17, 40, 65, 216–17, 222, 236–37, 255–56
Sullivan, Louis, 3, 168
Summers, Gerald, 82
superblocks, 155
surface of the work: Albers (Josef) and, 15, 209–16, 220, 230–41; Moholy-Nagy and, 8, 30, 34, 36–41, 45, 53. *See also* materials/materiality
surrealism, 282
Sweeney, James Johnson, 281

tactile sense. *See* touch/tactile sense
Taylor, Robert, 172
teaching. *See* pedagogy
Technometer (magazine), 188
Tecton Group, Highpoint apartments, 83

Teige, Karel, *The Minimum Dwelling*, 66–67, 93
Textile Design (exhibition, 1945), 258
theater, Moholy-Nagy and, 49–50
theories of art, architecture, and design: Albers (Anni), 15, 243, 247, 250–57, 259, 261, 263–64, 267–68, 270–71, 273; Albers (Josef), 212, 214, 231–33, 239, 241; Bayer, 16, 275, 278, 284, 286, 291, 299; exile's effect on, 7; Gropius, 88; Hilberseimer, 13, 155, 161, 163–64, 169, 173–78, 180–89, 191–203; minimal existence concept, 62–67; Moholy, 108–9; Moholy-Nagy, 22, 24–27, 31, 34, 36–43, 47–51, 55, 129–30, 151–52; reproduction as concept in, 39
Thomas, James Merle, 22
Three Modern Styles (exhibition, 1950), 258
totalization: of capitalism, 171; Hilberseimer's housing proposals and, 163, 171, 191; of the living environment, 65, 67, 88, 92–93. See also *Gesamtkunstwerk*
touch panels, 51
touch/tactile sense: Albers (Anni) and, 261, 263, 267; Albers (Josef) and, 13, 213, 215; Moholy-Nagy and, 51
trademarks, 40
translation, 7, 89–92
transnationalism, 5
transparency, Moholy-Nagy and, 27, 29–31, 34, 36, 44–45
transposition, 8–10, 21, 38
Trolit, 8, 36–39, 47
Tschichold, Jan, 27
typewriter studies, 15, 264–67, *264*, *265*
typification, 165–66, 172, 183–84, 186, 202–3, 324n16
typofacture, 215

Ullstein, Hermann, 246
Ullstein publishing house, 207, 228, 246–47
unit: Gropius and, 67; Hilberseimer and, 6, 12–13, 64, 66, 155, 157, 163–67, 171–72, 176, 181, 191–92, 202; Isokon and, 74; minimal dwelling and, 63, 66; modernism and, 63; as object of exile, 202–3; prefabrication and, 92; theoretical significance of, 13; in urban design, 12–13, 155, 157, 167, 176, 181. See also cells; standardization
United States: Albers (Anni) in, 223–24, 243, 246–48; Albers (Josef) in, 223–24, 246–48; Bayer in, 129, 277–78, 285, 319n13, 319n19; craft traditions of, 137; German exiles in, 127–30, 277–81, 296–99, 319n12, 319n19; the grid in, 155, 157, 160, 163, 168, 202; Gropius in, 125, 128–29, 319n19; Hilberseimer and, 167–69; Mies van der Rohe in, 128, 319n13, 319n19; modernism in, 2, 3, 12, 16, 89, 122, 127, 150, 223, 277, 298, 316n72, 318n5; Moholy-Nagy in, 125, 127–28, 319n13, 320n19, 320n22, 320n28. See also Chicago, Illinois
universalism, 4–5
University of Pennsylvania, 134–35
Urbain, John, 214–15
urban design: of Chicago, 13, 181, 195, 199–200; decentralization in, 180, 192–95, *194*, 200; defense considerations affecting, 193–95; the grid in, 12–13, 155, 157, 176; Hilberseimer and, 12–13, 155, 157, 160, 163–67, *164*, 173, 176–81, 191–203; Mies van der Rohe and, 155, 196; the unit in, 12–13, 155, 157, 167, 176, 181. See also garden city concept
urban sprawl, 196
US Defense Department, 299
US Education Department, 150
Useful Objects in Wartime (exhibition, 1942), 321n41
US Information Agency, 285, 318n11
US Naturalization Service, 128
US Office of Civilian Defense, 12, 128, 142–43, 150
US Office of War Information, 16, 277, 286

US Relocation Authority, 134
US Treasury Department, 225
US Veterans' Administration, 12, 138
US War Information Bureau, 128–29
US War Production Board, 135, 143, 321n41
US Wartime Commission for Higher Education, 138, 150

Velde, Henry van de, 66
Venesta, 57, 79, 82
Victoria, Charlotte, 51
viewer-work relationship: Albers (Josef) and, 216–17, 222, 228–30, 235–37, 240–41; Bauhaus pedagogy and, 52; Bayer and, 275, 285–86, 291, 293
Vinylite, 239, 330n91
visuality: Albers (Josef) and, 13, 15, 207–17, 220–22, 236–37, 241; Bayer's expanded vision and, 16, 275, 288, 291, 293–97; concept of, 211; materiality in relation to, 210–15; subjectivity and, 13, 15, 216–17, 222. See also anti-materiality; viewer-work relationship
Volk aus Vielen Völkern (*Nation of Nations*) (exhibition, 1957), 318n11
V-spring, 134

Wachsmann, Konrad, 318n11
Wagenfeld, Wilhelm, table lamps (with Carl J. Jucker), *102*, 103
Wagner, Martin, 185
Waldheim, Jack, Z-Chair, 137
Walter Gropius Bauhausbauten Dessau (*Walter Gropius Bauhaus Building Dessau*), 116
War Art (exhibition, 1942), 12, 147–49
Warburg, Edward, 246
Warhol, Andy, 234
War Services Project, 143, 277, 282
weaving: Albers (Anni) and, 5, 15–16, 243, 253–54, 257–61, 263–64, 270–71; materiality of, 243, 254, 257, 259–64, 267, 271
Webb, Michael, Suitaloon, 92–93
Weber, Nicholas Fox, 220, 225
Weissenhofsiedlung exhibition (Stuttgart, 1927), 63
welfare, 176
Wells, H. G., *Things to Come*, 45, 50, *50*, 307n91
Werkbund: and mass production, 40, 171; and modernism, 3; and nationalism, 5; Paris exhibition (1930), 16, 37, 44, 275, 277, 291; and standardization, 40; Weissenhof Settlement, 4
Wildberg, Anni, 51
Wingler, Hans Maria, *The Bauhaus*, 118
wooden springs, *133*, 134
"Wood Only": The Exhibition of Finnish Furniture (1933), 82
Works Progress Administration (WPA), 12, 16, 277, 282, 299
World War II: Americans' response to, 127–28, 251; Albers (Anni) and, 250–53, 268; Bayer and, 284; design contributions during, 2, 12, 16, 48, 127–28, 130–49, 247–50, 252–53, 277–84, 318n11; émigrés' attitude toward, 125
WPA. See Works Progress Administration
Wright, Frank Lloyd, 3, 167, 169, 193

Yale University, 2, 13, 207, 215, 247, 271
Yorke, F.R.S., 59, 81; dining area of the Isobar, London (with Marcel Breuer), *72–73*, 73; London Theatre Studio (with Marcel Breuer), 83

Zimmerman, Claire, 313n3
Zinns, Robert, Knock-Down Chair, 135
Zucker, Paul, 318n11

Photo Credits

Architectural Review (fig. 2.16 left, top and bottom)

The Art Institute of Chicago (fig. I.8, fig. 5.27)

The Art Institute of Chicago / Art Resource, NY (fig. 5.4, fig. 5.5, fig. 5.7 left and right, fig. 5.15, fig. 5.16, fig. 5.18, fig. 5.29)

© 2022 Artists Rights Society (ARS), New York / VG Bild-Kunst, Bonn (fig. 3.2, fig. 3.3, fig. 3.4, fig. 3.5, fig. 3.9, fig. 3.11, fig. 3.12, fig. 3.13, fig. 3.14, fig. 4.6, fig. 4.7 right, fig. 5.3, fig. 5.23)

© 2022 Artists Rights Society (ARS), New York / VG Bild-Kunst, Bonn. Photograph of glass negative: Jan Tichy (fig. 3.1)

Avanti Architects (fig. 2.1)

Bauhaus-Archiv, Berlin (fig. 2.3, fig. 2.15 bottom, fig. 2.18, fig. 4.3 left, fig. 4.4)

Bauhaus-Archiv, Berlin. © 2023 Artists Rights Society (ARS), New York / VG Bild-Kunst, Bonn (fig. I.3, fig. 6.10, fig. 7.7 right, fig. 8.3, fig. 8.8 top)

Bauhaus-Archiv, Berlin. © Hannes Rose, Munich (fig. 7.7 left)

Bauhaus-Archiv, Berlin. Photograph by Berliner Bild-Bericht (fig. 1.13)

Photograph by Berliner Bildbericht. Harvard Art Museums / Busch-Reisinger Museum, Gift of Ise Gropius, BRGA.45.65. Photo © President and Fellows of Harvard College © Artists Rights Society (ARS), New York / VG Bild-Kunst, Bonn (fig. 8.2 left)

Photograph by Bryan Boyer (fig. 5.28 right)

bpk, Berlin / Kupferstichkabinett, Staatliche Museen, Berlin, Germany. © 2022 The Moholy-Nagy Estate and Artists Rights Society (ARS), New York / VG Bild- Kunst, Bonn (fig. 1.1)

Christies (fig. 2.19 left)

Dell and Wainwright / RIBA Collections (fig. 2.14)

Photography courtesy of the Denver Art Museum (fig. 8.1, fig. 8.4, fig. 8.5, fig. 8.6, fig. 8.7, fig. 8.8 bottom, fig. 8.9, fig. 8.10, fig. 8.15)

Deutsches Architekturmuseum, Frankfurt am Main (fig. 2.7)

Elmhurst Art Museum (fig. 5.22)

Special Collections, Getty Research Institute (fig. 6.5)

Harvard Art Museums / Busch-Reisinger Museum, Gift of Lydia Dorner. Photo © President and Fellows of Harvard College (fig. 8.11)

Harvard Art Museums / Busch-Reisinger Museum, Gift of Ise Gropius. Photo © President and Fellows of Harvard College (fig. 2.11 left, fig. 6.13)

Harvard Art Museums / Busch-Reisinger Museum, Gift of Walter Gropius. Photo © President and Fellows of Harvard College (fig. 2.10 left, fig. 2.16 right, top and bottom)

Harvard Art Museums / Busch-Reisinger Museum, Purchase through the generosity of Claudia Oetker and Liliane Soriano, and Francis H. Burr Memorial Fund. Photo © President and Fellows of Harvard College (fig. 2.20 bottom)

Photo © President and Fellows of Harvard College. © 2022 Artists Rights Society (ARS), New York / VG Bild-Kunst, Bonn (fig. I.7, fig. 3.6, fig. 3.7, fig. 3.8, fig. 3.10)

Photograph by Markus Hawlik. © 2022 The Moholy-Nagy Estate and Artists Rights Society (ARS), New York / VG Bild- Kunst, Bonn (fig. 1.10)

Herbert Bayer Papers, WH2416, Western History Collection, The Denver Public Library (fig. 8.12, fig. 8.17, fig. 8.18, fig. 8.19, fig. 8.20)

The Hilla von Rebay Foundation, on extended loan to the Solomon R. Guggenheim Museum, New York. © 2022 The Moholy-Nagy Estate and Artists Rights Society (ARS), New York / VG Bild-Kunst, Bonn (fig. 1.18)

IIT Archives (Chicago) (fig. 4.1, fig. 4.2 top, fig. 4.3 right, fig. 4.5)

Institute of Design Collection, (photo ID# IDC_0003_0084_cover1), University of Illinois at Chicago Library, Special Collections (fig. 4.7 left)

© 2023 The Josef and Anni Albers Foundation / Artists Rights Society (ARS), New York (fig. 6.12, fig. 6.16)

© 2023 The Josef and Anni Albers Foundation / Artists Rights Society (ARS), New York. *Offset: Buch und Werbekunst*, vol. 7, 1926 (fig. 6.18)

© 2023 The Josef and Anni Albers Foundation / Artists Rights Society (ARS), New York. Photograph by Tim Nighswander / Imaging4Art (fig. I.2, fig. 6.1, fig. 6.2 left and right, fig. 6.3, fig. 6.4, fig. 6.7, fig. 6.8, fig. 6.9, fig. 6.11, fig. 6.14, fig. 6.17, fig. 6.19, fig. 6.20, fig. 6.21, fig. 6.22, fig. 6.23, fig. 6.24, fig. 6.25, fig. 7.4, fig. 7.6, fig. 7.8, fig. 7.9, fig. 7.10)

© 2023 The Josef and Anni Albers Foundation / Artists Rights Society (ARS), New York. Photographer unknown (fig. 6.15)

Courtesy of the Josef and Anni Albers Foundation (fig. 7.5)

The J. Paul Getty Museum (fig. 1.20)

The J. Paul Getty Museum. © 2022 The Moholy-Nagy Estate and Artists Rights Society (ARS), New York / VG Bild-Kunst, Bonn (fig. 1.17)

Kunstbibliothek, Berlin (fig. 1.4, fig. 1.8, fig. 2.2, fig. 2.8, fig. 2.21 top, fig. 4.2 bottom, fig. 5.8, fig. 5.9, fig. 5.10, fig. 5.12, fig. 5.13, fig. 5.14, fig. 5.19, fig. 5.20, fig. 5.21, fig. 5.24, fig. 5.25, fig. 5.26, fig. 6.6, fig. 8.2 right, fig. 8.13, fig. 8.14, fig. 8.16)

Kunstbibliothek, Berlin. © 2023 Artists Rights Society (ARS), New York / VG Bild-Kunst, Bonn (fig. 8.21)

Kunsthandel Fred Richter (fig. 1.6 right, fig. 1.7 right)

Ludwig Karl Hilberseimer Papers, Ryerson and Burnham Art and Architecture Archives, Art Institute of Chicago (fig. 5.1, fig. 5.2, fig. 5.17)

© 2022 The Moholy-Nagy Estate and Artists Rights Society (ARS), New York / VG Bild-Kunst, Bonn (fig. 1.5, fig. 1.6 left, fig. 1.7 left, fig. 1.11, fig. 1.19)

© 2022 The Moholy-Nagy Estate and Artists Rights Society (ARS), New York / VG Bild-Kunst, Bonn. Photo © President and Fellows of Harvard College (fig. 1.9)

© 2023 The Moholy-Nagy Estate and Artists Rights Society (ARS), New York / VG Bild-Kunst, Bonn (fig. I.1, fig. I.4, fig. 1.2, fig. 1.3, fig. 1.16)

Digital Image © The Museum of Modern Art / Licensed by SCALA / Art Resource, NY (fig. 7.2, fig. 7.3, fig. 7.11)

Pritchard Papers, Archives and Special Collections, University of East Anglia (fig. I.5, fig. 2.4, fig. 2.9, fig. 2.10 right, fig. 2.11 right, fig. 2.13, fig. 2.17, fig. 2.21 bottom)

Pritchard Papers, Archives and Special Collections, University of East Anglia. © *Architect and Building News* (fig. 2.5, fig. 2.12)

Pritchard Papers, Archives and Special Collections, University of East Anglia. © Sam Lambert (fig. 2.6)

Pritchard Papers, Archives and Special Collections, University of East Anglia. Photograph by Denisa Ilie (fig. 2.19 right, fig. 2.20 top, fig. 2.22 left and right)

Public domain (fig. 1.15)

RIBA Collections (fig. 2.15 top)

Solomon R. Guggenheim Founding Collection. © 2022 The Moholy-Nagy Estate and Artists Rights Society (ARS), New York / VG Bild- Kunst, Bonn (fig. I.6, fig. 1.21)

Solomon R. Guggenheim Founding Collection, by gift. © 2022 The Moholy-Nagy Estate and Artists Rights Society (ARS), New York / VG Bild-Kunst, Bonn (fig. 1.12)

Photo courtesy of Tate Modern (fig. 7.1)

Technische Universität Berlin (fig. 5.6, fig. 5.11)

Photograph by Daniel J. Wilson. © 2022 The Moholy-Nagy Estate and Artists Rights Society (ARS), New York / VG Bild-Kunst, Bonn (fig. 1.14)

Copyright © 2024 by Princeton University Press

Princeton University Press is committed to the protection of copyright and the intellectual property our authors entrust to us. Copyright promotes the progress and integrity of knowledge. Thank you for supporting free speech and the global exchange of ideas by purchasing an authorized edition of this book. If you wish to reproduce or distribute any part of it in any form, please obtain permission.

Requests for permission to reproduce material from this work should be sent to permissions@press.princeton.edu

Published by Princeton University Press, 41 William Street, Princeton, New Jersey 08540
In the United Kingdom: Princeton University Press, 99 Banbury Road, Oxford OX2 6JX

press.princeton.edu

Cover image: Marcel Breuer, plywood nesting chair, blueprint, 13 July 1937. Pritchard Papers, Archives and Special Collections, University of East Anglia. Photograph by Denisa Ilie.
Endpapers: based on a study made on the typewriter by Anni Albers, n.d., typewriter printing in blue ink on paper mounted on board. The Josef and Anni Albers Foundation, 1994.18.4.
Part title illustrations: p. 18, detail of fig. 1.5; p. 94, detail of fig. 5.1; p. 204, detail of fig. 8.21

All Rights Reserved

Library of Congress Cataloging-in-Publication Data

Names: Schuldenfrei, Robin, author.
Title: Objects in exile : modern art and design across borders, 1930-1960 / Robin Schuldenfrei.
Description: Princeton : Princeton University Press, [2024] | Includes index. | Includes bibliographical references.
Identifiers: LCCN 2023007295 (print) | LCCN 2023007296 (ebook) | ISBN 9780691232669 (hardback) | ISBN 9780691254951 (ebook)
Subjects: LCSH: Modernism (Aesthetics)--History--20th century. | Architecture, Modern--20th century. | Art, Modern--20th century. | Expatriate architects. | Expatriate artists. | BISAC: ART / History / Modern (late 19th Century to 1945) | DESIGN / Reference
Classification: LCC BH301.M54 S38 2024 (print) | LCC BH301.M54 (ebook) | DDC 111/.85--dc23/eng/20230705
LC record available at https://lccn.loc.gov/2023007295
LC ebook record available at https://lccn.loc.gov/2023007296

British Library Cataloging-in-Publication Data is available

Publication of this book has been aided by the Graham Foundation for Advanced Studies in the Fine Arts

Designed by Robin Schuldenfrei and Jeff Wincapaw

This book has been composed in Neue Haas Grotesk Pro

Printed on acid-free paper. ∞

Printed in China

10 9 8 7 6 5 4 3 2 1

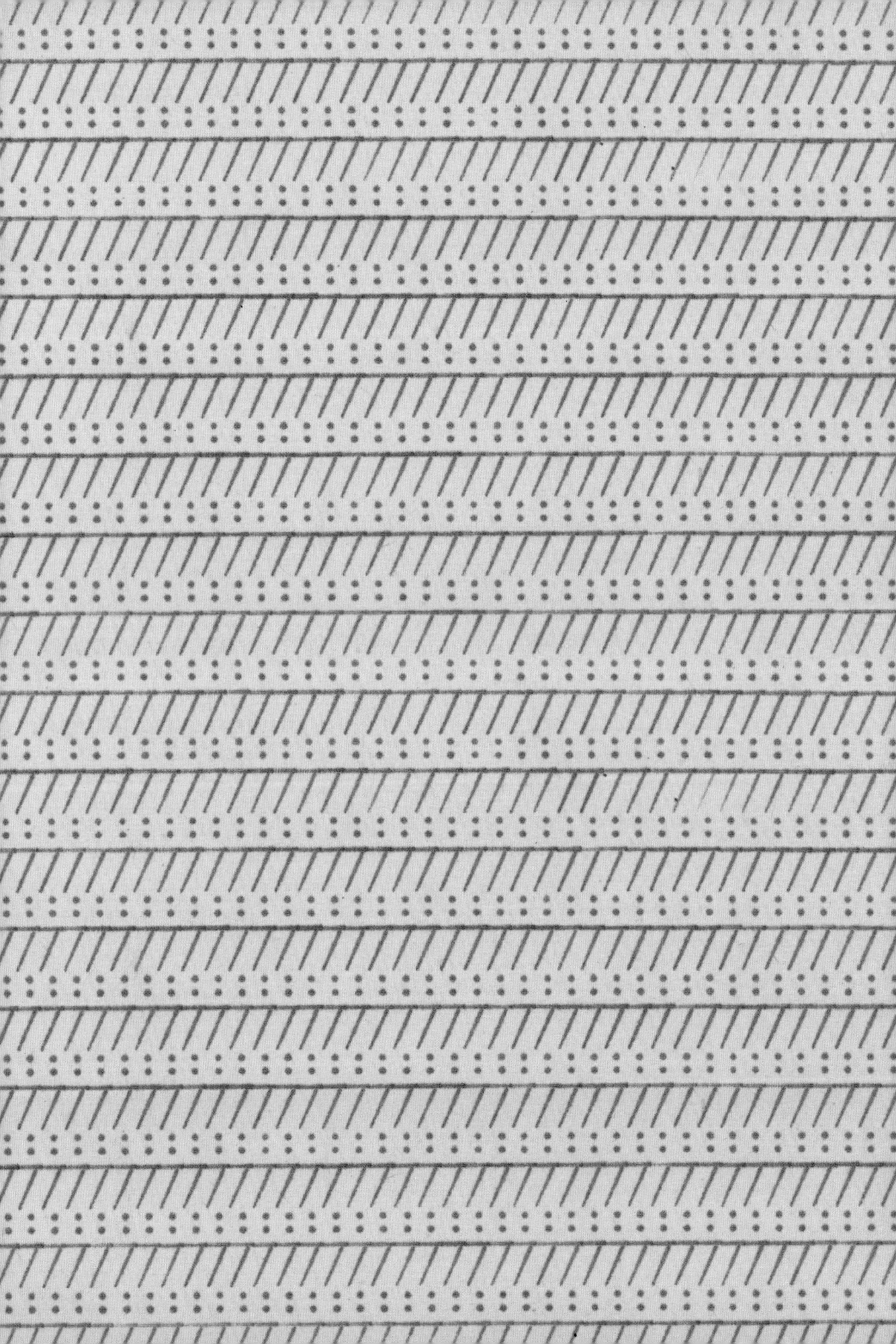

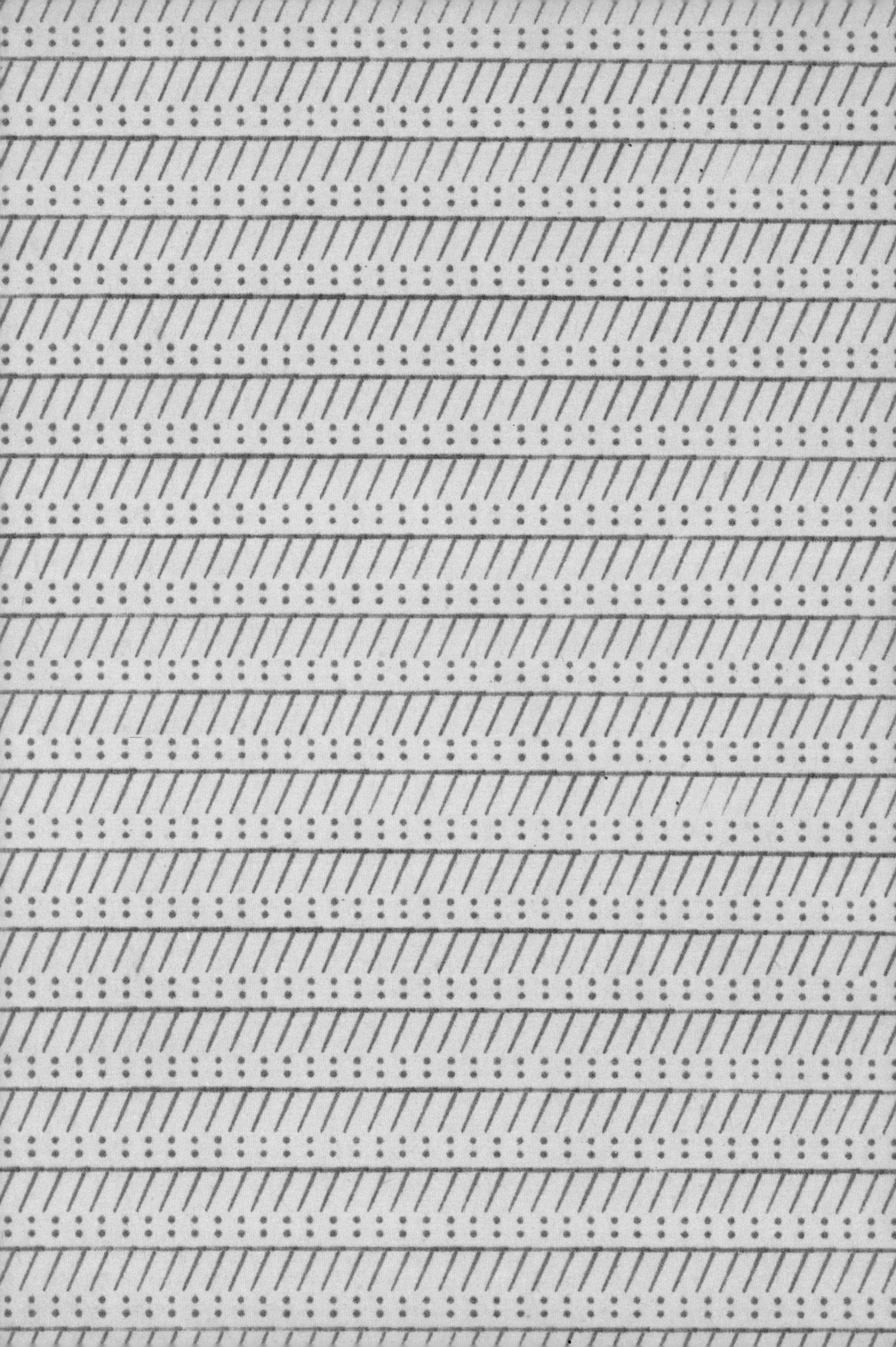